# SHAKESPEARE IN THE THEATRE
1701–1800

---

LONDON
1701–1750

# SHAKESPEARE IN THE THEATRE
## 1701-1800

A RECORD OF PERFORMANCES
IN LONDON
1701-1750

*By*
*Charles Beecher Hogan*

OXFORD
AT THE CLARENDON PRESS
1952

*Oxford University Press, Amen House, London E.C. 4*
GLASGOW NEW YORK TORONTO MELBOURNE WELLINGTON
BOMBAY CALCUTTA MADRAS CAPE TOWN
*Geoffrey Cumberlege, Publisher to the University*

PR
3097
.H6
v.1

PRINTED IN GREAT BRITAIN

# PREFACE

THE purpose of this book is introductory. For the past few years I have been engaged on an investigation of the treatment accorded to Shakespeare's plays on the eighteenth-century stage. The emphasis of this investigation does not fall on such matters as stage business, scenery, costumes, &c., but rather on what the actors saw in the text—the meaning of the text as conveyed, in the medium for which Shakespeare originally wrote, directly to an audience.

A fully documented source-book was, however, lacking. Information as to when Shakespeare's plays were acted, where, and by whom, was incomplete and frequently erroneous. My first concern, therefore, presently came to be facts and figures: the statistics, in short, which constitute this volume. I hope at a later date to produce a second volume that will continue the record of performances in London from 1751 to 1800, and others in which I shall set forth the eighteenth-century history of Shakespeare's plays in the principal provincial theatres of the British Isles and of America.

This book is divided into two parts. The first is a list of performances, arranged chronologically. Here I have incorporated the benefits allowed to actors and to other personages, and wherever possible, the nightly receipts. The second is an alphabetical grouping of the plays in which are given, in so far as they are available, the complete casts for every performance. This is followed by brief appendixes outlining the comparative popularity of Shakespeare's plays and the history of the London theatres, and by indexes of the actors and of the characters in the plays themselves.

C. B. H.

JONATHAN EDWARDS COLLEGE
    YALE UNIVERSITY

# ACKNOWLEDGEMENTS

Sir Leigh Ashton, Mr Tucker Brooke, Mrs Gabrielle Enthoven, Mr and Mrs Ifan Kyrle Fletcher, Mr Samuel B. Hemingway, Dr J. G. McManaway, Mr Allardyce Nicoll, Miss S. Rosenfeld, Mr Richard Southern, Mr G. W. Stone, Dr William Van Lennep, Mr C. B. Young: to these I am indebted for many courtesies and for much salutary advice. The libraries in which I have pursued my principal investigations—the Birmingham Public Library, the British Museum, the Bodleian, the Folger Shakespeare Library, Harvard, the Huntington Library, and Yale—have freely welcomed me and generously helped me. Mr and Mrs Arthur Cook have rechecked, with patience and efficiency, the details of many troublesome queries. To my parents goes my gratitude for their labours on my index; to Mrs S. Donahue my gratitude for her expert rendering of a fair copy out of the chaos of my working manuscript. To my wife my debt is without measure. This book is as much hers as it is mine.

# CONTENTS

| | |
|---|---|
| SOURCES | ix |
| CUE-TITLES AND ABBREVIATIONS | xiii |
| PART I. CALENDAR OF PERFORMANCES | 1 |
| PART II. THE PLAYS | 87 |
| APPENDIX A. SHAKESPEARE'S POPULARITY IN THE THEATRE, 1701–50 | 459 |
| APPENDIX B. ORDER OF POPULARITY OF SHAKESPEARE'S PLAYS, 1701–50 | 460 |
| APPENDIX C. LONDON THEATRES IN USE BETWEEN 1701 AND 1750 | 462 |
| INDEX I. ACTORS | 466 |
| INDEX II. CHARACTERS | 497 |

# SOURCES

VIRTUALLY none of the actual playbills used in the London theatres of the early eighteenth century has survived to the present day. The historian of the stage is, therefore, obliged to turn to the public announcements inserted in the newspapers. Until about 1725, and occasionally thereafter, these announcements are often incomplete, that is, they assign only a few parts or frequently none at all. But in subsequent years it became the custom of the theatres almost invariably to publish the newspaper bills in their entirety. In fact, the information they supply is in many instances far more complete than that given in the regular playhouse bill.[1] Of these playhouse bills I have located about a dozen dating before 1750; they are noted in Part II under their proper dates.

In assembling the material for this book I have had recourse chiefly to the collection of London newspapers in the British Museum brought together by the Rev. Charles Burney. I have also made use of the files of the *Daily Courant* owned by Yale and by the New York Historical Society. The former file covers the years 1702–9; the latter the years 1717–24. I may also note that all the issues of the *London Daily Post* for 1735 that are missing from the British Museum file are now at Yale. A complete collection of the Drury Lane and Covent Garden newspaper announcements for 1738 is at Harvard.

I have made full use of the manuscript transcriptions of the newspaper bills made in the 1880's by Frederick Latreille. This manuscript (British Museum, Add. MSS 32249–52) covers the years 1702–46, and is the most complete and the most accurate account ever written of the London stage during that period.

Burney's manuscript Theatrical Register has also been helpful. This catalogue was one of the principal sources drawn upon by Genest.[2] More often than not, however, it fails to record the complete casts, but it does record all the plays at least by title, theatre, and date. Another, and not dissimilar, manuscript account of the London stage was made in the early nineteenth century by James Winston; it is now at the Folger Shakespeare Library. This I have not used. Winston's accuracy is not always above suspicion.

Directly upon its establishment on November 4, 1734 the *London Daily Post* became the official organ for the advertisement of all the principal London theatres—a practice that was continued when the paper subsequently became, on March 10, 1744, the *General Advertiser*, and, on December 1, 1752, the *Public Advertiser*. Before 1734 the different theatres were from time to time in the habit of inserting their announcements in different newspapers; I have therefore listed the sources separately, by theatres.

---

[1] On this point I may anticipate my second volume. For example, the playbill for *The Merry Wives of Windsor* at Covent Garden on Jan. 11, 1760 lists seven characters; the bill in the *Public Advertiser* lists nineteen. The playbill for *Much Ado about Nothing* at Drury Lane on Jan. 27, 1764 lists eight characters; the bill in the *Public Advertiser* lists sixteen.
[2] Genest, ii. 256–7.

## SOURCES

**DRURY LANE**

| | |
|---|---|
| 1701 | Hotson |
| 1702–Apr. 1711 | DC |
| Apr. 1711–Aug. 1712 | DC and Sp |
| Sept.–Dec. 1712 | Sp |

Sp ceased publication on Saturday, Dec. 6. It is not known what plays were acted from Monday, Dec. 8 to Wednesday, Dec. 10, since DC did not resume its publication of the bills until Thursday, Dec. 11.

| | |
|---|---|
| Dec. 1712–Oct. 1719 | DC |
| Oct. 1719–Apr. 1720 | DP |

From Oct. 1719 to Apr. 1, 1720 the bills have been removed from the BM file of DP. All the clippings have, however, been pasted into TR.

| | |
|---|---|
| May 1720–Nov. 1726 | DC and DP |

From Apr. to Dec. 1722 the DP bills have been removed from the BM file and pasted into TR.

| | |
|---|---|
| Nov. 1726–Dec. 1731 | DP |

About half the bills for 1731 have been removed from the BM file and pasted into TR.

| | |
|---|---|
| Jan. 1732–Sept. 1733 | DP and TR |

Throughout this period a considerable number of bills have been removed from the BM file of DP. They have not, however, been pasted into TR, which for 1732 and 1733 consists of abbreviated manuscript entries only.

| | |
|---|---|
| Sept.–Nov. 1733 | DP and DA |
| Nov. 1733–Apr. 1734 | DJ and DA |
| Apr.–Nov. 1734 | DA |
| Nov. 1734–Dec. 1736 | LDP |
| 1737 | Harris, GEC, and TR |

The BM file of LDP for this year is lacking. A few bills are missing from Harris; some, but not all of these, are in GEC. For this year TR seldom gives more than the title of the play.

| | |
|---|---|
| 1738–41 | LDP |

A few issues of this paper for 1738 and 1739 are missing from the BM file. The bills are, however, supplied by Harris.

| | |
|---|---|
| 1742 | GEC |

The BM file of LDP for this year is lacking. All the bills, however, have been preserved, and are now in GEC.

| | |
|---|---|
| 1743–Mar. 1744 | LDP |
| Mar. 1744–50 | GA |

**COVENT GARDEN**

| | |
|---|---|
| 1732–Nov. 1733 | DJ |
| Nov. 1733–Nov. 1734 | DJ and DA |
| Nov. 1734–Dec. 1736 | LDP |
| 1737 | Harris, GEC and TR |

Same as DL for this year.

## SOURCES

| | |
|---|---|
| 1738–41 . . . . . . . . | LDP |
| Same as DL for these years. | |
| 1742 . . . . . . . . | GEC |
| Same as DL for this year. | |
| 1743–Mar. 1744 . . . . . . | LDP |
| Mar. 1744–50 . . . . . . . | GA |

### LINCOLN'S INN FIELDS

| | |
|---|---|
| 1702–5 . . . . . . . . | DC |
| 1714–Oct. 1719 . . . . . . | DC |
| Oct. 1719–Mar. 1721. . . . . . | DP |

The source of the bills from Oct. 1719 to Apr. 1, 1720 is the same as for DL, q.v.

| | |
|---|---|
| Mar. 1721–July 1726 . . . . . | DC and DP |

The source of the DP bills from Apr. to Dec. 1722 is the same as for DL, q.v.

| | |
|---|---|
| July–Aug. 1726 . . . . . . | DP |
| Sept. 1726–32 . . . . . . . | DJ |
| 1735–6 . . . . . . . . | LDP |
| 1737 . . . . . . . . | Harris and TR |
| Same as DL for this year, but no bills in GEC. | |
| 1742 . . . . . . . . | GEC and DA |
| Same as DL for this year. | |
| 1743 . . . . . . . . | LDP and DA |

### QUEEN'S

| | |
|---|---|
| 1705–10 . . . . . . . . | DC |

### GOODMAN'S FIELDS

| | |
|---|---|
| 1729–Apr. 1730 . . . . . . | DJ |
| Apr.–June 1730 . . . . . . | DJ and DP |
| June 1730–Dec. 1731 . . . . . | DP |
| 1732–3 . . . . . . . . | DA and DP |

For these years several issues of the BM file of DP are missing.

| | |
|---|---|
| Jan.–Nov. 1734 . . . . . . | DA |
| Nov. 1734–6 . . . . . . . | LDP |
| 1740–1 . . . . . . . . | LDP |
| 1742 . . . . . . . . | GEC |
| Same as DL for this year. | |

### HAYMARKET

| | |
|---|---|
| 1720–6 . . . . . . . . | DC |
| 1727–Mar. 1731 . . . . . . | DP |
| Mar. 1731–Sept. 1733 . . . . . | DP and DA |

xi

## SOURCES

| | |
|---|---|
| Oct. 1733–Nov. 1734. | DJ and DA |
| Nov. 1734–6 | LDP and DA |
| 1737 | DA |
| 1738–41 | LDP and DA |
| 1742 | DA |
| 1743–Mar. 1744 | LDP and DA |
| Mar.–Sept. 1744 | GA and DA |
| Sept.–Dec. 1744 | GA and DP |
| 1745–50 | GA and DA |

MINOR THEATRES

| | |
|---|---|
| 1712 | Sp |
| 1719–20 | DP |
| 1723 | DP |
| 1731 | DP and DA |
| 1731–50 | DA |

Wherever possible, I have listed the nightly receipts at the various theatres.[1] My sources are as follows:

DRURY LANE

| | |
|---|---|
| Apr. 28, 1738 | LDP, June 5, 1738 |
| Sept. 1747–Dec. 1750 | C–H |

Almost without exception the receipts listed in this manuscript are given in round numbers only.

COVENT GARDEN

| | |
|---|---|
| Dec. 1732–May 1733 | Latreille |
| Sept. 1735–Apr. 1736 | Egerton MS 2267, BM |
| Apr. 10, 1739 | Latreille |
| Sept. 1740–Apr. 1741 | Account Book, FSL |
| Sept. 1746–May 1747 | Egerton MS 2268, BM |
| Apr. 6, 1748 | GA, Apr. 11, 1748 |
| Sept. 1749–Apr. 1750 | Egerton MS 2269, BM |

LINCOLN'S INN FIELDS

| | |
|---|---|
| Feb. 1715–Jan. 1718 | Play-Accounts, FSL, and Egerton MS 2321, BM |
| Jan. 1720–May 1723 | Play-Accounts, FSL |
| Jan. 1720–May 1729 | Egerton MS 2322, BM |
| Sept. 1723–Nov. 1732 | Latreille |
| Sept. 1724–May 1725 | Egerton MS 2265, BM |
| Sept. 1726–June 1727 | Egerton MS 2266, BM |
| Oct. 1726–Feb. 1729 | Account Book, HTC |

[1] The variations in the amounts received at the box-office from night to night are, of course, not absolute, but comparative. The appearance of a favourite actor would tend to increase the receipts; so would a benefit, the presence of royalty, the popularity of the after-piece, &c.

# CUE-TITLES AND ABBREVIATIONS

| | |
|---|---|
| Avery and Scouten | *A Tentative Calendar of Daily Theatrical Performances in London, 1700–1701 to 1704–1705* (*PMLA*, 1948, lxiii. 114–80). |
| BM | British Museum |
| BT | Benefit, *or* for the benefit of |
| CG | Covent Garden Theatre |
| C–H | Manuscript diary kept by Richard Cross and William Hopkins, successively prompters at Drury Lane (in Folger Shakespeare Library) |
| DA | *The Daily Advertiser* |
| Davies | Thomas Davies, *Dramatic Miscellanies*, London, 1784 |
| DC | *The Daily Courant* |
| DJ | *The Daily Journal* |
| DL | Drury Lane Theatre |
| Downes | John Downes, *Roscius Anglicanus*, London, 1708 |
| DP | *The Daily Post* |
| Egerton | MSS 2265–9 (in British Museum) |
| FSL | Folger Shakespeare Library |
| GA | *The General Advertiser* |
| GEC | Gabrielle Enthoven Collection (in Victoria and Albert Museum) |
| Genest | John Genest, *Some Account of the English Stage*, Bath, 1832 |
| GF | Goodman's Fields Theatre |
| Griffin | Manuscript note-book kept by Benjamin Griffin, 1715–40 (Egerton MS 2320, in British Museum) |
| Harris | Harris Collection (in British Museum) |
| Harvard Account-Book | Manuscript account-book of Lincoln's Inn Fields, 1726–8 (in Harvard Theatre Collection) |
| Hay | Haymarket Theatre |
| Hotson | Leslie Hotson, *The Commonwealth and Restoration Stage*, Cambridge (Mass.), 1928 |
| HTC | Harvard Theatre Collection (in Houghton Library, Harvard University) |
| Jaggard | William Jaggard, *Shakespeare Bibliography*, Stratford-on-Avon, 1911 |
| Latreille | Manuscript compilation of London playbills, 1702–46, made by Frederick Latreille, *c.* 1885 (Add. MSS 32249–52, in British Museum) |
| LDP | *The London Daily Post* |
| LIF | Lincoln's Inn Fields Theatre |
| MacMillan | Dougald MacMillan, *Drury Lane Calendar 1747–1776*, Oxford, 1938 |
| MWJ | *Mist's Weekly Journal* |
| Nicoll | Allardyce Nicoll, *A History of Early Eighteenth Century Drama 1700–1750*, Cambridge, 1929 |

| | |
|---|---|
| Odell | George C. D. Odell, *Shakespeare from Betterton to Irving*, New York, 1920 |
| Play-A | Manuscript play-accounts of Lincoln's Inn Fields, 1714–23 (in Folger Shakespeare Library) |
| Sp | *The Spectator* |
| Spencer | Hazelton Spencer, *Shakespeare Improved*, Cambridge (Mass.), 1927 |
| TR | Manuscript 'Theatrical Register' made by Charles Burney (in British Museum, Department of Printed Books, 938. a–d) |

PART I

# CALENDAR OF PERFORMANCES

In the two principal sections of this book I depart from a custom usually observed by historians of the stage. This custom is to date performances, or a series of performances, by the theatrical season—the season of, say, 1730–1. But since I have limited myself to an account of one dramatist only I am not primarily concerned with general theatrical history. For this reason it has seemed simpler and clearer to make use of the ordinary calendar year, from January 1 to December 31.

In the eighteenth century the patent theatres usually opened in September and closed in late May. No performances were given on Christmas Eve, Christmas Day, the anniversary of the martyrdom of Charles I (January 30), Wednesdays and Fridays in Lent, and all of Holy Week. The theatres were also dark during periods of mourning for members of the royal family, on days when General Thanksgivings or Fasts were proclaimed, and, lastly, whenever the box-office receipts were so small that the audience was dismissed.[1] The average number of acting nights in a season was approximately 180. In the early years of the century the patent theatres (i.e. the 'Theatres Royal' in Drury Lane, Covent Garden, and Lincoln's Inn Fields, which operated under a patent from the crown), as well as the Queen's, which had no patent, sometimes reopened for a brief summer season. The other, unlicensed, theatres were in use irregularly throughout the entire year.

It may be pointed out that in the eighteenth century the theatres operated on a repertory system. Each theatre had its own company of actors, and a different play (and also a different farce, or after-piece) was performed each night. New plays and revivals were frequently acted on successive nights, but the size of the theatre-going public was too small to permit any great length of run.[2]

[1] The practice of dismissal was abandoned about 1740.
[2] For an admirably complete and condensed account of general eighteenth-century theatrical practice, see Dougald MacMillan's introduction to his *Drury Lane Calendar*, 1938, xi–xxxiii.

## 1701 DRURY LANE

Jan. 1 The Tempest
17 Timon of Athens
Feb. 7 The Tempest
Mar. 4 same
Apr. 12 Caius Marius

### LINCOLN'S INN FIELDS
May ? The Jew of Venice
> The first edition of the play was published on June 17, 1701; the actual date of its first performance is conjectured from this fact. No specific knowledge of the performance of any play by Shakespeare at this theatre in 1701 has as yet come to light.

## 1702 DRURY LANE

Apr. ? The Comical Gallant
> The first edition of the play was published in May; the actual date of its first performance is conjectured from this fact.

Oct. 30 King Lear *BT. Fairbank and others*
Nov. 21 Macbeth *BT. Wilks*

### LINCOLN'S INN FIELDS
Sept. 24 Cymbeline
> Although announced as by Shakespeare, this was D'Urfey's alteration, originally known as *The Injured Princess, or the Fatal Wager*.

Oct. 7 same
13 The Tempest *BT. Underhill*

## 1703 DRURY LANE

May 24 Timon of Athens
June 17 Macbeth
July 5 Timon of Athens *BT. Newman*
Oct. 9 King Lear
23 Hamlet *BT. Wilks*
27 King Lear *BT. Mills*
Nov. 13 Hamlet
27 Macbeth
Dec. 11 Timon of Athens
18 Caius Marius
21 King Lear

### LINCOLN'S INN FIELDS
Feb. ? Love Betrayed
> The first edition of the play was published on Mar. 1, 1703; the actual date of its first performance is conjectured from this fact. The advertisements for this theatre in DC are virtually non-existent for 1703. No play by Shakespeare is announced.

May 21 Othello
> Bill not in DC. See p. 346.

2

## 1704 DRURY LANE

- Jan. 1 Macbeth
- 25 same
- Feb. 8 Hamlet
- 10 Caius Marius
- 21 Timon of Athens
- 24 Caius Marius *BT. Mrs Rogers*
- 29 Macbeth
- Apr. 4 Richard III *BT. Cibber*
- 6 Hamlet *BT. Hall and Swinny*
- 25 Macbeth
- June 19 The Tempest *BT. Mrs Rogers*
- 27 Macbeth *BT. Baggs*
- July 5 Sauny the Scot *BT. Fairbank and Bickerstaff*
  Announced as *The Taming of a Shrew*.

- Aug. 23 Titus Andronicus
- Sept. 16 same
- Oct. 7 Hamlet
  The bill is misprinted Oct. 6.

- 20 Sauny the Scot
  Announced as *The Taming of the Shrew*.

- Nov. 4 Hamlet
- 15 King Lear
- 17 Titus Andronicus
- 25 Henry IV, Part I
- 28 same
  The bill is misprinted Nov. 27.

- Dec. 2 Macbeth
- 6 Timon of Athens
- 29 Macbeth

## LINCOLN'S INN FIELDS

- Jan. 27 Timon of Athens
- Feb. 14 Julius Caesar
- 19 Othello *BT. Dogget*
- Apr. 27 same
- May 18 The Merry Wives of Windsor *BT. Betterton*
  Genest (ii. 309) erroneously has May 16.

- Nov. 6 Henry IV, Part I
  Possibly postponed. The bills both for this performance and for Nov. 9 have 'Falstaff by Mr. Betterton, being the first time of his appearing on the Stage this Season'.

## 1704 LINCOLN'S INN FIELDS (cont.)

Nov. 9 Henry IV, Part I

> Betterton's version of *Henry IV, Part II*, was first acted this year. The date is, however, conjectural. At the revival of the play in 1720 the bill has 'Not acted these 16 years'—a statement (here, as in all eighteenth-century theatrical usage) that is by no means trustworthy. From Sept. through Dec. 1704 the bills for this theatre were printed in DC very irregularly, and the play might well have been produced during that period. Genest is inconsistent; he states (iii. 46) that in 1720 the play had not been acted for 17 years (a misreading of the bill), and (ii. 461) that Betterton probably first played Falstaff in *Part II* in 1700.

## 1705 DRURY LANE

Jan.  5 Henry IV, Part I
      26 Timon of Athens
      31 Hamlet
Apr. 17 Macbeth
July  7 Hamlet *BT. the box-keepers*
      13 King Lear
Nov.  6 Hamlet
      13 Macbeth
      28 Hamlet
Dec. 15 Henry IV, Part I
      19 same
      22 Caius Marius
      29 Macbeth

## LINCOLN'S INN FIELDS

Mar.  1 Love Betrayed *BT. Pack and Mrs Bradshaw*
        Announced as *The Agreeable Disappointment*.

       3 Othello *BT. Betterton*
Oct. 19 Timon of Athens

## QUEEN'S

Apr. 23 The Merry Wives of Windsor
May  3 Henry VIII
June  2 Othello
Dec. 13 The Merry Wives of Windsor
      22 Othello

## 1706 DRURY LANE

Jan.  1 Timon of Athens
Feb.  5 Macbeth
Mar.  5 The Tempest *BT. Estcourt*
Apr. 25 Hamlet
June 18 same *BT. the charge of repairing and fitting up the chapel in Russel-Court*
Dec. 26 The Tempest

## 1706 QUEEN'S

    Mar. 14  Julius Caesar
    Apr. 26  Measure for Measure *BT. Mrs Willis and Mrs Porter*

             The advertisement attributes the play to 'the famous Beaumont and Fletcher'.[1]

        30  King Lear *BT. Knapp, Mrs Baker, and Minns*
    Aug. 13  same
    Oct. 19  Hamlet
        23  The Jew of Venice
        26  Henry IV, Part I
        30  King Lear
    Nov. 6  Henry IV, Part I
    Dec. 4  same
        10  Hamlet
        26  Henry IV, Part I

## 1707 DRURY LANE

    Jan.  1  The Tempest
         9  Timon of Athens
        21  The Tempest
        23  Macbeth
        31  same
    Feb. 11  Timon of Athens
        13  The Tempest
    Apr. 16  Macbeth
    Oct. 29  Timon of Athens
    Nov. 20  The Tempest
        28  Macbeth
    Dec. 10  Timon of Athens
        27  The Tempest

## QUEEN'S

    Jan. 11  Hamlet
        14  Julius Caesar *BT. the encouragement of the comedians acting in the Hay-Market, and to enable them to keep the diversion of plays under a separate interest from operas*

        15  same
        28  Othello
    Feb. 15  Henry VIII
        18  Caius Marius *BT. Wilks*
        19  same
        27  Henry VIII
    Apr. 1  Julius Caesar *BT. Keene*
        28  Hamlet *BT. Mrs Bradshaw*
    June 18  same
        27  Timon of Athens *BT. Corey and Mrs Willis*

[1] Gildon's alteration. An advertisement in his *Love's Victim*, 1701, reads, 'Measure for Measure a Comedy alter'd from Beaumont [sic] and Fletcher by Mr. Gilden'.

1707 QUEEN'S (*cont.*)
    July  4  Sauny the Scot
              Announced as *The Taming of a Shrew.*

         16  Timon of Athens
    Aug.  5  Sauny the Scot
    Oct. 15  same
              Both performances announced as *The Taming of a Shrew.*

    Nov. 19  Henry IV, Part I
        22  Hamlet
    Dec. 27  Macbeth
        29  same

## 1708 DRURY LANE

    Jan.  1  King Lear
        15  Hamlet
        24  Henry IV, Part I
    Mar. 11  Henry VIII *BT. Betterton*
    Apr. 24  Macbeth
    June 11  Hamlet *BT. Corey and Fairbank*
        19  Sauny the Scot
              Announced as *The Taming of a Shrew.*

    July  1  Timon of Athens
        29  The Tempest
    Sept.  9  Hamlet
        14  Macbeth
    Oct.  9  Othello *BT. Thurmond*
        16  Macbeth
        21  King Lear
        28  [Henry IV, Part I]
              Bill in DC, but not acted on account of the death of Prince George, consort of Queen Anne (Genest, ii. 423).

## QUEEN'S

    Jan. 10  Macbeth *BT. Wilks*

## 1709 DRURY LANE

    Jan.  1  Henry IV, Part I
         6  Macbeth
        22  Hamlet
        26  Henry VIII
    Mar. 10  Henry IV, Part I
        24  Othello
    Apr. 27  King Lear *BT. Husband and Mrs Willis*
    May  7  Hamlet *BT. Mrs Moore*
        20  Macbeth

## 1709–1710

**1709 DRURY LANE** (*cont.*)
- June  2  Troilus and Cressida
-            3  Hamlet *BT. Cave Underhill*
- Dec. 10  Timon of Athens
-           22  Julius Caesar
-           29  Timon of Athens

**QUEEN'S**
- Sept. 15  Othello
-            20  Hamlet
- Nov.   4  same
-           28  Macbeth
-           30  same
- Dec. 17  same
-           27  same

**1710 DRURY LANE**
- Jan. 20  The Tempest
-           21  Othello *BT. Booth*
-           24  The Tempest
- Feb.   2  same
-           10  same
-           14  Hamlet *BT. Mrs Santlow*
-           18  Caius Marius *BT. Norris*
-           23  Hamlet
- Apr. 13  The Tempest
-           22  Julius Caesar *BT. Mrs Hodgson*
- May    5  Timon of Athens
-             9  Hamlet
-           12  The Tempest *BT. Cave Underhill*
-           17  Caius Marius *BT. the author of the farce* [The Twin Adventurers, also acted this night]

> The announcement concerning the BT. appears only in the *Tatler* of May 6–9, when it was advertised for May 11. DC of May 12 announces the postponement of the farce until May 17, but no further mention of a BT. is made anywhere. The author of the farce is unknown.

-           18  Othello *BT. Pervill and Sherman*
- Nov. 30  King Lear
- Dec.   2  Henry IV, Part I

**QUEEN'S**
- Jan.   2  Hamlet
-           28  Richard III
- Feb.   4  King Lear
- Mar. 20  Macbeth *BT. Mrs Rogers*
-           27  Richard III *BT. Mrs Porter*

7

1710 QUEEN'S (*cont.*)
    Apr. 24 Macbeth *BT. Bowen*
          27 Hamlet *BT. Mrs Powell and Hall*
    May 4 Henry IV, Part I *BT. Evans*
         13 Richard III
    June 22 Othello *BT. Cibber*
    July 26 Hamlet *BT. Mills*
    Nov. 11 same
         18 Macbeth

1711 DRURY LANE
    Jan. 13 Macbeth
         18 Othello
    Feb. 3 The Jew of Venice
         17 Timon of Athens
    Mar. 17 Caius Marius
         24 Hamlet
    Apr. 5 Macbeth
         24 Othello *BT. Booth*
         28 King Lear
    May 3 Hamlet *BT. Keene*
         8 Henry IV, Part I *BT. Bullock*
    June 22 Timon of Athens
    July 10 Sauny the Scot
            Announced as *The Taming of a Shrew.*
    Oct. 20 Macbeth
         27 Hamlet
         30 Timon of Athens
    Nov. 6 Henry IV, Part I
         10 King Lear
         27 Othello
    Dec. 22 Macbeth

1712 DRURY LANE
    Jan. 7 The Tempest
         8 same
         10 same
         11 same
         15 same
         17 same
         24 same
    Feb. 1 same
         6 Sauny the Scot
            Announced as *The Taming of a Shrew.*
         15 The Tempest
         26 King Lear
    Mar. 6 Macbeth

**1712 DRURY LANE** (*cont.*)

- Mar. 15 The Tempest
- Apr. 5 Julius Caesar
  - 7 Henry IV, Part I *BT. Powell*
  - 8 Julius Caesar
  - 21 The Tempest
  - 24 Julius Caesar
  - 25 Hamlet *BT. Booth*
- May 10 The Tempest
  - 12 Caius Marius *BT. Mrs Bradshaw*
  - 17 Timon of Athens
  - 22 Othello *BT. Pack*
- June 5 Macbeth *BT. Mrs Mills*
- July 4 Sauny the Scot
    Announced as *The Taming of a Shrew*.

- Oct. 4 Hamlet
  - 14 Othello
  - 23 King Lear
  - 25 Macbeth
- Nov. 4 Hamlet
  - 5 The Tempest
  - 15 Julius Caesar
  - 20 Caius Marius
  - 21 The Tempest
  - 22 Macbeth
- Dec. 11 Julius Caesar
  - 20 Hamlet
  - 26 The Tempest

**1713 DRURY LANE**

- Jan. 1 The Tempest
  - 8 King Lear
  - 20 Julius Caesar
  - 24 Macbeth
  - 27 Othello
- Feb. 6 The Tempest
  - 14 Richard III
  - 26 same
- Mar. 16 Julius Caesar *BT. Mills*
  - 26 Othello
- Apr. 6 Julius Caesar *BT. Penkethman*
  - 7 The Tempest
  - 27 Richard III *BT. Mrs Bicknell*
- May 4 Julius Caesar *BT. Keene*
  - 18 Henry IV, Part I *BT. Bullock*
- June 5 Macbeth *BT. Bickerstaff*
  - 18 Caius Marius *BT. Boman*
  - 23 The Tempest *BT. Mrs Mills and Mrs Saunders*

9

## 1713 DRURY LANE (cont.)

 Sept. 22 Macbeth
   26 Julius Caesar
 Oct. 3 Othello
   17 Hamlet
   27 Julius Caesar
   31 Caius Marius
 Nov. 5 The Tempest
   21 King Lear
 Dec. 8 Macbeth
   19 Hamlet
   26 The Tempest
   28 same

## 1714 DRURY LANE

 Jan. 2 Richard III
   14 Othello
   19 Macbeth
   23 Julius Caesar
 Feb. 27 Richard III
 Mar. 20 Hamlet
   30 The Tempest
 Apr. 12 Julius Caesar *BT. Johnson*
   17 Richard III
   23 Hamlet *BT. Mrs Mountfort*
   26 King Lear *BT. Keene*
 May 17 Timon of Athens *BT. Husband and Boman*
 June 2 Henry IV, Part I *BT. Corey and Cross*
   4 The Tempest *BT. Newman and Mrs Baker*
   16 Timon of Athens *BT. Mrs Powell and King, the box-keeper*
   18 Macbeth
 July 13 Sauny the Scot
    Announced as *The Taming of a Shrew*.
 Oct. 7 Othello
   9 Julius Caesar
   15 Richard III
   21 Macbeth
   30 Caius Marius
 Nov. 25 The Tempest
 Dec. 3 same
   4 Hamlet
   9 King Lear
   13 The Tempest
   18 King Lear

## 1715 DRURY LANE

 Jan. 1 The Tempest
   4 King Lear

## 1715 DRURY LANE (cont.)

- Jan. 15 Othello
- 20 The Tempest
- 22 Hamlet
- 24 Julius Caesar
- 27 Richard III
- Feb. 1 Hamlet
- 2 The Tempest
- 12 Henry IV, Part I
- 14 same
- 18 The Tempest
- 21 Caius Marius
- Mar. 26 Hamlet *BT. Mrs Mountfort*
- Apr. 18 The Tempest
- May 13 Julius Caesar *BT. Birkhead*
- 27 Hamlet *BT. Mrs Mills*
- June 10 The Tempest *BT. Chetwood, prompter, and King, box-keeper*
- July 12 same
- Aug. 16 same
- Nov. 12 Hamlet
- 17 Timon of Athens
- 18 The Tempest
- 22 Timon of Athens
- 24 Julius Caesar
- 29 King Lear
- Dec. 6 Richard III
- 22 Hamlet
- 27 Timon of Athens

## LINCOLN'S INN FIELDS

|  |  |  | £ | s. | d. |
|---|---|---|---|---|---|
| Feb. | 28 | The Jew of Venice | 63 | 16 | 6 |
| Mar. | 3 | Macbeth | 56 | 12 | 0 |
|  | 8 | same | 52 | 5 | 6 |
|  | 17 | same | 64 | 15 | 6 |
|  | 22 | The Jew of Venice | 27 | 8 | 0 |
|  | 24 | Timon of Athens *BT. Pack* | 158 | 11 | 6 |
|  | 28 | Macbeth | 28 | 12 | 6 |
| Apr. | 4 | Henry IV, Part I *BT. Hall* | 64 | 10 | 6 |
|  | 22 | Timon of Athens | 31 | 6 | 0 |
| June | 30 | Hamlet | 35 | 14 | 6 |
| July | 8 | The Jew of Venice *BT. Henry Rich, pit office-keeper* | 124 | 1 | 6 |
|  | 14 | Hamlet *BT. the gallery, box- and door-keepers* | 78 | 4 | 6 |
| Sept. | 27 | same . | 50 | 7 | 0 |
| Oct. | 18 | Macbeth | 26 | 16 | 6 |
|  | 29 | same | 30 | 2 | 0 |
| Nov. | 11 | Timon of Athens | 25 | 5 | 0 |
|  | 18 | The Jew of Venice | 12 | 19 | 0 |
| Dec. | 17 | Macbeth | 27 | 11 | 6 |

11

## 1716 DRURY LANE

- Jan. 6 The Tempest
- 7 Othello
- 10 Macbeth
- 13 Caius Marius
- 18 Othello
- Feb. 3 The Cobler of Preston
- 4 same
- 6 same *BT. the author* [*Charles Johnson*]
- 8 same
- 9 same
- 10 same
- 14 same
- 16 same
- 18 same
- 21 same
- 23 same
- 25 same
- 27 same
- 28 Timon of Athens
- Mar. 3 Henry IV, Part I
- 12 Hamlet *BT. Cibber*
- 22 Julius Caesar *BT. Booth*
- Apr. 5 The Cobler of Preston *BT. Penkethman*
- 6 same
- 21 Hamlet *BT. Bickerstaff*
- 25 The Tempest
- May 1 Othello *BT. Quin*
- 11 Henry IV, Part I *BT. Cross and Wilks's nephew* [*W. Wilks*]
- 16 Timon of Athens *BT. Birkhead*
- 24 Julius Caesar *BT. Boman*
- June 1 King Lear *BT. Thurmond*
- 5 Hamlet *BT. Wilks's brother, the office-keeper* [*W. Wilks Sr.*]
- 8 The Tempest *BT. Weller, Boman Jr., and Maddocks*
- July 31 same
- Aug. 7 same
- 23 same
- Oct. 2 Henry IV, Part I
- 6 Hamlet
- 13 Macbeth
- 18 Timon of Athens
- 20 Julius Caesar
- 25 The Cobler of Preston
- 26 same
- Nov. 19 Henry VIII
- 20 same
- 21 same
- 23 same
- 24 same

# 1716

**1716 DRURY LANE** (*cont.*)

| | | | | | |
|---|---|---|---|---|---|
| Dec. | 1 | Othello | | | |
| | 8 | Henry VIII | | | |
| | 26 | same | | | |
| | 28 | The Tempest | | | |

## LINCOLN'S INN FIELDS

| | | | £ | s. | d. |
|---|---|---|---|---|---|
| Jan. | 20 | The Jew of Venice | 11 | 17 | 6 |
| | 24 | The Cobler of Preston | 26 | 19 | 6 |
| | 25 | same | 21 | 16 | 6 |
| | 26 | same | 24 | 7 | 0 |
| | 27 | same | 26 | 18 | 0 |
| | 31 | same | 27 | 18 | 6 |
| Feb. | 1 | same | 18 | 19 | 6 |
| | 2 | same | 26 | 2 | 6 |
| | 3 | same | 15 | 13 | 6 |
| | 4 | same | 25 | 6 | 0 |
| | 16 | same | 31 | 12 | 0 |
| | 27 | same | 22 | 6 | 0 |
| Mar. | 1 | same | 45 | 13 | 6 |
| | 3 | same *BT. Keene* | 154 | 4 | 0 |
| | 10 | Every Body Mistaken | 31 | 10 | 0 |
| | 12 | same | 28 | 16 | 0 |
| | 13 | same *BT. the authors* [*William Taverner and Dr Brown*] | 114 | 17 | 0 |

The recipients of the BT. are named in Play-A, but not in DC. Dr Brown I have been unable to identify.

| | | | | | |
|---|---|---|---|---|---|
| | 15 | Henry IV, Part I *BT. Pack* | 137 | 3 | 0 |
| Apr. | 2 | The Cobler of Preston | 25 | 18 | 6 |
| | 5 | same *BT. Mrs Knight* | 51 | 10 | 6 |
| | 11 | Pyramus and Thisbe *BT. Leveridge* | 112 | 14 | 6 |
| | 13 | Macbeth *BT. Husband* | 52 | 5 | 6 |
| | 14 | The Cobler of Preston *BT. Mrs Hunt* | 44 | 8 | 6 |
| | 16 | [Hamlet *BT. Thurmond*] | | | |

Bill in DC, but 'No play by reason Mr. Thurmond did not lay down 20 Guineas in the Office for his benefit' (Play-A).

| | | | | | |
|---|---|---|---|---|---|
| | 17 | Henry IV, Part I *BT. Mrs Bullock* | 45 | 3 | 6 |
| | 19 | The Cobler of Preston *BT. Spiller* | 54 | 12 | 6 |
| | 21 | [Pyramus and Thisbe *BT. Shaw*] | | | |

Announced in DC of Apr. 18 and 19, but not in DC of Apr. 21, nor in Play-A. It was almost certainly not acted on this day: the bills for Oct. 25, 26, and 29 have, respectively, 'Never perform'd but once [twice, thrice]'.

| | | | | | |
|---|---|---|---|---|---|
| May | 2 | Timon of Athens *BT. Smith and Corey* | 86 | 5 | 6 |
| | 21 | The Cobler of Preston *BT. Mrs Spiller* | 27 | 13 | 6 |
| | 24 | Macbeth | 15 | 18 | 6 |

## 1716 LINCOLN'S INN FIELDS (cont.)

|  |  |  | £ | s. | d. |
|---|---|---|---|---|---|
| June | 20 | Sauny the Scot | 17 | 3 | 6 |
|  | 27 | same | 20 | 2 | 6 |

        Both performances announced as *The Taming of the Shrew*.

| July | 6 | The Cobler of Preston | 23 | 14 | 6 |
|---|---|---|---|---|---|
|  | 13 | same | 19 | 11 | 6 |
|  | 20 | The Jew of Venice *and* The Cobler of Preston | 18 | 16 | 6 |
|  | 25 | Sauny the Scot *BT.* Mrs Schoolding | 21 | 16 | 6 |

        Announced as *The Taming of the Shrew*.

| Aug. | 15 | The Cobler of Preston | 15 | 6 | 6 |
|---|---|---|---|---|---|
| Oct. | 6 | Hamlet | 57 | 17 | 6 |
|  | 17 | The Cobler of Preston | 25 | 12 | 0 |
|  | 20 | Henry IV, Part I | 47 | 2 | 0 |
|  | 22 | Sauny the Scot | 17 | 12 | 0 |

        Announced as *The Taming of the Shrew*.

|  | 25 | Pyramus and Thisbe | 49 | 3 | 6 |
|---|---|---|---|---|---|
|  | 26 | same | 30 | 0 | 0 |
|  | 27 | Julius Caesar | 48 | 9 | 0 |
|  | 29 | Pyramus and Thisbe | 29 | 6 | 0 |

        Genest (ii. 604) implies that this was the first performance. The bill for Apr. 11, however, has, 'A Comic Masque, never perform'd before'. And see note under Apr. 21, *supra*.

|  | 30 | Macbeth | 26 | 15 | 0 |
|---|---|---|---|---|---|
| Nov. | 8 | Julius Caesar | 29 | 18 | 6 |
|  | 10 | Hamlet | 48 | 16 | 0 |
|  | 21 | Pyramus and Thisbe | 32 | 18 | 6 |
|  | 22 | Timon of Athens *and* Pyramus and Thisbe | 48 | 18 | 6 |
| Dec. | 12 | Henry IV, Part I | 21 | 1 | 6 |
|  | 28 | The Cobler of Preston | 50 | 10 | 6 |
|  | 29 | Pyramus and Thisbe | 70 | 6 | 6 |

## 1717 DRURY LANE

| Jan. | 1 | Richard III |
|---|---|---|
|  | 5 | King Lear |
|  | 12 | Hamlet |
|  | 14 | Macbeth |
|  | 29 | Timon of Athens |
| Feb. | 1 | Macbeth |
|  | 12 | The Tempest |
|  | 21 | Henry VIII |
| Mar. | 4 | same |
| Apr. | 8 | Hamlet *BT. Johnson* |
|  | 22 | The Tempest |

## 1717 DRURY LANE (cont.)

|        |    |                                          |
|--------|---:|------------------------------------------|
| Apr.   | 27 | Julius Caesar *BT. Bickerstaff*          |
| May    |  2 | Othello *BT. Ryan*                       |
|        |  9 | Macbeth *BT. Quin*                       |
|        | 10 | Caius Marius *BT. Chetwood and Mrs Moore* |
|        | 21 | Henry IV, Part I *BT. Prince*            |
|        | 24 | Henry VIII *BT. Walker*                  |
| June   | 10 | The Tempest                              |
| Aug.   | 13 | Titus Andronicus                         |
|        | 16 | same                                     |
|        | 20 | same                                     |
|        | 23 | same                                     |
| Sept.  | 28 | Hamlet                                   |
| Oct.   |  5 | Henry VIII                               |
|        |  8 | Macbeth                                  |
|        | 11 | Timon of Athens                          |
|        | 15 | Henry IV, Part I                         |
|        | 22 | Othello                                  |
| Nov.   |  9 | Richard III                              |
|        | 14 | King Lear                                |
|        | 16 | Julius Caesar                            |
|        | 19 | Caius Marius                             |
| Dec.   |  2 | Henry VIII                               |
|        |  5 | The Tempest                              |
|        | 31 | Macbeth                                  |

## LINCOLN'S INN FIELDS

|        |    |                                                                   | £   | s. | d. |
|--------|---:|-------------------------------------------------------------------|----:|---:|---:|
| Jan.   |  1 | Macbeth                                                           |  66 |  4 | 6  |
|        |  3 | Julius Caesar                                                     |  33 |  5 | 6  |
|        | 25 | Pyramus and Thisbe                                                |  31 | 11 | 6  |
|        | 31 | same                                                              |  39 |  7 | 0  |
| Feb.   |  2 | Hamlet                                                            |  23 | 11 | 6  |
| Mar.   | 23 | Timon of Athens *and* Pyramus and Thisbe                          |  34 | 12 | 6  |
|        | 25 | Hamlet *BT. Pack*                                                 | 180 | 15 | 6  |
|        | 28 | Macbeth *BT. Bullock Sr.*                                         | receipts omitted |||
| Apr.   |  4 | Julius Caesar *BT. Leveridge*                            money:[1] |  47 |  0 | 0  |
|        | 25 | Hamlet *BT. Mrs Bullock*                                          | 105 |  4 | 6  |
| May    |  2 | Henry IV, Part I *BT. [C.] Bullock*                               |  76 | 18 | 0  |
|        |  3 | Julius Caesar *BT. Settle*                                        |  61 | 17 | 6  |

The recipient of the BT. is named in Play-A, but not in DC.

|        |    |                                                                   |    |    |    |
|--------|---:|-------------------------------------------------------------------|---:|---:|---:|
|        | 13 | Macbeth *BT. Smith*                                               | 57 |  4 | 0  |
|        | 16 | The Jew of Venice *BT. Griffin, Coker, and Mrs Robertson*         | 57 |  4 | 0  |
|        | 27 | Hamlet *BT. Henry Rich, pit office-keeper*                        | 58 |  6 | 6  |

[1] i.e. the box-office receipts only. Recipients of a BT. were always given tickets which they were allowed to sell privately. On this night these additional receipts are omitted by Play-A.

1717-1718

## 1717 LINCOLN'S INN FIELDS (cont.)

£ s. d.

June 12 Sauny the Scot *BT. Miss Smith and others* [*Kelloms, Schollar, Buck, Cross, and Williams*]     70 12 0
         Announced as *The Taming of the Shrew*. The additional recipients of the BT. are named in Play-A.

    25 The Cobler of Preston     16 0 6
July  5 same     18 18 6
Oct.  5 Cymbeline     receipts omitted
    9 same     "
    12 same     "
    25 same *BT. J. and C. M. Rich*     61 8 0
         The recipients of the BT. are named in Play-A, but not in DC.

    28 The Cobler of Preston
Nov.  7 Julius Caesar
    13 Sauny the Scot
         Genest (ii. 625) erroneously has Nov. 15.

    30 Cymbeline
Dec. 26 same
    31 The Cobler of Preston

## 1718 DRURY LANE

Jan.  2 Henry IV, Part I
Feb.  1 Hamlet
    8 Othello
Mar.  1 King Lear
    15 Richard III
Apr. 17 Henry VIII *BT*. [*F*.] *Leigh*
May  1 Macbeth *BT. Shepard, Williams, and Oates*
    2 Timon of Athens *BT. Shaw*
    16 Henry IV, Part I *BT. Castleman*
June 11 The Tempest
July  8 Titus Andronicus
Aug.  1 The Tempest
Sept. 20 Hamlet
    23 same
         This performance took place, by command, at Hampton Court (Play-A). Bill not in DC.

    25 King Lear
    27 Henry IV, Part I
    30 Henry VIII
Oct.  1 same
         At Hampton Court. See note under Sept. 23.

Nov. 13 Julius Caesar
    20 King Lear
    25 Othello
    27 Macbeth

## 1718–1719

### 1718 DRURY LANE (cont.)

Dec. 11 The Tempest
20 Hamlet

### LINCOLN'S INN FIELDS

|  |  |  | £ | s. | d. |
|---|---|---|---|---|---|
| Jan. | 3 | Macbeth *BT. J. and C. M. Rich* | 56 | 7 | 0 |

The recipients of the BT. are named in Play-A, but not in DC.

7 Henry IV, Part I — receipts omitted
10 Timon of Athens *BT. J. and C. M. Rich* — 48 12 6

The recipients of the BT. are named in Play-A, but not in DC.

24 The Jew of Venice — 47 4 6
Feb. 17 The Cobler of Preston
27 Timon of Athens *BT. Bullock Sr.*
Mar. 1 Julius Caesar *BT. Ryan*
3 Macbeth *BT. [J.] Leigh*
17 Julius Caesar *BT. Mrs Barbier*
Apr. 23 Cymbeline *BT. Corey and Ogden*
26 The Jew of Venice *BT. Babell*
May 3 The Cobler of Preston *BT. H. Bullock, Giffard, Egleton, and Mrs Robertson*
29 same *BT. the pit door-keepers and gallery box-keepers*
Sept. 30 Henry IV, Part I
Oct. 23 Cymbeline
Nov. 1 Julius Caesar
13 Macbeth
15 Cymbeline
25 Julius Caesar

Genest (ii. 650) erroneously has Nov. 27.

Dec. 13 Coriolanus
15 same
16 same
29 Macbeth

### 1719 DRURY LANE

Jan. 10 Henry IV, Part I
13 Macbeth
28 Julius Caesar
Feb. 9 The Tempest
12 Richard III
Mar. 30 The Tempest *BT. Mrs Santlow*
Apr. 4 Macbeth
6 Henry VIII *BT. Mrs Bicknell*
24 Julius Caesar *BT. Walker*

## 1719 DRURY LANE (cont.)

- May   6   Othello *BT. Birkhead*
-         7   Henry IV, Part I *BT. Williams and Oates*
-      15   Macbeth *BT. Topham*
- July 21   The Tempest
-      28   Titus Andronicus

    Genest (ii. 647) erroneously has June 28.

- Sept. 12   Hamlet
-       19   Macbeth
-       26   Richard III
- Oct. 10   Othello
-      22   Henry IV, Part I
- Nov. 11   The Invader of his Country
-      12   same
-      13   same *BT. the author [John Dennis]*
-      19   King Lear
-      24   Timon of Athens
-      28   Henry VIII
- Dec. 26   Macbeth

## LINCOLN'S INN FIELDS

- Jan.   2   The Jew of Venice
- Feb. 16   Macbeth
-      23   Cymbeline
-      26   Hamlet *BT. Ryan*
- Mar. 30   same
- Apr.   4   Henry IV, Part I *BT. Mons. and Mrs Moreau*
-      25   Julius Caesar *BT. Mrs Fletcher*
-      30   Hamlet *BT. Hall and Laguerre*
- May 12   Macbeth
- Oct.   2   Henry IV, Part I
-      13   Macbeth
-      17   Hamlet
- Nov. 14   Coriolanus

    Announced as *The Invader of his Country*.

-      16   Hamlet
-      19   Julius Caesar
- Dec. 10   Richard II
-      11   same
-      12   same *BT. the author [Lewis Theobald]*
-      14   same

    Play-A states that this performance was for Theobald's BT., which, since this was the fourth night, is unlikely.[1]

-      18   Macbeth

[1] Custom dictated the third, sixth, and ninth nights of a play's run as being for the BT. of the author.

## 1719–1720

**1719 LINCOLN'S INN FIELDS** (*cont.*)
- Dec. 19 Richard II
- 21 Sauny the Scot
- 29 same
  - Both performances announced as *The Taming of the Shrew*.

**1720 DRURY LANE**
- Jan. 2 Hamlet
- 5 Caius Marius
- 6 The Tempest
- 9 King Lear
- Feb. 11 Othello
- 13 Richard III
- Mar. 14 Hamlet *BT. Mills*
- 28 Henry VIII *BT. Mrs Thurmond*
- Apr. 7 King Lear *BT. Penkethman*
- 20 The Tempest
- 28 Othello *BT. Walker*
- 30 Hamlet *BT. [W.] Wilks*
- May 3 Macbeth *BT. Mrs Horton*
- 11 Henry VIII *BT. Corey and Williams*
- 19 Richard III *BT. Cross and Jones*
- 20 Timon of Athens *BT. Oates*
- June 24 The Tempest
- Aug. 9 same
- Sept. 17 Henry IV, Part I
- 24 Othello
- Oct. 1 King Lear
- 18 Timon of Athens
- 24 Othello
- Nov. 2 Macbeth
- 10 Hamlet
- 15 Henry IV, Part I
- 24 King Lear
- Dec. 3 Richard III
- 6 Caius Marius
- 8 Timon of Athens
- 15 Caius Marius
- 17 Henry IV, Part II
- 19 same
- 20 same
- 21 same
- 22 same
- 26 The Tempest
- 29 Macbeth
- 30 Henry IV, Part II
- 31 Hamlet

19

## 1720

### 1720 LINCOLN'S INN FIELDS

|  |  |  | £ | s. | d. |
|---|---|---|---|---|---|
| Jan. | 1 | Coriolanus | 33 | 5 | 6 |
|  |  | Announced as *The Invader of his Country*. | | | |
|  | 2 | Richard II | receipts omitted | | |
|  | 7 | Cymbeline | ,, | | |
|  | 20 | same | 29 | 16 | 6 |
|  | 25 | Richard II | receipts omitted | | |
| Feb. | 3 | Hamlet | 31 | 2 | 0 |
|  | 8 | Sauny the Scot | receipts omitted | | |
|  |  | Announced as *The Taming of the Shrew*. | | | |
|  | 9 | Henry IV, Part I | ,, | | |
|  | 15 | Macbeth | ,, | | |
|  | 20 | Hamlet | ,, | | |
|  | 26 | The Jew of Venice | 63 | 12 | 0 |
| Mar. | 12 | Othello *BT. Quin* | receipts omitted | | |
|  | 14 | Cymbeline *BT. Keene's widow* | ,, | | |
|  | 17 | Macbeth | ,, | | |
|  | 19 | Othello *BT. J. Rich* | 86 | 11 | 6 |
|  |  | The recipient of the BT. is named in Play-A, but not in DP. | | | |
|  | 22 | Hamlet *BT. Leveridge* | receipts omitted | | |
|  | 31 | The Cobler of Preston *BT. Spiller* | ,, | | |
| Apr. | 2 | Hamlet | ,, | | |
|  | 9 | Julius Caesar *BT. [J.] Leigh* | ,, | | |
|  | 18 | Macbeth | ,, | | |
|  | 29 | Henry IV, Part I *BT. Topham Jr. and Sandham's son* | ,, | | |
|  |  | Sandham's son is named in Play-A, but not in DP. | | | |
| May | 21 | Othello *BT. Hulett* | ,, | | |
|  | 30 | Hamlet *BT. Randal, Rowland, and Gallant, pit door-keepers* | ,, | | |
| June | 9 | Cymbeline *BT. Chris. Bullock and Pack* | ,, | | |
| Oct. | 1 | Hamlet | 52 | 9 | 0 |
|  | 15 | King Lear | 49 | 17 | 0 |
|  | 20 | Othello | 36 | 2 | 4½ |
|  | 22 | The Merry Wives of Windsor | 99 | 14 | 0 |
|  | 24 | same | 92 | 0 | 0 |
|  | 25 | same | 45 | 16 | 0 |
|  | 26 | same | 45 | 1 | 6 |
|  | 27 | Hamlet *BT. Chr. Bullock* | 76 | 15 | 6 |
|  | 29 | The Merry Wives of Windsor | 77 | 3 | 0 |
| Nov. | 1 | Julius Caesar | 29 | 11 | 6 |
|  | 3 | Cymbeline | 15 | 16 | 0 |
|  | 5 | King Lear | 68 | 14 | 6 |
|  | 8 | The Merry Wives of Windsor | 55 | 16 | 0 |
|  | 10 | Troilus and Cressida | 86 | 11 | 0 |

20

## 1720–1721

**1720 LINCOLN'S INN FIELDS** (*cont.*)

|  |  |  | £ | s. | d. |
|---|---|---|---|---|---|
| Nov. | 11 | Troilus and Cressida | 21 | 8 | 6 |
|  | 12 | same | 44 | 16 | 0 |
|  | 17 | The Merry Wives of Windsor | 65 | 19 | 6 |
|  | 19 | Macbeth | 38 | 14 | 0 |
|  | 24 | Coriolanus | 38 | 2 | 6 |
| Dec. | 3 | The Merry Wives of Windsor | 87 | 7 | 6 |
|  | 8 | Measure for Measure | 34 | 10 | 6 |
|  | 9 | same | 15 | 0 | 6 |
|  | 10 | same | 52 | 19 | 0 |
|  | 12 | same | 26 | 12 | 0 |
|  | 13 | same | 20 | 11 | 6 |
|  | 15 | The Merry Wives of Windsor | 78 | 19 | 6 |
|  | 21 | Titus Andronicus | 35 | 0 | 6 |
|  | 26 | Coriolanus | 92 | 14 | 0 |
|  | 29 | The Merry Wives of Windsor | 64 | 5 | 6 |
|  | 30 | Titus Andronicus | 29 | 15 | 0 |
|  | 31 | King Lear | 49 | 12 | 6 |

**1721 DRURY LANE**

Jan. 12 Henry VIII
    26 Julius Caesar
Feb. 21 King Lear
Mar. 4 Julius Caesar
    11 Othello
    16 Hamlet *BT. Mrs Booth*
Apr. 26 Julius Caesar *BT. Thurmond Sr.*
May 6 Caius Marius *BT. Birkhead*
    12 Hamlet *BT. [W.] Wilks [Sr.], the office-keeper*
    13 Henry VIII *BT. Boval and Mrs Moore*
    20 The Tempest *BT. Rogers and Theoph. Cibber*
    24 Timon of Athens *BT. Watson and Cross*
June 27 Titus Andronicus
Aug. 22 The Tempest
Sept. 16 Macbeth
    26 Henry IV, Part I
    30 Hamlet
Oct. 3 Julius Caesar
    7 King Lear
    10 Timon of Athens
    31 Henry VIII
Nov. 18 Othello
Dec. 1 Caius Marius
    9 Hamlet
    16 Macbeth
    19 Henry VIII
    26 Richard III
    30 King Lear

## 1721

### 1721 LINCOLN'S INN FIELDS   £ s. d.

| | | | | | |
|---|---|---|---|---|---|
| Jan. | 2 | Measure for Measure | 65 | 17 | 6 |
| | 5 | Othello | 25 | 13 | 0 |
| | 7 | Richard II | 86 | 9 | 0 |
| | 9 | Hamlet | 40 | 12 | 0 |
| | 14 | The Merry Wives of Windsor | 72 | 3 | 0 |
| | 23 | Measure for Measure | 53 | 7 | 0 |
| | 24 | King Lear *BT. C. Bullock* | 72 | 12 | 0 |
| | 26 | The Merry Wives of Windsor | 76 | 11 | 6 |
| | 27 | same *and* The Cobler of Preston | 42 | 15 | 0 |
| | 28 | Henry IV, Part I | 27 | 17 | 6 |
| Feb. | 1 | Macbeth | 20 | 16 | 6 |

   The performance was interrupted by a riot. See DP, Feb. 3; and Genest, iii. 57–9.

| | | | | | |
|---|---|---|---|---|---|
| | 4 | Richard II | 23 | 9 | 0 |
| | 7 | Titus Andronicus | 16 | 9 | 0 |
| | 9 | Much Ado about Nothing | 26 | 11 | 6 |
| | 10 | same | 13 | 9 | 6 |
| | 11 | same | 19 | 19 | 6 |
| | 16 | The Merry Wives of Windsor *BT. Pack* | 123 | 9 | 6 |
| | 18 | Troilus and Cressida | 23 | 5 | 0 |
| | 23 | Othello | 21 | 0 | 0 |
| | 27 | Hamlet *BT. a gentleman in trouble* | 79 | 2 | 0 |
| Mar. | 9 | The Merry Wives of Windsor *BT. C. M. Rich* | 130 | 10 | 6 |

   The recipient of the BT. is named in Play-A, but not in DP.

| | | | | | |
|---|---|---|---|---|---|
| | 11 | Richard III *BT. Ryan* | 79 | 17 | 0 |
| | 13 | same | 23 | 13 | 0 |
| | 16 | King Lear *BT. Mrs Seymour* | 101 | 6 | 0 |
| | 25 | Measure for Measure *BT. Keene's widow* | 58 | 15 | 6 |
| | 27 | Richard III *BT. Ryan* | 44 | 3 | 6 |
| | 28 | The Jew of Venice *BT. Longueville* | 42 | 9 | 0 |
| | 30 | The Merry Wives of Windsor *BT. J. Rich* | 123 | 14 | 6 |

   The recipient of the BT. is named in Play-A, but not in DP.

| | | | | | |
|---|---|---|---|---|---|
| Apr. | 10 | Coriolanus *BT. Bullock Sr.* | 53 | 16 | 6 |
| | 12 | King Lear *BT. J. Rich* | 34 | 17 | 0 |

   The recipient of the BT. is named in Play-A, but not in DP.

| | | | | | |
|---|---|---|---|---|---|
| | 28 | The Merry Wives of Windsor | 57 | 7 | 0 |
| May | 3 | same *BT. Mottley* | 67 | 9 | 6 |

   The recipient of the BT. is named in Play-A, but not in DP.

| | | | | | |
|---|---|---|---|---|---|
| | 15 | King Lear *BT. Pelling, Mrs Knapp, and Mrs Elsam* | 147 | 5 | 0 |
| | 25 | Julius Caesar *BT. Laurence and Wilson, box-keepers* | 148 | 16 | 0 |
| June | 8 | The Merry Wives of Windsor | 44 | 15 | 0 |

## 1721–1722

**1721 LINCOLN'S INN FIELDS** (*cont.*)

|  |  |  | £ | s. | d. |
|---|---|---|---:|---:|---:|
| Sept. | 23 | King Lear | 25 | 9 | 0 |
|  | 29 | Othello | 26 | 7 | 0 |
| Oct. | 7 | Richard III | 16 | 1 | 6 |
|  | 10 | Measure for Measure | 19 | 9 | 0 |
|  | 17 | The Jew of Venice | 14 | 8 | 6 |
|  | 21 | The Merry Wives of Windsor | 31 | 1 | 6 |
|  | 24 | Richard II | 11 | 14 | 6 |
|  | 26 | Macbeth | 14 | 5 | 0 |
|  | 28 | Henry IV, Part I | 30 | 7 | 0 |
|  | 31 | Coriolanus | 18 | 13 | 0 |
| Nov. | 3 | Henry IV, Part I | 19 | 10 | 6 |
|  | 10 | The Jew of Venice | 16 | 18 | 0 |
|  | 14 | Othello | 11 | 19 | 0 |
|  | 15 | The Merry Wives of Windsor | 29 | 18 | 6 |
|  | 17 | The Cobler of Preston | 20 | 1 | 6 |
|  | 25 | Hamlet | 38 | 17 | 6 |
|  | 27 | Measure for Measure | 11 | 8 | 0 |
|  | 30 | King Lear | 29 | 3 | 0 |
| Dec. | 7 | The Merry Wives of Windsor | 42 | 12 | 6 |
|  | 9 | Henry IV, Part I | 21 | 14 | 6 |
|  | 14 | Measure for Measure *BT. a widow in distress* | 142 | 10 | 6 |
|  | 16 | Richard III | 21 | 2 | 6 |
|  | 22 | Hamlet | 17 | 17 | 6 |
|  | 28 | The Merry Wives of Windsor | 57 | 5 | 6 |

**1722 DRURY LANE**

Jan. 2 Henry IV, Part I
　　 3 The Tempest
　　16 Julius Caesar
Feb. 1 Hamlet *BT. a gentleman reduc'd by the late general misfortune* [*i.e. the South Sea Bubble*]
Mar. 26 The Tempest
　　27 Othello *BT. Mrs Thurmond*
Apr. 24 Hamlet *BT. Shaw*
　　26 King Lear *BT.* [*W.*] *Wilks*
May 5 Henry IV, Part II *BT. Boman*
　　10 Macbeth *BT. Mrs Moore*
　　14 Richard III *BT. Theophilus Cibber*
　　22 Henry VIII *BT. Robinson*
　　　　Genest (iii. 71) erroneously has May 21.

　　29 Timon of Athens *BT. Symmons and May*
June 12 The Tempest
Sept. 15 Hamlet
　　22 Othello
　　25 Henry VIII
　　29 King Lear

1722

## 1722 DRURY LANE (cont.)

Oct. 19 Julius Caesar
Dec. 15 Hamlet
     26 Macbeth
     29 King Lear

## LINCOLN'S INN FIELDS

|  |  |  | £ | s. | d. |
|---|---|---|---|---|---|
| Jan. | 1 | Coriolanus | 35 | 7 | 0 |
|  | 4 | The Merry Wives of Windsor | 60 | 15 | 6 |
|  | 5 | The Jew of Venice | 29 | 3 | 0 |
|  | 10 | Othello | 11 | 3 | 0 |
|  | 16 | King Lear | 16 | 8 | 6 |
|  | 19 | The Merry Wives of Windsor | 34 | 10 | 0 |
|  | 29 | Hamlet | 27 | 13 | 0 |
| Feb. | 1 | The Merry Wives of Windsor | 79 | 14 | 0 |
| Mar. | 3 | same *BT. C. M. Rich* | 144 | 18 | 6 |

The recipient of the BT. is named in Play-A, but not in DC.

     26 same *BT. Chr. Bullock, who in great distress, has kept his chamber these two months, under a severe and expensive sickness*    117 14 0

| Apr. | 6 | Henry IV, Part I *BT. Walker* | 51 | 12 | 6 |
|---|---|---|---|---|---|
|  | 11 | The Merry Wives of Windsor *BT. Diggs* | 129 | 8 | 6 |
| May | 1 | same | 24 | 18 | 6 |
|  | 3 | The Cobler of Preston *BT. Cross* | 80 | 16 | 6 |
|  | 9 | Othello *BT. Beckingham* | 90 | 9 | 0 |
|  | 28 | The Merry Wives of Windsor *BT. Jones, Maine, and Tillman, gallery-keepers* | 83 | 1 | 0 |
| June | 2 | King Lear | 11 | 1 | 6 |
| Aug. | 1 | Titus Andronicus | receipts omitted |  |  |
| Sept. | 29 | Henry IV, Part I | 40 | 17 | 6 |
| Oct. | 4 | Richard III | 23 | 8 | 0 |
|  | 13 | Hamlet | 27 | 2 | 6 |
|  | 18 | Julius Caesar | 29 | 15 | 6 |
|  | 19 | The Merry Wives of Windsor | 31 | 19 | 6 |
|  | 20 | Macbeth | 34 | 13 | 6 |
|  | 25 | The Merry Wives of Windsor | 52 | 19 | 0 |
| Nov. | 1 | Othello | 18 | 6 | 0 |
|  | 2 | Measure for Measure | 21 | 17 | 0 |
|  | 3 | King Lear | 21 | 13 | 0 |
|  | 15 | Richard III | 31 | 2 | 6 |
|  | 16 | The Jew of Venice | 32 | 2 | 6 |
| Dec. | 8 | The Merry Wives of Windsor | 61 | 6 | 6 |
|  | 11 | Macbeth | 25 | 13 | 6 |
|  | 20 | King Lear | 15 | 5 | 0 |
|  | 29 | The Merry Wives of Windsor | 46 | 1 | 6 |

24

# 1723

**1723 DRURY LANE**

| | | |
|---|---|---|
| Jan. | 1 | Henry VIII |
| | 7 | The Tempest |
| | 9 | Love in a Forest |
| | 10 | same |
| | 11 | same *BT. the author* [*Charles Johnson*] |
| | 12 | same |
| | 14 | same |
| | 15 | same *BT. the author, a Free Mason* |
| Feb. | 13 | Julius Caesar |
| | 15 | Humfrey, Duke of Gloster |
| | 16 | same |
| | 18 | same *BT. the author* [*Ambrose Philips*] |
| | 19 | same |
| | 20 | same |
| | 21 | same *BT. the author* |
| | 22 | same |
| | 23 | same |
| | 25 | same *BT. the author* |
| Mar. | 9 | Richard III |
| Apr. | 15 | Macbeth |
| | 20 | Hamlet *BT. a person who has been a great sufferer in trade, and is now under confinement for debt* |
| May | 9 | Julius Caesar *BT. William Mills* |
| | 11 | Henry IV, Part I *BT. Harper* |
| | 14 | King Lear *BT. Mrs Willis and Mrs Wetherilt* |
| | 20 | Timon of Athens *BT. Watson and Corey* |
| | 27 | Macbeth *BT. King, box-keeper* |
| | 28 | Henry VIII *BT. Roberts, Wright, and Nailer* |
| June | 6 | The Tempest *BT. William Wilks* [*Sr.*], *the office-keeper* |
| July | 5 | An Historical Tragedy of the Civil Wars between the Houses of York and Lancaster in the Reign of King Henry the Sixth |
| Sept. | 24 | Julius Caesar |
| | 28 | Hamlet |
| Oct. | 5 | King Lear |
| | 8 | Henry IV, Part I |
| | 19 | Othello |
| | 22 | Henry VIII |
| | 29 | Macbeth |
| Nov. | 12 | Caius Marius |
| Dec. | 5 | Henry V |
| | 6 | same |
| | 7 | same |
| | 9 | same |
| | 10 | same |
| | 21 | Hamlet |
| | 26 | Henry V |
| | 28 | Macbeth |
| | 30 | Timon of Athens |

## 1723 LINCOLN'S INN FIELDS

|  |  |  | £ | s. | d. |
|---|---|---|---|---|---|
| Jan. | 10 | Julius Caesar | 22 | 9 | 0 |
|  | 12 | Henry IV, Part I | 27 | 9 | 0 |
|  | 14 | Measure for Measure | 15 | 12 | 6 |
|  | 15 | Othello | 22 | 13 | 6 |
|  | 25 | The Jew of Venice | 18 | 4 | 6 |
|  | 29 | Macbeth | 23 | 12 | 0 |
| Feb. | 9 | Hamlet | 37 | 17 | 0 |
|  | 11 | The Merry Wives of Windsor *BT. J. Rich* | 122 | 2 | 6 |

The recipient of the BT. is named in Play-A, but not in DC.

| Mar. | 21 | same *BT. Quin* | 140 | 17 | 6 |
|---|---|---|---|---|---|
| Apr. | 17 | Henry IV, Part I *BT. J. Rich* | 121 | 8 | 0 |

The recipient of the BT. is named in Play-A, but not in DC.

|  | 18 | Hamlet *BT. Mrs Cross* | 86 | 6 | 6 |
|---|---|---|---|---|---|
|  | 19 | Measure for Measure *BT. Diggs* | 88 | 12 | 0 |
|  | 20 | The Merry Wives of Windsor | 136 | 6 | 0 |
|  | 27 | same *BT. Newhouse and Mrs Rogeir* | 123 | 15 | 6 |
|  | 30 | Othello *BT. a gentleman under misfortunes* [*Webb*] | 105 | 9 | 0 |

The recipient of the BT. is named in Play-A, but not in DC.

| May | 3 | Troilus and Cressida *BT. Hippisley* | 84 | 7 | 0 |
|---|---|---|---|---|---|
|  | 8 | The Cobler of Preston *BT. Smith and Morgan* | 63 | 5 | 6 |
|  | 14 | Julius Caesar *BT. Ward, Chapman, and Mackenzie* | 93 | 15 | 6 |
|  | 18 | Macbeth *BT. Pelling, Giles, and the widow Rakestraw* | 67 | 9 | 0 |
|  | 21 | Henry IV, Part I *BT. Gallant and Maine* | 114 | 18 | 6 |
|  | 25 | Troilus and Cressida | 101 | 10 | 6 |
|  | 27 | King Lear *BT. Harrison* | 122 | 10 | 6 |
|  | 31 | The Merry Wives of Windsor *BT. Mrs Bubb* | 27 | 2 | 0 |

The recipient of the BT. is named in Play-A, but not in DC.

| Sept. | 30 | Macbeth | 42 | 19 | 0 |
|---|---|---|---|---|---|
| Oct. | 2 | Othello | 23 | 17 | 0 |
|  | 11 | Richard III | 53 | 16 | 0 |
|  | 19 | The Merry Wives of Windsor | 130 | 14 | 6 |
|  | 24 | Henry IV, Part I | 21 | 19 | 0 |
|  | 31 | Julius Caesar | 27 | 0 | 6 |
| Nov. | 14 | Hamlet | 33 | 16 | 0 |
|  | 21 | Troilus and Cressida | 11 | 9 | 6 |
|  | 22 | The Merry Wives of Windsor | 116 | 3 | 6 |
|  | 30 | King Lear | 64 | 2 | 6 |
| Dec. | 5 | Henry IV, Part I | 43 | 13 | 0 |
|  | 14 | The Merry Wives of Windsor | 131 | 16 | 0 |
|  | 31 | Julius Caesar | 13 | 2 | 6 |

# 1724

## 1724 DRURY LANE

- Jan. 1 Henry VIII
- 4 King Lear
- 7 The Tempest
- 11 Julius Caesar
- Feb. 7 Henry IV, Part I
- 8 Caius Marius
- Apr. 8 Henry VIII *BT. Johnson*
- 14 The Tempest
- 20 Othello *BT. Thurmond, dancing-master*
- 24 Hamlet *BT.* [*W.*] *Wilks*
- 27 King Lear *BT. Thurmond Sr.*
- May 5 Timon of Athens *BT. Oates*
- 6 Macbeth *BT. Robinson and Mrs Willis*
- 25 The Tempest *BT. the widow* [*F.*] *Leigh*
- Sept. 12 Hamlet
- 19 Julius Caesar
- 24 King Lear
- 26 Othello
- Oct. 3 Henry IV, Part I
- 22 Henry VIII
- 27 Macbeth
- 30 The Tempest
- Nov. 17 Timon of Athens
- 24 Caius Marius
- Dec. 19 Hamlet
- 29 Henry VIII

## LINCOLN'S INN FIELDS

|  |  |  | £ | s. | d. |
|---|---|---|---|---|---|
| Jan. | 1 | The Merry Wives of Windsor | 84 | 14 | 6 |
|  | 4 | Measure for Measure | 74 | 4 | 6 |
|  | 8 | The Merry Wives of Windsor | 160 | 19 | 0 |
|  | 16 | Measure for Measure | 127 | 4 | 0 |
|  | 22 | The Merry Wives of Windsor | 159 | 1 | 0 |
| Feb. | 10 | same | 151 | 19 | 6 |
|  | 13 | Measure for Measure | 114 | 4 | 0 |
| Mar. | 2 | The Merry Wives of Windsor *BT. Nivelon Jr.* | 72 | 10 | 0 |
|  | 7 | Henry IV, Part I | 115 | 2 | 6 |
|  | 19 | Titus Andronicus *BT. Quin* | 145 | 0 | 6 |

See note under Apr. 25.

|  |  |  |  |  |  |
|---|---|---|---|---|---|
|  | 24 | The Merry Wives of Windsor | 104 | 17 | 6 |
|  | 28 | King Lear *BT. Boheme* | 141 | 11 | 0 |
| Apr. | 9 | Measure for Measure *BT. Leveridge* | 140 | 18 | 6 |
|  | 23 | Hamlet *BT. Diggs* | 145 | 1 | 0 |
|  | 25 | Titus Andronicus | 35 | 5 | 0 |

Genest (iii. 145) states that this performance was for Quin's BT., and that it was 'again [as it was on Mar. 19, q.v.] said not to have been acted for 3 years'. Genest's

27

## 1724–1725

### 1724 LINCOLN'S INN FIELDS (*cont.*)

source was DC. The bill in DP makes no reference to any of the above information. The receipts clearly indicate that it was not a BT., certainly not Quin's. Latreille (ii. 121)—on what authority I do not know—deletes Quin's name, and inserts that of Hurst.

|  |  |  | £ | s. | d. |
|---|---|---|---|---|---|
| Apr. 28 | The Merry Wives of Windsor *BT. Wood, treasurer* | | 157 | 12 | 0 |
| 30 | Richard III *BT. Mrs Vincent* | | 105 | 1 | 0 |
| May 8 | The Cobler of Preston *BT. Ogden and Morgan* | | 116 | 15 | 0 |
| 13 | Macbeth *BT. Huddy and Lanyon* | | 124 | 5 | 0 |
| 15 | King Lear *BT. Hulett and Chapman* | | 75 | 7 | 6 |
| 20 | Henry IV, Part I *BT. Ward, Gwinn, and Merrivale* | | 114 | 7 | 0 |
| 29 | Measure for Measure *BT. Wilcox, Randal, and Miss Connelly* | | 127 | 7 | 6 |
| Sept. 28 | Macbeth | | 46 | 0 | 6 |
| Oct. 22 | Richard III | | 26 | 15 | 6 |
| 24 | The Merry Wives of Windsor | | 76 | 13 | 0 |
| 31 | King Lear | | 68 | 2 | 6 |
| Nov. 7 | Henry IV, Part I | | 61 | 11 | 0 |
| 13 | The Cobler of Preston | | 19 | 12 | 6 |
| 14 | Measure for Measure | | 30 | 3 | 0 |
| 18 | The Merry Wives of Windsor | | 33 | 8 | 6 |
| 23 | same | | 63 | 13 | 0 |
| 26 | Hamlet | | 50 | 10 | 0 |

### 1725 DRURY LANE

Jan. 2 Julius Caesar
 5 King Lear
 6 The Tempest
 21 Timon of Athens
 22 Hamlet
Feb. 6 Richard III
 18 Macbeth
Mar. 15 Hamlet *BT. Mrs Booth*
 18 Othello *BT. Mrs Thurmond*
 29 Timon of Athens
Apr. 1 Henry IV, Part I
 3 Julius Caesar
 13 Henry VIII
 26 Macbeth *BT. Corey and William Mills*
May 11 Timon of Athens *BT. Ferrers*
 24 The Tempest *BT. Mrs Willis, the widow Bowen, and the widow [F.] Leigh*
June 14 Othello
 18 Julius Caesar
Sept. 4 Othello
 11 Hamlet
 18 Henry IV, Part I

## 1725 DRURY LANE (*cont.*)

|  |  |
|---|---|
| Sept. 30 | Julius Caesar |
| Oct. 5 | Macbeth |
| 30 | The Tempest |
| Nov. 26 | Timon of Athens |
| Dec. 8 | Othello |
| 14 | Henry IV, Part I |
| 22 | King Lear |

## LINCOLN'S INN FIELDS

|  |  | £ | s. | d. |
|---|---|---|---|---|
| Jan. 1 | The Merry Wives of Windsor | 119 | 17 | 0 |
| 19 | Henry IV, Part I | 25 | 11 | 0 |
| 21 | The Merry Wives of Windsor | 174 | 8 | 0 |
| Feb. 8 | same | 149 | 18 | 0 |
| 11 | Measure for Measure | 131 | 7 | 6 |
| Mar. 11 | Julius Caesar *BT. Boheme* | 120 | 10 | 6 |
| 18 | Henry IV, Part I *BT. Quin* | 164 | 4 | 0 |
| 20 | Macbeth | 132 | 12 | 0 |
| Apr. 7 | Sauny the Scot *BT. Mr and Mrs Egleton* | 107 | 8 | 6 |
| 16 | The Merry Wives of Windsor *BT. Mr and Mrs Laguerre* | 98 | 15 | 6 |
| 20 | Henry IV, Part I *BT. Edward Lally* | 167 | 11 | 6 |
| 23 | King Lear *BT. Diggs* | 135 | 3 | 6 |
| 28 | Hamlet *BT. Hall and the prompter* [*Stede*] | 133 | 18 | 0 |
| May 1 | Richard III *BT. Hulett and Huddy* | 125 | 7 | 0 |
| 10 | The Merry Wives of Windsor *BT. Harrison, pit office-keeper, and Clarkson* | 177 | 0 | 6 |
| 18 | Sauny the Scot *BT. Lovelace and Taylor, box-keepers* | 149 | 1 | 0 |
| 22 | Julius Caesar *BT. Larsay, Sparling, Clarke, and Rogers* | 101 | 0 | 0 |
| 25 | King Lear *BT. Jones, Tillman, and Tyfer, gallery door-keepers* | 114 | 5 | 6 |
| Sept. 24 | same | 67 | 4 | 6 |
| Oct. 16 | Henry IV, Part I | 27 | 7 | 0 |
| 21 | The Merry Wives of Windsor | 104 | 2 | 0 |
| 28 | Hamlet | 32 | 15 | 0 |
| 30 | Henry VIII | 68 | 16 | 6 |
| Nov. 1 | same | 41 | 3 | 0 |
| 9 | Richard III | 25 | 3 | 0 |
| 19 | The Merry Wives of Windsor | 76 | 0 | 0 |
| Dec. 2 | Macbeth | 44 | 11 | 0 |
| 6 | Othello | 19 | 14 | 6 |
| 14 | Henry VIII | 25 | 1 | 0 |
| 15 | Julius Caesar | 24 | 3 | 0 |
| 30 | The Merry Wives of Windsor | 74 | 11 | 0 |
| 31 | Macbeth | 40 | 0 | 6 |

## 1726 DRURY LANE

- Jan. 1 Hamlet
- 6 The Tempest
- 26 Julius Caesar
- Feb. 12 Timon of Athens
- Mar. 10 Hamlet *BT. Mills*
- Apr. 16 Julius Caesar
- 18 Hamlet *BT. Williams*
- 27 Othello *BT. Thurmond Sr.*
- May 5 Macbeth *BT. Castleman, treasurer*
- 7 Henry IV, Part I *BT. [T.] Hallam, Robert Williams, and Miss Tynte*
- 23 Timon of Athens *BT. Mrs Willis and Wright*
- Sept. 3 Othello
- Nov. 3 Richard III
- 12 Hamlet
- 16 Macbeth
- Dec. 20 King Lear
- 22 Hamlet
- 28 Macbeth

## LINCOLN'S INN FIELDS

|  |  | £ | s. | d. |
|---|---|---|---|---|
| Jan. 5 Henry IV, Part I | | 23 | 17 | 0 |
| 15 The Merry Wives of Windsor | | 155 | 18 | 6 |
| 19 Measure for Measure | | 158 | 2 | 6 |
| 24 The Merry Wives of Windsor | | 167 | 3 | 0 |
| 29 Henry IV, Part I | | 136 | 11 | 0 |
| Feb. 3 Othello | | 138 | 14 | 0 |
| 16 King Lear | | 77 | 3 | 0 |
| 18 The Merry Wives of Windsor | | 86 | 2 | 0 |
| Mar. 7 Measure for Measure | | 51 | 17 | 6 |
| 14 The Merry Wives of Windsor | | 87 | 12 | 6 |
| 26 King Lear | | 103 | 13 | 0 |
| Apr. 12 Macbeth | | 100 | 2 | 0 |
| 22 Henry VIII *BT. Mrs Parker* | | 103 | 18 | 0 |
| 25 Hamlet *BT. Hippisley* | | 84 | 11 | 6 |

- Apr. 28 [The Merry Wives of Windsor *BT. an author, whose play is deferred till next season (Leonard Welsted)*]

  Bill in DC, but 'Dismissed' (Egerton MS 2321). This MS also identifies the author. Welsted's play, *The Dissembled Wanton*, came out at this theatre on Dec. 14, 1726.

| May 13 King Lear *BT. Milward, Mrs Moffett, and Mrs Smithies* | | 105 | 12 | 6 |
|---|---|---|---|---|
| 17 Henry IV, Part I *BT. Norris [Jr.], Houghton, and Vaughan* | | 84 | 3 | 0 |
| 18 The Cobler of Preston *BT. Morgan and Hulett* | | 102 | 9 | 6 |
| 25 Hamlet *BT. Ward and Gwinn* | | 115 | 19 | 0 |

1726–1727

1726 LINCOLN'S INN FIELDS (cont.)

|  |  |  | £ | s. | d. |
|---|---|---|---|---|---|
| Aug. | 12 | The Cobler of Preston | 28 | 10 | 6 |
|  | 16 | same | 11 | 1 | 0 |
| Sept. | 9 | Hamlet | 45 | 10 | 6 |
|  | 21 | Henry IV, Part I | 37 | 2 | 6 |
|  | 23 | King Lear | 103 | 17 | 6 |
|  | 26 | Macbeth | 54 | 6 | 6 |
|  | 30 | The Merry Wives of Windsor | 116 | 19 | 0 |
| Oct. | 17 | Richard III | 93 | 17 | 6 |
|  | 31 | Henry VIII | 45 | 6 | 6[1] |
| Nov. | 11 | Julius Caesar | 12 | 14 | 0 |
|  | 18 | King Lear | 18 | 3 | 0 |
| Dec. | 2 | The Merry Wives of Windsor | 48 | 8 | 6 |
|  | 29 | Richard III | 54 | 0 | 0 |

1727 DRURY LANE

Jan. 17 Richard III
24 The Tempest
Feb. 21 Henry IV, Part II
25 same
27 same
Mar. 14 same
Apr. 4 Macbeth
5 Julius Caesar
15 Hamlet *BT. Miss Tenoe*
29 Caius Marius *BT. Bridgwater*
May 22 The Tempest *BT. [T.] Hallam, Robert Williams, and Peploe*
31 Julius Caesar
Sept. 7 Othello
9 Henry IV, Part II
16 King Lear
23 Hamlet
30 Macbeth
Oct. 3 Julius Caesar
26 Henry VIII
27 same
28 same
31 same
Nov. 2 same
3 same
7 same
8 same
10 same
11 same

[1] From this date to Feb. 3, 1729 there are four sources for the receipts: the actual Account Book of the theatre for the season of 1726–7 (Egerton MS 2266); a contemporary, but incomplete Account Book for the seasons of 1726–9 (HTC); and two nineteenth-century compilations made by James Winston (Egerton MS 2322) and by Frederick Latreille (Add. MS 32251). The Harvard MS is in such frequent disagreement with the other MSS that I have not used it.

## 1727 DRURY LANE (cont.)

- Nov. 13 Henry VIII
- 15 same
- 16 same
- 17 same
- 24 same

> To this play was appended a pantomime representing the coronation of George II, which occurred on Oct. 11. See Genest, iii. 199–202.

- Dec. 29 The Tempest

### LINCOLN'S INN FIELDS

| | | | £ | s. | d. |
|---|---|---|---|---|---|
| Jan. | 4 | Hamlet | 35 | 13 | 0 |
| | 10 | Henry IV, Part I | 28 | 7 | 6 |
| | 14 | Measure for Measure | 51 | 0 | 0 |
| Feb. | 2 | Henry VIII | 34 | 6 | 6 |
| | 20 | The Merry Wives of Windsor | 208 | 10 | 6 |
| Mar. | 13 | Hamlet *BT. Ryan* | 134 | 9 | 0 |
| | 20 | Measure for Measure *BT. Nivelon* | 85 | 17 | 6 |
| Apr. | 3 | Macbeth *BT. Boheme* | 88 | 3 | 0 |
| | 11 | The Merry Wives of Windsor | 99 | 10 | 0 |
| | 17 | The Jew of Venice *BT. Mrs Berriman* | 74 | 4 | 0 |
| May | 15 | Hamlet *BT. Wm. Bullock [Jr.], Houghton, and Montigny* | 152 | 2 | 6 |
| | 22 | The Merry Wives of Windsor *BT. Steddy* | 137 | 12 | 6 |
| | 25 | Measure for Measure | 140 | 13 | 0 |
| June | 1 | King Lear | 59 | 4 | 6 |
| Sept. | 18 | Henry IV, Part I | 40 | 19 | 0 |
| | 29 | The Merry Wives of Windsor | 112 | 1 | 6 |
| Oct. | 6 | Othello | 78 | 14 | 6 |
| | 19 | King Lear | 28 | 15 | 0 |
| | 21 | Hamlet | 29 | 18 | 0 |
| Nov. | 9 | The Merry Wives of Windsor | 136 | 3 | 6 |
| | 13 | The Jew of Venice | 86 | 12 | 6 |
| | 17 | Macbeth | 31 | 2 | 0 |
| | 29 | The Merry Wives of Windsor | 91 | 12 | 0 |
| | 30 | The Jew of Venice | 83 | 19 | 0 |
| Dec. | 8 | Hamlet | 30 | 2 | 0 |
| | 21 | [Richard III] | | | |

> Bill in DJ, but 'Dismissed' (Egerton MS 2322).

| | | | | | |
|---|---|---|---|---|---|
| | 30 | King Lear | 56 | 6 | 0 |

## 1728 DRURY LANE

- Jan. 4 Julius Caesar
- Feb. 24 Hamlet
- May 8 Macbeth *BT. Shepard and Mrs Moore*
- 14 Henry VIII *BT. Mrs Burton, gallery box-keeper, and Mrs Shireburn*

## 1728

**1728 DRURY LANE** (cont.)

- May 23 Richard III *BT. Wrexham, who sustained great losses in the year 1720*
- Sept. 10 Henry IV, Part I
- 21 Hamlet
- 28 Henry VIII
- Oct. 12 Othello
- 18 Henry IV, Part II
- 29 Henry VIII
- Nov. 6 Richard III
- 20 same
- 28 Henry IV, Part I
- Dec. 3 Henry IV, Part II
- 6 Macbeth
- 11 Henry VIII
- 28 Othello
- 30 Henry IV, Part II

**LINCOLN'S INN FIELDS**

|  |  | £ | s. | d. |
|---|---|---|---|---|
| Jan. 3 | Richard III | 47 | 2 | 0 |
| Mar. 18 | Hamlet *BT. Mrs Barbier* | 161 | 10 | 0 |
| May 15 | same *BT. Rochetti and Mrs Laguerre* | 139 | 2 | 6 |
| 23 | The Jew of Venice *BT. Gwinn, Mrs Clarke, and Mrs Palin* | 151 | 7 | 0 |

Genest (iii. 227) erroneously has May 29.

|  |  | £ | s. | d. |
|---|---|---|---|---|
| Sept. 16 | King Lear | 32 | 11 | 0 |
| 30 | Macbeth | 64 | 7 | 0 |
| Oct. 7 | Othello | 41 | 11 | 0 |
| 14 | The Merry Wives of Windsor | 104 | 18 | 6 |
| Nov. 1 | Hamlet | 25 | 12 | 6 |
| 18 | [Henry IV, Part I] | | | |

Listed by Genest (iii. 238). On this night the theatre was dark.

|  |  | £ | s. | d. |
|---|---|---|---|---|
| 19 | Henry IV, Part I | 35 | 13 | 0 |
| 20 | Julius Caesar | 26 | 9 | 0 |
| 29 | [The Merry Wives of Windsor] | | | |

Bill in DJ, but 'Dismissed' (Latreille, ii. 279).

- Dec. 3 [Macbeth]

Bill in DJ, but 'Dismissed' (Harvard Account-book).

|  |  | £ | s. | d. |
|---|---|---|---|---|
| 19 | Hamlet | 27 | 15 | 1 |
| 28 | The Merry Wives of Windsor | 173 | 15 | 0 |

**HAYMARKET**

- Aug. 19 Richard III *BT. a decay'd tradesman*

## 1729 DRURY LANE

- Jan. 2 The Tempest
- 3 same
- 6 same
- 11 King Lear
- 28 Henry IV, Part I
- Feb. 5 Henry IV, Part II
- 12 The Tempest
- 20 Henry VIII
- Mar. 18 Hamlet *BT. Mrs Booth*
- 29 Othello *BT. Elrington*
- Apr. 11 Henry VIII *BT. Harper*
- 18 same
- 23 Timon of Athens *BT. Shepard and Rainton, the dancer*
- May 6 Macbeth *BT. Boman and Mrs Walter*
- 7 Henry IV, Part II *BT. Mrs Shireburn and Miss Brett*
- 26 Timon of Athens
- 28 The Tempest
- Sept. 20 Othello
- 23 Henry IV, Part II
- 25 Henry VIII
- Oct. 28 Macbeth
- 30 The Tempest
- Nov. 27 Timon of Athens
- Dec. 18 Henry VIII
- 30 Henry IV, Part II

## LINCOLN'S INN FIELDS

| | | | £ | s. | d. |
|---|---|---|---|---|---|
| Jan. | 13 | Measure for Measure *BT. a gentleman who has wrote for the stage [Matthew Concanen]* | 95 | 3 | 0 |

The recipient of the BT. is identified in Egerton MS 2322.

| | | | | | |
|---|---|---|---|---|---|
| | 22 | The Merry Wives of Windsor | 74 | 7 | 6 |
| | 23 | The Jew of Venice | 38 | 12 | 6 |
| | 31 | Macbeth | 38 | 17 | 6 |
| Feb. | 1 | Measure for Measure | 73 | 4 | 6 |
| | 3 | Othello | 59 | 4 | 6 |
| | 25 | Macbeth | 74 | 14 | 0 |
| Mar. | 13 | Othello | 65 | 4 | 0 |
| | 22 | Henry IV, Part I | 72 | 14 | 0 |
| Apr. | 9 | The Merry Wives of Windsor *BT. Hippisley* | 130 | 17 | 0 |
| | 23 | Hamlet *BT. Milward* | 148 | 11 | 0 |
| | 26 | Measure for Measure *BT. a gentlewoman [Mrs Stede] and her daughter, under misfortunes* | 125 | 4 | 0 |

The recipient of the BT. is identified in Latreille, ii. 284.

| | | | | | |
|---|---|---|---|---|---|
| | 28 | Macbeth *BT. Mrs Buchanan and Mrs Benson* | 158 | 4 | 6 |

## 1729–1730

**1729 LINCOLN'S INN FIELDS** (*cont.*)

|  |  |  | £ | s. | d. |
|---|---|---|---|---|---|
| May 12 | The Merry Wives of Windsor *BT. Houghton, Clarke, and Miss Palin* | | 196 | 19 | 6 |
| Sept. 12 | King Lear | | 61 | 18 | 6 |
| 22 | Hamlet | | 59 | 6 | 6 |
| Oct. 3 | Macbeth | | 58 | 15 | 6 |
| 10 | Henry IV, Part I | | 103 | 17 | 6 |
| 15 | The Merry Wives of Windsor | | 105 | 5 | 0 |
| Nov. 13 | Julius Caesar | | 30 | 2 | 6 |
| 15 | The Merry Wives of Windsor | | 44 | 4 | 6 |
| 17 | Hamlet | | 24 | 11 | 0 |
| 20 | Macbeth | | 75 | 0 | 0 |

The bill in DJ gives *The Rival Queens*. In Latreille (ii. 311) this is deleted and the above substituted.

| 22 | Measure for Measure | | 82 | 15 | 6 |
|---|---|---|---|---|---|
| 29 | Henry IV, Part I | | 68 | 15 | 0 |
| Dec. 16 | The Jew of Venice | | 58 | 13 | 0 |
| 30 | King Lear | | 47 | 3 | 6 |

**1730 DRURY LANE**

Jan. 6 [The Tempest]

Bill in DP, but 'Dismissed' (Latreille, ii. 301).

7 Othello
24 Hamlet
Feb. 12 Henry IV, Part II
May 2 Macbeth *BT. Castleman, the treasurer*
19 Henry VIII *BT. Wright*
Sept. 12 Hamlet
22 Henry VIII
29 Henry IV, Part II
Oct. 31 Timon of Athens
Nov. 10 Richard III
24 Macbeth
27 Henry VIII
28 King Lear
30 The Tempest
Dec. 1 Othello
4 Henry IV, Part II
17 The Tempest
18 Timon of Athens
31 Henry IV, Part I

**LINCOLN'S INN FIELDS**

| Jan. 1 | Macbeth | | 40 | 0 | 6 |
|---|---|---|---|---|---|
| 10 | The Merry Wives of Windsor | | 112 | 9 | 6 |
| 17 | Measure for Measure | | 78 | 7 | 6 |
| Feb. 7 | The Merry Wives of Windsor | | 137 | 9 | 6 |

## 1730

### 1730 LINCOLN'S INN FIELDS (cont.)

|  |  |  | £ | s. | d. |
|---|---|---|---|---|---|
| Apr. | 10 | The Merry Wives of Windsor *BT. Poitier, petit-maître* | 114 | 10 | 0 |
|  | 15 | Hamlet *BT. Leveridge* | 235 | 0 | 0 |
|  | 22 | Henry IV, Part I *BT. Mrs Wright and Mrs Vincent* | 136 | 6 | 0 |
| May | 7 | The Cobler of Preston *BT. Mr and Mrs Morgan* | 172 | 8 | 0 |
|  | 14 | Macbeth *BT. Houghton and the prompter [Stede]* | 144 | 4 | 6 |
|  | 15 | The Merry Wives of Windsor *BT. Eversman and Mrs Benson* | 126 | 1 | 6 |
|  | 28 | King Lear *BT. Wilmer and the widow Redfern, box-keepers* | 145 | 19 | 0 |
| Sept. | 16 | same | 58 | 8 | 0 |
|  | 21 | Macbeth | 56 | 1 | 6 |
|  | 25 | Henry IV, Part I | 104 | 17 | 0 |
| Oct. | 7 | The Jew of Venice | 54 | 17 | 6 |
|  | 9 | The Merry Wives of Windsor | 102 | 6 | 6 |
|  | 14 | Othello | 44 | 9 | 0 |
| Nov. | 7 | Measure for Measure | 99 | 4 | 0 |
|  | 13 | Hamlet | 30 | 14 | 0 |
|  | 21 | The Jew of Venice | 81 | 5 | 0 |
|  | 26 | The Merry Wives of Windsor | 91 | 11 | 6 |
| Dec. | 30 | Macbeth | 34 | 1 | 6 |

### HAYMARKET

June 27 Othello *BT. Paget and Rosco*
Dec. 17 same *BT. Royer*

### GOODMAN'S FIELDS

Jan. 9 Hamlet
   10 same
   21 same
Feb. 21 same
Mar. 17 The Merry Wives of Windsor *BT. W. Giffard*
   19 same
Apr. 20 Hamlet *BT. W. Williams*
   24 The Merry Wives of Windsor
May 14 Hamlet
   26 King Lear *BT. Theo. Lacy*
June 3 Othello *BT. Mynn and Burny Sr.*
   18 King Lear *BT. Bolton, Bevil, and Charlton*
   30 Hamlet *BT. Ravenscroft*
July 7 King Lear
   10 The Cobler of Preston
   13 same
   29 Hamlet
Sept. 25 same
Oct. 9 King Lear
   19 Othello

## 1730–1731

**1730 GOODMAN'S FIELDS** (*cont.*)

- Oct. 30   The Merry Wives of Windsor
- Nov. 4   Othello
  - 18   Hamlet
  - 25   Othello
- Dec. 8   King Lear
  - 10   The Merry Wives of Windsor
  - 18   Hamlet

**1731 DRURY LANE**

- Jan. 13   The Tempest
  - 16   Hamlet
- Feb. 1   Henry VIII
- Mar. 8   Henry IV, Part I
  - 16   Henry IV, Part II
- Apr. 6   Macbeth *BT. Essex*
- May 4   Henry VIII *BT. Chetwood and Miss Williams*
  - 17   Macbeth *BT. Jones, numberer, and Little, gallery box-keeper*
  - 18   Henry VIII
  - 19   Henry IV, Part II *BT. Wright*
- June 7   The Tempest
- Sept. 18   Hamlet
- Oct. 14   Henry IV, Part II
  - 21   Timon of Athens
- Nov. 13   Henry VIII
  - 15   Othello
  - 29   Henry VIII
- Dec. 1   Macbeth
  - 2   The Tempest
  - 6   Henry IV, Part II
  - 29   The Tempest

**LINCOLN'S INN FIELDS**

|  |  |  | £ | s. | d. |
|---|---|---|---|---|---|
| Jan. | 5 | Hamlet | 26 | 15 | 6 |
|  | 8 | The Merry Wives of Windsor | 39 | 4 | 0 |
|  | 28 | [King Lear] |  |  |  |
|  |  | Bill in DJ, but 'Dismissed' (Latreille, ii. 364). |  |  |  |
| Feb. | 1 | The Merry Wives of Windsor | 69 | 16 | 0 |
|  | 2 | Measure for Measure | 42 | 11 | 0 |
|  | 22 | The Jew of Venice | 77 | 11 | 0 |
| Mar. | 4 | The Merry Wives of Windsor | 150 | 1 | 6 |
|  | 8 | Othello | 67 | 6 | 6 |
|  | 13 | King Lear | 84 | 1 | 0 |
|  | 29 | The Merry Wives of Windsor *BT. Mrs Bullock* | 142 | 9 | 0 |
| Apr. | 28 | Hamlet *BT. Mr and Mrs Laguerre* | 162 | 8 | 6 |
| May | 17 | Measure for Measure *BT. Papillion and Mrs Kilby* | 126 | 7 | 6 |
|  | 19 | The Merry Wives of Windsor *BT. Newhouse and Mrs Cantrell* | 113 | 4 | 6 |

37

## 1731 LINCOLN'S INN FIELDS (cont.)

|   |   |   | £ | s. | d. |
|---|---|---|---|---|---|
| Sept. | 17 | Othello | 53 | 15 | 0 |
|  | 27 | Macbeth | 61 | 18 | 0 |
|  | 29 | Henry IV, Part I | 50 | 6 | 6 |
| Oct. | 4 | The Merry Wives of Windsor | 104 | 2 | 0 |
|  | 6 | King Lear | 47 | 2 | 0 |
|  | 20 | The Jew of Venice | 49 | 12 | 6 |
|  | 25 | The Cobler of Preston | 65 | 19 | 0 |
|  | 29 | Henry IV, Part I | 176 | 17 | 0 |
| Nov. | 13 | Measure for Measure | 55 | 6 | 0 |
|  | 15 | [Richard III] |  |  |  |

Bill in DJ, but 'Dismissed' (Latreille, iii. 19).

|  |  |  |  |  |  |
|---|---|---|---|---|---|
|  | 17 | Hamlet | 36 | 6 | 0 |
|  | 24 | The Merry Wives of Windsor | 50 | 0 | 0 |
| Dec. | 8 | same | 178 | 2 | 6 |
|  | 29 | Macbeth | 85 | 10 | 6 |
|  | 31 | Henry IV, Part I | 57 | 17 | 0 |

## HAYMARKET

Mar. 17 The Cobler of Preston *BT. Mrs Stevens*
Apr. 20 same *BT. a gentleman under great misfortunes*
May  3 Henry IV, Part I
      5 same

## GOODMAN'S FIELDS

Feb.  6 The Merry Wives of Windsor
      8 The Cobler of Preston
      9 same
     11 same
     12 same
     19 Hamlet
Mar. 16 Othello *BT. Lucas*
May  15 The Cobler of Preston *BT. Ravenscroft*
     20 Macbeth *BT. W. Giffard and Collett*
     21 The Cobler of Preston *BT. Mrs Morgan*
June  2 The Tempest *BT. Havard and Boucher, prompter*
Oct. 25 The Merry Wives of Windsor
Nov.  1 Henry IV, Part I
      2 same
     26 Othello
     30 same

## 1732 DRURY LANE

Jan.  4 Henry VIII
      6 Timon of Athens
     15 Henry IV, Part II
Feb. 12 Hamlet

## 1732

**1732 DRURY LANE** (*cont.*)

- Mar. 11 Hamlet *BT. Mrs Thurmond*
- Apr. 11 Henry VIII *BT. Shepard and Corey*
- 17 Henry IV, Part I *BT. Bridgwater*
- 18 Henry IV, Part II *BT. Lally*
- May 5 Macbeth *BT. Boman and Paget*
- Aug. 4 Othello
- 17 same
- Sept. 28 Macbeth
- Oct. 14 Richard III
- 17 Henry IV, Part I
- 19 Henry IV, Part II
- Nov. 11 Hamlet
- 13 Henry VIII
- 15 Henry IV, Part II
- 17 Richard III
- Dec. 4 Othello
- 13 [Henry VIII]
    Bill in DP, but 'Dismissed' (Latreille, iii. 57).
- 26 The Tempest

**LINCOLN'S INN FIELDS**

|  |  | £ | s. | d. |
|---|---|---|---|---|
| Jan. 15 | Measure for Measure | 45 | 14 | 6 |
| 24 | Othello | 72 | 10 | 6 |
| 25 | The Jew of Venice | 34 | 1 | 0 |
| 29 | Hamlet | 85 | 11 | 6 |
| Feb. 3 | Macbeth | 79 | 0 | 0 |
| 8 | King Lear | 62 | 4 | 0 |
| 12 | The Merry Wives of Windsor | 81 | 9 | 6 |
| Apr. 12 | same *BT. Mons. Sallé* | 79 | 14 | 6 |
| 13 | Othello *BT. M. Poitier, petit-maître* | 141 | 14 | 0 |
| May 3 | Hamlet *BT. Hulett and Penkethman [Jr.]* | 176 | 0 | 6 |
| 8 | Henry IV, Part I *BT. Ray and Ford* | 168 | 6 | 0 |
| 11 | The Cobler of Preston *BT. Lynham* | 152 | 10 | 0 |
| 12 | Macbeth *BT. Gallant, Gibbs, Mrs Atkins, and Mrs Redfern* | 161 | 14 | 6 |
| Sept. 22 | Hamlet | 69 | 15 | 6 |
| Oct. 4 | Othello | 96 | 11 | 6 |
| 6 | The Merry Wives of Windsor | 75 | 9 | 0 |
| 25 | Measure for Measure *BT. a person who has met with losses in trade* | 110 | 3 | 6 |

Latreille (iii. 77) says that the recipient of the BT. was Miss Norsa. This seems unlikely; Miss Norsa made her first appearance, at Covent Garden, on Dec. 16 of this year. Another member of her family perhaps had the BT.

| 27 | King Lear | 79 | 11 | 0 |
| 30 | Macbeth | 92 | 0 | 0 |

39

## 1732 LINCOLN'S INN FIELDS (cont.)

|  |  |  | £ | s. | d. |
|---|---|---|---|---|---|
| Nov. | 25 | Henry IV, Part I | 68 | 3 | 6 |
|  | 28 | The Merry Wives of Windsor | 51 | 1 | 6 |

## COVENT GARDEN

|  |  |  |  |  |  |
|---|---|---|---|---|---|
| Dec. 13 | King Lear | | 55 | 10 | 0 |

## GOODMAN'S FIELDS

Jan. 22 Othello
    29 Henry IV, Part I

        Genest (iii. 356) has '28 or 29'. The play on Jan. 28 was *The Old Bachelor*.

Feb. 1 same
    16 Othello
    26 Hamlet
    29 same
Mar. 4 The Merry Wives of Windsor
    6 Othello
    20 Richard III *BT. Delane*
    25 same
    30 Henry IV, Part I *BT. Huddy*
Apr. 14 Hamlet *BT. Bardin*
    17 Othello *BT. Mrs Haughton*
May 11 Richard III *BT. [R.] Williams*
    19 Othello *BT. Temple, box-keeper, and Gibbs, pit-keeper*
Oct. 2 Henry IV, Part I
    3 same
    11 The Merry Wives of Windsor
    13 Othello
    24 Hamlet
Nov. 16 Othello
    21 Hamlet
Dec. 1 Julius Caesar
    2 same
    4 same
    5 same
    6 same
    7 same
    8 same
    9 same
    11 same
    12 same
    13 same
    14 same
    20 Henry IV, Part I
    22 The Merry Wives of Windsor
    26 Julius Caesar

# 1733

1733 DRURY LANE
- Jan. 5 Hamlet
- 6 Henry IV, Part II
- 8 Hamlet
- 15 Macbeth
- 24 The Tempest
- 29 Hamlet
- Feb. 3 Henry IV, Part I
- 5 Henry VIII
- 12 Richard III
- 13 Hamlet
- Mar. 26 Henry VIII *BT. Mons. Desnoyer*
- Apr. 18 Timon of Athens *BT. Shepard*
- 25 Hamlet *BT. Fielding and Haughton*
- 30 King Lear *BT. A. Hallam and Mrs Walter*
- May 7 Henry IV, Part II *BT. Charke*

  Genest (iii. 372) assigns the BT. to Mrs Charke.

- 11 Hamlet
- 28 [Henry VIII]

  Bill in DP, but not acted (DP, May 29). See following note.

- 29 [The Tempest]

  Bill in DP, but not acted. *The Craftsman*, June 2: 'The revolt of the Performers has prevented any Plays being acted at Drury Lane this week.'

- Oct. 17 Richard III
- Nov. 2 same
- 14 Henry VIII
- 15 same
- 19 same
- 23 Timon of Athens
- 24 Henry VIII
- 26 The Tempest
- 27 same
- 28 same
- 29 same
- 30 same
- Dec. 3 same
- 19 same
- 27 Henry VIII
- 28 The Tempest

## COVENT GARDEN

|   |   |   | £ | s. | d. |
|---|---|---|---|---|---|
| Jan. | 12 | Measure for Measure | 36 | 7 | 6 |
|  | 13 | Othello | 61 | 7 | 0 |
|  | 18 | The Merry Wives of Windsor | 61 | 12 | 0 |
|  | 22 | Hamlet | 39 | 6 | 6 |
|  | 23 | The Merry Wives of Windsor | 119 | 0 | 6 |
|  | 25 | Macbeth | 88 | 8 | 0 |

## 1733

**1733 COVENT GARDEN** (*cont.*)

|   |   |   | £ | s. | d. |
|---|---|---|---|---|---|
| Apr. | 3 | Othello *BT. Chapman* | 137 | 15 | 0 |
|  | 9 | Hamlet | 48 | 17 | 0 |
|  | 10 | Henry IV, Part I | 26 | 10 | 0 |
|  | 16 | The Merry Wives of Windsor | 50 | 7 | 0 |
|  | 21 | King Lear *BT. Paget and Mrs Forrester* | 135 | 8 | 0 |
| May | 1 | Timon of Athens *BT. Wood, treasurer* | 275 | 12 | 0 |
|  | 3 | Macbeth *BT. Dupré and Mrs Pelling* | 142 | 8 | 0 |
|  | 19 | The Merry Wives of Windsor *BT. the author [of The Rape of Helen, also acted this night—John Durant Breval]* | 103 | 6 | 6 |
|  | 29 | Timon of Athens |  |  |  |
|  | 31 | Othello |  |  |  |
| Sept. | 15 | same |  |  |  |
|  | 22 | Hamlet |  |  |  |
|  | 29 | The Merry Wives of Windsor |  |  |  |
| Oct. | 11 | Macbeth |  |  |  |
| Nov. | 10 | Othello |  |  |  |
|  | 12 | Macbeth |  |  |  |
|  | 14 | King Lear |  |  |  |
|  | 17 | Hamlet |  |  |  |
|  | 19 | Measure for Measure |  |  |  |
|  | 20 | The Merry Wives of Windsor |  |  |  |
|  | 30 | Henry IV, Part I |  |  |  |
| Dec. | 15 | Richard III |  |  |  |
|  | 20 | Troilus and Cressida |  |  |  |
|  | 21 | The Merry Wives of Windsor |  |  |  |
|  | 26 | Richard III |  |  |  |

## HAYMARKET

Oct. 10 Henry IV, Part I
    12 Henry IV, Part II
    17 Hamlet
Nov. 12 Henry IV, Part I
    17 Hamlet
    21 Henry IV, Part I
    22 Henry IV, Part II
    26 Othello
Dec. 8 Henry IV, Part II

## GOODMAN'S FIELDS

Jan. 3 Julius Caesar
    22 same
Feb. 19 Macbeth *BT. Delane*
Mar. 8 Hamlet *BT. Mrs Roberts*
    17 King Lear *BT. Hulett*
Apr. 2 Othello *BT. Delane*

## 1733–1734

**1733 GOODMAN'S FIELDS** (*cont.*)

- Apr. 6 Julius Caesar *BT. W. Giffard*
- 9 Macbeth *BT. Huddy*
- 11 Richard III *BT. Mr and Mrs Hamilton*
- 12 same
- 18 Hamlet *BT. Norris [Jr.] and Mrs Bullock, the dancer*
- 23 King Lear *BT. Mrs Haughton*
- May 3 Henry IV, Part I *BT. Havard and Winstone*
- 7 Othello *BT. [W.] Bullock [Jr.] and Excell*
- 15 Julius Caesar *BT. Eversman*
- 16 Othello *BT. Dove, Morris, World, and Edward Giffard*
- 21 Hamlet *BT. Gibbs, pit-keeper*
- 22 Macbeth *BT. Temple and Boucher, box-keepers*
- Sept. 10 Julius Caesar
- 25 Henry IV, Part I
- 28 Hamlet
- Oct. 5 Othello
- 10 Julius Caesar
- 26 The Merry Wives of Windsor
- Nov. 10 King Lear
- Dec. 12 Hamlet

**1734 DRURY LANE**

- Jan. 1 The Tempest
- 22 Richard III
- 29 The Tempest
- Apr. 17 Henry IV, Part I
- 18 Henry IV, Part II *BT. Mills*
- 20 Henry VIII
- May 2 Henry IV, Part I
- 4 Henry IV, Part II *BT. the editor of Shakespeare [Lewis Theobald]*

  Theobald's edition, 'collated with the oldest copies, and corrected', was published in 1733.

- 13 Othello *BT. Mrs Charke*
- 15 The Tempest *BT. Chetwood*
- 17 Henry IV, Part I *BT. Paget*
- Sept. 10 Othello
- 24 Henry IV, Part I
- Oct. 4 same
- 14 Henry VIII
- 15 same
- 16 Othello
- 22 The Tempest
- 26 Richard III
- 28 same
- 29 Henry VIII
- Nov. 8 Julius Caesar

43

## 1734 DRURY LANE (cont.)

- Nov. 9 Julius Caesar
- 11 same
- 12 same
- 13 same
- 15 The Tempest
- Dec. 4 Julius Caesar
- 6 The Merry Wives of Windsor
- 7 same
- 9 same
- 10 same
- 11 same
- 18 same
- 27 Henry VIII
- 30 Henry IV, Part I

## COVENT GARDEN

- Jan. 1 Macbeth
- 3 Hamlet
- 5 Othello
- 7 Troilus and Cressida
- 14 King Lear
- 21 Henry IV, Part I
- 25 The Merry Wives of Windsor
- Feb. 6 Measure for Measure
- 8 The Jew of Venice
- 13 Macbeth
- 21 Hamlet
- Mar. 2 Othello
- 19 Macbeth *BT. Mrs Bullock*
- 21 Henry IV, Part I *BT. Mlle. Sallé*
- 28 Timon of Athens *BT. Walker*
- May 14 Hamlet *BT. the prompter* [*Stede*]
- 15 Timon of Athens *BT. Gwinn and Jarvis, house-keeper*
- 16 Richard III *BT. Aston, Thompson, and a gentleman under misfortunes* [*Sambre*]

    The recipient of the BT. is named in DA of May 15.

- 22 Othello
- 24 [Macbeth]

    Bill in DJ, but 'Dismissed' (Latreille, iii. 166).

- Sept. 18 Hamlet
- Oct. 9 See if You Like It
- 11 same
- 14 same *BT. the author of the new comedy* [*unidentified*]
- 19 Othello
- 21 same

## 1734

1734 COVENT GARDEN (*cont.*)

Oct. 23 Othello
 24 same
  Genest (iii. 456) has, 'Acted 4 times successively'. This is correct; Oct. 20 was a Sunday, and on Oct. 22 the theatre was dark.

 26 same
 31 Hamlet
Nov. 2 Othello
  *and* See if You Like It
 14 Henry IV, Part I
 18 Othello
Dec. 14 Hamlet
 19 Othello
 26 Richard III

## HAYMARKET

Jan. 16 Henry IV, Part I
 19 Henry IV, Part II
Feb. 1 Othello
May 27 Henry IV, Part I *BT. Hewson*
June 3 The Humours of Sir John Falstaff, Justice Shallow, and Ancient Pistol
 4 same
 5 same

## GOODMAN'S FIELDS

Jan. 9 Othello
 21 Julius Caesar
 25 Othello
 31 Macbeth
Feb. 1 same
 4 same
 14 Julius Caesar
 20 The Merry Wives of Windsor
Mar. 18 Richard III *BT. Hulett*
Apr. 1 Julius Caesar
 22 Hamlet
 29 Henry IV, Part I
May 8 Richard III *BT. Evans and Miss Cole*
 10 King Lear *BT. Jenkins*
Sept. 16 Hamlet
 20 Julius Caesar
Oct. 4 Othello
 9 The Merry Wives of Windsor
 16 Henry IV, Part I
 17 Hamlet

## 1734 GOODMAN'S FIELDS (cont.)

Nov. 7 Macbeth
8 same
29 King Lear
Dec. 6 Richard III
9 Macbeth
23 Hamlet

## VILLIERS ST., YORK BUILDINGS

Nov. 19 Othello BT. the author of the Mad Captain [also acted this night—Robert Drury]
29 same BT. Drury

## 1735 DRURY LANE

Jan. 7 Richard III
18 Julius Caesar
Feb. 5 Richard III BT. Hyde
7 Henry VIII
13 The Merry Wives of Windsor
14 The Tempest
22 Othello
25 A Cure for a Scold

> Genest (iii. 448) says that, preceding this new farce, *Richard III* was acted. *The Earl of Essex* was, however, acted in its stead. On the LDP bill is an N.B.: 'The Play of King Richard III advertis'd for this Day . . . is deferr'd.'

27 same
Mar. 1 same BT. the author of the farce [*James Worsdale*]
10 Hamlet BT. Mills
20 A Cure for a Scold BT. Mrs Thurmond
Apr. 11 Henry IV, Part II BT. Harper
May 5 A Cure for a Scold BT. the author of the farce
8 Henry IV, Part II BT. Salway and Miss Mann
13 The Merry Wives of Windsor BT. Oates
Sept. 1 Julius Caesar
6 Othello
11 Henry IV, Part I
18 Timon of Athens
27 King Lear
Oct. 1 Julius Caesar
21 Macbeth
22 same
25 Richard III
27 Henry VIII
31 The Tempest
Nov. 1 Hamlet
15 Henry IV, Part I

> Genest (iii. 474) erroneously gives *Henry IV, Part II*.

## 1735 DRURY LANE (cont.)

- Nov. 21 The Merry Wives of Windsor
- 24 King Lear
- 27 Macbeth
- Dec. 5 Hamlet
- 8 Timon of Athens
- 9 Julius Caesar
- 30 Henry VIII

## COVENT GARDEN

|  |  |  | £ | s. | d. |
|---|---|---|---|---|---|
| Jan. 20 | Henry IV, Part I |  |  |  |  |
| 24 | Othello |  |  |  |  |
| Feb. 11 | The Jew of Venice |  |  |  |  |
| Apr. 8 | Richard III *BT. Mrs Bullock* |  |  |  |  |
| 10 | King Lear *BT. Stephens* |  |  |  |  |
| 17 | Henry IV, Part I *BT. Glover* |  |  |  |  |
| May 9 | Othello *BT. Ridout, Wignell, and Dupré* |  |  |  |  |
| June 6 | King Lear |  |  |  |  |
| Sept. 12 | Hamlet |  | 55 | 19 | 0 |
| Oct. 3 | Othello |  | 42 | 8 | 6 |
| Nov. 14 | [Macbeth] |  |  |  |  |

Listed by Genest (iii. 479). On this night the theatre was dark. 'The Play of Macbeth was inserted in several of the Daily Papers yesterday, to have been perform'd at the Theatre in Covent Garden last night, which was impossible, on Account of the Decorations, &c. preparing for it' (LDP, Nov. 15).

|  |  | £ | s. | d. |
|---|---|---|---|---|
| 15 | Macbeth | 65 | 6 | 0 |
| 22 | Julius Caesar | 69 | 4 | 0 |
| Dec. 6 | Othello | 46 | 18 | 0 |
| 20 | King Lear | 70 | 7 | 6 |
| 27 | Macbeth | 90 | 3 | 6 |

## LINCOLN'S INN FIELDS

- Apr. 19 Othello *BT. the prompter* [*Stede*]

Genest (iii. 466) erroneously has 'the prompters'.

- May 7 King Lear *BT. Henry Chapman, coachmaker*
- Aug. 16 [Caius Marius]

Bill in LDP of Aug. 15, but not of Aug. 16. 'Apparently postponed' (Latreille, iii. 324).

- 22 Caius Marius

## GOODMAN'S FIELDS

- Jan. 4 Othello
- 29 The Merry Wives of Windsor
- Feb. 15 King Lear
- 27 Hamlet

47

## 1735 GOODMAN'S FIELDS (cont.)

- Mar. 13 Julius Caesar *BT. Wetherilt [Sr.] and Bardin*
- 27 Othello *BT. Huddy*
- Apr. 23 Macbeth *BT. Shepheard, treasurer*
- 29 Henry IV, Part I *BT. Eversman*
- Sept. 10 Othello
- 19 Hamlet
- Oct. 10 same *BT.* [Henry] *Carey, author of The Honest Yorkshire-man* [*also acted this night*]
- Nov. 11 The Merry Wives of Windsor
- 26 Henry V
- 27 same
- 28 same
- 29 same
- Dec. 1 same
- 2 same
- 3 same
- 5 Hamlet
- 8 Sauny the Scot
- 9 same
- 10 same
- 12 same
- 13 same
- 15 same

## VILLIERS ST., YORK BUILDINGS

- Mar. 19 Othello
- Sept. 18 The Cobler of Preston

## 1736 DRURY LANE

- Feb. 25 Timon of Athens
- Mar. 4 Othello
- 11 Henry IV, Part II *BT. Quin*
- 20 Hamlet *BT. Milward*
- Apr. 1 Henry IV, Part II *BT. Madem. Roland*
- 16 Julius Caesar *BT. Mrs Heron's executors*
- May 5 Henry VIII
- 10 Hamlet
- 13 Henry VIII *BT. Chetwood*
- 17 Henry IV, Part I *BT. a private gentleman*
- 19 Julius Caesar
- 20 Henry IV, Part II *BT. Winstone and Miss Cole*
- 21 The Merry Wives of Windsor *BT. Robinson, supervisor and sub-treasurer*
- 26 Richard III
- 29 Julius Caesar
- 31 Henry VIII
- Sept. 4 Hamlet

# 1736

1736 DRURY LANE (cont.

- Sept. 9 Macbeth
- 18 Richard III
- 21 Julius Caesar
- Oct. 5 Othello
- 7 Henry IV, Part I
- 9 Henry IV, Part II
- 19 Henry VIII
- 28 Julius Caesar
- Nov. 9 Hamlet
- 18 Macbeth
- 19 Timon of Athens
- 27 Henry IV, Part I
- Dec. 1 Richard III
- 4 Henry IV, Part II
- 16 Othello
- 20 Hamlet
- 23 Macbeth
- 27 Timon of Athens
- 30 Henry VIII

## COVENT GARDEN

Jan. 3 [Richard III]
    Bill in LDP, but 'Dismissed' (Latreille, iii. 287).

|  |  | £ | s. | d. |
|---|---|---|---|---|
| 8 | King Lear | 78 | 4 | 6 |
| 17 | Hamlet | 42 | 13 | 6 |
| 21 | Macbeth | 133 | 0 | 6 |
| Feb. 12 | The Jew of Venice | 58 | 18 | 6 |
| 18 | Macbeth | 73 | 19 | 6 |
| 24 | King Lear BT. Hyde | 110 | 17 | 6 |
| Mar. 13 | Hamlet | 72 | 13 | 0 |
| 18 | The Merry Wives of Windsor BT. Ryan | 140 | 12 | 0 |
| 30 | Othello BT. Stephens | 172 | 3 | 6 |
| Apr. 26 | Macbeth BT. Madem. D'Hervigni and Mrs Kilby | 138 | 4 | 0 |
| Oct. 20 | same |  |  |  |
| 23 | Hamlet |  |  |  |
| Nov. 8 | King Lear |  |  |  |
| Dec. 21 | [Macbeth] |  |  |  |

    Listed by Genest (iii. 503). The play this night was *The Beggar's Opera*.

## LINCOLN'S INN FIELDS

- Apr. 14 Henry IV, Part I BT. *Macklin, Bardin, and Turbutt*
- 16 Hamlet BT. *Aston and a gentleman under misfortunes*
- Nov. 18 Sauny the Scot
- 20 Henry IV, Part I
- 22 same
- Dec. 13 Hamlet

# 1736-1737

## 1736 GOODMAN'S FIELDS

Feb. 5 Henry V
  9 Hamlet
  23 Sauny the Scot
  27 Timon of Athens
  28 same
Mar. 5 same
Apr. 13 Henry V *BT. Monsieur Vallois*

## 1737 DRURY LANE

Jan. 3 Richard III
  6 The Merry Wives of Windsor
  10 King Lear
  13 Othello
  17 Henry IV, Part I
  21 Henry IV, Part II
  24 Julius Caesar
  27 Hamlet
Feb. 1 The Merry Wives of Windsor
   The bill for the above is in HTC. The play appears to have been changed from *The Conscious Lovers*, which is advertised for this night in Harris.

  3 same
  7 Macbeth
  10 The Tempest
  11 same
  12 same
  14 same
  15 same
  17 Julius Caesar
  21 Timon of Athens
  26 Henry VIII
  28 The Universal Passion
Mar. 1 same
  3 same *BT. the author* [James Miller]
  7 same
  8 same
  10 Measure for Measure *BT. Quin*
  14 The Universal Passion *BT. the author*
  21 same
  24 same
   Genest (iii. 496) says that this was BT. T. Cibber. This is erroneous: Cibber had his BT. on Mar. 22.

  28 same *BT. the author*
  31 same
Apr. 11 The Tempest
  14 same
  18 Henry IV, Part I

50

1737 DRURY LANE (cont.)
- Apr. 21 Measure for Measure
- 25 The Tempest
- 28 Julius Caesar *BT. Mons. Muilment and Miss Mann*
- May 19 Macbeth *BT. Leviez, Ray, and Raftor*
- 23 Hamlet *BT. a person in distress*
- Sept. 22 Henry IV, Part I
- 24 Hamlet
- Oct. 1 Richard III
- 6 Othello
- 20 Henry IV, Part II
- Nov. 1 Measure for Measure
- 10 Othello

## COVENT GARDEN
- Jan. 13 Hamlet
- Feb. 1 Macbeth
- 7 King Lear
- 15 Cymbeline
- 17 same
- 21 same
- 26 King John
- Mar. 1 same
- 3 same
- 5 same
- 8 same
- 14 Othello *BT. Delane*
- 21 Macbeth *BT. Swinny*
- 22 King John
- 24 The Merry Wives of Windsor *BT. Glover*
- 29 King John
- Apr. 14 Henry IV, Part I *BT. Stephens*
- 16 King John
- 21 Othello *BT. Mrs Stevens and Mrs Wright*
- 25 Hamlet *BT. Short*
- 29 The Merry Wives of Windsor *BT. Boman [Jr.] and Mr and Mrs James*
- May 5 Cymbeline *BT. Wood*
- 27 [King John]

Listed by Genest (iii. 506) as 'about 10th time—last bill [of the season]'. The theatre was, however, dark from May 23–8, and the season did not end until May 31. *King John* had been acted 8 times.

- Sept. 16 King John
- 28 King Lear
- Oct. 4 Macbeth
- Nov. 2 Much Ado about Nothing
- 3 same
- 7 same

# 1737-1738

## 1737 LINCOLN'S INN FIELDS

 Jan.  3  The Merry Wives of Windsor
    6  Hamlet
 May  2  same *BT. two citizens in distress*
 Sept.  7  Othello

## HAYMARKET

 Mar.  4  King John *BT. the author of the farce* [The Rival Milliners, also acted this night—Robert Drury] *and Miss Burgess*

## NEW WELLS, CLERKENWELL

 June 13  The Cobler of Preston
   14  same
   15  same
   16  same
   17  same
   18  same
   20  same
   21  same
   22  same
   23  same
   24  same

## 1738 DRURY LANE

 Jan.  4  Othello
   12  Henry IV, Part I
   13  Henry IV, Part II
   19  Julius Caesar
   23  Hamlet
   26  Measure for Measure
   31  Macbeth
 Feb.  8  Julius Caesar
   13  Richard III
   25  Othello
 Apr. 12  Measure for Measure *BT. Mrs Cibber*

| | | | £ | s. | d. |
|---|---|---|---|---|---|
|    28 | Julius Caesar *BT. a fund for erecting a monument to the memory of Shakespeare* | | 170 | 0 | 0 |

     This statue, designed by William Kent, was erected in Westminster Abbey in 1741. See COVENT GARDEN, Apr. 10, 1739.

 May  1  Hamlet *BT. Essex*
   3  The Merry Wives of Windsor *BT. Macklin and Turbutt*
   6  Henry VIII *BT. Haughton*
   11  Othello *BT. Hyde*
   18  The Merry Wives of Windsor *BT. Hobson, Beckham, Allen, and Miss Cole*

1738 DRURY LANE (cont.)
- May 22 Henry VIII *BT. Vallois and the two Miss Scots, scholars to Mr Vallois*
-      23 Richard III *BT. a family under misfortunes*
- Sept. 7 Hamlet
-      14 Henry IV, Part I
-      16 Henry IV, Part II
-      21 Julius Caesar
-      26 Othello
-      30 Richard III
- Oct. 13 Henry IV, Part II
-      20 Macbeth
-      23 Hamlet
- Nov. 13 Othello
-      17 Henry IV, Part I
-      20 Henry VIII
-      29 Julius Caesar
- Dec. 12 same
-      14 Hamlet *BT. Mrs Miller, widow of the late Jo. Miller, comedian*
-      19 Henry IV, Part I
-      22 Henry VIII

## COVENT GARDEN

- Jan. 3 Macbeth
-     17 Hamlet *BT. Hippisley*
- Feb. 2 King John
-     6 Richard II
-     7 same
-     8 same
-     9 same
-     10 same
-     11 same
-     13 Henry IV, Part I
-     14 Richard II
-     16 Henry IV, Part II
-     20 same
-     21 Richard II
-     23 Henry V
-     25 same
-     27 same
-     28 same
- Mar. 2 King John
-     6 Henry V
-     9 Richard II
-     13 Henry VI, Part I *BT. Delane*
-     20 Cymbeline *BT. Nivelon*
- Apr. 3 Henry V

### 1738–1739

**1738 COVENT GARDEN** (cont.)

- Apr. 5 Henry IV, Part I *BT. Bridgwater*
- 7 The Cobler of Preston *BT. Chapman*
- 8 King John *BT. Walker*
- 10 Othello *BT. Lalauze*
- 13 Hamlet
- 14 Macbeth *BT. Mrs Hallam*
- May 2 Richard II *BT. Wood, treasurer*
- 4 Henry V
- June 27 Othello
- Aug. 1 Marina
- 4 same
- 8 same *BT. the author* [George Lillo]
- Oct. 6 Macbeth
- 14 Hamlet
- 21 King Lear
- Nov. 29 King John
- 30 Richard II
- Dec. 1 same
- 2 Henry IV, Part I
- 4 Henry IV, Part II
- 5 Henry V
- 21 Richard II
- 22 Henry V
- 29 Macbeth

**1739 DRURY LANE**

- Jan. 1 Macbeth
- 25 Hamlet
- 31 Richard III
- Feb. 10 Henry VIII
- Mar. 6 Henry IV, Part I
- 8 King Lear *BT. Quin*
- 29 Julius Caesar
- Apr. 27 Henry VIII *BT. Wright*
- May 16 Hamlet *BT. Turbutt and Ridout*
- 17 Henry VIII
- Sept. 1 Hamlet
- 18 Macbeth
- 21 Othello
- Oct. 10 Julius Caesar
- 13 The Merry Wives of Windsor
- 17 Richard III
- 20 Henry VIII
- Nov. 19 Henry IV, Part I
- 20 Henry IV, Part II
- 26 Hamlet
- Dec. 11 Julius Caesar

**1739 DRURY LANE** (*cont.*)
- Dec. 13 Othello
- 17 Macbeth
- 20 Henry VIII
- 26 The Tempest
- 27 same

**COVENT GARDEN**
- Jan. 11 Henry V
- 20 Macbeth
- 23 The Jew of Venice
- Feb. 13 Hamlet
- 19 Richard II
- Mar. 3 King Lear
- 8 King John
- 19 Henry V *BT. Hippisley*
- Apr. 10 Hamlet *BT. a fund for erecting a monument to the memory of Shakespeare*   £ s. d.   82 16 0

  See DRURY LANE, Apr. 28, 1738.

- 25 The Merry Wives of Windsor *BT. Stephens*
- May 4 Henry IV, Part I *BT. Rosco, Villeneuve, and Desse*
- 25 Much Ado about Nothing *BT. Wilmer, Laurence, and Powell, box-keepers*
- June 5 [Macbeth]

  Listed by Genest (iii. 592). On this night the theatre was almost certainly dark. Bill in LDP of June 4, advertising the performance 'Tomorrow', but no bill at all on June 5.

- Sept. 27 Henry IV, Part I
- Oct. 22 King John
- 23 Richard II
- 25 Macbeth
- Nov. 17 Hamlet
- Dec. 6 Henry IV, Part II *BT. Hyde*
- 19 Othello *BT. a gentlewoman in distress*
- 31 Macbeth

**1740 DRURY LANE**
- Jan. 2 Henry VIII
- 4 The Tempest
- 14 Richard III
- 17 Julius Caesar
- 23 Hamlet
- Mar. 13 Julius Caesar *BT. Quin*
- 20 Timon of Athens *BT. Milward*
- 29 Macbeth *BT. Johnson*
- Apr. 7 Timon of Athens

1740 DRURY LANE (cont.)
- Apr. 23 The Merry Wives of Windsor BT. *Wright*
- 25 Henry IV, Part I BT. *Peirson, treasurer*
- 26 Hamlet BT. *Essex*
- 30 Henry VIII BT. *Mr and Mrs Chetwood*
- May 13 Macbeth BT. *Stoppelaer*
- 14 The Tempest BT. *Ridout, Raftor, and Mrs Bennet*
- 23 Hamlet BT. *Ray, Cole, and Vaughan*
- 30 Henry VIII
- Sept. 6 Hamlet
- 16 Richard III
- 27 Othello
- Oct. 4 Julius Caesar
- 13 Henry IV, Part I
- 14 Henry IV, Part II
- 15 The Merry Wives of Windsor
- Nov. 10 Henry VIII
- 26 Hamlet
- 27 Macbeth
- 28 The Tempest BT. *the brave and unfortunate crew [of the Prince of Orange], belonging to Capt. [John] Peddie, who (after having clear'd themselves by the most gallant behaviour from a Spanish privateer) were shipwreck'd in a tempest in Margate Road [on Nov. 1], and stood on the wreck upwards of twelve hours, with the sea beating over them, before they were relieved. And for the benefit of the widow of the boatswain killed in the engagement*

  For details of the above circumstances, see Capt. Peddie's letter to LDP, Nov. 17, 1740.

- Dec. 3 Macbeth
- 16 Othello
- 19 Julius Caesar
- 20 As You Like It
- 22 same
- 23 same
- 26 same
- 27 same
- 29 same
- 30 same
- 31 same

## COVENT GARDEN

- Jan. 1 Macbeth
- Feb. 6 Henry IV, Part II
- Mar. 10 Othello BT. *[T.] Cibber*
- 11 Henry V BT. *Delane*
- 27 The Merry Wives of Windsor BT. *Hippisley*
- Apr. 17 same
- 21 Macbeth BT. *Mrs Hallam*

## 1740–1741

**1740 COVENT GARDEN** (*cont.*)

|  |  |  | £ | s. | d. |
|---|---|---|---|---|---|
| May 10 | Macbeth | | | | |
| 29 | The Merry Wives of Windsor *BT. Boucher and Giles* | | | | |
| Sept. 26 | Macbeth | | 54 | 8 | 6 |
| Oct. 24 | Hamlet | | 31 | 0 | 0 |
| Nov. 5 | Macbeth | | 53 | 5 | 6 |

### GOODMAN'S FIELDS

Oct. 23 Othello
Nov. 14 same
    15 The Merry Wives of Windsor
    28 Henry IV, Part I
Dec. 4 Hamlet
    10 Macbeth
    18 Henry IV, Part I
    20 The Merry Wives of Windsor
    22 Hamlet
    27 Macbeth

**1741 DRURY LANE**

Jan. 1 As You Like It
    2 same
    3 same
    5 same
    7 same
    8 same
    9 same
    10 same
    12 same
    13 same
    14 same
    15 Twelfth Night
    17 same
    19 same
    20 same
    21 same
    22 same
    23 same
    26 Henry IV, Part I
    27 Henry IV, Part II
    28 As You Like It
    29 same
Feb. 5 Twelfth Night
    6 As You Like It
    12 Richard III
    14 The Merchant of Venice
    16 same

1741 DRURY LANE (cont.)
- Feb. 17 The Merchant of Venice
- 19 same
- 21 same
- 23 same
- 24 Julius Caesar BT. *a gentleman, who has wrote for the stage*
- 26 The Merchant of Venice
- 28 same
- Mar. 2 same
- 3 same
- 7 same
- 9 same
- 10 As You Like It BT. *Quin*
- 12 The Merchant of Venice
- 14 The Universal Passion BT. *Mrs Clive*
- 16 The Merchant of Venice
- 19 same
- 21 Hamlet BT. *Johnson*
- 30 Macbeth BT. *Mrs Roberts*
- Apr. 3 Julius Caesar
- 6 Henry IV, Part I BT. *[W.] Mills*
- 7 The Merchant of Venice BT. *Macklin*
- 10 same
- 14 As You Like It BT. *Mrs Pritchard*
- 17 The Universal Passion BT. *Wright*
- 18 Henry VIII BT. *Essex*
- 20 Twelfth Night BT. *Woodward*
- 21 Henry VIII
- 23 The Merchant of Venice
- 25 As You Like It
- 30 The Merchant of Venice
- May 5 Hamlet BT. *Chetwood*
- 11 As You Like It
- 13 Timon of Athens BT. *Cashell*
- 15 The Tempest BT. *Ray, Green, Beckham, Rogers, Mrs Penkethman, and a widow under misfortunes*
- 18 The Merchant of Venice
- 20 As You Like It
- Sept. 10 Othello
- 19 Hamlet
- Oct. 8 Macbeth
- 9 Henry IV, Part I
- 15 As You Like It
- 16 same
- 17 same
- 19 same
- 20 [same]
    Listed by Genest (iii. 643). The play this night was *Love Makes a Man*.

## 1741

**1741 DRURY LANE** (cont.)

Oct. 21 [As You Like It]
        Listed by Genest (iii. 643). The play this night was *The Twin Rivals*.
    26 Othello
    28 As You Like It
Nov. 2 The Merchant of Venice
    3 same
    7 same
    10 As You Like It
    11 The Comedy of Errors
    12 same
    13 same
    14 same
    16 Julius Caesar
    17 The Merchant of Venice
    18 Hamlet
    28 As You Like It
    30 Macbeth
Dec. 2 The Merchant of Venice
    10 The Comedy of Errors
    17 [Julius Caesar]
        Listed by Genest (iii. 643). The play this night was *The Twin Rivals*.
    19 Richard III
    21 As You Like It
    22 The Merchant of Venice
    28 Richard III
    31 Hamlet

## COVENT GARDEN

|  |  |  | £ | s. | d. |
|---|---|---|---|---|---|
| Jan. | 5 | The Merry Wives of Windsor | 136 | 17 | 6 |
|  | 7 | King Lear | 75 | 10 | 0 |
|  | 16 | The Merry Wives of Windsor | 90 | 7 | 0 |
|  | 20 | King Lear | 62 | 12 | 0 |
|  | 27 | Henry IV, Part I *BT. a person under misfortunes* | 59 | 4 | 6 |
| Feb. | 10 | The Merry Wives of Windsor | 140 | 2 | 0 |
| Mar. | 5 | Macbeth | 105 | 1 | 0 |
| Apr. | 9 | King John *BT. Bridgwater* | 88 | 16 | 0 |
| May | 4 | The Merry Wives of Windsor *BT. Cross, prompter, Anderson, Clarke, and White* |  |  |  |
| Oct. | 10 | same |  |  |  |
|  | 13 | Richard III |  |  |  |
|  | 14 | same |  |  |  |
|  | 15 | As You Like It |  |  |  |
|  | 16 | same |  |  |  |
|  | 17 | same |  |  |  |
|  | 19 | same |  |  |  |
|  | 20 | Hamlet |  |  |  |

59

# 1741

**1741 COVENT GARDEN** (*cont.*)

Oct. 28 As You Like It
Nov. 11 The Winter's Tale
 12 same
 13 same
 14 same

> Genest (iv. 4) erroneously has 'acted 5 times successively'.

 16 The Merry Wives of Windsor
Dec. 3 As You Like It
 8 Richard III
 9 Othello *BT. Christopher Perry*
 10 The Merry Wives of Windsor

## GOODMAN'S FIELDS

Jan. 15 The Winter's Tale
 16 same
 17 same
 19 same
 21 same

> The bill has 'the 4th Day', and the remaining bills have respectively the '5th, 6th, 7th Day'. The performance on Jan. 19 was advertised as 'Acted but Thrice'. Another play was perhaps acted on that night, but an error in the numbering of the 'Days' is equally possible.

 23 same
 24 same
 26 same
 29 Othello
Feb. 10 Richard III
 26 Hamlet
Mar. 7 All's Well that Ends Well *BT. Mrs Giffard*
 9 same
 10 same
 14 same
 17 same
 19 Timon of Athens *BT. Marshall*
 21 All's Well that Ends Well
 30 same
Apr. 3 same
 10 The Winter's Tale *BT. Mrs Steel*
 17 The Merry Wives of Windsor *BT. Major John Triquet (late of Spital-Fields), under misfortunes*
 21 Henry IV, Part I *BT. Cole, prompter*
 24 Hamlet *BT. Nelson and Marr*
Sept. 28 All's Well that Ends Well
Oct. 14 Hamlet
 15 The Merry Wives of Windsor
 19 Richard III

60

## 1741–1742

1741 **GOODMAN'S FIELDS** (*cont.*)
    Oct. 20 Richard III
         21 same
         22 same
         24 same
         26 same
         27 same
    Nov. 2 same
         23 same
         26 same
    Dec. 9 Hamlet
         15 Richard III
         23 same

## JAMES ST., HAYMARKET

May 11 The Cobler of Preston *BT. an unfortunate brother Mason*

1742 **DRURY LANE**
    Jan. 11 The Merchant of Venice
         16 As You Like It
         22 All's Well that Ends Well
         26 Hamlet
    Feb. 16 All's Well that Ends Well
         19 same
         20 same
         22 same
         23 same
         25 same
         26 same
         27 same
    Mar. 6 The Merchant of Venice
         9 As You Like It *BT. the widow Milward and her four children*
         11 same
         15 Hamlet *BT. Delane*
         18 The Merchant of Venice
         23 All's Well that Ends Well
    Apr. 8 As You Like It *BT. Mons. and Madem. Mechel*
         19 Macbeth
         23 The Merchant of Venice *BT. Mons. Muilment*
         24 Henry VIII *BT. Berry*
         27 Henry IV, Part I *BT. Shepard and Winstone*
         30 Richard III *BT. Turbutt and Leviez*
    May 3 Hamlet *BT. Havard, Arthur, and Ridout*
         6 Othello

            Genest (iii. 651) erroneously has May 5, on which night the theatre was dark.

         7 The Merchant of Venice
         20 As You Like It *BT. Raftor*

## 1742 DRURY LANE (*cont.*)

- May 28 King Lear
- 31 Richard III
- Sept. 11 The Merchant of Venice
- 14 As You Like It
- 23 The Merchant of Venice
- Oct. 13 Richard III
- 14 As You Like It
- 15 Richard III
- 23 same
- 25 The Merchant of Venice
- 26 King Lear
- 27 As You Like It
- 28 Richard III
- Nov. 5 same
- 9 King Lear
- 11 Richard III

> Genest (iv. 38) erroneously has Nov. 10, on which night, being a General Fast Day, the theatre was dark.

- 16 Hamlet
- 18 same
- 20 same
- 23 same
- 24 King Lear
- 25 Hamlet
- 27 The Merchant of Venice
- 29 Hamlet
- 30 As You Like It
- Dec. 2 Hamlet
- 4 same
- 10 same
- 13 King Lear
- 20 Richard III
- 21 As You Like It *BT. Gale*
- 30 Hamlet

## COVENT GARDEN

- Jan. 8 As You Like It
- 21 The Winter's Tale
- 22 As You Like It
- 29 The Merry Wives of Windsor
- Feb. 12 Henry IV, Part II
- 13 As You Like It
- 18 Hamlet
- 20 Henry IV, Part II
- Mar. 23 The Merry Wives of Windsor
- Apr. 21 same *BT. Mons. Dubuisson and Madame Bonneval*
- 23 As You Like It *BT. E. Roberts and Mons. Destrade*

## 1742

**1742 COVENT GARDEN** (*cont.*)

| | | |
|---|---|---|
| Apr. | 26 | Othello *BT. Stephens* |
| May | 5 | Macbeth *BT. Cashell and Marten* |
| | 7 | Henry IV, Part II *BT. Mullart and Laurence, box-keeper* |
| | 20 | Hamlet |
| Sept. | 22 | Othello |
| | 24 | same |
| | 27 | same |
| Oct. | 8 | Macbeth |
| | 13 | Richard III |
| | 14 | same |
| | 25 | Henry IV, Part I |
| | 26 | Henry IV, Part II |
| | 27 | The Merry Wives of Windsor |
| | 30 | Macbeth |
| Nov. | 11 | Hamlet |

Genest (iv. 41) erroneously has Nov. 10, on which night, being a General Fast Day, the theatre was dark.

| | | |
|---|---|---|
| | 20 | Julius Caesar |
| | 23 | Othello |
| | 25 | Measure for Measure |
| | 26 | same |
| Dec. | 2 | Othello |
| | 3 | The Merry Wives of Windsor |
| | 4 | Measure for Measure |
| | 6 | Richard III |
| | 11 | Henry IV, Part I |
| | 13 | Othello |
| | 15 | King Lear |
| | 16 | same |
| | 20 | Julius Caesar |
| | 29 | Henry IV, Part II |

## LINCOLN'S INN FIELDS

Dec. 27  Richard III

## GOODMAN'S FIELDS

| | | |
|---|---|---|
| Jan. | 15 | Hamlet |
| Mar. | 6 | Richard III |
| | 11 | King Lear |
| | 13 | same |
| | 18 | same *BT. Garrick* |
| | 20 | same |
| | 27 | same |
| | 30 | same |
| Apr. | 8 | same *BT. Blakes and Paget* |
| | 10 | same |
| | 21 | Richard III |

## 1742 GOODMAN'S FIELDS (cont.)

- May 1 King Lear
    - Genest (iv. 25) erroneously has Apr. 30, on which night the theatre was dark. Its only announcement is for the performance on May 1.
  - 5 Richard III
  - 12 King Lear
  - 14 Richard III
  - 19 King Lear
  - 21 Richard III

## JAMES ST., HAYMARKET
- Apr. 19 As You Like It *BT. Page*

## 1743 DRURY LANE
- Jan. 3 Richard III
  - 5 Hamlet
  - 6 As You Like It
  - 10 Richard III
  - 13 Hamlet *BT. Garrick*
  - 15 King Lear
  - 19 Richard III
  - 21 The Merchant of Venice *BT. the author of the Prologue [on Shakespeare and his writings] and Epilogue [on Shakespeare's women's characters, spoken this night—Thomas Cooke]*
  - 22 Hamlet
- Feb. 1 King Lear
  - 5 Hamlet
  - 10 Henry IV, Part I
  - 14 Richard III
- Mar. 5 Hamlet
  - 12 King Lear
- Apr. 15 The Merchant of Venice *BT. Neale and Turbutt*
  - 16 Richard III
- May 3 same
  - 20 The Merchant of Venice *BT. Bradshaw, box-keeper*
  - 23 As You Like It *BT. Fenn, stage-door-keeper, Fuller, Fullwood, and Walker, numberer*
- Oct. 25 King Lear
- Nov. 29 The Merry Wives of Windsor
- Dec. 13 King Lear
  - 15 Hamlet
  - 17 Richard III
  - 23 Hamlet
  - 31 King Lear

## COVENT GARDEN
- Jan. 1 Macbeth
  - 4 Measure for Measure

1743 COVENT GARDEN (cont.)

Jan. 17 King Lear
21 Henry IV, Part I
22 Julius Caesar
27 The Merry Wives of Windsor
28 Richard III
Feb. 1 Measure for Measure
3 Macbeth
5 Othello
7 Henry IV, Part II
8 King Lear
15 Julius Caesar
21 Measure for Measure
22 The Merry Wives of Windsor
24 Othello
Mar. 1 Macbeth
7 Richard III *BT. Quin*
8 Measure for Measure
12 Henry IV, Part I
22 The Merry Wives of Windsor *BT. Hippisley*
Apr. 4 Othello *BT. Chapman*
7 Macbeth *BT. Madem. Auguste and Woodward*
   The second recipient of the BT. was probably Mrs Woodward. See Apr. 11.
8 Richard III *BT. Mons. Picq and Signora Domitilla*
11 Measure for Measure *BT. Woodward*
28 King Lear *BT. Ridout, Mons. Dupré, Goodall, and Stede*
May 9 Hamlet *BT. Mines, Gwinn, and Verhuyck*
17 Othello
Sept. 21 Hamlet
28 Richard III
Nov. 5 Hamlet
14 Richard III
28 Othello
29 same
Dec. 3 Macbeth
8 Julius Caesar
10 Richard III *BT. a tradesman under misfortunes*
12 Henry IV, Part I
14 Hamlet
19 The Merry Wives of Windsor
27 King Lear
29 Macbeth

LINCOLN'S INN FIELDS

Jan. 3 Richard III
5 same
7 same

## 1743 LINCOLN'S INN FIELDS (cont.)

- Jan. 10 King Lear
- 14 Richard III
- 24 King Lear
- 26 same
- Feb. 2 All's Well that Ends Well
- 4 same
- Mar. 17 Henry IV, Part I *BT. W. Giffard*

## 1744 DRURY LANE

- Jan. 3 Richard III
- 7 Macbeth
- 9 same
- 10 same
- 11 same
- 14 same
- 16 same
- 18 same
- 20 same
- 21 same
- 26 same
- 27 Henry IV, Part II
- 31 Macbeth
- Feb. 11 Hamlet
- 14 King Lear
- 18 Richard III
- Mar. 3 Macbeth
- 5 Hamlet *BT. Garrick*
- 8 King Lear
- 10 Othello *BT. a gentleman under misfortunes*
- 27 Hamlet
- Apr. 7 Richard III
- 14 Macbeth
- 20 King Lear
- May 4 The Merchant of Venice *BT. Shepard*
- 7 Richard III
- 18 Hamlet
- 22 Henry IV, Part I *BT. Church, Baker, Saunders, Dunbar, Bride, Brooks, Peite, and Stephens, gallery box-keeper*
- 24 King Lear
- 31 Richard III
- Oct. 22 Hamlet
- 24 King Lear
- 30 Macbeth
- Nov. 3 Richard III
- 9 Hamlet
- Dec. 8 King Lear
- 10 Macbeth

## 1744

**1744 DRURY LANE** (*cont.*)

Dec. 13 Hamlet *BT. Sheridan*
    15 Richard III
    19 The Merchant of Venice
    20 same

## COVENT GARDEN

Jan.  2 Richard III
    3 Julius Caesar
    5 As You Like It
    6 same
    9 same
   10 same
   11 Henry IV, Part II
   12 Othello
   13 As You Like It
   14 Measure for Measure
   19 Julius Caesar *BT. Mrs Saunders, many years a comedian*
   20 The Merry Wives of Windsor
   21 As You Like It
   23 Measure for Measure
   24 Henry VIII
   25 same
   26 same
   27 same

Feb.  4 same
    9 Macbeth
   11 As You Like It
   18 The Merry Wives of Windsor
   25 As You Like It

Mar.  1 Henry IV, Part II
   13 The Merchant of Venice *BT. Mrs Clive*
   26 Richard III
   27 As You Like It *BT. Chapman*
   31 Hamlet

Apr.  2 Othello *BT. Mrs Pritchard*
    3 Hamlet
    4 Measure for Measure *BT. Cooke*
    5 Richard III
    6 The Merry Wives of Windsor *BT. Woodward*
    7 The Merchant of Venice *BT. Picq and Reinhold*
   12 Henry VIII *BT. [E.] Roberts and Mrs Stevens*
   13 Macbeth
   18 Julius Caesar *BT. Sheridan*
   19 Henry V *BT. Mr and Mrs Hale*
   20 same *BT. Stephens*
   26 The Merchant of Venice *BT. Ridout, Dupré, Goodall, and Madem. Fabres*

## 1744

### 1744 COVENT GARDEN (cont.)

- Apr. 27 Henry IV, Part II *BT. James and Rosco*
- May 1 Macbeth *BT. Philips*
-     10 Henry VIII
-     16 The Merry Wives of Windsor
-     23 As You Like It
-     25 Othello
- Sept. 26 As You Like It
- Oct. 1 Macbeth
-     8 Henry IV, Part I
-     12 Macbeth
-     16 Othello
-     20 Henry VIII
-     22 The Merry Wives of Windsor
-     24 Richard III
-     31 Julius Caesar
- Nov. 1 Measure for Measure
-     2 As You Like It
-     3 Othello
-     9 Henry IV, Part II
-     10 Julius Caesar
-     15 As You Like It
-     19 Macbeth
-     24 The Merry Wives of Windsor
- Dec. 1 Henry IV, Part II
-     13 King Lear *BT. Perry*
-     19 As You Like It
-     29 Henry VIII

### HAYMARKET

- Feb. 6 Othello
-     13 same
-     15 Richard III *BT. a person under misfortune*
-     20 Othello
-     23 same
- Mar. 2 same
- Apr. 26 same *BT. a brave soldier, that suffered extremely at the battle of Dettingen* [*Thomas Brown*]

  Brown is identified in DA of Apr. 7.

- June 29 Hamlet
- July 2 [same]

  Listed by Genest (iv. 77). On this night, a Monday, the theatre was dark. During this summer the company acted on Tuesdays and Fridays only.

-     3 Hamlet
-     6 same
- Sept. 11 Romeo and Juliet

68

1744–1745

1744 HAYMARKET (*cont.*)
    Sept. 12 Romeo and Juliet
         14 same
         17 same
         19 same
         22 Othello
         29 Romeo and Juliet
    Oct.  2 same
         13 same
    Nov.  1 same
         8 Cymbeline
         10 [same]
             Bill in DP, but not acted. On this night the theatre was closed by order of the Lord Chamberlain. See T. Cibber's letter in DP of Nov. 12, and Genest (iv. 171).
    Dec. 17 Romeo and Juliet *BT*. *Miss Jenny Cibber*

NEW WELLS, GOODMAN'S FIELDS
    Nov. 27 Hamlet
         28 same
    Dec.  5 Richard III
         6 same
         7 same
         8 same
         13 Hamlet
         20 Richard III

1745 DRURY LANE
    Jan.  1 The Merchant of Venice
         5 Hamlet
         12 Richard III
         18 The Merchant of Venice
         23 King Lear
         25 Macbeth
         28 Hamlet
    Feb.  4 The Merchant of Venice
         12 Richard III
         20 King John
         21 same
         22 same
         23 same
         25 same
         26 same
         28 same
    Mar.  2 same
         4 The Merchant of Venice
         5 Richard III
         7 Othello

## 1745 DRURY LANE (cont.)

- Mar. 9 Othello *BT. Garrick*
- 14 King Lear *BT. Mrs Giffard*
- Apr. 25 Othello *BT. Sheridan*
- 27 The Merchant of Venice *BT. Leviez, Desse, and Powell, deputy treasurer*
- May 13 same *BT. Wright, Fenn, stage-door-keeper, Saunders, and Payne*
- Oct. 1 Othello
- 12 Hamlet
- Nov. 22 Henry VIII
- 23 The Merchant of Venice
- 29 Hamlet
- Dec. 5 As You Like It
- 6 The Merchant of Venice
- 26 Henry VIII
- 31 As You Like It

## COVENT GARDEN

- Jan. 8 Richard III *BT. a person under misfortunes*
- 12 Henry IV, Part I
- 25 Pyramus and Thisbe
- 26 same
- 28 same
- 29 As You Like It
  *and* Pyramus and Thisbe
- 31 Pyramus and Thisbe
- Feb. 1 same
- 2 Julius Caesar
  *and* Pyramus and Thisbe
- 4 Pyramus and Thisbe
- 5 same
- 6 same
- 7 same
- 8 Henry IV, Part II
  *and* Pyramus and Thisbe
- 11 Pyramus and Thisbe
- 15 Papal Tyranny in the Reign of King John
- 16 same
- 18 same *BT. the author* [Colley Cibber]
- 19 same
- 20 same
- 21 same *BT. the author*
- 22 same
- 23 same
- 25 same *BT. the author*
- 26 same
- Mar. 2 Othello
  *and* Pyramus and Thisbe

## 1745

**1745 COVENT GARDEN** (*cont.*)

- Mar. 5 Henry VIII
  - *and* Pyramus and Thisbe
  - 12 Pyramus and Thisbe
  - 25 same *BT. Mrs Pritchard*
  - 30 same
- Apr. 1 Henry IV, Part II *BT. Hippisley*
  - 4 Papal Tyranny ... *BT. [T.] Cibber*
  - 6 Measure for Measure
  - 16 Henry VIII
    - *and* Pyramus and Thisbe *BT. Reinhold, Destrade, Rawlings, and Miss Bellamy*
  - 18 Othello *BT. Signora Campioni*
  - 20 Timon of Athens *BT. Mr and Mrs Hale*
  - 22 Richard III *BT. a gentlewoman under misfortunes*
    - Genest (iv. 164) erroneously has 'a Gentleman'.
  - 23 The Merchant of Venice *BT. Lalauze*
  - 24 As You Like It *BT. Leveridge*
  - 25 Henry V
    - *and* Pyramus and Thisbe *BT. Mrs Lampe and Mrs Vincent*
  - 26 Hamlet *BT. Cashell*
- May 4 Henry VIII
- Sept. 23 Hamlet
  - 25 As You Like It
  - 27 Pyramus and Thisbe
- Oct. 4 same
  - 11 same
  - 16 same
  - 28 same
  - 31 same
- Nov. 8 same
  - 15 Macbeth
  - 18 Henry V
  - 19 Pyramus and Thisbe
  - 22 Timon of Athens
  - 28 Richard III
    - *and* Pyramus and Thisbe
- Dec. 11 Henry V
  - 20 Pyramus and Thisbe
  - 21 Macbeth
  - 30 Timon of Athens

## NEW WELLS, GOODMAN'S FIELDS

- Jan. 19 Richard III
- Feb. 6 Othello *BT. an antient widow gentlewoman*
  - 14 The Tempest
  - 15 same

## 1745 NEW WELLS, GOODMAN'S FIELDS (cont.)

Feb. 16 The Tempest
18 same
19 same
20 same
21 same
22 same
23 same
Mar. 5 same
9 Macbeth
16 same
18 Richard III BT. *Cushing*
21 Othello BT. *Townly*
23 Hamlet BT. *a distrest family*
26 Henry IV, Part I BT. *Mrs Cushing*
28 The Merry Wives of Windsor BT. *Furnival*
Apr. 1 The Cobler of Preston BT. *L. Hallam*
15 The Tempest
17 Henry IV, Part I BT. *Paget*
26 The Cobler of Preston BT. *Ravenscroft and Beaumont*
30 Richard III BT. *a family under misfortunes*
May 2 King Lear
and The Cobler of Preston BT. *Kennedy*
7 Othello
9 King Lear
Nov. 27 Hamlet
29 Othello
30 [Henry IV, Part I]
  Listed by Genest (iv. 197). On this night the theatre was dark; its only announcement is for the performance on Dec. 2.

Dec. 2 Henry IV, Part I BT. *Howard, Powell, and others*
3 same
4 The Tempest
5 same
16 Richard III BT. *W. Hallam*
17 same
26 The Tempest
28 Hamlet

## SHEPHERD'S MARKET, MAYFAIR

Feb. 11 Othello
18 same
20 same

## 1746 DRURY LANE

Jan. 1 Henry VIII
8 Richard III

# 1746

1746 DRURY LANE (cont.)

- Jan. 9 Richard III
- 10 The Merchant of Venice
- 31 The Tempest
- Feb. 1 same
- 4 same
- 5 same
- 8 The Merchant of Venice
- 18 The Tempest
- Mar. 22 The Merchant of Venice *BT. Lowe*
- Apr. 9 Othello *BT. [L.] Sparks*
- 11 Measure for Measure *BT. Havard and Berry*
- 15 Twelfth Night *BT. Raftor and Miss Edwards*
- 18 same *BT. Neale and Winstone*
- 22 Richard III *BT. Goodfellow and Barrington*
- 29 same
- May 3 The Merchant of Venice *BT. Ray, Gray, and Dunbar, box-keeper*
- 7 Hamlet *BT. Shawford, Peacopp, house-keeper, Currier, and Fryar*
- 9 Henry IV, Part I *BT. Lee, Pilkington, Prichard, Saunders, and Emberton, stage-door-keeper*
- 19 The Tempest *BT. I. Sparks*
- Aug. 4 The Conspiracy Discovered
- 6 same
- 8 same
- 11 [same]

  Advertised in GA of Aug. 9, but not of Aug. 11. Almost certainly not acted.

- Sept. 23 The Merchant of Venice
- Oct. 4 Othello
- 7 same
- 9 same
- 11 same
- 14 same
- 17 same
- 18 same
- 21 same
- 28 same
- Nov. 7 Macbeth
- 8 same
- 10 same
- 11 same
- 12 The Merchant of Venice
- 24 Macbeth
- 26 Othello
- Dec. 5 same
- 27 Macbeth

73

## 1746 COVENT GARDEN

Jan. 1 Henry V
11 Henry IV, Part I
13 Henry IV, Part II
14 Macbeth
    *and* Pyramus and Thisbe
18 Pyramus and Thisbe
21 As You Like It
22 Macbeth
Feb. 3 The Merry Wives of Windsor
7 Pyramus and Thisbe
8 Papal Tyranny . . .
18 Pyramus and Thisbe
Mar. 6 Henry V
10 The Merchant of Venice *BT. Ryan*
13 Much Ado about Nothing *BT. Mrs Pritchard*
22 same
Apr. 1 All's Well that Ends Well
3 Othello *BT. Cashell*
7 Cymbeline *BT. Woodward*
10 same
14 Much Ado about Nothing *BT. Lalauze*

    Genest (iv. 193) erroneously has Apr. 13, a Sunday.

26 The Merchant of Venice *BT. James*
May 1 Henry V *BT. Stoppelaer*
June 11 King Lear
13 Hamlet
16 Richard III
20 Othello
27 Macbeth

| | | | £ | s. | d. |
|---|---|---|---|---|---|
| Sept. | 29 | Hamlet | 115 | 8 | 0 |
| Oct. | 20 | Richard III | 160 | 19 | 0 |
| | 22 | Hamlet | 186 | 18 | 0 |
| | 27 | King Lear | 190 | 6 | 0 |
| | 31 | Richard III | 188 | 8 | 6 |

    Genest (iv. 209), quoting Davies, say that 'Quin's Richard [on Oct. 20] scarcely drew a decent house, Garrick's [on this night] a crowded one'. The receipts indicate that Garrick's house was not materially superior to Quin's.

| Nov. | 10 | Hamlet | 178 | 1 | 6 |
|---|---|---|---|---|---|
| | 18 | The Merry Wives of Windsor | 54 | 9 | 6 |
| | 28 | Othello | 103 | 18 | 6 |
| Dec. | 4 | King Lear | 137 | 17 | 6 |
| | 6 | Henry IV, Part I | 189 | 7 | 0 |
| | 8 | same | 179 | 0 | 6 |
| | 9 | same | 177 | 11 | 6 |
| | 12 | same | 171 | 19 | 0 |

1746–1747

1746 COVENT GARDEN (*cont.*)                    £    s.   d.
    Dec. 13  Henry IV, Part I              153  16   0
          17  Measure for Measure             72   0   6
          19  As You Like It                  90  10   6
          29  Henry VIII                     110   3   0
          30  Richard III                    140  19   6
          31  Othello                        153  11   0

## HAYMARKET
Dec.  4  Othello

## NEW WELLS, GOODMAN'S FIELDS
Jan.  31  Hamlet *BT. Banberry*
Feb.  25  The Tempest *BT. Owen and Starkey*
Mar.   3  Richard III *BT. Paget*
Oct.  29  Henry IV, Part I
      30  same
Nov.   3  same
      10  same
      11  Richard III
Dec.   3  Hamlet
       4  same
       9  Othello
      17  Richard III
      26  same

## JAMES ST., HAYMARKET
Mar. 12  Henry V
Oct.  2  Othello *BT. Perry*

## BOWLING GREEN, SOUTHWARK
Oct. 20  Henry IV, Part I *BT. Paget*

1747 DRURY LANE
    Jan.  1  Othello
         15  Henry IV, Part I
         16  same
         17  same
         19  same
             Genest (iv. 203) has 'acted 4 times successively'. This
             is correct; Jan. 18 was a Sunday.

         29  The Merchant of Venice
    Feb.  4  Othello

# 1747

1747 DRURY LANE (*cont.*)

|  |  |  |  |  |  |
|---|---|---|---|---|---|
| Feb. | 6 | [Macbeth] | | | |

              Bill in GA of Feb. 5, advertising the performance 'Tomorrow'. The play was not acted; on Feb. 6 there is no announcement from DRURY LANE of any sort.

|  |  |  | £ | s. | d. |
|---|---|---|---|---|---|
|  | 9 | The Merchant of Venice | | | |
|  | 24 | Othello | | | |
|  | 27 | The Merchant of Venice *BT. Signora Padouana* | | | |
| Mar. | 14 | Macbeth *BT. Mrs Giffard* | | | |
|  | 16 | King John *BT. Delane* | | | |
|  | 24 | Hamlet *BT. Macklin* | | | |
|  | 28 | Julius Caesar *BT.* [L.] *Sparks* | | | |
| Apr. | 2 | same *BT. Mons. and Madem. Mechel* | | | |
|  | 4 | Othello *BT. Mrs Elmy* | | | |
|  | 10 | same *BT. the fund for the support of the Lock-Hospital, near Hyde-Park Corner* | | | |
|  | 11 | Hamlet | | | |
|  | 24 | [Henry V] | | | |

              Announced for Mrs Macklin's BT., but deferred (Genest, iv. 206). On this night the theatre was dark.

|  |  |  | £ | s. | d. |
|---|---|---|---|---|---|
|  | 29 | Hamlet *BT. Raftor, Dickinson, gallery office-keeper, and Mrs Dickinson, Burton's box-keeper*[1] | | | |
|  | 30 | Julius Caesar *BT. Mrs Mills* | | | |
| May | 1 | Macbeth *BT. Taswell, Ray, Leigh* [*Jr.*], *Miss Pitt, and Miss Royer* | | | |
|  | 16 | The Merchant of Venice *BT.* [W.] *Mills* | | | |
| Sept. | 15 | same | 150 | 0 | 0 |
|  | 22 | Hamlet | 160 | 0 | 0 |
|  | 26 | Othello | 160 | 0 | 0 |
| Oct. | 22 | same | 120 | 0 | 0 |
|  | 23 | Hamlet | 190 | 0 | 0 |
|  | 27 | The Merchant of Venice | 100 | 0 | 0 |
|  | 30 | King Lear | 190 | 0 | 0 |
| Nov. | 2 | As You Like It | 110 | 0 | 0 |
|  | 6 | Richard III | 190 | 0 | 0 |
|  | 14 | King Lear | 180 | 0 | 0 |
|  | 24 | Hamlet | 130 | 0 | 0 |
|  | 26 | As You Like It | 90 | 0 | 0 |
| Dec. | 11 | Othello | 130 | 0 | 0 |
|  | 16 | Henry V | 180 | 0 | 0 |
|  | 17 | same | 130 | 0 | 0 |
|  | 18 | same | 140 | 0 | 0 |
|  | 23 | King Lear | 180 | 0 | 0 |
|  | 26 | The Tempest | 160 | 0 | 0 |
|  | 28 | same | 150 | 0 | 0 |
|  | 29 | same | 100 | 0 | 0 |
|  | 31 | Henry V | 100 | 0 | 0 |

[1] i.e. the middle gallery box-keeper. An eccentric widow, Mrs Burton, had for many years held this office at Drury Lane.

## 1747 COVENT GARDEN

|  |  |  | £ | s. | d. |
|---|---|---|---|---|---|
| Jan. | 1 | As You Like It | 89 | 6 | 6 |
| Mar. | 3 | Henry VIII | 100 | 6 | 0 |
|  | 9 | As You Like It | 79 | 16 | 0 |
|  | 16 | The Merry Wives of Windsor | 154 | 12 | 0 |
|  | 28 | Henry IV, Part I | 112 | 0 | 0 |
| Apr. | 20 | Julius Caesar *BT. Woodward* | 140 | 12 | 6 |
|  | 23 | As You Like It *BT. Lalauze* | 110 | 8 | 6 |
| May | 14 | Henry VIII | 87 | 7 | 6 |
| Dec. | 9 | Hamlet |  |  |  |
|  | 28 | Richard III |  |  |  |

## NEW WELLS, GOODMAN'S FIELDS

Jan. 2 Henry IV, Part I
     5 Macbeth
     6 same
     8 same
     9 The Merry Wives of Windsor
    13 same
    14 Macbeth
    16 The Tempest
    19 same
    20 same
    28 Macbeth
    29 Hamlet *BT. Richard Starkey*
Feb. 6 Richard III *BT. Mrs Howard*
     9 The Tempest
    20 Othello
    26 The Tempest
Mar. 2 King Lear *BT. W. Hallam*
    12 Hamlet *BT. Lee*
    16 Macbeth *BT. Cushing*
    26 Richard III *BT. Law, Mrs Beckham, Mrs Moreau, Miss Baker, and Miss Jackson*
Apr. 4 The Tempest *BT. a gentleman under misfortunes*
     6 Henry IV, Part II *BT. Paget*
     7 Hamlet *BT. Goodfellow*

## BOWLING GREEN, SOUTHWARK

Oct. 22 Othello

## 1748 DRURY LANE

|  |  |  | £ | s. | d. |
|---|---|---|---|---|---|
| Jan. | 1 | The Merchant of Venice | 100 | 0 | 0 |
|  | 6 | Twelfth Night | 120 | 0 | 0 |
|  | 7 | same | 100 | 0 | 0 |
|  | 15 | Othello | 150 | 0 | 0 |
|  | 21 | Hamlet | 195 | 0 | 0 |
|  | 27 | Richard III | 195 | 0 | 0 |

## 1748

### 1748 DRURY LANE (cont.)

|  |  |  | £ | s. | d. |
|---|---|---|---|---|---|
| Feb. | 10 | Othello | 140 | 0 | 0 |
| Mar. | 1 | King Lear | 200 | 0 | 0 |
|  | 3 | Hamlet | 70 | 0 | 0 |
|  | 8 | As You Like It | 50 | 0 | 0 |
|  | 19 | Macbeth | 200 | 0 | 0 |
| Apr. | 2 | same *BT. Mrs Elmy* | 160 | 0 | 0 |
|  | 11 | The Tempest | 130 | 0 | 0 |
|  | 18 | Hamlet *BT. [L.] Sparks* | 150 | 0 | 0 |
|  | 20 | Othello *BT. Arne* | 140 | 0 | 0 |

Genest (iv. 242) erroneously has 'Mrs. Arne's bt.'.

|  |  |  | £ | s. | d. |
|---|---|---|---|---|---|
|  | 23 | King Lear *BT. the sufferers by the late fire* [on Mar. 25, in Exchange Alley, Cornhill] | 208 | 1 | 0 |
|  | 27 | Macbeth *BT. Pritchard, treasurer* | 180 | 0 | 0 |
|  | 30 | Richard III | receipts omitted |  |  |
| May | 9 | The Merchant of Venice *BT. Gray, Jones, box-office-keeper, Berrisford, box-keeper, Atkinson, pit door-keeper, and Goodwin* | 220 | 0 | 0 |
|  | 13 | Macbeth | 40 | 0 | 0 |
|  | 16 | As You Like It *BT. Dunbar, box-keeper, Warner and Foley, box-lobby-keepers, Prichard, upper-gallery office-keeper, and Saunders, stage-door-keeper* | 180 | 0 | 0 |
| Sept. | 24 | Hamlet | 150 | 0 | 0 |
|  | 29 | Richard III | 190 | 0 | 0 |
| Oct. | 4 | Othello | 150 | 0 | 0 |
|  | 8 | King Lear | 190 | 0 | 0 |
|  | 13 | Henry V | 120 | 0 | 0 |
|  | 14 | Hamlet | 170 | 0 | 0 |
|  | 26 | King Lear | 170 | 0 | 0 |
|  | 28 | Macbeth | 120 | 0 | 0 |
| Nov. | 3 | The Merchant of Venice | 30 | 0 | 0 |
|  | 9 | Twelfth Night | 50 | 0 | 0 |
|  | 14 | Much Ado about Nothing | 160 | 0 | 0 |
|  | 15 | same | 70 | 0 | 0 |
|  | 16 | same | 120 | 0 | 0 |
|  | 17 | same | 140 | 0 | 0 |
|  | 18 | same | 130 | 0 | 0 |
|  | 19 | same | 160 | 0 | 0 |
|  | 21 | same | 130 | 0 | 0 |
|  | 22 | same | 80 | 0 | 0 |
|  | 23 | Othello | 140 | 0 | 0 |
|  | 29 | Romeo and Juliet | 160 | 0 | 0 |
|  | 30 | Much Ado about Nothing | 185 | 0 | 0 |
| Dec. | 1 | Romeo and Juliet | 150 | 0 | 0 |
|  | 2 | same | 140 | 0 | 0 |
|  | 3 | same | 160 | 0 | 0 |
|  | 5 | same | 170 | 0 | 0 |

## 1748 DRURY LANE (cont.)

|  |  |  | £ | s. | d. |
|---|---|---|---|---|---|
| Dec. | 6 | Romeo and Juliet | 160 | 0 | 0 |
|  | 7 | same | 170 | 0 | 0 |
|  | 8 | same | 150 | 0 | 0 |
|  | 9 | same | 140 | 0 | 0 |
|  | 10 | same | 160 | 0 | 0 |
|  | 12 | same | 150 | 0 | 0 |
|  | 13 | same | 140 | 0 | 0 |
|  | 14 | same | 130 | 0 | 0 |
|  | 15 | same | 130 | 0 | 0 |
|  | 16 | Much Ado about Nothing | 90 | 0 | 0 |
|  | 17 | Hamlet | 170 | 0 | 0 |
|  | 19 | Macbeth | 170 | 0 | 0 |
|  | 20 | Romeo and Juliet | 140 | 0 | 0 |
|  | 23 | Richard III | 180 | 0 | 0 |
|  | 30 | Romeo and Juliet | 140 | 0 | 0 |
|  | 31 | King Lear | 150 | 0 | 0 |

## COVENT GARDEN

| | | | £ | s. | d. |
|---|---|---|---|---|---|
| Jan. | 9 | Othello | | | |
| | 11 | same | | | |
| | 12 | The Merry Wives of Windsor | | | |
| Feb. | 23 | Hamlet | | | |
| | 29 | Richard III *BT. Sowdon* | | | |
| Mar. | 21 | The Merry Wives of Windsor *BT. Beard* | | | |
| Apr. | 2 | Hamlet | | | |
| | 6 | Othello *BT. the relief of the unhappy sufferers by the late fire* [*on Mar. 25, in Exchange Alley, Cornhill*] | 218 | 12 | 4 |
| | 13 | Pyramus and Thisbe *BT. Mr and Mrs Dunstall, Mrs Lampe, and Miss* [*E.*] *Young* | | | |
| | 22 | Henry IV, Part I *BT. Quin* | | | |
| | 25 | same | | | |
| | 27 | Hamlet *BT. Marten and White, treasurer* | | | |
| Oct. | 3 | King Lear | | | |
| | 5 | same | | | |
| | 14 | The Merry Wives of Windsor | | | |
| | 17 | Henry IV, Part I | | | |
| | 28 | Othello | | | |
| | 31 | The Merry Wives of Windsor | | | |
| Nov. | 10 | same | | | |
| | 11 | As You Like It | | | |
| | 24 | Julius Caesar | | | |
| | 25 | same | | | |
| | 26 | Measure for Measure | | | |
| | 30 | same | | | |
| Dec. | 6 | Henry IV, Part I | | | |
| | 8 | Julius Caesar | | | |
| | 17 | The Merry Wives of Windsor | | | |

# 1748-1749

**1748 COVENT GARDEN** (*cont.*)
    Dec. 30  The Merry Wives of Windsor
         31  Measure for Measure

## HAYMARKET
    Apr. 20  Richard III *BT. a poor distress'd citizen's widow, and six children*
         30  Othello *BT. Adams and Scudamore*

## PHILLIPS'S BOOTH, BOWLING GREEN, SOUTHWARK
    Sept. 7  The Tempest
        8  same
        9  same
       10  same
       12  same

## BOWLING GREEN, SOUTHWARK
    Sept. 26  Richard III *BT. Mr and Mrs Morgan*
    Oct. 24  King Lear *BT. Mrs Morgan*

## TILED BOOTH, BOWLING GREEN, SOUTHWARK
    Oct. 31  The Jew of Venice *BT. Yeates Jr.*

**1749 DRURY LANE**

| | | | £ | s. | d. |
|---|---|---|---|---|---|
| Jan. | 5 | Hamlet | 170 | 0 | 0 |
| | 6 | Othello | 150 | 0 | 0 |
| | 7 | Twelfth Night | 160 | 0 | 0 |
| | 9 | Measure for Measure | 150 | 0 | 0 |
| | 10 | The Merchant of Venice | 120 | 0 | 0 |
| | 12 | Romeo and Juliet | 160 | 0 | 0 |
| | 16 | Macbeth | 99 | 0 | 0 |
| | 19 | Much Ado about Nothing | 120 | 0 | 0 |
| | 26 | Hamlet | 190 | 0 | 0 |
| Feb. | 1 | Romeo and Juliet | 120 | 0 | 0 |
| | 3 | Much Ado about Nothing | 80 | 0 | 0 |
| | 28 | same | 170 | 0 | 0 |
| Mar. | 2 | Romeo and Juliet | 160 | 0 | 0 |
| | 4 | Richard III *BT. Garrick* | 190 | 0 | 0 |

            The recipient of the BT. is named in C-H, but not in GA.

| | | | | | |
|---|---|---|---|---|---|
| | 6 | Macbeth | 120 | 0 | 0 |
| | 9 | Othello *BT. Barry* | 289 | 0 | 0 |
| | 29 | Hamlet *BT. Beard* | 275 | 0 | 0 |
| | 30 | Much Ado about Nothing *BT. Cooke* | 230 | 0 | 0 |
| Apr. | 1 | Romeo and Juliet *BT. Berry* | 160 | 0 | 0 |
| | 6 | Richard III | 170 | 0 | 0 |
| | 7 | Macbeth *BT. Blakes* | 140 | 0 | 0 |

## 1749

**1749 DRURY LANE** (cont.)

| | | | £ | s. | d. |
|---|---|---|---|---|---|
| Apr. | 14 | The Merchant of Venice BT. Leviez, ballet-master | 180 | 0 | 0 |
| | 29 | Much Ado about Nothing BT. Cross, prompter, and Burton | 139 | 0 | 0 |
| May | 10 | King Lear | 170 | 0 | 0 |
| | 18 | Much Ado about Nothing | 60 | 0 | 0 |
| Sept. | 21 | The Merchant of Venice | 70 | 0 | 0 |
| | 28 | Much Ado about Nothing | 180 | 0 | 0 |
| Oct. | 3 | Hamlet | 170 | 0 | 0 |
| | 5 | Much Ado about Nothing | 170 | 0 | 0 |
| | 13 | King Lear | 180 | 0 | 0 |
| | 17 | Macbeth | 130 | 0 | 0 |
| | 20 | The Merchant of Venice | 40 | 0 | 0 |
| | 27 | Hamlet | 160 | 0 | 0 |
| | 28 | Twelfth Night | 200 | 0 | 0 |
| Nov. | 2 | Othello | 180 | 0 | 0 |
| | 3 | Much Ado about Nothing | 140 | 0 | 0 |
| | 8 | King Lear | 160 | 0 | 0 |
| | 13 | Macbeth | 110 | 0 | 0 |
| | 16 | Richard III | 210 | 0 | 0 |
| | 20 | Hamlet | 130 | 0 | 0 |
| | 22 | Othello | 180 | 0 | 0 |
| | 24 | same | 160 | 0 | 0 |
| | 30 | Much Ado about Nothing | 120 | 0 | 0 |
| Dec. | 1 | Othello | 120 | 0 | 0 |
| | 30 | Macbeth | 100 | 0 | 0 |

**COVENT GARDEN**

| | | | £ | s. | d. |
|---|---|---|---|---|---|
| Jan. | 10 | Henry IV, Part I | | | |
| | 27 | The Merry Wives of Windsor | | | |
| Feb. | 27 | Henry IV, Part I BT. Quin | | | |
| Mar. | 2 | Henry IV, Part II | | | |
| | 11 | same | | | |
| | 16 | same | | | |
| | 18 | same | | | |
| | 31 | Measure for Measure BT. Lowe | | | |
| Apr. | 1 | The Merry Wives of Windsor | | | |
| | 8 | Henry IV, Part II | | | |
| | 13 | Henry IV, Part I | | | |
| May | 4 | Henry VIII | | | |
| | 5 | same | | | |
| Sept. | 27 | Hamlet | 77 | 8 | 6 |
| Oct. | 2 | Richard III | 164 | 13 | 0 |
| | 4 | Othello | 107 | 4 | 6 |
| | 12 | Macbeth | 156 | 1 | 0 |
| | 18 | The Merry Wives of Windsor | 76 | 15 | 0 |
| | 19 | Julius Cacsar | 69 | 10 | 6 |
| | 25 | Measure for Measure | 53 | 9 | 6 |

## 1749 COVENT GARDEN (*cont.*)

|  |  |  | £ | s. | d. |
|---|---|---|---|---|---|
| Oct. | 26 | Henry IV, Part I | 59 | 5 | 6 |
| Nov. | 8 | Henry IV, Part II | 67 | 9 | 6 |
|  | 13 | The Merry Wives of Windsor | 68 | 17 | 6 |
|  | 28 | Julius Caesar | 142 | 4 | 0 |
| Dec. | 6 | The Merry Wives of Windsor | 86 | 14 | 6 |
|  | 9 | Henry IV, Part II | 123 | 10 | 6 |
|  | 14 | Macbeth | 105 | 12 | 0 |
|  | 15 | Hamlet | 53 | 9 | 6 |
|  | 29 | The Merry Wives of Windsor | 108 | 4 | 0 |

## HAYMARKET

Jan. 28 Hamlet *BT. a family in great necessity*
Oct. 17 Othello *BT. Bruodin and Mrs Hutton*

## JAMES ST., HAYMARKET

Mar. 21 Richard III *BT. a person under misfortunes*

## CUSHING'S BOOTH, SMITHFIELD

Aug. 23 King John
    24 same
    25 same
    26 same
    28 same

## PHILLIPS'S BOOTH, SMITHFIELD

Aug. 23 The Tempest
    24 same
    25 same
    26 same
    28 same

## TILED BOOTH, BOWLING GREEN, SOUTHWARK

Oct. 16 Richard III *BT. Morgan*

## 1750 DRURY LANE

|  |  |  | £ | s. | d. |
|---|---|---|---|---|---|
| Jan. | 1 | The Tempest | 120 | 0 | 0 |
|  | 2 | same | 100 | 0 | 0 |
|  | 3 | Hamlet | 100 | 0 | 0 |
|  | 5 | The Tempest | 100 | 0 | 0 |
|  | 19 | same | 50 | 0 | 0 |
|  | 25 | King Lear | 180 | 0 | 0 |
|  | 27 | Much Ado about Nothing | 170 | 0 | 0 |
|  | 29 | Macbeth | 130 | 0 | 0 |
| Feb. | 12 | The Tempest | 100 | 0 | 0 |
|  | 19 | Richard III *BT. Garrick* | 220 | 0 | 0 |

The recipient of the BT. is named in C-H, but not in GA.

# 1750

**1750 DRURY LANE** (cont.)

|  |  |  | £ | s. | d. |
|---|---|---|---|---|---|
| Feb. | 22 | The Merchant of Venice *BT. a young gentlewoman, distress'd by the bankruptcy of her guardian* | 210 | 0 | 0 |
|  | 23 | Much Ado about Nothing | 160 | 0 | 0 |
| Mar. | 10 | Othello *BT. Barry* | 280 | 0 | 0 |
|  | 15 | Hamlet *BT. Mrs Clive* | 240 | 0 | 0 |
|  | 29 | Much Ado about Nothing *BT. Mr and Mrs Havard* | 160 | 0 | 0 |
| Apr. | 19 | Hamlet *BT. Palmer and Shuter* | 150 | 0 | 0 |
|  | 23 | Macbeth *BT. Cross, prompter, and Burton* | 154 | 0 | 0 |
|  | 27 | The Tempest *BT. Leviez, ballet-master* | 150 | 0 | 0 |
| May | 4 | The Merchant of Venice *BT. Hobson* | 200 | 0 | 0 |
| Sept. | 8 | same | 110 | 0 | 0 |
|  | 22 | The Merry Wives of Windsor | 110 | 0 | 0 |
|  | 25 | Hamlet | 180 | 0 | 0 |
|  | 28 | Romeo and Juliet | 180 | 0 | 0 |
|  | 29 | same | 130 | 0 | 0 |
| Oct. | 1 | same | 170 | 0 | 0 |
|  | 2 | same | 150 | 0 | 0 |
|  | 3 | same | 120 | 0 | 0 |
|  | 4 | same | 100 | 0 | 0 |
|  | 5 | same | 90 | 0 | 0 |
|  | 6 | same | 100 | 0 | 0 |
|  | 8 | same | 100 | 0 | 0 |
|  | 9 | same | 100 | 0 | 0 |
|  | 10 | same | 90 | 0 | 0 |
|  | 11 | same | 120 | 0 | 0 |
|  | 12 | same | 160 | 0 | 0 |
|  | 15 | As You Like It | 50 | 0 | 0 |
| Nov. | 1 | King Lear | 160 | 0 | 0 |
|  | 7 | Much Ado about Nothing | 100 | 0 | 0 |
|  | 8 | Richard III | 180 | 0 | 0 |
|  | 13 | Macbeth | 160 | 0 | 0 |
|  | 16 | same | 120 | 0 | 0 |
|  | 21 | Romeo and Juliet | 190 | 0 | 0 |
|  | 23 | Much Ado about Nothing | 80 | 0 | 0 |
|  | 26 | Romeo and Juliet | 160 | 0 | 0 |
|  | 29 | Hamlet | 120 | 0 | 0 |
| Dec. | 6 | As You Like It *BT. a distress'd citizen's widow with eight children* [Elizabeth Fletcher] | 280 | 0 | 0 |
|  |  | The recipient of the BT. is identified in GA of Dec. 10. |  |  |  |
|  | 18 | Romeo and Juliet | 120 | 0 | 0 |

## COVENT GARDEN

|  |  |  | £ | s. | d. |
|---|---|---|---|---|---|
| Jan. | 1 | Richard III | 147 | 7 | 0 |
|  | 3 | Henry IV, Part I | 122 | 7 | 6 |
|  | 12 | Julius Caesar | 116 | 14 | 6 |
|  | 15 | Measure for Measure | 110 | 12 | 0 |
|  | 16 | Henry V | 85 | 3 | 0 |

# 1750

## 1750 COVENT GARDEN (cont.)

|  |  |  | £ | s. | d. |
|---|---|---|---|---|---|
| Jan. | 17 | Henry IV, Part II | 122 | 16 | 0 |
|  | 24 | The Merry Wives of Windsor | 89 | 8 | 6 |
| Feb. | 15 | Hamlet | 165 | 10 | 0 |
|  | 19 | Henry V | 169 | 1 | 0 |
|  | 24 | same | 137 | 4 | 0 |
| Mar. | 1 | Romeo and Juliet | 155 | 18 | 6 |
|  | 3 | same | 165 | 14 | 6 |
|  | 5 | same | 125 | 6 | 6 |
|  | 6 | same | 117 | 16 | 0 |
|  | 8 | same | 105 | 7 | 6 |

Genest (iv. 305) has 'acted 5 times successively'. This is correct: on a Thurs., Sat., Mon., Tues., and Thurs. in Lent. See p. 1.

|  |  |  | £ | s. | d. |
|---|---|---|---|---|---|
|  | 13 | Macbeth | 85 | 10 | 6 |
|  | 19 | Henry IV, Part I *BT. Ryan* | 151 | 7 | 6 |
|  | 26 | The Merry Wives of Windsor *BT. [L.] Sparks* | 153 | 9 | 0 |
|  | 27 | A Cure for a Scold *BT. Lowe* | 152 | 13 | 0 |
| Apr. | 2 | Richard III *BT. Lee* | 150 | 3 | 0 |
|  | 16 | Macbeth *BT. Bencraft* | 133 | 12 | 0 |
|  | 18 | Romeo and Juliet *BT. Lalauze* | 151 | 2 | 0 |
|  | 26 | A Cure for a Scold *BT. Dunstall and Oates, harlequin* | 143 | 17 | 6 |
| Sept. | 28 | Romeo and Juliet |  |  |  |
|  | 29 | same |  |  |  |
| Oct. | 1 | same |  |  |  |
|  | 2 | same |  |  |  |
|  | 3 | same |  |  |  |
|  | 4 | same |  |  |  |
|  | 5 | same |  |  |  |
|  | 6 | same |  |  |  |
|  | 8 | same |  |  |  |
|  | 9 | same |  |  |  |
|  | 10 | same |  |  |  |
|  | 11 | same |  |  |  |
|  | 17 | Othello |  |  |  |
|  | 18 | The Merchant of Venice |  |  |  |
|  | 22 | The Merry Wives of Windsor |  |  |  |
|  | 25 | Hamlet |  |  |  |
|  | 26 | Richard III |  |  |  |
| Nov. | 8 | Macbeth |  |  |  |
|  | 12 | Henry IV, Part I |  |  |  |
|  | 13 | same |  |  |  |
|  | 14 | same |  |  |  |
|  | 15 | same |  |  |  |
|  | 16 | The Merchant of Venice |  |  |  |
|  | 22 | Henry IV, Part II |  |  |  |
|  | 23 | same |  |  |  |

1750 COVENT GARDEN (cont.)
- Nov. 24 Julius Caesar
- 26 same
- 27 same
- 29 Henry V
- 30 same
- Dec. 3 Othello
- 4 Measure for Measure
- 6 The Merry Wives of Windsor
- 7 [Romeo and Juliet]

    Listed by Genest (iv. 333). On this night the theatre was dark; its only announcement is for the performance on the 8th.

- 8 Romeo and Juliet
- 11 Hamlet
- 15 Romeo and Juliet
- 17 same
- 27 Julius Caesar

## HAYMARKET
Mar. 15 Richard III *BT. a tradesman in distress*

## JAMES ST., HAYMARKET
July 23 Othello *BT. a brother [Mason] indisposed*

# PART II
# THE PLAYS

FOLLOWING, in alphabetical order, are the thirty-four plays by Shakespeare that were seen in the London theatres between 1701 and 1750.[1] All adaptations appear under the heading of the original play, whether they have a different title or not. All different titles are, however, included in the general alphabetical listing and are cross-referenced.

For each play I have given, whenever such information is available from a published prompt copy, a brief summary of what rearrangements were made of the original text. This information includes, of course, the adaptations of entire plays. All references are to W. J. Craig's one-volume 'Oxford' *Shakespeare*, edition of 1943. In the summaries, the acts, scenes, and lines of each original play are indicated by italics.

In the left-hand column of each page will be found a transcript of the playbill for the first performance in each calendar year. The order in which the characters are listed in the original bill has been maintained.[2] In the right-hand column, in small type, will be found the changes in the cast that took place in subsequent performances throughout that year. These changes are not cumulative; each one refers independently to the full bill on the left. Occasionally so many changes took place that it has seemed best to give a complete new transcript of the bill, in, of course, the left-hand column. Any subsequent changes in respect to this bill appear opposite it in the right-hand column. Each time a change in a cast occurs an asterisk appears after the character in question.

The names of the characters have been spelled in accordance with modern usage. Thus, in Dryden and Davenant's adaptation of *The Tempest*, Trinculo is Trincalo; in *Hamlet*, Osric is usually Ostrick, &c. Variant spellings in the names of the performers: Pinkeman, Pinkethman, Penkethman, &c., have been regularized, as has the name Shakespeare. I have also corrected silently the occasional listing of an actress as either 'Miss' or 'Mrs', in favour of the style she most generally used.[3]

I have not thought it necessary to copy from the bills statements regarding the first appearance of an actor in any given part. The bills in this case speak for themselves, and in any event, these statements are sometimes erroneous. I have, however, noted the first appearance of a performer, either on the stage or on the London stage.

Unless stated to the contrary, it is to be understood that what was acted was Shakespeare's original play.

---

[1] I have excluded all 'adaptations' that are not based directly upon Shakespeare's written text. The most notable of these is Dryden's *All for Love*, admittedly an imitation of *Antony and Cleopatra*, but in no sense an actual adaptation of it.

[2] In the bills the male characters are almost invariably listed first. This procedure I have adhered to, even when the bills, as is sometimes the case (albeit very rarely), depart from it. For a brief history of the arrangement of the characters in eighteenth-century playbills, see Genest, vii. 57–8.

[3] In the eighteenth century the title of 'Miss' was not uncommonly given a vulgar connotation, and many unmarried women preferred the more respectable 'Mistress'.

# ALL'S WELL THAT ENDS WELL

No acting versions were published before 1750.

## 1741 GOODMAN'S FIELDS

*Mar. 7*

| | |
|---|---|
| KING* | Crisp |
| DUKE* | Nelson |
| BERTRAM | Giffard |
| LAFEU | Paget |
| PAROLLES | Peterson |
| CLOWN | Yates |
| DUMAIN SR. | Blakes |
| STEWARD | Dunstall |
| COUNTESS | Mrs Steel |
| WIDOW | Mrs Yates |
| DIANA | Miss Hippisley |
| MARIANA | Mrs Dunstall |
| HELENA | Mrs Giffard |

*Mar. 9.* No parts assigned

*Mar. 10, 14, 17, 21, 30; Apr. 3*

| | |
|---|---|
| HELENA | Mrs Giffard |

No other parts assigned

*Sept. 28*

| | |
|---|---|
| KING | Marshall |
| DUKE | Pattenden |

## 1742 DRURY LANE

*Jan. 22*

| | |
|---|---|
| KING* | Milward |
| BERTRAM | [W.] Mills |
| LAFEU | Berry |
| CLOWN | Macklin |
| DUKE | Woodburn |
| DUMAIN SR. | Havard |
| DUMAIN JR. | Ridout |
| SOLDIER | |
| [INTERPRETER] | Winstone |
| STEWARD | Turbutt |
| PAROLLES | [T.] Cibber |
| DIANA | Mrs Ridout |
| WIDOW | Mrs Cross |
| MARIANA | Mrs Marshall |
| COUNTESS | Mrs Butler |
| HELENA* | Mrs Woffington |

[Genest (iii. 645) says that Mrs Woffington was taken ill 'as she stood at the scenes ready to come on—this was in the 1st act—the part was read'. This is incorrect; see note under Feb. 16.]

*Feb. 16*

| | |
|---|---|
| KING | Delane |
| HELENA | read (probably by Mrs Mills) |

[It was on this night, and not on Jan. 22, that Mrs Woffington was unable to appear. An undated clipping from LDP in GEC reads, 'Last Night, in the First Act of All's Well ... Mrs Woffington was taken so violently ill, that she fainted away.... After a proper Apology being made, The Audience ... waited till another Person dress'd to read the Part.' The date of this clipping is Feb. 17, since it also refers to other arrangements at the theatre, all of which were fulfilled in the course of the week of Feb. 15–20. Mrs Woffington had first been taken ill *after* Jan. 22, and the bills announce several deferments of *All's Well* for this reason. Genest (iii. 645) says that 'the play was advertised for the following Friday, when if Mrs Woffington would not be well enough; Mrs Mills would be prepared in the part'. The Friday in question was not Jan. 29, but Feb. 19, q.v., on which day Mrs Woffington was in fact well enough to perform Helena, for the second time.]

*Feb. 19, 20, 22, 23, 25, 26, 27; Mar. 23*

| | |
|---|---|
| KING | Delane |

88

## ALL'S WELL THAT ENDS WELL

### 1743 LINCOLN'S INN FIELDS
*Feb. 2, 4*

| PAROLLES | [T.] Cibber |
| KING | W. Giffard |
| BERTRAM | Giffard |
| LAFEU | Peterson |
| CLOWN | Dunstall |
| DUKE | Blakey |
| DUMAIN SR. | Mozeen |
| DUMAIN JR. | Freeman |
| STEWARD | Julian |
| WIDOW | Mrs Bambridge |
| MARIANA | Mrs Dunstall |
| COUNTESS | Mrs Butler |
| DIANA | Mrs Chetwood |
| HELENA | Mrs Giffard |

### 1746 COVENT GARDEN
*Apr. 1*

| KING | Cashell |
| BERTRAM | Hale |
| LAFEU | Bridgwater |
| PAROLLES | Woodward |
| CLOWN | Chapman |
| DUKE | Bencraft |
| STEWARD | Marten |
| DUMAIN SR. | Ridout |
| DUMAIN JR. | Gibson |
| SOLDIER | |
| [INTERPRETER] | Arthur |
| PAGE | Miss Morrison |
| 1ST GENTLEMAN | Anderson |
| 2ND GENTLEMAN | Hayman |
| COUNTESS | Mrs Horton |
| DIANA | Miss Hippisley |
| WIDOW | Mrs James |
| MARIANA | Mrs Bland |
| HELENA | Mrs Pritchard |

## AS YOU LIKE IT

Adapted as LOVE IN A FOREST, by Charles Johnson. In five acts.

1723   W. Chetwood and Tho. Edlin.

Act I, scene i follows the original almost verbatim to *120*. The concluding dialogue between Oliver and Charles (who is here a fencer) is much expanded. Scene ii is *I. ii*, altered. The fencing match is preceded by *Richard II, I. iii. 7–8*;

## AS YOU LIKE IT

*I. i. 30–66*, abridged; *I. iii. 42–5, 117*, and by *Much Ado about Nothing*, *V. i. 84, 76*. Scene iii is *I. iii* of the original, reduced.

Act II, scene i is *II. iii*, verbatim. About 10 new lines are added: Le Beau tells Orlando that he is banished. Scene ii is *II. ii*, verbatim. Scene iii is *II. i*, somewhat reduced; Jaques has the Lord's speeches. Scene iv is *II. iv*, omitting *22–70*. Silvius has Corin's speeches. Then follow *II. vi*, verbatim, and *II. vii*, which is slightly altered: *45–87* are cut, and Amiens speaks of the arrival of the players.

Act III is one uninterrupted scene. It begins with *III. ii. 1–10, 94–121* (Celia here has Touchstone's speeches), *182–287*, practically verbatim. The following dialogue, *288–314*, consists chiefly of *I. i. 245–82* of *Much Ado about Nothing*. The original is then resumed, *315–end*, a little reduced. Then follows *III. iii*, drastically altered. The act ends with *III. iv*, in which the speeches are occasionally rearranged.

Act IV begins with a rewriting into dialogue (between Rosalind and Jaques) of Berowne's speeches in *Love's Labour's Lost*, *III. i. 183–215* and *IV. iii. 22–76*. It continues with *IV. i. 44–end*, reduced. The 'damask cheek' from *Twelfth Night*, *II. iv. 107–17*, is introduced. Then follows *IV. ii*, verbatim, and *IV. iii. 77–170*. A new dialogue then recounts the death of Oliver, and the marriage of Jaques and Celia. The act ends with *V. ii. 22–end*, somewhat reduced.

Act V begins with *V. iv. 1–34*, verbatim. Then follows the mock play (with its introductory dialogue) from *A Midsummer-Night's Dream*, *V. i. 61–371*, considerably reduced. The original is resumed at *V. iv. 115*, and continues almost verbatim, save for the omission of *185–203*.

See Genest, iii. 100–2; Odell, i. 244–7.

'As it is acted at the Theatre-Royal in Aungier-Street, Dublin.'
1741   Dublin: A. Reilly.

This version follows the original throughout. No scenes are rearranged. There are numerous excisions, the most important being:
Act I. ii. 67–97.
Act II. v. 15–22, 25–30, 38–60; vii. 35–87.
Act III. ii. 37–77; iii. 64–end.
Act IV. i. 1–40, 53–69.
Act V. ii. 101–19; iii, entire; iv. 115–22, 132–53.
In II. i the 1st Lord's speeches are given to Jacques.

That this was the version used in the London theatres seems certain. Quin, who appeared in Ireland in the summer of 1741, is listed in the dramatis personae as Jaques (which part he performed in London). It is probable that he brought the Drury Lane prompt copy with him.

No other acting versions were published before 1750.

[*as* LOVE IN A FOREST]

1723 DRURY LANE

*Jan. 9, 10, 11, 12, 14, 15*
  DUKE FREDERICK Williams
  ALBERTO    Booth

## AS YOU LIKE IT [as LOVE IN A FOREST]

### 1723 DRURY LANE (cont.)
*Jan. 9, &c. (cont.)*

| | |
|---|---|
| JAQUES | Cibber |
| AMIENS | Corey |
| OLIVER | Thurmond |
| ORLANDO | Wilks |
| ROBERTO | Roberts |
| ADAM | Mills |
| LE BEAU | Theo. Cibber |
| CHARLES | W. Mills |
| ROSALIND | Mrs Booth |
| CELIA | Mrs Thurmond |
| HYMEN | Miss Lindar |

*In the mock play*

| | |
|---|---|
| PYRAMUS | Penkethman |
| WALL | Norris |
| LION | Wilson |
| MOONSHINE | Ray |
| THISBE | *Mr* Miller |

[The bills give neither the parts nor the actors' names. The above assignment is taken from the printed text. Mr Miller is there misprinted Mrs Miller.]

[*The original*]

### 1740 DRURY LANE
*Dec. 20, 22, 23, 26, 27, 29, 30, 31*

| | |
|---|---|
| DUKE SENIOR | [W.] Mills |
| DUKE FREDERICK | Wright |
| JAQUES | Quin |
| ORLANDO | Milward |
| AMIENS | Lowe |
| TOUCHSTONE | Chapman |
| OLIVER | Cashell |
| ADAM | Berry |
| SILVIUS | Woodward |
| LE BEAU | Ridout |
| JAQUES DE BOIS | Turbutt |
| CORIN | Taswell |
| CHARLES | Winstone |
| WILLIAM | Ray |
| PHEBE | Mrs Bennet |
| AUDREY | Mrs Egerton |
| CELIA | Mrs Clive |
| ROSALIND | Mrs Pritchard |

[The bill has, 'Not acted these Forty Years—Written by Shakespeare'. Genest's remark (iii. 627), 'The original play had probably never been acted since the Restoration', is almost certainly correct.]

AS YOU LIKE IT

## 1741 DRURY LANE

*Jan. 1, 2, 3, 5, 7, 8, 9, 10, 12, 13, 14, 28, 29*

| | |
|---|---|
| DUKE SENIOR | [W.] Mills |
| DUKE FREDERICK* | Wright |
| JAQUES* | Quin |
| ORLANDO | Milward |
| AMIENS | Lowe |
| TOUCHSTONE* | Chapman |
| OLIVER* | Cashell |
| ADAM | Berry |
| SILVIUS* | Woodward |
| LE BEAU | Ridout |
| JAQUES DE BOIS | Turbutt |
| CORIN | Taswell |
| CHARLES | Winston |
| WILLIAM | Ray |
| PHEBE | Mrs Bennet |
| AUDREY | Mrs Egerton |
| CELIA | Mrs Clive |
| ROSALIND* | Mrs Pritchard |

[The playhouse bill for Jan. 9 is in HTC. It is also reproduced in Odell, i. 262.]

*Feb. 6; Mar. 10; Apr. 14, 25; May 11, 20*

| | |
|---|---|
| SILVIUS | Green |

*Oct. 15, 16, 17, 19, 28; Nov. 10, 28; Dec. 21*

| | |
|---|---|
| DUKE FREDERICK | Ward |
| JAQUES | [T.] Cibber |
| TOUCHSTONE | Macklin |
| OLIVER | Havard |
| SILVIUS | Green |
| ROSALIND | Mrs Woffington |

## COVENT GARDEN

*Oct. 15*

| | |
|---|---|
| DUKE SENIOR | Stephens |
| DUKE FREDERICK | Rosco |
| JAQUES | Ryan |
| ORLANDO | Hale |
| TOUCHSTONE* | Chapman |
| AMIENS* | Salway |
| OLIVER | Cashell |
| ADAM | Bridgwater |
| SILVIUS* | Woodward |
| LE BEAU* | Gibson |
| JAQUES DE BOIS* | Stevens |
| CORIN* | James |
| CHARLES* | Marten |
| WILLIAM* | Vaughan |
| PHEBE | Mrs Wright |
| AUDREY* | Miss Hilliard |
| CELIA | Mrs Vincent |
| ROSALIND | Mrs Pritchard |

*Oct. 16, 17, 19, 28*

| | |
|---|---|
| SILVIUS | Goodall |

*Dec. 3*

| | |
|---|---|
| TOUCHSTONE | Woodward |
| AMIENS | [E.] Roberts |
| SILVIUS | Goodall |

omitted
  LE BEAU, JAQUES DE BOIS, CORIN, CHARLES, WILLIAM, AUDREY

92

## AS YOU LIKE IT

### 1742 DRURY LANE
*Jan. 16*

| | |
|---|---|
| DUKE SENIOR | [W.] Mills |
| DUKE FREDERICK | Ward |
| JAQUES | [T.] Cibber |
| ORLANDO | Milward |
| AMIENS | Lowe |
| TOUCHSTONE | Macklin |
| OLIVER | Havard |
| ADAM | Berry |
| SILVIUS | Green |
| LE BEAU | Ridout |
| JAQUES DE BOIS | Turbutt |
| CORIN | Taswell |
| CELIA | Mrs Clive |
| PHEBE | Mrs Bennet |
| AUDREY | Mrs Egerton |
| ROSALIND | Mrs Woffington |

*Mar. 9, 11*

| | |
|---|---|
| DUKE SENIOR* | Ridout |
| DUKE FREDERICK | Winstone |
| JAQUES* | [T.] Cibber |
| ORLANDO | [W.] Mills |
| AMIENS* | Lowe |
| TOUCHSTONE | Macklin |
| OLIVER | Havard |
| ADAM | Berry |
| SILVIUS | Green |
| LE BEAU | Woodburn |
| JAQUES DE BOIS | Turbutt |
| CORIN* | Taswell |
| CHARLES* | Raftor |
| WILLIAM* | Ray |
| CELIA | Mrs Clive |
| PHEBE | Mrs Bennet |
| AUDREY* | Mrs Egerton |
| ROSALIND | Mrs Woffington |

*Apr. 8*

| | |
|---|---|
| JAQUES | Cross |

*May 20*

| | |
|---|---|
| JAQUES | Cross |
| AMIENS | Beard |
| CORIN | Arthur |
| WILLIAM | Raftor |
| omitted | |
| CHARLES | |

*Sept. 14; Oct. 14, 27; Nov. 30*

| | |
|---|---|
| DUKE SENIOR | Blakes |
| JAQUES | Cross |
| CHARLES | Arthur |
| AUDREY | Mrs Horsington |

*Dec. 21*

| | |
|---|---|
| DUKE SENIOR | Blakes |
| JAQUES | Cross |
| CHARLES | Arthur |
| AUDREY | Mrs Ridout |

### COVENT GARDEN
*Jan. 8, 22*

| | |
|---|---|
| DUKE SENIOR | Stephens |
| DUKE FREDERICK | Rosco |
| JAQUES | Ryan |
| ORLANDO | Hale |
| AMIENS* | [E.] Roberts |
| TOUCHSTONE | Chapman |
| OLIVER | Cashell |

*Feb. 13*

| | |
|---|---|
| AMIENS | Salway |

*Apr. 23*

| | |
|---|---|
| CELIA | Mrs Hale |

93

## 1742 COVENT GARDEN (cont.)
*Jan. 8, 22 (cont.)*

| | |
|---|---|
| ADAM | Bridgwater |
| SILVIUS | Goodall |
| PHEBE | Mrs Wright |
| CELIA* | Mrs Vincent |
| ROSALIND | Mrs Pritchard |

## JAMES ST., HAYMARKET
*Apr. 19*

| | |
|---|---|
| ROSALIND | *Mr* Page |

No other parts assigned

## 1743 DRURY LANE
*Jan. 6*

| | |
|---|---|
| DUKE SENIOR | Blakes |
| DUKE FREDERICK | Winstone |
| JAQUES | Cross |
| ORLANDO | [W.] Mills |
| AMIENS | Lowe |
| TOUCHSTONE | Macklin |
| OLIVER | Havard |
| ADAM | Berry |
| SILVIUS | Green |
| LE BEAU | Woodburn |
| JAQUES DE BOIS* | Turbutt |
| CORIN | Taswell |
| CHARLES | Arthur |
| WILLIAM | Ray |
| CELIA | Mrs Clive |
| PHEBE | Mrs Bennet |
| AUDREY | Mrs Horsington |
| ROSALIND | Mrs Woffington |

*May 23*

| | |
|---|---|
| JAQUES DE BOIS | Marr |

## 1744 COVENT GARDEN
*Jan. 5, 6, 9, 10, 13, 21; Feb. 11, 25; Mar. 27; May 23*

| | |
|---|---|
| JAQUES | Quin |
| TOUCHSTONE* | Chapman |
| DUKE SENIOR* | Stephens |
| DUKE FREDERICK | Rosco |
| OLIVER | Cashell |
| ADAM | Bridgwater |
| ORLANDO | Hale |
| CORIN | James |
| CHARLES | Marten |
| SILVIUS* | Goodall |

*Sept. 26*

| | |
|---|---|
| TOUCHSTONE | Woodward |
| DUKE SENIOR | Ridout |
| CELIA | Mrs Vincent |

*Nov. 2, 15*

| | |
|---|---|
| DUKE SENIOR | Ridout |
| SILVIUS | Hayman |
| CELIA | Mrs Vincent |

*Dec. 19*

| | |
|---|---|
| DUKE SENIOR | Ridout |
| SILVIUS | Hayman |

## AS YOU LIKE IT

### 1744 COVENT GARDEN (cont.)
*Jan. 5, &c. (cont.)*

| | |
|---|---|
| AMIENS | Beard |
| CELIA* | Mrs Clive |
| PHEBE | Miss Hippisley |
| ROSALIND | Mrs Pritchard |

### 1745 DRURY LANE
*Dec. 5*

| | |
|---|---|
| DUKE SENIOR* | Blakes |
| DUKE FREDERICK | Marshall |
| JAQUES | L. Sparks |
| ORLANDO* | [W.] Mills |
| AMIENS | Lowe |
| TOUCHSTONE | Macklin |
| ADAM | Berry |
| OLIVER | Havard |
| SILVIUS | Goodfellow |
| LE BEAU | Woodburn |
| JAQUES DE BOIS | Usher |
| CORIN* | Vaughan |
| CHARLES | I. Sparks |
| WILLIAM | Ray |
| CELIA | Mrs Clive |
| PHEBE | Mrs Bennet |
| ROSALIND | Mrs Woffington |

*Dec. 31*

| | |
|---|---|
| DUKE SENIOR | Bridges |
| ORLANDO | Blakes |
| CORIN | Taswell |

### COVENT GARDEN
*Jan. 29; Apr. 24*

| | |
|---|---|
| JAQUES* | Quin |
| TOUCHSTONE* | Chapman |
| DUKE SENIOR | Ridout |
| DUKE FREDERICK | Rosco |
| OLIVER | Cashell |
| ADAM | Bridgwater |
| ORLANDO | Hale |
| AMIENS | Beard |
| CORIN | James |
| SILVIUS | Hayman |
| CHARLES | Marten |
| PHEBE | Miss Hippisley |
| CELIA* | Mrs Clive |
| ROSALIND | Mrs Pritchard |

*Sept. 25*

| | |
|---|---|
| JAQUES | Ryan |
| TOUCHSTONE | Woodward |
| CELIA | Mrs Vincent |
| added | |
|   LE BEAU | Gibson |
|   WILLIAM | Vaughan |
|   JAQUES DE BOIS | Anderson |
|   AUDREY | Mrs James |

## 1746 COVENT GARDEN
*Jan. 21*

| | |
|---|---|
| JAQUES* | Ryan |
| TOUCHSTONE* | Woodward |
| ORLANDO* | Hale |
| AMIENS | Beard |
| DUKE SENIOR | Ridout |
| DUKE FREDERICK | Rosco |
| LE BEAU* | Gibson |
| OLIVER | Cashell |
| ADAM | Bridgwater |
| CHARLES | Marten |
| CORIN | James |
| WILLIAM* | Vaughan |
| JAQUES DE BOIS* | Anderson |
| SILVIUS | Hayman |
| CELIA | Mrs Vincent |
| PHEBE* | Mrs Rowley |
| AUDREY* | Mrs James |
| ROSALIND | Mrs Pritchard |

*Dec. 19*

| | |
|---|---|
| JAQUES | Quin |
| TOUCHSTONE | Chapman |
| ORLANDO | Havard |
| PHEBE | Miss Hippisley |

omitted
   LE BEAU, WILLIAM, JAQUES DE BOIS, AUDREY

## 1747 DRURY LANE
*Nov. 2*

| | |
|---|---|
| DUKE SENIOR* | [W.] Mills |
| DUKE FREDERICK | Winstone |
| JAQUES | [L.] Sparks |
| ORLANDO* | Blakes |
| AMIENS | Lowe |
| TOUCHSTONE | Macklin |
| OLIVER* | Havard |
| ADAM | Berry |
| SILVIUS* | Mozeen |
| LE BEAU* | Bransby |
| JAQUES DE BOIS* | Usher |
| CORIN* | Taswell |
| CHARLES* | I. Sparks |
| WILLIAM* | Shuter |
| PHEBE* | Mrs Bennet |
| AUDREY* | Mrs Horsington |
| CELIA | Mrs Clive |
| ROSALIND* | Mrs Woffington |

*Nov. 26*

| | |
|---|---|
| DUKE SENIOR | Blakes |
| ORLANDO | Havard |
| OLIVER | Mozeen |
| ROSALIND | Mrs Pritchard |

omitted
   SILVIUS, LE BEAU, JAQUES DE BOIS, CORIN, CHARLES, WILLIAM, PHEBE, AUDREY

## COVENT GARDEN
*Jan. 1*

| | |
|---|---|
| JAQUES | Quin |
| TOUCHSTONE | Chapman |
| ORLANDO | Havard |
| AMIENS | Beard |
| DUKE SENIOR* | Ridout |

*Mar. 9*

| | |
|---|---|
| OLIVER | Anderson |

*Apr. 23*
omitted
   DUKE SENIOR, DUKE FREDERICK, OLIVER, ADAM, CORIN, SILVIUS, CHARLES, PHEBE

## AS YOU LIKE IT

### 1747 COVENT GARDEN (cont.)
*Jan. 1 (cont.)*

| | |
|---|---|
| DUKE FREDERICK* | Rosco |
| OLIVER* | Cashell |
| ADAM* | Bridgwater |
| CORIN* | James |
| SILVIUS* | Davies |
| CHARLES* | Marten |
| CELIA | Mrs Vincent |
| PHEBE* | Miss Hippisley |
| ROSALIND | Mrs Pritchard |

### 1748 DRURY LANE
*Mar. 8*

| | |
|---|---|
| DUKE SENIOR* | Blakes |
| DUKE FREDERICK | Winstone |
| JAQUES | [L.] Sparks |
| ORLANDO* | Havard |
| AMIENS | Lowe |
| TOUCHSTONE | Macklin |
| OLIVER* | Mozeen |
| ADAM | Berry |
| CELIA | Mrs Clive |
| ROSALIND | Mrs Pritchard |

*May 16*

| | |
|---|---|
| DUKE SENIOR | [W.] Mills |
| ORLANDO | Blakes |
| OLIVER | Havard |

### COVENT GARDEN
*Nov. 11*

| | |
|---|---|
| JAQUES | Quin |
| ORLANDO | Ryan |
| TOUCHSTONE | Arthur |
| OLIVER | Anderson |
| AMIENS | Lowe |
| CELIA | Mrs Ridout |
| ROSALIND | Mrs Woffington |

### 1750 DRURY LANE
*Oct. 15*

| | |
|---|---|
| DUKE SENIOR | Blakes |
| DUKE FREDERICK | Winstone |
| JAQUES | Berry |
| ORLANDO | Palmer |
| AMIENS | Beard |
| ADAM | Havard |
| SILVIUS | Mozeen |
| CORIN | Shuter |
| LE BEAU | Scrase |
| CHARLES* | Vaughan |

*Dec. 6*

| | |
|---|---|
| CHARLES added | Layfield |
| OLIVER | Burton |

## AS YOU LIKE IT

### 1750 DRURY LANE (*cont.*)
Oct. 15 (*cont.*)

| | |
|---|---|
| TOUCHSTONE | Woodward |
| JAQUES DE BOIS | Simpson |
| WILLIAM | Vaughan |
| PHEBE | Mrs Bennet |
| AUDREY | Mrs James |
| CELIA | Mrs Clive |
| ROSALIND | Mrs Pritchard |

[Vaughan doubled CHARLES and WILLIAM.]

## CAIUS MARIUS

Thomas Otway's alteration of ROMEO AND JULIET, q.v.

## THE COBLER OF PRESTON

Christopher Bullock's alteration of THE TAMING OF THE SHREW, q.v.

## THE COBLER OF PRESTON

Charles Johnson's alteration of THE TAMING OF THE SHREW, q.v.

## THE COMEDY OF ERRORS

Adapted as EVERY BODY MISTAKEN, by William Taverner and Dr Brown. In three acts.
    1716   Not published.

Adapted as SEE IF YOU LIKE IT, anonymously. In two acts.
    1734   Not published.
No acting versions of the original were published before 1750.

### [*as* EVERY BODY MISTAKEN]
### 1716 LINCOLN'S INN FIELDS
Mar. 10, 12, 13. No parts assigned

### [*as* SEE IF YOU LIKE IT]
### 1734 COVENT GARDEN
Oct. 9, 11, 14; Nov. 2

| | |
|---|---|
| THE PRINCIPAL PARTS BY | Stoppelaer |
| | Chapman |
| | Aston |
| | Mullart |
| | Ridout |
| | James |

# THE COMEDY OF ERRORS [as SEE IF YOU LIKE IT]

## 1734 COVENT GARDEN (cont.)
Oct. 9, &c. (cont.)

   Miss Norsa
   Miss Bincks

[The bill has 'A Comedy of Two Acts, Taken from Plautus and Shakespeare'. 'This piece was no doubt founded on the Comedy of Errors, that being the only play which Shakespeare has borrowed from Plautus' (Genest, iii. 456).]

[*The original*]

## 1741 DRURY LANE
*Nov. 11, 12, 13, 14; Dec. 10*

| | |
|---|---|
| ANTIPHOLUS OF SYRACUSE | Milward |
| ANTIPHOLUS OF EPHESUS | [W.] Mills |
| AEGEON | Berry |
| DROMIO OF SYRACUSE | Macklin |
| DROMIO OF EPHESUS | Arthur |
| DUKE | Winstone |
| BALTHAZAR | Ridout |
| ANGELO | Havard |
| PINCH | Neale |
| 1ST MERCHANT | Turbutt |
| 2ND MERCHANT | Ward |
| MESSENGER | Taswell |
| OFFICER | Woodburn |
| ABBESS | Mrs Macklin |
| LUCIANA | Mrs Mills |
| COURTESAN | Mrs Bennet |
| ADRIANA | Mrs Woffington |

# THE COMICAL GALLANT

John Dennis's alteration of THE MERRY WIVES OF WINDSOR, q.v.

# THE CONSPIRACY DISCOVERED

An anonymous alteration of HENRY V, q.v.

# CORIOLANUS

Adapted as THE INVADER OF HIS COUNTRY, by John Dennis. In five acts.

1720 J. Pemberton.

Act I begins with about 80 new lines that recount the events in *I. iv*. Then follow *I. vi. 15–39*: *I. ix. 11–15*; *I. vi. 47–75*; *I. viii. 1–16*, expanded; *I. ix. 1–9, 60–73*. The act ends with about 50 new lines: Coriolanus expresses his distaste for the Roman populace.

Act II, scene i consists of *I. iii. 1–47*, much expanded and rewritten; and *II. i. 187–223*, wholly rewritten. Scene ii consists of *II. i. 224–87* and *II. ii. 137–58*, somewhat revised. Scene iii is *II. iii*, the parts of the Citizens being much expanded.

Act III, scene i is *III. i. 1–29, 160–269, 280–92, 306–end*, virtually verbatim. Scene ii is *III. ii. 1–39, 93–end*; *III. iii. 1–40, 57–end*, virtually verbatim, and *IV. i*, entirely rewritten: the scene is chiefly between Coriolanus and Virgilia, not Volumnia.

Act IV, scene i begins with *IV. iv*, almost verbatim, and *IV. v. 1–54*, somewhat altered. About 70 new lines are then inserted: Aufidius hears of Coriolanus's expulsion from Rome. The scene continues with *IV. v. 55–153*, slightly altered, and with about 60 new lines: Coriolanus and Aufidius plan the invasion of Rome. The scene ends with a continuation of *IV. v. 154–end*, much expanded. Scene ii is *IV. vi*, considerably reduced and altered.

Act V begins with *IV. vii*, wholly rewritten. Then follows *V. iii*, considerably altered and enlarged. The remainder of the act is new: about 275 lines, in which Coriolanus and Aufidius quarrel, Coriolanus kills Aufidius, and he in turn is killed by the tribunes.

See Genest, iii. 2–5; Odell, i. 239–41.

No acting versions of the original were published before 1750.

## 1718 LINCOLN'S INN FIELDS

*Dec. 13, 15, 16.* No parts assigned

[*as* THE INVADER OF HIS COUNTRY]

## 1719 DRURY LANE

*Nov. 11, 12, 13*

| | |
|---|---|
| CORIOLANUS | Booth |
| AUFIDIUS | Mills |
| MENENIUS | Corey |
| COMINIUS | Thurmond |
| SICINIUS | W. Wilks |
| JUNIUS BRUTUS | Walker |
| CLUENTIUS | Boman Sr. |
| LARTIUS | Williams |
| AEDILE | Oates |
| 1ST CITIZEN | Bickerstaff |
| 2ND CITIZEN | Penkethman |
| 3RD CITIZEN | Johnson |
| 4TH CITIZEN | Miller |
| 5TH CITIZEN | Norris |

## CORIOLANUS [as THE INVADER OF HIS COUNTRY]

### 1719 DRURY LANE (cont.)
*Nov. 11, 12, 13 (cont.)*

| 6TH CITIZEN | Cross |
| 1ST SERVANT | Penkethman |
| 2ND SERVANT | Norris |
| 3RD SERVANT | Miller |
| VOLUMNIA | Mrs Porter |
| VIRGILIA | Mrs Thurmond |

[The bills give neither the parts nor the actors' names. The above assignment is taken from the printed text. Penkethman, Miller, and Norris doubled as CITIZENS and SERVANTS.]

### [The original]
### LINCOLN'S INN FIELDS
*Nov. 14.* No parts assigned

[The bill has 'written by Shakespeare'. This was almost certainly the case. Despite its being announced as *The Invader of his Country*, the production appears to have been an attempt to discredit Dennis, whose alteration had just come out at Drury Lane. In Play-A the title is given as *Coriolanus*.]

### 1720 LINCOLN'S INN FIELDS
*Jan. 1; Nov. 24.* No parts assigned

[On Jan. 1 the play is announced as *The Invader of his Country*; on Nov. 24 as *Coriolanus*.]

*Dec. 26*

| CORIOLANUS | Quin |
| 1ST CITIZEN | Bullock Sr. |
| 2ND CITIZEN | Pack |
| 3RD CITIZEN | Griffin |
| 4TH CITIZEN | Spiller |
| 5TH CITIZEN | Ch. Bullock |

[Genest (iii. 55) suggests that Quin acted CORIOLANUS. The part does not, however, appear in the bill, which lists only the CITIZENS, as the COMIC PARTS.]

### 1721 LINCOLN'S INN FIELDS

*Apr. 10*

| 1ST CITIZEN | Bullock Sr. |
| 2ND CITIZEN | Spiller |
| 3RD CITIZEN* | Griffin |
| 4TH CITIZEN* | Pack |
| 5TH CITIZEN | Hall |
| 6TH CITIZEN | H. Bullock |

[In the bill the CITIZENS are called the COMIC PARTS OF THE MOBB, and are named respectively, Rob-Sack the Miller, Mend-Soul the Cobler, Nitt the Taylor, Burn-Crust the Baker, Fatt-Dab the Cook, and Wash-Ball the Barber.]

*Oct. 31*

3RD CITIZEN   C. Bullock
omitted
4TH CITIZEN

[In the bill the CITIZENS are called the the COMIC PARTS.]

101

## CORIOLANUS

**1722 LINCOLN'S INN FIELDS**
*Jan. 1.* No parts assigned

## A CURE FOR A SCOLD

James Worsdale's alteration of THE TAMING OF THE SHREW, q.v.

## CYMBELINE

Adapted as THE INJURED PRINCESS, by Thomas D'Urfey. In five acts.

1682  R. Bentley and M. Magnes.

Act I, scene i consists of *I. i. 84–158*, followed by *I. iii* and *II. i*. Everything is much altered. The scene concludes with about 40 new lines, recounting the Queen's resolve to poison Eugenia. Scene ii is *I. iv*, almost verbatim, but slightly enlarged (not, as Spencer says, 315, reduced).

Act II begins with about 75 new lines: Pisanio pleads before Cymbeline on behalf of Ursaces. This is followed by *I. v. 4–44*, much reduced. Scene ii is *I. vi*, somewhat altered. Scene iii is a brief new scene in which the Queen proffers the poison to Pisanio. Scene iv is *II. ii*, practically verbatim, followed by *II. iii. 1–14, 82–end*, much reduced.

Act III, scene i is *II. iv*; scene ii is *II. v*; scene iii is *III. iii* and *iv*. With occasional alterations this act follows the original with considerable fidelity.

Act IV, scene i consists of about 50 new lines: the Queen's anger at Eugenia's escape. Scene ii is *III. vi*, slightly altered. Scene iii is new: Cloten puts out Pisanio's eyes for having aided Clarinna. Scene iv is *IV. ii*, much reduced.

Act V, scene i is *V. i*, somewhat altered. Scene ii is *V. ii*, expanded; it ends with a long new scene, in which Shattillion tries to escape, but is killed by Ursaces. Scene iii is *V. v*, reduced almost exactly by half.

See Genest, i. 331–4; Odell, i. 67–70; Spencer, 313–18.

No acting versions of the original were published before 1750.

[*as altered by* D'URFEY]

**1702 LINCOLN'S INN FIELDS**
*Sept. 24; Oct. 7.* No parts assigned
[Bills in DC of Sept. 23 and Oct. 6 respectively.]

**1717 LINCOLN'S INN FIELDS**
*Oct. 5, 9, 12, 25; Nov. 30; Dec. 26.* No parts assigned

**1718 LINCOLN'S INN FIELDS**
*Apr. 23*                                *Oct. 23; Nov. 15.* No parts assigned

| CYMBELINE | [J.] Leigh |
| URSACES | Keene |
| PISANIO | Corey |
| SHATTILLION | [C.] Bullock |

CYMBELINE [*as altered by* D'Urfey]

## 1718 LINCOLN'S INN FIELDS (*cont.*)
*Apr. 23 (cont.)*
| | |
|---|---|
| BELARIUS | Ogden |
| ARVIRAGUS | Smith |
| IACHIMO | Spiller |
| QUEEN | Mrs Knight |
| EUGENIA | Mrs Thurmond |

## 1719 LINCOLN'S INN FIELDS
*Feb. 23.* No parts assigned

## 1720 LINCOLN'S INN FIELDS
*Jan. 7*
| | |
|---|---|
| CYMBELINE* | [J.] Leigh |
| URSACES | Ryan |
| PISANIO | Boheme |
| CLOTEN* | H. Bullock |
| IACHIMO* | Spiller |
| SHATTILLION | Ch. Bullock |
| BELARIUS* | Ogden |
| PALLADOUR* | Egleton |
| ARVIRAGUS* | Smith |
| LUCIUS* | Diggs |
| QUEEN | Mrs Giffard |
| EUGENIA | Mrs Bullock |
| CLARINNA* | Mrs Gulick |

*Jan. 20.* No parts assigned

*Mar. 14*
| | |
|---|---|
| CLARINNA | Mrs Jevon |

omitted
    CLOTEN, LUCIUS

*June 9*
| | |
|---|---|
| CYMBELINE | Quin |
| IACHIMO | Pack |
| ARVIRAGUS | Boheme |

omitted
    CLOTEN, BELARIUS, PALLADOUR, LUCIUS, CLARINNA

[The assignment of Boheme to ARVIRAGUS seems to be a misprint, since he also appears in this bill as PISANIO. Doubling these parts is not possible.]

*Nov. 3*
omitted
    CLOTEN, BELARIUS, PALLADOUR, ARVIRAGUS, LUCIUS, CLARINNA

## 1737 COVENT GARDEN
*Feb. 15, 17, 21; May 5*
| | |
|---|---|
| CYMBELINE | Ryan |
| URSACES | Delane |
| PISANIO | Bridgwater |
| SHATTILLION | Walker |
| BELARIUS | Stephens |
| ARVIRAGUS | A. Hallam |
| LUCIUS | Aston |
| IACHIMO | James |
| BEAUPRE | Salway |
| DON MICHAEL | Neale |
| CLOTEN | Chapman |
| QUEEN | Mrs Hallam |
| EUGENIA | Mrs Templer |
| CLARINNA | Mrs Kilby |

[The bill has, 'Written by Shakespeare. Revis'd with Alterations.']

103

CYMBELINE [as altered by D'Urfey]

## 1738 COVENT GARDEN
*Mar. 20*

| | |
|---|---|
| CYMBELINE | Ryan |
| URSACES | Delane |
| SHATTILLION | Walker |
| PISANIO | Bridgwater |
| CLOTEN | Chapman |
| BELARIUS | Stephens |
| PALLADOUR | Stevens |
| ARVIRAGUS | [A.] Hallam |
| IACHIMO | James |
| BEAUPRE | Salway |
| DON MICHAEL | Neale |
| LUCIUS | Aston |
| QUEEN | Mrs Hallam |
| EUGENIA | Mrs Templer |
| CLARINNA | Mrs Kilby |

[*The original*]

## 1744 HAYMARKET
*Nov. 8*

| | |
|---|---|
| POSTHUMUS | [T.] Cibber |
| IMOGEN | Miss J. Cibber |

[The bill gives neither the parts nor the actors' names. The assignment of Cibber is suggested by Genest (iv. 172); that of Miss Cibber is taken from T. Cibber, *A Seriocomic Apology* [1748], 80. The bill in DP contains an elaborate outline of the plot; it is unmistakably Shakespeare's.]

## 1746 COVENT GARDEN
*Apr. 7, 10*

| | |
|---|---|
| CYMBELINE | Cashell |
| POSTHUMUS | Ryan |
| IACHIMO | Hale |
| BELARIUS | Johnson |
| GUIDERIUS | Woodward |
| ARVIRAGUS | Beard |
| CLOTEN | Chapman |
| CORNELIUS | Rosco |
| PISANIO | Bridgwater |
| LUCIUS | Ridout |
| PHILARIO | Anderson |
| CAPTAIN | Bencraft |
| LORD | Carr |
| FRENCH GENTLEMAN | Hayman |
| QUEEN | Mrs James |
| HELEN | Mrs Bland |
| IMOGEN | Mrs Pritchard |

# EVERY BODY MISTAKEN

William Taverner's and Dr Brown's alteration of THE COMEDY OF ERRORS, q.v.

# HAMLET

'As it is now Acted by Her Majesties Servants.'

    1703   Rich. Wellington.

This version follows the original throughout, save that many lines are excised. Entirely eliminated are: Polonius's advice to Laertes (*I. iii. 58–81*) [for many years Polonius was portrayed as a low comedy character]; 12 lines from 'Angels and ministers of grace' (*I. iv. 40–51*); the scene between Polonius and Reynaldo (*II. i. 1–74*); the Norwegian ambassadors (*II. ii. 40–85*); 'rugged Pyrrhus' (*II. ii. 481–95*); the advice to the players (*III. ii. 1–51*); Hamlet and the Norwegian captain (*IV. iv. 1–66*).

'As it is now Acted by his Majesty's Servants.'

    1718   J. Darby.

This version is similar to the above, save that all of 'Angels and ministers of grace' and all of the advice to the players are retained. The first part of the interview of Hamlet with Rosencrantz and Guildenstern (*II. ii. 228–383*) is drastically reduced. The play ends at 'flights of angels' (*V. ii. 374*).

'As it is now Acted by his Majesty's Servants.'

    1723   J. Darby.
    1734   J. Tonson.
    1737   W. Feales.
    1747   J. and P. Knapton [&c.].
    1750   J. and P. Knapton [&c.].

All these versions are identical with Darby's 1718 edition.

## 1703 DRURY LANE

*Oct. 23; Nov. 13.* No parts assigned

## 1704 DRURY LANE

*Feb. 8; Apr. 6; Oct. 7.* No parts assigned

*Nov. 4*
    GRAVEDIGGER   Estcourt
    No other parts assigned

## 1705 DRURY LANE

*Jan. 31*
    POLONIUS   Dogget
    No other parts assigned

*July 7.* No parts assigned

## 1705 DRURY LANE (cont.)
*Nov. 6, 28*
    OPHELIA    Mrs Mountfort
    No other parts assigned

## 1706 DRURY LANE
*Apr. 25; June 18.* No parts assigned

### QUEEN'S
*Oct. 19.* No parts assigned
*Dec. 10*
    KING    Keene
    HAMLET    Betterton
    HORATIO    Verbruggen
    LAERTES    Booth
    OPHELIA    Mrs Bracegirdle

## 1707 QUEEN'S
*Jan. 11*
    HAMLET    Wilks
    KING    Keene
    HORATIO*    Verbruggen
    LAERTES    Booth
    GRAVEDIGGER    Johnson
    OSRIC*    Bowen
    OPHELIA*    Mrs Bracegirdle

*Apr. 28*
    HAMLET    Wilks
    OPHELIA    Mrs Bradshaw
    No other parts assigned

*June 18*
    OSRIC    Norris
    OPHELIA    Mrs Bradshaw
    added
        GHOST    Mills
        POLONIUS    Cross

*Nov. 22*
    HORATIO    Mills
    OPHELIA    Mrs Bradshaw

## 1708 DRURY LANE
*Jan. 15*
    KING    Keene
    HAMLET    Wilks
    HORATIO    Mills
    LAERTES    Powell
    GHOST    Booth
    POLONIUS*    Johnson
    OSRIC*    Cibber
    GRAVEDIGGER    Estcourt
    QUEEN    Mrs Knight
    OPHELIA*    Mrs Mountfort

*June 11*
    POLONIUS    Cross
    OSRIC    Norris
    OPHELIA    Mrs Bradshaw

## 1708 DRURY LANE (cont.)
*Sept. 9*

| | |
|---|---|
| HAMLET | Thurmond |
| KING | Keene |
| LAERTES | Powell |
| HORATIO | Husband |
| POLONIUS | Cross |
| GRAVEDIGGER | Johnson |
| OSRIC | Thurmond Jr. |
| QUEEN | Mrs Powell |
| OPHELIA | Mrs Bradshaw |

## 1709 DRURY LANE
*Jan. 22*

| | |
|---|---|
| HAMLET | Wilks |
| KING | Keene |
| HORATIO | Mills |
| GHOST | Booth |
| GRAVEDIGGER* | Estcourt |
| POLONIUS | Cross |
| QUEEN | Mrs Knight |
| OPHELIA | Mrs Bradshaw |

*May 7*
added

| | |
|---|---|
| LAERTES | Powell |
| MARCELLUS | Bickerstaff |
| OSRIC | Cibber |

*June 3*

| | |
|---|---|
| GRAVEDIGGER | Underhill |

added

| | |
|---|---|
| LAERTES | Powell |
| MARCELLUS | Bickerstaff |
| OSRIC | Cibber |

## QUEEN'S
*Sept. 20*

| | |
|---|---|
| HAMLET | Betterton |

No other parts assigned

*Nov. 4*

| | |
|---|---|
| HAMLET | Wilks |
| KING | Husband |
| POLONIUS | Cross |
| LAERTES | Thurmond |
| HORATIO | Mills |
| OSRIC | Bowen |
| GRAVEDIGGER | Johnson |
| QUEEN | Mrs Porter |
| OPHELIA | Mrs Cross |

## 1710 DRURY LANE
*Feb. 14; May 9*

| | |
|---|---|
| HAMLET | Powell |
| OPHELIA | Mrs Santlow |

No other parts assigned

*Feb. 23*
added

| | |
|---|---|
| HORATIO | Booth |
| GRAVEDIGGER | Cave Underhill |

## 1710 QUEEN'S
*Jan. 2*
    HAMLET     Wilks
    No other parts assigned

*Apr. 27.* No parts assigned

*July 26*
    HAMLET     Wilks
    HORATIO     Mills
    GRAVEDIGGER     Dogget
    No other parts assigned

*Nov. 11*
    HAMLET     Wilks
    KING     Keene
    LAERTES     Booth
    HORATIO     Mills
    OSRIC     Bowen
    GRAVEDIGGER     Johnson
    QUEEN     Mrs Porter
    OPHELIA     Mrs Santlow

## 1711 DRURY LANE
*Mar. 24*
    HAMLET     Wilks
    KING     Keene
    HORATIO     Mills
    GHOST*     Boman
    GRAVEDIGGER     Johnson
    QUEEN     Mrs Knight
    OPHELIA*     Mrs Santlow

*May 3*
    GHOST     Booth
    OPHELIA     Mrs Bradshaw
    added
        LAERTES     Powell
        OSRIC     Bowen

*Oct. 27*
    GHOST     Booth
    added
        LAERTES     Powell
        OSRIC     Bowen

## 1712 DRURY LANE
*Apr. 25.* No parts assigned

*Oct. 4*
    HAMLET     Wilks
    KING     Keene
    HORATIO     Mills
    GHOST     Booth
    GRAVEDIGGER     Johnson
    OPHELIA     Mrs Mountfort
    QUEEN     Mrs Knight

*Nov. 4; Dec. 20*
    added
        LAERTES     Powell
        POLONIUS     Cross
        OSRIC     Bowen

## 1713 DRURY LANE
*Oct. 17; Dec. 19.* No parts assigned

HAMLET

## 1714 DRURY LANE
*Mar. 20.* No parts assigned

*Apr. 23; Dec. 4*
| | |
|---|---|
| HAMLET | Wilks |
| GHOST | Booth |
| OPHELIA | Mrs Mountfort |

No other parts assigned

## 1715 DRURY LANE
*Jan. 22; Feb. 1*
| | |
|---|---|
| KING* | Evans |
| HAMLET | Wilks |
| GHOST | Booth |
| GRAVEDIGGER | Johnson |
| QUEEN | Mrs Porter |
| OPHELIA* | Mrs Mountfort |

*Mar. 26*
added
| | |
|---|---|
| HORATIO | Mills |
| LAERTES | Ryan |

[The assignment of LAERTES is in the bill in DC of Mar. 25 only.]

*May 27*
| | |
|---|---|
| KING | Bickerstaff |

added
| | |
|---|---|
| HORATIO | Mills |
| LAERTES | Ryan |

*Nov. 12*
| | |
|---|---|
| OPHELIA | Mrs Santlow |

added
| | |
|---|---|
| HORATIO | Mills |

omitted
KING

*Dec. 22*
| | |
|---|---|
| KING | Bickerstaff |
| OPHELIA | Mrs Santlow |

added
| | |
|---|---|
| HORATIO | Mills |

## LINCOLN'S INN FIELDS
*June 30; July 14; Sept. 27.* No parts assigned

## 1716 DRURY LANE
*Mar. 12.* No parts assigned

*Apr. 21*
| | |
|---|---|
| HAMLET | Wilks |
| KING* | Bickerstaff |
| HORATIO | Mills |
| GHOST | Booth |
| LAERTES* | Ryan |
| GRAVEDIGGER | Johnson |
| QUEEN | Mrs Porter |
| OPHELIA | Mrs Santlow |

*June 5*
omitted
  KING, LAERTES

*Oct. 6*
added
| | |
|---|---|
| POLONIUS | Cross |

109

## HAMLET

### 1716 LINCOLN'S INN FIELDS
*Oct. 6*

| HAMLET | Elrington |

No other parts assigned

*Nov. 10*

| HAMLET | Elrington |
| KING | Keene |
| HORATIO | [J.] Leigh |
| LAERTES | Corey |
| GHOST | Smith |
| 1ST GRAVEDIGGER | Hall |
| 2ND GRAVEDIGGER | Spiller |
| QUEEN | Mrs Knight |
| OPHELIA | Mrs Cross |

### 1717 DRURY LANE
*Jan. 12*

| HAMLET | Wilks |
| GHOST | Booth |
| KING | Bickerstaff |
| HORATIO | Mills |
| LAERTES | Ryan |
| POLONIUS | Cross |
| OSRIC | Bowen |
| 1ST GRAVEDIGGER | Johnson |
| QUEEN | Mrs Porter |
| OPHELIA | Mrs Santlow |

[In the acting version published by J. Darby in 1718 the cast is the same as that of this performance, with the following additions:

| ROSENCRANTZ | [W.] Wilks |
| GUILDENSTERN | Quin |
| MARCELLUS | Shepard |
| LUCIANUS | Norris |
| 2ND GRAVEDIGGER | [F.] Leigh |

*Apr. 8*

| HAMLET | Wilks |
| GHOST* | Boman |
| GRAVEDIGGER | Johnson |
| QUEEN | Mrs Porter |
| OPHELIA* | Mrs Mountfort |

*Sept. 28*

| GHOST | Booth |
| OPHELIA | Mrs Santlow |

### LINCOLN'S INN FIELDS
*Feb. 2*

| HAMLET | Elrington |

*Apr. 25*

| OPHELIA | Mrs Thurmond |

110

# HAMLET

## 1717 LINCOLN'S INN FIELDS (cont.)

### Feb. 2 (cont.)
| | |
|---|---|
| KING | Keene |
| HORATIO | [J.] Leigh |
| LAERTES* | Corey |
| GHOST | Smith |
| POLONIUS* | Griffin |
| 1ST GRAVEDIGGER* | Spiller |
| 2ND GRAVEDIGGER* | Hall |
| QUEEN | Mrs Knight |
| OPHELIA* | Mrs Cross |

### May 27
omitted
    LAERTES, POLONIUS, GRAVEDIGGERS

### Mar. 25
| | |
|---|---|
| HAMLET | Elrington |

No other parts assigned

## 1718 DRURY LANE

### Feb. 1
| | |
|---|---|
| HAMLET | Wilks |
| HORATIO | Mills |
| GHOST | Booth |
| GRAVEDIGGER | Johnson |
| QUEEN | Mrs Porter |
| OPHELIA | Mrs Santlow |

### Sept. 20
added
    OSRIC  Cibber

### Sept. 23. No parts assigned
[Bill not in DC. See p. 16.]

### Dec. 20
added
    KING  Thurmond
    OSRIC  Cibber

## 1719 DRURY LANE

### Sept. 12
| | |
|---|---|
| HAMLET | Wilks |
| KING | Thurmond |
| HORATIO | Mills |
| GHOST | Booth |
| OSRIC | Cibber |
| GRAVEDIGGER | Johnson |
| QUEEN | Mrs Porter |
| OPHELIA | Mrs Booth |

## LINCOLN'S INN FIELDS

### Feb. 26
| | |
|---|---|
| HAMLET | Ryan |

No other parts assigned

### Mar. 30
| | |
|---|---|
| HAMLET | Ryan |
| KING | Quin |
| HORATIO | [J.] Leigh |
| POLONIUS | Griffin |

## 1719 LINCOLN'S INN FIELDS (cont.)

*Mar. 30 (cont.)*

| | |
|---|---|
| 1ST GRAVEDIGGER | Hall |
| 2ND GRAVEDIGGER | Spiller |
| [FRANCISCO | Boheme] |
| QUEEN | Mrs Knight |
| OPHELIA | Miss Willis |

[FRANCISCO is not in the bill. Davies (iii. 5) says that at about this time Boheme made his first appearance on the stage in this part. That he acted FRANCISCO is not unlikely, but his first recorded appearance (Genest, ii. 650) was at this theatre on Jan. 16, 1719.]

*Apr. 30.* No parts assigned

*Oct. 17*

| | |
|---|---|
| HAMLET | Ryan |
| KING | Quin |
| HORATIO | [J.] Leigh |
| POLONIUS | Griffin |
| OSRIC | Ch. Bullock |
| 1ST GRAVEDIGGER | Bullock [Sr.] |
| 2ND GRAVEDIGGER | Spiller |
| QUEEN* | Mrs Spiller |
| OPHELIA | Miss Willis |

*Nov. 16*

| | |
|---|---|
| QUEEN added | Mrs Giffard |
| GHOST | Boheme |
| LAERTES | Egleton |

## 1720 DRURY LANE

*Jan. 2*

| | |
|---|---|
| HAMLET | Wilks |
| KING* | Thurmond |
| HORATIO | Mills |
| GHOST | Booth |
| LAERTES* | Walker |
| OSRIC* | Miller |
| GRAVEDIGGER | Johnson |
| QUEEN* | Mrs Porter |
| OPHELIA | Mrs Booth |

*Mar. 14*

| | |
|---|---|
| OSRIC | Cibber |
| omitted | |
| KING, LAERTES | |

*Apr. 30*

| | |
|---|---|
| HAMLET | Wilks |

No other parts assigned

*Nov. 10*

| | |
|---|---|
| OSRIC | Cibber |
| QUEEN | Mrs Thurmond |
| omitted | |
| KING | |

*Dec. 31*

| | |
|---|---|
| OSRIC | Cibber |
| omitted | |
| KING | |

## LINCOLN'S INN FIELDS

*Feb. 3*

| | |
|---|---|
| HAMLET | Ryan |
| KING | Quin |
| HORATIO* | [J.] Leigh |
| POLONIUS* | Griffin |
| GHOST | Boheme |
| 1ST GRAVEDIGGER* | Bullock Sr. |

*Feb. 20*

omitted
    GRAVEDIGGERS

*Mar. 22.* No parts assigned

*Apr. 2*

| | |
|---|---|
| HAMLET | Ryan |

No other parts assigned

112

# HAMLET

## 1720 LINCOLN'S INN FIELDS (cont.)

### Feb. 3 (cont.)

| | |
|---|---|
| 2ND GRAVEDIGGER* | Spiller |
| QUEEN | Mrs Giffard |
| OPHELIA | Miss Stone |

### Apr. 2 (cont.)

[It was perhaps on this night that Mrs Mountfort 'pushed on the stage before the person who played' Ophelia (Genest, ii. 659), and acted the part. This was shortly before Mrs Mountfort's death, which occurred on May 3, 1720 (MWJ, May 7). She died partially insane.]

### May 30

added
| | |
|---|---|
| LAERTES | Ogden |
| OSRIC | C. Bullock |

omitted
POLONIUS, 2ND GRAVEDIGGER

### Oct. 1

| | |
|---|---|
| HORATIO | Ogden |

added
| | |
|---|---|
| LAERTES | Egleton |

### Oct. 27

added
| | |
|---|---|
| LAERTES | Egleton |
| OSRIC | Chr. Bullock |

## 1721 DRURY LANE

### Mar. 16; May 12

| | |
|---|---|
| HAMLET | Wilks |
| GHOST | Booth |
| KING | Thurmond |
| HORATIO | Mills |
| OSRIC* | Cibber |
| GRAVEDIGGER | Johnson |
| QUEEN | Mrs Porter |
| OPHELIA | Mrs Booth |

### Sept. 30

| | |
|---|---|
| OSRIC | Miller |

added
| | |
|---|---|
| POLONIUS | Griffin |

### Dec. 9

added
| | |
|---|---|
| POLONIUS | Griffin |

## LINCOLN'S INN FIELDS

### Jan. 9

| | |
|---|---|
| HAMLET | Ryan |
| KING | Quin |
| HORATIO* | [J.] Leigh |
| LAERTES* | Egleton |
| OSRIC* | C. Bullock |
| GHOST | Boheme |
| POLONIUS* | Griffin |
| 1ST GRAVEDIGGER | Bullock Sr. |
| 2ND GRAVEDIGGER | Spiller |
| QUEEN* | Mrs Giffard |
| OPHELIA | Miss Stone |

### Feb. 27

omitted
LAERTES, OSRIC

### Nov. 25

| | |
|---|---|
| HORATIO | Walker |
| QUEEN | Mrs Seymour |

omitted
OSRIC, POLONIUS

### Dec. 22

| | |
|---|---|
| HORATIO | Walker |
| QUEEN | Mrs Seymour |

omitted
POLONIUS

HAMLET

### 1722 DRURY LANE
*Feb. 1; Apr. 24*

| | |
|---|---|
| HAMLET | Wilks |
| GHOST | Booth |
| KING | Thurmond |
| HORATIO | Mills |
| POLONIUS | Griffin |
| LAERTES | [W.] Wilks |
| OSRIC* | Cibber |
| GRAVEDIGGER | Johnson |
| QUEEN | Mrs Porter |
| OPHELIA | Mrs Booth |

*Sept. 15; Dec. 15*

| | |
|---|---|
| OSRIC | [T.] Cibber |

### LINCOLN'S INN FIELDS
*Jan. 29*

| | |
|---|---|
| HAMLET | Ryan |
| KING | Quin |
| HORATIO* | Walker |
| LAERTES* | Egleton |
| GHOST | Boheme |
| OSRIC* | W. Bullock [Jr.] |
| 1ST GRAVEDIGGER | Bullock Sr. |
| 2ND GRAVEDIGGER | Spiller |
| QUEEN | Mrs Seymour |
| OPHELIA* | Miss Stone |

*Oct. 13*

| | |
|---|---|
| HORATIO | [J.] Leigh |
| LAERTES | Walker |
| OSRIC | Egleton |
| OPHELIA | Mrs Cross |

### 1723 DRURY LANE
*Apr. 20; Sept. 28; Dec. 21*

| | |
|---|---|
| HAMLET | Wilks |
| GHOST | Booth |
| KING | Thurmond |
| HORATIO | Mills |
| POLONIUS | Griffin |
| LAERTES | [W.] Wilks |
| OSRIC | [T.] Cibber |
| GRAVEDIGGER | Johnson |
| QUEEN | Mrs Porter |
| OPHELIA | Mrs Booth |

### LINCOLN'S INN FIELDS
*Feb. 9*

| | |
|---|---|
| HAMLET | Ryan |
| KING | Quin |
| HORATIO* | Walker |
| LAERTES* | Egleton |
| GHOST | Boheme |
| 1ST GRAVEDIGGER | Bullock Sr. |
| 2ND GRAVEDIGGER* | H. Bullock |

*Apr. 18*

| | |
|---|---|
| HORATIO | [J.] Leigh |
| LAERTES | Walker |
| QUEEN | Mrs Boheme [i.e. formerly Mrs Seymour] |

added
| | |
|---|---|
| POLONIUS | Hippisley |
| OSRIC | Egleton |

HAMLET

## 1723 LINCOLN'S INN FIELDS (cont.)

*Feb. 9 (cont.)*
| | |
|---|---|
| QUEEN* | Mrs Seymour |
| OPHELIA* | Mrs Cross |

*Nov. 14*
| | |
|---|---|
| HORATIO | [J.] Leigh |
| LAERTES | Walker |
| 2ND GRAVEDIGGER | Spiller |
| QUEEN | Mrs Knight |
| OPHELIA | Mrs Sterling |
| added | |
|   POLONIUS | Hippisley |
|   OSRIC | Egleton |

## 1724 DRURY LANE

*Apr. 24*
| | |
|---|---|
| HAMLET | Wilks |
| GHOST | Booth |
| KING | Thurmond |
| HORATIO | Mills |
| POLONIUS | Griffin |
| LAERTES* | [W.] Wilks |
| OSRIC* | Theo. Cibber |
| GRAVEDIGGER | Johnson |
| QUEEN | Mrs Porter |
| OPHELIA* | Mrs Thurmond |

*Sept. 12; Dec. 19*
| | |
|---|---|
| OPHELIA | Mrs Booth |
| omitted | |
|   LAERTES, OSRIC | |

## LINCOLN'S INN FIELDS

*Apr. 23*
| | |
|---|---|
| HAMLET | Ryan |
| KING | Quin |
| GHOST | Boheme |
| HORATIO | Diggs |
| LAERTES | Walker |
| POLONIUS | Hippisley |
| OSRIC | Egleton |
| QUEEN* | Mrs Knight |
| OPHELIA* | Mrs Sterling |

*Nov. 26*
| | |
|---|---|
| QUEEN | Mrs Parker |
| OPHELIA | Mrs Vincent |
| added | |
|   1ST GRAVEDIGGER | Bullock Sr. |
|   2ND GRAVEDIGGER | Spiller |

## 1725 DRURY LANE

*Jan. 22*
| | |
|---|---|
| HAMLET | Wilks |
| GHOST | Booth |
| KING | Thurmond |
| HORATIO | Mills |
| POLONIUS | Griffin |
| GRAVEDIGGER | Johnson |
| QUEEN | Mrs Porter |
| OPHELIA | Mrs Booth |

*Mar. 15*
| | |
|---|---|
| added | |
|   OSRIC | [T.] Cibber |
| *Sept. 11* | |
| added | |
|   LAERTES | Williams |
|   OSRIC | [T.] Cibber |

## 1725 LINCOLN'S INN FIELDS

*Apr. 28*

| | |
|---|---|
| HAMLET | Ryan |
| KING | Quin |
| GHOST | Boheme |
| POLONIUS | Hippisley |
| HORATIO | Diggs |
| LAERTES | Walker |
| OSRIC | Egleton |
| 1ST GRAVEDIGGER* | Hall |
| 2ND GRAVEDIGGER | Spiller |
| QUEEN* | Mrs Egleton |
| OPHELIA | Mrs Vincent |

*Oct. 28*

| | |
|---|---|
| 1ST GRAVEDIGGER | Bullock [Sr.] |
| QUEEN | Mrs Parker |

## 1726 DRURY LANE

*Jan. 1; Mar. 10; Apr. 18*

| | |
|---|---|
| HAMLET | Wilks |
| KING | Thurmond |
| GHOST* | Booth |
| HORATIO | Mills |
| POLONIUS | Griffin |
| LAERTES | Williams |
| OSRIC | [T.] Cibber |
| GRAVEDIGGER | Johnson |
| QUEEN | Mrs Porter |
| OPHELIA | Mrs Booth |

*Nov. 12; Dec. 22*

| | |
|---|---|
| GHOST | Bridgwater |

### LINCOLN'S INN FIELDS

*Apr. 25*

| | |
|---|---|
| HAMLET | Ryan |
| KING | Quin |
| GHOST | Boheme |
| POLONIUS | Hippisley |
| HORATIO | Diggs |
| LAERTES | Walker |
| OSRIC | Egleton |
| QUEEN | Mrs Parker |
| OPHELIA | Mrs Vincent |

*May 25*
added

| | |
|---|---|
| 1ST GRAVEDIGGER | Bullock [Sr.] |
| 2ND GRAVEDIGGER | Spiller |

*Sept. 9.* No parts assigned

## 1727 DRURY LANE

*Apr. 15*

| | |
|---|---|
| HAMLET | Wilks |
| GHOST | Booth |
| KING* | Thurmond |
| HORATIO | Mills |
| POLONIUS | Griffin |
| LAERTES | Williams |

*Sept. 23*

| | |
|---|---|
| KING | Wm. Mills |

added

| | |
|---|---|
| 2ND GRAVEDIGGER | Ray |

HAMLET

## 1727 DRURY LANE (cont.)
*Apr. 15 (cont.)*

| | |
|---|---|
| OSRIC | [T.] Cibber |
| 1ST GRAVEDIGGER | Johnson |
| QUEEN | Mrs Porter |
| OPHELIA | Mrs Booth |

## LINCOLN'S INN FIELDS
*Jan. 4*

| | |
|---|---|
| HAMLET | Ryan |
| KING | Quin |
| GHOST* | Boheme |
| POLONIUS | Hippisley |
| HORATIO* | Diggs |
| LAERTES | Walker |
| OSRIC* | W. Bullock [Jr.] |
| 1ST GRAVEDIGGER | Bullock [Sr.] |
| 2ND GRAVEDIGGER | Spiller |
| QUEEN* | Mrs Berriman |
| OPHELIA* | Mrs Vincent |

*Mar. 13*

| | |
|---|---|
| OPHELIA | Mrs Rice |
| omitted OSRIC | |

*May 15*

| | |
|---|---|
| GHOST | Hulett |
| HORATIO added | Milward |
| BERNARDO | Houghton |

*Oct. 21*

| | |
|---|---|
| HORATIO | Milward |
| QUEEN | Mrs Buchanan |

*Dec. 8*

| | |
|---|---|
| HORATIO | Milward |
| OSRIC | Chapman |

## 1728 DRURY LANE
*Feb. 24; Sept. 21*

| | |
|---|---|
| HAMLET | Wilks |
| KING | William Mills |
| GHOST | Bridgwater |
| HORATIO | Mills |
| POLONIUS | Griffin |
| LAERTES | Williams |
| OSRIC | [T.] Cibber |
| 1ST GRAVEDIGGER | Johnson |
| 2ND GRAVEDIGGER | Ray |
| QUEEN | Mrs Porter |
| OPHELIA | Mrs Booth |

## LINCOLN'S INN FIELDS
*Mar. 18*

| | |
|---|---|
| HAMLET | Ryan |
| OPHELIA | Miss Fenton |

No other parts assigned

*May 15*

| | |
|---|---|
| KING | Quin |
| HAMLET | Ryan |
| GHOST* | Milward |

*Nov. 1*

| | |
|---|---|
| GHOST | Boheme |
| HORATIO | Milward |
| OPHELIA | Mrs Vincent |

117

## HAMLET

### 1728 LINCOLN'S INN FIELDS (cont.)

*May 15 (cont.)*

| | |
|---|---|
| POLONIUS | Hippisley |
| LAERTES | Walker |
| HORATIO* | Ogden |
| OSRIC | Chapman |
| 1ST GRAVEDIGGER | Bullock [Sr.] |
| 2ND GRAVEDIGGER | Spiller |
| QUEEN* | Mrs Berriman |
| OPHELIA* | Miss Fenton |

*Dec. 19*

| | |
|---|---|
| GHOST | Boheme |
| HORATIO | Milward |
| QUEEN | Mrs Buchanan |
| OPHELIA | Mrs Vincent |

### 1729 DRURY LANE

*Mar. 18*

| | |
|---|---|
| HAMLET | Wilks |
| KING | Wm. Mills |
| GHOST | Bridgwater |
| HORATIO | Mills |
| POLONIUS | Griffin |
| LAERTES | Williams |
| OSRIC | [T.] Cibber |
| 1ST GRAVEDIGGER | Johnson |
| 2ND GRAVEDIGGER | Ray |
| QUEEN | Mrs Porter |
| OPHELIA | Mrs Thurmond |

### LINCOLN'S INN FIELDS

*Apr. 23*

| | |
|---|---|
| HAMLET | Ryan |
| KING | Quin |
| GHOST* | Chapman |
| HORATIO | Milward |
| POLONIUS | Hippisley |
| LAERTES | Walker |
| 1ST GRAVEDIGGER | Bullock [Sr.] |
| 2ND GRAVEDIGGER | Penkethman [Jr.] |
| QUEEN | Mrs Berriman |
| OPHELIA* | Miss Holliday |

*Sept. 22; Nov. 17*

| | |
|---|---|
| GHOST | Boheme |
| OPHELIA | Mrs Vincent |

added

| | |
|---|---|
| OSRIC | Chapman |

[On Nov. 17 Penkethman [Jr.] made his first appearance at Goodman's Fields (Genest, iii. 274), but his name is here retained as the 2ND GRAVE-DIGGER.]

### 1730 DRURY LANE

*Jan. 24*

| | |
|---|---|
| HAMLET | Wilks |
| KING | Wm. Mills |
| GHOST | Bridgwater |
| HORATIO | Mills |
| POLONIUS* | Griffin |
| LAERTES | Williams |
| OSRIC | [T.] Cibber |

*Sept. 12*

omitted
POLONIUS

## 1730 DRURY LANE (cont.)

*Jan. 24 (cont.)*
| | |
|---|---|
| GRAVEDIGGER | Johnson |
| QUEEN | Mrs Porter |
| OPHELIA | Mrs Booth |

## LINCOLN'S INN FIELDS

*Apr. 15*
| | |
|---|---|
| 1ST GRAVEDIGGER* | Leveridge |
| HAMLET | Ryan |
| KING | Quin |
| GHOST | Boheme |
| POLONIUS | Hippisley |
| LAERTES | Walker |
| HORATIO | Milward |
| OSRIC | Chapman |
| QUEEN | Mrs Berriman |
| OPHELIA | Mrs Vincent |

*Nov. 13*
| | |
|---|---|
| 1ST GRAVEDIGGER added | Bullock [Sr.] |
| 2ND GRAVEDIGGER | Ray |

## GOODMAN'S FIELDS

*Jan. 9, 10*
| | |
|---|---|
| HAMLET* | Giffard |
| GHOST* | Smith |
| KING | W. Giffard |
| POLONIUS* | Collett |
| LAERTES* | W. Williams |
| HORATIO | Huddy |
| OSRIC* | W. Bullock [Jr.] |
| GUILDENSTERN* | R. Williams |
| 1ST GRAVEDIGGER* | Penkethman [Jr.] |
| 2ND GRAVEDIGGER* | [G.] Hallam |
| QUEEN | Mrs Haughton |
| OPHELIA | Mrs Giffard |

[GUILDENSTERN is omitted from all subsequent performances.]

*Jan. 21; Sept. 25*
| | |
|---|---|
| 2ND GRAVEDIGGER | R. Williams |

*Feb. 21*
| | |
|---|---|
| 2ND GRAVEDIGGER omitted | R. Williams |
| GHOST | |

*Apr. 20*
| | |
|---|---|
| HAMLET | A Gentleman [unidentified] |
| POLONIUS | Penkethman [Jr.] |
| 2ND GRAVEDIGGER | W. Williams |

[Penkethman [Jr.] doubled POLONIUS and the 1ST GRAVEDIGGER. This was W. Williams's BT., and his assignment to the 2ND GRAVEDIGGER would therefore appear to be correct, but the part is an unlikely one to be doubled with LAERTES. The name is perhaps a misprint for R. Williams.]

*May 14; June 30; July 29*
| | |
|---|---|
| OSRIC | Bardin |
| 2ND GRAVEDIGGER | R. Williams |

*Nov. 18*
| | |
|---|---|
| GHOST | Rosco |
| LAERTES | Bardin |
| 2ND GRAVEDIGGER added | R. Williams |
| ROSENCRANTZ | R. Williams |

[R. Williams doubled ROSENCRANTZ and the 2ND GRAVEDIGGER.]

119

# HAMLET

## 1730 GOODMAN'S FIELDS (cont.)

*Dec. 18*

| | |
|---|---|
| GHOST | Rosco |
| LAERTES | Bardin |
| 1ST GRAVEDIGGER | Morgan |
| 2ND GRAVEDIGGER | R. Williams |

## 1731 DRURY LANE

*Jan. 16*

| | |
|---|---|
| HAMLET | Wilks |

No other parts assigned

*Sept. 18*

| | |
|---|---|
| HAMLET | Wilks |
| KING | William Mills |
| HORATIO | Mills |
| GHOST | Bridgwater |
| POLONIUS | Griffin |
| LAERTES | A. Hallam |
| OSRIC | Theophilus Cibber |
| GRAVEDIGGER | Johnson |
| QUEEN | Mrs Thurmond |
| OPHELIA | Mrs Booth |

## LINCOLN'S INN FIELDS

*Jan. 5; Apr. 28*

| | |
|---|---|
| HAMLET | Ryan |
| KING* | Quin |
| GHOST* | Hulett |
| POLONIUS | Hippisley |
| LAERTES | Walker |
| HORATIO | Milward |
| OSRIC | Chapman |
| 1ST GRAVEDIGGER | Bullock [Sr.] |
| 2ND GRAVEDIGGER | Ray |
| QUEEN* | Mrs Berriman |
| OPHELIA | Mrs Vincent |

*Nov. 17*

| | |
|---|---|
| KING | Hulett |
| GHOST | Quin |
| QUEEN | Mrs Hallam [i.e. formerly Mrs Berriman] |

## GOODMAN'S FIELDS

*Feb. 19*

| | |
|---|---|
| HAMLET | Giffard |
| KING | W. Giffard |
| GHOST | Rosco |
| POLONIUS | Collett |
| LAERTES | Bardin |
| HORATIO | Huddy |
| OSRIC | [W.] Bullock [Jr.] |

HAMLET

### 1731 GOODMAN'S FIELDS (*cont.*)
*Feb. 19 (cont.)*
| | |
|---|---|
| 1ST GRAVEDIGGER | Morgan |
| 2ND GRAVEDIGGER | R. Williams |
| QUEEN | Mrs Haughton |
| OPHELIA | Mrs Giffard |

### 1732 DRURY LANE
*Feb. 12; Mar. 11*

| | |
|---|---|
| HAMLET* | Wilks |
| KING | Wm. Mills |
| HORATIO* | Mills |
| GHOST | Bridgwater |
| POLONIUS | Griffin |
| LAERTES | A. Hallam |
| OSRIC | Theoph. Cibber |
| GRAVEDIGGER | Johnson |
| QUEEN* | Mrs Thurmond |
| OPHELIA | Mrs Booth |

*Nov. 11*

| | |
|---|---|
| HAMLET | Mills |
| HORATIO | Watson |
| QUEEN | Mrs Butler |

### LINCOLN'S INN FIELDS
*Jan. 29.* No parts assigned

*May 3*

| | |
|---|---|
| HAMLET | Ryan |
| GHOST | Quin |
| KING* | Hulett |
| POLONIUS | Hippisley |
| LAERTES* | Walker |
| HORATIO* | Milward |
| OSRIC* | Chapman |
| 1ST GRAVEDIGGER | Penkethman [Jr.] |
| 2ND GRAVEDIGGER* | Ray |
| QUEEN | Mrs Hallam |
| OPHELIA | Miss Bincks |

*Sept. 22*

| | |
|---|---|
| KING | Milward |
| LAERTES | Chapman |
| HORATIO | Walker |
| 2ND GRAVEDIGGER | Bullock [Sr.] |
| omitted | |
| OSRIC | |

### GOODMAN'S FIELDS
*Feb. 26*

| | |
|---|---|
| HAMLET | Giffard |
| KING* | W. Giffard |
| GHOST | Delane |
| LUCIANUS* | Norris [Jr.] |
| HORATIO* | Huddy |
| POLONIUS | Collett |
| LAERTES* | Bardin |
| OSRIC | [W.] Bullock [Jr.] |

*Feb. 29*

| | |
|---|---|
| OPHELIA | Mrs Roberts |

*Apr. 14*
added
| | |
|---|---|
| MARCELLUS | Havard |

omitted
LUCIANUS

*Oct. 24; Nov. 21*

| | |
|---|---|
| KING | Hulett |
| HORATIO | Rosco |

121

## 1732 GOODMAN'S FIELDS (cont.)

*Feb. 26 (cont.)*

| | |
|---|---|
| 1ST GRAVEDIGGER* | Miller |
| 2ND GRAVEDIGGER | Morgan |
| QUEEN | Mrs Haughton |
| OPHELIA* | Mrs Giffard |

*Oct. 24, &c. (cont.)*

| | |
|---|---|
| LAERTES | W. Giffard |
| 1ST GRAVEDIGGER | Pearce |
| omitted | |
|    LUCIANUS | |

## 1733 DRURY LANE

*Jan. 5, 29; Apr. 25; May 11.* The bills for these performances are missing

*Jan. 8*

| | |
|---|---|
| HAMLET | Mills |
| KING | Wm. Mills |
| GHOST | Bridgwater |
| HORATIO | Roberts |
| POLONIUS | Griffin |
| LAERTES | A. Hallam |
| OSRIC | Oates |
| GRAVEDIGGER | Johnson |
| QUEEN | Mrs Butler |
| OPHELIA | Mrs Booth |

[Genest (iii. 366) says that the bills for Jan. 5 and 8 were identical.]

*Feb. 13.* No parts assigned

## COVENT GARDEN

*Jan. 22*

| | |
|---|---|
| HAMLET | Ryan |
| KING* | Milward |
| GHOST* | Quin |
| POLONIUS | Hippisley |
| LAERTES* | Chapman |
| 1ST GRAVEDIGGER | Bullock [Sr.] |
| 2ND GRAVEDIGGER | Ray |
| QUEEN* | Mrs Hallam |
| OPHELIA | Miss Bincks |

*Apr. 9*

added

| | |
|---|---|
| HORATIO | Walker |

*Sept. 22*

| | |
|---|---|
| KING | Quin |
| GHOST | Salway |
| LAERTES | Walker |
| QUEEN | Mrs Buchanan |

added

| | |
|---|---|
| HORATIO | Hale |

*Nov. 17*

| | |
|---|---|
| KING | Quin |
| GHOST | Chapman |
| LAERTES | Walker |

added

| | |
|---|---|
| HORATIO | Hale |
| OSRIC | Neale |

## HAYMARKET

*Oct. 17*

| | |
|---|---|
| HAMLET | Mills |
| KING | Milward |
| GHOST | Boman |

*Nov. 17*

| | |
|---|---|
| OSRIC | Charke |
| omitted | |
|    MARCELLUS | |

# HAMLET

## 1733 HAYMARKET (cont.)
*Oct. 17 (cont.)*

| | |
|---|---|
| LAERTES | A. Hallam |
| HORATIO | Oates |
| MARCELLUS* | Berry |
| POLONIUS | Griffin |
| OSRIC* | [T.] Cibber |
| GRAVEDIGGER | Johnson |
| QUEEN | Mrs Butler |
| OPHELIA | Mrs Pritchard |

## GOODMAN'S FIELDS
*Mar. 8*

| | |
|---|---|
| HAMLET | Giffard |
| GHOST | Delane |
| KING | Hulett |
| HORATIO | Rosco |
| POLONIUS* | Collett |
| LAERTES* | W. Giffard |
| OSRIC* | [W.] Bullock [Jr.] |
| 1ST GRAVEDIGGER* | Morgan |
| 2ND GRAVEDIGGER | Pearce |
| QUEEN | Mrs Haughton |
| OPHELIA* | Mrs Giffard |

*Apr. 18; May 21*

| | |
|---|---|
| POLONIUS added | Norris [Jr.] |
|   LUCIANUS | Penkethman [Jr.] |

*Sept. 28*

| | |
|---|---|
| LAERTES | Bardin |
| OSRIC | R. Wetherilt |

*Dec. 12*

| | |
|---|---|
| LAERTES | Bardin |
| OSRIC | A Gentleman [unidentified; first appearance on the stage] |
| 1ST GRAVEDIGGER | Penkethman [Jr.] |
| OPHELIA | Mrs Hamilton |
| added | |
|   MARCELLUS | Havard |
|   ROSENCRANTZ | Harbin |
|   GUILDENSTERN | Hamilton |
|   BERNARDO | Jenkins |
|   FRANCISCO | Moore |
|   PLAYER QUEEN | Mrs Monlass |

## 1734 COVENT GARDEN
*Jan. 3*

| | |
|---|---|
| HAMLET | Ryan |
| KING | Quin |
| GHOST | Chapman |
| POLONIUS | Hippisley |
| LAERTES | Walker |
| HORATIO | Hale |
| OSRIC | Neale |
| 1ST GRAVEDIGGER* | Bullock [Sr.] |
| 2ND GRAVEDIGGER* | Ray |
| QUEEN | Mrs Hallam |
| OPHELIA | Miss Bincks |

*Feb. 21*

| | |
|---|---|
| 1ST GRAVEDIGGER | Morgan |

*May 14*

| | |
|---|---|
| 1ST GRAVEDIGGER omitted | Leveridge |
|   2ND GRAVEDIGGER | |

## HAMLET

### 1734 COVENT GARDEN (cont.)

*Sept. 18*

| | |
|---|---|
| HAMLET | Ryan |
| KING | Marshall |
| GHOST* | Walker |
| POLONIUS | Hippisley |
| LAERTES | A. Hallam |
| HORATIO | Hale |
| OSRIC | Chapman |
| 1ST GRAVEDIGGER | Morgan |
| 2ND GRAVEDIGGER | Mullart |
| QUEEN | Mrs Hallam |
| OPHELIA | Miss Bincks |

*Oct. 31; Dec. 14*

| | |
|---|---|
| GHOST | Stephens |

### GOODMAN'S FIELDS

*Apr. 22.* No parts assigned

*Sept. 16*

| | |
|---|---|
| HAMLET | Giffard |
| GHOST | Delane |
| KING | Hulett |
| HORATIO* | Rosco |
| POLONIUS* | Lyon |
| LAERTES* | Bardin |
| MARCELLUS* | Havard |
| ROSENCRANTZ* | Harbin |
| GUILDENSTERN* | Hamilton |
| BERNARDO* | Jenkins |
| FRANCISCO* | Moore |
| 1ST GRAVEDIGGER | Penkethman [Jr.] |
| 2ND GRAVEDIGGER* | Pearce |
| QUEEN | Mrs Haughton |
| OPHELIA | Mrs Hamilton |

*Oct. 17*

omitted
    HORATIO, POLONIUS, LAERTES, MARCELLUS, ROSENCRANTZ, GUILDENSTERN, BERNARDO, FRANCISCO

*Dec. 23*

| | |
|---|---|
| 2ND GRAVEDIGGER | Ray |

### 1735 DRURY LANE

*Mar. 10*

| | |
|---|---|
| HAMLET* | Mills |
| KING* | Milward |
| GHOST* | Quin |
| OSRIC | [T.] Cibber |
| POLONIUS | Griffin |
| LAERTES | W. Mills |
| GRAVEDIGGER | Johnson |
| HORATIO | Este |
| GUILDENSTERN* | Winstone |
| ROSENCRANTZ* | Cross |
| MARCELLUS* | Berry |

*Nov. 1; Dec. 5*

| | |
|---|---|
| HAMLET | Milward |
| KING | Quin |
| GHOST | Mills |

omitted
    GUILDENSTERN, ROSENCRANTZ, MARCELLUS, PLAYER KING, PLAYER QUEEN

## 1735 DRURY LANE (cont.)
*Mar. 10 (cont.)*

| PLAYER KING* | Turbutt |
| PLAYER QUEEN* | Mrs Cross |
| QUEEN | Mrs Butler |
| OPHELIA | Mrs Clive |

## COVENT GARDEN
*Sept. 12*

| HAMLET | Ryan |
| KING | Walker |
| POLONIUS | Hippisley |
| LAERTES | A. Hallam |
| HORATIO | Hale |
| OSRIC | Chapman |
| GHOST | Stephens |
| 1ST GRAVEDIGGER | Bridgwater |
| 2ND GRAVEDIGGER | Mullart |
| QUEEN | Mrs Hallam |
| OPHELIA | Miss Bincks |

## GOODMAN'S FIELDS
*Feb. 27*

| HAMLET | Giffard |
| GHOST | Delane |
| KING | Hulett |
| HORATIO | Rosco |
| POLONIUS | Lyon |
| LAERTES | Bardin |
| OSRIC | [R.] Wetherilt |
| MARCELLUS | Havard |
| ROSENCRANTZ | Harbin |
| GUILDENSTERN | Hamilton |
| BERNARDO | Jenkins |
| FRANCISCO | Moore |
| 1ST GRAVEDIGGER | Penkethman [Jr.] |
| 2ND GRAVEDIGGER | Ray |
| QUEEN | Mrs Haughton |
| OPHELIA | Mrs Hamilton |

*Sept. 19*

| HAMLET | Giffard |
| KING | W. Giffard |
| POLONIUS | Lyon |
| LAERTES* | Bardin |
| HORATIO* | Rosco |

*Oct. 10*

| HORATIO | Havard |
| MARCELLUS | Richardson |
| GHOST | Rosco |
| omitted | |
| GRAVEDIGGERS | |

125

HAMLET

### 1735 GOODMAN'S FIELDS (cont.)

*Sept. 19 (cont.)*

| | |
|---|---|
| MARCELLUS* | Havard |
| OSRIC* | Woodward |
| GUILDENSTERN | Hamilton |
| BERNARDO | Dove |
| FRANCISCO* | Presgrave |
| GHOST* | Hulett |
| 1ST GRAVEDIGGER* | Penkethman [Jr.] |
| 2ND GRAVEDIGGER* | Wetherilt Sr. |
| QUEEN | Mrs Haughton |
| OPHELIA | Mrs Hamilton |

*Dec. 5*

| | |
|---|---|
| LAERTES | Richardson |
| HORATIO | Havard |
| MARCELLUS | Woodward |
| FRANCISCO | Ray |
| GHOST | Rosco |
| omitted | |
| OSRIC, GRAVEDIGGERS | |

### 1736 DRURY LANE

*Mar. 20; May 10*

| | |
|---|---|
| HAMLET | Milward |
| KING | Quin |
| POLONIUS | Griffin |
| LAERTES* | W. Mills |
| OSRIC* | [T.] Cibber |
| HORATIO | Este |
| GHOST* | Mills |
| 1ST GRAVEDIGGER | Johnson |
| 2ND GRAVEDIGGER* | Salway |
| QUEEN | Mrs Butler |
| OPHELIA | Mrs Clive |

*Sept. 4*

| | |
|---|---|
| 2ND GRAVEDIGGER | Macklin |

*Nov. 9*

| | |
|---|---|
| OSRIC | Macklin |
| 2ND GRAVEDIGGER | Macklin |

[It is probable that the assignment of Macklin on this night to the 2ND GRAVEDIGGER is a misprint.]

*Dec. 20*

| | |
|---|---|
| LAERTES | [T.] Cibber |
| OSRIC | Macklin |
| GHOST | Boman |
| omitted | |
| 2ND GRAVEDIGGER | |

### COVENT GARDEN

*Jan. 17; Mar. 13*

| | |
|---|---|
| HAMLET | Ryan |
| KING* | Walker |
| POLONIUS | Hippisley |
| LAERTES | A. Hallam |
| OSRIC | Chapman |
| GHOST | Delane |
| 1ST GRAVEDIGGER | Bridgwater |
| 2ND GRAVEDIGGER | Mullart |
| QUEEN | Mrs Hallam |
| OPHELIA | Miss Bincks |

*Oct. 23*

| | |
|---|---|
| KING | Paget |
| added | |
| HORATIO | Marshall |

### LINCOLN'S INN FIELDS

*Apr. 16*

| | |
|---|---|
| HAMLET | Aston |
| KING | Paget |
| POLONIUS | Hippisley |

## 1736 LINCOLN'S INN FIELDS (cont.)
*Apr. 16 (cont.)*

| | |
|---|---|
| LAERTES | Ridout |
| OSRIC | Clarke |
| HORATIO | Boman [Jr.] |
| ROSENCRANTZ | Houghton |
| GUILDENSTERN | W. Hallam |
| LUCIANUS | James |
| FRANCISCO | Bencraft |
| GHOST | Stephens |
| 1ST GRAVEDIGGER | Bullock Sr. |
| 2ND GRAVEDIGGER | Mullart |
| QUEEN | Mrs Forrester |
| OPHELIA | Miss Male |

*Dec. 13.* No parts assigned

## GOODMAN'S FIELDS
*Feb. 9*

| | |
|---|---|
| HAMLET | Giffard |
| KING | W. Giffard |
| POLONIUS | Lyon |
| LAERTES | Richardson |
| OSRIC | Woodward |
| HORATIO | Havard |
| GUILDENSTERN | Hamilton |
| BERNARDO | Dove |
| GHOST | Rosco |
| 1ST GRAVEDIGGER | Penkethman [Jr.] |
| 2ND GRAVEDIGGER | Ray |
| QUEEN | Mrs Haughton |
| OPHELIA | Mrs Hamilton |

## 1737 DRURY LANE
*Jan. 27*

| | |
|---|---|
| HAMLET | Milward |
| KING* | Quin |
| GHOST | Boman |
| POLONIUS | Griffin |
| LAERTES* | [W.] Mills |
| HORATIO* | Este |
| OSRIC | Macklin |
| 1ST GRAVEDIGGER | Johnson |
| QUEEN | Mrs Butler |
| OPHELIA | Mrs Clive |

[Genest (iii. 492) erroneously assigns the GHOST to Quin, and OPHELIA to Mrs Cibber.]

*May 23*

| | |
|---|---|
| KING | Berry |

*Sept. 24*

| | |
|---|---|
| KING | [W.] Mills |
| LAERTES | Wright |
| HORATIO added | Havard |
| 2ND GRAVEDIGGER | Ray |

## 1737 COVENT GARDEN
*Jan. 13*

| | | | |
|---|---|---|---|
| HAMLET | Ryan | *Apr. 25* | |
| KING | Walker | HORATIO | Paget |
| GHOST | Delane | | |
| OSRIC | Chapman | | |
| HORATIO* | Marshall | | |
| POLONIUS | Hippisley | | |
| LAERTES | A. Hallam | | |
| 1ST GRAVEDIGGER | Bridgwater | | |
| 2ND GRAVEDIGGER | Mullart | | |
| QUEEN | Mrs Hallam | | |
| OPHELIA | Miss Bincks | | |

### LINCOLN'S INN FIELDS
*Jan. 6.* No parts assigned

*May 2*

| | |
|---|---|
| HAMLET | Giffard |
| KING | Johnson |
| GHOST | Rosco |
| POLONIUS | Lyon |
| LAERTES | Wright |
| HORATIO | Havard |
| OSRIC | Woodward |
| 1ST GRAVEDIGGER | Penkethman [Jr.] |
| 2ND GRAVEDIGGER | Wetherilt [Sr.] |
| QUEEN | Mrs Roberts |
| OPHELIA | Mrs Hamilton |

## 1738 DRURY LANE
*Jan. 23; Sept. 7*

| | | | |
|---|---|---|---|
| HAMLET | Milward | *May 1; Oct. 23; Dec. 14* | |
| GHOST | Quin | added | |
| KING | [W.] Mills | 2ND GRAVEDIGGER | Ray |
| LAERTES | Wright | | |
| OSRIC | Macklin | | |
| POLONIUS | Griffin | | |
| HORATIO | Havard | | |
| 1ST GRAVEDIGGER | Johnson | | |
| QUEEN | Mrs Butler | | |
| OPHELIA | Mrs Clive | | |

### COVENT GARDEN
*Jan. 17; Apr. 13*

| | | | |
|---|---|---|---|
| HAMLET | Ryan | *Oct. 14* | |
| GHOST | Delane | HORATIO | Hale |

HAMLET

## 1738 COVENT GARDEN (cont.)

*Jan. 17, &c. (cont.)*

| | |
|---|---|
| KING | Bridgwater |
| LAERTES | [A.] Hallam |
| OSRIC | Chapman |
| POLONIUS | Hippisley |
| HORATIO* | Walker |
| 1ST GRAVEDIGGER | Rosco |
| 2ND GRAVEDIGGER | Mullart |
| QUEEN | Mrs Hallam |
| OPHELIA | Mrs Vincent |

## 1739 DRURY LANE

*Jan. 25; Sept. 1; Nov. 26*

| | |
|---|---|
| HAMLET | Milward |
| GHOST | Quin |
| KING | [W.] Mills |
| POLONIUS | Griffin |
| LAERTES* | Wright |
| OSRIC | Macklin |
| HORATIO | Havard |
| 1ST GRAVEDIGGER | Johnson |
| 2ND GRAVEDIGGER* | Ray |
| QUEEN | Mrs Butler |
| OPHELIA | Mrs Clive |

*May 16*

| | |
|---|---|
| LAERTES | Ridout |
| added | |
| PLAYER KING | Taswell |
| omitted | |
| 2ND GRAVEDIGGER | |

## COVENT GARDEN

*Feb. 13; Apr. 10*

| | |
|---|---|
| HAMLET | Ryan |
| GHOST | Delane |
| KING* | Bridgwater |
| LAERTES | [A.] Hallam |
| OSRIC* | Chapman |
| POLONIUS | Hippisley |
| HORATIO | Hale |
| 1ST GRAVEDIGGER* | Rosco |
| 2ND GRAVEDIGGER* | Mullart |
| QUEEN | Mrs Hallam |
| OPHELIA | Mrs Vincent |

*Nov. 17*

| | |
|---|---|
| KING | Rosco |
| OSRIC | Neale |
| omitted | |
| GRAVEDIGGERS | |

## 1740 DRURY LANE

*Jan. 23*

| | |
|---|---|
| HAMLET | Milward |
| GHOST | Quin |
| KING | [W.] Mills |
| POLONIUS* | Griffin |
| LAERTES | Wright |

*Apr. 26; May 23; Sept. 6*

| | |
|---|---|
| POLONIUS | Taswell |

*Nov. 26*

| | |
|---|---|
| POLONIUS | Taswell |
| HORATIO | Cashell |

## HAMLET

### 1740 DRURY LANE (cont.)
*Jan. 23 (cont.)*

| | |
|---|---|
| OSRIC | Macklin |
| HORATIO* | Havard |
| 1ST GRAVEDIGGER | Johnson |
| 2ND GRAVEDIGGER | Ray |
| QUEEN | Mrs Butler |
| OPHELIA | Mrs Clive |

### COVENT GARDEN
*Oct. 24*

| | |
|---|---|
| HAMLET | Ryan |
| GHOST | Delane |
| KING | Bridgwater |
| POLONIUS | Hippisley |
| LAERTES | [A.] Hallam |
| OSRIC | Neale |
| HORATIO | Hale |
| ROSENCRANTZ | Gibson |
| GUILDENSTERN | Anderson |
| PLAYER KING | Arthur |
| LUCIANUS | James |
| FRANCISCO | Bencraft |
| PRIEST | Harrington |
| PLAYER QUEEN | Mrs Mullart |
| OPHELIA | Mrs Vincent |
| QUEEN | Mrs Woodward |

### GOODMAN'S FIELDS
*Dec. 4*              *Dec. 22.* No parts assigned

| | |
|---|---|
| HAMLET | Giffard |
| GHOST | Walker |
| KING | Paget |
| POLONIUS | Julian |
| LAERTES | Marshall |
| OSRIC | Peterson |
| HORATIO | W. Giffard |
| 1ST GRAVEDIGGER | Yates |
| 2ND GRAVEDIGGER | Dunstall |
| QUEEN | Mrs Steel |
| OPHELIA | Miss Hippisley |

### 1741 DRURY LANE
*Mar. 21; May 5*            *Sept. 19*

| | | | |
|---|---|---|---|
| HAMLET | Milward | GHOST | Delane |
| GHOST* | Quin | LAERTES | Ward |

130

## 1741 DRURY LANE (cont.)

*Mar. 21, &c. (cont.)*

| | |
|---|---|
| KING | [W.] Mills |
| POLONIUS | Taswell |
| LAERTES* | Ridout |
| OSRIC | Macklin |
| HORATIO | Havard |
| 1ST GRAVEDIGGER | Johnson |
| 2ND GRAVEDIGGER | Ray |
| QUEEN | Mrs Butler |
| OPHELIA | Mrs Clive |

*Sept. 19 (cont.)*
added

| | |
|---|---|
| ROSENCRANTZ | Ridout |
| GUILDENSTERN | Winstone |
| PLAYER KING | Turbutt |
| PLAYER QUEEN | Mrs Bennet |

*Nov. 18; Dec. 31*

| | |
|---|---|
| GHOST | Delane |

added

| | |
|---|---|
| ROSENCRANTZ | Woodburn |
| GUILDENSTERN | Green |
| PLAYER KING | Turbutt |
| PLAYER QUEEN | Mrs Bennet |

## COVENT GARDEN

*Oct. 20*

| | |
|---|---|
| HAMLET | Ryan |
| KING | Bridgwater |
| GHOST | Stephens |
| POLONIUS | Hippisley |
| LAERTES | Hale |
| HORATIO | Cashell |
| OSRIC | Woodward |
| ROSENCRANTZ | Gibson |
| GUILDENSTERN | Stevens |
| PLAYER KING | Mullart |
| MARCELLUS | Harrington |
| FRANCISCO | Bencraft |
| LUCIANUS | James |
| PLAYER QUEEN | Mrs Mullart |
| OPHELIA | Mrs Vincent |
| QUEEN | Mrs Pritchard |

## GOODMAN'S FIELDS

*Feb. 26*

| | |
|---|---|
| HAMLET | Giffard |
| GHOST* | Walker |
| KING | Paget |
| POLONIUS | Julian |
| LAERTES | Marshall |
| OSRIC | Peterson |
| HORATIO | W. Giffard |
| 1ST GRAVEDIGGER | Yates |
| 2ND GRAVEDIGGER | Dunstall |
| QUEEN | Mrs Steel |
| OPHELIA | Miss Hippisley |

*Apr. 24.* No parts assigned

*Oct. 14*

| | |
|---|---|
| GHOST | A Gentleman [unidentified] |
| HAMLET | Giffard |

No other parts assigned

*Dec. 9*

| | |
|---|---|
| GHOST | Garrick |

added

| | |
|---|---|
| ROSENCRANTZ | Vaughan |
| GUILDENSTERN | Naylor |
| MARCELLUS | Blakes |

131

## 1742 DRURY LANE

*Jan. 26*

| | |
|---|---|
| HAMLET* | read by [T.] Cibber |
| KING | [W.] Mills |
| GHOST* | Delane |
| LAERTES* | Ridout |
| HORATIO* | Havard |
| POLONIUS* | Taswell |
| ROSENCRANTZ | Woodburn |
| GUILDENSTERN | Green |
| OSRIC* | Macklin |
| PLAYER KING* | Turbutt |
| 1ST GRAVEDIGGER* | Johnson |
| 2ND GRAVEDIGGER | Ray |
| PLAYER QUEEN | Mrs Bennet |
| QUEEN* | Mrs Butler |
| OPHELIA | Mrs Clive |

[In the bill HAMLET is assigned to Milward, but he 'was unable to perform, and Cibber Jun. read the part' (Genest, iii. 647). Milward died on Feb. 6.]

*Mar. 15*

| | |
|---|---|
| HAMLET | Delane |
| GHOST | Berry |

*May 3*

| | |
|---|---|
| HAMLET | Havard |
| GHOST | Berry |
| HORATIO | Cross |
| POLONIUS | Arthur |
| PLAYER KING | Taswell |

*Nov. 16, 18, 20, 23, 25, 29; Dec. 2, 4, 10, 30*

| | |
|---|---|
| HAMLET | Garrick |
| LAERTES | [A.] Hallam |
| OSRIC | Neale |
| 1ST GRAVEDIGGER | Macklin |
| QUEEN | Mrs Pritchard |
| added | |
|   LUCIANUS | Yates |

## COVENT GARDEN

*Feb. 18*

| | |
|---|---|
| HAMLET | Ryan |
| KING | Bridgwater |
| GHOST* | Stephens |
| LAERTES | Hale |
| HORATIO* | Cashell |
| POLONIUS | Hippisley |
| ROSENCRANTZ* | Gibson |
| GUILDENSTERN* | Stevens |
| OSRIC | Woodward |
| MARCELLUS* | Harrington |
| LUCIANUS* | James |
| 1ST GRAVEDIGGER | Rosco |
| 2ND GRAVEDIGGER | Stoppelaer |
| OPHELIA | Mrs Vincent |
| QUEEN* | Mrs Pritchard |

*May 20*

omitted
  HORATIO, ROSENCRANTZ, GUILDENSTERN, MARCELLUS, LUCIANUS

*Nov. 11*

| | |
|---|---|
| GHOST | Quin |
| QUEEN | Mrs Woodward |

omitted
  ROSENCRANTZ, GUILDENSTERN, MARCELLUS, LUCIANUS

## GOODMAN'S FIELDS

*Jan. 15*

| | |
|---|---|
| GHOST | Garrick |
| HAMLET | Giffard |
| KING | Paget |
| LAERTES | Marshall |

## HAMLET

### 1742 GOODMAN'S FIELDS (cont.)
*Jan. 15 (cont.)*

| | |
|---|---|
| HORATIO | W. Giffard |
| POLONIUS | Julian |
| ROSENCRANTZ | Vaughan |
| GUILDENSTERN | Naylor |
| OSRIC | Peterson |
| MARCELLUS | Blakes |
| 1ST GRAVEDIGGER | Yates |
| 2ND GRAVEDIGGER | Dunstall |
| QUEEN | Mrs Steel |
| OPHELIA | Miss Hippisley |

### 1743 DRURY LANE
*Jan. 5, 13, 22; Feb. 5; Mar. 5*

| | |
|---|---|
| HAMLET | Garrick |
| KING | [W.] Mills |
| GHOST | Delane |
| LAERTES* | [A.] Hallam |
| HORATIO | Havard |
| OSRIC | Neale |
| POLONIUS | Taswell |
| LUCIANUS* | Yates |
| ROSENCRANTZ | Woodburn |
| GUILDENSTERN | Green |
| PLAYER KING* | Turbutt |
| 1ST GRAVEDIGGER* | Macklin |
| 2ND GRAVEDIGGER | Ray |
| QUEEN* | Mrs Pritchard |
| OPHELIA* | Mrs Clive |
| PLAYER QUEEN | Mrs Bennet |

*Dec. 15, 23*

| | |
|---|---|
| LAERTES | Blakes |
| PLAYER KING | W. Giffard |
| 1ST GRAVEDIGGER | Yates |
| QUEEN | Mrs Roberts |
| OPHELIA | Mrs Woffington |
| added | |
|   MARCELLUS | Turbutt |
| omitted | |
|   LUCIANUS | |

### COVENT GARDEN
*May 9*

| | |
|---|---|
| HAMLET | Ryan |
| KING | Bridgwater |
| GHOST | Stephens |
| LAERTES | Hale |
| HORATIO | Cashell |
| OSRIC | Woodward |
| POLONIUS | Hippisley |
| 1ST GRAVEDIGGER | Rosco |
| 2ND GRAVEDIGGER | Stoppelaer |
| QUEEN | Mrs Woodward |
| OPHELIA | Mrs Vincent |

## 1743 COVENT GARDEN (*cont.*)

### Sept. 21; Nov. 5

| | |
|---|---|
| HAMLET | Ryan |
| KING | Bridgwater |
| GHOST* | Stephens |
| LAERTES* | Chapman |
| HORATIO* | Cashell |
| OSRIC | Woodward |
| POLONIUS | Hippisley |
| BERNARDO | Gibson |
| ROSENCRANTZ | Ridout |
| GUILDENSTERN | Anderson |
| PLAYER KING* | Harrington |
| MARCELLUS | Carr |
| FRANCISCO | Bencraft |
| LUCIANUS | James |
| 1ST GRAVEDIGGER | Rosco |
| 2ND GRAVEDIGGER* | Dunstall |
| QUEEN* | Mrs Woodward |
| OPHELIA* | Mrs Vincent |
| PLAYER QUEEN | Mrs Mullart |

### Dec. 14

| | |
|---|---|
| GHOST | Quin |
| LAERTES | Cashell |
| HORATIO | Hale |
| 2ND GRAVEDIGGER | Stoppelaer |
| QUEEN | Mrs James |
| OPHELIA | Mrs Clive |

added
  PRIEST   Hayman
omitted
  PLAYER KING

## 1744 DRURY LANE

### Feb. 11; Mar. 5, 27; May 18

| | |
|---|---|
| HAMLET* | Garrick |
| KING* | [W.] Mills |
| GHOST | Delane |
| POLONIUS | Taswell |
| LAERTES | Blakes |
| OSRIC | Neale |
| MARCELLUS* | Turbutt |
| ROSENCRANTZ | Woodburn |
| GUILDENSTERN | Green |
| HORATIO | Havard |
| PLAYER KING* | W. Giffard |
| 1ST GRAVEDIGGER | Yates |
| 2ND GRAVEDIGGER | Ray |
| QUEEN* | Mrs Roberts |
| OPHELIA | Mrs Woffington |
| PLAYER QUEEN* | Mrs Bennet |

[The bill for May 18 is missing.]

### Oct. 22

| | |
|---|---|
| KING | Bridges |
| PLAYER KING | Turbutt |
| QUEEN | Mrs Bennet |
| PLAYER QUEEN | Mrs Yates |

[Turbutt doubled MARCELLUS and the PLAYER KING.]

### Nov. 9

| | |
|---|---|
| KING | Bridges |
| QUEEN | Mrs Bennet |
| PLAYER QUEEN | Mrs Yates |

added
  BERNARDO   Winstone
omitted
  PLAYER KING

### Dec. 13

| | |
|---|---|
| HAMLET | Sheridan |
| KING | Bridges |
| MARCELLUS | Usher |
| QUEEN | Mrs Bennet |
| PLAYER QUEEN | Mrs Yates |

added
  BERNARDO   Winstone
omitted
  PLAYER KING

## 1744 COVENT GARDEN
### Mar. 31; Apr. 3

| | |
|---|---|
| HAMLET | Sheridan [first appearance, Mar. 31, in London] |
| GHOST | Quin |
| KING | Bridgwater |
| HORATIO | Hale |
| POLONIUS | Hippisley |
| LAERTES | Cashell |
| OSRIC | Woodward |
| BERNARDO | Gibson |
| MARCELLUS | Carr |
| ROSENCRANTZ | Ridout |
| GUILDENSTERN | Anderson |
| FRANCISCO | Bencraft |
| PRIEST | Hayman |
| LUCIANUS | James |
| 1ST GRAVEDIGGER | Rosco |
| 2ND GRAVEDIGGER | Stoppelaer |
| PLAYER QUEEN | Mrs Mullart |
| QUEEN | Mrs Pritchard |
| OPHELIA | Mrs Clive |

## HAYMARKET
### June 29; July 3, 6

| | |
|---|---|
| HAMLET | A Young Gentleman [probably Goodfellow; first appearance, June 29, on the stage] |
| GHOST | Macklin |
| KING | Townly |
| LAERTES | Marr |
| HORATIO | Simpson |
| POLONIUS | Mallin |
| MARCELLUS | Holt |
| ROSENCRANTZ | Nelson |
| GUILDENSTERN | Jervis |
| OSRIC | Penington |
| BERNARDO | Reeves |
| FRANCISCO | Smith |
| 1ST GRAVEDIGGER | Macklin |
| 2ND GRAVEDIGGER | Vaughan |
| QUEEN | Mrs Macklin |
| PLAYER QUEEN | Miss Taylor |

## HAMLET

### 1744 HAYMARKET (cont.)
*June 29, &c. (cont.)*

OPHELIA      A Young Lady [unidentified]

[Macklin doubled the GHOST and the 1ST GRAVEDIGGER.]

### NEW WELLS, GOODMAN'S FIELDS
*Nov. 27, 28; Dec. 13*

HAMLET      Goodfellow
No other parts assigned

### 1745 DRURY LANE
*Jan. 5, 28*

| | |
|---|---|
| HAMLET* | Garrick |
| KING | Bridges |
| GHOST | Delane |
| POLONIUS | Taswell |
| LAERTES* | Blakes |
| OSRIC | Neale |
| MARCELLUS | Turbutt |
| ROSENCRANTZ* | Woodburn |
| GUILDENSTERN* | Green |
| HORATIO | Havard |
| BERNARDO | Winstone |
| LUCIANUS | Yates |
| 1ST GRAVEDIGGER | Macklin |
| 2ND GRAVEDIGGER | Ray |
| PLAYER QUEEN | Mrs Yates |
| QUEEN | Mrs Bennet |
| OPHELIA* | Mrs Woffington |

*Oct. 12*

| | |
|---|---|
| HAMLET | A Young Actor [Stevens (Latreille, iv. 285)] |
| LAERTES | Marshall |
| ROSENCRANTZ | Simpson |
| GUILDENSTERN | Goodfellow |

*Nov. 29*

| | |
|---|---|
| HAMLET | Stevens [misprinted 'Stephens'] |
| LAERTES | Marshall |
| ROSENCRANTZ | Simpson |
| GUILDENSTERN | Goodfellow |
| OPHELIA | Mrs Clive |

### COVENT GARDEN
*Apr. 26*

| | |
|---|---|
| HAMLET* | Cashell |
| KING | Bridgwater |
| HORATIO | Hale |
| POLONIUS | Hippisley |
| LAERTES* | Chapman |
| OSRIC | Woodward |
| BERNARDO | Gibson |
| MARCELLUS | Carr |
| ROSENCRANTZ* | Ridout |
| GUILDENSTERN | Anderson |
| FRANCISCO | Bencraft |
| PRIEST | Hayman |
| LUCIANUS | James |
| 1ST GRAVEDIGGER | Rosco |
| 2ND GRAVEDIGGER | Stoppelaer |

*Sept. 23*

| | |
|---|---|
| HAMLET | Ryan |
| LAERTES | Cashell |
| ROSENCRANTZ | Paddick |
| GHOST | Johnson |
| OPHELIA | Mrs Vincent |

## 1745 COVENT GARDEN (cont.)
*Apr. 26 (cont.)*

| | |
|---|---|
| GHOST* | Quin |
| QUEEN | Mrs Pritchard |
| OPHELIA* | Mrs Clive |
| PLAYER QUEEN | Mrs James |

## NEW WELLS, GOODMAN'S FIELDS
*Mar. 23*

| | |
|---|---|
| HAMLET | Goodfellow |
| GHOST | Dance |

No other parts assigned

*Nov. 27*

| | |
|---|---|
| HAMLET | Furnival |
| KING* | Paget |
| GHOST* | Lee |
| POLONIUS | Julian |
| HORATIO | Cushing |
| OSRIC | Blakey |
| LUCIANUS | L. Hallam |
| LAERTES | Kennedy |
| 1ST GRAVEDIGGER | Morgan |
| 2ND GRAVEDIGGER | Dove |
| QUEEN | Mrs Bambridge |
| PLAYER QUEEN | Mrs Cushing |
| OPHELIA | Mrs Phillips |

*Dec. 28*

| | |
|---|---|
| KING | Roberts |
| GHOST | Paget |

## 1746 DRURY LANE
*May 7*

| | |
|---|---|
| HAMLET | Giffard |
| KING | Bridges |
| GHOST | Delane |
| POLONIUS | Taswell |
| LAERTES | Marshall |
| HORATIO | Havard |
| LUCIANUS | Yates |
| MARCELLUS | Bransby |
| ROSENCRANTZ | Simpson |
| GUILDENSTERN | Usher |
| OSRIC | Neale |
| BERNARDO | Winstone |
| 1ST GRAVEDIGGER | Macklin |
| 2ND GRAVEDIGGER | Ray |
| QUEEN | Mrs Bennet |
| PLAYER QUEEN | Mrs Yates |
| OPHELIA | Mrs Clive |

## 1746 COVENT GARDEN

*June 13*

| | |
|---|---|
| HAMLET | Garrick |
| GHOST | Johnson |
| KING | Bridgwater |
| HORATIO | Cashell |
| POLONIUS | Paget |
| LAERTES | Chapman |
| OSRIC | Master Shuter |
| 1ST GRAVEDIGGER | Morgan |
| 2ND GRAVEDIGGER | Stoppelaer |
| QUEEN | Mrs Horton |
| OPHELIA | Mrs Vincent |

*Sept. 29*

| | |
|---|---|
| HAMLET* | Ryan |
| GHOST | Cashell |
| KING | Bridgwater |
| HORATIO | Havard |
| POLONIUS | Hippisley |
| LAERTES | Ridout |
| OSRIC | Woodward |
| BERNARDO* | Gibson |
| MARCELLUS | Carr |
| ROSENCRANTZ | Bencraft |
| GUILDENSTERN | Anderson |
| FRANCISCO | Paddick |
| LUCIANUS | James |
| PLAYER KING* | Marten |
| 1ST GRAVEDIGGER | Morgan |
| 2ND GRAVEDIGGER | Stoppelaer |
| OPHELIA | Mrs Vincent |
| PLAYER QUEEN | Mrs James |
| QUEEN | Mrs Pritchard |

*Oct. 22; Nov. 10*

| | |
|---|---|
| HAMLET | Garrick |
| BERNARDO | Kennedy |
| PLAYER KING | Gibson |

## NEW WELLS, GOODMAN'S FIELDS

*Jan. 31*

| | |
|---|---|
| HAMLET | Banberry [first appearance on the stage] |
| HORATIO | Cushing |
| 1ST GRAVEDIGGER | Morgan |
| 2ND GRAVEDIGGER | Dove |
| OPHELIA | Mrs Phillips |

[Genest (iv. 198) has 'Banbury'; the bills in both DA and GA spell the name as above.]

*Dec. 3, 4*

| | |
|---|---|
| HAMLET | Goodfellow |
| KING | Paget |

## HAMLET

### 1746 NEW WELLS, GOODMAN'S FIELDS (cont.)
*Dec. 3, &c. (cont.)*

| | |
|---|---|
| POLONIUS | [G.] Hallam |
| LAERTES | Wignell |
| HORATIO | Cushing |
| OSRIC | Shuter |
| GUILDENSTERN | Lee |
| ROSENCRANTZ | Cartwright |
| 1ST GRAVEDIGGER | L. Hallam |
| 2ND GRAVEDIGGER | Dove |
| GHOST | Burton |
| QUEEN | Mrs Bambridge |
| OPHELIA | Mrs Cushing |

### 1747 DRURY LANE
*Mar. 24*

| | |
|---|---|
| HAMLET | Barry |
| KING | Bridges |
| GHOST | Delane |
| HORATIO | [W.] Mills |
| POLONIUS | Taswell |
| LAERTES | Blakes |
| GRAVEDIGGER | Macklin |
| QUEEN | Mrs Furnival |
| OPHELIA | Mrs Clive |

*Apr. 11*

| | | *Apr. 29* | |
|---|---|---|---|
| HAMLET* | Barry | HAMLET | Giffard |
| KING | Bridges | 2ND GRAVEDIGGER | Raftor |
| GHOST | Delane | | |
| HORATIO | [W.] Mills | | |
| POLONIUS | Taswell | | |
| LAERTES | Blakes | | |
| OSRIC | Neale | | |
| LUCIANUS | Yates | | |
| ROSENCRANTZ | Simpson | | |
| GUILDENSTERN | Usher | | |
| MARCELLUS | Bransby | | |
| BERNARDO | Winstone | | |
| FRANCISCO | Leigh [Jr.] | | |
| 1ST GRAVEDIGGER | Macklin | | |
| 2ND GRAVEDIGGER* | Ray | | |
| QUEEN | Mrs Furnival | | |
| PLAYER QUEEN | Mrs Yates | | |
| OPHELIA | Mrs Clive | | |

*Sept. 22* | | *Oct. 23* | |
|---|---|---|---|
| HAMLET* | Barry | HAMLET | Garrick |

## 1747 DRURY LANE (cont.)
*Sept. 22 (cont.)*

| | |
|---|---|
| KING | [L.] Sparks |
| GHOST | Delane |
| HORATIO | Havard |
| POLONIUS | Taswell |
| LAERTES | Blakes |
| OSRIC | Neale |
| LUCIANUS | Yates |
| ROSENCRANTZ | Simpson |
| GUILDENSTERN | Usher |
| 1ST GRAVEDIGGER | Macklin |
| 2ND GRAVEDIGGER | Ray |
| MARCELLUS | Bransby |
| BERNARDO | Marr |
| PLAYER KING | Winstone |
| PLAYER QUEEN | Mrs Yates |
| QUEEN* | Mrs Bennet |
| OPHELIA | Mrs Clive |

*Nov. 24*

| | |
|---|---|
| QUEEN | Mrs Pritchard |

## COVENT GARDEN
*Dec. 9*

| | |
|---|---|
| HAMLET | Ryan |
| KING | Bridges |
| HORATIO | Ridout |
| GHOST | Giffard |
| POLONIUS | Paget |
| LAERTES | Gibson |
| ROSENCRANTZ | Bencraft |
| GUILDENSTERN | Storer |
| BERNARDO | Kennedy |
| MARCELLUS | Anderson |
| LUCIANUS | James |
| FRANCISCO | Paddick |
| PLAYER KING | Rosco |
| 1ST GRAVEDIGGER | Morgan |
| 2ND GRAVEDIGGER | Stoppelaer |
| OSRIC | [T.] Cibber |
| QUEEN | Mrs Horton |
| PLAYER QUEEN | Mrs Bland |
| OPHELIA | Mrs Storer |

## NEW WELLS, GOODMAN'S FIELDS
*Jan. 29*

| | |
|---|---|
| HAMLET | Cushing |
| KING | Paget |
| POLONIUS | [G.] Hallam |
| LAERTES | Wignell |

*Mar. 12*

| | |
|---|---|
| HAMLET | Lee |
| POLONIUS | Shuter |
| OPHELIA | Miss Budgell |

No other parts assigned

HAMLET

## 1747 NEW WELLS, GOODMAN'S FIELDS (cont.)

*Jan. 29 (cont.)*

| | |
|---|---|
| HORATIO | Furnival |
| OSRIC | Shuter |
| GHOST | Lee |
| 1ST GRAVEDIGGER | L. Hallam |
| 2ND GRAVEDIGGER | Dove |
| QUEEN | Mrs Bambridge |
| OPHELIA | Mrs Cushing |

*Apr. 7*

| | |
|---|---|
| HAMLET | Goodfellow |
| OPHELIA | Miss Budgell |

No other parts assigned

## 1748 DRURY LANE

*Jan. 21*

| | |
|---|---|
| HAMLET* | Garrick |
| KING | [L.] Sparks |
| GHOST | Delane |
| HORATIO | Havard |
| POLONIUS | Taswell |
| LAERTES | Blakes |
| OSRIC | Neale |
| 1ST GRAVEDIGGER | Macklin |
| 2ND GRAVEDIGGER | Ray |
| OPHELIA | Mrs Clive |
| QUEEN | Mrs Pritchard |

*Mar. 3; Apr. 18*

| | |
|---|---|
| HAMLET | Barry |

[HAMLET is erroneously assigned to Garrick on Mar. 3 by Genest (iv. 239), and on Apr. 18 by MacMillan (254).]

*Sept. 24*

| | |
|---|---|
| HAMLET* | Barry |
| KING* | [L.] Sparks |
| GHOST | Berry |
| HORATIO | Havard |
| POLONIUS | Taswell |
| LAERTES | Blakes |
| OSRIC | Woodward |
| LUCIANUS | James |
| ROSENCRANTZ | Simpson |
| GUILDENSTERN | Usher |
| MARCELLUS | Bransby |
| PLAYER KING | Winstone |
| 1ST GRAVEDIGGER | Yates |
| 2ND GRAVEDIGGER* | Vaughan |
| PLAYER QUEEN | Mrs Yates |
| OPHELIA | Mrs Clive |
| QUEEN | Mrs Pritchard |

*Oct. 14*

| | |
|---|---|
| HAMLET | Garrick |
| 2ND GRAVEDIGGER | Ray |

*Dec. 17*

| | |
|---|---|
| HAMLET | Garrick |
| KING | Bridges |
| 2ND GRAVEDIGGER | Ray |

## COVENT GARDEN

*Feb. 23*

| | |
|---|---|
| HAMLET | Ryan |
| KING | Bridges |
| GHOST | Giffard |

*Apr. 2.* No parts assigned

*Apr. 27*

omitted
    ROSENCRANTZ, GUILDENSTERN,

141

HAMLET

## 1748 COVENT GARDEN (cont.)

### Feb. 23 (cont.)

| | |
|---|---|
| HORATIO | Rosco |
| POLONIUS | Paget |
| LAERTES | Gibson |
| OSRIC | [T.] Cibber |
| 1ST GRAVEDIGGER | Morgan |
| 2ND GRAVEDIGGER | Stoppelaer |
| ROSENCRANTZ* | Bencraft |
| GUILDENSTERN* | Storer |
| BERNARDO* | Collins |
| MARCELLUS | Anderson |
| LUCIANUS* | James |
| FRANCISCO* | Paddick |
| PLAYER KING* | Dunstall |
| QUEEN | Mrs Horton |
| PLAYER QUEEN* | Mrs Bland |
| OPHELIA | Mrs Storer |

### Apr. 27 (cont.)

BERNARDO, LUCIANUS, FRANCISCO, PLAYER KING, PLAYER QUEEN

## 1749 DRURY LANE

### Jan. 5

| | |
|---|---|
| HAMLET* | Garrick |
| KING | Bridges |
| GHOST | Berry |
| HORATIO | Havard |
| POLONIUS* | Taswell |
| LAERTES | Blakes |
| OSRIC | Woodward |
| LUCIANUS* | James |
| ROSENCRANTZ* | Simpson |
| GUILDENSTERN* | Usher |
| MARCELLUS* | Bransby |
| PLAYER KING* | Winstone |
| 1ST GRAVEDIGGER | Yates |
| 2ND GRAVEDIGGER* | Ray |
| PLAYER QUEEN* | Mrs Yates |
| OPHELIA* | Mrs Clive |
| QUEEN | Mrs Pritchard |

### Jan. 26

| | |
|---|---|
| HAMLET | Barry |
| 2ND GRAVEDIGGER | Vaughan |

[MacMillan (254) erroneously assigns the 2ND GRAVEDIGGER to Ray.]

### Mar. 29

| | |
|---|---|
| HAMLET | Barry |
| POLONIUS | James |
| OPHELIA | Mrs Cibber |

omitted
    LUCIANUS, ROSENCRANTZ, GUILDENSTERN, MARCELLUS, PLAYER KING, PLAYER QUEEN

### Oct. 3

| | |
|---|---|
| HAMLET | Barry |

added
    BERNARDO     Marr
omitted
    MARCELLUS

### Oct. 27

added
    BERNARDO     Marr
omitted
    MARCELLUS

### Nov. 20

| | |
|---|---|
| HAMLET | Barry |

omitted
    LUCIANUS, ROSENCRANTZ, GUILDENSTERN, MARCELLUS, PLAYER KING, PLAYER QUEEN

HAMLET

## 1749 COVENT GARDEN

*Sept. 27*

| | |
|---|---|
| HAMLET | Ryan |
| KING | [L.] Sparks |
| GHOST | Delane |
| HORATIO | Ridout |
| POLONIUS | Arthur |
| LAERTES | Gibson |
| OSRIC | Cushing |
| 1ST GRAVEDIGGER | Dunstall |
| 2ND GRAVEDIGGER | Stoppelaer |
| ROSENCRANTZ* | Bencraft |
| GUILDENSTERN* | Bransby |
| MARCELLUS* | Anderson |
| BERNARDO* | Oates |
| PLAYER KING* | Redman |
| PLAYER QUEEN* | Mrs Bambridge |
| QUEEN | Mrs Horton |
| OPHELIA | Mrs Vincent |

*Dec. 15*
omitted
ROSENCRANTZ, GUILDENSTERN, MAR-CELLUS, BERNARDO, PLAYER KING, PLAYER QUEEN

## HAYMARKET

*Jan. 28.* No parts assigned

## 1750 DRURY LANE

*Jan. 3*

| | |
|---|---|
| HAMLET* | Barry |
| KING | Bridges |
| GHOST* | Sowdon |
| HORATIO* | Havard |
| POLONIUS* | Taswell |
| LAERTES* | Blakes |
| OSRIC* | Woodward |
| 1ST GRAVEDIGGER* | Yates |
| 2ND GRAVEDIGGER* | Ray |
| OPHELIA | Mrs Clive |
| QUEEN | Mrs Pritchard |

*Mar. 15*

| | |
|---|---|
| HAMLET | Garrick |
| GHOST | Berry |

omitted
POLONIUS, LAERTES, OSRIC, GRAVE-DIGGERS
[MacMillan (254) erroneously assigns the GHOST to Sowdon.]

*Apr. 19*

| | |
|---|---|
| GHOST | Berry |
| HORATIO | Palmer |

added
| | |
|---|---|
| LUCIANUS | James |

*Sept. 25; Nov. 29*

| | |
|---|---|
| HAMLET | Garrick |
| GHOST | Berry |

added
| | |
|---|---|
| LUCIANUS | James |
| ROSENCRANTZ | Simpson |
| GUILDENSTERN | Scrase |
| BERNARDO | Marr |
| PLAYER KING | Winstone |
| PLAYER QUEEN | Mrs Yates |

## 1750 COVENT GARDEN
*Feb. 15*

| HAMLET | Ryan |
| --- | --- |
| KING | [L.] Sparks |
| GHOST | Delane |
| HORATIO | Ridout |
| POLONIUS | Arthur |
| LAERTES | Gibson |
| OSRIC | Cushing |
| 1ST GRAVEDIGGER | Dunstall |
| 2ND GRAVEDIGGER | Stoppelaer |
| QUEEN | Mrs Horton |
| OPHELIA | Mrs Vincent |

*Oct. 25; Dec. 11*

| HAMLET | Barry |
| --- | --- |
| KING | [L.] Sparks |
| HORATIO | Ridout |
| GHOST | Ryan |
| ROSENCRANTZ | Usher |
| GUILDENSTERN | Bransby |
| MARCELLUS | Anderson |
| BERNARDO | [R.] Elrington |
| LAERTES | Gibson |
| OSRIC | Dyer |
| PLAYER KING | Redman |
| 1ST GRAVEDIGGER | Dunstall |
| 2ND GRAVEDIGGER | Stoppelaer |
| POLONIUS | Macklin |
| QUEEN | Mrs Woffington |
| PLAYER QUEEN | Mrs Bambridge |
| OPHELIA | Mrs Cibber |

# HENRY IV, PART I

'As it is Acted at the Theatre in Little-Lincolns-Inn-Fields.'

1700   R. W[ellington?].

This version follows the original throughout, save for excisions. The most important of these are:

Act I. i. *3–6, 9–16, 18–30;* ii. *117–22, 225–9.*
Act II. iii. *49–67;* iv. *9–18, 436–44, 448–58.*
Act III. i. *140–end* (Hotspur, Mortimer, and their wives); ii. *50–87.*
Act IV. iv entire (the Archbishop of York).
Act V. i. *3–8;* iv. *1–58;* v. *5–10, 16–33.*

See Genest, ii. 219–20; Odell, i. 84–5; Spencer, 360–1.

No other acting versions were published before 1750.

## 1704 DRURY LANE
*Nov. 25, 28*

    FALSTAFF          Estcourt
No other parts assigned

### LINCOLN'S INN FIELDS
*Nov. 6, 9*

    FALSTAFF          Betterton
No other parts assigned
    [Bills in DC of Nov. 4 and Nov. 8 respectively.]

## 1705 DRURY LANE
*Jan. 5; Dec. 15*          *Dec. 19.* No parts assigned

    FALSTAFF          Estcourt
No other parts assigned

## 1706 QUEEN'S
*Oct. 26; Nov. 6; Dec. 4, 26*

    FALSTAFF          Betterton
    HENRY            Keene
    PRINCE OF WALES  Wilks
    NORTHUMBERLAND  Boman
    HOTSPUR          Verbruggen
    GLENDOWER       Husband
    DOUGLAS          Mills
    VERNON           Booth

## 1707 QUEEN'S
*Nov. 19*

    FALSTAFF          Betterton
    HENRY            Keene
    PRINCE OF WALES  Wilks
    HOTSPUR          Booth
    WORCESTER       Cibber
    GLENDOWER       Husband
    DOUGLAS          Mills

## 1708 DRURY LANE
*Jan. 24.* No parts assigned

## 1709 DRURY LANE
*Jan. 1*                      *Mar. 10.* No parts assigned

    FALSTAFF          Betterton
    HENRY            Keene
    PRINCE OF WALES  Wilks
    HOTSPUR          Powell
    VERNON           Booth

## 1709 DRURY LANE (cont.)
*Jan. 1 (cont.)*

| | |
|---|---|
| GLENDOWER | Cibber |
| DOUGLAS | Husband |
| 1ST CARRIER | Johnson |
| 2ND CARRIER | Bullock |
| FRANCIS | Norris |
| HOSTESS | Mrs Powell |

## 1710 DRURY LANE
*Dec. 2*

| | |
|---|---|
| FALSTAFF | Estcourt |
| HENRY | Keene |
| PRINCE OF WALES | Wilks |
| HOTSPUR | Booth |
| 1ST CARRIER | Johnson |
| 2ND CARRIER | Bullock |
| FRANCIS | Norris |
| LADY PERCY | Mrs Santlow |

## QUEEN'S
*May 4*

| | |
|---|---|
| FALSTAFF | Evans |

No other parts assigned

## 1711 DRURY LANE
*May 8*

| | |
|---|---|
| FALSTAFF | Estcourt |
| HOTSPUR | Booth |
| HENRY | Keene |
| PRINCE OF WALES | Wilks |
| DOUGLAS | Mills |
| VERNON* | [C.] Bullock |
| 1ST CARRIER | Johnson |
| 2ND CARRIER | Bullock [Sr.] |
| FRANCIS | Norris |
| LADY PERCY* | Mrs Bradshaw |

*Nov. 6*

LADY PERCY Mrs Santlow
omitted
VERNON
[Sp retains Mrs Bradshaw as LADY PERCY.]

## 1712 DRURY LANE
*Apr. 7*

| | |
|---|---|
| FALSTAFF | Powell |

No other parts assigned

## 1713 DRURY LANE
*May 18*

| FALSTAFF | Bullock [Sr.] |
| HOTSPUR | Booth |
| HENRY | Keene |
| PRINCE OF WALES | Wilks |
| DOUGLAS | Mills |
| 1ST CARRIER | Johnson |
| 2ND CARRIER | [F.] Leigh |

## 1714 DRURY LANE
*June 2*

| HENRY | Keene |
| PRINCE OF WALES | Wilks |
| HOTSPUR | Booth |
| DOUGLAS | Mills |
| FALSTAFF | Bullock [Sr.] |
| 1ST CARRIER | Johnson |
| 2ND CARRIER | [F.] Leigh |
| FRANCIS | Norris |
| LADY PERCY | Mrs Santlow |
| HOSTESS | Mrs Willis |

## 1715 DRURY LANE
*Feb. 12, 14*

| HENRY | Mills |
| PRINCE OF WALES | Wilks |
| HOTSPUR | Elrington |
| FALSTAFF | Evans |
| 1ST CARRIER | Johnson |
| 2ND CARRIER | Penkethman |
| FRANCIS | Norris |
| LADY PERCY | Mrs Santlow |
| HOSTESS | Mrs Willis |

### LINCOLN'S INN FIELDS
*Apr. 4*

| FALSTAFF | Hall |

No other parts assigned

## 1716 DRURY LANE
*Mar. 3*

| FALSTAFF | Mills |
| HENRY* | Boman |
| PRINCE OF WALES | Wilks |
| HOTSPUR | Booth |
| 1ST CARRIER | Johnson |

*May 11; Oct. 2*

| HENRY | Thurmond |

## 1716 DRURY LANE (cont.)
*Mar. 3 (cont.)*

| | |
|---|---|
| 2ND CARRIER | Miller |
| FRANCIS | Norris |
| LADY PERCY | Mrs Santlow |
| HOSTESS | Mrs Willis |

## LINCOLN'S INN FIELDS
*Mar. 15.* No parts assigned

*Apr. 17*

| | |
|---|---|
| HENRY | Keene |
| FALSTAFF | Bullock Sr. |

No other parts assigned

*Oct. 20; Dec. 12*

| | |
|---|---|
| HOTSPUR | Elrington |
| HENRY | Keene |
| PRINCE OF WALES | [J.] Leigh |
| FALSTAFF | Bullock Sr. |
| FRANCIS | Spiller |
| POINS | [C.] Bullock |
| 1ST CARRIER | Knapp |
| 2ND CARRIER | Griffin |

[The assignment of FRANCIS, POINS, CARRIERS is conjectural. In the bills they are called the COMIC PARTS.]

## 1717 DRURY LANE
*May 21; Oct. 15*

| | |
|---|---|
| FALSTAFF | Mills |
| HENRY | Thurmond |
| PRINCE OF WALES | Wilks |
| HOTSPUR | Booth |
| 1ST CARRIER | Johnson |
| 2ND CARRIER | Miller |
| FRANCIS | Norris |
| HOSTESS | Mrs Willis |

## LINCOLN'S INN FIELDS
*May 2*

| | |
|---|---|
| HENRY | Keene |
| PRINCE OF WALES | [J.] Leigh |
| HOTSPUR | Elrington |
| FALSTAFF | Bullock Sr. |

No other parts assigned

# HENRY IV, PART I

## 1718 DRURY LANE

*Jan. 2*

| | |
|---|---|
| FALSTAFF | Mills |
| HENRY | Thurmond |
| PRINCE OF WALES | Wilks |
| HOTSPUR* | Booth |
| 1ST CARRIER | Johnson |
| 2ND CARRIER | Miller |
| FRANCIS | Norris |
| HOSTESS | Mrs Willis |

*May 16*

added
| | |
|---|---|
| LADY PERCY | Mrs Santlow |

*Sept. 27*
| | |
|---|---|
| HOTSPUR | Elrington |

added
| | |
|---|---|
| LADY PERCY | Mrs Santlow |

## LINCOLN'S INN FIELDS

*Jan. 7*

| | |
|---|---|
| HOTSPUR | Quin |
| HENRY | Keene |
| PRINCE OF WALES | [J.] Leigh |
| NORTHUMBERLAND | Schoolding |
| WESTMORLAND | Ogden |
| WORCESTER | Corey |
| MORTIMER | Williams |
| GLENDOWER | Husband |
| DOUGLAS | Smith |
| FALSTAFF | Bullock Sr. |
| FRANCIS | Spiller |

*Sept. 30*

| | |
|---|---|
| FALSTAFF | Evans |
| HENRY | Ogden |
| PRINCE OF WALES | [J.] Leigh |
| HOTSPUR | Quin |
| WORCESTER | Corey |
| VERNON | Ryan |
| DOUGLAS | Smith |
| FRANCIS | Spiller |
| LADY PERCY | Mrs Bullock |

## 1719 DRURY LANE

*Jan. 10*

| | |
|---|---|
| HOTSPUR* | Elrington |
| HENRY | Thurmond |
| PRINCE OF WALES | Wilks |
| FALSTAFF | Mills |
| 1ST CARRIER | Johnson |
| 2ND CARRIER | Miller |
| FRANCIS | Norris |
| LADY PERCY* | Mrs Santlow |
| HOSTESS | Mrs Hunt |

*May 7*

| | |
|---|---|
| HOTSPUR | Booth |

added
| | |
|---|---|
| DOUGLAS | Williams |
| VERNON | Oates |

*Oct. 22*

| | |
|---|---|
| HOTSPUR | Booth |
| LADY PERCY | Mrs Booth [i.e. formerly Mrs Santlow] |

added
| | |
|---|---|
| DOUGLAS | Williams |
| VERNON | Walker |

## 1719 LINCOLN'S INN FIELDS
*Apr. 4.* No parts assigned

*Oct. 2*

| | |
|---|---|
| FALSTAFF | Bullock [Sr.] |
| HENRY | Ogden |
| PRINCE OF WALES | [J.] Leigh |
| HOTSPUR | Quin |
| WORCESTER | Boheme |
| DOUGLAS | Smith |
| VERNON | Ryan |
| POINS | C. Bullock |
| 1ST CARRIER | Griffin |
| 2ND CARRIER | H. Bullock |
| LADY PERCY | Mrs Bullock |
| HOSTESS | Mrs Cook |

[The bill has 'LADY PERCY, Mrs Bullock; HOSTESS, Mrs Cook; LADY PERCY, Mrs Spiller'. Mrs Bullock regularly acted the part; she may, however, have been unable to perform on this night.]

## 1720 DRURY LANE
*Sept. 17*

| | |
|---|---|
| HOTSPUR | Booth |
| HENRY | Thurmond |
| PRINCE OF WALES | Wilks |
| FALSTAFF | Mills |
| VERNON | Walker |
| 1ST CARRIER | Johnson |
| 2ND CARRIER | Miller |
| FRANCIS | Norris |
| LADY PERCY | Mrs Booth |
| HOSTESS | Mrs Willis |

*Nov. 15*
added
GLENDOWER  Cibber

## LINCOLN'S INN FIELDS
*Feb. 9*

| | |
|---|---|
| FALSTAFF | Bullock Sr. |
| HENRY | Ogden |
| PRINCE OF WALES | [J.] Leigh |
| HOTSPUR | Quin |
| WORCESTER | Boheme |
| VERNON | Egleton |
| DOUGLAS | Smith |
| POINS | Ch. Bullock |
| FRANCIS | Spiller |
| LADY PERCY | Mrs Bullock |
| HOSTESS | Mrs Cook |

*Apr. 29.* No parts assigned

## 1721 DRURY LANE
*Sept. 26*

| | |
|---|---|
| HOTSPUR | Booth |
| HENRY | Thurmond |
| PRINCE OF WALES | Wilks |
| FALSTAFF | Mills |
| 1ST CARRIER | Johnson |
| 2ND CARRIER | Miller |
| FRANCIS | Norris |
| LADY PERCY | Mrs Booth |
| HOSTESS | Mrs Willis |

## LINCOLN'S INN FIELDS
*Jan. 28*

| | |
|---|---|
| HOTSPUR | Ryan |
| HENRY | Quin |
| PRINCE OF WALES | [J.] Leigh |
| WORCESTER | Boheme |
| FALSTAFF | Bullock Sr. |
| FRANCIS | Spiller |
| LADY PERCY | Mrs Bullock |

*Oct. 28*

| | |
|---|---|
| FALSTAFF | Quin |
| HENRY | Boheme |
| PRINCE OF WALES | Ryan |
| HOTSPUR | Walker |
| VERNON* | Egleton |
| FRANCIS* | Spiller |
| LADY PERCY | Mrs Bullock |
| HOSTESS | Mrs Egleton |

*Nov. 3*
omitted
    VERNON, FRANCIS

*Dec. 9*
omitted
    VERNON

## 1722 DRURY LANE
*Jan. 2*

| | |
|---|---|
| HOTSPUR | Booth |
| HENRY | Thurmond |
| PRINCE OF WALES | Wilks |
| FALSTAFF | Mills |
| 1ST CARRIER | Johnson |
| 2ND CARRIER | Miller |
| FRANCIS | Norris |
| LADY PERCY | Mrs Booth |
| HOSTESS | Mrs Willis |

## HENRY IV, PART I

### 1722 LINCOLN'S INN FIELDS

*Apr. 6*

| | |
|---|---|
| HOTSPUR | Walker |
| HENRY | Boheme |
| PRINCE OF WALES* | Ryan |
| FALSTAFF | Quin |
| FRANCIS | Spiller |
| LADY PERCY* | Mrs Spiller |
| HOSTESS | Mrs Egleton |

*Sept. 29*

| | |
|---|---|
| PRINCE OF WALES | [J.] Leigh |
| LADY PERCY | Mrs Bullock |
| added | |
| 1ST CARRIER | Bullock [Sr.] |
| 2ND CARRIER | Phipps |

### 1723 DRURY LANE

*May 11; Oct. 8*

| | |
|---|---|
| FALSTAFF | Harper |
| HENRY | Thurmond |
| PRINCE OF WALES | Wilks |
| HOTSPUR | Booth |
| 1ST CARRIER | Johnson |
| 2ND CARRIER | Miller |
| FRANCIS | Norris |
| LADY PERCY | Mrs Booth |
| HOSTESS | Mrs Willis |

### LINCOLN'S INN FIELDS

*Jan. 12*

| | |
|---|---|
| FALSTAFF | Quin |
| HENRY | Boheme |
| PRINCE OF WALES | Ryan |
| HOTSPUR | Walker |
| 1ST CARRIER | Bullock [Sr.] |
| 2ND CARRIER* | Phipps |
| FRANCIS | Hippisley |
| LADY PERCY | Mrs Bullock |
| HOSTESS | Mrs Egleton |

*Apr. 17; Dec. 5.* No parts assigned

*May 21*

| | |
|---|---|
| 2ND CARRIER | Hall |

*Oct. 24*

| | |
|---|---|
| FALSTAFF | Quin |
| HENRY | [J.] Leigh |
| PRINCE OF WALES | Ryan |
| HOTSPUR | Boheme |
| VERNON | Egleton |
| 1ST CARRIER | Bullock [Sr.] |
| 2ND CARRIER | Hall |
| FRANCIS | Spiller |
| LADY PERCY | Mrs Vincent |
| HOSTESS | Mrs Egleton |

### 1724 DRURY LANE

*Feb. 7; Oct. 3.* No parts assigned

152

## HENRY IV, PART I

### 1724 LINCOLN'S INN FIELDS
*Mar. 7; Nov. 7.* No parts assigned

*May 20*

| | |
|---|---|
| HOTSPUR | Walker |
| HENRY | Boheme |
| PRINCE OF WALES | Ryan |
| VERNON | Ward |
| WORCESTER | Ogden |
| MORTIMER | Merrivale |
| FRANCIS | Spiller |
| FALSTAFF | Quin |
| 1ST CARRIER | Bullock Sr. |
| 2ND CARRIER | Hall |
| HOSTESS | Mrs Egleton |
| LADY PERCY | Mrs Vincent |

### 1725 DRURY LANE
*Apr. 1; Dec. 14.* No parts assigned

*Sept. 18*

| | |
|---|---|
| HOTSPUR | Booth |
| HENRY | Thurmond |
| PRINCE OF WALES | Wilks |
| FALSTAFF | Harper |
| 1ST CARRIER | Johnson |
| 2ND CARRIER | Miller |
| FRANCIS | Norris |
| LADY PERCY | Mrs Booth |
| HOSTESS | Mrs Willis |

### LINCOLN'S INN FIELDS

*Jan. 19*

| | |
|---|---|
| FALSTAFF | Quin |
| HENRY | Boheme |
| PRINCE OF WALES | Ryan |
| HOTSPUR | Walker |
| 1ST CARRIER | Bullock [Sr.] |
| 2ND CARRIER | Hall |
| FRANCIS | Spiller |
| LADY PERCY | Mrs Bullock |
| HOSTESS* | Mrs Egleton |

*Mar. 18; Apr. 20*

| | |
|---|---|
| FALSTAFF | Quin |

No other parts assigned

*Oct. 16*

| | |
|---|---|
| HOSTESS | Mrs Cook |

### 1726 DRURY LANE
*May 7*

| | |
|---|---|
| HOTSPUR | Booth |
| PRINCE OF WALES | Giffard |

153

## 1726 DRURY LANE (cont.)

*May 7 (cont.)*

| | |
|---|---|
| HENRY | Thurmond |
| FALSTAFF | Harper |
| 1ST CARRIER | Johnson |
| 2ND CARRIER | Miller |
| FRANCIS | Norris |
| HOSTESS | Mrs Willis |

## LINCOLN'S INN FIELDS

*Jan. 5*

| | |
|---|---|
| FALSTAFF | Quin |
| HENRY | Boheme |
| PRINCE OF WALES | Ryan |
| HOTSPUR | Walker |
| 1ST CARRIER | Bullock [Sr.] |
| 2ND CARRIER | Hall |
| FRANCIS* | Spiller |
| LADY PERCY* | Mrs Vincent |
| HOSTESS | Mrs Egleton |

*Jan. 29.* No parts assigned

*May 17*

| | |
|---|---|
| FRANCIS added | Norris [Jr.] |
| VERNON | Houghton |

*Sept. 21*

| | |
|---|---|
| LADY PERCY | Mrs Bullock |

## 1727 LINCOLN'S INN FIELDS

*Jan. 10; Sept. 18*

| | |
|---|---|
| FALSTAFF | Quin |
| HENRY | Boheme |
| PRINCE OF WALES | Ryan |
| HOTSPUR | Walker |
| 1ST CARRIER | Bullock [Sr.] |
| 2ND CARRIER | Hall |
| FRANCIS | Spiller |
| LADY PERCY | Mrs Bullock |
| HOSTESS | Mrs Egleton |

## 1728 DRURY LANE

*Sept. 10*

| | |
|---|---|
| HOTSPUR | Elrington |
| HENRY | Mills |
| PRINCE OF WALES | Wilks |
| FALSTAFF | Harper |
| 1ST CARRIER | Johnson |
| 2ND CARRIER | Miller |
| FRANCIS | Norris |
| LADY PERCY | Mrs Booth |
| HOSTESS | Mrs Willis |

*Nov. 28*

| | |
|---|---|
| HOTSPUR | Elrington |

No other parts assigned

## 1728 LINCOLN'S INN FIELDS
*Nov. 19*

| | |
|---|---|
| FALSTAFF | Quin |
| HENRY | Boheme |
| PRINCE OF WALES | Ryan |
| HOTSPUR | Walker |
| 1ST CARRIER | Bullock [Sr.] |
| 2ND CARRIER | Hall |
| FRANCIS | Spiller |
| LADY PERCY | Mrs Benson |
| HOSTESS | Mrs Egleton |

## 1729 DRURY LANE
*Jan. 28*

| | |
|---|---|
| HOTSPUR | Elrington |
| HENRY | Mills |
| PRINCE OF WALES | Wilks |
| GLENDOWER | Cibber |
| DOUGLAS | Williams |
| BLUNT | Wm. Mills |
| VERNON | Bridgwater |
| FALSTAFF | Harper |
| POINS | Watson |
| 1ST CARRIER | Johnson |
| 2ND CARRIER | Miller |
| FRANCIS | Norris |
| LADY PERCY | Mrs Booth |
| HOSTESS | Mrs Willis |

## LINCOLN'S INN FIELDS
*Mar. 22.* No parts assigned

*Oct. 10; Nov. 29*

| | |
|---|---|
| FALSTAFF | Quin |
| HENRY | Boheme |
| PRINCE OF WALES | Ryan |
| HOTSPUR | Walker |
| WORCESTER | Hulett |
| LADY PERCY | Mrs Bullock |
| HOSTESS | Mrs Egleton |

## 1730 DRURY LANE
*Dec. 31*

HOTSPUR   The Gentleman who oblig'd the House by his Performance [of Lothario, &c.] last year [Highmore (Genest, iii. 254, 286)]

No other parts assigned

## HENRY IV, PART I

### 1730 LINCOLN'S INN FIELDS
*Apr. 22*  
    FALSTAFF         Quin  
  No other parts assigned

*Sept. 25.* No parts assigned

### 1731 DRURY LANE
*Mar. 8*  
    HOTSPUR          A Gentleman [Highmore (Genest, iii. 254, 286, 289)]  
    HENRY            Mills  
    PRINCE OF WALES  Wilks  
    GLENDOWER      Cibber  
    FALSTAFF         Harper  
    LADY PERCY      Mrs Booth

### LINCOLN'S INN FIELDS
*Sept. 29*  
    FALSTAFF         Quin  
    HENRY            Milward  
    PRINCE OF WALES  Ryan  
    HOTSPUR          Walker  
    WORCESTER      Hulett  
    POINS             Chapman  
    WESTMORLAND    Ogden  
    FRANCIS          Hippisley  
    LADY PERCY      Mrs Bullock  
    HOSTESS         Mrs Egleton

*Oct. 29.* No parts assigned

*Dec. 31*  
    FALSTAFF    Quin  
  No other parts assigned

### HAYMARKET
*May 3, 5*  
    FALSTAFF         A Gentleman [unidentified]  
    PRINCE OF WALES  Giffard  
    HOTSPUR          Rosco  
    LADY PERCY      Mrs Giffard  
  No other parts assigned

    [Bill for May 3 in DP of May 1.]

### GOODMAN'S FIELD
*Nov. 1, 2*  
    FALSTAFF         W. Giffard  
    HENRY            Huddy  
    PRINCE OF WALES  Giffard  
    WORCESTER      Smith  
    HOTSPUR          Rosco

## 1731 GOODMAN'S FIELDS (cont.)
*Nov. 1, 2 (cont.)*

| | |
|---|---|
| NORTHUMBERLAND | [R.] Williams |
| VERNON | Bardin |
| BLUNT | Havard |
| BARDOLPH | Collett |
| FRANCIS | Morgan |
| 1ST CARRIER | [W.] Bullock [Jr.] |
| 2ND CARRIER | Beckham |
| LADY PERCY | Mrs Purden |
| HOSTESS | Mrs Palmer |

## 1732 DRURY LANE

*Apr. 17*

| | |
|---|---|
| HENRY | Mills |
| PRINCE OF WALES* | Wilks |
| GLENDOWER* | Cibber |
| HOTSPUR | Bridgwater |
| FALSTAFF | Harper |
| NORTHUMBERLAND | Boman |
| WORCESTER | Corey |
| DOUGLAS* | W. Mills |
| VERNON | A. Hallam |
| POINS | Watson |
| MORTIMER* | Paget |
| BLUNT | Oates |
| FRANCIS | R. Wetherilt |
| 1ST CARRIER | Johnson |
| 2ND CARRIER* | [T.] Cibber |
| HOSTESS | Mrs Willis |
| LADY PERCY | Mrs Booth |

*Oct. 17*

| | |
|---|---|
| PRINCE OF WALES | William Mills |
| GLENDOWER | [T.] Cibber |
| DOUGLAS | Roberts |
| MORTIMER | Berry |
| 2ND CARRIER | Jones |

## LINCOLN'S INN FIELDS

*May 8*

| | |
|---|---|
| FALSTAFF | Quin |
| HENRY | Milward |
| PRINCE OF WALES | Ryan |
| HOTSPUR | Walker |
| WORCESTER | Hulett |
| POINS | Chapman |
| WESTMORLAND | Ogden |
| FRANCIS | Hippisley |
| 1ST CARRIER | Bullock [Sr.] |
| 2ND CARRIER | Ray |
| LADY PERCY | Mrs Bullock |
| HOSTESS | Mrs Egleton |

*Nov. 25.* No parts assigned

## 1732 GOODMAN'S FIELDS

*Jan. 29; Feb. 1*

| | |
|---|---|
| FALSTAFF | A Gentleman [unidentified. DA, Jan. 20, states that he was the same person who played FALSTAFF at the Haymarket 'some time since', i.e. May 3, 1731] |
| HOTSPUR | Delane |
| HENRY | Huddy |
| PRINCE OF WALES | Giffard |
| WORCESTER | Smith |
| MORTIMER | Rosco |
| NORTHUMBERLAND | [R.] Williams |
| VERNON | Bardin |
| BLUNT | Havard |
| BARDOLPH | Collett |
| 1ST CARRIER | Miller |
| 2ND CARRIER | Morgan |
| FRANCIS | Norris [Jr.] |
| LADY PERCY | Mrs Purden |
| HOSTESS | Mrs Palmer |

*Mar. 30*

added
WESTMORLAND   [W.] Bullock [Jr.]

*Oct. 2, 3*

| | |
|---|---|
| FALSTAFF | Hulett |
| HOTSPUR | Delane |
| HENRY | Huddy |
| PRINCE OF WALES | Giffard |
| WORCESTER | W. Giffard |
| MORTIMER | Havard |
| WESTMORLAND | Smith |
| VERNON | Bardin |
| DOUGLAS | Winstone |
| BLUNT | Rosco |
| BARDOLPH | Collett |
| 1ST CARRIER | Morgan |
| 2ND CARRIER | [W.] Bullock [Jr.] |
| FRANCIS | Norris [Jr.] |
| LADY PERCY* | Miss Vaughan |
| HOSTESS | Mrs Morgan |

*Dec. 20*

LADY PERCY   Mrs Purden

158

## HENRY IV, PART I

### 1733 DRURY LANE
*Feb. 3*

| | |
|---|---|
| HENRY | Mills |
| PRINCE OF WALES | Wm. Mills |
| HOTSPUR | Bridgwater |
| FALSTAFF | Harper |
| 1ST CARRIER | Johnson |
| 2ND CARRIER | Miller |
| NORTHUMBERLAND | Boman |
| WORCESTER | Roberts |
| DOUGLAS | Fielding |
| VERNON | A. Hallam |
| BLUNT | Oates |
| LADY PERCY | Mrs Booth |
| HOSTESS | Mrs Willis |

### COVENT GARDEN

*Apr. 10*

| | |
|---|---|
| FALSTAFF | Quin |
| HENRY* | Milward |
| PRINCE OF WALES | Ryan |
| HOTSPUR | Walker |
| WORCESTER* | Paget |
| POINS* | Chapman |
| VERNON | Houghton |
| BLUNT | Salway |
| FRANCIS | Hippisley |
| 1ST CARRIER | Bullock [Sr.] |
| 2ND CARRIER | Hall |
| LADY PERCY | Mrs Bullock |
| HOSTESS* | Mrs Egleton |

*Nov. 30*

| | |
|---|---|
| HENRY | Chapman |
| WORCESTER | Aston |
| POINS | Hale |
| HOSTESS | Mrs Martin |
| added | |
| GLENDOWER | [J.] Lacy |

### HAYMARKET

*Oct. 10*

| | |
|---|---|
| HOTSPUR | Milward |
| HENRY | Mills |
| PRINCE OF WALES | W. Mills |
| FALSTAFF* | Harper |
| GLENDOWER | [T.] Cibber |
| WORCESTER | Berry |
| VERNON | A. Hallam |
| 1ST CARRIER | Johnson |
| 2ND CARRIER | Miller |
| FRANCIS | Master Arne |
| NORTHUMBERLAND* | Boman |
| DOUGLAS* | Winstone |

*Nov. 12*

| | |
|---|---|
| FALSTAFF | read by [T.] Cibber |
| omitted | |
| NORTHUMBERLAND, DOUGLAS, BLUNT, WESTMORLAND, BARDOLPH, POINS | |

[Harper's name is in the bill, but late in the afternoon of this day he was committed to Bridewell at the instance of the Drury Lane manager, under the Vagrant Act, and FALSTAFF was read by [T.] Cibber (DP, Nov. 13). It is not stated who took Cibber's place as GLENDOWER. Harper was released on Nov. 20; Genest (iii. 405–6) gives an account of these circumstances.]

159

## 1733 HAYMARKET (cont.)

*Oct. 10 (cont.)*

| | |
|---|---|
| BLUNT* | Oates |
| WESTMORLAND* | Ridout |
| BARDOLPH* | Shepard |
| POINS* | Harrington |
| LADY PERCY | Miss Mann |
| HOSTESS | Mrs Shireburn |

*Nov. 21*

| | |
|---|---|
| FALSTAFF | Harper |

No other parts assigned

[The bill has, 'All the other Parts as usual.']

## GOODMAN'S FIELDS

*May 3*

| | |
|---|---|
| HOTSPUR | Delane |
| PRINCE OF WALES | Giffard |
| FALSTAFF | Hulett |
| HENRY | Huddy |
| WORCESTER* | W. Giffard |
| MORTIMER | Havard |
| WESTMORLAND* | Cole |
| VERNON | Bardin |
| DOUGLAS* | Winstone |
| BLUNT | Rosco |
| BARDOLPH | Collett |
| 1ST CARRIER | Morgan |
| 2ND CARRIER* | [W.] Bullock [Jr.] |
| FRANCIS* | Norris [Jr.] |
| LADY PERCY* | Mrs Christian |
| HOSTESS | Mrs Morgan |

*Sept. 25*

| | |
|---|---|
| WORCESTER | Dawson |
| WESTMORLAND | Moore |
| DOUGLAS | Harbin |
| 2ND CARRIER | R. Wetherilt |
| FRANCIS | Penkethman [Jr.] |
| LADY PERCY | Mrs Hamilton |

## 1734 DRURY LANE

*Apr. 17*

| | |
|---|---|
| HOTSPUR | Milward |
| HENRY | Mills |
| PRINCE OF WALES | W. Mills |
| FALSTAFF* | Harper |
| GLENDOWER* | [T.] Cibber |
| WORCESTER* | Berry |
| VERNON* | Cross |
| 1ST CARRIER | Johnson |
| 2ND CARRIER | Miller |
| FRANCIS* | Master Arne |
| LADY PERCY* | Miss Mann |
| HOSTESS* | Mrs Shireburn |

*May 2*

| | |
|---|---|
| FALSTAFF | Hyde |
| omitted | |
| GLENDOWER | |

*May 17*

| | |
|---|---|
| FALSTAFF | Paget |
| LADY PERCY | A Young Gentle-woman [unidentified] |

omitted
GLENDOWER

*Sept. 24; Dec. 30*

| | |
|---|---|
| FALSTAFF | Quin |
| LADY PERCY | Miss Holliday |

added

| | |
|---|---|
| NORTHUMBERLAND | Boman |
| BLUNT | Salway |
| MORTIMER | Hewitt |
| DOUGLAS | Winstone |
| WESTMORLAND | Turbutt |

HENRY IV, PART I

1734 DRURY LANE (cont.)

*Sept. 24, &c.* (cont.)
 BARDOLPH  Shepard
 POINS  Macklin
 GADSHILL  Este
 PETO  Raftor

*Oct. 4*
 FALSTAFF  Quin
 omitted
  WORCESTER, VERNON, FRANCIS, LADY PERCY, HOSTESS

## COVENT GARDEN

*Jan. 21*
 FALSTAFF*  Quin
 HENRY*  Chapman
 PRINCE OF WALES  Ryan
 HOTSPUR  Walker
 WORCESTER  Aston
 POINS  Hale
 VERNON*  Houghton
 GLENDOWER*  [J.] Lacy
 FRANCIS  Hippisley
 LADY PERCY  Mrs Bullock
 HOSTESS  Mrs Martin

*Mar. 21.* No parts assigned

*Nov. 14*
 FALSTAFF  Vaughan [first appearance on the stage]
 HENRY  Bridgwater
 VERNON  A. Hallam
 GLENDOWER  Marshall
 added
  BLUNT  Ridout
  1ST CARRIER  Morgan
  2ND CARRIER  Mullart

## HAYMARKET

*Jan. 16.* No parts assigned

*May 27*
 HOTSPUR  Hewson
 HENRY  Hewitt
 PRINCE OF WALES  Macklin
 FALSTAFF  Paget
 WORCESTER  Ridout
 VERNON  Cross
 DOUGLAS  Winstone
 WESTMORLAND  Turbutt
 BLUNT  Machen
 BARDOLPH  Topham
 FRANCIS  [T.] Hallam
 LADY PERCY  Miss Mann
 HOSTESS  Mrs Dyer

## GOODMAN'S FIELDS

*Apr. 29.* No parts assigned

*Oct. 16*
 FALSTAFF  Hulett
 HOTSPUR  Delane

HENRY IV, PART I

## 1734 GOODMAN'S FIELDS (cont.)
*Oct. 16 (cont.)*

|  |  |
|---|---|
| HENRY | Huddy |
| PRINCE OF WALES | Giffard |
| PRINCE JOHN | Woodward |
| WORCESTER | W. Giffard |
| MORTIMER | Havard |
| WESTMORLAND | Moore |
| VERNON | Bardin |
| DOUGLAS | Harbin |
| BLUNT | Rosco |
| POINS | Hamilton |
| BARDOLPH | Monlass |
| 1ST CARRIER | Lyon |
| 2ND CARRIER | R. Wetherilt |
| FRANCIS | Penkethman [Jr.] |
| LADY PERCY | Mrs Hamilton |
| HOSTESS | Mrs Wetherilt |

## 1735 DRURY LANE
*Sept. 11*

|  |  |
|---|---|
| FALSTAFF | Quin |
| HENRY | Mills |
| PRINCE OF WALES | W. Mills |
| HOTSPUR | Milward |
| WORCESTER | Berry |
| NORTHUMBERLAND | Poman |
| VERNON | Cross |
| BLUNT | Salway |
| DOUGLAS | Winstone |
| WESTMORLAND | Turbutt |
| FRANCIS | Leigh [Jr.] |
| BARDOLPH | Shepard |
| GADSHILL | Este |
| PETO | Raftor |
| 1ST CARRIER | Johnson |
| 2ND CARRIER | Miller |
| LADY PERCY | Miss Holliday |
| HOSTESS | Mrs Cross |

*Nov. 15*

added
GLENDOWER    [T.] Cibber

## COVENT GARDEN
*Jan. 20*

|  |  |
|---|---|
| FALSTAFF | Vaughan |
| HOTSPUR | Walker |
| HENRY | Bridgwater |
| PRINCE OF WALES | Ryan |
| WORCESTER | Aston |

162

## HENRY IV, PART I

**1735 COVENT GARDEN** (*cont.*)

*Jan. 20 (cont.)*

| | |
|---|---|
| POINS | Hale |
| MORTIMER | Houghton |
| WESTMORLAND | Wignell |
| VERNON | A. Hallam |
| BLUNT | Ridout |
| GLENDOWER | Marshall |
| FRANCIS | Hippisley |
| 1ST CARRIER | Mullart |
| 2ND CARRIER | Morgan |
| LADY PERCY | Mrs Bullock |
| HOSTESS | Mrs Martin |

*Apr. 17*

| | |
|---|---|
| FALSTAFF | Bridgwater |
| HENRY | Stephens |
| PRINCE OF WALES | A. Hallam |
| HOTSPUR | Walker |
| FRANCIS | Hippisley |
| 1ST CARRIER | Mullart |
| 2ND CARRIER | Morgan |
| LADY PERCY | Mrs Bullock |
| HOSTESS | Mrs Martin |

## GOODMAN'S FIELDS

*Apr. 29*

| | |
|---|---|
| FALSTAFF | Hulett |
| HENRY | Huddy |
| PRINCE OF WALES | Giffard |
| HOTSPUR | Delane |
| FRANCIS | Penkethman [Jr.] |
| PRINCE JOHN | Miss Norris |
| WORCESTER | W. Giffard |
| MORTIMER | Havard |
| WESTMORLAND | Moore |
| VERNON | Bardin |
| DOUGLAS | Harbin |
| BLUNT | Rosco |
| POINS | Hamilton |
| BARDOLPH | Monlass |
| 1ST CARRIER | Lyon |
| 2ND CARRIER | R. Wetherilt |
| LADY PERCY | Mrs Hamilton |
| HOSTESS | Mrs Wetherilt |

HENRY IV, PART I

## 1736 DRURY LANE
*May 17.* No parts assigned

*Oct. 7*

| | |
|---|---|
| FALSTAFF | Quin |
| HENRY | Mills |
| PRINCE OF WALES | W. Mills |
| HOTSPUR | Milward |
| GLENDOWER* | [T.] Cibber |
| 1ST CARRIER | Johnson |
| 2ND CARRIER | Miller |
| LADY PERCY | Miss Holliday |
| HOSTESS | Mrs Cross |

*Nov. 27*
added
   FRANCIS  Macklin
omitted
   GLENDOWER

## LINCOLN'S INN FIELDS
*Apr. 14*

| | |
|---|---|
| FALSTAFF | Harper |
| HENRY | [T.] Cibber |
| PRINCE OF WALES | W. Mills |
| HOTSPUR | Milward |
| 1ST CARRIER | Miller |
| 2ND CARRIER | Macklin |
| LADY PERCY | Miss Mann |

*Nov. 20, 22*

| | |
|---|---|
| HOTSPUR | The Gentleman who perform'd the Part of Cato [at this theatre, Oct. 28. He is unidentified] |
| HENRY | Johnson |
| FALSTAFF | W. Giffard |
| PRINCE OF WALES | Giffard |
| WORCESTER | Hewitt |
| VERNON | Havard |
| BLUNT | Rosco |
| GLENDOWER | Lyon |
| DOUGLAS | Richardson |
| MORTIMER | Nelson |
| POINS | Woodward |
| BARDOLPH | Dove |
| FRANCIS | Penkethman [Jr.] |
| LADY PERCY | Mrs Marshall |
| HOSTESS | Mrs Wetherilt |

[Genest seems not to have had access to the bill. He suggests (iii. 484, 506) that Hulett acted Falstaff. Hulett died in the autumn of 1735; Genest mistakenly says that he died in 1736.]

164

## 1737 DRURY LANE
*Jan. 17; Apr. 18*

| | |
|---|---|
| FALSTAFF | Quin |
| HENRY | Berry |
| PRINCE OF WALES | W. Mills |
| HOTSPUR | Milward |
| GLENDOWER | [T.] Cibber |
| FRANCIS | Macklin |
| 1ST CARRIER | Johnson |
| 2ND CARRIER | Miller |
| LADY PERCY | Miss Holliday |
| HOSTESS | Mrs Cross |

*Sept. 22*

| | |
|---|---|
| FALSTAFF | Quin |
| HENRY | Wright |
| PRINCE OF WALES | [W.] Mills |
| HOTSPUR | Milward |
| WORCESTER | Havard |
| NORTHUMBERLAND | Boman |
| WESTMORLAND | Turbutt |
| DOUGLAS | Furnival |
| VERNON | Cross |
| BLUNT | Hill |
| BARDOLPH | Ray |
| FRANCIS | Macklin |
| 1ST CARRIER | Johnson |
| 2ND CARRIER | Miller |
| LADY PERCY | Mrs Mills |
| HOSTESS | Mrs Roberts |

## COVENT GARDEN
*Apr. 14*

| | |
|---|---|
| FALSTAFF | Stephens |
| HENRY | Bridgwater |
| PRINCE OF WALES | Ryan |
| HOTSPUR | Walker |
| VERNON | A. Hallam |
| WORCESTER | Aston |
| GLENDOWER | Boman [Jr.] |
| POINS | A. Ryan |
| DOUGLAS | Paget |
| BLUNT | Ridout |
| FRANCIS | Hippisley |
| 1ST CARRIER | Mullart |
| 2ND CARRIER | James |
| LADY PERCY | Mrs Templer |

## HENRY IV, PART I

### 1738 DRURY LANE
*Jan. 12*

| | |
|---|---|
| FALSTAFF | Quin |
| HENRY | Wright |
| PRINCE OF WALES | [W.] Mills |
| HOTSPUR | Milward |
| WORCESTER | Havard |
| NORTHUMBERLAND* | Boman |
| WESTMORLAND | Turbutt |
| DOUGLAS | Furnival |
| VERNON | Cross |
| BLUNT* | Hill |
| BARDOLPH | Ray |
| FRANCIS | Macklin |
| 1ST CARRIER | Johnson |
| 2ND CARRIER* | Miller |
| LADY PERCY | Mrs Mills |
| HOSTESS* | Mrs Roberts |

*Sept. 14*

| | |
|---|---|
| 2ND CARRIER | Macklin |

added

| | |
|---|---|
| GLENDOWER | [T.] Cibber |

omitted

NORTHUMBERLAND

[Harper's name is in the bill as the 2ND CARRIER, but 'Harper ill Macklin did ye Carrier for him' (Griffin). Macklin presumably doubled FRANCIS.]

*Nov. 17*

| | |
|---|---|
| BLUNT | Ridout |
| 2ND CARRIER | Woodward |
| HOSTESS | Mrs Cross |

omitted

NORTHUMBERLAND

*Dec. 19*

| | |
|---|---|
| BLUNT | Ridout |
| 2ND CARRIER | Woodward |
| HOSTESS | Mrs Cross |

added

| | |
|---|---|
| POINS | Winstone |
| PETO | Raftor |

### COVENT GARDEN
*Feb. 13; Apr. 5*

| | |
|---|---|
| HOTSPUR | Delane |
| HENRY | Johnson |
| PRINCE OF WALES | Ryan |
| WORCESTER | Rosco |
| GLENDOWER | Chapman |
| WESTMORLAND* | Aston |
| DOUGLAS | Hale |
| MORTIMER | Stevens |
| VERNON | [A.] Hallam |
| BLUNT | Salway |
| POINS | A. Ryan |
| GADSHILL | Bencraft |
| BARDOLPH | W. Hallam |
| FRANCIS | Hippisley |
| 1ST CARRIER | Mullart |
| 2ND CARRIER | James |
| FALSTAFF | Bridgwater |
| LADY PERCY | Mrs Ware |
| HOSTESS | Mrs Martin |

*Dec. 2*

| | |
|---|---|
| WESTMORLAND | Hill |

166

## HENRY IV, PART I

### 1738 NEW WELLS, CLERKENWELL
*Apr. 12, 18, 21*

[These performances are listed by Scouten and Hughes in their calendar of performances before 1750 of both parts of *Henry IV* (*Journal of English and Germanic Philology*, xliii. 23–41). Their information for the three performances in question is based on Winston's MS record of plays acted in London (now FSL). This record is a compilation made in the early nineteenth century, and for the New Wells, Clerkenwell, Winston does not indicate his source. I have made an exhaustive search in all the primary sources, and have found no mention of these performances. Until further evidence comes to light, they must therefore be rejected.]

### 1739 DRURY LANE
*Mar. 6*

| FALSTAFF | Quin |
| HENRY | Wright |
| PRINCE OF WALES | [W.] Mills |
| HOTSPUR | Milward |
| WORCESTER | Havard |
| NORTHUMBERLAND | Taswell |
| WESTMORLAND | Turbutt |
| DOUGLAS* | Furnival |
| VERNON* | Cross |
| BLUNT | Ridout |
| BARDOLPH | Ray |
| POINS* | Winstone |
| PETO* | Raftor |
| FRANCIS | Macklin |
| 1ST CARRIER | Johnson |
| 2ND CARRIER | Woodward |
| LADY PERCY | Mrs Mills |
| HOSTESS* | Mrs Cross |

*Nov. 19*

| DOUGLAS | Winstone |
| VERNON | Cashell |
| HOSTESS | Mrs Grace |

added
   GLENDOWER   Chapman
omitted
   POINS, PETO

### COVENT GARDEN
*May 4*

| HENRY | Johnson |
| PRINCE OF WALES | Ryan |
| HOTSPUR | Delane |
| WORCESTER | Roberts |
| WESTMORLAND | Arthur |
| DOUGLAS | Hale |
| VERNON | [A.] Hallam |
| BLUNT | Salway |
| GLENDOWER* | Chapman |
| POINS | A. Ryan |
| GADSHILL | Bencraft |
| BARDOLPH* | Dove |
| FRANCIS | Hippisley |
| 1ST CARRIER | James |
| 2ND CARRIER | Mullart |

*Sept. 27*

| BARDOLPH | Littleton |
| FALSTAFF | Stephens |

added
   NORTHUMBERLAND   Mullart
   PETO   Anderson
omitted
   GLENDOWER

[The assignment of Mullart to both NORTHUMBERLAND and the 2ND CARRIER appears to be a misprint.]

HENRY IV, PART I

## 1739 COVENT GARDEN (*cont.*)

*May 4 (cont.)*

| | |
|---|---|
| FALSTAFF* | Rosco |
| LADY PERCY | Mrs Ware |
| HOSTESS | Mrs Martin |

## 1740 DRURY LANE

*Apr. 25*

| | |
|---|---|
| FALSTAFF | Quin |
| HENRY | Wright |
| PRINCE OF WALES | [W.] Mills |
| HOTSPUR | Milward |
| WORCESTER | Havard |
| NORTHUMBERLAND | Taswell |
| WESTMORLAND | Turbutt |
| DOUGLAS* | Winstone |
| VERNON | Cashell |
| BLUNT | Ridout |
| FRANCIS | Macklin |
| BARDOLPH | Ray |
| 1ST CARRIER | Johnson |
| 2ND CARRIER | Woodward |
| GLENDOWER | Chapman |
| LADY PERCY | Mrs Mills |
| HOSTESS* | Mrs Grace [a misprint; she had become Mrs Macklin in the autumn of 1739] |

*Oct. 13*

| | |
|---|---|
| DOUGLAS | Stevens |
| HOSTESS | Mrs Macklin [i.e. formerly Mrs Grace] |
| added | |
| POINS | Winstone |

## GOODMAN'S FIELDS

*Nov. 28*

| | |
|---|---|
| HENRY | Peterson |
| PRINCE OF WALES | Giffard |
| HOTSPUR | Walker |
| FALSTAFF | Paget |
| WORCESTER | Blakes |
| DOUGLAS | Nelson |
| VERNON | W. Giffard |
| MORTIMER | Marr |
| GLENDOWER | Wallis |
| BARDOLPH | Dunstall |
| CARRIER | Julian |
| FRANCIS | Yates |
| HOSTESS | Mrs Yates |
| LADY PERCY | Mrs Giffard |

*Dec. 18.* No parts assigned

HENRY IV, PART I

## 1741 DRURY LANE
*Jan. 26*

| | |
|---|---|
| FALSTAFF* | Quin |
| HENRY* | Wright |
| PRINCE OF WALES | [W.] Mills |
| HOTSPUR | Milward |
| WORCESTER* | Havard |
| VERNON* | Cashell |
| NORTHUMBERLAND* | Taswell |
| WESTMORLAND* | Turbutt |
| BLUNT* | Ridout |
| POINS* | Winstone |
| BARDOLPH* | Ray |
| 1ST CARRIER | Johnson |
| 2ND CARRIER* | Woodward |
| GLENDOWER* | Chapman |
| FRANCIS | Macklin |
| HOSTESS | Mrs Macklin |
| LADY PERCY | Mrs Mills |

*Apr. 6*

omitted
    WORCESTER, VERNON, NORTHUMBER-
    LAND, WESTMORLAND, BLUNT, POINS,
    BARDOLPH

*Oct. 9*

| | |
|---|---|
| FALSTAFF | A Citizen of London [unidentified] |
| HENRY | Berry |
| WORCESTER | Winstone |
| VERNON | Havard |
| 2ND CARRIER | Arthur |

added
| | |
|---|---|
| PRINCE JOHN | Green |
| DOUGLAS | Ward |
| PETO | Raftor |
| GADSHILL | Leigh [Jr.] |

omitted
    POINS, GLENDOWER

## COVENT GARDEN
*Jan. 27*

| | |
|---|---|
| HENRY | Stephens |
| PRINCE OF WALES | Ryan |
| HOTSPUR | Delane |
| FALSTAFF | Bridgwater |
| WORCESTER | Rosco |
| VERNON | [A.] Hallam |
| WESTMORLAND | Arthur |
| PRINCE JOHN | Clarke |
| BLUNT | Salway |
| POINS | Gibson |
| BARDOLPH | Stoppelaer |
| DOUGLAS | Hale |
| PETO | Anderson |
| GADSHILL | Bencraft |
| 1ST CARRIER | Mullart |
| 2ND CARRIER | James |
| FRANCIS | Hippisley |
| LADY PERCY | Mrs Ware |
| HOSTESS | Mrs Martin |

## GOODMAN'S FIELDS
*Apr. 21*

| | |
|---|---|
| FALSTAFF | A Gentleman [unidentified] |

No other parts assigned

169

## 1742 DRURY LANE
*Apr. 27*

| | |
|---|---|
| FALSTAFF | Shepard |
| HENRY | Berry |
| PRINCE OF WALES | [W.] Mills |
| HOTSPUR | Delane |
| WORCESTER | Winstone |
| PRINCE JOHN | Green |
| VERNON | Havard |
| DOUGLAS | Woodburn |
| NORTHUMBERLAND | Taswell |
| WESTMORLAND | Turbutt |
| BLUNT | Ridout |
| BARDOLPH | Ray |
| PETO | Raftor |
| FRANCIS | Macklin |
| 1ST CARRIER | Johnson |
| 2ND CARRIER | Arthur |
| LADY PERCY | Mrs Mills |
| HOSTESS | Mrs Macklin |

## COVENT GARDEN
*Oct. 25*

| | |
|---|---|
| FALSTAFF | Quin |
| HENRY | Stephens |
| PRINCE OF WALES | Ryan |
| HOTSPUR | Hale |
| WORCESTER | Rosco |
| WESTMORLAND | Harrington |
| VERNON | Gibson |
| NORTHUMBERLAND | Carr |
| DOUGLAS | Anderson |
| POINS* | Anderson |
| BARDOLPH | Marten |
| BLUNT | Salway |
| 1ST CARRIER | Chapman |
| 2ND CARRIER | Woodward |
| FRANCIS | Hippisley |
| LADY PERCY | Mrs Hale |
| HOSTESS | Mrs James |

*Dec. 11*

| | |
|---|---|
| POINS | Cashell |

[Anderson doubled DOUGLAS and POINS. His assignment to POINS may, however, be a misprint. See Dec. 11.]

## 1743 DRURY LANE
*Feb. 10*

| | |
|---|---|
| HOTSPUR | Whittingham [first appearance on the stage] |
| HENRY | Havard |
| PRINCE OF WALES | [W.] Mills |
| FALSTAFF | Berry |
| PRINCE JOHN | Marr |
| WORCESTER | Winstone |
| VERNON | Blakes |
| NORTHUMBERLAND | Taswell |
| DOUGLAS | Woodburn |
| GLENDOWER | Turbutt |
| BLUNT | Green |
| BARDOLPH | Ray |
| PETO | Raftor |
| GADSHILL | Leigh [Jr.] |
| 1ST CARRIER | Morgan |
| 2ND CARRIER | Arthur |
| FRANCIS | Yates |
| LADY PERCY | Mrs Mills |
| HOSTESS | Mrs Cross |

## COVENT GARDEN
*Jan. 21*

| | | | |
|---|---|---|---|
| FALSTAFF | Quin | | |
| HENRY | Stephens | | |
| PRINCE OF WALES | Ryan | | |
| HOTSPUR | Hale | | |
| WORCESTER | Rosco | | |
| WESTMORLAND* | Harrington | | |
| VERNON | Gibson | | |
| NORTHUMBERLAND | Carr | | |
| DOUGLAS | Anderson | | |
| POINS* | Cashell | | |
| BARDOLPH | Marten | | |
| BLUNT* | Salway | | |
| 1ST CARRIER | Chapman | | |
| 2ND CARRIER | Woodward | | |
| FRANCIS | Hippisley | | |
| LADY PERCY | Mrs Hale | | |
| HOSTESS | Mrs Mullart | | |

*Mar. 12*

| | |
|---|---|
| BLUNT | Ridout |
| omitted POINS | |

*Dec. 12*

| | |
|---|---|
| WESTMORLAND | Hayman |
| BLUNT | Ridout |

## 1743 LINCOLN'S INN FIELDS
*Mar. 17*

| | |
|---|---|
| HENRY | Peterson |
| PRINCE OF WALES | Giffard |
| HOTSPUR | W. Giffard |
| FALSTAFF | A Citizen of London [unidentified] |

No other parts assigned

## 1744 DRURY LANE
*May 22*

| | |
|---|---|
| HOTSPUR | Delane |
| HENRY | Havard |
| PRINCE OF WALES | Giffard |
| FALSTAFF | Berry |
| PRINCE JOHN | Miss Cole |
| VERNON | Blakes |
| WORCESTER | Winstone |
| NORTHUMBERLAND | Taswell |
| DOUGLAS | Woodburn |
| GLENDOWER | Turbutt |
| BLUNT | Green |
| BARDOLPH | Ray |
| PETO | Collins |
| GADSHILL | Dunstall |
| FRANCIS | Yates |
| 1ST CARRIER | Morgan |
| 2ND CARRIER | Arthur |
| LADY PERCY | Mrs Ridout |
| HOSTESS | Mrs Cross |

## COVENT GARDEN
*Oct. 8*

| | |
|---|---|
| FALSTAFF | Quin |
| HENRY | Cashell |
| PRINCE OF WALES | Ryan |
| HOTSPUR | Hale |
| WORCESTER | Rosco |
| WESTMORLAND | Hayman |
| VERNON | Gibson |
| NORTHUMBERLAND | Carr |
| DOUGLAS | Anderson |
| POINS | Chapman |
| BLUNT | Ridout |
| BARDOLPH | Marten |
| 1ST CARRIER | Woodward |

## 1744 COVENT GARDEN (cont.)
*Oct. 8 (cont.)*

| 2ND CARRIER | Arthur |
| FRANCIS | Hippisley |
| LADY PERCY | Mrs Hale |
| HOSTESS | Mrs Mullart |

## 1745 COVENT GARDEN
*Jan. 12*

| FALSTAFF | Quin |
| HENRY | Cashell |
| PRINCE OF WALES | Ryan |
| HOTSPUR | Hale |
| WORCESTER | Rosco |
| WESTMORLAND | Hayman |
| VERNON | Gibson |
| NORTHUMBERLAND | Carr |
| DOUGLAS | Anderson |
| POINS | Chapman |
| BLUNT | Ridout |
| BARDOLPH | Marten |
| 1ST CARRIER | Woodward |
| 2ND CARRIER | Arthur |
| FRANCIS | Hippisley |
| LADY PERCY | Mrs Hale |
| HOSTESS | Mrs Mullart |

## NEW WELLS, GOODMAN'S FIELDS
*Mar. 26*

| FALSTAFF | Dance |

No other parts assigned

*Apr. 17*

| FALSTAFF | Dance |
| VERNON | Paget |
| HOTSPUR | Goodfellow |

No other parts assigned

*Dec. 2, 3*

| FALSTAFF | Paget |
| HENRY | Furnival |
| PRINCE OF WALES | Cushing |
| HOTSPUR | Lee |
| NORTHUMBERLAND | Dove |
| WORCESTER | Julian |
| BLUNT | Shepard |
| POINS | Kennedy |
| PETO | Blakey |
| BARDOLPH | G. Hallam |

## HENRY IV, PART I

### 1745 NEW WELLS, GOODMAN'S FIELDS (cont.)
*Dec. 2, 3 (cont.)*

| | |
|---|---|
| 1ST CARRIER | Dove |
| 2ND CARRIER | Morgan |
| FRANCIS | L. Hallam |
| LADY PERCY | Mrs [L.] Hallam |
| HOSTESS | Mrs Bambridge |

[Dove doubled NORTHUMBERLAND and the 1ST CARRIER.]

### 1746 DRURY LANE
*May 9*

| | |
|---|---|
| HOTSPUR | Lee |
| HENRY | Havard |
| PRINCE OF WALES | Giffard |
| FALSTAFF | Dance |
| FRANCIS | Yates |
| PRINCE JOHN | Marr |
| VERNON | Blakes |
| WORCESTER | Winstone |
| BLUNT | Goodfellow |
| DOUGLAS | Usher |
| BARDOLPH | Ray |
| PETO | Collins |
| GADSHILL | Leigh [Jr.] |
| 1ST CARRIER | Barrington |
| 2ND CARRIER | I. Sparks |
| LADY PERCY | Mrs Mills |
| HOSTESS | Mrs Cross |

### COVENT GARDEN

*Jan. 11*

| | |
|---|---|
| HENRY | Cashell |
| PRINCE OF WALES | Ryan |
| HOTSPUR* | Hale |
| FALSTAFF* | Bridgwater |
| 1ST CARRIER* | Woodward |
| 2ND CARRIER | Arthur |
| FRANCIS* | Hippisley |
| WORCESTER | Rosco |
| WESTMORLAND | Hayman |
| VERNON | Gibson |
| NORTHUMBERLAND | Carr |
| DOUGLAS | Anderson |
| POINS | Chapman |
| BLUNT | Ridout |
| BARDOLPH | Marten |
| LADY PERCY* | Mrs Hale |
| HOSTESS | Mrs James |

*Dec. 6*

| | |
|---|---|
| HOTSPUR | Garrick |
| FALSTAFF | Quin |
| LADY PERCY | Mrs Vincent |

*Dec. 8, 9, 12, 13*

| | |
|---|---|
| HOTSPUR | Garrick |
| FALSTAFF | Quin |
| 1ST CARRIER | Hippisley |
| FRANCIS | Woodward |
| LADY PERCY | Mrs Vincent |
| added | |
| GLENDOWER | Havard |
| MORTIMER | Davies |
| PRINCE JOHN | Mrs Rowley |
| GADSHILL | Bencraft |

## HENRY IV, PART I

### 1746 NEW WELLS, GOODMAN'S FIELDS
*Oct. 29, 30*                               *Nov. 3, 10*

| | | | |
|---|---|---|---|
| HOTSPUR | Lee | VERNON | Cartwright |
| HENRY | Furnival | | |
| PRINCE OF WALES | Cushing | | |
| WORCESTER | Pinner | | |
| VERNON* | Lynham | | |
| NORTHUMBERLAND | G. Hallam | | |
| BLUNT | Edwards | | |
| POINS | Baker | | |
| BARDOLPH | Miles | | |
| GADSHILL | Orpin | | |
| PETO | Simons | | |
| 1ST CARRIER | Dove | | |
| 2ND CARRIER | Beckham | | |
| FRANCIS | L. Hallam | | |
| FALSTAFF | Paget | | |
| LADY PERCY | Mrs [L.] Hallam | | |
| HOSTESS | Mrs Beckham | | |

### BOWLING GREEN, SOUTHWARK
*Oct. 20*

| | |
|---|---|
| HOTSPUR | Lee |
| HENRY | Furnival |
| PRINCE OF WALES | Cushing |
| FRANCIS | Phillips |
| FALSTAFF | Paget |
| HOSTESS | Mrs Phillips |

### 1747 DRURY LANE
*Jan. 15*                               *Jan. 17, 19*

| | | | |
|---|---|---|---|
| HOTSPUR | Barry | added | |
| HENRY | [L.] Sparks | WESTMORLAND | Bransby |
| PRINCE OF WALES | Giffard | SHERIFF | Gray |
| FALSTAFF | Berry | omitted | |
| FRANCIS | Yates | PRINCE JOHN | |
| PRINCE JOHN* | Miss Cole | | |
| VERNON | Blakes | | |
| WORCESTER | Winstone | | |
| NORTHUMBERLAND | Bridges | | |
| DOUGLAS | Mozeen | | |
| GLENDOWER | [T.] Cibber | | |
| BLUNT | Usher | | |
| BARDOLPH | Ray | | |
| PETO | Collins | | |
| GADSHILL | Leigh [Jr.] | | |
| 1ST CARRIER | Barrington | | |
| 2ND CARRIER | I. Sparks | | |

175

## 1747 DRURY LANE (*cont.*)

*Jan. 15 (cont.)*

| | |
|---|---|
| HOSTESS | Mrs Cross |
| LADY PERCY | Mrs Woffington |

*Jan. 16*

| | |
|---|---|
| HOTSPUR | Barry |
| HENRY | [L.] Sparks |
| PRINCE OF WALES | Giffard |
| FALSTAFF | Berry |
| GLENDOWER | [T.] Cibber |
| LADY PERCY | Mrs Woffington |

No other parts assigned

## COVENT GARDEN

*Mar. 28*

| | |
|---|---|
| FALSTAFF | Quin |
| HENRY | Cashell |
| PRINCE OF WALES | Ryan |
| HOTSPUR | Havard |
| FRANCIS | Woodward |
| WORCESTER | Rosco |
| WESTMORLAND | Kennedy |
| VERNON | Gibson |
| NORTHUMBERLAND | Carr |
| DOUGLAS | Anderson |
| POINS | Chapman |
| BARDOLPH | Marten |
| BLUNT | Ridout |
| PRINCE JOHN | Mrs Rowley |
| GADSHILL | Bencraft |
| 1ST CARRIER | Morgan |
| 2ND CARRIER | Arthur |
| LADY PERCY | Mrs Vincent |
| HOSTESS | Mrs James |

## NEW WELLS, GOODMAN'S FIELDS

*Jan. 2*

| | |
|---|---|
| FALSTAFF | A Gentleman [unidentified] |
| HENRY | Furnival |
| PRINCE OF WALES | Cushing |
| WORCESTER | Wignell |
| VERNON | Shuter |
| NORTHUMBERLAND | [G.] Hallam |
| BLUNT | Edwards |
| FRANCIS | L. Hallam |
| HOTSPUR | Lee |

# HENRY IV, PART I

## 1747 NEW WELLS, GOODMAN'S FIELDS (cont.)

*Jan. 2 (cont.)*

| | |
|---|---|
| LADY PERCY | Mrs [L.] Hallam |
| HOSTESS | Mrs Bambridge |

[The bill has, 'In which will be reviv'd that excellent Scene between Falstaff and the Prince of Wales, which Shakespeare himself was so extremely fond of.' This was almost certainly the play extempore in Act II, scene iv. Davies (i. 239) says that this scene was 'generally left out on the stage.... It has been occasionally revived, but never produced the effect which the admirers of Shakespeare expected ... [since] it is not heightened with incident.']

## 1748 COVENT GARDEN

*Apr. 22*

| | |
|---|---|
| FALSTAFF | Quin |
| HENRY | Bridges |
| PRINCE OF WALES | Giffard |
| GADSHILL | Bencraft |
| PETO | Stoppelaer |
| BARDOLPH | Marten |
| FRANCIS | James |
| 1ST CARRIER | Morgan |
| 2ND CARRIER | Collins |
| PRINCE JOHN | Miss [E.] Hippisley |
| WESTMORLAND | Storer |
| BLUNT* | Ridout |
| SHERIFF | Dunstall |
| WORCESTER* | Rosco |
| VERNON | Gibson |
| DOUGLAS | Anderson |
| HOTSPUR | Ryan |
| HOSTESS | Mrs James |
| LADY PERCY | Mrs Hale |

*Apr. 25*

| | |
|---|---|
| BLUNT | Rosco |
| WORCESTER | Paget |

*Oct. 17*

| | |
|---|---|
| FALSTAFF | Quin |
| HENRY | [L.] Sparks |
| PRINCE OF WALES | Ryan |
| PRINCE JOHN | Miss [E.] Hippisley |
| WESTMORLAND | Holtom |
| NORTHUMBERLAND | Paget |
| BLUNT | Ridout |
| DOUGLAS | Anderson |
| VERNON | Gibson |
| WORCESTER* | Dance |
| 1ST CARRIER | Arthur |
| 2ND CARRIER | Dunstall |
| FRANCIS | Collins |

*Dec. 6*

| | |
|---|---|
| WORCESTER | Kirby |

## 1748 COVENT GARDEN (cont.)

*Oct. 17 (cont.)*

| | |
|---|---|
| GADSHILL | Bencraft |
| BARDOLPH | Marten |
| PETO | Stoppelaer |
| SHERIFF | Oates |
| TRAVELLER | Smith |
| HOTSPUR | Delane |
| HOSTESS | Mrs Bambridge |
| LADY PERCY | Mrs Woffington |

[The playhouse bill for this performance is in Harris. It is also reproduced in Wilkinson's *Memoirs*, i. 31.]

## 1749 COVENT GARDEN

*Jan. 10; Feb. 27*

| | |
|---|---|
| FALSTAFF | Quin |
| HENRY | [L.] Sparks |
| PRINCE OF WALES | Ryan |
| PRINCE JOHN | Miss [E.] Hippisley |
| WESTMORLAND* | Holtom |
| NORTHUMBERLAND* | Paget |
| BLUNT | Ridout |
| DOUGLAS | Anderson |
| VERNON | Gibson |
| WORCESTER* | Arthur |
| 1ST CARRIER* | Cushing |
| 2ND CARRIER | Dunstall |
| FRANCIS | Collins |
| GADSHILL | Bencraft |
| BARDOLPH | Marten |
| PETO* | Stoppelaer |
| SHERIFF | Oates |
| TRAVELLER* | Smith |
| HOTSPUR | Delane |
| HOSTESS | Mrs Bambridge |
| LADY PERCY* | Mrs Woffington |

*Apr. 13*

| | |
|---|---|
| LADY PERCY | Miss Bellamy |

*Oct. 26*

| | |
|---|---|
| NORTHUMBERLAND | Redman |
| WORCESTER | Bransby |
| 1ST CARRIER | Arthur |
| LADY PERCY | Mrs Vincent |

omitted
    WESTMORLAND, PETO, TRAVELLER

[The bill for Feb. 27 has, 'In which will be reviv'd a Scene not acted these Thirty Years.' This was perhaps the play extempore in Act II, scene iv. See NEW WELLS, GOODMAN'S FIELDS, Jan. 2, 1747.]

## 1750 COVENT GARDEN

*Jan. 3*

| | |
|---|---|
| FALSTAFF | Quin |
| HENRY | [L.] Sparks |
| PRINCE OF WALES | Ryan |

*Mar. 19*

| | |
|---|---|
| LADY PERCY | Mrs Woffington |

omitted
    PRINCE JOHN, WORCESTER, NORTHUM-

## 1750 COVENT GARDEN (cont.)

*Jan. 3 (cont.)*

| | |
|---|---|
| PRINCE JOHN* | Miss [E.] Hippisley |
| WORCESTER* | Bransby |
| NORTHUMBERLAND* | Redman |
| BLUNT* | Ridout |
| DOUGLAS* | Anderson |
| VERNON* | Gibson |
| 1ST CARRIER | Arthur |
| 2ND CARRIER | Dunstall |
| FRANCIS | Collins |
| GADSHILL* | Bencraft |
| BARDOLPH* | Marten |
| SHERIFF* | Oates |
| HOTSPUR* | Delane |
| HOSTESS* | Mrs Bambridge |
| LADY PERCY* | Mrs Vincent |

*Mar. 19 (cont.)*

BERLAND, BLUNT, DOUGLAS, VERNON, GADSHILL, BARDOLPH, SHERIFF, HOSTESS

*Nov. 12, 13, 14, 15*

| | |
|---|---|
| BLUNT | [R.] Elrington |
| HOTSPUR | Barry |
| HOSTESS | Mrs Macklin |

added

| | |
|---|---|
| MORTIMER | Dyer |
| GLENDOWER | Ridout |
| WESTMORLAND | Usher |

omitted

SHERIFF

## HENRY IV, PART II

Adapted by Thomas Betterton. In five acts.

   1720  W. Chetwood.

Act I, scene i is *I. ii*; scene ii is *I. iii*; and scene iii is *II. i*. There are minor excisions throughout; otherwise the dialogue is verbatim.

Act II, scene i is *II. ii*, virtually verbatim. *II. iii* is omitted. Scene ii is *II. iv. 24–end*, somewhat shortened.

Act III, scene i is *III. ii*. Scene ii is *IV. i. ii. iii*, without interruption, but with slight excisions.

Act IV, scene i begins with the King's soliloquy in *III. i. 1–31*, slightly revised. Then follow *IV. iv. 12–end* and *IV. v*, almost verbatim. Scene ii is *V. iii*, slightly reduced. Scene iii is *V. ii. 14–end*, almost verbatim.

Act V, scene i is *V. v. 6–end*. Scene ii is *Henry V, I. i* and *ii*, shortened, and *II. ii. 19–end*, also somewhat shortened.

See Genest, iii. 47–8; Odell, i. 85–6; Spencer, 359–60.

Adapted as THE HUMOURS OF SIR JOHN FALSTAFF, JUSTICE SHALLOW, AND ANCIENT PISTOL, anonymously. In one act.

   1734  Not published.

No acting versions of the original were published before 1750

[*as altered by* BETTERTON]

## 1704 LINCOLN'S INN FIELDS

*n.d.* No parts assigned

   [The bills are missing. See p. 4.]

## HENRY IV, PART II [as altered by BETTERTON]

### 1720 DRURY LANE
*Dec. 17, 19, 20, 21, 22, 30*

| | |
|---|---|
| HENRY | Booth |
| PRINCE OF WALES | Wilks |
| PRINCE JOHN | Walker |
| PRINCE HUMPHREY | Oates |
| CLARENCE | Theo. Cibber |
| WESTMORLAND | Williams |
| LORD CHIEF JUSTICE | Boman |
| ARCHBISHOP OF CANTERBURY | Corey |
| BISHOP OF ELY | Rogers |
| ARCHBISHOP OF YORK | Thurmond |
| MOWBRAY | W. Mills |
| HASTINGS | Watson |
| POINS | W. Wilks |
| FALSTAFF | Mills |
| SHALLOW | Cibber |
| SILENCE | Miller |
| BARDOLPH | Shepard |
| PISTOL | Norris |
| DAVY | Wright |
| FEEBLE | Penkethman |
| SHADOW | Ray |
| WART | Cole |
| MOULDY | Wilson |
| BULLCALF | Wetherilt [Sr.] |
| FALSTAFF'S PAGE | Miss Lindar |
| HOSTESS | Mrs Willis |
| DOLL TEARSHEET | Miss Willis |

[The bills give neither the parts nor the actors' names. The above assignment is from the printed text. The bills have 'Written by Shakespeare, And Revis'd by the late Mr Betterton. Not acted these 16 (Genest, iii. 46, erroneously has 17) years.']

### 1722 DRURY LANE
*May 5*

| | |
|---|---|
| HENRY | Booth |
| PRINCE OF WALES | Wilks |
| FALSTAFF | Mills |
| SHALLOW | Cibber |

No other parts assigned

### 1727 DRURY LANE
*Feb. 21, 25*

| | |
|---|---|
| HENRY | Booth |
| PRINCE OF WALES | Williams |
| PRINCE JOHN | Wm. Mills |

*Feb. 27; Mar. 14.* No parts assigned
*Sept. 9*

| | |
|---|---|
| PISTOL | Norris |

180

HENRY IV, PART II [as altered by BETTERTON]

## 1727 DRURY LANE (cont.)
*Feb. 21, &c. (cont.)*

| | |
|---|---|
| PRINCE HUMPHREY | Oates |
| WESTMORLAND | Bridgwater |
| HASTINGS | Watson |
| LORD CHIEF JUSTICE | Boman |
| FALSTAFF | Harper |
| SHALLOW | Cibber |
| SILENCE | Miller |
| FEEBLE | Griffin |
| BARDOLPH | Shepard |
| PISTOL* | Theophilus Cibber |
| FALSTAFF'S PAGE | Miss Robinson Jr. |
| HOSTESS | Mrs Wetherilt |
| DOLL TEARSHEET | Miss Lindar |

## 1728 DRURY LANE
*Oct. 18; Dec. 3, 30*

| | |
|---|---|
| HENRY | Elrington |
| SHALLOW | Cibber |

No other parts assigned

## 1729 DRURY LANE
*Feb. 5.* No parts assigned

*May 7*

| | |
|---|---|
| HENRY | Mills |
| PRINCE OF WALES* | Wilks |
| PRINCE JOHN | Wm. Mills |
| WESTMORLAND | Bridgwater |
| LORD CHIEF JUSTICE | Boman |
| ARCHBISHOP OF YORK | Roberts |
| ARCHBISHOP OF CANTERBURY | Corey |
| HASTINGS | Watson |
| FALSTAFF | Harper |
| SHALLOW | Cibber |
| POINS | Oates |
| BARDOLPH | Shepard |
| FEEBLE | Griffin |
| FALSTAFF'S PAGE* | Miss Brett |
| PISTOL | [T.] Cibber |
| SILENCE | Miller |
| HOSTESS | Mrs Wetherilt |
| DOLL TEARSHEET | Mrs Shireburn |

*Sept. 23; Dec. 30*

| | |
|---|---|
| PRINCE OF WALES | Williams |
| FALSTAFF'S PAGE | Miss Robinson [Jr.] |

181

HENRY IV, PART II [as altered by BETTERTON]

## 1730 DRURY LANE
*Feb. 12*
|  |  |
|---|---|
| HENRY | Mills |
| PRINCE OF WALES | Williams |
| PRINCE JOHN | Wm. Mills |
| WESTMORLAND | Bridgwater |
| LORD CHIEF JUSTICE | Boman |
| ARCHBISHOP OF YORK | Roberts |
| ARCHBISHOP OF CANTERBURY | Corey |
| HASTINGS | Watson |
| FALSTAFF | Harper |
| SHALLOW | Cibber |
| POINS | Oates |
| BARDOLPH | Shepard |
| FEEBLE* | Griffin |
| FALSTAFF'S PAGE | Miss Robinson [Jr.] |
| PISTOL* | Norris |
| SILENCE* | Miller |
| HOSTESS | Mrs Wetherilt |
| DOLL TEARSHEET | Mrs Shireburn |

*Sept. 29*
|  |  |
|---|---|
| PISTOL | [T.] Cibber |
| SILENCE | Griffin |
| omitted |  |
| FEEBLE |  |

*Dec. 4.* No parts assigned

## 1731 DRURY LANE
*Mar. 16; Oct. 14*
|  |  |
|---|---|
| HENRY | Mills |
| PRINCE OF WALES | W. Mills |
| FALSTAFF | Harper |
| SHALLOW | Cibber |
| PISTOL | [T.] Cibber |
| SILENCE | Griffin |

*May 19*
added
|  |  |
|---|---|
| PRINCE JOHN | Marshall |
| WESTMORLAND | Bridgwater |
| LORD CHIEF JUSTICE | Boman |
| ARCHBISHOP OF YORK | Paget |
| ARCHBISHOP OF CANTERBURY | Corey |
| HASTINGS | Watson |
| POINS | Oates |
| BARDOLPH | Shepard |
| FEEBLE | Oates |
| FALSTAFF'S PAGE | Miss Robinson [Jr.] |
| HOSTESS | Mrs Wetherilt |
| DOLL TEARSHEET | Mrs Shireburn |

[Oates doubled POINS and FEEBLE.]

*Dec. 6*
|  |  |
|---|---|
| SHALLOW | Cibber |

No other parts assigned

## 1732 DRURY LANE
*Jan. 15*
|  |  |
|---|---|
| HENRY | Mills |
| SHALLOW | Cibber |

HENRY IV, PART II [as altered by BETTERTON]

## 1732 DRURY LANE (cont.)

*Jan. 15 (cont.)*

| | |
|---|---|
| LORD CHIEF JUSTICE | Boman |
| PISTOL | [T.] Cibber |

[The bill for this performance is missing. The above assignment is taken, complete, from TR.]

*Apr. 18*

| | |
|---|---|
| SHALLOW | Cibber |

No other parts assigned

*Oct. 19; Nov. 15*

| | |
|---|---|
| SHALLOW | Cibber |
| HENRY | Mills |
| PRINCE OF WALES | Wm. Mills |
| FALSTAFF | Harper |
| SILENCE | Griffin |
| PISTOL | [T.] Cibber |

## 1733 DRURY LANE

*Jan. 6*

| | |
|---|---|
| SHALLOW | Cibber |

No other parts assigned

[The bill for this performance is missing. The above assignment is taken from TR.]

*May 7*

| | |
|---|---|
| SHALLOW | Cibber |
| PISTOL | [T.] Cibber |
| HENRY | Mills |
| PRINCE OF WALES | W. Mills |
| FALSTAFF | Harper |
| SILENCE | Miller |
| FEEBLE | Griffin |

[Bill in DP of May 4. DP of May 7 missing.]

## HAYMARKET

*Oct. 12*

| | |
|---|---|
| HENRY | Mills |
| PRINCE OF WALES | William Mills |
| FALSTAFF | Harper |
| SHALLOW | Johnson |
| PISTOL | [T.] Cibber |
| SILENCE | Miller |
| PRINCE JOHN | A. Hallam |
| LORD CHIEF JUSTICE | Boman |
| POINS | Oates |
| BARDOLPH | Shepard |
| ARCHBISHOP OF YORK | Milward |

*Nov. 22; Dec. 8*

omitted WESTMORLAND, MOWBRAY, PRINCE HUMPHREY, HASTINGS, SHADOW, WART, MOULDY, BULLCALF, FALSTAFF'S PAGE

## HENRY IV, PART II [as altered by BETTERTON]

### 1733 HAYMARKET (cont.)
*Oct. 12 (cont.)*

| | |
|---|---|
| FEEBLE | Griffin |
| WESTMORLAND* | Winstone |
| MOWBRAY* | Berry |
| PRINCE HUMFHREY* | Oates |
| HASTINGS* | Ridout |
| SHADOW* | Mawley |
| WART* | Peploe |
| MOULDY* | [G.] Hallam |
| BULLCALF* | Gray |
| FALSTAFF'S PAGE* | Miss Brett |
| HOSTESS | Mrs Shireburn |
| DOLL TEARSHEET | Miss Mann |

[Oates doubled POINS and PRINCE HUMPHREY.]

### 1734 DRURY LANE
*Apr. 18*

| | |
|---|---|
| HENRY | Mills |
| PRINCE OF WALES | W. Mills |
| PRINCE JOHN | A. Hallam |
| PRINCE HUMPHREY* | Cross |
| SHALLOW | Johnson |
| ARCHBISHOP OF YORK | Milward |
| LORD CHIEF JUSTICE* | Boman |
| POINS | Oates |
| SILENCE | Miller |
| BARDOLPH | Shepard |
| FEEBLE | Griffin |
| FALSTAFF | Harper |
| PISTOL | [T.] Cibber |
| HOSTESS | Mrs Shireburn |
| DOLL TEARSHEET | Miss Mann |

*May 4*
omitted PRINCE HUMPHREY, LORD CHIEF JUSTICE

### HAYMARKET
*Jan. 19*

| | |
|---|---|
| HENRY | Mills |
| PRINCE OF WALES | W. Mills |
| FALSTAFF | Harper |
| SHALLOW | Johnson |
| PISTOL | [T.] Cibber |
| SILENCE | Miller |
| PRINCE JOHN | A. Hallam |
| LORD CHIEF JUSTICE | Boman |
| POINS | Oates |

HENRY IV, PART II [*as altered by* BETTERTON]

## 1734 HAYMARKET (*cont.*)
*Jan. 19 (cont.)*

| | |
|---|---|
| BARDOLPH | Shepard |
| ARCHBISHOP OF YORK | Milward |
| FEEBLE | Griffin |
| HOSTESS | Mrs Shireburn |
| DOLL TEARSHEET | Miss Mann |

[*as* THE HUMOURS OF SIR JOHN FALSTAFF, JUSTICE SHALLOW, AND ANCIENT PISTOL]

## HAYMARKET
*June 3, 4*

| | |
|---|---|
| PISTOL | Mrs Charke |
| FALSTAFF | Turbutt |
| SHALLOW | James |
| BARDOLPH | Jones |
| FEEBLE | Tench |
| HOSTESS | Mrs Monlass |
| DOLL TEARSHEET | Mrs Talbot |

*June 5*
added

| | |
|---|---|
| HENRY | Este |
| LORD CHIEF JUSTICE | Cole |
| SILENCE | [T.] Hallam |
| DRAWER | Thompson |
| SHADOW | Master Arne |
| MOULDY | Monlass |

[*as altered by* BETTERTON]

## 1735 DRURY LANE
*Apr. 11; May 8*

| | |
|---|---|
| HENRY | Mills |
| PRINCE OF WALES | W. Mills |
| PRINCE JOHN | Salway |
| LORD CHIEF JUSTICE | Boman |
| ARCHBISHOP OF YORK | Milward |
| ARCHBISHOP OF CANTERBURY | Corey |
| FALSTAFF | Harper |
| PISTOL | [T.] Cibber |
| SHALLOW | Johnson |
| SILENCE | Miller |
| FEEBLE | Griffin |
| BARDOLPH | Shepard |
| POINS | Oates |
| FALSTAFF'S PAGE | Miss Cole |
| HOSTESS | Mrs Cross |
| DOLL TEARSHEET | Miss Mann |

185

## HENRY IV, PART II
*[The original]*

### 1736 DRURY LANE
*Mar. 11; Apr. 1*

| | |
|---|---|
| FALSTAFF | Quin |
| HENRY | Mills |
| PRINCE OF WALES | W. Mills |
| PRINCE JOHN* | Salway |
| ARCHBISHOP OF YORK | Milward |
| LORD CHIEF JUSTICE | Boman |
| PISTOL | [T.] Cibber |
| SHALLOW | Johnson |
| SILENCE | Miller |
| FEEBLE | Griffin |
| BARDOLPH | Shepard |
| POINS | Oates |
| FALSTAFF'S PAGE | Miss Cole |
| HOSTESS | Mrs Cross |
| DOLL TEARSHEET* | Miss Mann |

*May 20*

| | |
|---|---|
| DOLL TEARSHEET added | Miss Dancey |
| WESTMORLAND | Winstone |

*Oct. 9; Dec. 4*

| | |
|---|---|
| PRINCE JOHN added | Este |
| WESTMORLAND | Winstone |

[The bill has, 'Written by Shakespeare. In which will be restor'd Scenes, Soliloquies, and other Circumstances, originally in the Part of Falstaff, which have been for many Years omitted.']

### 1737 DRURY LANE
*Jan. 21*

| | |
|---|---|
| FALSTAFF | Quin |
| HENRY | Milward |
| PRINCE OF WALES | W. Mills |
| PRINCE JOHN* | Este |
| ARCHBISHOP OF YORK* | Berry |
| LORD CHIEF JUSTICE | Boman |
| WESTMORLAND | Winstone |
| PISTOL | [T.] Cibber |
| SHALLOW | Johnson |
| SILENCE | Miller |
| FEEBLE | Griffin |
| BARDOLPH* | Shepard |
| POINS* | Oates |
| FALSTAFF'S PAGE | Miss Cole |
| HOSTESS* | Mrs Cross |
| DOLL TEARSHEET* | Miss Mann |

*Oct. 20*

| | |
|---|---|
| PRINCE JOHN | Havard |
| ARCHBISHOP OF YORK | Wright |
| BARDOLPH | Ray |
| POINS | Macklin |
| HOSTESS | Mrs Roberts |
| DOLL TEARSHEET | Miss Brett |

### 1738 DRURY LANE
*Jan. 13*

| | |
|---|---|
| FALSTAFF | Quin |
| HENRY | Milward |
| PRINCE OF WALES | [W.] Mills |
| PRINCE JOHN | Havard |
| ARCHBISHOP OF YORK | Wright |

*Sept. 16*

| | |
|---|---|
| SILENCE | Griffin |
| POINS | Cross |
| HOSTESS | Mrs Cross |
| DOLL TEARSHEET | Miss Mann |

['Harper's name in for Silence Griffin Played it' (Griffin). Harper was ill. See

186

HENRY IV, PART II

## 1738 DRURY LANE (cont.)

**Jan. 13 (cont.)**

| | |
|---|---|
| LORD CHIEF JUSTICE | Boman |
| WESTMORLAND | Winstone |
| PISTOL | [T.] Cibber |
| SHALLOW | Johnson |
| SILENCE* | Miller |
| FEEBLE | Woodward |
| BARDOLPH | Ray |
| POINS* | Macklin |
| FALSTAFF'S PAGE | Miss Cole |
| HOSTESS* | Mrs Roberts |
| DOLL TEARSHEET* | Miss Brett |

**Sept. 16 (cont.)**

Henry IV, Part I at this theatre, Sept. 14, 1738.]

**Oct. 13**

| | |
|---|---|
| FALSTAFF | Quin |
| HENRY | Milward |
| PRINCE OF WALES | [W.] Mills |
| PISTOL | [T.] Cibber |
| SHALLOW | Cibber Sr. |

No other parts assigned

## COVENT GARDEN

**Feb. 16, 20**

| | |
|---|---|
| HENRY | Delane |
| PRINCE OF WALES | Ryan |
| PRINCE JOHN | [A.] Hallam |
| LORD CHIEF JUSTICE | Stephens |
| WESTMORLAND* | Aston |
| MORTON | Stevens |
| ARCHBISHOP OF YORK | Chapman |
| MOWBRAY | Rosco |
| LORD BARDOLPH | Hale |
| HASTINGS* | Ridout |
| FALSTAFF | Bridgwater |
| POINS | Salway |
| BARDOLPH | W. Hallam |
| SHALLOW | Hippisley |
| SILENCE | Neale |
| FEEBLE | Penkethman [Jr.] |
| SHADOW | Bencraft |
| BULLCALF | Mullart |
| WART | Yates |
| MOULDY | Stoppelaer |
| PISTOL | James |
| HOSTESS | Mrs James |
| DOLL TEARSHEET | Miss Dancey |

[The bill has, 'The Above Play of King Henry IV. is the Genuine Play of Shakespeare, and not that alter'd by Mr. Betterton, and so frequently acted at the other Theatre.']

**Dec. 4**

| | |
|---|---|
| WESTMORLAND | Roberts |
| HASTINGS added | Hill |
| NORTHUMBERLAND | Johnson |

187

HENRY IV, PART II

[*as altered by* BETTERTON]

## 1739 DRURY LANE
*Nov. 20*

| | |
|---|---|
| FALSTAFF | Quin |
| HENRY | Milward |
| PRINCE OF WALES | [W.] Mills |
| PRINCE JOHN | Havard |
| ARCHBISHOP OF YORK | Wright |
| LORD CHIEF JUSTICE | Berry |
| WESTMORLAND | Winstone |
| FRENCH AMBASSADOR | Turbutt |
| HASTINGS | Ridout |
| PISTOL | Yates |
| SHALLOW | Johnson |
| SILENCE | Griffin |
| FEEBLE | Woodward |
| BARDOLPH | Ray |
| POINS | Cashell |
| FALSTAFF'S PAGE | Miss Cole |
| HOSTESS | Mrs Grace |
| DOLL TEARSHEET | Mrs Bennet |

[*The original*]

## COVENT GARDEN
*Dec. 6*

| | |
|---|---|
| HENRY | Delane |
| PRINCE OF WALES | Ryan |
| FALSTAFF | Hyde |
| SHALLOW | Hippisley |
| SILENCE | Neale |
| PRINCE JOHN | [A.] Hallam |
| LORD CHIEF JUSTICE | Stephens |
| NORTHUMBERLAND | Johnson |
| WESTMORLAND | Roberts |
| POINS | Salway |
| ARCHBISHOP OF YORK | Rosco |
| LORD BARDOLPH | Hale |
| FEEBLE | James |
| PISTOL | [T.] Cibber |
| HOSTESS | Mrs James |
| DOLL TEARSHEET | Miss Dancey |

[*as altered by* BETTERTON]

## 1740 DRURY LANE
*Oct. 14*

| | |
|---|---|
| FALSTAFF | Quin |
| HENRY | Milward |

188

HENRY IV, PART II [*as altered by* BETTERTON]

## 1740 DRURY LANE (cont.)
*Oct. 14* (cont.)

| | |
|---|---|
| PRINCE OF WALES | [W.] Mills |
| PRINCE JOHN | Havard |
| ARCHBISHOP OF YORK | Wright |
| FRENCH AMBASSADOR | Turbutt |
| LORD CHIEF JUSTICE | Berry |
| WESTMORLAND | Winstone |
| HASTINGS | Ridout |
| PISTOL | Woodward |
| SHALLOW | Johnson |
| SILENCE | Taswell |
| FEEBLE | Ray |
| BARDOLPH | Shepard |
| POINS | Cashell |
| FALSTAFF'S PAGE | Miss Cole |
| HOSTESS | Mrs Macklin |
| DOLL TEARSHEET | Mrs Bennet |

[*The original*]

## COVENT GARDEN
*Feb. 6*

| | |
|---|---|
| HENRY | Delane |
| PRINCE OF WALES | Ryan |
| FALSTAFF | Bridgwater |
| SHALLOW | Hippisley |
| SILENCE | Neale |
| PRINCE JOHN | [A.] Hallam |
| LORD CHIEF JUSTICE | Stephens |
| NORTHUMBERLAND | Johnson |
| WESTMORLAND | Roberts |
| POINS | Salway |
| ARCHBISHOP OF YORK | Rosco |
| LORD BARDOLPH | Hale |
| MORTON | Gibson |
| COLEVILE | Anderson |
| FEEBLE | James |
| PISTOL | [T.] Cibber |
| HOSTESS | Mrs James |
| DOLL TEARSHEET | Mrs Cross |

[*as altered by* BETTERTON]

## 1741 DRURY LANE
*Jan. 27*

| | |
|---|---|
| FALSTAFF | Quin |
| HENRY | Milward |
| PRINCE OF WALES | [W.] Mills |

189

HENRY IV, PART II [*as altered by* BETTERTON]

## 1741 DRURY LANE (*cont.*)
*Jan. 27 (cont.)*

| | |
|---|---|
| PRINCE JOHN | Havard |
| ARCHBISHOP OF YORK | Wright |
| FRENCH AMBASSADOR | Turbutt |
| LORD CHIEF JUSTICE | Berry |
| WESTMORLAND | Winstone |
| HASTINGS | Ridout |
| PISTOL | Woodward |
| SHALLOW | Johnson |
| SILENCE | Taswell |
| FEEBLE | Ray |
| BARDOLPH | Shepard |
| POINS | Cashell |
| FALSTAFF'S PAGE | Miss Cole |
| HOSTESS | Mrs Macklin |
| DOLL TEARSHEET | Mrs Bennet |

[*The original*]

## 1742 COVENT GARDEN
*Feb. 12, 20*

| | |
|---|---|
| SHALLOW | Cibber Sr. |

No other parts assigned

*May 7*

| | |
|---|---|
| SHALLOW | Hippisley |
| HENRY | Stephens |
| PRINCE OF WALES | Ryan |
| PRINCE JOHN | Hale |
| ARCHBISHOP OF YORK | Chapman |
| LORD CHIEF JUSTICE | Rosco |
| WESTMORLAND | Gibson |
| MOWBRAY | Cashell |
| HASTINGS | Harrington |
| SILENCE | Salway |
| PISTOL* | James |
| BARDOLPH* | Stoppelaer |
| FALSTAFF'S PAGE* | Miss Mullart |
| FALSTAFF* | Bridgwater |
| HOSTESS* | Mrs James |
| DOLL TEARSHEET | Miss Hilliard |

*Oct. 26*

| | |
|---|---|
| PISTOL | Woodward |
| BARDOLPH | Marten |
| FALSTAFF | Quin |

omitted
    FALSTAFF'S PAGE

*Dec. 29*

| | |
|---|---|
| PISTOL | Woodward |
| BARDOLPH | Marten |
| FALSTAFF | Quin |
| HOSTESS | Mrs Mullart |

omitted
    FALSTAFF'S PAGE

## 1743 COVENT GARDEN
*Feb. 7*

| | |
|---|---|
| FALSTAFF | Quin |
| HENRY | Stephens |
| PRINCE OF WALES | Ryan |
| PRINCE JOHN | Hale |

## HENRY IV, PART II

## 1743 COVENT GARDEN (cont.)
*Feb. 7 (cont.)*

| | |
|---|---|
| ARCHBISHOP OF YORK | Chapman |
| LORD CHIEF JUSTICE | Rosco |
| WESTMORLAND | Gibson |
| MOWBRAY | Cashell |
| HASTINGS | Harrington |
| SILENCE | Salway |
| PISTOL | Woodward |
| BARDOLPH | Marten |
| SHALLOW | Hippisley |
| HOSTESS | Mrs Mullart |
| DOLL TEARSHEET | Miss Hilliard |

[*as altered by* BETTERTON]

## 1744 DRURY LANE
*Jan. 27*

| | |
|---|---|
| SHALLOW | Cibber Sr. |
| HENRY | Delane |
| PRINCE OF WALES | [W.] Mills |
| PRINCE JOHN | Havard |
| ARCHBISHOP OF YORK | Turbutt |
| ARCHBISHOP OF CANTERBURY | Woodburn |
| LORD CHIEF JUSTICE | Bridges |
| HASTINGS | Blakes |
| GOWER | Usher |
| SILENCE | Neale |
| PISTOL | Yates |
| POINS | W. Giffard |
| BARDOLPH | Ray |
| SCROOP | Arthur |
| WESTMORLAND | Winstone |
| CAMBRIDGE | Taswell |
| GREY | Dunstall |
| FALSTAFF | Berry |
| HOSTESS | Mrs Cross |
| DOLL TEARSHEET | Mrs Bennet |

[*The original*]

## COVENT GARDEN

*Jan. 11; Mar. 1*

| | |
|---|---|
| FALSTAFF | Quin |
| HENRY* | Stephens |
| PRINCE OF WALES | Ryan |
| PRINCE JOHN | Hale |
| ARCHBISHOP OF YORK | Chapman |
| PISTOL* | Woodward |

*Apr. 27*

| | |
|---|---|
| PISTOL | James |
| HOSTESS | Mrs James |

*Nov. 9; Dec. 1*

| | |
|---|---|
| HENRY | Cashell |
| MOWBRAY | Arthur |
| DOLL TEARSHEET | Mrs Dunstall |

## HENRY IV, PART II

### 1744 COVENT GARDEN (*cont.*)
*Jan. 11; Mar. 1* (*cont.*)

| LORD CHIEF JUSTICE | Rosco |
| WESTMORLAND | Gibson |
| MOWBRAY* | Cashell |
| HASTINGS | Carr |
| GOWER | Anderson |
| SILENCE | Stoppelaer |
| POINS | Hayman |
| BARDOLPH | Marten |
| SHALLOW | Hippisley |
| HOSTESS* | Mrs Mullart |
| DOLL TEARSHEET* | Miss Hilliard |

### 1745 COVENT GARDEN
*Feb. 8*

| FALSTAFF | Quin |
| HENRY | Cashell |
| PRINCE OF WALES | Ryan |
| PRINCE JOHN | Hale |
| LORD CHIEF JUSTICE | Rosco |
| WESTMORLAND | Gibson |
| MOWBRAY | Arthur |
| HASTINGS | Carr |
| GOWER | Anderson |
| SILENCE | Stoppelaer |
| ARCHBISHOP OF YORK | Chapman |
| PISTOL* | Woodward |
| POINS* | Hayman |
| BARDOLPH | Marten |
| SHALLOW | Hippisley |
| HOSTESS* | Mrs Mullart |
| DOLL TEARSHEET | Mrs Dunstall |

*Apr. 1*

| PISTOL | [T.] Cibber |
| HOSTESS added | Mrs James |
| LORD BARDOLPH | Ridout |
| POINS omitted | |

### 1746 COVENT GARDEN
*Jan. 13*

| HENRY | Cashell |
| PRINCE OF WALES | Ryan |
| PRINCE JOHN | Hale |
| ARCHBISHOP OF YORK | Chapman |
| FALSTAFF | Bridgwater |
| SHALLOW | Hippisley |
| LORD CHIEF JUSTICE | Rosco |
| WESTMORLAND | Gibson |
| MOWBRAY | Arthur |
| HASTINGS | Carr |
| GOWER | Anderson |
| LORD BARDOLPH | Ridout |

## 1746 COVENT GARDEN (cont.)
*Jan. 13 (cont.)*

| | |
|---|---|
| SILENCE | Stoppelaer |
| BARDOLPH | Marten |
| PISTOL | [T.] Cibber |
| HOSTESS | Mrs James |
| DOLL TEARSHEET | Mrs Dunstall |

## 1747 NEW WELLS, GOODMAN'S FIELDS
*Apr. 6*

| | |
|---|---|
| FALSTAFF | Paget |
| FALSTAFF'S PAGE | Master Paget |

No other parts assigned

[GA lists only FALSTAFF; DA lists only FALSTAFF'S PAGE.]

## 1749 COVENT GARDEN
*Mar. 2*

| | |
|---|---|
| FALSTAFF | Quin |
| HENRY | Delane |
| PRINCE OF WALES | Ryan |
| ARCHBISHOP OF YORK | Bridgwater |
| MOWBRAY* | Paget |
| HASTINGS | Anderson |
| CLARENCE | Miss [E.] Hippisley |
| WESTMORLAND | Gibson |
| COLEVILE | Oates |
| PRINCE JOHN | Ridout |
| SHALLOW | Arthur |
| SILENCE | Stoppelaer |
| BARDOLPH | Marten |
| POINS* | Cushing |
| BULLCALF | Dunstall |
| FEEBLE | Collins |
| MOULDY | Bencraft |
| PISTOL* | [T.] Cibber |
| HOSTESS | Mrs Bambridge |
| DOLL TEARSHEET | Mrs Dunstall |

*Mar. 11, 16, 18; Apr. 8*
added

| | |
|---|---|
| LORD CHIEF JUSTICE | [L.] Sparks |

*Nov. 8; Dec. 9*

| | |
|---|---|
| MOWBRAY | Redman |
| POINS | Bransby |
| PISTOL | Cushing |

added

| | |
|---|---|
| PRINCE HUMPHREY | Baker |
| LORD CHIEF JUSTICE | [L.] Sparks |
| SHADOW | Hacket |

## 1750 COVENT GARDEN
*Jan. 17*

| | |
|---|---|
| HENRY* | Delane |
| PRINCE OF WALES | Ryan |
| ARCHBISHOP OF YORK | Bridgwater |
| MOWBRAY | Redman |
| HASTINGS | Anderson |

*Nov. 22*

| | |
|---|---|
| HENRY | Gibson |
| WESTMORLAND | Usher |
| COLEVILE | [R.] Elrington |
| HOSTESS | Mrs Macklin |

added

| | |
|---|---|
| PETO | Atkins |

HENRY IV, PART II

## 1750 COVENT GARDEN (cont.)

Jan. 17 (cont.)

| | |
|---|---|
| WESTMORLAND* | Gibson |
| PRINCE JOHN | Ridout |
| PRINCE HUMPHREY | Baker |
| CLARENCE* | Miss [E.] Hippisley |
| POINS | Bransby |
| COLEVILE* | Oates |
| LORD CHIEF JUSTICE | [L.] Sparks |
| SILENCE | Stoppelaer |
| BARDOLPH | Marten |
| SHALLOW | Arthur |
| BULLCALF | Dunstall |
| FEEBLE | Collins |
| MOULDY | Bencraft |
| SHADOW | Hacket |
| PISTOL | Cushing |
| FALSTAFF | Quin |
| DOLL TEARSHEET | Miss Haughton |
| HOSTESS* | Mrs Bambridge |

Nov. 23

| | |
|---|---|
| HENRY | Gibson |
| WESTMORLAND | Usher |
| CLARENCE | Bennet |
| COLEVILE | [R.] Elrington |
| HOSTESS | Mrs Macklin |
| added | |
| PETO | Atkins |

# HENRY V

Adapted by Aaron Hill. In five acts.

1723  W. Chetwood and J. Watts.

Act I opens with the *Chorus* to *II. 1–19*, used as dialogue and somewhat enlarged. This is followed by *I. i. 24–66*; *I. ii. 9–12, 86–110, 221–97*; *III. iii. 5–49*. All this material is slightly altered and occasionally reduced. Then follow 175 new lines: the conspiracy is plotted, and Harriet, Scroop's niece, vows to revenge her seduction by Henry.

Act II, scene i is *II. iv. 1–75*; *III. v. 3–35*; *II. iv. 75–144*, considerably altered, and about 30 new lines: the Dauphin and Harriet discuss the conspiracy. Scene ii is new: Harriet poisons Katharine's mind against Henry. Katharine is given the speech on Ceremony: *IV. i. 254–300*, reduced.

Act III, scene i is also new: Katharine expresses her hatred for Henry. Scene ii is *V. ii. 1–46* and *I. ii. 207–13*, altered. The rest is new: Katharine discovers she has already met and fallen in love with Henry; the kings refuse mutual offers of peace (Henry here has *IV. iii. 96–101*); Katharine resolves to warn Henry about the conspiracy.

Act IV opens with about 250 new lines: Henry learns of the conspiracy and placates Harriet, who stabs herself. Then comes *II. ii. 14–127*, a little reduced. About 50 new lines follow: Katharine promises to marry Henry.

Act V is *III. vii. 1–38, 145–end*, verbatim. Henry and York then speak the *Chorus* to *IV. 1–42*, virtually verbatim. Then follow the Crispin speech: *IV. iii.*

*19–62*, verbatim; about 20 new lines: Henry gives directions for the battle; and *IV. ii. 14–end*, somewhat reduced. A song by the Genius of England is here inserted, and is followed by *IV. v*, complete; *IV. vi. 3–34*; *IV. vii. 74–8*—all verbatim. The act concludes with about 50 new lines: the French capitulate, and Katharine is given to Henry.

See Genest, iii. 129–31; Odell, i. 252–3.

Adapted as THE CONSPIRACY DISCOVERED, anonymously. In one act.
   1746 Not published.

No acting versions of the original were published before 1750.

### [as altered by HILL]

## 1723 DRURY LANE

*Dec. 5, 6, 7, 9, 26*

| | | |
|---|---|---|
| HENRY | Booth | |
| DAUPHIN | Wilks | |
| KING OF FRANCE | Thurmond | |
| EXETER | Mills | |
| YORK | Corey | |
| SCROOP | Williams | |
| BOURBON | Bridgwater | |
| ORLEANS | Watson | |
| CAMBRIDGE | W. Mills | |
| GREY | Oates | |
| FRENCH OFFICER* | Roberts | |
| KATHARINE | Mrs Oldfield | |
| HARRIET | Mrs Thurmond | |
| CHARLOTTE* | Mrs Campbell | |

*Dec. 10*
omitted
FRENCH OFFICER, CHARLOTTE
[The bill assigns the parts.]

[The bills give neither the parts nor the actors' names. The above assignment is taken from the printed text.]

## 1735 GOODMAN'S FIELDS

*Nov. 26, 27, 28, 29; Dec. 1, 2, 3*

| | |
|---|---|
| HENRY | Johnson |
| DAUPHIN | Giffard |
| KING OF FRANCE | W. Giffard |
| BOURBON | Richardson |
| ORLEANS | Woodward |
| EXETER | Rosco |
| YORK | Lyon |
| SCROOP | Havard |
| CAMBRIDGE | Hamilton |
| GREY | Ray |
| KATHARINE | Mrs Giffard |
| HARRIET | Mrs Roberts |
| CHARLOTTE | Miss Tollett |

[Genest (iii. 482) infers that this was the original. The bill has, 'Written by Aaron Hill, esq.']

HENRY V [*as altered by* HILL]

## 1736 GOODMAN'S FIELDS
*Feb. 5; Apr. 13*

| | |
|---|---|
| HENRY | Johnson |
| DAUPHIN | Giffard |
| KING OF FRANCE | W. Giffard |
| BOURBON | Richardson |
| ORLEANS | Woodward |
| EXETER | Rosco |
| YORK | Lyon |
| SCROOP | Havard |
| CAMBRIDGE | Hamilton |
| GREY | Ray |
| KATHARINE | Mrs Giffard |
| HARRIET | Mrs Roberts |
| CHARLOTTE | Miss Tollett |

[*The original*]

## 1738 COVENT GARDEN
*Feb. 23, 25, 27, 28; Mar. 6; Apr. 3; Dec. 5, 22*
*May 4*

| | |
|---|---|
| HENRY | Delane |
| ARCHBISHOP OF CANTERBURY | Chapman |
| EXETER | Stephens |
| GLOUCESTER* | Ridout |
| BEDFORD | A. Ryan |
| WESTMORLAND* | Aston |
| CAMBRIDGE* | Houghton |
| SCROOP | Arthur |
| GREY | Stevens |
| GOWER | Hale |
| FLUELLEN | Hippisley |
| PISTOL | James |
| MACMORRIS | Neale |
| JAMY* | Lyon |
| WILLIAMS | Rosco |
| BATES | Mullart |
| NYM | Stoppelaer |
| BARDOLPH | W. Hallam |
| BOY | Miss Ferguson |
| KING OF FRANCE | Johnson |
| DAUPHIN | [A.] Hallam |
| BURGUNDY | Walker |
| CONSTABLE | Bridgwater |
| CHORUS* | Ryan |
| HOSTESS | Mrs Mullart |
| ISABEL | Mrs James |
| KATHARINE | Mrs Ware |

| | |
|---|---|
| GLOUCESTER | Hill |
| WESTMORLAND | Roberts |
| CAMBRIDGE | Anderson |
| omitted | |
| JAMY | |

[On Dec. 5 the CHORUS is omitted. This is almost certainly a misprint.]

196

## 1739 COVENT GARDEN
*Jan. 11; Mar. 19*

| | |
|---|---|
| HENRY | Delane |
| ARCHBISHOP OF CANTERBURY | Chapman |
| FLUELLEN | Hippisley |
| PISTOL | James |
| KING OF FRANCE | Johnson |
| DAUPHIN | [A.] Hallam |
| BURGUNDY | Walker |
| CONSTABLE | Bridgwater |
| EXETER | Stephens |
| GLOUCESTER | Hill |
| BEDFORD | A. Ryan |
| WESTMORLAND | Roberts |
| CAMBRIDGE | Anderson |
| SCROOP | Arthur |
| GREY | Stevens |
| GOWER | Hale |
| MACMORRIS | Neale |
| WILLIAMS | Rosco |
| BATES | Mullart |
| NYM | Stoppelaer |
| BARDOLPH | W. Hallam |
| BOY | Miss Ferguson |
| CHORUS | Ryan |
| ISABEL | Mrs James |
| KATHARINE | Mrs Ware |
| HOSTESS | Mrs Mullart |

## 1740 COVENT GARDEN
*Mar. 11*

| | |
|---|---|
| HENRY | Delane |
| FLUELLEN | Hippisley |
| KING OF FRANCE | Johnson |
| DAUPHIN | [A.] Hallam |
| BURGUNDY | Harrington |
| CONSTABLE | Bridgwater |
| EXETER | Stephens |
| GLOUCESTER | Clarke |
| BEDFORD | A. Ryan |
| WESTMORLAND | Roberts |
| CAMBRIDGE | Anderson |
| SCROOP | Arthur |
| GREY | Gibson |
| GOWER | Hale |
| MACMORRIS | Neale |
| WILLIAMS | Rosco |

## 1740 COVENT GARDEN (cont.)
*Mar. 11 (cont.)*

| | |
|---|---|
| BATES | Mullart |
| NYM | Stoppelaer |
| BARDOLPH | Oates |
| BOY | Miss Ferguson |
| PISTOL | [T.] Cibber |
| ISABEL | Mrs James |
| KATHARINE | Mrs Ware |
| HOSTESS | Mrs Mullart |

## 1744 COVENT GARDEN
*Apr. 19, 20*

| | |
|---|---|
| HENRY | Hale |
| FLUELLEN | Hippisley |
| PISTOL | Woodward |
| KING OF FRANCE | Cashell |
| DAUPHIN | Goodall |
| ARCHBISHOP OF CANTERBURY | Chapman |
| EXETER | Stephens |
| WILLIAMS | Rosco |
| CONSTABLE | Bridgwater |
| BURGUNDY | Gibson |
| FRENCH SOLDIER | Destrade |
| CHORUS | Ryan |
| ISABEL | Mrs James |
| KATHARINE | Mrs Hale |

## 1745 COVENT GARDEN
*Apr. 25*

| | |
|---|---|
| HENRY | Hale |
| EXETER | Ridout |
| ARCHBISHOP OF CANTERBURY | Chapman |
| FLUELLEN | Hippisley |
| KING OF FRANCE* | Cashell |
| DAUPHIN | Woodward |
| CONSTABLE | Bridgwater |
| FRENCH SOLDIER | Destrade |
| PISTOL | [T.] Cibber |
| CHORUS | Ryan |
| ISABEL | Mrs Bland |
| KATHARINE* | Mrs Vincent |
| HOSTESS | Mrs James |

*Nov. 18*

| | |
|---|---|
| KATHARINE added | Mrs Hale |
| WILLIAMS | Rosco |

*Dec. 11*

| | |
|---|---|
| KING OF FRANCE | Johnson |
| KATHARINE added | Mrs Hale |
| WILLIAMS | Rosco |

## HENRY V

### [as THE CONSPIRACY DISCOVERED]
### 1746 DRURY LANE
*Aug. 4, 6, 8.* No parts assigned

[The subtitle is FRENCH POLICY DEFEATED. The bill has, 'In One Act (taken from Shakespeare) With a Representation of the Trials of the Lords for High-Treason, in the Reign of King Henry V'. This adaptation was almost certainly occasioned by the trial, which began at Westminster Hall on July 28, of Lords Kilmarnock, Cromarty, and Balmerino for participation in the Rebellion of '45.]

### [*The original*]
### COVENT GARDEN

*Jan. 1; Mar. 6*

| | |
|---|---|
| HENRY | Hale |
| EXETER | Ridout |
| ARCHBISHOP OF CANTERBURY | Chapman |
| FLUELLEN | Hippisley |
| PISTOL* | [T.] Cibber |
| WILLIAMS | Rosco |
| KING OF FRANCE | Johnson |
| DAUPHIN* | Woodward |
| CONSTABLE | Bridgwater |
| BURGUNDY | Gibson |
| FRENCH SOLDIER | Destrade |
| CHORUS | Ryan |
| ISABEL | Mrs Bland |
| KATHARINE | Mrs Hale |
| HOSTESS | Mrs James |

*May 1*

| | |
|---|---|
| PISTOL | Woodward |
| DAUPHIN added | Hayman |
| NYM | Stoppelaer |

### [*as altered by* HILL]
### JAMES ST., HAYMARKET
*Mar. 12.* No parts assigned

[The bill has, 'An Historical Play, not acted these Twenty Years'.]

### [*The original*]
### 1747 DRURY LANE

*Dec. 16*

| | |
|---|---|
| HENRY | Barry |
| ARCHBISHOP OF CANTERBURY | Delane |
| EXETER | Berry |
| BISHOP OF ELY | Winstone |
| KING OF FRANCE | [W.] Mills |
| DAUPHIN | Havard |
| CONSTABLE | [L.] Sparks |
| BURGUNDY | Blakes |

*Dec. 17, 18, 31*

| | |
|---|---|
| GLOUCESTER | Marr |
| BEDFORD added | Usher |
| HOSTESS | Mrs Macklin |

199

## 1747 DRURY LANE (cont.)
### Dec. 16 (cont.)

| | |
|---|---|
| MONTJOY | Lee |
| FLUELLEN | Macklin |
| PISTOL | Yates |
| GLOUCESTER* | Usher |
| BEDFORD* | Marr |
| WESTMORLAND | Simpson |
| GOWER | Bransby |
| SALISBURY | Burton |
| CAMBRIDGE | Raftor |
| SCROOP | Mozeen |
| GREY | Ray |
| GOVERNOR OF HARFLEUR | Taswell |
| MACMORRIS | Barrington |
| JAMY | Neale |
| NYM | Arthur |
| BARDOLPH | I. Sparks |
| BOY | Miss Yates |
| CHORUS | Garrick |
| ISABEL | Mrs Bennet |
| KATHARINE | Mrs Green |

[Genest (iv. 235) assigns GLOUCESTER to Marr, and BEDFORD to Usher. This is perhaps correct; the assignment in the bill might be a misprint. See Dec. 17.]

## 1748 DRURY LANE
### Oct. 13

| | |
|---|---|
| HENRY | Barry |
| ARCHBISHOP OF CANTERBURY | Bridges |
| EXETER | Berry |
| BISHOP OF ELY | Winstone |
| KING OF FRANCE | [W.] Mills |
| DAUPHIN | Havard |
| CONSTABLE | [L.] Sparks |
| BURGUNDY | Blakes |
| MONTJOY | Lee |
| GOWER | Bransby |
| MACMORRIS | James |
| JAMY | Neale |
| NYM | Taswell |
| BARDOLPH | Ray |
| BOY | Miss Yates |
| FLUELLEN | Yates |
| PISTOL | Woodward |

## 1748 DRURY LANE (cont.)
*Oct. 13 (cont.)*

| | |
|---|---|
| CHORUS | Garrick |
| ISABEL | Mrs Mills |
| KATHARINE | Mrs Green |
| HOSTESS | Miss Pitt |

## 1750 COVENT GARDEN
*Jan. 16*

| | |
|---|---|
| HENRY | Delane |
| EXETER | Ridout |
| ARCHBISHOP OF CANTERBURY | [L.] Sparks |
| WILLIAMS | Bransby |
| KING OF FRANCE | Gibson |
| DAUPHIN | Lee |
| CONSTABLE | Bridgwater |
| BURGUNDY | [Tho.] Lacy |
| FLUELLEN | Arthur |
| PISTOL | Dyer |
| CHORUS* | Ryan |
| ISABEL | Mrs Horton |
| KATHARINE | Mrs Barrington |
| HOSTESS | Mrs Bambridge |

*Feb. 19*
added
| | |
|---|---|
| MACMORRIS | Barrington |
| JAMY | Dunstall |

*Feb. 24*
added
| | |
|---|---|
| MONTJOY | Baker |
| MACMORRIS | Barrington |
| JAMY | Dunstall |

omitted
CHORUS

*Nov. 29*

| | |
|---|---|
| HENRY | Barry |
| EXETER | Ridout |
| ARCHBISHOP OF CANTERBURY | [L.] Sparks |
| SALISBURY | Bencraft |
| WESTMORLAND | [R.] Elrington |
| BISHOP OF ELY | Bransby |
| CAMBRIDGE* | Anderson |
| SCROOP | Cushing |
| GREY | Redman |
| KING OF FRANCE | Gibson |
| DAUPHIN | Usher |
| BURGUNDY | [Tho.] Lacy |
| CONSTABLE | Bridgwater |
| MONTJOY | Baker |
| FLUELLEN | Macklin |
| MACMORRIS | Barrington |
| JAMY | Dunstall |
| BARDOLPH | Marten |
| NYM | Stoppelaer |
| BOY | Miss Morrison |
| PISTOL | Dyer |

*Nov. 30*
added
| | |
|---|---|
| WILLIAMS | Bransby |
| GOWER | Anderson |
| CHORUS | Ryan |

omitted
CAMBRIDGE

## 1750 COVENT GARDEN (cont.)

*Nov. 29 (cont.)*

| ISABEL | Mrs Bambridge |
| KATHARINE | Miss Haughton |
| HOSTESS | Mrs Macklin |

# HENRY VI, PART I

No acting versions were published before 1750.

## 1738 COVENT GARDEN

*Mar. 13*

| TALBOT | Delane |
| GLOUCESTER | Ryan |
| YORK | Stephens |
| DAUPHIN | [A.] Hallam |
| REIGNIER | Bridgwater |
| HENRY | A. Ryan |
| BEDFORD | Johnson |
| BISHOP OF WINCHESTER | Chapman |
| SUFFOLK | Walker |
| EXETER | Aston |
| SOMERSET | Hale |
| WARWICK | Rosco |
| SALISBURY | Lyon |
| JOHN TALBOT | Stevens |
| VERNON | Bencraft |
| BASSET | Anderson |
| LUCY | Arthur |
| BURGUNDY | Ridout |
| ALENÇON | Salway |
| MARGARET | Mrs Ware |
| COUNTESS | Mrs James |
| JOAN LA PUCELLE | Mrs Hallam |

# HENRY VI, PART II

Adapted as HUMFREY, DUKE OF GLOSTER, by Ambrose Philips. In five acts.

1723   J. Roberts.

This version is a rewriting of the first three acts. Its general outline is not dissimilar to the original. About 35 lines, a few of them slightly altered, are Shakespeare's. They are: *I. i. 159–63; II. iv. 32–6; III. ii. 168–73;* and *III. iii. 8–29.*

See Genest, iii. 102–4; Odell, i. 248–50.

HENRY VI, PART II [as HUMFREY, DUKE OF GLOSTER]

## 1723 DRURY LANE
*Feb. 15, 16, 18, 19, 20, 21, 22, 23, 25*

| | |
|---|---|
| GLOUCESTER | Booth |
| YORK | Mills |
| SALISBURY | Thurmond |
| WARWICK | Williams |
| CARDINAL | Cibber |
| SUFFOLK | Watson |
| BUCKINGHAM | [W.] Mills |
| MARGARET | Mrs Oldfield |
| ELEANOR | Mrs Porter |

[The bills give neither the parts nor the actors' names. The above assignment is taken from the printed text.]

# HENRY VI, PART III

Adapted as AN HISTORICAL TRAGEDY OF THE CIVIL WARS BETWEEN THE HOUSES OF YORK AND LANCASTER IN THE REIGN OF KING HENRY THE SIXTH, by Theophilus Cibber. In five acts.

1724 W. Chetwood.

[The above is the title as given in the bill. In the title of the first edition, published about 1722 by J. Walthoe, the words 'BETWEEN THE HOUSES OF YORK AND LANCASTER' are omitted. Walthoe's edition gives no cast. The title of Chetwood's edition is merely 'KING HENRY VI'.]

Act I consists of *Henry VI, Part II, V. i. 56–end of play*, much expanded and altered, with the exception of *V. ii*, which is virtually verbatim. Here, and elsewhere throughout the play, Cibber occasionally borrows from Crowne's alteration, *The Misery of Civil War*, 1680.

Act II is *I. i. 44–end*, expanded; *I. ii. 22–54*, almost verbatim; a brief new scene, in which York bids farewell to Rutland; *I. iii* and *iv*, much altered.

Act III begins with *II. i*, slightly reduced. Then follow *II. iii* and *iv*, almost verbatim; *v. 1–54*, expanded, *125–end*, mostly rewritten; and *II. vi*, somewhat reduced. The act ends with *III. ii*, considerably altered.

Act IV begins with an expansion of Warwick's speeches in *III. iii. 186–98, 256–65*. This is followed by *IV. i. 87–114*, verbatim. Two new scenes follow: Margaret encourages Henry (she here speaks Clifford's lines in *II. ii. 19–42*), and the Prince of Wales speaks of his love for Lady Anne, Warwick's daughter. Then come *IV. iii. 1–58*, virtually verbatim; and *IV. iv*, in which the dialogue is between Lady Grey and a Gentleman, instead of between the Queen and Rivers.

Act V begins with *IV. vi*, much altered; *IV. vii. 1–6, 78–end*, verbatim; *IV. viii. 1–8*, slightly expanded. A new scene of about 150 lines follows: the Prince of Wales makes love to Lady Anne. Margaret then has Henry's speech before Harfleur in *Henry V, III. i. 7–33*. This is followed by *V. iv. 39–end*, slightly reduced. Then comes a brief new scene: Warwick inspires the Prince of Wales. The act ends with *V. ii. 1–28*; *V. v*; and *V. vii. 1–14, 37, 41–end*, all virtually verbatim.

See Genest, iii. 110–13; Odell, i. 250–2.

### HENRY VI, PART III
[*as altered by* T. CIBBER]

## 1723 DRURY LANE
*July 5*

| | |
|---|---|
| HENRY | Roberts |
| PRINCE OF WALES | [T.] Cibber |
| CLIFFORD | Boman |
| YOUNG CLIFFORD | [W.] Wilks |
| YORK | Savage |
| EDWARD | Oates |
| GEORGE | Parlour |
| RICHARD | Wilson |
| WARWICK | Bridgwater |
| MARGARET | Mrs Campbell |
| LADY GREY | Mrs Seal |
| LADY ELIZABETH | Mrs Davison |
| LADY ANNE | Mrs Brett |

[The bill gives neither the parts nor the actors' names. The above assignment is taken from the printed text.]

# HENRY VIII

'As it is acted . . . at the Theatres of London and Dublin'.

1734   Dublin: S. Powell.

This version follows the original throughout. No scenes are rearranged. There are numerous excisions, the most important being:
*The Prologue.*
*Act I. iii. 1–15.*
*Act II. i. 1–55, 137–end.*
*Act III. i. 1–14.*
*Act IV. i* entire, save for the dumb show of the Coronation.
*Act V. i. 1–55.*
*The Epilogue.*

No other acting versions were published before 1750.

## 1705 QUEEN'S
*May 3.* No parts assigned

[Bill in DC of May 1. Avery and Scouten (171) question this performance, since it occurred during the May-Fair, when the theatres were usually closed, and since the performance on Feb. 15, 1707 at this theatre was announced as 'Never Acted there before'.]

## 1707 QUEEN'S
*Feb. 15, 27*

| | |
|---|---|
| HENRY | Betterton |
| NORFOLK | Mills |
| BUCKINGHAM | Booth |

## 1707 QUEEN'S (cont.)
*Feb. 15, 27 (cont.)*

| | |
|---|---|
| WOLSEY | Verbruggen |
| SUFFOLK | Boman |
| SURVEYOR | Keene |
| SANDS | Bullock |
| GUILDFORD | Pack |
| SURREY | Cibber |
| CROMWELL | Husband |
| QUEEN KATHARINE | Mrs Barry |
| ANNE BULLEN | Mrs Bradshaw |

## 1708 DRURY LANE
*Mar. 11*

| | |
|---|---|
| HENRY | Betterton |

No other parts assigned

## 1709 DRURY LANE
*Jan. 26*

| | |
|---|---|
| HENRY | Betterton |
| NORFOLK | Mills |
| BUCKINGHAM | Booth |
| WOLSEY | Keene |
| SURREY | Powell |
| SANDS | Bullock |
| CRANMER | Cibber |
| GARDINER | Johnson |
| QUEEN KATHARINE | Mrs Knight |
| ANNE BULLEN | Mrs Bradshaw |

## 1716 DRURY LANE
*Nov. 19, 20, 21, 23, 24; Dec. 8, 26.* No parts assigned

## 1717 DRURY LANE
*Feb. 21; Mar. 4; May 24; Oct. 5; Dec. 2.* No parts assigned

## 1718 DRURY LANE
*Apr. 17; Sept. 30; Oct. 1.* No parts assigned

[Bill for Oct. 1 not in DC. See p. 16.]

## 1719 DRURY LANE
*Apr. 6; Nov. 28.* No parts assigned

## 1720 DRURY LANE
*Mar. 28; May 11.* No parts assigned

## 1721 DRURY LANE
*Jan. 12.* No parts assigned

*May 13; Oct. 31; Dec. 19*
| | |
|---|---|
| HENRY | Booth |
| QUEEN KATHARINE | Mrs Porter |

No other parts assigned

## 1722 DRURY LANE
*May 22*
| | |
|---|---|
| HENRY | Booth |
| WOLSEY | Cibber |
| BUCKINGHAM | Wilks |
| CRANMER | Mills |
| GARDINER | Johnson |
| SANDS | Miller |
| ? | Thurmond* |
| ? | Williams* |
| ? | Penkethman* |
| ? | Norris* |
| QUEEN KATHARINE | Mrs Porter |
| OLD LADY | Mrs Willis |

*Sept. 25*
omitted THURMOND, WILLIAMS, PENKETHMAN, NORRIS

[The only part assigned in the bill is QUEEN KATHARINE. It has otherwise, 'The Principal Parts by, etc.' The above assignment is based, where known, on bills of this play in later seasons. The only name not listed at all is Mrs Willis, but Davies (i. 422) says that she acted the OLD LADY for 'many years'.]

## 1723 DRURY LANE
*Jan. 1; May 28; Oct. 22*
| | |
|---|---|
| HENRY | Booth |
| WOLSEY | Cibber |
| BUCKINGHAM | Wilks |
| CRANMER | Mills |
| GARDINER | Johnson |
| SANDS | Miller |
| QUEEN KATHARINE | Mrs Porter |

[These bills correspond to that of May 22, 1722. The four names questioned thereunder are here omitted.]

## 1724 DRURY LANE
*Jan. 1.* No parts assigned

*Apr. 8*

| | |
|---|---|
| HENRY | Booth |
| WOLSEY | Cibber |
| BUCKINGHAM* | Wilks |
| CRANMER | Mills |
| GARDINER | Johnson |
| QUEEN KATHARINE | Mrs Porter |
| ANNE BULLEN* | Mrs Horton |

[The bill assigns the parts.]

*Oct. 22; Dec. 29*
omitted
    BUCKINGHAM, ANNE BULLEN

## 1725 DRURY LANE
*Apr. 13*

| | |
|---|---|
| HENRY | Booth |
| WOLSEY | Cibber |
| CRANMER | Mills |
| GARDINER | Johnson |

No other parts assigned

### LINCOLN'S INN FIELDS
*Oct. 30; Nov. 1; Dec. 14.* No parts assigned

## 1726 LINCOLN'S INN FIELDS
*Apr. 22*

| | |
|---|---|
| HENRY | Quin |
| WOLSEY | Boheme |
| BUCKINGHAM | Ryan |
| CROMWELL | Walker |
| QUEEN KATHARINE | Mrs Parker |
| ANNE BULLEN | Mrs Bullock |

*Oct. 31.* No parts assigned

## 1727 DRURY LANE
*Oct. 26, 27, 28, 31; Nov. 2, 3, 7, 8, 10, 11, 13, 15, 16, 17, 24*

| | |
|---|---|
| HENRY | Booth |
| WOLSEY | Cibber |
| CRANMER | Mills |
| GARDINER | Johnson |
| QUEEN KATHARINE | Mrs Porter |

[Genest (iii. 197) says that Wilks acted BUCKINGHAM. It is probable that he did, but his name appears in no bill. This revival included an elaborate pantomime representing the coronation of Anne Bullen. George II had been crowned on Oct. 11 of this year.]

# HENRY VIII

## 1727 LINCOLN'S INN FIELDS
*Feb. 2*

| | |
|---|---|
| HENRY | Quin |
| BUCKINGHAM | Ryan |
| WOLSEY | Boheme |
| QUEEN KATHARINE | Mrs Berriman |
| ANNE BULLEN | Mrs Bullock |

## 1728 DRURY LANE
*May 14; Sept. 28; Oct. 29*   *Dec. 11.* No parts assigned

| | |
|---|---|
| HENRY | Harper |
| WOLSEY | Cibber |
| CRANMER | Mills |
| GARDINER | Johnson |
| QUEEN KATHARINE | Mrs Porter |

## 1729 DRURY LANE
*Feb. 20.* No parts assigned

*Apr. 11*   *Apr. 18; Sept. 25; Dec. 18*
  omitted BUCKINGHAM, NORFOLK, SUFFOLK, SURREY, SANDS

| | |
|---|---|
| HENRY | Harper |
| WOLSEY | Cibber |
| CRANMER | Mills |
| GARDINER | Johnson |
| BUCKINGHAM* | Bridgwater |
| NORFOLK* | Wm. Mills |
| SUFFOLK* | Boman |
| SURREY* | Williams |
| SANDS* | Miller |
| QUEEN KATHARINE | Mrs Porter |
| ANNE BULLEN | Mrs Horton |

## 1730 DRURY LANE
*May 19; Sept. 22*   *Nov. 27.* No parts assigned

| | |
|---|---|
| HENRY | Harper |
| WOLSEY | Cibber |
| CRANMER | Mills |
| GARDINER | Johnson |
| QUEEN KATHARINE | Mrs Porter |
| ANNE BULLEN | Mrs Horton |

## 1731 DRURY LANE
*Feb. 1; Nov. 29.* No parts assigned

*May 4*   *May 18*
  added

| | |   | | |
|---|---|---|---|---|
| HENRY | Harper |   | BUCKINGHAM | Bridgwater |
| WOLSEY | Cibber |   | NORFOLK | W. Mills |
| CRANMER | Mills |   | | |

208

## HENRY VIII

### 1731 DRURY LANE (cont.)

*May 4 (cont.)*

| | |
|---|---|
| GARDINER | Johnson |
| QUEEN KATHARINE | Mrs Porter |
| ANNE BULLEN | Mrs Horton |

*May 18 (cont.)*

| | |
|---|---|
| SURREY | [T.] Cibber |
| CROMWELL | Watson |

*Nov. 13*

| | |
|---|---|
| SANDS | Griffin |
| QUEEN KATHARINE | Mrs Horton |
| ANNE BULLEN | Mrs Butler |

[The DP bill assigns no parts. The above assignment is from Genest (iii. 326), who adds 'rest as before'. Genest's source was a bill from the Field collection, now lost.]

### 1732 DRURY LANE

*Jan. 4; Apr. 11.* The bills for these performances are missing

*Nov. 13*

| | |
|---|---|
| HENRY | Harper |
| WOLSEY | Cibber |
| BUCKINGHAM | Bridgwater |
| SURREY | [T.] Cibber |
| CRANMER | Mills |
| GARDINER | Johnson |
| NORFOLK | Wm. Mills |
| SUFFOLK | Boman |
| LORD CHANCELLOR | Shepard |
| LORD CHAMBERLAIN | Berry |
| SANDS | Griffin |
| ABERGAVENNY | Fielding |
| CROMWELL | Watson |
| QUEEN KATHARINE | Mrs Horton |
| ANNE BULLEN | Mrs Butler |

### 1733 DRURY LANE

*Feb. 5*

| | |
|---|---|
| HENRY | Harper |
| WOLSEY | Cibber |
| BUCKINGHAM | Bridgwater |
| CRANMER | Mills |
| SURREY | [T.] Cibber |
| GARDINER | Johnson |
| SANDS | Griffin |
| ANNE BULLEN | Mrs Butler |
| QUEEN KATHARINE | Mrs Porter |

[The bill for this performance is missing. The above assignment is from Genest (iii. 368).]

HENRY VIII

### 1733 DRURY LANE (cont.)

*Mar. 26.* No parts assigned

*Nov. 14*

| | |
|---|---|
| HENRY | [W.] Giffard |
| BUCKINGHAM | Bridgwater |
| WOLSEY | Roberts |
| CRANMER | Paget |
| NORFOLK | Hewitt |
| SUFFOLK | Richardson |
| GARDINER | Aston |
| SURREY | Marshall |
| SANDS | Norris [Jr.] |
| CAMPEIUS | Mullart |
| LORD CHAMBERLAIN | Corey |
| CROMWELL | Raftor |
| SURVEYOR | Turbutt |
| QUEEN KATHARINE | Mrs Horton |
| ANNE BULLEN | Miss Holliday |

*Nov. 15, 19, 24; Dec. 27*

added
| | |
|---|---|
| BUTTS | Topham |
| OLD LADY | Mrs Willis |

### 1734 DRURY LANE

*Apr. 20*

| | |
|---|---|
| HENRY | Harper |
| WOLSEY | Mills |
| SURREY | [T.] Cibber |
| CRANMER | Milward |
| GARDINER | Johnson |
| BUCKINGHAM | Bridgwater |
| NORFOLK | Hewitt |
| SUFFOLK | Richardson |
| SANDS | Miller |
| BUTTS | Griffin |
| CROMWELL | Cross |
| CAMPEIUS | Mullart |
| SURVEYOR | Oates |
| LORD CHAMBERLAIN | Berry |
| QUEEN KATHARINE | Mrs Horton |
| ANNE BULLEN | Mrs Heron |

*Oct. 14, 15*

| | |
|---|---|
| HENRY* | Harper |
| WOLSEY | Mills |
| BUCKINGHAM | W. Mills |
| SURREY | [T.] Cibber |
| CRANMER | Milward |
| GARDINER | Johnson |
| SANDS | Miller |
| NORFOLK* | Hewitt |
| SUFFOLK* | Boman |

*Oct. 29*

omitted
NORFOLK, SUFFOLK, LORD CHAMBERLAIN, CAMPEIUS, ABERGAVENNY, CAPUCIUS, CROMWELL, BUTTS, SURVEYOR

*Dec. 27*

| | |
|---|---|
| HENRY | Quin |

210

## 1734 DRURY LANE (cont.)
*Oct. 14, 15 (cont.)*

| | |
|---|---|
| LORD CHAMBERLAIN* | Corey |
| CAMPEIUS* | Shepard |
| ABERGAVENNY* | Salway |
| CAPUCIUS* | Turbutt |
| CROMWELL* | Cross |
| BUTTS* | Griffin |
| SURVEYOR* | Oates |
| QUEEN KATHARINE | Mrs Thurmond |
| ANNE BULLEN | Miss Holliday |

## 1735 DRURY LANE
*Feb. 7*

| | |
|---|---|
| HENRY | Quin |
| WOLSEY | Mills |
| BUCKINGHAM | W. Mills |
| SURREY | [T.] Cibber |
| CRANMER | Milward |
| SANDS | Miller |
| GARDINER | Johnson |
| NORFOLK* | Hewitt |
| SUFFOLK | Boman |
| LORD CHAMBERLAIN* | Corey |
| CAMPEIUS | Shepard |
| ABERGAVENNY | Salway |
| CAPUCIUS* | Turbutt |
| CROMWELL | Cross |
| BUTTS* | Griffin |
| SURVEYOR* | Oates |
| QUEEN KATHARINE* | Mrs Porter |
| ANNE BULLEN | Miss Holliday |

*Oct. 27; Dec. 30*

| | |
|---|---|
| NORFOLK | Berry |
| LORD CHAMBERLAIN | Winstone |
| QUEEN KATHARINE | Mrs Thurmond |
| omitted | |
|     CAPUCIUS, BUTTS, SURVEYOR | |

## 1736 DRURY LANE
*May 5, 13, 31*

| | |
|---|---|
| HENRY | Quin |
| WOLSEY* | Mills |
| BUCKINGHAM | W. Mills |
| SURREY | [T.] Cibber |
| CRANMER* | Milward |
| GARDINER | Johnson |
| SANDS | Miller |
| NORFOLK* | Berry |
| SUFFOLK | Boman |
| LORD CHAMBERLAIN | Winstone |
| ABERGAVENNY* | Salway |
| CAMPEIUS | Shepard |

*Oct. 19*

| | |
|---|---|
| ABERGAVENNY | Este |

*Dec. 30*

| | |
|---|---|
| WOLSEY | Milward |
| CRANMER | Berry |
| NORFOLK | Este |
| ABERGAVENNY | Hill |

211

## 1736 DRURY LANE (cont.)
### May 5, &c. (cont.)

| | |
|---|---|
| CROMWELL | Cross |
| QUEEN KATHARINE | Mrs Thurmond |
| ANNE BULLEN | Miss Holliday |

## 1737 DRURY LANE
### Feb. 26

| | |
|---|---|
| HENRY | Quin |
| WOLSEY | Milward |
| BUCKINGHAM | W. Mills |
| SURREY | [T.] Cibber |
| CRANMER | Berry |
| SANDS | Miller |
| GARDINER | Johnson |
| QUEEN KATHARINE | Mrs Porter |
| ANNE BULLEN | Miss Holliday |

## 1738 DRURY LANE
### May 6, 22

| | |
|---|---|
| HENRY | Quin |
| WOLSEY | Milward |
| BUCKINGHAM | [W.] Mills |
| CRANMER | Wright |
| GARDINER | Johnson |
| SANDS* | Miller |
| NORFOLK | Havard |
| SUFFOLK | Boman |
| LORD CHAMBERLAIN | Winstone |
| ABERGAVENNY* | Hill |
| CAMPEIUS* | Turbutt |
| CROMWELL | Cross |
| QUEEN KATHARINE | Mrs Roberts |
| ANNE BULLEN* | Mrs Bennet |

[The DA bill also includes SURREY—[T.] Cibber, and assigns ANNE BULLEN to Mrs Mills.]

### Nov. 20; Dec. 22

| | |
|---|---|
| SANDS | Griffin |
| ABERGAVENNY | Ridout |
| CAMPEIUS | Shepard |
| ANNE BULLEN added | Mrs Mills |
| LOVELL | Ray |

## 1739 DRURY LANE
### Feb. 10. No parts assigned
### Apr. 27

| | |
|---|---|
| HENRY | Quin |
| WOLSEY | Milward |
| BUCKINGHAM | [W.] Mills |
| CRANMER | Wright |
| GARDINER | Johnson |
| SANDS | Griffin |
| LOVELL | Ray |

### May 17

| | |
|---|---|
| CAMPEIUS | Turbutt |

### Oct. 20

| | |
|---|---|
| CROMWELL | Cashell |

### Dec. 20

| | |
|---|---|
| CROMWELL | Cashell |
| ANNE BULLEN added | Mrs Pritchard |
| SURREY | Chapman |

## 1739 DRURY LANE (cont.)

*Apr. 27 (cont.)*

| | |
|---|---|
| NORFOLK | Havard |
| SUFFOLK | Ridout |
| LORD CHAMBERLAIN | Winstone |
| ABERGAVENNY | Raftor |
| CAMPEIUS* | Shepard |
| CROMWELL* | Cross |
| QUEEN KATHARINE | Mrs Roberts |
| ANNE BULLEN* | Mrs Mills |

## 1740 DRURY LANE

*Jan. 2*

| | |
|---|---|
| HENRY | Quin |
| WOLSEY | Milward |
| BUCKINGHAM | [W.] Mills |
| CRANMER | Wright |
| GARDINER | Johnson |
| SANDS* | Griffin |
| LOVELL* | Ray |
| NORFOLK* | Havard |
| SUFFOLK* | Ridout |
| LORD CHAMBERLAIN* | Winstone |
| ABERGAVENNY* | Raftor |
| CAMPEIUS* | Shepard |
| CROMWELL | Cashell |
| SURREY* | Chapman |
| QUEEN KATHARINE | Mrs Roberts |
| ANNE BULLEN* | Mrs Pritchard |

*Apr. 30*

| | |
|---|---|
| SURREY | [W.] Mills |
| omitted | |

SANDS, LOVELL, NORFOLK, SUFFOLK, LORD CHAMBERLAIN, ABERGAVENNY, CAMPEIUS

*May 30*

| | |
|---|---|
| SURREY | [W.] Mills |
| ANNE BULLEN | Mrs Mills |
| omitted | |

SANDS, LOVELL, NORFOLK, SUFFOLK, LORD CHAMBERLAIN, ABERGAVENNY, CAMPEIUS

[In these two performances Mills doubled BUCKINGHAM and SURREY.]

*Nov. 10*

| | |
|---|---|
| SANDS | Marten |

## 1741 DRURY LANE

*Apr. 18, 21*

| | |
|---|---|
| HENRY | Quin |
| WOLSEY | Milward |
| BUCKINGHAM | [W.] Mills |
| SURREY | Chapman |
| CRANMER | Wright |
| GARDINER | Johnson |
| SANDS | Marten |
| LOVELL | Ray |
| NORFOLK | Havard |
| SUFFOLK | Ridout |
| LORD CHAMBERLAIN | Winstone |
| ABERGAVENNY | Raftor |
| CAMPEIUS | Shepard |
| CROMWELL | Cashell |
| QUEEN KATHARINE | Mrs Roberts |
| ANNE BULLEN | Mrs Pritchard |

## HENRY VIII

### 1742 DRURY LANE
*Apr. 24*

| | |
|---|---|
| HENRY | Berry |
| WOLSEY | [W.] Mills |
| BUCKINGHAM | Winston |
| GARDINER | Johnson |
| CRANMER | Turbutt |
| NORFOLK | Havard |
| SUFFOLK | Ridout |
| LORD CHAMBERLAIN | Woodburn |
| CAMPEIUS | Shepard |
| ABERGAVENNY | Raftor |
| CROMWELL | Cross |
| SANDS | Neale |
| SURVEYOR | Taswell |
| LOVELL | Ray |
| OLD LADY | Mrs Egerton |
| ANNE BULLEN | Mrs Ridout |
| QUEEN KATHARINE | Mrs Roberts |

### 1744 COVENT GARDEN
*Jan. 24, 25, 26, 27; Feb. 4;*
*Apr. 12; May 10*

| | |
|---|---|
| HENRY | Quin |
| WOLSEY | Ryan |
| BUCKINGHAM | Hale |
| CRANMER | Bridgwater |
| NORFOLK | Cashell |
| SUFFOLK* | Stephens |
| SURREY | Gibson |
| GARDINER | Hippisley |
| LORD CHAMBERLAIN* | Ridout |
| CROMWELL* | Goodall |
| CAMPEIUS | Chapman |
| SANDS | Woodward |
| SURVEYOR* | Rosco |
| ABERGAVENNY | Anderson |
| BUTTS | Stoppelaer |
| ANNE BULLEN* | Mrs Stevens |
| OLD LADY | Mrs Mullart |
| QUEEN KATHARINE | Mrs Pritchard |

*Oct. 20*

| | |
|---|---|
| SUFFOLK | Arthur |

*Dec. 29*

| | |
|---|---|
| SUFFOLK | Arthur |
| LORD CHAMBERLAIN | Rosco |
| CROMWELL | Ridout |
| SURVEYOR | Marten |
| ANNE BULLEN | Mrs Horton |

### 1745 DRURY LANE
*Nov. 22*

| | |
|---|---|
| HENRY | Berry |
| WOLSEY | L. Sparks |
| BUCKINGHAM* | [W.] Mills |
| NORFOLK | Havard |
| SURREY | Marshall |

*Dec. 26*

| | |
|---|---|
| BUCKINGHAM | Winston |
| LORD CHAMBERLAIN | Woodburn |
| BRANDON | Bransby |

[Bransby doubled BRANDON and CAPUCIUS.]

214

## 1745 DRURY LANE (cont.)

*Nov. 22 (cont.)*

| | |
|---|---|
| CRANMER | Bridges |
| SUFFOLK | Blakes |
| SANDS | Neale |
| ABERGAVENNY | Mozeen |
| LORD CHAMBERLAIN* | Winstone |
| CROMWELL | Stevens |
| CAMPEIUS | Turbutt |
| GARDINER | Taswell |
| SURVEYOR | Goodfellow |
| LOVELL | Ray |
| BRANDON* | Woodburn |
| SERGEANT | Usher |
| BUTTS | I. Sparks |
| CAPUCIUS | Bransby |
| GUILDFORD | Marr |
| PORTER | Barrington |
| ANNE BULLEN | Mrs Ridout |
| OLD LADY | Mrs Cross |
| QUEEN KATHARINE | Mrs Giffard |

## COVENT GARDEN

*Mar. 5*

| | |
|---|---|
| HENRY | Quin |
| WOLSEY | Ryan |
| BUCKINGHAM | Hale |
| CRANMER | Bridgwater |
| NORFOLK | Cashell |
| SUFFOLK | Arthur |
| SURREY | Gibson |
| GARDINER | Hippisley |
| LORD CHAMBERLAIN | Rosco |
| CROMWELL | Ridout |
| CAMPEIUS | Chapman |
| SANDS | Woodward |
| SURVEYOR | Marten |
| ABERGAVENNY | Anderson |
| BUTTS | Stoppelaer |
| ANNE BULLEN* | Mrs Horton |
| OLD LADY* | Mrs Mullart |
| QUEEN KATHARINE | Mrs Pritchard |

*Apr. 16*

| | |
|---|---|
| ANNE BULLEN | Miss Bellamy |
| OLD LADY | Mrs James |

*May 4*

| | |
|---|---|
| OLD LADY | Mrs James |

## 1746 DRURY LANE

*Jan. 1*

| | |
|---|---|
| HENRY | Berry |
| WOLSEY | L. Sparks |

## 1746 DRURY LANE (cont.)

*Jan. 1 (cont.)*

| | |
|---|---|
| BUCKINGHAM | Winstone |
| NORFOLK | Havard |
| SURREY | Marshall |
| CRANMER | Bridges |
| SUFFOLK | Blakes |
| SANDS | Neale |
| ABERGAVENNY | Mozeen |
| LORD CHAMBERLAIN | Woodburn |
| CROMWELL | Stevens |
| CAMPEIUS | Goodfellow |
| GARDINER | Taswell |
| SURVEYOR | Goodfellow |
| LOVELL | Ray |
| BRANDON | Bransby |
| SERGEANT | Usher |
| BUTTS | I. Sparks |
| CAPUCIUS | Bransby |
| GUILDFORD | Marr |
| PORTER | Barrington |
| ANNE BULLEN | Mrs Bennet |
| OLD LADY | Mrs Cross |
| QUEEN KATHARINE | Mrs Giffard |

[Goodfellow doubled CAMPEIUS and the SURVEYOR; Bransby doubled BRANDON and CAPUCIUS.]

## COVENT GARDEN

*Dec. 29*

| | |
|---|---|
| HENRY | Quin |
| WOLSEY | Ryan |
| BUCKINGHAM | Havard |
| CRANMER | Bridgwater |
| NORFOLK | Cashell |
| SUFFOLK | Arthur |
| SURREY | Gibson |
| GARDINER | Hippisley |
| LORD CHAMBERLAIN | Rosco |
| CROMWELL | Ridout |
| CAMPEIUS | Chapman |
| SANDS | Woodward |
| SURVEYOR | Marten |
| ABERGAVENNY | Anderson |
| BUTTS | Stoppelaer |
| ANNE BULLEN | Mrs Horton |
| OLD LADY | Mrs James |
| QUEEN KATHARINE | Mrs Pritchard |

## 1747 COVENT GARDEN
*Mar. 3*

| | | | |
|---|---|---|---|
| HENRY | Quin | *May 14* | |
| WOLSEY | Ryan | NORFOLK | Cashell |
| BUCKINGHAM | Havard | | |
| CRANMER | Bridgwater | | |
| NORFOLK* | Davies | | |
| SUFFOLK | Arthur | | |
| SURREY | Gibson | | |
| GARDINER | Hippisley | | |
| LORD CHAMBERLAIN | Rosco | | |
| CROMWELL | Ridout | | |
| CAMPEIUS | Chapman | | |
| SANDS | Woodward | | |
| SURVEYOR | Marten | | |
| ABERGAVENNY | Anderson | | |
| BUTTS | Stoppelaer | | |
| ANNE BULLEN | Mrs Horton | | |
| OLD LADY | Mrs James | | |
| QUEEN KATHARINE | Mrs Pritchard | | |

## 1749 COVENT GARDEN
*May 4, 5*

| | |
|---|---|
| HENRY | Quin |
| WOLSEY | Ryan |
| BUCKINGHAM | Delane |
| NORFOLK | [L.] Sparks |
| CROMWELL | Ridout |
| SUFFOLK | Arthur |
| SURREY | Gibson |
| ABERGAVENNY | Oates |
| GUILDFORD | Cushing |
| LORD CHANCELLOR | Marten |
| CAMPEIUS | Dunstall |
| SANDS | Collins |
| LOVELL | Holtom |
| LORD CHAMBERLAIN | Anderson |
| BUTTS | Stoppelaer |
| CRANMER | Bridgwater |
| GARDINER | [T.] Cibber |
| PATIENCE | Miss Allen |
| ANNE BULLEN | Miss Bellamy |
| QUEEN KATHARINE | Mrs Woffington |

# HUMFREY, DUKE OF GLOSTER

Ambrose Philip's alteration of HENRY VI, PART II, q.v.

217

## THE HUMOURS OF SIR JOHN FALSTAFF

An anonymous alteration of HENRY IV, PART II, q.v.

## THE INJURED PRINCESS

Thomas D'Urfey's alteration of CYMBELINE, q.v. [This title was never used in the bills, which invariably announce the play as CYMBELINE]

## THE INVADER OF HIS COUNTRY

John Dennis's alteration of CORIOLANUS, q.v.

## THE JEW OF VENICE

George Granville, Baron Lansdowne's alteration of
THE MERCHANT OF VENICE, q.v.

## JULIUS CAESAR

'As it is now Acted By His Majesty's Company of Comedians at the Theatre-Royal.'

    1719  W. Chetwood.

This version follows the original verbatim; the excisions are trivial. Act II ends at *II. ii*, and Act III opens at *II. iii*. In Act V Casca has Titinius's speeches. The concluding scene, following Brutus's death (*V. v. 52–end*), is considerably reduced.

'As it is now Acted by his Majesty's Servants.'

    1729  J. Tonson.
    1734  J. Tonson.

Both these versions are identical with Chetwood's 1719 edition.

[An edition published in Dublin by James Dalton, 1750, 'As it is acted at the Theatre-Royal in Smock-Alley', is a reading edition, verbatim throughout.]

### 1704 LINCOLN'S INN FIELDS
*Feb. 14.* No parts assigned

### 1706 QUEEN'S
*Mar. 14.* No parts assigned

### 1707 QUEEN'S

*Jan. 14, 15*

| | | | |
|---|---|---|---|
| CAESAR | Booth | | |
| OCTAVIUS | Mills | | |
| ANTONY | Wilks | | |
| BRUTUS | Betterton | | |
| CASSIUS | Verbruggen | | |
| CASCA | Keene | | |
| LIGARIUS | Boman | | |
| DECIUS | Husband | | |

*Apr. 1*

| | |
|---|---|
| CALPHURNIA | Mrs Bradshaw |
| PORTIA | Mrs Boman |
| added | |
| 5TH CITIZEN | Cibber |

## 1707 QUEEN'S (cont.)

*Jan. 14, 15 (cont.)*

| | |
|---|---|
| CINNA THE POET | Bowen |
| 1ST CITIZEN | Johnson |
| 2ND CITIZEN | Bullock |
| 3RD CITIZEN | Norris |
| 4TH CITIZEN | Cross |
| CALPHURNIA* | Mrs Barry |
| PORTIA* | Mrs Bracegirdle |

[Genest (ii. 363) has 'Cinna (probably the Poet, not the Conspirator)'. This is correct; DC has as above.]

## 1709 DRURY LANE

*Dec. 22*

| | |
|---|---|
| BRUTUS | Booth |
| CASSIUS | Powell |

No other parts assigned

## 1710 DRURY LANE

*Apr. 22*

| | |
|---|---|
| CAESAR | Keene |
| BRUTUS | Booth |
| CASSIUS | Powell |
| CALPHURNIA | Mrs Knight |
| PORTIA | Mrs Bradshaw |

## 1712 DRURY LANE

*Apr. 5, 8, 24; Nov. 15; Dec. 11.* No parts assigned

## 1713 DRURY LANE

*Jan. 20; Sept. 26; Oct. 27.* No parts assigned

*Mar. 16; Apr. 6; May 4*

| | |
|---|---|
| CAESAR | Mills |
| ANTONY | Wilks |
| BRUTUS | Booth |
| CASSIUS | Powell |
| CASCA | Keene |
| 1ST CITIZEN | Johnson |
| 2ND CITIZEN | Penkethman |
| 3RD CITIZEN | Bullock |
| 4TH CITIZEN | Norris |
| 5TH CITIZEN | Cross |
| 6TH CITIZEN | [F.] Leigh |

## 1714 DRURY LANE
*Jan. 23; Apr. 12; Oct. 9.* No parts assigned

[Bill for Apr. 12 in DC of Apr. 10.]

## 1715 DRURY LANE
*Jan. 24*                          *May 13; Nov. 24.* No parts assigned
    CASSIUS    Elrington
    CAESAR    Mills
    BRUTUS    Booth
    ANTONY    Wilks
    PORTIA    Mrs Porter

## 1716 DRURY LANE
*Mar. 22; May 24; Oct. 20.* No parts assigned

### LINCOLN'S INN FIELDS
*Oct. 27; Nov. 8*
    BRUTUS    Keene
    CASSIUS    Elrington
No other parts assigned

## 1717 DRURY LANE
*Apr. 27; Nov. 16.* No parts assigned

### LINCOLN'S INN FIELDS
*Jan. 3; Apr. 4; May 3*                    *Nov. 7.* No parts assigned
    BRUTUS    Keene
    CASSIUS    Elrington
No other parts assigned

## 1718 DRURY LANE
*Nov. 13*
    CAESAR    Mills
    BRUTUS    Booth
    ANTONY    Wilks
    PORTIA    Mrs Porter
    CALPHURNIA    Mrs Horton

## JULIUS CAESAR

## 1718 LINCOLN'S INN FIELDS
*Mar. 1*

| CASSIUS | Ryan |
| CAESAR | [J.] Leigh |
| BRUTUS | Keene |
| ANTONY | Quin |
| CASCA | Corey |
| CALPHURNIA | Mrs Knight |
| PORTIA | Mrs Rogers |

*Mar. 17.* No parts assigned

*Nov. 1*

| BRUTUS | Quin |
| CASSIUS | Ryan |

No other parts assigned

*Nov. 25*

| BRUTUS | Quin |
| CASSIUS | Ryan |
| ANTONY | [J.] Leigh |
| CAESAR | Ogden |
| OCTAVIUS | Diggs |
| CALPHURNIA | Mrs Knight |
| PORTIA | Mrs Bullock |

## 1719 DRURY LANE
*Jan. 28*

| CAESAR | Mills |
| BRUTUS | Booth |
| CASSIUS | Elrington |
| ANTONY | Wilks |
| PORTIA | Mrs Porter |
| CALPHURNIA | Mrs Horton |

*Apr. 24.* No parts assigned

[In the acting version published by Chetwood in 1719 the cast is the same as that of this performance, with the following additions:

| OCTAVIUS | Walker |
| CASCA | Bickerstaff |
| FLAVIUS | Boman |
| DECIUS | Shepard |
| METELLUS | W. Wilks |
| MESSALA | W. Mills |
| CINNA | Wilson |
| PINDARUS | Oates |
| SOOTHSAYER | Williams |
| TREBONIUS | Boman Jr. |
| ANTONY'S SERVANT | Ray |
| IST CITIZEN | Johnson |

## 1719 DRURY LANE (cont.)
*Jan. 28 (cont.)*
    2ND CITIZEN    Miller
    3RD CITIZEN    Norris
    4TH CITIZEN    Cross
    LUCIUS    Norris Jr.]

## LINCOLN'S INN FIELDS
*Apr. 25.* No parts assigned
*Nov. 19*
    BRUTUS    Quin
    CASSIUS    Ryan
    CAESAR    Ogden
    OCTAVIUS    Diggs
    ANTONY    [J.] Leigh
    CASCA    Harper
    TREBONIUS    Smith
    LIGARIUS    Boheme
    DECIUS    Ch. Bullock
    CALPHURNIA    Mrs Giffard
    PORTIA    Mrs Forrester

## 1720 LINCOLN'S INN FIELDS
*Apr. 9*
    CAESAR*    Ogden
    BRUTUS    Quin
    CASSIUS    Ryan
    ANTONY    [J.] Leigh
    No other parts assigned

*Nov. 1*
    CAESAR    Boheme
    added
        OCTAVIUS    Diggs
        CASCA    Ogden
        CALPHURNIA    Mrs Giffard
        PORTIA    Mrs Spiller

## 1721 DRURY LANE
*Jan. 26; Mar. 4.* No parts assigned
*Apr. 26*
    CAESAR    Thurmond
    BRUTUS    Booth
    CASSIUS    Mills
    ANTONY    Wilks
    OCTAVIUS*    Walker
    1ST CITIZEN    Johnson
    2ND CITIZEN    Norris
    3RD CITIZEN    Miller
    CALPHURNIA    Mrs Horton
    PORTIA    Mrs Thurmond

*Oct. 3*
    OCTAVIUS    Williams

## 1721 LINCOLN'S INN FIELDS
*May 25*

| | |
|---|---|
| CAESAR | Boheme |
| BRUTUS | Quin |
| CASSIUS | Ryan |
| ANTONY | [J.] Leigh |
| CASCA | Ogden |
| 1ST CITIZEN | Bullock [Sr.] |
| 2ND CITIZEN | Hall |
| 3RD CITIZEN | Griffin |
| 4TH CITIZEN | H. Bullock |
| CALPHURNIA | Mrs Giffard |
| PORTIA | Mrs Seymour |

## 1722 DRURY LANE
*Jan. 16; Oct. 19*

| | |
|---|---|
| CAESAR | Thurmond |
| BRUTUS | Booth |
| CASSIUS | Mills |
| ANTONY | Wilks |
| OCTAVIUS | Williams |
| 1ST CITIZEN | Johnson |
| 2ND CITIZEN | Norris |
| 3RD CITIZEN | Miller |
| 4TH CITIZEN | Harper |
| CALPHURNIA | Mrs Horton |
| PORTIA | Mrs Porter |

## LINCOLN'S INN FIELDS
*Oct. 18*

| | |
|---|---|
| CAESAR | [J.] Leigh |
| BRUTUS | Quin |
| CASSIUS | Boheme |
| ANTONY | Walker |
| CASCA | Ogden |
| 1ST CITIZEN | Spiller |
| 2ND CITIZEN | Bullock Sr. |
| 3RD CITIZEN | Hall |
| 4TH CITIZEN | Morgan |
| 5TH CITIZEN | Phipps |
| CALPHURNIA | Mrs Seymour |
| PORTIA | Mrs Bullock |

## JULIUS CAESAR

### 1723 DRURY LANE
*Feb. 13*

|  |  |
|---|---|
| CAESAR | Thurmond |
| BRUTUS | Booth |
| CASSIUS | Mills |
| ANTONY | Wilks |
| OCTAVIUS | Williams |
| 1ST CITIZEN | Johnson |
| 2ND CITIZEN | Norris |
| 3RD CITIZEN | Miller |
| 4TH CITIZEN | Harper |
| PORTIA* | Mrs Porter |

*May 9.* No parts assigned
*Sept. 24*

|  |  |
|---|---|
| PORTIA added | Mrs Thurmond |
| CALPHURNIA | Mrs Horton |

### LINCOLN'S INN FIELDS
*Jan. 10*

|  |  |
|---|---|
| BRUTUS | Quin |
| CASSIUS | Boheme |
| CAESAR | [J.] Leigh |
| ANTONY | Walker |
| CASCA* | Hulett |
| 1ST CITIZEN | Bullock Sr. |
| 2ND CITIZEN | Hippisley |
| 3RD CITIZEN | Hall |
| 4TH CITIZEN | Morgan |
| 5TH CITIZEN | H. Bullock |
| 6TH CITIZEN* | Phipps |
| CALPHURNIA* | Mrs Seymour |
| PORTIA* | Mrs Bullock |

[In the bill the CITIZENS are called the COMIC PARTS.]

*May 14*

|  |  |
|---|---|
| CALPHURNIA | Mrs Boheme [i.e. formerly Mrs Seymour] |

omitted
   CASCA, 6TH CITIZEN

*Oct. 31; Dec. 31*

|  |  |
|---|---|
| 6TH CITIZEN | Spiller |
| CALPHURNIA | Mrs Knight |
| PORTIA | Mrs Spicer [first appearance, Oct. 31, on the stage] |

omitted
   CASCA

### 1724 DRURY LANE
*Jan. 11; Sept. 19*

|  |  |
|---|---|
| CAESAR | Thurmond |
| BRUTUS | Booth |
| CASSIUS | Mills |
| ANTONY | Wilks |
| OCTAVIUS | Williams |
| 1ST CITIZEN | Johnson |
| 2ND CITIZEN | Norris |
| 3RD CITIZEN | Miller |
| 4TH CITIZEN | Harper |
| PORTIA | Mrs Thurmond |
| CALPHURNIA | Mrs Horton |

## 1725 DRURY LANE

*Jan. 2*

| | |
|---|---|
| CAESAR | Thurmond |
| BRUTUS | Booth |
| CASSIUS | Mills |
| ANTONY | Wilks |
| OCTAVIUS | Williams |
| 1ST CITIZEN* | Johnson |
| 2ND CITIZEN* | Norris |
| 3RD CITIZEN* | Miller |
| 4TH CITIZEN* | Harper |
| PORTIA | Mrs Thurmond |
| CALPHURNIA | Mrs Horton |

*Apr. 3.* No parts assigned

*June 18; Sept. 30*
added
   CASCA    Corey
omitted
   CITIZENS

## LINCOLN'S INN FIELDS

*Mar. 11; May 22*

| | |
|---|---|
| CAESAR | Ryan |
| BRUTUS | Quin |
| CASSIUS | Boheme |
| ANTONY | Walker |
| 1ST CITIZEN | Bullock Sr. |
| 2ND CITIZEN | Hippisley |
| 3RD CITIZEN | Spiller |
| 4TH CITIZEN | Hall |
| 5TH CITIZEN | Morgan |
| CALPHURNIA* | Mrs Egleton |
| PORTIA | Mrs Bullock |

*Dec. 15*

| | |
|---|---|
| CALPHURNIA | Mrs Harold |

## 1726 DRURY LANE

*Jan. 26; Apr. 16*

| | |
|---|---|
| CAESAR | Thurmond |
| BRUTUS | Booth |
| CASSIUS | Mills |
| ANTONY | Wilks |
| OCTAVIUS | Williams |
| CASCA | Corey |
| 1ST CITIZEN | Johnson |
| 2ND CITIZEN | Miller |
| 3RD CITIZEN | Harper |
| 4TH CITIZEN | Norris |
| CALPHURNIA | Mrs Horton |
| PORTIA | Mrs Thurmond |

## 1726 LINCOLN'S INN FIELDS
*Nov. 11*

| | |
|---|---|
| CAESAR | Ryan |
| BRUTUS | Quin |
| CASSIUS | Boheme |
| ANTONY | Walker |
| 1ST CITIZEN | Bullock [Sr.] |
| 2ND CITIZEN | Hippisley |
| 3RD CITIZEN | Spiller |
| 4TH CITIZEN | Hall |
| 5TH CITIZEN | Morgan |
| CALPHURNIA | Mrs Egleton |
| PORTIA | Mrs Bullock |

## 1727 DRURY LANE
*Apr. 5; May 31.* No parts assigned

*Oct. 3*

| | |
|---|---|
| CAESAR | Williams |
| BRUTUS | Booth |
| CASSIUS | Mills |
| ANTONY | Wilks |
| OCTAVIUS | Watson |
| 1ST CITIZEN | Johnson |
| 2ND CITIZEN | Miller |
| 3RD CITIZEN | Harper |
| 4TH CITIZEN | Norris |
| CALPHURNIA | Mrs Butler |
| PORTIA | Mrs Thurmond |

## 1728 DRURY LANE
*Jan. 4*

| | |
|---|---|
| CAESAR | Williams |
| BRUTUS | Booth |
| CASSIUS | Mills |
| ANTONY | Wilks |
| OCTAVIUS | Watson |
| DECIUS | Bridgwater |
| MESSALA | Wm. Mills |
| CASCA | Corey |
| 1ST CITIZEN | Johnson |
| 2ND CITIZEN | Miller |
| 3RD CITIZEN | Harper |
| 4TH CITIZEN | Norris |
| CALPHURNIA | Mrs Butler |
| PORTIA | Mrs Thurmond |

## JULIUS CAESAR

### 1728 LINCOLN'S INN FIELDS
*Nov. 20*

| | |
|---|---|
| CAESAR | Ryan |
| BRUTUS | Quin |
| CASSIUS | Boheme |
| ANTONY | Walker |
| OCTAVIUS | Milward |
| 1ST CITIZEN | Bullock [Sr.] |
| 2ND CITIZEN | Hippisley |
| 3RD CITIZEN | Spiller |
| 4TH CITIZEN | Hall |
| 5TH CITIZEN | Morgan |
| CALPHURNIA | Mrs Buchanan |
| PORTIA | Mrs Bullock |

### 1729 LINCOLN'S INN FIELDS
*Nov. 13*

| | |
|---|---|
| CAESAR | Ryan |
| BRUTUS | Quin |
| CASSIUS | Boheme |
| ANTONY | Walker |
| OCTAVIUS | Milward |
| 1ST CITIZEN | Bullock [Sr.] |
| 2ND CITIZEN | Hippisley |
| 3RD CITIZEN | Hall |
| 4TH CITIZEN | Morgan |
| 5TH CITIZEN | H. Bullock |
| CALPHURNIA | Mrs Buchanan |
| PORTIA | Mrs Bullock |

### 1732 GOODMAN'S FIELDS
*Dec. 1*

| | |
|---|---|
| CAESAR | Huddy |
| OCTAVIUS | Rosco |
| ANTONY | Giffard |
| BRUTUS | Delane |
| CASCA | W. Giffard |
| TREBONIUS | Smith |
| LIGARIUS | Jenkins |
| DECIUS | Bardin |
| METELLUS | Winstone |
| CINNA | [R.] Williams |
| LUCIUS | Master Huddy |
| SOOTHSAYER | James |
| 1ST CITIZEN | Morgan |
| 2ND CITIZEN | Norris [Jr.] |
| 3RD CITIZEN | Collett |

*Dec. 2*
added

| | |
|---|---|
| CASSIUS | Hulett |

*Dec. 4, 5, 6, 7, 8, 9, 11, 12, 13, 14, 26*
added

| | |
|---|---|
| CASSIUS | Hulett |
| 8TH CITIZEN | [R.] Wetherilt |
| 9TH CITIZEN | Lyon |

## 1732 GOODMAN'S FIELDS (cont.)

*Dec. 1 (cont.)*

| | |
|---|---|
| 4TH CITIZEN | [W.] Bullock [Jr.] |
| 5TH CITIZEN | Wetherilt Sr. |
| 6TH CITIZEN | Pearce |
| 7TH CITIZEN | Stoppelaer |
| CALPHURNIA | Mrs Williamson |
| PORTIA | Mrs Thurmond |

## 1733 GOODMAN'S FIELDS

*Jan. 3, 22*

| | |
|---|---|
| CAESAR | Huddy |
| OCTAVIUS | Rosco |
| ANTONY | Giffard |
| BRUTUS | Delane |
| CASSIUS | Hulett |
| CASCA | W. Giffard |
| TREBONIUS* | Smith |
| LIGARIUS | Jenkins |
| DECIUS | Bardin |
| METELLUS | Winstone |
| CINNA | [R.] Williams |
| LUCIUS* | Master Huddy |
| SOOTHSAYER | James |
| 1ST CITIZEN | Morgan |
| 2ND CITIZEN | Norris [Jr.] |
| 3RD CITIZEN* | Collett |
| 4TH CITIZEN* | [W.] Bullock [Jr.] |
| 5TH CITIZEN | Wetherilt Sr. |
| 6TH CITIZEN | Pearce |
| 7TH CITIZEN | Stoppelaer |
| 8TH CITIZEN | [R.] Wetherilt |
| 9TH CITIZEN | Lyon |
| CALPHURNIA* | Mrs Williamson |
| PORTIA | Mrs Thurmond |

*Sept. 10*

| | |
|---|---|
| CAESAR | Huddy |
| BRUTUS | Delane |
| CASSIUS | Hulett |
| ANTONY | Giffard |
| OCTAVIUS* | A Gentleman [unidentified; first appearance on the stage] |
| CASCA | Lyon |
| DECIUS* | Rosco |
| TREBONIUS | Havard |

*Apr. 6*

| | |
|---|---|
| TREBONIUS | Evans |
| LUCIUS | Master Giffard |
| CALPHURNIA | Mrs M. Giffard [first appearance on the stage] |

omitted
    4TH CITIZEN

*May 15*

| | |
|---|---|
| TREBONIUS | Evans |
| LUCIUS | Master Giffard |

omitted
    3RD CITIZEN

*Oct. 10*

| | |
|---|---|
| OCTAVIUS | Rosco |
| DECIUS | Bardin |

omitted
    2ND CITIZEN

## 1733 GOODMAN'S FIELDS (cont.)
*Sept. 10 (cont.)*

| | |
|---|---|
| METELLUS | R. Wetherilt |
| LIGARIUS | Jenkins |
| CINNA | [R.] Williams |
| SOOTHSAYER | James |
| LUCIUS | Master Giffard |
| 1ST CITIZEN | Morgan |
| 2ND CITIZEN* | Norris [Jr.] |
| 3RD CITIZEN | Collett |
| 4TH CITIZEN | Penkethman [Jr.] |
| 5TH CITIZEN | Wetherilt Sr. |
| 6TH CITIZEN | Pearce |
| 7TH CITIZEN | Stoppelaer |
| CALPHURNIA | Mrs Haughton |
| PORTIA | Mrs Thurmond |

## 1734 DRURY LANE
*Nov. 8, 9, 11, 12, 13; Dec. 4*

| | |
|---|---|
| CAESAR | Wm. Mills |
| BRUTUS | Quin |
| CASSIUS | Mills |
| ANTONY | Milward |
| CASCA | [T.] Cibber |
| OCTAVIUS | Salway |
| DECIUS | Hewitt |
| MESSALA | Corey |
| ARTEMIDORUS | Shepard |
| FLAVIUS | Berry |
| METELLUS | Turbutt |
| CINNA | Este |
| POPILIUS | Woodburn |
| TREBONIUS | Winstone |
| LEPIDUS | Cole |
| LIGARIUS | Boman |
| LUCILIUS | Leigh [Jr.] |
| PINDARUS | Oates |
| CAESAR'S SERVANT | Raftor |
| ANTONY'S SERVANT | Cross |
| LUCIUS | Master Arne |
| 1ST CITIZEN | Johnson |
| 2ND CITIZEN | Miller |
| 3RD CITIZEN | Harper |
| 4TH CITIZEN | Griffin |
| 5TH CITIZEN | Macklin |
| | and others |
| CALPHURNIA | Mrs Butler |
| PORTIA | Mrs Thurmond |

JULIUS CAESAR

## 1734 GOODMAN'S FIELDS
*Jan. 21*

| | |
|---|---|
| CAESAR | Huddy |
| OCTAVIUS | Rosco |
| ANTONY | Giffard |
| BRUTUS | Delane |
| CASSIUS | Hulett |
| CASCA | W. Giffard |
| TREBONIUS | Havard |
| LIGARIUS | Jenkins |
| DECIUS | Bardin |
| METELLUS | Moore |
| CINNA | Ayres |
| LUCIUS | Master Giffard |
| SOOTHSAYER | Harbin |
| 1ST CITIZEN | Penkethman [Jr.] |
| 2ND CITIZEN | Lyon |
| 3RD CITIZEN | Wetherilt [Sr.] |
| 4TH CITIZEN | Monlass |
| CALPHURNIA | Mrs Haughton |
| PORTIA* | Mrs Thurmond |

*Feb. 14; Apr. 1.* No parts assigned
*Sept. 20*

| | |
|---|---|
| PORTIA added | Mrs Roberts |
| 5TH CITIZEN | Norris [Jr.] |

## 1735 DRURY LANE
*Jan. 18*

| | |
|---|---|
| CAESAR | W. Mills |
| BRUTUS | Quin |
| CASSIUS | Mills |
| ANTONY | Milward |
| CASCA | [T.] Cibber |
| OCTAVIUS | Salway |
| DECIUS | Hewitt |
| MESSALA | Corey |
| ARTEMIDORUS | Shepard |
| FLAVIUS | Berry |
| METELLUS | Turbutt |
| CINNA | Este |
| POPILIUS | Woodburn |
| TREBONIUS | Winston |
| LEPIDUS | Cole |
| LIGARIUS | Boman |
| LUCILIUS | Leigh [Jr.] |
| PINDARUS | Oates |
| CAESAR'S SERVANT | Raftor |
| ANTONY'S SERVANT | Cross |
| LUCIUS | Master Arne |
| 1ST CITIZEN | Johnson |
| 2ND CITIZEN | Miller |
| 3RD CITIZEN | Harper |

230

## JULIUS CAESAR

**1735 DRURY LANE** (*cont.*)

*Jan. 18* (*cont.*)

| | |
|---|---|
| 4TH CITIZEN | Griffin |
| 5TH CITIZEN | Macklin |
| | and others |
| CALPHURNIA | Mrs Butler |
| PORTIA | Mrs Thurmond |

*Sept. 1*

| | |
|---|---|
| CAESAR | W. Mills |
| OCTAVIUS* | Salway |
| BRUTUS | Quin |
| CASSIUS | Mills |
| ANTONY | Milward |
| CASCA | [T.] Cibber |
| 1ST CITIZEN | Johnson |
| 2ND CITIZEN | Miller |
| 3RD CITIZEN | Harper |
| 4TH CITIZEN | Griffin |
| CALPHURNIA* | Mrs Cantrell |
| PORTIA | Mrs Thurmond |

*Oct. 1*

| | |
|---|---|
| CALPHURNIA | Mrs Butler |

*Dec. 9*

| | |
|---|---|
| CALPHURNIA | Mrs Butler |
| omitted | |
| OCTAVIUS | |

## COVENT GARDEN

*Nov. 22*

| | |
|---|---|
| CAESAR | Bridgwater |
| BRUTUS | Delane |
| CASSIUS | Ryan |
| ANTONY | Walker |
| OCTAVIUS | A. Hallam |
| CASCA | Stephens |
| TREBONIUS | Marshall |
| CINNA | Houghton |
| DECIUS | Paget |
| METELLUS | Ridout |
| LIGARIUS | Aston |
| SOOTHSAYER | Hind |
| 1ST CITIZEN | Hippisley |
| 2ND CITIZEN | Chapman |
| 3RD CITIZEN | Neale |
| 4TH CITIZEN | Mullart |
| 5TH CITIZEN | Smith |
| 6TH CITIZEN | [W.] Hallam |
| | and others |
| CALPHURNIA | Mrs Hallam |
| PORTIA | Mrs Buchanan |

## 1735 GOODMAN'S FIELDS
*Mar. 13*

| | |
|---|---|
| CAESAR | Huddy |
| ANTONY | Giffard |
| CASSIUS | Hulett |
| CASCA | W. Giffard |
| DECIUS | Bardin |
| OCTAVIUS | Rosco |
| TREBONIUS | Havard |
| SOOTHSAYER | Harbin |
| BRUTUS | Delane |
| 1ST CITIZEN | Penkethman [Jr.] |
| 2ND CITIZEN | Lyon |
| 3RD CITIZEN | Wetherilt [Sr.] |
| 4TH CITIZEN | Norris [Jr.] |
| 5TH CITIZEN | Monlass |
| CALPHURNIA | Mrs Haughton |
| PORTIA | Mrs Roberts |

## 1736 DRURY LANE
*Apr. 16; May 19, 29; Sept. 21; Oct. 28*

| | |
|---|---|
| CAESAR | W. Mills |
| BRUTUS | Quin |
| CASSIUS | Mills |
| ANTONY | Milward |
| CASCA | [T.] Cibber |
| 1ST CITIZEN | Johnson |
| 2ND CITIZEN | Miller |
| 3RD CITIZEN | Harper |
| 4TH CITIZEN | Griffin |
| CALPHURNIA | Mrs Butler |
| PORTIA | Mrs Thurmond |

## 1737 DRURY LANE
*Jan. 24; Feb. 17; Apr. 28*

| | |
|---|---|
| CAESAR | Berry |
| BRUTUS | Quin |
| CASSIUS | Milward |
| ANTONY | W. Mills |
| CASCA | [T.] Cibber |
| 1ST CITIZEN | Johnson |
| 2ND CITIZEN | Miller |
| 3RD CITIZEN | Harper |
| 4TH CITIZEN | Griffin |
| CALPHURNIA | Mrs Butler |
| PORTIA | Mrs Thurmond |

## 1738 DRURY LANE
*Jan. 19*

| | |
|---|---|
| CAESAR | [W.] Mills |
| BRUTUS | Quin |
| CASSIUS | Milward |
| OCTAVIUS* | Hill |
| ANTONY | Wright |
| CASCA* | [T.] Cibber |
| 1ST CITIZEN | Johnson |
| 2ND CITIZEN* | Miller |
| 3RD CITIZEN* | Harper |
| 4TH CITIZEN | Griffin |
| CALPHURNIA | Mrs Butler |
| PORTIA* | Mrs Furnival |

*Feb. 8*

| | |
|---|---|
| PORTIA | Mrs Roberts |

*Apr. 28*

| | |
|---|---|
| CASCA | Winstone |
| PORTIA | Mrs Porter |
| added | |
| 5TH CITIZEN | Macklin |

*Sept. 21*

| | |
|---|---|
| 2ND CITIZEN | Macklin |
| PORTIA | Mrs Roberts |

*Nov. 29; Dec. 12*

| | |
|---|---|
| OCTAVIUS | Havard |
| CASCA | Winstone |
| 2ND CITIZEN | Macklin |
| 3RD CITIZEN | Woodward |
| PORTIA | Mrs Roberts |
| added | |
| TREBONIUS | Ridout |
| ARTEMIDORUS | Shepard |

[On Nov. 29 PORTIA is omitted.]

## 1739 DRURY LANE
*Mar. 29*

| | |
|---|---|
| CAESAR | [W.] Mills |
| BRUTUS | Quin |
| CASSIUS | Milward |
| ANTONY | Wright |
| OCTAVIUS | Havard |
| CASCA* | Winstone |
| TREBONIUS | Ridout |
| ARTEMIDORUS | Shepard |
| 1ST CITIZEN | Johnson |
| 2ND CITIZEN | Griffin |
| 3RD CITIZEN | Macklin |
| 4TH CITIZEN | Woodward |
| 5TH CITIZEN | Reed |
| CALPHURNIA | Mrs Butler |
| PORTIA | Mrs Roberts |

*Oct. 10*

| | |
|---|---|
| added | |
| 6TH CITIZEN | Yates |

*Dec. 11*

| | |
|---|---|
| CASCA | Berry |
| added | |
| MESSALA | Cashell |
| METELLUS | Turbutt |
| 6TH CITIZEN | Yates |

## 1740 DRURY LANE
*Jan. 17*

| | |
|---|---|
| CAESAR | [W.] Mills |
| BRUTUS | Quin |
| CASSIUS | Milward |
| ANTONY | Wright |
| OCTAVIUS* | Havard |
| CASCA | Berry |

*Mar. 13*

| | |
|---|---|
| added | |
| DECIUS | Cashell |
| 7TH CITIZEN | Ray |
| omitted | |
| TREBONIUS, ARTEMIDORUS, MESSALA, METELLUS, CINNA, 2ND, 5TH, 6TH CITIZENS | |

## 1740 DRURY LANE (cont.)

*Jan. 17 (cont.)*

| | |
|---|---|
| TREBONIUS* | Winstone |
| ARTEMIDORUS* | Shepard |
| MESSALA* | Cashell |
| METELLUS* | Turbutt |
| CINNA* | Ridout |
| 1ST CITIZEN | Johnson |
| 2ND CITIZEN* | Griffin |
| 3RD CITIZEN | Macklin |
| 4TH CITIZEN* | Woodward |
| 5TH CITIZEN* | Yates |
| 6TH CITIZEN* | Reed |
| CALPHURNIA | Mrs Butler |
| PORTIA | Mrs Roberts |

*Oct. 4*

| | |
|---|---|
| 2ND CITIZEN | Chapman |
| 6TH CITIZEN added | Marten |
| LIGARIUS | Taswell |

*Dec. 19*

| | |
|---|---|
| OCTAVIUS | Woodward |
| 2ND CITIZEN | Chapman |
| 4TH CITIZEN | Hough |
| 5TH CITIZEN | Vaughan |
| 6TH CITIZEN added | Marten |
| DECIUS | Cashell |
| LIGARIUS | Taswell |
| MESSALA omitted | |

[The playhouse bill for this performance is in FSL.]

## 1741 DRURY LANE

*Feb. 24*

| | |
|---|---|
| CAESAR | [W.] Mills |
| BRUTUS | Quin |
| CASSIUS | Milward |
| ANTONY | Wright |
| OCTAVIUS | Havard |
| CASCA* | Winstone |
| DECIUS | Cashell |
| LIGARIUS | Taswell |
| ARTEMIDORUS | Shepard |
| METELLUS | Turbutt |
| CINNA | Ridout |
| 1ST CITIZEN | Johnson |
| 2ND CITIZEN | Macklin |
| 3RD CITIZEN | Chapman |
| 4TH CITIZEN | Vaughan |
| 5TH CITIZEN | Marten |
| 6TH CITIZEN* | Hough |
| PORTIA | Mrs Roberts |
| CALPHURNIA | Mrs Butler |

*Nov. 16*

| | |
|---|---|
| CAESAR | Berry |
| BRUTUS | Delane |
| CASSIUS | Milward |
| ANTONY | [W.] Mills |
| CASCA | [T.] Cibber |
| OCTAVIUS | Havard |
| DECIUS | Winstone |

*Apr. 3*

| | |
|---|---|
| CASCA | Berry |
| 6TH CITIZEN added | Woodward |
| TREBONIUS | Winstone |

## 1741 DRURY LANE (cont.)
*Nov. 16 (cont.)*

| | |
|---|---|
| LIGARIUS | Taswell |
| ARTEMIDORUS | Shepard |
| TREBONIUS | Ward |
| METELLUS | Turbutt |
| PINDARUS | Raftor |
| 1ST CITIZEN | Johnson |
| 2ND CITIZEN | Macklin |
| 3RD CITIZEN | Neale |
| 4TH CITIZEN | Arthur |
| CALPHURNIA | Mrs Butler |
| PORTIA | Mrs Roberts |

## 1742 COVENT GARDEN
*Nov. 20; Dec. 20*

| | |
|---|---|
| BRUTUS | Quin |
| CASSIUS | Ryan |
| CAESAR | Bridgwater |
| ANTONY | Hale |
| OCTAVIUS | Gibson |
| CASCA | Cashell |
| TREBONIUS | Rosco |
| DECIUS | Ridout |
| METELLUS | Carr |
| SOOTHSAYER | Marten |
| 1ST CITIZEN | Hippisley |
| 2ND CITIZEN | Chapman |
| 3RD CITIZEN | Woodward |
| 4TH CITIZEN | James |
| CALPHURNIA | Mrs Woodward |
| PORTIA | Mrs Horton |

## 1743 COVENT GARDEN
*Jan. 22; Feb. 15*

| | |
|---|---|
| BRUTUS | Quin |
| CASSIUS | Ryan |
| CAESAR | Bridgwater |
| ANTONY | Hale |
| OCTAVIUS | Gibson |
| CASCA | Cashell |
| TREBONIUS | Rosco |
| DECIUS | Ridout |
| METELLUS | Carr |
| SOOTHSAYER | Marten |
| 1ST CITIZEN | Hippisley |
| 2ND CITIZEN | Chapman |

*Dec. 8*
added

| | |
|---|---|
| CINNA | Anderson |
| LEPIDUS | Bencraft |
| 5TH CITIZEN | Stoppelaer |
| 6TH CITIZEN | Vaughan |

## 1743 COVENT GARDEN (cont.)

*Jan. 22, &c. (cont.)*

| | |
|---|---|
| 3RD CITIZEN | Woodward |
| 4TH CITIZEN | James |
| CALPHURNIA | Mrs Woodward |
| PORTIA | Mrs Horton |

## 1744 COVENT GARDEN

*Jan. 3, 19*

| | |
|---|---|
| BRUTUS* | Quin |
| CASSIUS | Ryan |
| CAESAR | Bridgwater |
| ANTONY | Hale |
| OCTAVIUS | Gibson |
| CASCA | Cashell |
| TREBONIUS | Rosco |
| DECIUS | Ridout |
| METELLUS | Carr |
| SOOTHSAYER | Marten |
| CINNA | Anderson |
| LEPIDUS | Bencraft |
| 1ST CITIZEN | Hippisley |
| 2ND CITIZEN | Chapman |
| 3RD CITIZEN | Woodward |
| 4TH CITIZEN | James |
| 5TH CITIZEN* | Stoppelaer |
| 6TH CITIZEN | Vaughan |
| CALPHURNIA | Mrs James |
| PORTIA* | Mrs Horton |

*Apr. 18*

| | |
|---|---|
| BRUTUS | Sheridan |
| PORTIA | Mrs Pritchard |

*Oct. 31*

| | |
|---|---|
| 5TH CITIZEN | Smith |
| PORTIA | Mrs Pritchard |

*Nov. 10*

| | |
|---|---|
| PORTIA | Mrs Pritchard |
| added | |
| 7TH CITIZEN | Smith |

## 1745 COVENT GARDEN

*Feb. 2*

| | |
|---|---|
| BRUTUS | Quin |
| CASSIUS | Ryan |
| CAESAR | Bridgwater |
| ANTONY | Hale |
| OCTAVIUS | Gibson |
| CASCA | Cashell |
| TREBONIUS | Rosco |
| CINNA | Anderson |
| LEPIDUS | Bencraft |
| DECIUS | Ridout |
| METELLUS | Carr |
| SOOTHSAYER | Marten |
| 1ST CITIZEN | Hippisley |
| 2ND CITIZEN | Chapman |
| 3RD CITIZEN | Woodward |
| 4TH CITIZEN | James |

## JULIUS CAESAR

### 1745 COVENT GARDEN (cont.)
*Feb. 2 (cont.)*

| | |
|---|---|
| 5TH CITIZEN | Stoppelaer |
| 6TH CITIZEN | Smith |
| 7TH CITIZEN | Vaughan |
| CALPHURNIA | Mrs James |
| PORTIA | Mrs Pritchard |

### 1747 DRURY LANE
*Mar. 28; Apr. 2*

| | |
|---|---|
| BRUTUS | Delane |
| CASSIUS | [L.] Sparks |
| OCTAVIUS | Blakes |
| CASCA | Berry |
| CAESAR | [W.] Mills |
| DECIUS | Bridges |
| TREBONIUS | Winstone |
| METELLUS | Usher |
| MESSALA | Bransby |
| LIGARIUS | Taswell |
| CINNA | Marr |
| ANTONY'S SERVANT | Ray |
| LUCILIUS | Leigh [Jr.] |
| PINDARUS | Raftor |
| PUBLIUS | Wright |
| 1ST CITIZEN | Neale |
| 2ND CITIZEN | Yates |
| 3RD CITIZEN | Collins |
| 4TH CITIZEN | Barrington |
| ANTONY★ | Barry |
| CALPHURNIA | Mrs Bennet |
| PORTIA★ | Mrs Furnival |

*Apr. 30*

| | |
|---|---|
| ANTONY | Giffard |
| PORTIA | Mrs Mills |
| added | |
| SOOTHSAYER | I. Sparks |

### COVENT GARDEN
*Apr. 20*

| | |
|---|---|
| BRUTUS | Quin |
| CASSIUS | Ryan |
| ANTONY | Havard |
| CAESAR | Bridgwater |
| 1ST CITIZEN | Hippisley |
| 2ND CITIZEN | Chapman |
| 3RD CITIZEN | Woodward |
| CALPHURNIA | Mrs James |
| PORTIA | Mrs Pritchard |

## 1748 COVENT GARDEN
*Nov. 24, 25; Dec. 8*

| | |
|---|---|
| BRUTUS | Quin |
| CASSIUS | Ryan |
| ANTONY | Delane |
| CAESAR | Bridgwater |
| CASCA | [L.] Sparks |
| TREBONIUS | Anderson |
| LIGARIUS | Holtom |
| LEPIDUS | Bencraft |
| DECIUS | Ridout |
| OCTAVIUS | Gibson |
| METELLUS | Paddick |
| CINNA | Paget |
| PINDARUS | Oates |
| 1ST CITIZEN | Collins |
| 2ND CITIZEN | Dunstall |
| 3RD CITIZEN | Stoppelaer |
| 4TH CITIZEN | Arthur |
| CALPHURNIA | Mrs Horton |
| PORTIA | Mrs Woffington |

## 1749 COVENT GARDEN
*Oct. 19; Nov. 28*

| | |
|---|---|
| BRUTUS | Quin |
| CASSIUS | Ryan |
| CAESAR | Bridgwater |
| CASCA | [L.] Sparks |
| TREBONIUS | Anderson |
| METELLUS | Bransby |
| DECIUS | Ridout |
| LEPIDUS | Bencraft |
| ANTONY | Delane |
| OCTAVIUS | Gibson |
| LIGARIUS | Holtom |
| CINNA | Redman |
| PINDARUS | Oates |
| 1ST CITIZEN | Collins |
| 2ND CITIZEN | Dunstall |
| 3RD CITIZEN | Stoppelaer |
| 4TH CITIZEN | Arthur |
| CALPHURNIA | Mrs Horton |
| PORTIA | Mrs Woffington |

## 1750 COVENT GARDEN
*Jan. 12*

| | |
|---|---|
| BRUTUS | Quin |
| CASSIUS | Ryan |
| CAESAR* | Bridgwater |
| CASCA* | [L.] Sparks |
| TREBONIUS | Anderson |
| METELLUS | Bransby |
| DECIUS* | Ridout |
| LEPIDUS | Bencraft |
| ANTONY* | Delane |
| OCTAVIUS | Gibson |
| LIGARIUS* | Holtom |
| CINNA | Redman |
| PINDARUS* | Oates |
| 1ST CITIZEN | Collins |
| 2ND CITIZEN | Dunstall |
| 3RD CITIZEN | Stoppelaer |
| 4TH CITIZEN | Arthur |
| CALPHURNIA* | Mrs Horton |
| PORTIA | Mrs Woffington |

*Nov. 24, 26, 27; Dec. 27*

| | |
|---|---|
| CAESAR | [L.] Sparks |
| CASCA | Ridout |
| DECIUS | [R.] Elrington |
| ANTONY | Barry |
| LIGARIUS | Usher |
| CALPHURNIA | Mrs Bambridge |

added
| | |
|---|---|
| PUBLIUS | Roberts |
| 5TH CITIZEN | Barrington |

omitted
PINDARUS

# KING JOHN

Adapted as PAPAL TYRANNY IN THE REIGN OF KING JOHN, by Colley Cibber. In five acts.

    1745    J. Watts.

    A virtually complete rewriting. The general structure of the original is followed with reasonable fidelity, and an occasional line retained: *III. i. 136*; *III. ii. 95–6*, &c. The correspondence of the acts is as follows: Act I consists of *II* (*I* being omitted entirely); Act II of *III. i–iii*; Act III of *III. iv* and *IV. i*; Act IV of *V. ii* and *IV. ii* (in that order); Act V of *IV. iii* and *v*.

    See Genest, iv. 158–62; Odell, i. 347–53.
    No acting versions of the original were published before 1750.

## 1737 COVENT GARDEN
*Feb. 26; Mar. 1, 3, 5, 8, 22, 29; Sept. 16*
*Apr. 16*

| | |
|---|---|
| JOHN | Delane |
| ARTHUR | Miss Bincks |
| BASTARD | Walker |
| HUBERT | Bridgwater |
| KING PHILIP | Ryan |
| DAUPHIN | A. Hallam |
| PANDULPH | Chapman |
| PRINCE HENRY | A. Ryan |
| AUSTRIA | Mullart |
| CITIZEN OF ANGERS | Rosco |
| LADY FALCONBRIDGE | Mrs Martin |

## 1737 COVENT GARDEN (cont.)

*Feb. 26, &c. (cont.)*

| | |
|---|---|
| SALISBURY | Stephens |
| PEMBROKE | Aston |
| ESSEX | Ridout |
| CHATILLON | Salway |
| AUSTRIA* | Boman [Jr.] |
| FALCONBRIDGE | Clarke |
| CITIZEN OF ANGERS* | Paget |
| ELINOR | Mrs James |
| LADY FALCONBRIDGE* | Mrs Mullart |
| CONSTANCE | Mrs Hallam |
| BLANCH | Mrs Horton |

[The bill for Apr. 16 is missing.]

## HAYMARKET

*Mar. 4*

| | |
|---|---|
| ARTHUR | Miss Burgess |

No other parts assigned

[The bill has 'As originally written by Shakespeare. Supervised, Read over, Revised, and Unalter'd'.]

## 1738 COVENT GARDEN

*Feb. 2*

| | |
|---|---|
| JOHN | Delane |
| ARTHUR | Mrs Vincent |
| BASTARD | Walker |
| HUBERT | Bridgwater |
| KING PHILIP | Ryan |
| DAUPHIN | [A.] Hallam |
| PANDULPH | Chapman |
| SALISBURY | Stephens |
| PEMBROKE* | Aston |
| ESSEX* | Ridout |
| PRINCE HENRY | A. Ryan |
| CHATILLON | Salway |
| AUSTRIA | Mullart |
| FALCONBRIDGE | Clarke |
| CITIZEN OF ANGERS | Rosco |
| ELINOR | Mrs James |
| LADY FALCONBRIDGE* | Mrs Martin |
| CONSTANCE | Mrs Hallam |
| BLANCH | Mrs Stevens |

*Mar. 2; Apr. 8*

| | |
|---|---|
| LADY FALCONBRIDGE | Mrs Mullart |

*Nov. 29*

| | |
|---|---|
| PEMBROKE | Hill |
| ESSEX | Arthur |
| LADY FALCONBRIDGE | Mrs Mullart |

# KING JOHN

## 1739 COVENT GARDEN
*Mar. 8*

| | |
|---|---|
| JOHN | Delane |
| ARTHUR | Mrs Vincent |
| BASTARD* | Walker |
| HUBERT | Bridgwater |
| KING PHILIP | Ryan |
| DAUPHIN | [A.] Hallam |
| PANDULPH* | Chapman |
| SALISBURY | Stephens |
| PEMBROKE* | Hill |
| ESSEX | Arthur |
| PRINCE HENRY | A. Ryan |
| CHATILLON | Salway |
| AUSTRIA | Mullart |
| FALCONBRIDGE | Clarke |
| CITIZEN OF ANGERS | Rosco |
| ELINOR | Mrs James |
| LADY FALCONBRIDGE* | Mrs Mullart |
| CONSTANCE | Mrs Hallam |
| BLANCH | Mrs Stevens |

*Oct. 22*

| | |
|---|---|
| BASTARD | Hale |
| PANDULPH | Roberts |
| PEMBROKE | Harrington |
| LADY FALCONBRIDGE | Mrs Cross |

## 1741 COVENT GARDEN
*Apr. 9*

| | |
|---|---|
| JOHN | Delane |
| ARTHUR | Mrs Vincent |
| BASTARD | Hale |
| HUBERT | Bridgwater |
| KING PHILIP | Ryan |
| DAUPHIN | [A.] Hallam |
| PANDULPH | Roberts |
| CONSTANCE | Mrs Mullart |
| BLANCH | Mrs Stevens |

## 1745 DRURY LANE
*Feb. 20, 21, 22, 23, 25, 26, 28; Mar. 2*

| | |
|---|---|
| JOHN | Garrick |
| BASTARD | Delane |
| KING PHILIP | Havard |
| HUBERT | Berry |
| DAUPHIN | Blakes |
| PANDULPH | Macklin |
| SALISBURY | [W.] Mills |
| PEMBROKE | Mozeen |
| ESSEX | Ray |
| AUSTRIA | Winstone |
| PRINCE HENRY | Green |

## 1745 DRURY LANE (cont.)

**Feb. 20, &c. (cont.)**

| | |
|---|---|
| CHATILLON | Turbutt |
| CITIZEN OF ANGERS | Bridges |
| FALCONBRIDGE | Simpson |
| ENGLISH HERALD | Usher |
| FRENCH HERALD | Woodburn |
| ARTHUR | Miss Macklin |
| ELINOR | Mrs Bennet |
| BLANCH | Miss Minors |
| LADY FALCONBRIDGE | Mrs Cross |
| CONSTANCE | Mrs Cibber |

[as PAPAL TYRANNY IN THE REIGN OF KING JOHN]

## COVENT GARDEN

*Feb. 15, 16, 18, 19, 20, 21, 22, 23, 25, 26*   *Apr. 4*

| | | | |
|---|---|---|---|
| JOHN | Quin | PANDULPH | Gibson |
| ARTHUR | Miss J. Cibber | ABBOT OF ANGERS | Marten |
| SALISBURY | Ridout | | |
| PEMBROKE | Rosco | | |
| ARUNDEL | Anderson | | |
| BASTARD | Ryan | | |
| HUBERT | Bridgwater | | |
| KING PHILIP | Hale | | |
| DAUPHIN | [T.] Cibber | | |
| MELUN | Cashell | | |
| PANDULPH* | Cibber [Sr.] | | |
| ABBOT OF ANGERS* | Gibson | | |
| GOVERNOR OF ANGERS | Carr | | |
| CONSTANCE | Mrs Pritchard | | |
| BLANCH | Miss Bellamy | | |

[For the first three performances the bills give neither the parts nor the actors' names. In the printed text 'Angers' is spelled 'Algiers', and BLANCH is assigned to Mrs Bellamy. Otherwise the cast agrees with that in the subsequent bills in GA.]

## 1746 COVENT GARDEN

*Feb. 8*

| | |
|---|---|
| JOHN | Cashell |
| BASTARD | Ryan |
| HUBERT | Bridgwater |
| KING PHILIP | Hale |

## KING JOHN [as PAPAL TYRANNY]

### 1746 COVENT GARDEN (cont.)
*Feb. 8 (cont.)*

| | |
|---|---|
| DAUPHIN | [T.] Cibber |
| PANDULPH | Johnson |
| SALISBURY | Ridout |
| PEMBROKE | Rosco |
| ABBOT OF ANGERS | Marten |
| ARUNDEL | Anderson |
| MELUN | Gibson |
| GOVERNOR OF ANGERS | Carr |
| ARTHUR | Miss Morrison |
| BLANCH | Miss Hippisley |
| CONSTANCE | Mrs Pritchard |

[The original]

### 1747 DRURY LANE
*Mar. 16*

| | |
|---|---|
| JOHN | Delane |
| BASTARD | [L.] Sparks |
| KING PHILIP | Giffard |
| HUBERT | Berry |
| DAUPHIN | Blakes |
| PANDULPH | Macklin |
| SALISBURY | [W.] Mills |
| PEMBROKE | Mozeen |
| ESSEX | Ray |
| AUSTRIA | Winstone |
| PRINCE HENRY | Miss Cole |
| CHATILLON | Bransby |
| CITIZEN OF ANGERS | Bridges |
| FALCONBRIDGE | Simpson |
| ENGLISH HERALD | Usher |
| FRENCH HERALD | Marr |
| ARTHUR | Miss Macklin |
| ELINOR | Mrs Bennet |
| BLANCH | Miss Minors |
| LADY FALCONBRIDGE | Miss Pitt |
| CONSTANCE | Mrs Giffard |

### 1749 CUSHING'S BOOTH, SMITHFIELD
*Aug. 23, 24, 25, 26, 28*

| | |
|---|---|
| JOHN | Redman |
| HUBERT | Simpson |
| BASTARD | Pinner |
| CHATILLON | Walker |
| PEMBROKE | Johnson |

# KING JOHN

## 1749 CUSHING'S BOOTH, SMITHFIELD (cont.)
*Aug. 23, &c. (cont.)*

| | |
|---|---|
| PANDULPH | White |
| ARTHUR | Miss Yates |
| CONSTANCE | Mrs Cushing |

# KING LEAR

Adapted by Nahum Tate. In five acts.

1681   E. Flesher.

Act I opens with Edmund's soliloquy (*I. ii. 1–16*, altered), followed by a versifying of *I. i. 1–35*, with new dialogue: both Gloucester and Kent already believe in Edgar's disobedience. Then comes *I. i. 36–200, 244–50*, with many verbal changes, followed by a new scene: Edgar and Cordelia mutually declare their love. This is followed by *I. ii. 180–end*, and *I. ii. 29–64, 115–22*, versified; and by *I. iv. 4–95, 209–96, 318–35*, almost verbatim, but considerably reduced. The Fool is entirely omitted. The act ends with the curse on Goneril (*I. iv. 299–313*, altered).

Act II consists of *II. i. 16–87*; *II. ii. 1–48*; *II. i. 88–end*; *II. ii. 51–end*; *II. iii* entire; and *II. iv. 1–290*. Throughout, the original has been followed with considerable fidelity, but everything is much reduced.

Act III, scene i is *III. ii. 1–73*, almost verbatim. Scene ii begins with 25 new lines: Edmund soliloquizes on Regan's and Goneril's guilty love for him. Then follow *III. iii. 1–26*, expanded, and about 65 new lines: Cordelia determines to aid her father, and Edmund, overhearing her, plans to pursue and assault her. Scene iii is *III. iv* abridged, with a few speeches from *III. vi* inserted, followed by about 130 new lines: Edgar saves Cordelia from Edmund's ruffians, and they renew their pledges of love. Scene iv is *III. vii. 1–87*, expanded. The blinding of Gloucester occurs off stage.

Act IV, scene i is new: Edmund and Regan make love and learn of the revolt of the peasants against them. Scene ii is *IV. i*, almost verbatim, followed by about 50 new lines: Cordelia, Kent, and Edgar plan to aid Lear (Cordelia here has the 'rank fumiter' from *IV. iv. 1–6*). Scene iii is a revision of *IV. v*: here Goneril has Regan's lines, and the letter is omitted. Scene iv is *IV. vi*, almost verbatim, but reduced. Scene v is *IV. vii. 26–84*, somewhat abridged, with 14 new lines at the end: Cordelia prays for victory over her sisters.

Act V, scene i opens with a brief new dialogue: Goneril's intention to poison Regan. Then follows *V. i. 55–end*, much altered. Scene ii opens with *V. ii*, expanded, followed by *V. iii. 1–3, 27–69*, reduced, and by 50 new lines: Edgar challenges Edmund, and Lear asks pardon of Cordelia and Kent. The scene ends with *V. iii. 9–26*, altered. Scene iii is *V. iii. 108–62*, reduced, and a new dialogue: Goneril and Regan are discovered to have poisoned one another. Scene iv is new: Lear kills the soldiers who come to kill him and Cordelia; news is brought of the deaths of Edmund, Goneril and Regan; Cordelia and Edgar are reunited; Lear, Kent, and Gloucester decide to spend the rest of their lives together in retirement and meditation.

See Genest, v. 194–200; Odell, i. 53–6; Spencer, 242–9.

## KING LEAR
### [as altered by TATE]

## 1702 DRURY LANE
*Oct. 30.* No parts assigned

## 1703 DRURY LANE
*Oct. 9; Dec. 21.* No parts assigned

*Oct. 27*
| | |
|---|---|
| LEAR | Mills |

No other parts assigned

## 1704 DRURY LANE
*Nov. 15.* No parts assigned

## 1705 DRURY LANE
*July 13.* No parts assigned

## 1706 QUEEN'S
*Apr. 30; Aug. 13.* No parts assigned
   [Bill for Aug. 13 in DC of Aug. 12.]

*Oct. 30*
| | |
|---|---|
| LEAR | Betterton |
| EDGAR | Verbruggen |
| EDMUND | Mills |
| GLOUCESTER | Freeman |
| KENT | Minns |
| GENTLEMAN USHER | probably Bowen |
| 1ST RUFFIAN | Kent |
| 2ND RUFFIAN | Peer |
| CORDELIA | Mrs Bracegirdle |

   [DC assigns LEAR to Betterton, but omits all the others. The above cast is given by Genest (ii. 357) 'from a copy of Lear, which had been the Prompter's book; and must belong to this season as Mills and Mrs Bracegirdle acted together'. That is, this was Mills's first season at this theatre, and Mrs Bracegirdle's last season on the stage.]

## 1708 DRURY LANE
*Jan. 1*
| | |
|---|---|
| LEAR | Powell |

No other parts assigned

*Oct. 21*
| | |
|---|---|
| LEAR | Betterton |
| EDGAR | Wilks |
| EDMUND | Mills |
| GLOUCESTER | Cibber |
| GENTLEMAN USHER | Penkethman |
| CORDELIA | Mrs Bradshaw |
| GONERIL | Mrs Kent |
| REGAN | Mrs Finch |

245

## KING LEAR [as altered by TATE]

### 1709 DRURY LANE
*Apr. 27*

| LEAR | Betterton |
| EDGAR | Wilks |
| EDMUND | Husband |
| GLOUCESTER | Cibber |
| KENT | Keene |
| ALBANY | Bickerstaff |
| CORNWALL | Fairbank |
| GENTLEMAN USHER | Penkethman |
| CORDELIA | A Young Gentlewoman [probably Miss Willis] |

[This performance was for the BT. of Miss Willis's mother. Miss Willis herself, with her mother, was regularly engaged the following season at the Queen's. ALBANY, CORNWALL, GENTLEMAN USHER appear only in the advance advertisement in DC of Apr. 25. Penkethman's part is there referred to as 'The Fox'.]

### 1710 DRURY LANE
*Nov. 30*

| LEAR | Powell |
| EDGAR | Wilks |
| GLOUCESTER | Cibber |
| EDMUND | Mills |
| KENT | Keene |
| GENTLEMAN USHER | Penkethman |
| CORDELIA | Mrs Rogers |

### QUEEN'S
*Feb. 4*

| LEAR | Betterton |
| EDGAR | Wilks |
| EDMUND | Mills |
| CORDELIA | Mrs Rogers |

No other parts assigned

### 1711 DRURY LANE
*Apr. 28*

| LEAR | Powell |
| EDGAR | Wilks |
| GLOUCESTER | Cibber |
| EDMUND | Mills |
| KENT | Keene |
| GENTLEMAN USHER | Penkethman |
| CORDELIA* | Mrs Rogers |

[DC omits EDGAR.]

*Nov. 10*

| CORDELIA | Mrs Sherburn |

246

KING LEAR [*as altered by* TATE]

## 1712 DRURY LANE
*Feb. 26.* No parts assigned

*Oct. 23*
| | |
|---|---|
| LEAR | Powell |
| EDGAR | Wilks |
| GLOUCESTER | Cibber |
| EDMUND | Mills |
| KENT | Keene |
| GENTLEMAN USHER | Penkethman |
| CORDELIA | Mrs Bradshaw |

## 1713 DRURY LANE
*Jan. 8*
| | |
|---|---|
| LEAR | Powell |
| EDGAR | Wilks |
| GLOUCESTER | Cibber |
| KENT | Keene |
| EDMUND | Mills |
| GENTLEMAN USHER | Penkethman |
| CORDELIA | Mrs Bradshaw |

*Nov. 21.* No parts assigned

## 1714 DRURY LANE
*Apr. 26*
| | |
|---|---|
| LEAR | Booth |
| EDGAR | Wilks |
| GLOUCESTER* | Cibber |
| KENT* | Keene |
| EDMUND | Mills |
| GENTLEMAN USHER* | Penkethman |
| CORDELIA* | Mrs Bradshaw |

*Dec. 9*
CORDELIA   Mrs Santlow
omitted
   GLOUCESTER, KENT, GENTLEMAN USHER

*Dec. 18*
CORDELIA   Mrs Santlow
omitted
   GLOUCESTER, GENTLEMAN USHER

## 1715 DRURY LANE
*Jan. 4; Nov. 29*
| | |
|---|---|
| LEAR | Booth |
| EDGAR | Wilks |
| EDMUND | Mills |
| CORDELIA | Mrs Santlow |

No other parts assigned

## 1716 DRURY LANE
*June 1.* No parts assigned

## 1717 DRURY LANE
*Jan. 5*
| | |
|---|---|
| LEAR | Booth |
| EDGAR | Wilks |
| EDMUND | Mills |

*Nov. 14.* No parts assigned

## 1717 DRURY LANE (cont.)
*Jan. 5 (cont.)*

| | |
|---|---|
| GLOUCESTER | Quin |
| KENT | Bickerstaff |
| GENTLEMAN USHER | Penkethman |
| CORDELIA | Mrs Santlow |

## 1718 DRURY LANE
*Mar. 1*

| | |
|---|---|
| LEAR | Booth |
| EDGAR | Wilks |
| EDMUND | Mills |
| GLOUCESTER | Cibber |
| KENT* | Thurmond |
| GENTLEMAN USHER | Penkethman |
| CORDELIA | Mrs Santlow |

*Sept. 25*
added

| | |
|---|---|
| ALBANY | Boman |
| CORNWALL | Walker |

*Nov. 20*
omitted
KENT

## 1719 DRURY LANE
*Nov. 19*

| | |
|---|---|
| LEAR | Booth |
| EDGAR | Wilks |
| EDMUND | Mills |
| GLOUCESTER | Cibber |
| GENTLEMAN USHER | Penkethman |
| CORDELIA | Mrs Booth |

## 1720 DRURY LANE
*Jan. 9; Apr. 7; Oct. 1; Nov. 24*

| | |
|---|---|
| LEAR | Booth |
| EDGAR | Wilks |
| EDMUND | Mills |
| GLOUCESTER | Thurmond |
| GENTLEMAN USHER | Penkethman |
| CORDELIA | Mrs Booth |

## LINCOLN'S INN FIELDS
*Oct. 15*

| | |
|---|---|
| LEAR | Boheme |
| GLOUCESTER | Quin |
| EDGAR | Ryan |
| KENT | Ogden |
| EDMUND | [J.] Leigh |
| GENTLEMAN USHER | Spiller |
| CORDELIA | Mrs Seymour |
| GONERIL* | Mrs Giffard |
| REGAN* | Mrs Parker |

*Nov. 5*
omitted
GONERIL, REGAN

*Dec. 31*
added

| | |
|---|---|
| ALBANY | Diggs |
| CORNWALL | Egleton |

omitted
GONERIL, REGAN

248

## KING LEAR [as altered by TATE]

### 1721 DRURY LANE
*Feb. 21*

| | |
|---|---|
| LEAR | Booth |
| EDGAR | Wilks |
| EDMUND | Mills |
| GLOUCESTER | Thurmond |
| CORDELIA | Mrs Booth |

*Oct. 7*
added
| | |
|---|---|
| GENTLEMAN USHER | Penkethman |

*Dec. 30*
added
| | |
|---|---|
| KENT | Williams |
| GENTLEMAN USHER | Penkethman |

### LINCOLN'S INN FIELDS
*Jan. 24*

| | |
|---|---|
| LEAR | Boheme |
| GLOUCESTER | Quin |
| EDGAR | Ryan |
| KENT* | Ogden |
| EDMUND* | [J.] Leigh |
| CORNWALL* | Egleton |
| GENTLEMAN USHER* | Spiller |
| CORDELIA* | Mrs Seymour |

*Mar. 16*
omitted
 KENT, CORNWALL, GENTLEMAN USHER

*Apr. 12*
| | |
|---|---|
| EDMUND | Egleton |
omitted
 KENT, CORNWALL

*May 15*
| | |
|---|---|
| GENTLEMAN USHER | Pack |
| CORDELIA | Mrs Knapp |
omitted
 KENT, CORNWALL

*Sept. 23; Nov. 30*
| | |
|---|---|
| EDMUND | Walker |
omitted
 KENT

### 1722 DRURY LANE
*Apr. 26*

| | |
|---|---|
| LEAR | Booth |
| EDGAR | Wilks |
| EDMUND* | [W.] Wilks |
| GLOUCESTER* | Cibber |
| KENT | Williams |
| GENTLEMAN USHER | Penkethman |
| CORDELIA | Mrs Booth |

*Sept. 29; Dec. 29*
| | |
|---|---|
| EDMUND | Mills |
| GLOUCESTER | Thurmond |
[DP omits KENT.]

### LINCOLN'S INN FIELDS
*Jan. 16*

| | |
|---|---|
| LEAR | Boheme |
| GLOUCESTER | Quin |
| EDGAR | Ryan |
| EDMUND | Walker |
| CORNWALL | Egleton |
| CORDELIA | Mrs Seymour |

*June 2*
added
| | |
|---|---|
| ALBANY | Diggs |
| GENTLEMAN USHER | Spiller |

*Nov. 3*
added
| | |
|---|---|
| ALBANY | Diggs |
| GENTLEMAN USHER | Morgan |

249

## KING LEAR [as altered by TATE]

### 1722 LINCOLN'S INN FIELDS (cont.)
*Dec. 20*
added
  KENT        [J.] Leigh
  ALBANY       Diggs
  GENTLEMAN USHER   Morgan

### 1723 DRURY LANE
*May 14; Oct. 5*

| | |
|---|---|
| LEAR | Booth |
| EDGAR | Wilks |
| EDMUND | Mills |
| GLOUCESTER | Thurmond |
| KENT | Williams |
| GENTLEMAN USHER | Penkethman |
| CORDELIA | Mrs Booth |

### LINCOLN'S INN FIELDS
*May 27*          *Nov. 30.* No parts assigned

| | |
|---|---|
| LEAR | Boheme |
| GLOUCESTER | Quin |
| EDGAR | Ryan |
| EDMUND | Walker |
| KENT | [J.] Leigh |
| CORNWALL | Egleton |
| ALBANY | Diggs |
| GENTLEMAN USHER | Morgan |
| CORDELIA | Mrs Boheme |

### 1724 DRURY LANE
*Jan. 4*          *Apr. 27*

| | | | |
|---|---|---|---|
| LEAR | Booth | CORDELIA | Mrs Thurmond |
| EDGAR | Wilks | | |
| EDMUND | Mills | *Sept. 24* | |
| GLOUCESTER | Thurmond | GENTLEMAN USHER | Theo. Cibber |
| KENT | Williams | | |
| GENTLEMAN USHER* | Penkethman | | |
| CORDELIA* | Mrs Booth | | |

### LINCOLN'S INN FIELDS
*Mar. 28*          *May 15*

| | | | |
|---|---|---|---|
| LEAR | Boheme | KENT | Hulett |
| GLOUCESTER | Quin | ALBANY | Chapman |
| EDGAR | Ryan | added | |
| KENT* | Ogden |  CORNWALL | Egleton |
| EDMUND | Walker | | |
| ALBANY* | Diggs | | |

*Oct. 31.* No parts assigned

250

KING LEAR [as altered by TATE]

## 1724 LINCOLN'S INN FIELDS (cont.)
*Mar. 28 (cont.)*
| | |
|---|---|
| GENTLEMAN USHER | Spiller |
| CORDELIA | Mrs Brett |

[The playhouse bill for this performance is in HTC.]

## 1725 DRURY LANE
*Jan. 5*
| | |
|---|---|
| LEAR | Booth |
| EDGAR | Wilks |
| EDMUND | Mills |
| GLOUCESTER | Thurmond |
| KENT | Williams |
| GENTLEMAN USHER | Theo. Cibber |
| CORDELIA | Mrs Booth |
| GONERIL* | Mrs Heron |
| REGAN* | Mrs Seal |

*Dec. 22*
omitted
   GONERIL, REGAN

## LINCOLN'S INN FIELDS
*Apr. 23; May 25*
| | |
|---|---|
| LEAR | Boheme |
| GLOUCESTER | Quin |
| EDGAR | Ryan |
| KENT | Ogden |
| EDMUND | Walker |
| ALBANY | Diggs |
| GENTLEMAN USHER | Spiller |
| CORDELIA* | Mrs Moffett |

*Sept. 24*
| | |
|---|---|
| CORDELIA added | Mrs Parker |
| CORNWALL | Egleton |

## 1726 DRURY LANE
*Dec. 20*
| | |
|---|---|
| LEAR | Mills |
| EDGAR | Wilks |
| EDMUND | Wm. Mills |
| GLOUCESTER | Thurmond |
| KENT | Williams |
| GENTLEMAN USHER | [T.] Cibber |
| CORDELIA | Mrs Booth |
| GONERIL | Mrs Heron |
| REGAN | Mrs Butler |

251

### KING LEAR [as altered by TATE]

#### 1726 LINCOLN'S INN FIELDS
*Feb. 16; Mar. 26; Sept. 23.* No parts assigned

*May 13*

| | |
|---|---|
| LEAR | Boheme |
| GLOUCESTER | Quin |
| EDGAR | Ryan |
| EDMUND | Walker |
| KENT | Ogden |
| ALBANY | Diggs |
| CORNWALL | Milward |
| GENTLEMAN USHER* | Morgan |
| CORDELIA | Mrs Younger |

*Nov. 18*

| | |
|---|---|
| GENTLEMAN USHER | Spiller |

#### 1727 DRURY LANE
*Sept. 16*

| | |
|---|---|
| LEAR | Booth |
| EDGAR | Wilks |
| EDMUND | Mills |
| GLOUCESTER | Cibber |
| KENT | Williams |
| GENTLEMAN USHER | [T.] Cibber |
| CORDELIA | Mrs Booth |
| GONERIL | Mrs Grace |
| REGAN | Mrs Butler |

#### LINCOLN'S INN FIELDS
*June 1; Dec. 30.* No parts assigned

*Oct. 19*

| | |
|---|---|
| LEAR | Boheme |
| GLOUCESTER | Quin |
| EDGAR | Ryan |
| EDMUND | Walker |
| KENT | Ogden |
| ALBANY | Milward |
| CORNWALL | Chapman |
| GENTLEMAN USHER | Spiller |
| CORDELIA | Mrs Younger |

#### 1728 LINCOLN'S INN FIELDS
*Sept. 16*

| | |
|---|---|
| LEAR | Boheme |
| GLOUCESTER | Quin |
| EDGAR | Ryan |
| EDMUND | Walker |
| KENT | Ogden |
| ALBANY | Milward |

252

KING LEAR [*as altered by* TATE]

## 1728 LINCOLN'S INN FIELDS (cont.)
*Sept. 16 (cont.)*

| | |
|---|---|
| CORNWALL | Chapman |
| GENTLEMAN USHER | Spiller |
| CORDELIA | Mrs Younger |

## 1729 DRURY LANE
*Jan. 11*

| | |
|---|---|
| LEAR | Mills |
| EDGAR | Elrington |
| EDMUND | Wm. Mills |
| GLOUCESTER | Roberts |
| KENT | Williams |
| GENTLEMAN USHER | [T.] Cibber |
| CORDELIA | Mrs Booth |
| GONERIL | Mrs Grace |
| REGAN | Mrs Shireburn |

## LINCOLN'S INN FIELDS
*Sept. 12; Dec. 30*

| | |
|---|---|
| LEAR | Boheme |
| GLOUCESTER | Quin |
| EDGAR | Ryan |
| EDMUND | Walker |
| KENT | Hulett |
| ALBANY | Milward |
| CORNWALL | Chapman |
| GENTLEMAN USHER | Morgan |
| GONERIL | Mrs Buchanan |
| REGAN | Mrs Templer |
| CORDELIA | Mrs Younger |

## 1730 DRURY LANE
*Nov. 28*

| | |
|---|---|
| LEAR | Mills |
| EDGAR | Wilks |
| EDMUND | Wm. Mills |
| GLOUCESTER | Cibber |
| KENT | Williams |
| GENTLEMAN USHER | [T.] Cibber |
| GONERIL | Mrs Grace |
| REGAN | Mrs Shireburn |
| CORDELIA | Mrs Booth |

## KING LEAR [as altered by TATE]

### 1730 LINCOLN'S INN FIELDS
*May 28; Sept. 16*

| | |
|---|---|
| LEAR | Boheme |
| GLOUCESTER | Quin |
| EDGAR | Ryan |
| EDMUND | Walker |
| KENT | Hulett |
| ALBANY | Milward |
| CORNWALL | Chapman |
| GENTLEMAN USHER | Morgan |
| GONERIL | Mrs Buchanan |
| REGAN | Mrs Templer |
| CORDELIA | Mrs Younger |

### GOODMAN'S FIELDS
*May 26*

| | |
|---|---|
| LEAR* | Huddy |
| EDGAR | Giffard |
| GLOUCESTER | W. Giffard |
| EDMUND* | Theo. Lacy |
| KENT | Bardin |
| ALBANY | R. Williams |
| CORNWALL* | Machen |
| BURGUNDY* | [W.] Bullock [Jr.] |
| GENTLEMAN USHER* | Penkethman [Jr.] |
| GONERIL* | Mrs Seal |
| REGAN* | Mrs Thomas |
| CORDELIA | Mrs Giffard |

*June 18*

| | |
|---|---|
| LEAR | A Gentleman for his Diversion, that lately play'd Hamlet [at this theatre, Apr. 20. He is unidentified.] |
| EDMUND | W. Williams |
| BURGUNDY | Pearce |
| GONERIL | Mrs Thomas |
| REGAN | Mrs Palmer |

*July 7*

| | |
|---|---|
| EDMUND | W. Williams |
| BURGUNDY | Pearce |
| GONERIL | Mrs Thomas |
| REGAN | Mrs Palmer |

*Oct. 9*

| | |
|---|---|
| LEAR | A Gentleman who never appeared on this Stage before [unidentified] |
| EDMUND | W. Williams |
| GONERIL | Mrs Woodward |
| REGAN | Mrs Palmer |

*Dec. 8*

| | |
|---|---|
| EDMUND | W. Williams |
| CORNWALL | Rosco |
| BURGUNDY | Collett |
| GENTLEMAN USHER | [W.] Bullock [Jr.] |
| GONERIL | Mrs Thomas |
| REGAN | Mrs Palmer |

### 1731 LINCOLN'S INN FIELDS
*Mar. 13*

| | |
|---|---|
| LEAR | Quin |

No other parts assigned

## KING LEAR [as altered by TATE]

### 1731 LINCOLN'S INN FIELDS (cont.)

**Oct. 6**

| | |
|---|---|
| LEAR | Quin |
| GLOUCESTER | Hulett |
| EDGAR | Ryan |
| EDMUND | Walker |
| ALBANY | Milward |
| CORNWALL | Chapman |
| GENTLEMAN USHER | Penkethman [Jr.] |
| KENT | Ogden |
| GONERIL | Mrs Buchanan |
| REGAN | Mrs Templer |
| CORDELIA | Mrs Younger |

### 1732 LINCOLN'S INN FIELDS

**Feb. 8**

| | |
|---|---|
| LEAR | Quin |
| GLOUCESTER* | Hulett |
| EDGAR | Ryan |
| EDMUND | Walker |
| ALBANY* | Milward |
| CORNWALL* | Chapman |
| GENTLEMAN USHER | Penkethman [Jr.] |
| GONERIL | Mrs Buchanan |
| REGAN | Mrs Templer |
| CORDELIA | Mrs Younger |

**Oct. 27**

| | |
|---|---|
| GLOUCESTER | Milward |
| ALBANY | Salway |
| CORNWALL | [J.] Lacy |
| added | |
| KENT | Chapman |

### COVENT GARDEN

**Dec. 13**

| | |
|---|---|
| LEAR | Quin |
| GLOUCESTER | Milward |
| EDGAR | Ryan |
| EDMUND | Walker |
| KENT | Chapman |
| ALBANY | Salway |
| CORNWALL | [J.] Lacy |
| GENTLEMAN USHER | Penkethman [Jr.] |
| GONERIL | Mrs Buchanan |
| REGAN | Mrs Templer |
| CORDELIA | Mrs Younger |

KING LEAR [as altered by TATE]

## 1733 DRURY LANE
*Apr. 30*

| | |
|---|---|
| LEAR | Mills |
| EDGAR | A. Hallam |
| EDMUND | Wm. Mills |
| GENTLEMAN USHER | [T.] Cibber |
| GLOUCESTER | Roberts |
| KENT | Berry |
| ALBANY | Oates |
| CORNWALL | Fielding |
| CORDELIA | Mrs Booth |
| GONERIL | Mrs Grace |
| REGAN | Mrs Shireburn |

## COVENT GARDEN
*Apr. 21*

| | |
|---|---|
| EDGAR | Ryan |
| GLOUCESTER* | Milward |
| KENT | Chapman |
| EDMUND | Walker |
| GENTLEMAN USHER* | Aston |
| LEAR* | Paget |
| CORDELIA* | A Young Gentlewoman [unidentified; first appearance on the stage] |
| GONERIL | Mrs Buchanan |
| REGAN | Mrs Forrester |

*Nov. 14*

| | |
|---|---|
| GLOUCESTER | Aston |
| GENTLEMAN USHER | Neale |
| LEAR | Quin |
| CORDELIA | Mrs Younger |
| added | |
| ALBANY | Salway |
| CORNWALL | [J.] Lacy |

## GOODMAN'S FIELDS
*Mar. 17; Nov. 10*

| | |
|---|---|
| LEAR | Delane |
| GLOUCESTER | Hulett |
| EDGAR | Giffard |
| EDMUND | Rosco |
| CORNWALL | Havard |
| ALBANY | Bardin |
| KENT | Huddy |
| GENTLEMAN USHER | Penkethman [Jr.] |
| REGAN | Mrs Morgan |
| GONERIL* | Mrs Haughton |
| CORDELIA | Mrs Giffard |

*Apr. 23*

| | |
|---|---|
| GONERIL | Mrs Williamson |

256

## KING LEAR [as altered by TATE]

### 1734 COVENT GARDEN
*Jan. 14*

| | |
|---|---|
| LEAR | Quin |
| EDGAR | Ryan |
| GLOUCESTER | Aston |
| EDMUND | Walker |
| KENT | Chapman |
| ALBANY | Salway |
| CORNWALL | [J.] Lacy |
| GENTLEMAN USHER | Neale |
| GONERIL | Mrs Buchanan |
| REGAN | Mrs Templer |
| CORDELIA | Mrs Younger |

### GOODMAN'S FIELDS
*May 10*

| | |
|---|---|
| LEAR | Delane |
| GLOUCESTER | Hulett |
| EDGAR | Giffard |
| EDMUND | Rosco |
| KENT | Huddy |
| BURGUNDY | Hamilton |
| GENTLEMAN USHER | Penkethman [Jr.] |
| CORDELIA | Mrs Giffard |
| GONERIL | Mrs Haughton |
| REGAN | Mrs Monlass |

*Nov. 29* added

| | |
|---|---|
| ALBANY | Bardin |
| CORNWALL | Havard |

### 1735 DRURY LANE
*Sept. 27; Nov. 24*

| | |
|---|---|
| LEAR | Quin |
| GLOUCESTER | Mills |
| EDGAR | Milward |
| EDMUND | W. Mills |
| KENT | Berry |
| GENTLEMAN USHER | [T.] Cibber |
| CORDELIA | Miss Holliday |

### COVENT GARDEN
*Apr. 10*

| | |
|---|---|
| LEAR | Stephens |
| EDGAR | A. Hallam |
| GLOUCESTER | Bridgwater |
| EDMUND | Walker |
| KENT | Chapman |
| CORNWALL | Aston |
| ALBANY | Hale |

*June 6.* No parts assigned

*Dec. 20.* The bill for this performance is missing

## KING LEAR [as altered by TATE]

### 1735 COVENT GARDEN (cont.)
*Apr. 10 (cont.)*

| | |
|---|---|
| GENTLEMAN USHER | Neale |
| GONERIL | Mrs Buchanan |
| REGAN | Mrs Templer |
| CORDELIA | Mrs Horton |

### LINCOLN'S INN FIELDS
*May 7*

| | |
|---|---|
| LEAR | Stephens |
| EDGAR | A. Hallam |
| GLOUCESTER | Bridgwater |
| EDMUND | Walker |
| KENT | Chapman |
| CORNWALL | Aston |
| ALBANY | Hale |
| GENTLEMAN USHER | Neale |
| GONERIL | Mrs Buchanan |
| REGAN | Mrs Templer |
| CORDELIA | Mrs Horton |

### GOODMAN'S FIELDS
*Feb. 15*

| | |
|---|---|
| LEAR | Delane |
| GLOUCESTER | Hulett |
| EDGAR | Giffard |
| EDMUND | Rosco |
| KENT | Huddy |
| BURGUNDY | Hamilton |
| GENTLEMAN USHER | Penkethman [Jr.] |
| CORDELIA | Mrs Giffard |
| GONERIL | Mrs Haughton |
| REGAN | Mrs Monlass |

### 1736 COVENT GARDEN
*Jan. 8*

| | |
|---|---|
| LEAR* | Delane |
| EDGAR | Ryan |
| GLOUCESTER | Bridgwater |
| EDMUND | Walker |
| CORNWALL | Aston |
| ALBANY | Paget |
| KENT* | Boman [Jr.] |
| GENTLEMAN USHER | Neale |
| GONERIL* | Mrs Buchanan |
| REGAN | Mrs Templer |
| CORDELIA | Mrs Horton |

*Feb. 24*

| | |
|---|---|
| LEAR | Hyde |

[Genest (iii. 479) erroneously assigns LEAR to Delane. This was Hyde's BT., and he had been announced in the part uninterruptedly since Feb. 18.]

*Nov. 8*

| | |
|---|---|
| KENT | Chapman |
| GONERIL | Mrs Mullart |

258

## KING LEAR [as altered by TATE]

### 1737 DRURY LANE
*Jan. 10*

| | |
|---|---|
| LEAR | Quin |
| GLOUCESTER | Berry |
| EDGAR | Milward |
| EDMUND | W. Mills |
| KENT | Winstone |
| GENTLEMAN USHER | [T.] Cibber |
| CORDELIA | Miss Holliday |

### COVENT GARDEN
*Feb. 7*

| | |
|---|---|
| LEAR | Delane |
| GLOUCESTER | Bridgwater |
| EDGAR | Ryan |
| EDMUND | Walker |
| CORDELIA | Mrs Horton |

*Sept. 28*
added

| | |
|---|---|
| KENT | Rosco |
| GENTLEMAN USHER | Penkethman [Jr.] |

### 1738 COVENT GARDEN
*Oct. 21*

| | |
|---|---|
| LEAR | Delane |
| EDGAR | Ryan |
| GLOUCESTER | Bridgwater |
| KENT | Rosco |
| ALBANY | Hale |
| CORNWALL | Hill |
| BURGUNDY | A. Ryan |
| GENTLEMAN USHER | Penkethman [Jr.] |
| EDMUND | Walker |
| CORDELIA | Mrs Horton |
| GONERIL | Mrs Mullart |
| REGAN | Mrs Templer |

### 1739 DRURY LANE
*Mar. 8*

| | |
|---|---|
| LEAR | Quin |
| EDGAR | Milward |
| GLOUCESTER | Wright |
| EDMUND | [W.] Mills |
| KENT | Winstone |
| GENTLEMAN USHER | [T.] Cibber |
| ALBANY | Havard |
| CORNWALL | Turbutt |
| GONERIL | Mrs Furnival |
| REGAN | Mrs Cross |
| CORDELIA | Mrs Mills |

KING LEAR [as altered by TATE]

## 1739 COVENT GARDEN
*Mar. 3*

| | |
|---|---|
| LEAR | Delane |
| EDGAR | Ryan |
| GLOUCESTER | Bridgwater |
| ALBANY | Hale |
| CORNWALL | Hill |
| BURGUNDY | A. Ryan |
| KENT | Rosco |
| GENTLEMAN USHER | Penkethman [Jr.] |
| EDMUND | Walker |
| CORDELIA | Mrs Horton |
| GONERIL | Mrs Mullart |
| REGAN | Mrs Templer |

[The playhouse bill for this performance is in FSL.]

## 1741 COVENT GARDEN
*Jan. 7, 20*

| | |
|---|---|
| LEAR | Delane |
| EDGAR | Ryan |
| GLOUCESTER | Bridgwater |
| EDMUND | Hale |
| ALBANY | Gibson |
| CORNWALL | [A.] Hallam |
| BURGUNDY | Bencraft |
| KENT | Rosco |
| GENTLEMAN USHER | Neale |
| GONERIL | Mrs Mullart |
| REGAN | Miss Burgess |
| CORDELIA | Mrs Woffington |

## 1742 DRURY LANE
*May 28*

| | |
|---|---|
| LEAR | Garrick |
| GLOUCESTER | Berry |
| EDGAR | Havard |
| EDMUND | [W.] Mills |
| KENT | Winstone |
| CORNWALL* | Ridout |
| ALBANY | Turbutt |
| GENTLEMAN USHER | Neale |
| GONERIL | Mrs Bennet |
| REGAN | Mrs Cross |
| CORDELIA | Mrs Woffington |

*Oct. 26; Nov. 9, 24*

| | |
|---|---|
| CORNWALL added | Blakes |
| BURGUNDY | Ray |

*Dec. 13*

| | |
|---|---|
| CORNWALL added | Blakes |
| BURGUNDY | Marr |

260

## KING LEAR [as altered by TATE]

### 1742 COVENT GARDEN
*Dec. 15, 16*

| | |
|---|---|
| LEAR | Quin |
| EDGAR | Ryan |
| GLOUCESTER | Bridgwater |
| EDMUND | Hale |
| KENT | Rosco |
| ALBANY | Gibson |
| CORNWALL | Cashell |
| BURGUNDY | Bencraft |
| GENTLEMAN USHER | Woodward |
| GONERIL | Mrs Woodward |
| REGAN | Mrs Mullart |
| CORDELIA | Mrs Cibber |

### GOODMAN'S FIELDS
*Mar. 11, 13, 18, 20*

| | |
|---|---|
| LEAR | Garrick |

No other parts assigned

*Mar. 27, 30*

| | |
|---|---|
| LEAR | Garrick |
| GLOUCESTER* | Marshall |
| EDGAR | Giffard |
| KENT | Paget |
| EDMUND* | W. Giffard |
| GENTLEMAN USHER | Yates |
| ALBANY* | Peterson |
| CORNWALL* | Blakes |
| BURGUNDY | Marr |
| PHYSICIAN | Dunstall |
| OLD MAN | Julian |
| GONERIL* | Mrs Bambridge |
| REGAN | Mrs Yates |
| ARANTE | Miss [E.] Hippisley |
| CORDELIA | Mrs Giffard |

*Apr. 8*

| | |
|---|---|
| GLOUCESTER | Blakes |
| CORNWALL | Dighton |
| GONERIL | Mrs Bishop |

*Apr. 10; May 1*

| | |
|---|---|
| CORNWALL | Dighton |
| GONERIL | Mrs Bishop |

*May 12*

| | |
|---|---|
| CORNWALL | Dighton |

*May 19*

| | |
|---|---|
| EDMUND | Peterson |
| ALBANY | Dighton |

### 1743 DRURY LANE
*Jan. 15*

| | |
|---|---|
| LEAR | Garrick |
| EDGAR* | Havard |
| EDMUND | [W.] Mills |
| KENT | Winstone |
| ALBANY | Turbutt |
| CORNWALL | Blakes |
| GENTLEMAN USHER | Neale |
| BURGUNDY* | Marr |

*Feb. 1; Mar. 12*
added

| | |
|---|---|
| GLOUCESTER | Berry |

*Dec. 13, 31*

| | |
|---|---|
| EDGAR | Giffard |
| BURGUNDY | Ray |
| CORDELIA | Mrs Giffard |

added

| | |
|---|---|
| GLOUCESTER | Bridges |

## KING LEAR [as altered by TATE]

### 1743 DRURY LANE (cont.)
*Jan. 15 (cont.)*

| | |
|---|---|
| GONERIL | Mrs Bennet |
| REGAN | Mrs Cross |
| CORDELIA* | Mrs Woffington |

*Oct. 25*

| | |
|---|---|
| LEAR | Delane |
| EDGAR | Giffard |
| GLOUCESTER | Bridges |
| EDMUND | W. Giffard |
| KENT | Winstone |
| CORNWALL | Blakes |
| ALBANY | Cross |
| BURGUNDY | Ray |
| GENTLEMAN USHER | Neale |
| OLD MAN | Taswell |
| GONERIL | Mrs Bennet |
| REGAN | Mrs Cross |
| ARANTE | Mrs Horsington |
| CORDELIA | Mrs Giffard |

### COVENT GARDEN
*Jan. 17; Feb. 8*

| | |
|---|---|
| LEAR | Quin |
| EDGAR | Ryan |
| EDMUND | Hale |
| GLOUCESTER | Bridgwater |
| ALBANY | Gibson |
| CORNWALL* | Cashell |
| BURGUNDY | Bencraft |
| KENT | Rosco |
| GENTLEMAN USHER | Woodward |
| GONERIL* | Mrs Woodward |
| REGAN | Mrs Mullart |
| CORDELIA* | Mrs Cibber |

*Apr. 28*

| | |
|---|---|
| CORNWALL | Ridout |

*Dec. 27*

| | |
|---|---|
| GONERIL | Mrs James |
| CORDELIA | Mrs Vincent |

### LINCOLN'S INN FIELDS
*Jan. 10, 24, 26*

| | |
|---|---|
| LEAR | A Gentleman [unidentified] |
| GLOUCESTER | [T.] Cibber |
| EDGAR | Giffard |
| KENT | Peterson |
| EDMUND | W. Giffard |
| ALBANY | Mozeen |
| CORNWALL | Dighton |
| BURGUNDY | Freeman |

KING LEAR [as altered by TATE]

## 1743 LINCOLN'S INN FIELDS (cont.)

*Jan. 10, &c. (cont.)*

| | |
|---|---|
| GENTLEMAN USHER | Blakey |
| GONERIL | Mrs Bambridge |
| REGAN | Mrs E. Giffard |
| ARANTE | Miss Scott |
| CORDELIA | Mrs Giffard |

[The bills have, 'With Restorations from Shakespeare'.]

## 1744 DRURY LANE

*Feb. 14; Mar. 8; Apr. 20; May 24*   *Oct. 24; Dec. 8*

| | | | |
|---|---|---|---|
| LEAR | Garrick | EDMUND | Havard |
| EDGAR | Giffard | | |
| GLOUCESTER | Bridges | | |
| EDMUND* | [W.] Mills | | |
| KENT | Winstone | | |
| CORNWALL | Blakes | | |
| ALBANY | Turbutt | | |
| BURGUNDY | Ray | | |
| GENTLEMAN USHER | Neale | | |
| GONERIL | Mrs Bennet | | |
| REGAN | Mrs Cross | | |
| CORDELIA | Mrs Giffard | | |

### COVENT GARDEN

*Dec. 13*

| | |
|---|---|
| LEAR | Perry |
| EDGAR | Ryan |
| GLOUCESTER | Bridgwater |
| EDMUND | Hale |
| KENT | Rosco |
| ALBANY | Gibson |
| CORNWALL | Cashell |
| GENTLEMAN USHER | Woodward |
| BURGUNDY | Bencraft |
| GONERIL | Mrs James |
| REGAN | Mrs Mullart |
| CORDELIA | Mrs Vincent |

[The bill has, 'With Restorations from Shakespeare'.]

## 1745 DRURY LANE

*Jan. 23*                                *Mar. 14*

| | | | |
|---|---|---|---|
| LEAR | Garrick | BURGUNDY | Simpson |
| EDGAR | Giffard | | |
| GLOUCESTER | Bridges | | |
| EDMUND | Havard | | |
| KENT | Winstone | | |

## KING LEAR [as altered by TATE]

### 1745 DRURY LANE (cont.)
*Jan. 23 (cont.)*

| | |
|---|---|
| ALBANY | Turbutt |
| CORNWALL | Blakes |
| GENTLEMAN USHER | Neale |
| BURGUNDY* | Ray |
| GONERIL | Mrs Bennet |
| REGAN | Mrs Cross |
| CORDELIA | Mrs Giffard |

### NEW WELLS, GOODMAN'S FIELDS

*May 2*

| | |
|---|---|
| LEAR | Goodfellow |

No other parts assigned

*May 9.* No parts assigned
[Bill in DA of May 8.]

### 1746 COVENT GARDEN
*June 11*

| | |
|---|---|
| LEAR | Garrick |
| EDGAR | Ryan |
| GLOUCESTER | Bridgwater |
| EDMUND | Cashell |
| KENT | Chapman |
| ALBANY | Oates |
| CORNWALL | Burton |
| BURGUNDY | Paddick |
| GENTLEMAN USHER | Philips |
| GONERIL | Miss Haughton |
| REGAN | Mrs Bland |
| CORDELIA | Mrs Vincent |

*Oct. 27*

| | |
|---|---|
| LEAR | Garrick |
| EDGAR | Ryan |
| GLOUCESTER | Havard |
| EDMUND | Cashell |
| KENT* | Chapman |
| ALBANY | Gibson |
| CORNWALL | Ridout |
| BURGUNDY | Bencraft |
| GENTLEMAN USHER | Woodward |
| GONERIL | Mrs James |
| REGAN | Mrs Bland |
| CORDELIA* | Mrs Vincent |

*Dec. 4*

| | |
|---|---|
| KENT | Rosco |
| CORDELIA | Mrs Cibber |

### 1747 DRURY LANE
*Oct. 30*

| | |
|---|---|
| LEAR | Garrick |
| GLOUCESTER | Berry |

*Nov. 14*

| | |
|---|---|
| EDMUND | Lee |
| REGAN | Mrs Yates |

264

## KING LEAR [as altered by TATE]

### 1747 DRURY LANE (cont.)

*Oct. 30 (cont.)*

| | |
|---|---|
| EDGAR | Havard |
| EDMUND* | [W.] Mills |
| KENT | Winstone |
| ALBANY | Mozeen |
| CORNWALL | Blakes |
| GENTLEMAN USHER | Neale |
| BURGUNDY | Marr |
| GONERIL | Mrs Bennet |
| REGAN* | Mrs Cross |
| CORDELIA | Mrs Cibber |

*Dec. 23*

| | |
|---|---|
| EDMUND | Lee |

### NEW WELLS, GOODMAN'S FIELDS

*Mar. 2*

| | |
|---|---|
| LEAR | Goodfellow |
| EDGAR | Cushing |
| GLOUCESTER | Furnival |
| EDMUND | Lee |
| KENT | Paget |
| GENTLEMAN USHER | L. Hallam |
| BURGUNDY | Miles |
| CORNWALL | Shuter |
| ALBANY | Wignell |
| OLD MAN | [G.] Hallam |
| CAPTAIN | W. Hallam |
| GONERIL | Mrs Bambridge |
| REGAN | Mrs Cushing |
| ARANTE | Mrs Dove |
| CORDELIA | Miss Budgell |

### 1748 DRURY LANE

*Mar. 1*

| | |
|---|---|
| LEAR | Garrick |
| GLOUCESTER | Berry |
| EDGAR | Havard |
| EDMUND | Lee |
| KENT | Winstone |
| ALBANY* | Mozeen |
| CORNWALL | Blakes |
| GENTLEMAN USHER | Neale |
| BURGUNDY | Marr |
| GONERIL* | Mrs Bennet |
| REGAN* | Miss Minors |
| CORDELIA | Mrs Cibber |

*Apr. 23*

| | |
|---|---|
| REGAN | Mrs Yates |

*Oct. 8, 26*

| | |
|---|---|
| ALBANY | Usher |
| GONERIL | Mrs Mills |
| REGAN | Mrs Cross |

*Dec. 31*

| | |
|---|---|
| ALBANY | Usher |
| REGAN | Mrs Cross |

265

KING LEAR [*as altered by* TATE]

## 1748 COVENT GARDEN
*Oct. 3, 5*

| | |
|---|---|
| LEAR | Quin |
| EDGAR | Ryan |
| GLOUCESTER | Bridgwater |
| KENT | Gibson |
| EDMUND | Ridout |
| CORNWALL | Bencraft |
| ALBANY | Anderson |
| BURGUNDY | Paddick |
| GENTLEMAN USHER | Cushing |
| GONERIL | Miss Haughton |
| REGAN | Mrs Ridout |
| CORDELIA | Mrs Ward [first appearance in London] |

### BOWLING GREEN, SOUTHWARK
*Oct. 24.* No parts assigned
[Bill in DA of Oct. 22.]

## 1749 DRURY LANE
*May 10*

| | |
|---|---|
| LEAR | Garrick |
| GLOUCESTER | Berry |
| EDGAR | Havard |
| EDMUND* | Lee |
| KENT | Winston |
| ALBANY | Usher |
| CORNWALL | Blakes |
| GENTLEMAN USHER* | Neale |
| BURGUNDY | Marr |
| GONERIL | Mrs Bennet |
| REGAN | Mrs Cross |
| CORDELIA* | Mrs Cibber |

*Oct. 13*

| | |
|---|---|
| EDMUND | Palmer |
| CORDELIA | Mrs Ward |

*Nov. 8*

| | |
|---|---|
| EDMUND | Palmer |
| GENTLEMAN USHER | Shuter |
| CORDELIA | Mrs Ward |

## 1750 DRURY LANE
*Jan. 25*

| | |
|---|---|
| LEAR | Garrick |
| GLOUCESTER | Berry |
| EDGAR | Havard |
| EDMUND | Palmer |
| KENT | Winstone |
| ALBANY* | Usher |
| CORNWALL | Blakes |
| GENTLEMAN USHER | Shuter |
| BURGUNDY | Marr |

*Nov. 1*

| | |
|---|---|
| ALBANY | Mozeen |
| CORDELIA | Miss Bellamy |

266

KING LEAR [*as altered by* TATE]

1750 DRURY LANE (*cont.*)

*Jan.* 25 (*cont.*)
    GONERIL          Mrs Bennet
    REGAN            Mrs Cross
    CORDELIA*      Mrs Ward

## LOVE BETRAYED, or THE AGREEABLE DISAPPOINTMENT

William Burnaby's alteration of TWELFTH NIGHT, q.v.

## LOVE IN A FOREST

Charles Johnson's alteration of AS YOU LIKE IT, q.v.

## MACBETH

Adapted by Sir William Davenant. In five acts.

1674 P. Chetwin.

The play follows the general structure of the original, but throughout there are numerous verbal 'improvements'.

Act I gives the wounded Sergeant's speeches to Seyton, and Ross's to Macduff. Angus is omitted. The original is followed until *v*, which opens with about 40 new lines: Lady Macbeth consoles Lady Macduff for the absence of her husband. The original is then resumed. In *vi* is a brief new dialogue between Lady Macbeth and Macduff concerning his wife.

Act II has the following changes: the dagger soliloquy is considerably reduced; the Porter is omitted; in *iv* Seyton has the Old Man's speeches, and Lennox has Ross's; at the end of the act a new scene is inserted in which the Witches meet Macduff and Lady Macduff on the heath and predict their fortunes.

Act III contains a new scene between *i* and *ii*: about 75 new lines, in which Macduff expresses his suspicions of Macbeth. Banquo is killed off stage in *iii*. In *iv* Seyton has Ross's speeches. Another new scene follows in which Macduff, on his way to England, takes farewell of his wife. *Scenes v* (which is about half again as long as the original) and *vi* (in which Seyton has the Lord's speeches) are transposed.

Act IV opens with the incantation, to which about 20 new lines are added. The apparitions are omitted; their prophecies are spoken by Hecate. The 'show of eight Kings' is retained. In the succeeding dialogue Seyton has Lennox's speeches, and in *ii* Lennox has Ross's speeches. This scene ends at 77, i.e. the murder of Macduff's son is not shown. *Scene iii* proceeds to *159*, omitting Malcolm's description of his intemperance (*61–100*); continues with a new scene of about 75 lines in which Macbeth speaks of his reluctance to leave his wife, who, already partially insane, heaps reproaches on him; and resumes at *159*. In this last scene Lennox has Ross's speeches.

## MACBETH

Act V, scene i ends at 57. Seyton has the Doctor's speeches. Scene ii is new: Fleance and Donalbain join forces to revenge their fathers. *Scene iii* is slightly reduced, and *iv* slightly enlarged. Scene v is *v*. In *vi* Lennox has Young Siward's speeches, and, like him, is killed. Macbeth dies on the stage; at the end his sword is brought forward.

See Genest, i. 139–42; Odell, i. 28–30; Spencer, 157–67.

No acting versions of the original were published before 1750.

[*as altered by* DAVENANT]

### 1702 DRURY LANE
*Nov. 21.* No parts assigned
[Bill in DC of Nov. 19.]

### 1703 DRURY LANE
*June 17; Nov. 27.* No parts assigned

### 1704 DRURY LANE
*Jan. 1, 25; Feb. 29; Apr. 25; June 27; Dec. 2, 29.* No parts assigned

### 1705 DRURY LANE
*Apr. 17; Nov. 13; Dec. 29.* No parts assigned

### 1706 DRURY LANE
*Feb. 5.* No parts assigned

### 1707 DRURY LANE
*Jan. 23, 31; Apr. 16.* No parts assigned

*Nov. 28*

| | |
|---|---|
| MACBETH | Powell |

No other parts assigned

### QUEEN'S
*Dec. 27, 29*

| | |
|---|---|
| MACBETH | Betterton |
| DUNCAN | Keene |
| MACDUFF | Wilks |
| BANQUO | Mills |
| LENNOX | Booth |
| SIWARD | Husband |
| SEYTON | Corey |
| HECATE | Johnson |
| 1ST WITCH | Norris |
| 2ND WITCH | Bullock |
| 3RD WITCH | Bowen |
| LADY MACBETH | Mrs Barry |
| LADY MACDUFF | Mrs Rogers |

## MACBETH [as altered by DAVENANT]

### 1708 DRURY LANE
*Apr. 24*

| | |
|---|---|
| MACBETH | Betterton |
| DUNCAN | Keene |
| MACDUFF | Powell |
| BANQUO | Mills |
| LENNOX | Booth |
| LADY MACBETH | Mrs Barry |

*Sept. 14*

| | |
|---|---|
| DUNCAN | Keene |
| MACBETH | Powell |
| MACDUFF | Thurmond |
| FLEANCE | Miss Norris |
| HECATE | Johnson |
| 1ST WITCH | [F.] Leigh |
| 2ND WITCH | Fairbank |
| 3RD WITCH | Cross |
| LADY MACBETH | Mrs Knight |
| LADY MACDUFF | Mrs Rogers |

*Oct. 16*

| | |
|---|---|
| MACBETH | Betterton |
| DUNCAN | Keene |
| MACDUFF | Wilks |
| LENNOX | Booth |
| BANQUO | Mills |
| HECATE | Johnson |
| 1ST WITCH | Penkethman |
| 2ND WITCH | Bullock |
| 3RD WITCH | Norris |
| LADY MACBETH | Mrs Knight |
| LADY MACDUFF | Mrs Rogers |

### QUEEN'S
*Jan. 10*

| | |
|---|---|
| MACBETH | Betterton |

No other parts assigned

[In the Davenant version published by Tonson in 1710, 'As it is now Acted at the Queens-Theatre', the cast is as follows:

| | |
|---|---|
| DUNCAN | Keene |
| MALCOLM | Corey |
| DONALBAIN | [C.] Bullock |
| LENNOX | Captain Griffin |
| MACBETH | Betterton |
| BANQUO | Mills |
| MACDUFF | Wilks |
| SIWARD | Husband |
| SEYTON | Bickerstaff |

## MACBETH [as altered by DAVENANT]

### 1708 QUEEN'S (cont.)
*Jan. 10 (cont.)*

| | |
|---|---|
| FLEANCE | Mrs B. Porter |
| 1ST MURDERER | Fairbank |
| 2ND MURDERER | Cross |
| HECATE | Johnson |
| LADY MACBETH | Mrs Knight |
| LADY MACDUFF | Mrs Rogers |

This would appear to be a Drury Lane cast of 1709 or 1710. Mrs Knight never acted at Queen's. On the other hand, Griffin retired in 1708.]

### 1709 DRURY LANE
*Jan. 6*

| | |
|---|---|
| MACBETH | Betterton |
| MACDUFF | Wilks |
| DUNCAN | Keene |
| MALCOLM* | Corey |
| LENNOX | Booth |
| SEYTON* | Bickerstaff |
| 1ST WITCH | Penkethman |
| 2ND WITCH | Bullock |
| 3RD WITCH | Norris |
| HECATE | Johnson |
| LADY MACBETH | Mrs Knight |
| LADY MACDUFF | Mrs Rogers |

*May 20*

added
  BANQUO  Mills
omitted
  MALCOLM, SEYTON

### QUEEN'S
*Nov. 28, 30; Dec. 27*

| | |
|---|---|
| LADY MACBETH | Mrs Barry |

No other parts assigned

*Dec. 17*

| | |
|---|---|
| MACBETH | Betterton |
| LADY MACBETH | Mrs Barry |

No other parts assigned

### 1710 QUEEN'S
*Mar. 20; Apr. 24.* No parts assigned

*Nov. 18*

| | |
|---|---|
| MACBETH | Mills |
| MACDUFF | Wilks |
| DUNCAN | Boman |
| BANQUO | Husband |
| LENNOX | Thurmond |
| SEYTON | Bickerstaff |
| HECATE | Johnson |
| 1ST WITCH | Dogget |
| 2ND WITCH | Penkethman |

270

MACBETH [as altered by DAVENANT]

## 1710 QUEEN'S (cont.)

*Nov. 18 (cont.)*

| | |
|---|---|
| 3RD WITCH | Bullock |
| LADY MACBETH | Mrs Knight |
| LADY MACDUFF | Mrs Porter |

## 1711 DRURY LANE

*Jan. 13*

| | |
|---|---|
| MACBETH | Mills |
| MACDUFF | Wilks |
| BANQUO* | Husband |
| LENNOX* | Thurmond |
| HECATE | Johnson |
| 1ST WITCH | Dogget |
| 2ND WITCH | Penkethman |
| 3RD WITCH | Bullock |
| LADY MACBETH | Mrs Knight |
| LADY MACDUFF | Mrs Porter |

*Apr. 5*

| | |
|---|---|
| LENNOX | Booth |
| omitted | |
| BANQUO | |

*Oct. 20; Dec. 22*

| | |
|---|---|
| BANQUO | Powell |
| LENNOX | Booth |
| added | |
| DUNCAN | Keene |
| SEYTON | Elrington |

[The DC bill of Oct. 20 omits BANQUO, SEYTON.]

## 1712 DRURY LANE

*Mar. 6; Oct. 25; Nov. 22.* No parts assigned

*June 5*

| | |
|---|---|
| MACBETH | Mills |
| MACDUFF | Wilks |
| BANQUO | Powell |
| LENNOX | Booth |
| HECATE | Johnson |
| 1ST WITCH | Dogget |
| 2ND WITCH | Penkethman |
| 3RD WITCH | Bullock |

## 1713 DRURY LANE

*Jan. 24; Sept. 22; Dec. 8.* No parts assigned

*June 5*

| | |
|---|---|
| DUNCAN | Keene |
| MACBETH | Mills |
| MACDUFF | Wilks |
| LENNOX | Booth |
| BANQUO | Bickerstaff |
| MALCOLM | [C.] Bullock |
| SEYTON | Corey |
| HECATE | Johnson |
| 1ST WITCH | Penkethman |
| 2ND WITCH | Norris |

271

## MACBETH [as altered by DAVENANT]

### 1713 DRURY LANE (cont.)
*June 5 (cont.)*

| | |
|---|---|
| 3RD WITCH | Bullock [Sr.] |
| LADY MACBETH | Mrs Knight |
| LADY MACDUFF | Mrs Porter |

[Johnson's part is specified not as HECATE, but as one of the WITCHES.]

### 1714 DRURY LANE
*Jan. 19; Oct. 21.* No parts assigned
[Bill for Oct. 21 in DC of Oct. 20.]

*June 18*

| | |
|---|---|
| DUNCAN | Keene |
| MACBETH | Mills |
| MACDUFF | Wilks |
| LENNOX | Booth |
| BANQUO | Powell |
| HECATE | Johnson |
| 1ST WITCH | Bullock [Sr.] |
| 2ND WITCH | Norris |
| 3RD WITCH | [F.] Leigh |
| LADY MACBETH | Mrs Knight |
| LADY MACDUFF | Mrs Porter |

### 1715 LINCOLN'S INN FIELDS
*Mar. 3, 8, 17, 28; Oct. 18, 29; Dec. 17.*
No parts assigned

### 1716 DRURY LANE
*Jan. 10*

| | |
|---|---|
| MACBETH | Mills |
| MACDUFF | Wilks |
| BANQUO | Booth |
| LADY MACBETH | Mrs Porter |

No other parts assigned

*Oct. 13*
added
| | |
|---|---|
| LADY MACDUFF | Mrs Horton |

### LINCOLN'S INN FIELDS
*Apr. 13; May 24; Oct. 30.* No parts assigned

### 1717 DRURY LANE
*Jan. 14; Feb. 1; May 9; Oct. 8.* No parts assigned
*Dec. 31*

| | |
|---|---|
| MACBETH | Mills |
| MACDUFF | Wilks |

## MACBETH [as altered by DAVENANT]

### 1717 DRURY LANE (cont.)
*Dec. 31 (cont.)*

| | |
|---|---|
| BANQUO | Booth |
| HECATE | Johnson |
| 1ST WITCH | Penkethman |
| 2ND WITCH | Norris |
| 3RD WITCH | [F.] Leigh |
| LADY MACBETH | Mrs Porter |
| LADY MACDUFF | Mrs Horton |

### LINCOLN'S INN FIELDS
*Jan. 1.* No parts assigned

*Mar. 28*

| | |
|---|---|
| MACBETH | Keene |
| MACDUFF | Elrington |

No other parts assigned

*May 13*
added
LENNOX   Smith

### 1718 DRURY LANE
*May 1*

| | |
|---|---|
| MACBETH | Mills |
| MACDUFF* | Wilks |
| BANQUO | Booth |
| HECATE | Johnson |
| 1ST WITCH | Penkethman |
| 2ND WITCH | Norris |
| 3RD WITCH | [F.] Leigh |
| LADY MACBETH | Mrs Porter |
| LADY MACDUFF | Mrs Horton |

*Nov. 27*

| | |
|---|---|
| MACDUFF | Elrington |

### LINCOLN'S INN FIELDS
*Jan. 3.* No parts assigned

*Mar. 3*

| | |
|---|---|
| MACBETH | Keene |
| MACDUFF | [J.] Leigh |

No other parts assigned

*Nov. 13; Dec. 29*

| | |
|---|---|
| MACBETH | Quin |
| MACDUFF | [J.] Leigh |
| BANQUO | Ryan |
| LENNOX | Smith |
| SEYTON | Corey |
| LADY MACBETH | Mrs Knight |
| LADY MACDUFF | Mrs Bullock |

## MACBETH [as altered by DAVENANT]

### 1719 DRURY LANE

*Jan. 13*

| | |
|---|---|
| MACBETH | Mills |
| MACDUFF* | Elrington |
| BANQUO | Booth |
| HECATE | Johnson |
| 1ST WITCH | Penkethman |
| 2ND WITCH | Norris |
| 3RD WITCH* | [F.] Leigh |
| LADY MACBETH | Mrs Porter |
| LADY MACDUFF* | Mrs Horton |

*Apr. 4; May 15.* No parts assigned

*Sept. 19*

| | |
|---|---|
| MACDUFF | Wilks |
| 3RD WITCH | Shepard |

*Dec. 26*

| | |
|---|---|
| MACDUFF | Wilks |
| 3RD WITCH | Shepard |
| LADY MACDUFF | Mrs Thurmond |

### LINCOLN'S INN FIELDS

*Feb. 16*

| | |
|---|---|
| MACBETH | Quin |
| MACDUFF | [J.] Leigh |
| BANQUO | Ryan |
| LENNOX | Smith |
| SEYTON* | Corey |
| LADY MACBETH* | Mrs Knight |
| LADY MACDUFF* | Mrs Bullock |

*May 12.* No parts assigned

*Oct. 13*

| | |
|---|---|
| LADY MACBETH | Mrs Bullock |
| LADY MACDUFF | Mrs Spiller |
| added | |
|   DUNCAN | Ogden |
|   1ST WITCH | Bullock [Sr.] |
|   2ND WITCH | C. Bullock |
|   3RD WITCH | Griffin |
|   1ST MURDERER | Spiller |
|   2ND MURDERER | Harper |
| omitted | |
|   SEYTON | |

*Dec. 18*

| | |
|---|---|
| SEYTON | Boheme |
| LADY MACBETH | Mrs Bullock |
| LADY MACDUFF | Mrs Spiller |
| added | |
|   DUNCAN | Ogden |
|   MALCOLM | Egleton |

### 1720 DRURY LANE

*May 3; Dec. 29*

| | |
|---|---|
| MACBETH | Mills |
| MACDUFF | Wilks |
| BANQUO | Booth |
| HECATE | Johnson |
| 1ST WITCH | Penkethman |
| 2ND WITCH | Norris |
| 3RD WITCH | Shepard |
| LADY MACBETH* | Mrs Porter |
| LADY MACDUFF | Mrs Thurmond |

*Nov. 2*

| | |
|---|---|
| LADY MACBETH | Mrs Horton |

## MACBETH [as altered by DAVENANT]

### 1720 LINCOLN'S INN FIELDS

*Feb. 15*

| MACBETH | Quin |
|---|---|
| MACDUFF* | [J.] Leigh |
| BANQUO* | Ryan |
| DUNCAN | Ogden |
| MALCOLM | Egleton |
| LENNOX | Smith |
| SEYTON | Boheme |
| LADY MACBETH | Mrs Bullock |

*Nov. 19*

| MACBETH | Quin |
|---|---|
| MACDUFF | Ryan |
| BANQUO | [J.] Leigh |
| 1ST WITCH | Bullock Sr. |
| 2ND WITCH | Griffin |
| 3RD WITCH | Morgan |
| LADY MACBETH | Mrs Bullock |
| LADY MACDUFF | Mrs Seymour |

*Mar. 17*

| MACDUFF | Ryan |
|---|---|
| BANQUO | [J.] Leigh |

added

| LADY MACDUFF | Mrs Gulick |
|---|---|

*Apr. 18*

added

| LADY MACDUFF | Mrs Seymour |
|---|---|

### 1721 DRURY LANE

*Sept. 16*

| MACBETH | Mills |
|---|---|
| MACDUFF | Wilks |
| BANQUO | Booth |
| HECATE | Johnson |
| 1ST WITCH | Penkethman |
| 2ND WITCH | Norris |
| 3RD WITCH | Shepard |
| LADY MACBETH | Mrs Porter |
| LADY MACDUFF* | Mrs Thurmond |

*Dec. 16*

| LADY MACDUFF | Mrs Horton |
|---|---|

### LINCOLN'S INN FIELDS

*Feb. 1*

| MACBETH | Quin |
|---|---|
| MACDUFF | Ryan |
| BANQUO | [J.] Leigh |
| MALCOLM | Egleton |
| SEYTON | Boheme |
| 1ST WITCH | Bullock Sr. |
| 2ND WITCH* | Griffin |
| 3RD WITCH | Morgan |
| LADY MACBETH* | Mrs Bullock |
| LADY MACDUFF* | Mrs Seymour |

*Oct. 26*

| 2ND WITCH | Phipps |
|---|---|
| LADY MACBETH | Mrs Seymour |
| LADY MACDUFF | Mrs Bullock |

added

| LENNOX | Hulett |
|---|---|
| HECATE | Hall |

275

MACBETH [*as altered by* DAVENANT]

## 1722 DRURY LANE
*May 10; Dec. 26*

| | |
|---|---|
| MACBETH | Mills |
| MACDUFF | Wilks |
| BANQUO | Booth |
| HECATE | Johnson |
| 1ST WITCH | Penkethman |
| 2ND WITCH | Norris |
| 3RD WITCH | Shepard |
| LADY MACBETH | Mrs Porter |
| LADY MACDUFF | Mrs Horton |

## LINCOLN'S INN FIELDS
*Oct. 20; Dec. 11*

| | |
|---|---|
| DUNCAN | Boheme |
| MACBETH | Quin |
| MACDUFF | Ryan |
| BANQUO | [J.] Leigh |
| LENNOX | Walker |
| MALCOLM | Egleton |
| HECATE | Hall |
| 1ST WITCH | Bullock Sr. |
| 2ND WITCH | Morgan |
| 3RD WITCH | Phipps |
| LADY MACBETH | Mrs Seymour |
| LADY MACDUFF | Mrs Bullock |

## 1723 DRURY LANE
*Apr. 15; May 27; Oct. 29*     Dec. 28. No parts assigned

| | |
|---|---|
| MACBETH | Mills |
| MACDUFF | Wilks |
| BANQUO | Booth |
| HECATE | Johnson |
| 1ST WITCH | Penkethman |
| 2ND WITCH | Norris |
| 3RD WITCH | Shepard |
| LADY MACBETH | Mrs Porter |
| LADY MACDUFF | Mrs Horton |

[The assignment for Apr. 15 is from the advance advertisement in DP of Apr. 11. The bill in DP of Apr. 15 is the same, but has 'Comic Parts by Johnson, Penkethman and Norris', and omits Shepard. The remaining bills are as above.]

## MACBETH [as altered by DAVENANT]

### 1723 LINCOLN'S INN FIELDS

*Jan. 29*

| | |
|---|---|
| DUNCAN* | Boheme |
| MACBETH | Quin |
| MACDUFF | Ryan |
| BANQUO* | [J.] Leigh |
| MALCOLM* | Egleton |
| LENNOX | Walker |
| HECATE* | Hippisley |
| 1ST WITCH | Bullock Sr. |
| 2ND WITCH | Morgan |
| 3RD WITCH* | Phipps |
| LADY MACBETH* | Mrs Seymour |
| LADY MACDUFF* | Mrs Bullock |

*May 18*

| | |
|---|---|
| HECATE | Hall |
| 3RD WITCH | Hippisley |
| LADY MACBETH | Mrs Boheme [i.e. formerly Mrs Seymour] |

*Sept. 30*

| | |
|---|---|
| BANQUO | Boheme |
| HECATE | Hall |
| 3RD WITCH | Hippisley |
| LADY MACBETH | Mrs Knight |
| LADY MACDUFF | Mrs Wilson |

added
    MURDERER    Spiller
omitted
    DUNCAN, MALCOLM

### 1724 DRURY LANE

*May 6; Oct. 27*

| | |
|---|---|
| MACBETH | Mills |
| MACDUFF | Wilks |
| BANQUO | Booth |
| HECATE | Johnson |
| 1ST WITCH | Penkethman |
| 2ND WITCH | Norris |
| 3RD WITCH | Griffin |
| LADY MACBETH | Mrs Porter |
| LADY MACDUFF | Mrs Horton |

[The bill for Oct. 27 is misprinted. HECATE is omitted, and Johnson is assigned Penkethman's part of the 1ST WITCH.]

### LINCOLN'S INN FIELDS

*May 13*

| | |
|---|---|
| MACBETH | Quin |
| DUNCAN* | Huddy |
| MACDUFF | Ryan |
| BANQUO | Boheme |
| LENNOX | Walker |
| HECATE | Hall |
| 1ST WITCH | Bullock Sr. |
| 2ND WITCH | Hippisley |
| 3RD WITCH | Morgan |
| MURDERER | Spiller |
| LADY MACBETH* | Mrs Knight |
| LADY MACDUFF | Mrs Purden |

*Sept. 28*

| | |
|---|---|
| DUNCAN | Ogden |
| LADY MACBETH | Mrs Bullock |

added
    SEYTON    Hulett

MACBETH [as altered by DAVENANT]

## 1725 DRURY LANE

*Feb. 18*

| | |
|---|---|
| MACBETH | Mills |
| MACDUFF | Wilks |
| BANQUO | Booth |
| HECATE | Johnson |
| 1ST WITCH | Norris |
| 2ND WITCH | Griffin |
| 3RD WITCH | [T.] Hallam |
| LADY MACBETH | Mrs Porter |
| LADY MACDUFF | Mrs Horton |

*Apr. 26*
added

| | |
|---|---|
| MALCOLM | Will. Mills |
| SEYTON | Corey |

*Oct. 5*
added

| | |
|---|---|
| MALCOLM | Will. Mills |
| LENNOX | Thurmond |
| SEYTON | Corey |

## LINCOLN'S INN FIELDS

*Mar. 20.* No parts assigned

*Dec. 2*

| | |
|---|---|
| MACBETH | Quin |
| MACDUFF | Ryan |
| BANQUO | Boheme |
| LENNOX | Walker |
| 1ST WITCH | Bullock Sr. |
| 2ND WITCH | Hippisley |
| 3RD WITCH | Morgan |
| HECATE | Hall |
| MURDERER | Spiller |
| LADY MACBETH | Mrs Parker |
| LADY MACDUFF* | Mrs Bullock |

*Dec. 31*

| | |
|---|---|
| LADY MACDUFF | Mrs Moffett |

## 1726 DRURY LANE

*May 5*

| | |
|---|---|
| MACBETH | Mills |
| MACDUFF | Wilks |
| BANQUO* | Booth |
| HECATE | Johnson |
| 1ST WITCH | Norris |
| 2ND WITCH | Griffin |
| 3RD WITCH | [T.] Hallam |
| LADY MACBETH | Mrs Porter |
| LADY MACDUFF | Mrs Horton |

*Nov. 16*

| | |
|---|---|
| BANQUO | Williams |

added

| | |
|---|---|
| LENNOX | Thurmond |

*Dec. 28*

| | |
|---|---|
| BANQUO | Williams |

added

| | |
|---|---|
| MALCOLM | Wm. Mills |
| LENNOX | Thurmond |

## LINCOLN'S INN FIELDS

*Apr. 12.* No parts assigned

*Sept. 26*

| | |
|---|---|
| MACBETH | Quin |
| MACDUFF | Ryan |
| BANQUO | Boheme |
| LENNOX | Walker |

278

## MACBETH [*as altered by* DAVENANT]

### 1726 LINCOLN'S INN FIELDS (cont.)
*Sept. 26 (cont.)*

| | |
|---|---|
| HECATE | Hall |
| 1ST WITCH | Bullock [Sr.] |
| 2ND WITCH | Hippisley |
| 3RD WITCH | Morgan |
| MURDERER | Spiller |
| LADY MACBETH | Mrs Parker |
| LADY MACDUFF | Mrs Bullock |

### 1727 DRURY LANE
*Apr. 4.* No parts assigned

*Sept. 30*

| | |
|---|---|
| MACBETH | Mills |
| MACDUFF | Wilks |
| BANQUO | Williams |
| MALCOLM | Wm. Mills |
| LENNOX | [T.] Cibber |
| HECATE | Johnson |
| 1ST WITCH | Norris |
| 2ND WITCH | Griffin |
| 3RD WITCH | [T.] Hallam |
| LADY MACBETH | Mrs Porter |
| LADY MACDUFF | Mrs Horton |

### LINCOLN'S INN FIELDS
*Apr. 3*

| | |
|---|---|
| MACBETH | Quin |
| MACDUFF | Ryan |
| BANQUO* | Diggs |
| LENNOX | Walker |
| HECATE | Hall |
| 1ST WITCH | Bullock [Sr.] |
| 2ND WITCH | Hippisley |
| 3RD WITCH | Morgan |
| MURDERER | Spiller |
| LADY MACBETH | Mrs Berriman |
| LADY MACDUFF | Mrs Bullock |

*Nov. 17*

| | |
|---|---|
| BANQUO added | Boheme |
| MALCOLM | Milward |

### 1728 DRURY LANE
*May 8*

| | |
|---|---|
| MACBETH | Mills |
| MACDUFF | Wilks |
| BANQUO | Williams |
| MALCOLM | Wm. Mills |

279

## MACBETH [as altered by DAVENANT]

### 1728 DRURY LANE (cont.)
*May 8 (cont.)*

| | |
|---|---|
| LENNOX | [T.] Cibber |
| SEYTON | Corey |
| HECATE | Johnson |
| 1ST WITCH | Norris |
| 2ND WITCH | Griffin |
| 3RD WITCH | Shepard |
| LADY MACBETH | Mrs Porter |
| LADY MACDUFF | Mrs Horton |

*Dec. 6*

| | |
|---|---|
| MACBETH | Mills |
| MACDUFF | Elrington |
| LADY MACBETH | Mrs Porter |

No other parts assigned

### LINCOLN'S INN FIELDS
*Sept. 30*

| | |
|---|---|
| MACBETH | Quin |
| MACDUFF | Ryan |
| BANQUO | Boheme |
| LENNOX | Walker |
| MALCOLM | Milward |
| HECATE | Hall |
| 1ST WITCH | Bullock [Sr.] |
| 2ND WITCH | Hippisley |
| 3RD WITCH | H. Bullock |
| MURDERER | Spiller |
| LADY MACBETH | Mrs Berriman |
| LADY MACDUFF | Mrs Bullock |

### 1729 DRURY LANE
*May 6*

| | |
|---|---|
| DUNCAN* | Boman |
| MACBETH | Mills |
| MACDUFF | Wilks |
| BANQUO* | Bridgwater |
| MALCOLM* | W. Mills |
| LENNOX* | [T.] Cibber |
| SEYTON* | Corey |
| HECATE* | Johnson |
| 1ST WITCH* | Shepard |
| 2ND WITCH* | Norris |
| 3RD WITCH* | Griffin |
| LADY MACBETH | Mrs Porter |
| LADY MACDUFF | Mrs Horton |

*Oct. 28*

BANQUO  Williams
omitted
    DUNCAN, MALCOLM, LENNOX, SEYTON,
    HECATE, WITCHES

## MACBETH [as altered by DAVENANT]

### 1729 LINCOLN'S INN FIELDS
*Jan. 31; Feb. 25*

| | |
|---|---|
| MACBETH | Quin |
| MACDUFF | Ryan |
| BANQUO* | Milward |
| LENNOX | Walker |
| MALCOLM* | Chapman |
| HECATE | Hall |
| 1ST WITCH | Bullock [Sr.] |
| 2ND WITCH | Hippisley |
| 3RD WITCH* | H. Bullock |
| LADY MACBETH* | Mrs Berriman |
| LADY MACDUFF* | Mrs Buchanan |

*Apr. 28*

| | |
|---|---|
| LADY MACBETH | Mrs Buchanan |
| LADY MACDUFF | Mrs Benson |

*Oct. 3*

| | |
|---|---|
| BANQUO | Boheme |
| MALCOLM | Milward |
| 3RD WITCH | Morgan |
| added | |
| SIWARD | Hulett |
| SEYTON | Chapman |

*Nov. 20.* No parts assigned
[Bill not in DJ. See p. 35.]

### 1730 DRURY LANE
*May 2; Nov. 24*

| | |
|---|---|
| MACBETH | Mills |
| MACDUFF | Wilks |
| BANQUO | Williams |
| HECATE | Johnson |
| 1ST WITCH | Norris |
| 2ND WITCH | Griffin |
| 3RD WITCH | [T.] Hallam |
| LADY MACBETH | Mrs Porter |
| LADY MACDUFF | Mrs Horton |

### LINCOLN'S INN FIELDS
*Jan. 1*

| | |
|---|---|
| MACBETH | Quin |
| MACDUFF | Ryan |
| BANQUO* | Boheme |
| LENNOX | Walker |
| SIWARD* | Hulett |
| SEYTON* | Chapman |
| MALCOLM* | Milward |
| HECATE | Hall |
| 1ST WITCH | Bullock [Sr.] |
| 2ND WITCH* | Morgan |
| 3RD WITCH | H. Bullock |
| LADY MACBETH | Mrs Berriman |
| LADY MACDUFF | Mrs Buchanan |

*May 14*

| | |
|---|---|
| SIWARD | Houghton |
| added | |
| DUNCAN | Ogden |
| MURDERER | Hippisley |

*Sept. 21*

| | |
|---|---|
| added | |
| MURDERER | Hippisley |

*Dec. 30*

| | |
|---|---|
| BANQUO | Milward |
| SEYTON | Hulett |
| MALCOLM | Chapman |
| 2ND WITCH | Penkethman [Jr.] |
| added | |
| DUNCAN | Ogden |
| MURDERER | Hippisley |
| omitted | |
| SIWARD | |

MACBETH [as altered by DAVENANT]

## 1731 DRURY LANE
*Apr. 6.* No parts assigned

*May 17*

| | |
|---|---|
| MACBETH | Mills |
| MACDUFF | Wilks |
| BANQUO | Bridgwater |
| LENNOX* | [T.] Cibber |
| MALCOLM* | A. Hallam |
| SEYTON* | Corey |
| HECATE | Johnson |
| 1ST WITCH | Griffin |
| 2ND WITCH* | Shepard |
| 3RD WITCH | R. Wetherilt |
| LADY MACBETH* | Mrs Porter |
| LADY MACDUFF* | Mrs Horton |

*Dec. 1*

| | |
|---|---|
| 2ND WITCH | [T.] Hallam |
| LADY MACBETH | Mrs Horton |
| LADY MACDUFF | Mrs Thurmond |

omitted
    LENNOX, MALCOLM, SEYTON

## LINCOLN'S INN FIELDS
*Sept. 27*

| | |
|---|---|
| MACBETH | Quin |
| DUNCAN | Ogden |
| MACDUFF | Ryan |
| BANQUO | Milward |
| LENNOX | Walker |
| SEYTON | Hulett |
| MALCOLM | Chapman |
| HECATE | Hall |
| 1ST WITCH | Ray |
| 2ND WITCH* | Penkethman [Jr.] |
| 3RD WITCH | H. Bullock |
| MURDERER* | Hippisley |
| LADY MACBETH | Mrs Hallam |
| LADY MACDUFF* | Mrs Bullock |

*Dec. 29*

| | |
|---|---|
| 2ND WITCH | Hippisley |
| LADY MACDUFF | Mrs Buchanan |

omitted
    MURDERER

## GOODMAN'S FIELDS
*May 20*

| | |
|---|---|
| MACBETH | W. Giffard |
| MACDUFF | Giffard |
| HECATE | Rosco |
| 1ST WITCH | Collett |
| 2ND WITCH | Morgan |
| 3RD WITCH | Pearce |

No other parts assigned

MACBETH [as altered by DAVENANT]

## 1732 DRURY LANE
*May 5*

| | | | |
|---|---|---|---|
| DUNCAN | Boman | | |
| MACBETH | Mills | | |
| MACDUFF* | Wilks | | |
| BANQUO* | Paget | | |
| LENNOX* | [T.] Cibber | | |
| MALCOLM | A. Hallam | | |
| SEYTON | Corey | | |
| SIWARD* | Watson | | |
| HECATE | Johnson | | |
| 1ST WITCH | Griffin | | |
| 2ND WITCH | [R.] Wetherilt | | |
| 3RD WITCH* | [T.] Hallam | | |
| LADY MACBETH | Mrs Horton | | |
| LADY MACDUFF | Mrs Butler | | |

*Sept. 28*

| | |
|---|---|
| MACDUFF | [T.] Cibber |
| BANQUO | Bridgwater |
| LENNOX | Roberts |
| 3RD WITCH | Shepard |
| added | |
| 1ST MURDERER | Harper |
| 2ND MURDERER | Jones |
| omitted | |
| SIWARD | |

## LINCOLN'S INN FIELDS
*Feb. 3*

| | |
|---|---|
| MACBETH | Quin |
| DUNCAN* | Ogden |
| MACDUFF | Ryan |
| BANQUO | Milward |
| LENNOX | Walker |
| SEYTON* | Hulett |
| MALCOLM | Chapman |
| HECATE | Hall |
| 1ST WITCH | Ray |
| 2ND WITCH | Penkethman [Jr.] |
| 3RD WITCH | H. Bullock |
| MURDERER | Hippisley |
| LADY MACBETH* | Mrs Hallam |
| LADY MACDUFF | Mrs Buchanan |

*May 12*

| | |
|---|---|
| LADY MACBETH | Mrs Bullock |

*Oct. 30*

| | |
|---|---|
| DUNCAN | Paget |
| SEYTON | [J.] Lacy |

## 1733 DRURY LANE
*Jan. 15*

| | |
|---|---|
| MACBETH | Mills |

No other parts assigned

[The bill for this performance is missing. The above assignment is taken from TR.]

## COVENT GARDEN
*Jan. 25*

| | |
|---|---|
| MACBETH | Quin |
| DUNCAN* | Paget |
| MACDUFF | Ryan |

*May 3*

| | |
|---|---|
| LADY MACBETH | Mrs Hallam |
| omitted | |
| DUNCAN, SEYTON | |

MACBETH [as altered by DAVENANT]

## 1733 COVENT GARDEN (cont.)

Jan. 25 (cont.)

| | |
|---|---|
| BANQUO* | Milward |
| LENNOX* | Walker |
| SEYTON* | [J.] Lacy |
| MALCOLM | Chapman |
| HECATE | Hall |
| 1ST WITCH | Ray |
| 2ND WITCH | Neale |
| 3RD WITCH* | H. Bullock |
| MURDERER | Hippisley |
| LADY MACBETH* | Mrs Bullock |
| LADY MACDUFF | Mrs Buchanan |

Oct. 11; Nov. 12

| | |
|---|---|
| DUNCAN | Dawson |
| BANQUO | Walker |
| LENNOX | Hale |
| 3RD WITCH | Dyer |
| LADY MACBETH | Mrs Hallam |
| omitted | |
| SEYTON | |

## GOODMAN'S FIELDS

Feb. 19

| | |
|---|---|
| MACBETH | Delane |
| MACDUFF | Giffard |
| BANQUO | Hulett |
| DUNCAN | Huddy |
| MALCOLM | Bardin |
| DONALBAIN* | Woodward |
| LENNOX | Rosco |
| SIWARD* | Winstone |
| SEYTON* | Corey |
| 1ST WITCH | Morgan |
| 2ND WITCH | Norris [Jr.] |
| 3RD WITCH | Penkethman [Jr.] |
| HECATE* | Lyon |
| 1ST MURDERER* | Wetherilt [Sr.] |
| 2ND MURDERER* | Pearce |
| LADY MACBETH | Mrs Roberts |
| LADY MACDUFF | Mrs Giffard |

Apr. 9

omitted
    DONALBAIN, SIWARD, SEYTON, HECATE, MURDERERS

May 22. No parts assigned

## 1734 COVENT GARDEN

Jan. 1; Feb. 13

| | |
|---|---|
| MACBETH | Quin |
| MALCOLM | Chapman |
| MACDUFF | Ryan |
| BANQUO | Walker |
| DUNCAN | Dawson |
| LENNOX | Hale |
| SEYTON | [J.] Lacy |
| SIWARD | Aston |
| HECATE | Hall |
| 1ST WITCH | Ray |
| 2ND WITCH | Morgan |

Mar. 19

LADY MACBETH   Mrs Bullock

[DJ omits SEYTON, SIWARD throughout.]

MACBETH [as altered by DAVENANT]

## 1734 COVENT GARDEN (cont.)
*Jan. 1, &c. (cont.)*

| | |
|---|---|
| 3RD WITCH | Neale |
| MURDERER | Hippisley |
| LADY MACBETH* | Mrs Hallam |
| LADY MACDUFF | Mrs Buchanan |

## GOODMAN'S FIELDS
*Jan. 31; Feb. 1*

| | |
|---|---|
| MACBETH | Delane |
| MACDUFF | Giffard |
| BANQUO | Hulett |
| DUNCAN | Huddy |
| MALCOLM | Bardin |
| DONALBAIN | Woodward |
| LENNOX | Rosco |
| SEYTON | Havard |
| SIWARD* | Harbin |
| FLEANCE* | Master Giffard |
| 1ST MURDERER* | Wetherilt [Sr.] |
| HECATE | Lyon |
| 1ST WITCH | Penkethman [Jr.] |
| 2ND WITCH | Jenkins |
| 3RD WITCH* | Monlass |
| LADY MACBETH | Mrs Roberts |
| LADY MACDUFF | Mrs Hamilton |

*Feb. 4*
added
| | |
|---|---|
| 4TH WITCH | Pearce |

*Nov. 7*
| | |
|---|---|
| 3RD WITCH | Ray |
added
| | |
|---|---|
| 4TH WITCH | Stoppelaer |
omitted
    SIWARD, FLEANCE, 1ST MURDERER

*Nov. 8; Dec. 9*
| | |
|---|---|
| 3RD WITCH | Norris [Jr.] |
added
| | |
|---|---|
| 4TH WITCH | Stoppelaer |
| 2ND MURDERER | Pearce |
omitted
    FLEANCE

## 1735 DRURY LANE
*Oct. 21, 22; Nov. 27*

| | |
|---|---|
| MACBETH | Mills |
| MACDUFF | Milward |
| BANQUO | W. Mills |
| LENNOX | [T.] Cibber |
| DUNCAN | Boman |
| MALCOLM | Cross |
| SIWARD | Winstone |
| SEYTON | Berry |
| MURDERER | Harper |
| 1ST WITCH | Miller |
| 2ND WITCH | Griffin |
| 3RD WITCH | Shepard |
| HECATE | Johnson |
| LADY MACBETH | Mrs Butler |
| LADY MACDUFF | Miss Holliday |

285

## MACBETH [as altered by DAVENANT]

### 1735 COVENT GARDEN
*Nov. 15*

| | |
|---|---|
| MACBETH | Delane |
| MALCOLM | A. Hallam |
| MACDUFF | Ryan |
| BANQUO* | Walker |
| LENNOX* | Stephens |
| DUNCAN* | Bridgwater |
| SIWARD | Marshall |
| SEYTON | Aston |
| MURDERER | Hippisley |
| LADY MACBETH | Mrs Hallam |
| LADY MACDUFF | Mrs Buchanan |

*Dec. 27*

| | |
|---|---|
| BANQUO | Bridgwater |
| LENNOX | Walker |
| DUNCAN | Paget |
| added | |
| 1ST WITCH | Mullart |
| 2ND WITCH | Neale |
| 3RD WITCH | James |

### GOODMAN'S FIELDS
*Apr. 23*

| | |
|---|---|
| MACBETH | Delane |
| MACDUFF | Giffard |
| BANQUO | Hulett |
| DUNCAN | Huddy |
| MALCOLM | Bardin |
| DONALBAIN | Jenkins |
| LENNOX | Rosco |
| SEYTON | Havard |
| SIWARD | Harbin |
| HECATE | Lyon |
| 1ST WITCH | Penkethman [Jr.] |
| 2ND WITCH | Norris [Jr.] |
| 3RD WITCH | Excell |
| 4TH WITCH | Stoppelaer |
| 1ST MURDERER | Wetherilt [Sr.] |
| 2ND MURDERER | Monlass |
| LADY MACBETH | Mrs Haughton |
| LADY MACDUFF | Mrs Hamilton |

### 1736 DRURY LANE
*Sept. 9*

| | |
|---|---|
| MACBETH* | Mills |
| MACDUFF | Milward |
| BANQUO | W. Mills |
| LENNOX | [T.] Cibber |
| HECATE | Johnson |
| DUNCAN | Boman |
| MALCOLM | Cross |
| SIWARD | Winstone |
| SEYTON | Berry |
| MURDERER | Harper |
| 1ST WITCH | Miller |

*Nov. 18*

| | |
|---|---|
| LADY MACBETH | Mrs Porter |

*Dec. 23*

| | |
|---|---|
| MACBETH | Quin |

[Genest's note on this performance (iii. 491) is misleading. He says that Mills's name was 'perhaps in the bill'. Under the entry for Dec. 4, 1736, Genest, quoting Davies (i. 319) states that Henry in *Henry IV, Part II*, was Mills's 'last part—after which he was announced for Macbeth, and Davies saw him hurrying to the playhouse

286

MACBETH [as altered by DAVENANT]

## 1736 DRURY LANE (cont.)

*Sept. 9 (cont.)*

| | |
|---|---|
| 2ND WITCH | Griffin |
| 3RD WITCH | Shepard |
| LADY MACBETH* | Mrs Butler |
| LADY MACDUFF | Miss Holliday |

*Dec. 23 (cont.)*

between 5 and 6; but he was taken ill and Quin was obliged to supply his place'. Mills died on Dec. 17, and his name is not in the bill for Dec. 23. Genest misinterprets Davies: it was Quin whom Davies saw hurrying to the playhouse.]

## COVENT GARDEN

*Jan. 21*

| | |
|---|---|
| LADY MACBETH | Mrs Porter |

No other parts assigned

*Feb. 18*

| | |
|---|---|
| MACBETH | Delane |
| MACDUFF | Ryan |
| BANQUO* | Bridgwater |
| LENNOX* | Walker |
| DUNCAN* | Paget |
| MALCOLM | A. Hallam |
| SIWARD* | Boman [Jr.] |
| SEYTON | Aston |
| MURDERER | Hippisley |
| 1ST WITCH | Mullart |
| 2ND WITCH | Neale |
| 3RD WITCH | James |
| LADY MACBETH | Mrs Hallam |
| LADY MACDUFF* | Mrs Buchanan |

*Apr. 26*

| | |
|---|---|
| BANQUO | Walker |
| LENNOX | Stephens |
| DUNCAN | Bridgwater |
| LADY MACDUFF | Mrs Kilby |

*Oct. 20*

| | |
|---|---|
| BANQUO | Walker |
| LENNOX | Stephens |
| DUNCAN | Bridgwater |
| SIWARD | Marshall |

added

| | |
|---|---|
| HECATE | Paget |

## 1737 DRURY LANE

*Feb. 7*

| | |
|---|---|
| MACBETH | Quin |
| MACDUFF | Milward |
| BANQUO | W. Mills |
| LENNOX | [T.] Cibber |
| DUNCAN | Boman |
| MALCOLM | Cross |
| SIWARD | Winstone |
| SEYTON | Berry |
| HECATE | Johnson |
| 1ST MURDERER | Harper |
| 1ST WITCH | Miller |
| 2ND WITCH | Griffin |
| 3RD WITCH | Shepard |
| LADY MACDUFF | Miss Holliday |
| LADY MACBETH | Mrs Butler |

*May 19*

added

| | |
|---|---|
| 2ND MURDERER | Turbutt |

287

## MACBETH [as altered by DAVENANT]

### 1737 COVENT GARDEN
*Feb. 1*

| | |
|---|---|
| MACBETH | Delane |
| MACDUFF | Ryan |
| BANQUO | Walker |
| LENNOX | Stephens |
| DUNCAN | Bridgwater |
| MALCOLM | A. Hallam |
| SIWARD* | Boman [Jr.] |
| SEYTON* | Aston |
| HECATE* | Paget |
| MURDERER* | Hippisley |
| 1ST WITCH* | Mullart |
| 2ND WITCH* | James |
| 3RD WITCH* | Neale |
| LADY MACDUFF* | Mrs Bellamy |
| LADY MACBETH | Mrs Hallam |

*Mar. 21*

LADY MACDUFF   Mrs Stevens
omitted
    SIWARD, SEYTON, HECATE, MURDERER, WITCHES

*Oct. 4.* The bill for this performance is missing

### 1738 DRURY LANE
*Jan. 31*

| | |
|---|---|
| MACBETH | Quin |
| MACDUFF | Milward |
| BANQUO | [W.] Mills |
| LENNOX | Wright |
| DUNCAN | Boman |
| MALCOLM | Cross |
| SIWARD | Winstone |
| SEYTON | Havard |
| 1ST MURDERER | Harper |
| 2ND MURDERER | Turbutt |
| HECATE | Johnson |
| 1ST WITCH* | Miller |
| 2ND WITCH | Griffin |
| 3RD WITCH | Ray |
| LADY MACBETH | Mrs Butler |
| LADY MACDUFF | Mrs Mills |

*Oct. 20*

| | |
|---|---|
| 1ST WITCH | Macklin |

[The bill has, 'Written by Shakespeare'. Genest (iii. 529) believes that it was, however, Davenant's version. This is correct; the original was not acted until Garrick restored it, at this theatre, on Jan. 7, 1744.]

### COVENT GARDEN
*Jan. 3*

| | |
|---|---|
| MACBETH | Delane |
| MACDUFF | Ryan |

*Apr. 14*

added
    DONALBAIN   A. Ryan

## MACBETH [as altered by DAVENANT]

### 1738 COVENT GARDEN (cont.)

*Jan. 3 (cont.)*

| | |
|---|---|
| DUNCAN* | Bridgwater |
| MALCOLM | A. Hallam |
| BANQUO* | Walker |
| LENNOX | Stephens |
| SIWARD | Hale |
| SEYTON* | Aston |
| HECATE* | Rosco |
| 1ST WITCH* | Mullart |
| 2ND WITCH | James |
| 3RD WITCH | Penkethman [Jr.] |
| MURDERER | Hippisley |
| LADY MACBETH | Mrs Hallam |
| LADY MACDUFF | Mrs Stevens |

*Oct. 6*

| | |
|---|---|
| DUNCAN | Rosco |
| BANQUO | Bridgwater |
| SEYTON | Arthur |
| HECATE | Mullart |
| 1ST WITCH | Neale |
| added | |
| DONALBAIN | A. Ryan |

*Dec. 29*

| | |
|---|---|
| DUNCAN | Roberts |
| BANQUO | Bridgwater |
| SEYTON | Arthur |
| HECATE | Mullart |
| 1ST WITCH | Neale |
| added | |
| DONALBAIN | A. Ryan |

### 1739 DRURY LANE

*Jan. 1*

| | |
|---|---|
| MACBETH | Quin |
| MACDUFF | Milward |
| BANQUO | [W.] Mills |
| LENNOX | Wright |
| DUNCAN* | Boman |
| MALCOLM* | Cross |
| SIWARD* | Winstone |
| SEYTON* | Havard |
| 1ST MURDERER | Turbutt |
| 2ND MURDERER | Cole |
| HECATE | Johnson |
| 1ST WITCH | Macklin |
| 2ND WITCH | Griffin |
| 3RD WITCH | Shepard |
| LADY MACBETH | Mrs Butler |
| LADY MACDUFF* | Mrs Mills |

*Sept. 18*

| | |
|---|---|
| DUNCAN | Winstone |
| MALCOLM | Havard |
| SIWARD | Ridout |
| SEYTON | Berry |

*Dec. 17*

| | |
|---|---|
| DUNCAN | Winstone |
| MALCOLM | Havard |
| SIWARD | Ridout |
| SEYTON | Berry |
| LADY MACDUFF | Mrs Pritchard |

### COVENT GARDEN

*Jan. 20*

| | |
|---|---|
| MACBETH | Delane |
| MACDUFF | Ryan |
| BANQUO | Bridgwater |
| LENNOX | Stephens |
| DUNCAN | Roberts |
| MALCOLM | [A.] Hallam |
| DONALBAIN* | A. Ryan |
| SIWARD | Hale |
| SEYTON | Arthur |
| MURDERER | Hippisley |

*Oct. 25*

| | |
|---|---|
| 1ST WITCH | Mullart |

*Dec. 31*

| | |
|---|---|
| 1ST WITCH | Mullart |
| omitted | |
| DONALBAIN | |

## MACBETH [as altered by DAVENANT]

### 1739 COVENT GARDEN (cont.)
*Jan. 20 (cont.)*

| | |
|---|---|
| HECATE | Rosco |
| 1ST WITCH* | Penkethman [Jr.] |
| 2ND WITCH | James |
| 3RD WITCH | Neale |
| LADY MACBETH | Mrs Hallam |
| LADY MACDUFF | Mrs Stevens |

### 1740 DRURY LANE
*Mar. 29*

| | |
|---|---|
| MACBETH | Quin |
| MACDUFF | Milward |
| BANQUO | [W.] Mills |
| LENNOX | Wright |
| DUNCAN | Winstone |
| MALCOLM* | Havard |
| SIWARD | Ridout |
| SEYTON | Berry |
| 1ST MURDERER | Turbutt |
| 2ND MURDERER* | Reed |
| HECATE | Johnson |
| 1ST WITCH | Macklin |
| 2ND WITCH | Shepard |
| 3RD WITCH* | Reed |
| LADY MACBETH | Mrs Butler |
| LADY MACDUFF* | Mrs Pritchard |

[Reed doubled the 2ND MURDERER and the 3RD WITCH.]

*May 13*

| | |
|---|---|
| 2ND MURDERER | Woodburn |
| 3RD WITCH | Ray |
| LADY MACDUFF | Mrs Mills |

*Nov. 27; Dec. 3*

| | |
|---|---|
| MALCOLM | Cashell |
| 2ND MURDERER | Taswell |
| 3RD WITCH | Ray |

### COVENT GARDEN
*Jan. 1*

| | |
|---|---|
| MACBETH | Delane |
| MACDUFF* | Ryan |
| BANQUO | Bridgwater |
| LENNOX | Stephens |
| DUNCAN | Roberts |
| MALCOLM* | [A.] Hallam |
| SIWARD* | Hale |
| SEYTON | Arthur |
| HECATE | Rosco |
| 1ST WITCH | James |
| 2ND WITCH | Neale |
| 3RD WITCH | Mullart |
| MURDERER | Hippisley |
| LADY MACBETH* | Mrs Hallam |
| LADY MACDUFF | Mrs Stevens |

*Apr. 21*

| | |
|---|---|
| MACDUFF | [A.] Hallam |
| MALCOLM | A. Ryan |
| SIWARD | Gibson |
| added | |
| DONALBAIN | Clarke |

*May 10.* No parts assigned

*Sept. 26; Nov. 5*

| | |
|---|---|
| LADY MACBETH | Mrs Horton |
| added | |
| DONALBAIN | Gibson |

MACBETH [*as altered by* DAVENANT]

## 1740 GOODMAN'S FIELDS
*Dec. 10*

| | |
|---|---|
| MACBETH | Marshall |
| MACDUFF | Giffard |
| BANQUO | Walker |
| LENNOX | Peterson |
| DUNCAN | Paget |
| MALCOLM | W. Giffard |
| SIWARD | Crofts |
| SEYTON | Blakes |
| HECATE | Yates |
| 1ST WITCH | Julian |
| 2ND WITCH | Dunstall |
| 3RD WITCH | Vaughan |
| LADY MACBETH | Mrs Steel |
| LADY MACDUFF | Mrs Lamball |

*Dec. 27.* No parts assigned

## 1741 DRURY LANE
*Mar. 30*

| | |
|---|---|
| MACBETH* | Quin |
| MACDUFF | Milward |
| BANQUO | [W.] Mills |
| LENNOX* | Wright |
| DUNCAN | Winstone |
| MALCOLM | Havard |
| SIWARD | Ridout |
| SEYTON | Berry |
| 1ST MURDERER | Turbutt |
| 2ND MURDERER | Taswell |
| HECATE | Johnson |
| 1ST WITCH | Macklin |
| 2ND WITCH | Shepard |
| 3RD WITCH | Ray |
| LADY MACBETH* | Mrs Roberts |
| LADY MACDUFF | Mrs Mills |

*Oct. 8; Nov. 30*

| | |
|---|---|
| MACBETH | Delane |
| LENNOX | [T.] Cibber |
| LADY MACBETH | Mrs Butler |
| added | |
| DONALBAIN | Green |
| FLEANCE | Miss Cole |

## COVENT GARDEN
*Mar. 5*

| | |
|---|---|
| MACBETH | Delane |
| MACDUFF | Ryan |
| DUNCAN | Roberts |
| BANQUO | Hale |
| LENNOX | Stephens |
| MALCOLM | [A.] Hallam |
| DONALBAIN | Clarke |
| SIWARD | Gibson |
| SEYTON | Arthur |
| MURDERER | Hippisley |

MACBETH [*as altered by* DAVENANT]

## 1741 COVENT GARDEN (*cont.*)
*Mar. 5 (cont.)*

| | |
|---|---|
| IST WITCH | Mullart |
| 2ND WITCH | James |
| 3RD WITCH | Neale |
| HECATE | Rosco |
| LADY MACDUFF | Mrs Stevens |
| LADY MACBETH | Mrs Porter |

## 1742 DRURY LANE
*Apr. 19*

| | |
|---|---|
| MACBETH | Delane |
| MACDUFF | Havard |
| BANQUO | [W.] Mills |
| LENNOX | Ridout |
| DUNCAN | Winstone |
| MALCOLM | Cross |
| SEYTON | Berry |
| DONALBAIN | Green |
| SIWARD | Woodburn |
| FLEANCE | Miss Cole |
| IST MURDERER | Turbutt |
| 2ND MURDERER | Taswell |
| HECATE | Johnson |
| IST WITCH | Macklin |
| 2ND WITCH | Shepard |
| 3RD WITCH | Ray |
| LADY MACBETH | Mrs Butler |
| LADY MACDUFF | Mrs Mills |

## COVENT GARDEN
*May 5*

| | |
|---|---|
| MACBETH | Cashell |
| MACDUFF | Ryan |
| BANQUO | Bridgwater |
| LENNOX | Stephens |
| DUNCAN | Harrington |
| MALCOLM | Chapman |
| SEYTON | Gibson |
| DONALBAIN | Clarke |
| IST MURDERER | Hippisley |
| 2ND MURDERER | Marten |
| HECATE | Rosco |
| IST WITCH | Woodward |
| 2ND WITCH | James |
| 3RD WITCH | Bencraft |
| LADY MACBETH | Mrs Horton |
| LADY MACDUFF | Mrs Stevens |

MACBETH [as altered by DAVENANT]

## 1742 COVENT GARDEN (cont.)

*Oct. 8, 30*

| | |
|---|---|
| MACBETH | Quin |
| MACDUFF | Ryan |
| DUNCAN | Gibson |
| BANQUO | Bridgwater |
| MALCOLM | Hale |
| DONALBAIN | Anderson |
| SIWARD | Cashell |
| LENNOX | Stephens |
| SEYTON | Harrington |
| 1ST MURDERER | Stoppelaer |
| 2ND MURDERER | Bencraft |
| 1ST WITCH | Hippisley |
| 2ND WITCH | Marten |
| 3RD WITCH | James |
| HECATE | Rosco |
| LADY MACDUFF | Mrs Hale |
| LADY MACBETH | Mrs Horton |

## 1743 COVENT GARDEN

*Jan. 1; Feb. 3; Mar. 1; Apr. 7*

| | |
|---|---|
| MACBETH | Quin |
| MACDUFF | Ryan |
| DUNCAN | Gibson |
| BANQUO | Bridgwater |
| MALCOLM | Hale |
| DONALBAIN | Anderson |
| LENNOX | Stephens |
| SIWARD | Cashell |
| SEYTON* | Harrington |
| HECATE | Rosco |
| 1ST MURDERER | Stoppelaer |
| 2ND MURDERER* | Bencraft |
| 1ST WITCH | Hippisley |
| 2ND WITCH* | Marten |
| 3RD WITCH | James |
| LADY MACDUFF | Mrs Stevens |
| LADY MACBETH | Mrs Horton |

*Dec. 3, 29*

| | |
|---|---|
| SEYTON | Ridout |
| 2ND MURDERER | Marten |
| 2ND WITCH | Woodward |

[*The original*]

## 1744 DRURY LANE

*Jan. 7, 9, 10, 11, 14, 16, 18, 20, 21, 26, 31; Mar. 3; Apr. 14*

| | |
|---|---|
| MACBETH | Garrick |
| MACDUFF | Giffard |
| DUNCAN* | [W.] Mills |
| BANQUO | Havard |

*Oct. 30; Dec. 10*

| | |
|---|---|
| DUNCAN | Berry |
| LENNOX | Turbutt |
| ANGUS | Simpson |
| 1ST WITCH | Phillips |
| LADY MACDUFF | Mrs Ridout |

293

## 1744 DRURY LANE (cont.)

*Jan. 7, &c. (cont.)*

| | |
|---|---|
| MALCOLM | Blakes |
| DONALBAIN | Green |
| LENNOX* | W. Giffard |
| SIWARD | Winstone |
| SEYTON | Ray |
| HECATE* | Berry |
| ROSS | Bridges |
| YOUNG SIWARD | Cross |
| FLEANCE | Miss Cole |
| ANGUS* | Turbutt |
| DOCTOR | Taswell |
| 1ST WITCH* | Arthur |
| 2ND WITCH | Neale |
| 3RD WITCH | Yates |
| LADY MACDUFF* | Mrs Mills |
| GENTLEWOMAN | Mrs Bennet |
| LADY MACBETH | Mrs Giffard |

*Oct. 30, &c. (cont.)*

omitted
HECATE

[*as altered by* DAVENANT]

## COVENT GARDEN

*Feb. 9*

| | |
|---|---|
| MACBETH* | Quin |
| MACDUFF | Ryan |
| DUNCAN* | Gibson |
| BANQUO | Bridgwater |
| MALCOLM | Hale |
| DONALBAIN | Anderson |
| LENNOX* | Stephens |
| SIWARD | Cashell |
| SEYTON* | Ridout |
| HECATE* | Rosco |
| 1ST MURDERER | Marten |
| 2ND MURDERER* | Stoppelaer |
| 1ST WITCH | Hippisley |
| 2ND WITCH | Woodward |
| 3RD WITCH | James |
| LADY MACDUFF | Mrs Stevens |
| LADY MACBETH* | Mrs Horton |

*Apr. 13; May 1*

| | |
|---|---|
| MACBETH | Sheridan |
| 2ND MURDERER | Bencraft |
| LADY MACBETH | Mrs Pritchard |

*Oct. 1, 12; Nov. 19*

| | |
|---|---|
| DUNCAN | Rosco |
| LENNOX | Ridout |
| SEYTON | Gibson |
| HECATE | Arthur |
| 2ND MURDERER | Bencraft |
| LADY MACBETH | Mrs Pritchard |

[*The original*]

## 1745 DRURY LANE

*Jan. 25*

| | |
|---|---|
| MACBETH | Garrick |
| DUNCAN | Berry |
| MACDUFF | Giffard |

## 1745 DRURY LANE (cont.)
### Jan. 25 (cont.)

| | |
|---|---|
| MALCOLM | Blakes |
| BANQUO | Havard |
| ROSS | Bridges |
| LENNOX | Turbutt |
| SIWARD | Winstone |
| DONALBAIN | Green |
| 1ST WITCH | Macklin |
| 2ND WITCH | Neale |
| 3RD WITCH | Yates |
| YOUNG SIWARD | Cross |
| FLEANCE | Miss Cole |
| SEYTON | Ray |
| ANGUS | Simpson |
| DOCTOR | Taswell |
| LADY MACDUFF | Mrs Mills |
| GENTLEWOMAN | Mrs Bennet |
| LADY MACBETH | Mrs Giffard |

[*as altered by* DAVENANT]

## COVENT GARDEN
### Nov. 15          Dec. 21

| | |   | | |
|---|---|---|---|---|
| MACBETH | Cashell | | 3RD WITCH | Hippisley |
| MACDUFF | Ryan |
| BANQUO | Bridgwater |
| MALCOLM | Hale |
| DUNCAN | Gibson |
| LENNOX | Ridout |
| SIWARD | Rosco |
| DONALBAIN | Anderson |
| SEYTON | Carr |
| FLEANCE | Miss Morrison |
| HECATE | Arthur |
| 1ST WITCH | Woodward |
| 2ND WITCH | James |
| 3RD WITCH* | Dunstall |
| 1ST MURDERER | Bencraft |
| 2ND MURDERER | Marten |
| LADY MACBETH | Mrs Pritchard |
| LADY MACDUFF | Mrs Hale |

## NEW WELLS, GOODMAN'S FIELDS
### Mar. 9

LADY MACBETH   Mrs Carlisle
No other parts assigned

[This assignment appears only in the advance bill in DA of Mar. 7.]

### Mar. 16. No parts assigned

295

## MACBETH
### [The original]

### 1746 DRURY LANE
*Nov. 7, 8*

|  |  |
|---|---|
| MACBETH | Barry |
| DUNCAN | Bridges |
| MALCOLM | [Tho.] Lacy |
| BANQUO | [W.] Mills |
| LENNOX | [L.] Sparks |
| MACDUFF | Delane |
| SEYTON | Blakes |
| HECATE | Berry |
| SIWARD | Winstone |
| DONALBAIN | Miss Cole |
| 1ST WITCH | Macklin |
| 2ND WITCH | Yates |
| 3RD WITCH | Neale |
| DOCTOR* | Goodfellow |
| 1ST MURDERER | Taswell |
| 2ND MURDERER | Bransby |
| FLEANCE* | Master Wilks |
| CAPTAIN | Usher |
| LADY MACDUFF | Mrs Mills |
| GENTLEWOMAN | Miss Minors |
| LADY MACBETH* | Mrs Macklin |

*Nov. 10, 11, 24*
    LADY MACBETH   Mrs Furnival

*Dec. 27*
    LADY MACBETH   Mrs Furnival
omitted
    DOCTOR, FLEANCE

### [as altered by DAVENANT]
### COVENT GARDEN
*Jan. 14, 22*

|  |  |
|---|---|
| MACBETH | Cashell |
| MACDUFF | Ryan |
| BANQUO | Bridgwater |
| MALCOLM | Hale |
| DUNCAN | Gibson |
| LENNOX | Ridout |
| SIWARD | Rosco |
| DONALBAIN | Anderson |
| SEYTON | Carr |
| FLEANCE | Miss Morrison |
| HECATE | Arthur |
| 1ST WITCH | Hippisley |
| 2ND WITCH | Woodward |
| 3RD WITCH | James |
| 1ST MURDERER | Bencraft |
| 2ND MURDERER | Marten |
| LADY MACBETH | Mrs Pritchard |
| LADY MACDUFF | Mrs Hale |

## MACBETH

*[The original]*

### 1746 COVENT GARDEN (cont.)
*June 27*

| | |
|---|---|
| MACBETH | Garrick |
| MACDUFF | Ryan |
| MALCOLM | Chapman |
| BANQUO | Cashell |
| LENNOX | Marr |
| SEYTON | Philips |
| SIWARD | Oates |
| DONALBAIN | Kennedy |
| FLEANCE | Miss Morrison |
| HECATE | Paget |
| 1ST WITCH | Marten |
| 2ND WITCH | Morgan |
| 3RD WITCH | Master Shuter |
| MURDERER | Stoppelaer |
| LADY MACDUFF | Miss Haughton |
| GENTLEWOMAN | Miss Ferguson |
| LADY MACBETH | Mrs Horton |

### 1747 DRURY LANE

*Mar. 14*

| | |
|---|---|
| MACBETH* | Barry |
| DUNCAN | Bridges |
| MALCOLM* | [Tho.] Lacy |
| BANQUO | [W.] Mills |
| LENNOX | [L.] Sparks |
| MACDUFF | Giffard |
| SEYTON | Blakes |
| HECATE | Berry |
| SIWARD | Winstone |
| DONALBAIN | Miss Cole |
| 1ST WITCH | Macklin |
| 2ND WITCH | Yates |
| 3RD WITCH | Neale |
| 1ST MURDERER* | Taswell |
| 2ND MURDERER | Bransby |
| CAPTAIN | Usher |
| LADY MACDUFF | Mrs Mills |
| GENTLEWOMAN | Miss Minors |
| LADY MACBETH* | Mrs Giffard |

*May 1*

| | |
|---|---|
| MACBETH | Delane |
| MALCOLM | Cross |
| 1ST MURDERER | Simpson |
| LADY MACBETH | Mrs Furnival |

### NEW WELLS, GOODMAN'S FIELDS

*Jan. 5, 6, 8, 14, 28*

| | |
|---|---|
| MACBETH* | Goodfellow |
| MACDUFF | Furnival |

*Mar. 16*

| | |
|---|---|
| MACBETH | Cushing |
| DUNCAN | Cross |

MACBETH

## 1747 NEW WELLS, GOODMAN'S FIELDS (cont.)

*Jan. 5, &c. (cont.)*

| | |
|---|---|
| BANQUO | Paget |
| DUNCAN* | Holmes |
| 1ST WITCH | [G.] Hallam |
| 2ND WITCH | Shuter |
| 3RD WITCH* | Banks |
| MALCOLM | Lee |
| DONALBAIN | Mrs Moreau |
| LENNOX* | Cushing |
| HECATE | L. Hallam |
| FLEANCE | Master Morgan |
| SIWARD* | Hart |
| SEYTON | Wignell |
| DOCTOR* | Miles |
| 1ST MURDERER | Dove |
| 2ND MURDERER | Baker |
| LADY MACDUFF | Mrs Bambridge |
| GENTLEWOMAN* | Mrs Beckham |
| LADY MACBETH | Miss Budgell |

*Mar. 16 (cont.)*

| | |
|---|---|
| 3RD WITCH | W. Hallam |
| LENNOX | Costollo |

omitted
    SIWARD, DOCTOR, GENTLEWOMAN

## 1748 DRURY LANE

*Mar. 19*

| | |
|---|---|
| MACBETH* | Garrick |
| DUNCAN* | [L.] Sparks |
| MACDUFF* | Delane |
| MALCOLM | Blakes |
| BANQUO* | Havard |
| ROSS | Lee |
| LENNOX* | Mozeen |
| SIWARD | Winstone |
| DONALBAIN | Miss Cole |
| HECATE | Berry |
| 1ST WITCH* | Arthur |
| 2ND WITCH | Neale |
| 3RD WITCH | Yates |
| YOUNG SIWARD* | Bransby |
| FLEANCE* | Master Cross |
| SEYTON* | Ray |
| ANGUS* | Simpson |
| DOCTOR* | Taswell |
| GENTLEWOMAN* | Miss Minors |
| LADY MACDUFF* | Mrs Mills |
| LADY MACBETH | Mrs Pritchard |

*Apr. 2*

| | |
|---|---|
| MACBETH | Barry |
| LADY MACDUFF | Mrs Elmy |

omitted
    YOUNG SIWARD, FLEANCE, SEYTON, ANGUS, DOCTOR, GENTLEWOMAN

[The playhouse bill for this performance is in the Garrick Club. It omits only FLEANCE, GENTLEWOMAN.]

*Apr. 27; May 13*

| | |
|---|---|
| MACBETH | Barry |

omitted
    YOUNG SIWARD, FLEANCE, SEYTON, ANGUS, DOCTOR, GENTLEWOMAN

*Oct. 28*

| | |
|---|---|
| MACBETH | Barry |
| DUNCAN | [W.] Mills |
| MACDUFF | Havard |
| BANQUO | Sowdon |
| LENNOX | Palmer |
| 1ST WITCH | Bridges |
| GENTLEWOMAN | Mrs Yates |

*Dec. 19*

| | |
|---|---|
| DUNCAN | [W.] Mills |
| MACDUFF | Havard |
| BANQUO | Sowdon |
| LENNOX | Palmer |
| 1ST WITCH | Bridges |
| GENTLEWOMAN | Mrs Yates |

MACBETH

## 1749 DRURY LANE
*Jan. 16*

| | |
|---|---|
| MACBETH | Barry |
| DUNCAN | [W.] Mills |
| MACDUFF | Havard |
| MALCOLM | Blakes |
| BANQUO | Sowdon |
| ROSS* | Lee |
| LENNOX* | Palmer |
| SIWARD* | Winstone |
| DONALBAIN* | Miss Cole |
| HECATE* | Berry |
| 1ST WITCH | Bridges |
| 2ND WITCH* | Neale |
| 3RD WITCH | Yates |
| YOUNG SIWARD* | Bransby |
| FLEANCE* | Master Cross |
| SEYTON* | Ray |
| ANGUS* | Simpson |
| DOCTOR* | Taswell |
| LADY MACDUFF | Mrs Mills |
| GENTLEWOMAN* | Mrs Yates |
| LADY MACBETH | Mrs Pritchard |

*Mar. 6*

| | |
|---|---|
| DOCTOR | Burton |

*Apr. 7*
omitted
   ROSS, LENNOX, SIWARD, DONALBAIN, YOUNG SIWARD, FLEANCE, SEYTON, ANGUS, DOCTOR, GENTLEWOMAN

*Oct. 17; Nov. 13*

| | |
|---|---|
| ROSS | King |
| LENNOX | Barnet |
| DONALBAIN | Master Mattocks |
| YOUNG SIWARD | Palmer |

*Dec. 30*

| | |
|---|---|
| ROSS | King |
| LENNOX | Barnet |
| DONALBAIN | Master Mattocks |
| 2ND WITCH | Shuter |
| YOUNG SIWARD | Palmer |
| omitted | |
|    HECATE | |

[*as altered by* DAVENANT]

## COVENT GARDEN
*Oct. 12; Dec. 14*

| | |
|---|---|
| MACBETH | Quin |
| MACDUFF | Ryan |
| DUNCAN | [L.] Sparks |
| BANQUO | Delane |
| MALCOLM | Anderson |
| DONALBAIN | Bennet |
| FLEANCE | Miss Morrison |
| SIWARD | Bransby |
| LENNOX | Ridout |
| SEYTON | Gibson |
| HECATE | Arthur |
| 1ST MURDERER | Bencraft |
| 2ND MURDERER | Marten |
| 1ST WITCH | Dunstall |
| 2ND WITCH | Collins |
| 3RD WITCH | Cushing |
| LADY MACDUFF | Mrs Barrington |
| LADY MACBETH | Mrs Woffington |

299

## MACBETH

[*The original*]

### 1750 DRURY LANE

*Jan. 29*

| | |
|---|---|
| MACBETH* | Barry |
| DUNCAN* | [W.] Mills |
| MACDUFF | Havard |
| MALCOLM | Blakes |
| BANQUO | Sowdon |
| ROSS* | King |
| LENNOX* | Barnet |
| SIWARD | Winstone |
| DONALBAIN | Master Mattocks |
| 1ST WITCH | Bridges |
| 2ND WITCH | Yates |
| 3RD WITCH | Shuter |
| YOUNG SIWARD* | Palmer |
| FLEANCE* | Master Cross |
| SEYTON* | Ray |
| ANGUS* | Simpson |
| DOCTOR* | Taswell |
| GENTLEWOMAN* | Mrs Yates |
| LADY MACDUFF | Mrs Mills |
| LADY MACBETH | Mrs Pritchard |

*Apr. 23*

| | |
|---|---|
| DUNCAN | Barnet |
| LENNOX | Ackman |

*Nov. 13*

| | |
|---|---|
| MACBETH | Garrick |
| DUNCAN | Berry |
| LENNOX | Scrase |
| DOCTOR added | Wilder |
| HECATE omitted | Layfield |
| ROSS | |

*Nov. 16*

| | |
|---|---|
| MACBETH | Garrick |
| DUNCAN | Berry |
| LENNOX added | Scrase |
| HECATE omitted | Layfield |

ROSS, YOUNG SIWARD, FLEANCE, SEYTON, ANGUS, DOCTOR, GENTLEWOMAN

[*as altered by* DAVENANT]

### COVENT GARDEN

*Mar. 13; Apr. 16*

| | |
|---|---|
| MACBETH | Quin |
| MACDUFF | Ryan |
| DUNCAN* | [L.] Sparks |
| BANQUO* | Bridgwater |
| MALCOLM | Anderson |
| DONALBAIN | Bennet |
| FLEANCE | Miss Morrison |
| SIWARD | Bransby |
| LENNOX | Ridout |
| SEYTON* | Gibson |
| HECATE | Arthur |
| 1ST MURDERER | Bencraft |
| 2ND MURDERER | Marten |
| 1ST WITCH | Dunstall |
| 2ND WITCH | Collins |
| 3RD WITCH | Cushing |
| LADY MACDUFF | Mrs Barrington |
| LADY MACBETH | Mrs Woffington |

*Nov. 8*

| | |
|---|---|
| DUNCAN | Gibson |
| BANQUO | [L.] Sparks |
| SEYTON | Usher |

# MARINA

George Lillo's alteration of PERICLES, q.v.

# MEASURE FOR MEASURE

Adapted by Charles Gildon. In five acts.

1700   D. Brown.

Act I opens with about 75 new lines in which are summarized the events of *I*. A few lines of the original are retained: *I. ii. 180*; *I. iv. 57–9*, &c. This is followed by *II. i. 1–40*, much altered, and by *I. ii. 18–end*, abridged. The act ends with the first part of Purcell's masque, *The Loves of Dido and Aeneas*. In this act, as elsewhere throughout the play, Gildon borrows occasionally from Davenant's earlier alteration of the original, *The Law against Lovers*.

Act II, scene i is *II. iv*, slightly altered. Scene ii consists chiefly of the second part of the masque. Scene iii is *I. iii*, rewritten, and *II. iii. 1–9*, verbatim. About 90 new lines follow: Claudio tells the Duke that he is lawfully married to Juliet. The scene closes with *II. iii. 19–end*, much rewritten.

Act III, scene i is *III. i*, considerably altered; it is in verse throughout. Scene ii is the third part of the masque.

Act IV, scene i is new: Angelo tempts Isabella by promising her some jewels. Scene ii is *IV. i*, almost verbatim. Scene iii is *IV. ii. 66–130*, slightly altered, followed by about 100 new lines: Claudio bids farewell to Juliet. The scene ends with *IV. iii. 119–57*, altered.

Act V opens with *IV. iv*, much reduced, followed by *V. i. 1–74, 106–26, 168–233*, all somewhat altered and occasionally expanded. A brief new scene follows: the Duke confronts Angelo with the jewels. Then comes *V. i. 376–end*, somewhat reduced. The play ends with the fourth part of the masque.

See Genest, ii. 221–3; Odell, i. 72–4; Spencer, 330–4.

'As it is Acted at the Theatre-Royal in Lincolns-Inn-Fields.'

1722   J. Tonson.

This version follows the original throughout, save for excisions. The most important of these are:

Act I. ii. 1–124; iv. 30–44, 51–5.
Act II. i. 39–end; ii. 84–7, 113–23.
Act IV. i. 9–17; iii. 1–21.
Act V. i. 537–end.

Act III consists of one scene only. In Act IV there is no interruption between scenes ii and iii. The only interpolation appears to be 8 new lines at the end of the play in praise of good kings.

[as altered by GILDON]

1706 QUEEN'S
Apr. 26. No parts assigned

MEASURE FOR MEASURE

[*The original*]
## 1720 LINCOLN'S INN FIELDS
*Dec. 8, 9, 10, 12, 13*

| | |
|---|---|
| DUKE | Quin |
| ANGELO | Boheme |
| CLAUDIO | Ryan |
| ISABELLA | Mrs Seymour |

[In the acting version published by Tonson in 1722 the cast is the same as that of this performance, with the following additions:

| | |
|---|---|
| ESCALUS | Diggs |
| LUCIO | C. Bullock |
| PROVOST | Egleton |
| FRIAR THOMAS | Orfeur |
| ELBOW | Hall |
| CLOWN | Spiller |
| ABHORSON | Morgan |
| BARNARDINE | H. Bullock |
| MARIANA | Mrs Spiller |
| JULIET | Miss Stone |
| MRS OVERDONE | Mrs Gulick] |

## 1721 LINCOLN'S INN FIELDS
*Jan. 2, 23; Mar. 25*

| | |
|---|---|
| DUKE | Quin |
| ANGELO | Boheme |
| CLAUDIO | Ryan |
| ISABELLA | Mrs Seymour |

No other parts assigned

*Oct. 10; Nov. 27*
added
| | |
|---|---|
| LUCIO | C. Bullock |

*Dec. 14*
added
| | |
|---|---|
| LUCIO | C. Bullock |
| ESCALUS | Diggs |

[DP omits ESCALUS.]

## 1722 LINCOLN'S INN FIELDS
*Nov. 2*

| | |
|---|---|
| DUKE | Quin |
| ANGELO | Boheme |
| CLAUDIO | Ryan |
| LUCIO | Egleton |
| ISABELLA | Mrs Seymour |

## 1723 LINCOLN'S INN FIELDS
*Jan. 14*

| | |
|---|---|
| DUKE | Quin |
| ANGELO | Boheme |
| CLAUDIO | Ryan |
| LUCIO | Egleton |
| ISABELLA* | Mrs Seymour |

*Apr. 19*
| | |
|---|---|
| ISABELLA | Mrs Boheme [i.e. formerly Mrs Seymour] |

added
| | |
|---|---|
| ESCALUS | Diggs |

302

## 1724 LINCOLN'S INN FIELDS
*Jan. 4, 16; Feb. 13; Nov. 14.* No parts assigned

*Apr. 9*
DUKE   Quin
ANGELO   Boheme
CLAUDIO   Ryan
ISABELLA   Mrs Parker
No other parts assigned

*May 29*
added
LUCIO   Egleton
PROVOST   Diggs

## 1725 LINCOLN'S INN FIELDS
*Feb. 11.* No parts assigned

## 1726 LINCOLN'S INN FIELDS
*Jan. 19; Mar. 7.* No parts assigned

## 1727 LINCOLN'S INN FIELDS
*Jan. 14; Mar. 20; May 25.* No parts assigned

## 1729 LINCOLN'S INN FIELDS
*Jan. 13*
DUKE   Quin
ANGELO*   Milward
ESCALUS*   Ogden
CLAUDIO   Ryan
LUCIO*   Chapman
PROVOST*   Pitt
ISABELLA*   Mrs Buchanan

*Feb. 1*
omitted
ESCALUS, LUCIO, PROVOST

*Apr. 26*
ISABELLA   Mrs Berriman
added
CLOWN   Hippisley
BARNARDINE   H. Bullock
MARIANA   Miss Holliday

*Nov. 22*
ANGELO   Boheme
omitted
ESCALUS, LUCIO, PROVOST

## 1730 LINCOLN'S INN FIELDS
*Jan. 17; Nov. 7.* No parts assigned

## 1731 LINCOLN'S INN FIELDS
*May 17*
DUKE   Quin
ANGELO   Milward
ESCALUS   Ogden
CLAUDIO   Ryan
LUCIO   Chapman
PROVOST   Hulett
ISABELLA   Mrs Berriman
MARIANA   Mrs Kilby

*Feb. 2; Nov. 13.* No parts assigned
[On Feb. 2 Genest (iii. 310) has, 'Angelo – Ryan:—perhaps a mistake in the manuscript bill—Ryan usually acted Claudio'.]

## 1732 LINCOLN'S INN FIELDS
*Jan. 15.* No parts assigned
*Oct. 25*

| | |
|---|---|
| DUKE | Quin |
| ANGELO | Milward |
| ESCALUS | [J.] Lacy |
| CLAUDIO | Ryan |
| LUCIO | Chapman |
| PROVOST | Paget |
| CLOWN | Hippisley |
| MARIANA | Miss Holliday |
| ISABELLA | Mrs Hallam |

## 1733 COVENT GARDEN
*Jan. 12*

| | |
|---|---|
| DUKE | Quin |
| ANGELO* | Milward |
| ESCALUS | [J.] Lacy |
| CLAUDIO | Ryan |
| LUCIO | Chapman |
| PROVOST* | Paget |
| CLOWN | Hippisley |
| MARIANA* | Miss Holliday |
| ISABELLA | Mrs Hallam |

*Nov. 19*

| | |
|---|---|
| ANGELO | Walker |
| PROVOST | Wignell |
| MARIANA | Mrs Templer |

## 1734 COVENT GARDEN
*Feb. 6.* No parts assigned

## 1737 DRURY LANE
*Mar. 10; Apr. 21*

| | |
|---|---|
| DUKE | Quin |
| ANGELO | Milward |
| ESCALUS* | Berry |
| CLAUDIO | [W.] Mills |
| LUCIO | [T.] Cibber |
| PROVOST* | Shepard |
| CLOWN | Miller |
| ELBOW | Harper |
| BARNARDINE | Ray |
| MARIANA* | Miss Holliday |
| ISABELLA | Mrs Cibber |

*Nov. 1*

| | |
|---|---|
| ESCALUS | Wright |
| PROVOST | Havard |
| MARIANA | Mrs Mills [i.e. formerly Miss Holliday] |

added

| | |
|---|---|
| FRIAR PETER | Winstone |
| FRIAR THOMAS | Cole |
| JULIET | Miss Brett |
| MRS OVERDONE | Mrs Marshall |

## 1738 DRURY LANE
*Jan. 26; Apr. 12*

| | |
|---|---|
| DUKE | Quin |
| ANGELO | Milward |
| CLAUDIO | [W.] Mills |
| LUCIO | [T.] Cibber |

304

## 1738 DRURY LANE (cont.)

*Jan. 26, &c. (cont.)*

| | |
|---|---|
| ESCALUS | Wright |
| FRIAR PETER | Winstone |
| FRIAR THOMAS | Cole |
| PROVOST | Havard |
| CLOWN | Miller |
| ELBOW | Harper |
| BARNARDINE | Ray |
| ISABELLA | Mrs Cibber |
| MARIANA | Mrs Mills |
| JULIET | Miss Tollett |
| MRS OVERDONE | Mrs Marshall |

## 1742 COVENT GARDEN

*Nov. 25, 26; Dec. 4*

| | |
|---|---|
| DUKE | Quin |
| CLAUDIO | Ryan |
| LUCIO | Chapman |
| ESCALUS | Rosco |
| ANGELO | Cashell |
| CLOWN | Hippisley |
| PROVOST | Ridout |
| ABHORSON | Bencraft |
| BARNARDINE | Evans |
| MARIANA | Mrs Hale |
| JULIET | Miss Hilliard |
| FRANCISCA | Mrs Bland |
| MRS OVERDONE | Mrs Martin |
| ISABELLA | Mrs Cibber |

## 1743 COVENT GARDEN

*Jan. 4; Feb. 1, 21; Mar. 8*

| | |
|---|---|
| DUKE | Quin |
| CLAUDIO | Ryan |
| LUCIO* | Chapman |
| ESCALUS | Rosco |
| ANGELO | Cashell |
| CLOWN | Hippisley |
| PROVOST | Ridout |
| ABHORSON | Bencraft |
| BARNARDINE | Evans |
| MARIANA | Mrs Hale |
| JULIET | Miss Hilliard |
| FRANCISCA | Mrs Bland |
| MRS OVERDONE | Mrs Martin |
| ISABELLA | Mrs Cibber |

*Apr. 11*

| | |
|---|---|
| LUCIO | Woodward |

## 1744 COVENT GARDEN
*Jan. 14, 23*

| | |
|---|---|
| DUKE | Quin |
| CLAUDIO | Ryan |
| LUCIO | Chapman |
| ESCALUS | Rosco |
| ANGELO | Cashell |
| CLOWN | Hippisley |
| PROVOST | Ridout |
| ABHORSON | Bencraft |
| BARNARDINE | Stoppelaer |
| MARIANA | Mrs Hale |
| JULIET* | Miss Hilliard |
| FRANCISCA* | Mrs Mullart |
| MRS OVERDONE | Mrs Martin |
| ISABELLA | Mrs Pritchard |

*Apr. 4*

| | |
|---|---|
| FRANCISCA | Mrs Bland |

*Nov. 1*

| | |
|---|---|
| JULIET | Mrs Bland |

[The playhouse bill for Jan. 14 is in FSL.]

## 1745 COVENT GARDEN
*Apr. 6*

| | |
|---|---|
| DUKE | Quin |
| CLAUDIO | Ryan |
| LUCIO | Chapman |
| CLOWN | Hippisley |
| ANGELO | Cashell |
| ESCALUS | Rosco |
| PROVOST | Ridout |
| ABHORSON | Bencraft |
| BARNARDINE | Stoppelaer |
| MARIANA | Mrs Hale |
| JULIET | Mrs Bland |
| FRANCISCA | Mrs Rowley |
| MRS OVERDONE | Mrs Martin |
| ISABELLA | Mrs Pritchard |

## 1746 DRURY LANE
*Apr. 11*

| | |
|---|---|
| DUKE | Berry |
| ANGELO | Havard |
| ESCALUS | Winstone |
| CLAUDIO | [W.] Mills |
| CLOWN | Barrington |
| LUCIO | Macklin |
| FRIAR PETER | Bridges |
| FRIAR THOMAS | Simpson |
| PROVOST | Blakes |

## 1746 DRURY LANE (*cont.*)
*Apr. 11 (cont.)*

| | |
|---|---|
| ABHORSON | Collins |
| ELBOW | I. Sparks |
| BARNARDINE | Ray |
| MARIANA | Mrs Bennet |
| JULIET | Miss Pitt |
| MRS OVERDONE | Mrs Bridges |
| FRANCISCA | Miss Cole |
| ISABELLA | Mrs Woffington |

## COVENT GARDEN
*Dec. 17*

| | |
|---|---|
| DUKE | Quin |
| CLAUDIO | Ryan |
| ANGELO | Cashell |
| LUCIO | Chapman |
| CLOWN | Hippisley |
| ESCALUS | Rosco |
| PROVOST | Ridout |
| ABHORSON | Bencraft |
| BARNARDINE | Stoppelaer |
| MARIANA | Mrs Hale |
| JULIET | Mrs Rowley |
| FRANCISCA | Mrs Bland |
| MRS OVERDONE | Mrs Martin |
| ISABELLA | Mrs Cibber |

## 1748 COVENT GARDEN
*Nov. 26, 30; Dec. 31*

| | |
|---|---|
| DUKE | Quin |
| CLAUDIO | Ryan |
| ANGELO | [L.] Sparks |
| LUCIO | Cushing |
| ESCALUS | Gibson |
| PROVOST | Ridout |
| ABHORSON | Bencraft |
| BARNARDINE | Stoppelaer |
| CLOWN | Arthur |
| ELBOW | Marten |
| MARIANA | Mrs Hale |
| JULIET | Miss Haughton |
| FRANCISCA | Miss Copin |
| MRS OVERDONE | Mrs Bambridge |
| ISABELLA | Mrs Woffington |

[LUCIO appears as above. Genest (iv. 276) has, 'Lucio is omitted'.]

## MEASURE FOR MEASURE

### 1749 DRURY LANE
*Jan. 9*

| | |
|---|---|
| DUKE | Berry |
| ANGELO | Havard |
| ESCALUS | Winstone |
| CLAUDIO | Lee |
| CLOWN | Yates |
| FRIAR PETER | Usher |
| FRIAR THOMAS | Simpson |
| PROVOST | Blakes |
| ELBOW | Taswell |
| LUCIO | Woodward |
| ABHORSON | Vaughan |
| BARNARDINE | Ray |
| MARIANA | Mrs Bennet |
| JULIET | Mrs Simpson |
| MRS OVERDONE | Mrs Bridges |
| FRANCISCA | Miss Cole |
| ISABELLA | Mrs Cibber |

### COVENT GARDEN
*Mar. 31*

| | |
|---|---|
| DUKE | Quin |
| CLAUDIO | Ryan |
| ANGELO | [L.] Sparks |
| LUCIO | Cushing |
| ISABELLA | Mrs Woffington |

*Oct. 25*
added

| | |
|---|---|
| ESCALUS | Gibson |
| PROVOST | Ridout |
| ABHORSON | Bencraft |
| BARNARDINE | Dunstall |
| CLOWN | Arthur |
| ELBOW | Marten |
| MARIANA | Mrs Barrington |
| JULIET | Miss Haughton |
| FRANCISCA | Miss [E.] Hippisley |
| MRS OVERDONE | Mrs Bambridge |

### 1750 COVENT GARDEN
*Jan. 15; Dec. 4*

| | |
|---|---|
| DUKE | Quin |
| CLAUDIO | Ryan |
| ESCALUS | Gibson |
| PROVOST | Ridout |
| ABHORSON | Bencraft |
| BARNARDINE | Stoppelaer |
| CLOWN | Arthur |
| ELBOW | Marten |
| ANGELO | [L.] Sparks |
| LUCIO | Cushing |
| MARIANA | Mrs Barrington |
| JULIET | Miss Haughton |
| FRANCISCA | Miss [E.] Hippisley |
| MRS OVERDONE | Mrs Bambridge |
| ISABELLA | Mrs Woffington |

# THE MERCHANT OF VENICE

Adapted as THE JEW OF VENICE, by George Granville, Baron Lansdowne. In five acts.

1701 Ber. Lintott.

Act I, scene i is *I. i. 77–end*, somewhat reduced and occasionally altered. Scene ii is *I. ii*, much reduced. Scene iii is *I. iii*, slightly reduced.

Act II begins with *II. v. 11–end*, considerably reduced. This is followed without interruption by *II. vi. 26–end*, also reduced. Then follows a brief new scene: Shylock, Antonio, and Bassanio feast together. At its end Bassanio has Lorenzo's speech in *V. i. 70–88*. The act concludes with a masque of *Peleus and Thetis*. (From this act are omitted *II. i–iv, vii–ix*.)

Act III, scene i is *III. ii*, somewhat rewritten. Scene ii is *III. iii*, only slightly altered. Inserted in it are Shylock's speech in *III. i. 56–78*, and an assemblage into one speech of his dialogue with Tubal, *III. i. 90–end*.

Act IV is *IV. i*, somewhat reduced and slightly altered. *IV. ii* is omitted.

Act V is *V. i*, somewhat expanded, but with occasional omissions, notably *25–88*.

See Genest, ii. 243–5; Odell, i. 76–9; Spencer, 340–3.

No acting versions of the original were published before 1750.

## [as THE JEW OF VENICE]

### 1701 LINCOLN'S INN FIELDS
*n.d., probably May*

| | |
|---|---|
| BASSANIO | Betterton |
| ANTONIO | Verbruggen |
| GRATIANO | Booth |
| LORENZO | Baily |
| SHYLOCK | Dogget |
| DUKE | Harris |
| PORTIA | Mrs Bracegirdle |
| NERISSA | Mrs Boman |
| JESSICA | Mrs Porter |

[The bill for this (the first) performance is missing. The above assignment is taken from the printed text.]

### 1706 QUEEN'S
*Oct. 23.* No parts assigned

### 1711 DRURY LANE
*Feb. 3*

| | |
|---|---|
| SHYLOCK | Dogget |
| BASSANIO | Booth |
| ANTONIO | Mills |
| GRATIANO | C. Bullock |
| LORENZO | Ryan |
| DUKE | Corey |

THE MERCHANT OF VENICE [*as* THE JEW OF VENICE]

## 1711 DRURY LANE (*cont.*)
*Feb. 3 (cont.)*
    PORTIA    Mrs Bradshaw
    NERISSA    Mrs Bicknell
    JESSICA    Mrs Sherburn

## 1715 LINCOLN'S INN FIELDS
*Feb. 28; Mar. 22; Nov. 18.* No parts assigned

*July 8*
    PORTIA    Mrs Thurmond
No other parts assigned

## 1716 LINCOLN'S INN FIELDS
*Jan. 20; July 20.* No parts assigned

## 1717 LINCOLN'S INN FIELDS
*May 16*
    SHYLOCK    Griffin
    PORTIA    Mrs Thurmond
No other parts assigned

## 1718 LINCOLN'S INN FIELDS
*Jan. 24; Apr. 26.* No parts assigned

## 1719 LINCOLN'S INN FIELDS
*Jan. 2*
    SHYLOCK    Griffin
No other parts assigned

## 1720 LINCOLN'S INN FIELDS
*Feb. 26*
    SHYLOCK    Griffin
    BASSANIO    [J.] Leigh
    ANTONIO    Ryan
    GRATIANO    Ch. Bullock
    PORTIA    Mrs Spiller
    NERISSA    Mrs Bullock
    JESSICA    Miss Stone

## 1721 LINCOLN'S INN FIELDS
*Mar. 28.* No parts assigned

*Oct. 17*
    SHYLOCK    Boheme
    ANTONIO    Ryan
    BASSANIO    Walker

*Nov. 10*
    JESSICA    Miss Stone

# THE MERCHANT OF VENICE [as THE JEW OF VENICE]

## 1721 LINCOLN'S INN FIELDS (cont.)
*Oct. 17 (cont.)*
| | |
|---|---|
| GRATIANO | C. Bullock |
| PORTIA | Mrs Seymour |
| NERISSA | Mrs Bullock |
| JESSICA* | Mrs Parlour |

## 1722 LINCOLN'S INN FIELDS
*Jan. 5*
| | |
|---|---|
| SHYLOCK | Boheme |
| BASSANIO | Walker |
| ANTONIO | Ryan |
| GRATIANO* | C. Bullock |
| PORTIA | Mrs Seymour |
| NERISSA | Mrs Bullock |

*Nov. 16*
| | |
|---|---|
| GRATIANO added | Egleton |
| JESSICA | Mrs Rogeir |

## 1723 LINCOLN'S INN FIELDS
*Jan. 25*
| | |
|---|---|
| SHYLOCK | Boheme |
| ANTONIO | Ryan |
| BASSANIO | Walker |
| GRATIANO | Egleton |
| PORTIA | Mrs Seymour |
| NERISSA | Mrs Bullock |
| JESSICA | Mrs Rogeir |

## 1727 LINCOLN'S INN FIELDS
*Apr. 17*          *Nov. 13, 30.* No parts assigned
| | |
|---|---|
| ANTONIO | Ryan |
| BASSANIO | Walker |
| GRATIANO | Berriman |
| PORTIA | Mrs Berriman |
| NERISSA | Mrs Bullock |
| JESSICA | Mrs Laguerre |

## 1728 LINCOLN'S INN FIELDS
*May 23*
| | |
|---|---|
| SHYLOCK | Ogden |
| ANTONIO | Ryan |
| BASSANIO | Walker |
| GRATIANO | Milward |
| PORTIA | Mrs Berriman |
| NERISSA | Mrs Bullock |
| JESSICA | Mrs Palin |

# THE MERCHANT OF VENICE [*as* THE JEW OF VENICE]

## 1729 LINCOLN'S INN FIELDS
*Jan. 23; Dec. 16*. No parts assigned

## 1730 LINCOLN'S INN FIELDS
*Oct. 7*                                *Nov. 21*. No parts assigned

| | |
|---|---|
| BASSANIO | Walker |
| ANTONIO | Ryan |
| GRATIANO | Milward |
| SHYLOCK | Boheme |
| LORENZO | Houghton |
| DUKE | Ogden |
| PORTIA | Mrs Berriman |
| NERISSA | Mrs Bullock |
| JESSICA | Miss Holliday |

## 1731 LINCOLN'S INN FIELDS
*Feb. 22.* No parts assigned

*Oct. 20*

| | |
|---|---|
| BASSANIO | Walker |
| ANTONIO | Ryan |
| GRATIANO | Milward |
| SHYLOCK | Ogden |
| LORENZO | Houghton |
| PORTIA | Mrs Hallam |
| NERISSA | Mrs Bullock |
| JESSICA | Miss Holliday |

## 1732 LINCOLN'S INN FIELDS
*Jan. 25.* No parts assigned

## 1734 COVENT GARDEN
*Feb. 8.* No parts assigned

## 1735 COVENT GARDEN
*Feb. 11*

| | |
|---|---|
| DUKE | Hale |
| BASSANIO | Walker |
| ANTONIO | Ryan |
| SHYLOCK | Aston |
| LORENZO | Houghton |
| GRATIANO | Chapman |
| SALERIO | Wignell |
| PORTIA | Mrs Hallam |
| NERISSA | Mrs Bullock |
| JESSICA | Miss Bincks |

[Additions from the original, incorporating SOLANIO and SALARINO, may have been used in this performance. In Lansdowne's alteration there is no such character as SALERIO.]

## THE MERCHANT OF VENICE [*as* THE JEW OF VENICE]

### 1736 COVENT GARDEN
*Feb. 12.* No parts assigned

### 1739 COVENT GARDEN
*Jan. 23*

| BASSANIO | Walker |
| ANTONIO | Ryan |
| GRATIANO | Chapman |
| SHYLOCK | Arthur |
| NERISSA | Mrs Bellamy |
| PORTIA | Mrs Hallam |

[*The original*]

### 1741 DRURY LANE
*Feb. 14, 16, 17, 19, 21, 23, 26, 28;*
*Mar. 2, 3, 7, 9, 12, 16, 19*

| ANTONIO* | Quin |
| BASSANIO | Milward |
| GRATIANO | [W.] Mills |
| SHYLOCK | Macklin |
| LAUNCELOT* | Chapman |
| GOBBO | Johnson |
| SOLANIO | Berry |
| MOROCCO* | Cashell |
| LORENZO* | Havard |
| ARRAGON* | Turbutt |
| DUKE | Winstone |
| TUBAL | Taswell |
| SALARINO | Ridout |
| PORTIA | Mrs Clive |
| NERISSA* | Mrs Pritchard |
| JESSICA* | Miss Woodman |

*Apr. 7, 10, 23, 30; May 18*
omitted
    ARRAGON

*Nov. 2, 3, 7, 17; Dec. 2*

| ANTONIO | Delane |
| LAUNCELOT | Neale |
| MOROCCO | Woodburn |
| LORENZO | Lowe |
| NERISSA | Mrs Woffington |

added
    BALTHAZAR  Green
omitted
    ARRAGON

*Dec. 22*

| ANTONIO | Delane |
| LAUNCELOT | Neale |
| MOROCCO | Woodburn |
| LORENZO | Lowe |
| NERISSA | Mrs Woffington |
| JESSICA | Mrs Ridout [i.e. formerly Miss Woodman] |

added
    BALTHAZAR  Green
omitted
    ARRAGON

### 1742 DRURY LANE
*Jan. 11*

| ANTONIO | Delane |
| BASSANIO* | Milward |
| GRATIANO | [W.] Mills |
| SHYLOCK | Macklin |
| LAUNCELOT | Neale |
| GOBBO* | Johnson |
| SOLANIO | Berry |
| MOROCCO | Woodburn |
| BALTHAZAR | Green |

*Mar. 6, 18*

| BASSANIO | Havard |

*Apr. 23*

| BASSANIO | Havard |
| NERISSA | Mrs Bennet |

*May 7*

| BASSANIO | Havard |
| GOBBO | Ray |
| LORENZO | Cross |
| NERISSA | Mrs Bennet |

## 1742 DRURY LANE (cont.)

**Jan. 11 (cont.)**

| | |
|---|---|
| DUKE | Winstone |
| TUBAL | Taswell |
| SALARINO* | Ridout |
| LORENZO* | Lowe |
| PORTIA | Mrs Clive |
| NERISSA* | Mrs Woffington |
| JESSICA | Mrs Ridout |

**Sept. 11, 23**

| | |
|---|---|
| BASSANIO | Havard |
| SALARINO | Turbutt |
| NERISSA | Mrs Bennet |
| omitted | |
| GOBBO | |

**Oct. 25**

| | |
|---|---|
| BASSANIO | Havard |
| SALARINO | Blakes |
| NERISSA | Mrs Bennet |
| omitted | |
| GOBBO | |

**Nov. 27**

| | |
|---|---|
| BASSANIO | Havard |
| GOBBO | Ray |
| SALARINO | Blakes |
| NERISSA | Mrs Bennet |

## 1743 DRURY LANE

**Jan. 21**

| | |
|---|---|
| ANTONIO | Delane |
| BASSANIO | Havard |
| GRATIANO | [W.] Mills |
| SHYLOCK | Macklin |
| LAUNCELOT | Neale |
| SOLANIO* | Berry |
| MOROCCO* | Woodburn |
| BALTHAZAR | Green |
| DUKE | Winstone |
| TUBAL | Taswell |
| SALARINO | Blakes |
| LORENZO | Lowe |
| GOBBO | Ray |
| NERISSA | Mrs Bennet |
| JESSICA | Mrs Ridout |
| PORTIA | Mrs Clive |

**Apr. 15; May 20**

| | |
|---|---|
| SOLANIO | Cross |
| omitted | |
| MOROCCO | |

## 1744 DRURY LANE

**May 4**

| | |
|---|---|
| SHYLOCK* | Shepard |
| ANTONIO | Delane |
| BASSANIO | Havard |
| GRATIANO | [W.] Mills |
| LAUNCELOT | Neale |
| GOBBO | Ray |
| MOROCCO | Woodburn |
| LORENZO* | Cross |
| NERISSA | Mrs Bennet |

**Dec. 19**

| | |
|---|---|
| SHYLOCK | Macklin |
| LORENZO | Lowe |
| added | |
| TUBAL | Taswell |
| SOLANIO | Berry |
| SALARINO | Blakes |
| BALTHAZAR | Green |

**Dec. 20**

| | |
|---|---|
| SHYLOCK | Macklin |
| LORENZO | Lowe |

## THE MERCHANT OF VENICE

### 1744 DRURY LANE (cont.)

*May 4 (cont.)*
| | |
|---|---|
| JESSICA | Mrs Ridout |
| PORTIA | Mrs Woffington |

*Dec. 20 (cont.)*
added
| | |
|---|---|
| TUBAL | Taswell |
| SOLANIO | Berry |
| SALARINO | Blakes |
| DUKE | Winstone |
| BALTHAZAR | Green |

### COVENT GARDEN

*Mar. 13*
| | |
|---|---|
| ANTONIO | Quin |
| BASSANIO | Hale |
| GRATIANO | Ryan |
| SHYLOCK* | Rosco |
| LAUNCELOT | Chapman |
| GOBBO* | James |
| LORENZO | Beard |
| SALARINO* | Ridout |
| SOLANIO | Gibson |
| DUKE | Marten |
| TUBAL* | Stoppelaer |
| NERISSA | Mrs Pritchard |
| JESSICA* | Miss Edwards [first appearance on the stage, i.e. as an actress, not a singer] |
| PORTIA | Mrs Clive |

*Apr. 7*
| | |
|---|---|
| SHYLOCK | James |
| GOBBO | Anderson |
| JESSICA | Mrs Vincent |

*Apr. 26*
| | |
|---|---|
| SHYLOCK | Ridout |
| GOBBO | Anderson |
| SALARINO | Goodall |
| TUBAL | Dunstall |
| JESSICA | Mrs Vincent |

### 1745 DRURY LANE

*Jan. 1, 18; Mar. 4*
| | |
|---|---|
| SHYLOCK | Macklin |
| ANTONIO | Delane |
| BASSANIO | Havard |
| GRATIANO | [W.] Mills |
| LAUNCELOT | Neale |
| LORENZO | Lowe |
| GOBBO | Ray |
| MOROCCO | Woodburn |
| TUBAL* | Taswell |
| SOLANIO | Berry |
| SALARINO | Blakes |
| DUKE | Winstone |
| BALTHAZAR* | Green |
| NERISSA | Mrs Bennet |
| JESSICA* | Mrs Ridout |
| PORTIA* | Mrs Woffington |

*Feb. 4*
| | |
|---|---|
| JESSICA | Miss Minors |

*Apr. 27*
| | |
|---|---|
| TUBAL | Vaughan |
| BALTHAZAR | Simpson |

*May 13*
| | |
|---|---|
| BALTHAZAR | Simpson |

*Nov. 23*
| | |
|---|---|
| PORTIA | Mrs Clive |
| omitted | |
| BALTHAZAR | |

*Dec. 6*
| | |
|---|---|
| TUBAL | Vaughan |
| PORTIA | Mrs Clive |
| omitted | |
| BALTHAZAR | |

315

## 1745 COVENT GARDEN
*Apr. 23*

| | |
|---|---|
| SHYLOCK | Lalauze |
| ANTONIO | Cashell |
| BASSANIO | Hale |
| GRATIANO | Ryan |
| LAUNCELOT | Chapman |
| LORENZO | Hayman |
| MOROCCO | Carr |
| GOBBO | Arthur |
| BALTHAZAR | Anderson |
| SALARINO | Ridout |
| SOLANIO | Gibson |
| DUKE | Marten |
| TUBAL | Stoppelaer |
| JESSICA | Mrs Vincent |
| NERISSA | Mrs Pritchard |
| PORTIA | Mrs Clive |

## 1746 DRURY LANE
*Jan. 10*

| | |
|---|---|
| SHYLOCK | Macklin |
| ANTONIO | Delane |
| BASSANIO* | Havard |
| GRATIANO* | L. Sparks |
| LAUNCELOT | Neale |
| LORENZO | Lowe |
| GOBBO | Ray |
| MOROCCO* | Woodburn |
| TUBAL* | Taswell |
| DUKE* | Winstone |
| SALARINO* | Blakes |
| SOLANIO | Berry |
| BALTHAZAR* | Simpson |
| NERISSA | Mrs Bennet |
| JESSICA* | Miss Minors |
| PORTIA | Mrs Clive |

*Feb. 8*

| | |
|---|---|
| GRATIANO | [W.] Mills |

*Mar. 22*

| | |
|---|---|
| GRATIANO | [W.] Mills |
| JESSICA | Miss Edwards |

*May 3*

| | |
|---|---|
| GRATIANO | [W.] Mills |
| JESSICA | Mrs Ridout |

omitted
   MOROCCO, TUBAL, DUKE, SALARINO, BALTHAZAR

*Sept. 23; Nov. 12*

| | |
|---|---|
| BASSANIO | [W.] Mills |
| MOROCCO | Bridges |
| JESSICA | Mrs Ridout |

### COVENT GARDEN
*Mar. 10*

| | |
|---|---|
| SHYLOCK* | Ryan |
| ANTONIO | Cashell |
| BASSANIO | Hale |
| GRATIANO* | [T.] Cibber |
| LORENZO | Beard |
| LAUNCELOT | Chapman |
| SALARINO | Ridout |
| MOROCCO | Carr |

*Apr. 26*

| | |
|---|---|
| SHYLOCK | James |
| GRATIANO | Anderson |

omitted
   LEONARDO

316

THE MERCHANT OF VENICE

## 1746 COVENT GARDEN (cont.)
*Mar. 10 (cont.)*

| | |
|---|---|
| LEONARDO* | Anderson |
| GOBBO | Arthur |
| BALTHAZAR | Hayman |
| SOLANIO | Gibson |
| DUKE | Marten |
| TUBAL | Stoppelaer |
| JESSICA | Mrs Vincent |
| NERISSA | Miss Hippisley |
| PORTIA | Mrs Pritchard |

## 1747 DRURY LANE
*Jan. 29*

| | |
|---|---|
| SHYLOCK | Macklin |
| ANTONIO | Delane |
| BASSANIO* | [W.] Mills |
| GRATIANO* | [L.] Sparks |
| LAUNCELOT | Neale |
| MOROCCO* | Bridges |
| DUKE | Winstone |
| SOLANIO | Berry |
| SALARINO | Blakes |
| GOBBO | Ray |
| TUBAL | Taswell |
| BALTHAZAR | Simpson |
| JESSICA | Mrs Ridout |
| NERISSA | Mrs Bennet |
| PORTIA | Mrs Clive |

*Feb. 9, 27; May 16*
added
LORENZO  Lowe

*Sept. 15; Oct. 27*

| | |
|---|---|
| BASSANIO | Havard |
| GRATIANO | [W.] Mills |
| MOROCCO | [I.] Sparks |

added
LORENZO  Lowe

## 1748 DRURY LANE
*Jan. 1; May 9*

| | |
|---|---|
| SHYLOCK* | Macklin |
| ANTONIO* | Delane |
| BASSANIO | Havard |
| GRATIANO* | [W.] Mills |
| LORENZO* | Lowe |
| LAUNCELOT | Neale |
| MOROCCO* | [I.] Sparks |
| DUKE | Winstone |
| SOLANIO* | Berry |
| SALARINO | Blakes |
| GOBBO | Ray |
| TUBAL | Taswell |
| BALTHAZAR* | Simpson |
| JESSICA* | Mrs Ridout |
| NERISSA | Mrs Bennet |
| PORTIA | Mrs Clive |

*Nov. 3*

| | |
|---|---|
| SHYLOCK | Yates |
| ANTONIO | Berry |
| GRATIANO | Palmer |
| LORENZO | Beard |
| SOLANIO | King |
| JESSICA | Miss Cole |

omitted
MOROCCO, BALTHAZAR

317

## THE MERCHANT OF VENICE
### [as THE JEW OF VENICE]
### 1748 TILED BOOTH, BOWLING GREEN, SOUTHWARK
Oct. 31. No parts assigned

[*The original*]

### 1749 DRURY LANE
*Jan. 10*

| | |
|---|---|
| SHYLOCK | Yates |
| ANTONIO | Berry |
| BASSANIO | Havard |
| GRATIANO | Palmer |
| LORENZO | Beard |
| LAUNCELOT | Neale |
| SOLANIO | King |
| DUKE* | Winstone |
| SALARINO | Blakes |
| GOBBO* | Ray |
| TUBAL* | Taswell |
| JESSICA | Miss Cole |
| NERISSA | Mrs Bennet |
| PORTIA | Mrs Clive |

*Apr. 14*
omitted
    DUKE, GOBBO, TUBAL

*Sept. 21; Oct. 20*
omitted
    DUKE

### 1750 DRURY LANE
*Feb. 22*

| | |
|---|---|
| SHYLOCK | Yates |
| ANTONIO | Berry |
| BASSANIO | Havard |
| GRATIANO* | [W.] Mills |
| LORENZO* | Beard |
| LAUNCELOT | Shuter |
| SOLANIO* | King |
| SALARINO* | Blakes |
| GOBBO* | Ray |
| TUBAL* | Taswell |
| JESSICA* | Miss Cole |
| NERISSA | Mrs Bennet |
| PORTIA | Mrs Clive |

*May 4*
  GRATIANO  Palmer
  LORENZO  Cross
omitted
    GOBBO, TUBAL

*Sept. 8*
  JESSICA    Miss Minors
omitted
    GRATIANO, SOLANIO, SALARINO, GOBBO, TUBAL

### COVENT GARDEN
*Oct. 18; Nov. 16*

| | |
|---|---|
| SHYLOCK | Macklin |
| ANTONIO | [L.] Sparks |
| BASSANIO | Ryan |
| GRATIANO | Dyer |
| LORENZO | Lowe |
| LAUNCELOT | Arthur |
| SALARINO | Ridout |

### 1750 COVENT GARDEN (*cont.*)

*Oct. 18, &c. (cont.)*

| SOLANIO | Gibson |
| DUKE | Anderson |
| TUBAL | Cushing |
| JESSICA | Mrs Ridout |
| NERISSA | Mrs Vincent |
| PORTIA | Mrs Woffington |

## THE MERRY WIVES OF WINDSOR

Adapted as THE COMICAL GALLANT, by John Dennis. In five acts.

1702   A. Baldwin.

Act I begins with a new scene: Fenton has the Host's aid in winning Anne Page; she promises her love to him; and Fenton is revealed as the instigator of all the plots in the play. Then follow *I. i. 195–268*, somewhat reduced; *I. iii. 32–90*; *II. ii. 1–31*; and *I. iii. 91–110*, all verbatim. A brief new scene follows: the Host incites Caius to fight Evans. The act closes with *II. i*, somewhat enlarged and with some of the speeches rearranged.

Act II, scene i is *II. iii*, verbatim. Scene ii is a complete rewriting of *II. ii*, much expanded. Ford's soliloquy at the end of the scene is retained verbatim. Scene iii is *III. i*, slightly reduced.

Act III begins with *III. iii. 1–91*, practically verbatim. Then follows a much enlarged and drastically rewritten version of the remainder of the scene. Mrs Page, disguised as a soldier, makes love to Mrs Ford, while Falstaff watches from behind a curtain. When he emerges the 'soldier's' boasts terrify him. The women leave and Falstaff speaks an expanded version of *IV. v. 96–107*. The act ends with *III. iii. 137–end*, reduced and revised.

Act IV begins with a brief new scene: Ford becomes suspicious of Falstaff. Then follows *III. v*, much reduced and omitting Mrs Quickly. A long new scene follows in which Ford is told about the 'soldier'; the Host reveals the whole truth to Ford; and Anne Page and Fenton discuss the arrangements for Herne's Oak. Then follow *III. iv. 22–70*, reduced, and *I. i. 269–end*, almost verbatim.

Act V consists of *IV. iv* and the better part of *V*, much enlarged and mostly rewritten.

See Genest, ii. 248–50; Odell, i. 80–1; Spencer, 346–9.

No acting versions of the original were published before 1750. [An edition published in Dublin by A. Bradley, 1730, 'As it is Acted at the Theatres', is a reading edition, verbatim throughout.]

### [*as* THE COMICAL GALLANT]

1702   DRURY LANE

*n.d., probably Apr.*

| FALSTAFF | Powell |

[The bill for this (the first) performance is missing. The printed text contains no cast of characters; the assignment of FALSTAFF is suggested by Genest (ii. 250).]

## THE MERRY WIVES OF WINDSOR
[*The original*]
### 1704 LINCOLN'S INN FIELDS
*May 18.* No parts assigned

[Bill in DC of May 15. Downes (47) lists a performance at Court at about this time. The date is unclear; Avery and Scouten (148) suggest Apr. 24, 1704. The cast is as follows:

| | |
|---|---|
| FALSTAFF | Betterton |
| EVANS | Dogget |
| PAGE | Verbruggen |
| FORD | Powell |
| CAIUS | Penkethman |
| HOST | Bullock |
| MRS PAGE | Mrs Barry |
| MRS FORD | Mrs Bracegirdle |
| ANNE PAGE | Mrs Bradshaw] |

### 1705 QUEEN'S
*Apr. 23; Dec. 13.* No parts assigned

### 1720 LINCOLN'S INN FIELDS
*Oct. 22, 24, 25, 26, 29; Nov. 8, 17*

| | | | |
|---|---|---|---|
| FALSTAFF | Quin | | *Dec. 3* |
| FORD | Ryan | | omitted |
| PAGE | Ogden | | PISTOL |
| SHALLOW | Boheme | | *Dec. 15, 29* |
| SLENDER | Ch. Bullock | | |
| EVANS | Griffin | CAIUS | Pack |
| CAIUS* | Harper | | |
| FENTON | Egleton | | |
| HOST | Bullock Sr. | | |
| PISTOL* | Spiller | | |
| MRS FORD | Mrs Cross | | |
| MRS PAGE | Mrs Seymour | | |
| ANNE PAGE | Miss Stone | | |
| MRS QUICKLY | Mrs Giffard | | |

### 1721 LINCOLN'S INN FIELDS
*Jan. 14, 26, 27; June 8; Dec. 7.* No parts assigned

*Feb. 16; Mar. 9, 30; Apr. 28; May 3*         *Oct. 21*

| | | | |
|---|---|---|---|
| FALSTAFF | Quin | CAIUS | Spiller |
| FORD | Ryan | EVANS | Phipps |
| PAGE* | Ogden | MRS QUICKLY | Mrs Egleton [i.e. formerly Mrs Giffard] |
| FENTON | Egleton | omitted | |
| SLENDER | Ch. Bullock | PISTOL | |
| SHALLOW | Boheme | | |
| CAIUS* | Harper | | |

[The above are the changes as given in the bill in DP. The bill in DC assigns

320

## THE MERRY WIVES OF WINDSOR

### 1721 LINCOLN'S INN FIELDS (cont.)

*Feb. 16, &c. (cont.)*

| | |
|---|---|
| EVANS* | Griffin |
| HOST | Bullock Sr. |
| PISTOL* | Spiller |
| MRS FORD | Mrs Cross |
| MRS PAGE | Mrs Seymour |
| ANNE PAGE | Miss Stone |
| MRS QUICKLY* | Mrs Giffard |

[Bill for May 3 from DC; the bill in DP assigns no parts.]

*Oct. 21 (cont.)*

Spiller to both CAIUS and PISTOL, which is almost certainly a mistake. It also erroneously retains the name of Mrs Giffard instead of Mrs Egleton.]

*Nov. 15*

| | |
|---|---|
| PAGE | Diggs |
| CAIUS | Spiller |
| EVANS | Phipps |
| MRS QUICKLY | Mrs Egleton [i.e. formerly Mrs Giffard] |

omitted
PISTOL

[The bills in both DP and DC are as above, but they both erroneously retain the name of Mrs Giffard.]

*Dec. 28*

| | |
|---|---|
| FALSTAFF | Quin |

No other parts assigned

### 1722 LINCOLN'S INN FIELDS

*Jan. 4*

| | |
|---|---|
| FALSTAFF | Quin |
| FORD | Ryan |
| PAGE | Diggs |
| FENTON | Egleton |
| SLENDER* | C. Bullock |
| SHALLOW | Boheme |
| EVANS* | Phipps |
| HOST | Bullock Sr. |
| CAIUS* | Spiller |
| MRS FORD | Mrs Cross |
| MRS PAGE | Mrs Seymour |
| ANNE PAGE* | Miss Stone |
| MRS QUICKLY | Mrs Egleton |

*Jan. 19; Feb. 1; Mar. 3, 26*

| | |
|---|---|
| SLENDER | W. Bullock [Jr.] |

*Apr. 11; May 1, 28; Oct. 19, 25*

| | |
|---|---|
| SLENDER | W. Bullock [Jr.] |
| ANNE PAGE | Mrs Rogeir |

*Dec. 8, 29*

| | |
|---|---|
| SLENDER | W. Bullock [Jr.] |
| EVANS | Hippisley |
| CAIUS | Hall |
| ANNE PAGE | Mrs Rogeir |

### 1723 LINCOLN'S INN FIELDS

*Feb. 11*

| | |
|---|---|
| FALSTAFF | Quin |
| FORD | Ryan |
| PAGE | Diggs |
| FENTON* | Egleton |
| SHALLOW | Boheme |
| EVANS | Hippisley |
| HOST | Bullock Sr. |
| CAIUS | Hall |
| MRS FORD | Mrs Cross |
| MRS PAGE* | Mrs Seymour |

*Mar. 21*

| | |
|---|---|
| MRS PAGE | Mrs Bullock |

*Apr. 20; Oct. 19; Nov. 22; Dec. 14.*
No parts assigned

*Apr. 27*

| | |
|---|---|
| FALSTAFF | Quin |

No other parts assigned

*May 31*

| | |
|---|---|
| MRS PAGE | Mrs Boheme [i.e. formerly Mrs Seymour] |

## THE MERRY WIVES OF WINDSOR

### 1723 LINCOLN'S INN FIELDS (cont.)

*Feb. 11 (cont.)*

| | |
|---|---|
| ANNE PAGE | Mrs Rogier |
| MRS QUICKLY | Mrs Egleton |

*May 31 (cont.)*

added
    SLENDER   Egleton
omitted
    FENTON

[DC assigns MRS PAGE to Mrs Bullock.]

### 1724 LINCOLN'S INN FIELDS

*Jan. 1, 8, 22; Feb. 10; Mar. 2, 24; Oct. 24; Nov. 23.* No parts assigned

*Apr. 28*

| | |
|---|---|
| FALSTAFF | Quin |
| EVANS | Hippisley |
| SHALLOW | Boheme |
| FORD | Ryan |
| PAGE | Diggs |
| SLENDER | Egleton |
| CAIUS | Spiller |
| MRS FORD* | Mrs Cross |
| MRS PAGE | Mrs Parker |
| ANNE PAGE* | Mrs Rogeir |
| MRS QUICKLY | Mrs Egleton |

*Nov. 18*

| | |
|---|---|
| MRS FORD | Mrs Moffett |
| ANNE PAGE | Mrs Laguerre [i.e. formerly Mrs Rogeir] |

added

| | |
|---|---|
| HOST | Bullock Sr. |

### 1725 LINCOLN'S INN FIELDS

*Jan. 1, 21; Feb. 8; Apr. 16; Oct. 21; Nov. 19; Dec. 30.* No parts assigned

*May 10*

| | |
|---|---|
| FALSTAFF | Quin |
| EVANS | Hippisley |
| SHALLOW | Boheme |
| FORD | Ryan |
| PAGE | Diggs |
| SLENDER | Egleton |
| CAIUS | Spiller |
| MRS FORD | Mrs Moffett |
| MRS PAGE | Mrs Plomer |
| ANNE PAGE | Mrs Laguerre |
| MRS QUICKLY | Mrs Egleton |

### 1726 LINCOLN'S INN FIELDS

*Jan. 15, 24; Feb. 18; Mar. 14; Sept. 30; Dec. 2.* No parts assigned

## 1727 LINCOLN'S INN FIELDS
*Feb. 20; Apr. 11; Sept. 29; Nov. 9, 29.*
No parts assigned

*May 22*

| | |
|---|---|
| FALSTAFF | Quin |
| FORD | Ryan |
| PAGE | Ogden |
| SHALLOW | Boheme |
| EVANS | Hippisley |
| SLENDER | W. Bullock [Jr.] |
| HOST | Bullock [Sr.] |
| MRS FORD | Mrs Vincent |
| MRS PAGE | Mrs Berriman |
| MRS QUICKLY | Mrs Egleton |

## 1728 LINCOLN'S INN FIELDS
*Oct. 14.* No parts assigned

*Dec. 28*

| | |
|---|---|
| FALSTAFF | Quin |
| FORD | Ryan |
| PAGE | Ogden |
| SHALLOW | Berriman |
| EVANS | Hippisley |
| FENTON | Chapman |
| SLENDER | Clarke |
| HOST | Bullock [Sr.] |
| MRS FORD | Mrs Younger |
| MRS PAGE | Mrs Bullock |
| MRS QUICKLY | Mrs Egleton |
| ANNE PAGE | Miss Holliday |

## 1729 LINCOLN'S INN FIELDS
*Jan. 22; Oct. 15; Nov. 15.* No parts assigned

*Apr. 9*

| | |
|---|---|
| FALSTAFF | Quin |
| FORD | Ryan |
| PAGE | Ogden |
| SHALLOW | Berriman |
| EVANS | Hippisley |
| SLENDER | Clarke |
| FENTON* | Chapman |
| HOST | Bullock [Sr.] |
| MRS FORD | Mrs Younger |
| MRS PAGE | Mrs Bullock |
| ANNE PAGE* | Miss Holliday |
| MRS QUICKLY | Mrs Egleton |

*May 12*

| | |
|---|---|
| FENTON | Houghton |
| ANNE PAGE added | Mrs Palin |
| CAIUS | Hall |

### THE MERRY WIVES OF WINDSOR

## 1730 LINCOLN'S INN FIELDS
*Jan. 10; Feb. 7; Oct. 9; Nov. 26.* No parts assigned

*Apr. 10*

| | |
|---|---|
| FALSTAFF | Quin |

No other parts assigned

*May 15*

| | |
|---|---|
| FALSTAFF | Quin |
| FORD | Ryan |
| PAGE | Ogden |
| SHALLOW | Boheme |
| EVANS | Hippisley |
| SLENDER | Clarke |
| FENTON | Chapman |
| HOST | Bullock [Sr.] |
| MRS FORD | Mrs Younger |
| MRS PAGE | Mrs Benson |
| ANNE PAGE | Miss Holliday |
| MRS QUICKLY | Mrs Egleton |

## GOODMAN'S FIELDS

*Mar. 17, 19*

| | |
|---|---|
| FALSTAFF | W. Giffard |
| FORD | Giffard |
| EVANS* | Penkethman [Jr.] |
| SHALLOW | Collett |
| PAGE | Huddy |
| CAIUS | Bardin |
| FENTON | [Theo.] Lacy |
| HOST | R. Williams |
| PISTOL | Pearce |
| BARDOLPH | Machen |
| SLENDER | [W.] Bullock [Jr.] |
| MRS FORD | Mrs Giffard |
| MRS PAGE | Mrs Haughton |
| ANNE PAGE | Mrs Mountfort |
| MRS QUICKLY | Mrs Kirk |

*Apr. 24*

| | |
|---|---|
| EVANS | Eaton |

*Oct. 30*

| | |
|---|---|
| FALSTAFF | W. Giffard |
| FORD | Giffard |
| PAGE | Rosco |
| SHALLOW | Collett |
| EVANS* | Eaton |
| HOST | Huddy |
| SLENDER | [W.] Bullock [Jr.] |
| FENTON* | Barret |

*Dec. 10*

| | |
|---|---|
| EVANS | Pearce |
| FENTON | Havard |

## THE MERRY WIVES OF WINDSOR

### 1730 GOODMAN'S FIELDS (cont.)
*Oct. 30 (cont.)*

| | |
|---|---|
| SIMPLE | Master Woodward |
| CAIUS | Bardin |
| MRS FORD | Mrs Giffard |
| MRS PAGE | Mrs Haughton |
| MRS QUICKLY | Mrs Palmer |
| ANNE PAGE | Mrs Mountfort |

### 1731 LINCOLN'S INN FIELDS
*Jan. 8; Mar. 29; Dec. 8*  *Feb. 1; Mar. 4; May 19; Oct. 4; Nov. 24.* No parts assigned

| | |
|---|---|
| FALSTAFF | Quin |
| FORD | Ryan |
| PAGE | Ogden |
| SHALLOW | Chapman |
| EVANS | Hippisley |
| SLENDER | Clarke |
| FENTON | Houghton |
| HOST | Bullock [Sr.] |
| MRS FORD | Mrs Younger |
| MRS PAGE | Mrs Bullock |
| ANNE PAGE | Miss Holliday |
| MRS QUICKLY | Mrs Egleton |

### GOODMAN'S FIELDS
*Feb. 6*

| | |
|---|---|
| FALSTAFF | W. Giffard |
| FORD | Giffard |
| PAGE | Rosco |
| SHALLOW | Collett |
| EVANS* | Pearce |
| HOST* | Huddy |
| SLENDER | [W.] Bullock [Jr.] |
| FENTON | Havard |
| SIMPLE | Master Woodward |
| CAIUS | Bardin |
| MRS FORD | Mrs Giffard |
| MRS PAGE | Mrs Haughton |
| MRS QUICKLY* | Mrs Palmer |
| ANNE PAGE* | Miss Smith |

*Oct. 25*

| | |
|---|---|
| EVANS | A Gentleman [unidentified] |
| HOST | Morgan |
| MRS QUICKLY | Mrs Morgan |
| ANNE PAGE | Mrs Purden |

### 1732 LINCOLN'S INN FIELDS
*Feb. 12; Nov. 28.* No parts assigned

*Apr. 12*

| | |
|---|---|
| FALSTAFF | Quin |
| FORD | Ryan |
| PAGE* | Ogden |

*Oct. 6*

| | |
|---|---|
| PAGE | Paget |
| MRS PAGE added | Mrs Hallam |
| SHALLOW | Chapman |
| CAIUS | Hall |

325

## THE MERRY WIVES OF WINDSOR

### 1732 LINCOLN'S INN FIELDS (cont.)

*Apr. 12 (cont.)*

| | |
|---|---|
| EVANS | Hippisley |
| MRS FORD | Mrs Younger |
| MRS PAGE* | Mrs Bullock |

*Oct. 6 (cont.)*

| | |
|---|---|
| HOST | Bullock [Sr.] |
| FENTON | Houghton |
| ANNE PAGE | Miss Holliday |
| MRS QUICKLY | Mrs Egleton |

### GOODMAN'S FIELDS

*Mar. 4*

| | |
|---|---|
| FALSTAFF* | The Gentleman who perform'd it in HARRY THE FOURTH [at this theatre, Jan. 29. He is unidentified] |
| FORD | Giffard |
| PAGE | Rosco |
| SHALLOW* | Collett |
| SLENDER | [W.] Bullock [Jr.] |
| FENTON* | Havard |
| CAIUS | Bardin |
| HOST* | Morgan |
| RUGBY* | [R.] Williams |
| SIMPLE | Master Woodward |
| EVANS* | Norris [Jr.] |
| MRS FORD* | Mrs Giffard |
| MRS PAGE | Mrs Haughton |
| ANNE PAGE | Mrs Purden |
| MRS QUICKLY | Mrs Morgan |

[DP assigns MRS FORD to Mrs Roberts.]

*Oct. 11*

| | |
|---|---|
| FALSTAFF | Hulett |
| SHALLOW | Norris [Jr.] |
| HOST | Huddy |
| EVANS | Pearce |
| omitted | |
| FENTON, RUGBY | |

*Dec. 22*

| | |
|---|---|
| FALSTAFF | Hulett |
| SHALLOW | Norris [Jr.] |
| EVANS | Pearce |
| MRS FORD | Mrs Roberts |
| omitted | |
| FENTON, RUGBY | |

### 1733 COVENT GARDEN

*Jan. 18*

| | |
|---|---|
| FALSTAFF | Quin |
| EVANS | Hippisley |
| SHALLOW* | Chapman |
| FORD | Ryan |
| PAGE* | Paget |
| SLENDER | Neale |
| CAIUS | Hall |
| HOST | Bullock [Sr.] |
| FENTON | Houghton |
| MRS FORD* | Mrs Templer |
| MRS PAGE | Mrs Bullock |
| ANNE PAGE* | Mrs Horsington |
| MRS QUICKLY* | Mrs Egleton |

*Jan. 23*

| | |
|---|---|
| MRS FORD | Mrs Younger |
| ANNE PAGE | Miss Holliday |

*Apr. 16*

| | |
|---|---|
| ANNE PAGE | Mrs Laguerre |

*May 19.* No parts assigned

*Sept. 29*

| | |
|---|---|
| SHALLOW | Dyer |
| PAGE | Aston |
| ANNE PAGE | Miss Norsa |
| MRS QUICKLY | Mrs Martin |

*Nov. 20; Dec. 21*

| | |
|---|---|
| PAGE | Aston |
| ANNE PAGE | Miss Norsa |
| MRS QUICKLY | Mrs Martin |

## THE MERRY WIVES OF WINDSOR

### 1733 GOODMAN'S FIELDS
*Oct. 26*

| | |
|---|---|
| FALSTAFF | Hulett |
| FORD | Giffard |
| PAGE | Huddy |
| SHALLOW | Rosco |
| EVANS | Pearce |
| SLENDER | R. Wetherilt |
| CAIUS | Bardin |
| HOST | Morgan |
| SIMPLE | Woodward |
| MRS FORD | Mrs Roberts |
| MRS PAGE | Mrs Haughton |
| ANNE PAGE | Mrs Hamilton |
| MRS QUICKLY | Mrs Morgan |

### 1734 DRURY LANE
*Dec. 6, 7, 9, 10, 11*

| | |
|---|---|
| FALSTAFF | Quin |
| SHALLOW | Johnson |
| SLENDER | [T.] Cibber |
| CAIUS | Harper |
| HOST | Miller |
| BARDOLPH* | Shepard |
| NYM* | Jones |
| PISTOL* | [T.] Hallam |
| RUGBY* | Leigh [Jr.] |
| SIMPLE* | Master Arne |
| ROBIN* | Master Green |
| FENTON | Este |
| EVANS | Griffin |
| FORD | Milward |
| PAGE | Berry |
| ANNE PAGE | Miss Holliday |
| MRS QUICKLY | Mrs Shireburn |
| MRS FORD | Mrs Heron |
| MRS PAGE | Mrs Butler |

*Dec. 18*

omitted BARDOLPH, NYM, PISTOL, RUGBY, SIMPLE, ROBIN

### COVENT GARDEN
*Jan. 25.* No parts assigned

### GOODMAN'S FIELDS
*Feb. 20; Oct. 9.* No parts assigned

327

## 1735 DRURY LANE

*Feb. 13*

| | |
|---|---|
| FALSTAFF | Quin |
| SHALLOW | Johnson |
| SLENDER | [T.] Cibber |
| CAIUS | Harper |
| HOST | Miller |
| BARDOLPH | Shepard |
| NYM* | Jones |
| PISTOL* | [T.] Hallam |
| RUGBY | Leigh [Jr.] |
| SIMPLE* | Master Arne |
| ROBIN* | Master Green |
| FENTON | Este |
| EVANS | Griffin |
| FORD | Milward |
| PAGE | Berry |
| ANNE PAGE | Miss Holliday |
| MRS QUICKLY | Mrs Cross |
| MRS FORD* | Mrs Heron |
| MRS PAGE | Mrs Butler |

[Mrs Cross's former name, Shireburn, appears in the bill. She had, however, married Cross about a fortnight earlier.]

*May 13*

| | |
|---|---|
| FALSTAFF | Quin |

No other parts assigned

*Nov. 21*

| | |
|---|---|
| NYM | Raftor |
| PISTOL | Cross |
| SIMPLE | Master Green |
| ROBIN | Miss Cole |
| MRS FORD | Mrs Cantrell |

## GOODMAN'S FIELDS

*Jan. 29.* No parts assigned

*Nov. 11*

| | |
|---|---|
| FALSTAFF | W. Giffard |
| FORD | Giffard |
| CAIUS | Bardin |
| PAGE | Rosco |
| SHALLOW | Norris [Jr.] |
| FENTON | Havard |
| HOST | Lyon |
| SLENDER | Woodward |
| SIMPLE | Hamilton |
| BARDOLPH | Dove |
| EVANS | Lowder |
| MRS FORD | Mrs Roberts |
| MRS PAGE | Mrs Haughton |
| ANNE PAGE | Mrs M. Giffard |
| MRS QUICKLY | Mrs Wetherilt |

## 1736 DRURY LANE
*May 21*

| | |
|---|---|
| FALSTAFF | Quin |
| FORD | Milward |
| EVANS | Griffin |
| CAIUS | Harper |
| PAGE | Berry |
| SHALLOW | Johnson |
| SLENDER | [T.] Cibber |
| FENTON | Este |
| HOST | Miller |
| BARDOLPH | Shepard |
| MRS FORD | Mrs Cantrell |
| MRS PAGE | Mrs Butler |
| ANNE PAGE | Miss Holliday |
| MRS QUICKLY | Mrs Cross |

## COVENT GARDEN
*Mar. 18*

| | |
|---|---|
| FALSTAFF | Delane |
| FORD | Ryan |
| EVANS | Hippisley |
| CAIUS | Mullart |
| PAGE | A. Hallam |
| SHALLOW | Chapman |
| SLENDER | Clarke |
| FENTON | Master [A.] Ryan |
| MRS FORD | Mrs Horton |
| MRS PAGE | Mrs Buchanan |
| ANNE PAGE | Miss Norsa |
| MRS QUICKLY | Mrs Mullart |

## 1737 DRURY LANE
*Jan. 6; Feb. 1, 3*

| | |
|---|---|
| FALSTAFF | Quin |
| SHALLOW | Johnson |
| SLENDER | [T.] Cibber |
| CAIUS | Miller |
| HOST | Harper |
| EVANS | Macklin |
| FORD | Milward |
| PAGE | Berry |
| BARDOLPH | Shepard |
| NYM | Raftor |
| PISTOL | Cross |
| RUGBY | Leigh [Jr.] |
| SIMPLE | Master Green |
| ROBIN | Miss Cole |

## 1737 DRURY LANE (cont.)

*Jan. 6, &c. (cont.)*

| | |
|---|---|
| FENTON | Este |
| MRS FORD | Mrs Thurmond |
| MRS PAGE | Mrs Butler |
| ANNE PAGE | Miss Holliday |
| MRS QUICKLY | Mrs Cross |

[The playhouse bill for Feb. 1 is in HTC.]

## COVENT GARDEN

*Mar. 24*

| | |
|---|---|
| FALSTAFF | Delane |
| SHALLOW | Chapman |
| EVANS | Hippisley |
| FORD | Ryan |
| PAGE | A. Hallam |
| SLENDER* | Clarke |
| CAIUS | Mullart |
| FENTON | Master A. Ryan |
| MRS FORD | Mrs Horton |
| MRS PAGE | Mrs Hallam |
| ANNE PAGE | Miss Bincks |
| MRS QUICKLY* | Mrs Mullart |

*Apr. 29*

| | |
|---|---|
| SLENDER | James |
| MRS QUICKLY added | Mrs James |
| HOST | Boman [Jr.] |

## LINCOLN'S INN FIELDS

*Jan. 3.* The bill for this performance is missing

## 1738 DRURY LANE

*May 3, 18*

| | |
|---|---|
| FALSTAFF | Quin |
| FORD | Milward |
| EVANS | Macklin |
| SHALLOW | Johnson |
| CAIUS | Miller |
| SLENDER | Woodward |
| HOST | Harper |
| BARDOLPH | Ray |
| NYM | Raftor |
| PISTOL | Cross |
| RUGBY | Leigh [Jr.] |
| SIMPLE | Master Green |
| ROBIN | Miss Cole |
| FENTON | Hill |
| PAGE | Winstone |
| ANNE PAGE | Miss Brett |
| MRS QUICKLY | Mrs Grace |
| MRS FORD | Mrs Roberts |
| MRS PAGE | Mrs Butler |

## THE MERRY WIVES OF WINDSOR

### 1739 DRURY LANE
*Oct. 13*

| | |
|---|---|
| FALSTAFF | Quin |
| SHALLOW | Johnson |
| CAIUS | Penkethman [Jr.] |
| SLENDER | Woodward |
| HOST | Turbutt |
| FORD | Milward |
| PAGE | Winstone |
| EVANS | Macklin |
| BARDOLPH | Ray |
| NYM | Raftor |
| PISTOL | Yates |
| RUGBY | Leigh [Jr.] |
| SIMPLE | Master Green |
| ROBIN | Miss Cole |
| FENTON | Ridout |
| MRS FORD | Mrs Roberts |
| MRS PAGE | Mrs Butler |
| ANNE PAGE | Mrs Chetwood |
| MRS QUICKLY | Mrs Grace |

### COVENT GARDEN
*Apr. 25*

| | |
|---|---|
| FALSTAFF | Stephens |
| FORD | Ryan |
| PAGE | [A.] Hallam |
| SHALLOW | Chapman |
| EVANS | Hippisley |
| SLENDER | Neale |
| CAIUS | Mullart |
| FENTON | A. Ryan |
| SIMPLE | Bencraft |
| PISTOL | James |
| NYM | Stoppelaer |
| BARDOLPH | Dove |
| HOST | Bullock [Sr.] |
| MRS FORD | Mrs Horton |
| MRS PAGE | Mrs Hallam |
| ANNE PAGE | Mrs Vincent |
| MRS QUICKLY | Mrs Mullart |

### 1740 DRURY LANE
*Apr. 23*

| | |
|---|---|
| FALSTAFF | Quin |

No other parts assigned

331

## 1740 DRURY LANE (cont.)

### Oct. 15

| | |
|---|---|
| FALSTAFF | Quin |
| FORD | Milward |
| SHALLOW | Johnson |
| CAIUS | Taswell |
| PAGE | Winstone |
| EVANS | Macklin |
| SLENDER | Woodward |
| HOST | Turbutt |
| BARDOLPH | Ray |
| NYM | Raftor |
| PISTOL | Stevens |
| RUGBY | Leigh [Jr.] |
| SIMPLE | Green |
| ROBIN | Miss Cole |
| FENTON | Ridout |
| MRS FORD | Mrs Roberts |
| MRS PAGE | Mrs Butler |
| ANNE PAGE | Mrs Wright |
| MRS QUICKLY | Mrs Macklin |

## COVENT GARDEN

### Mar. 27

| | |
|---|---|
| FALSTAFF | Stephens |
| FORD | Ryan |
| CAIUS* | Mullart |
| SLENDER | Neale |
| SHALLOW | Arthur |
| PAGE | [A.] Hallam |
| FENTON | A. Ryan |
| HOST | Rosco |
| PISTOL* | James |
| SIMPLE | Bencraft |
| EVANS | Hippisley |
| MRS FORD | Mrs Horton |
| MRS PAGE | Mrs Bellamy |
| ANNE PAGE | Mrs Vincent |
| MRS QUICKLY | Mrs Mullart |

### Apr. 17. No parts assigned

### May 29

| | |
|---|---|
| CAIUS | James |
| PISTOL | Clarke |

## GOODMAN'S FIELDS

### Nov. 15

| | |
|---|---|
| FALSTAFF | Paget |
| FORD | Giffard |
| SHALLOW | Julian |
| CAIUS | Blakes |
| PAGE | Naylor |

### Dec. 20. No parts assigned

## 1740 GOODMAN'S FIELDS (cont.)
*Nov. 15 (cont.)*

| | |
|---|---|
| EVANS | Yates |
| SLENDER | Vaughan |
| HOST | Dunstall |
| MRS FORD | Mrs Dunstall |
| MRS PAGE | Mrs Middleton |
| ANNE PAGE | Miss Hippisley |
| MRS QUICKLY | Mrs Yates |

## 1741 COVENT GARDEN
*Jan. 5, 16; Feb. 10.* No parts assigned

*May 4*

| | |
|---|---|
| FALSTAFF | Stephens |
| FORD | Ryan |
| CAIUS | Mullart |
| EVANS | Hippisley |
| SLENDER* | Clarke |
| SIMPLE | Bencraft |
| SHALLOW* | Arthur |
| PAGE* | [A.] Hallam |
| HOST | Rosco |
| PISTOL | James |
| FENTON* | Anderson |
| MRS FORD | Mrs Horton |
| MRS PAGE | Mrs Bellamy |
| ANNE PAGE | Mrs Vincent |
| MRS QUICKLY* | Mrs Cross |

*Oct. 10; Nov. 16; Dec. 10*

| | |
|---|---|
| SLENDER | Woodward |
| SHALLOW | Chapman |
| PAGE | Cashell |
| FENTON | Gibson |
| MRS QUICKLY | Mrs Mullart |

### GOODMAN'S FIELDS
*Apr. 17*

| | |
|---|---|
| FALSTAFF | Paget |
| FORD | Giffard |
| EVANS | Yates |
| MRS QUICKLY* | Mrs Yates |

No other parts assigned

[Bill in DA of Apr. 16. LDP assigns no parts.]

*Oct. 15*

omitted
   MRS QUICKLY

## 1742 COVENT GARDEN
*Jan. 29; Mar. 23; Apr. 21*

| | |
|---|---|
| FALSTAFF* | Stephens |
| FORD | Ryan |
| SHALLOW | Chapman |
| SLENDER | Woodward |
| PAGE | Cashell |

*Oct. 27*

| | |
|---|---|
| FALSTAFF | Quin |
| MRS QUICKLY | Mrs James |

added

| | |
|---|---|
| BARDOLPH | Harrington |
| ROBIN | Miss Morrison |

333

## THE MERRY WIVES OF WINDSOR

### 1742 COVENT GARDEN (cont.)

*Jan. 29, &c. (cont.)*

| | |
|---|---|
| FENTON | Gibson |
| CAIUS | Stoppelaer |
| HOST | Rosco |
| PISTOL | James |
| SIMPLE | Bencraft |
| EVANS | Hippisley |
| MRS FORD | Mrs Horton |
| MRS PAGE | Mrs Bellamy |
| ANNE PAGE | Mrs Vincent |
| MRS QUICKLY* | Mrs Mullart |

*Dec. 3*

| | |
|---|---|
| FALSTAFF | Quin |
| MRS QUICKLY added | Mrs James |
| BARDOLPH | Harrington |
| ROBIN | Miss Mullart |

### 1743 DRURY LANE

*Nov. 29*

| | |
|---|---|
| FALSTAFF | Delane |
| FORD | Giffard |
| PAGE | Winstone |
| SHALLOW | Taswell |
| EVANS | Yates |
| CAIUS | Blakes |
| SLENDER | Neale |
| HOST | Turbutt |
| FENTON | W. Giffard |
| SIMPLE | Green |
| RUGBY | Collins |
| BARDOLPH | Ray |
| NYM | Morgan |
| PISTOL | Cross |
| ROBIN | Miss Cole |
| MRS PAGE | Mrs Bennet |
| ANNE PAGE | Mrs Ridout |
| MRS QUICKLY | Mrs Cross |
| MRS FORD | Mrs Woffington |

### COVENT GARDEN

*Jan. 27*

| | |
|---|---|
| FALSTAFF | Quin |
| FORD | Ryan |
| SHALLOW | Chapman |
| SLENDER | Woodward |
| PAGE | Cashell |
| FENTON | Gibson |
| CAIUS | Stoppelaer |
| HOST | Rosco |
| PISTOL* | Mullart |
| SIMPLE | Bencraft |
| BARDOLPH* | Harrington |

*Feb. 22*

| | |
|---|---|
| BARDOLPH | Marten |
| MRS PAGE | Mrs Walter [i.e. formerly Mrs Bellamy] |

*Mar. 22*

| | |
|---|---|
| BARDOLPH | Marten |
| MRS PAGE | Mrs Walter [i.e. formerly Mrs Bellamy] |
| MRS QUICKLY | Mrs Mullart |

*Dec. 19*

| | |
|---|---|
| PISTOL | James |
| BARDOLPH | Marten |

334

## 1743 COVENT GARDEN (cont.)

*Jan. 27 (cont.)*

| | |
|---|---|
| ROBIN | Miss Morrison |
| EVANS | Hippisley |
| MRS FORD | Mrs Horton |
| MRS PAGE* | Mrs Bellamy |
| ANNE PAGE | Mrs Vincent |
| MRS QUICKLY* | Mrs James |

*Dec. 19 (cont.)*

| | |
|---|---|
| MRS PAGE | Mrs Walter [i.e. formerly Mrs Bellamy] |
| MRS QUICKLY | Mrs Mullart |

## 1744 COVENT GARDEN

*Jan. 20; Feb. 18*

| | |
|---|---|
| FALSTAFF | Quin |
| FORD | Ryan |
| PAGE | Cashell |
| SHALLOW | Chapman |
| EVANS | Hippisley |
| CAIUS* | Stoppelaer |
| SLENDER | Woodward |
| HOST | Rosco |
| FENTON | Gibson |
| SIMPLE | Bencraft |
| BARDOLPH | Marten |
| PISTOL* | James |
| ROBIN* | Miss Morrison |
| MRS PAGE* | Mrs Walter |
| ANNE PAGE | Mrs Vincent |
| MRS QUICKLY | Mrs Mullart |
| MRS FORD* | Mrs Horton |

*Apr. 6; May 16*

| | |
|---|---|
| CAIUS | James |
| PISTOL | Vaughan |

*Oct. 22; Nov. 24*

| | |
|---|---|
| MRS PAGE | Mrs Hale |
| MRS FORD | Mrs Pritchard |
| omitted | |
| ROBIN | |

## 1745 NEW WELLS, GOODMAN'S FIELDS

*Mar. 28*

| | |
|---|---|
| FALSTAFF | Dance |
| FORD | Furnival |

No other parts assigned

## 1746 COVENT GARDEN

*Feb. 3*

| | |
|---|---|
| FORD | Ryan |
| FALSTAFF* | Bridgwater |
| SHALLOW | Chapman |
| EVANS | Hippisley |
| SLENDER | Woodward |
| PAGE | Cashell |
| HOST | Rosco |
| CAIUS | Stoppelaer |
| PISTOL | James |
| SIMPLE | Vaughan |

*Nov. 18*

| | |
|---|---|
| FALSTAFF | Quin |

## 1746 COVENT GARDEN (cont.)
*Feb. 3 (cont.)*

| BARDOLPH | Marten |
| FENTON | Gibson |
| MRS PAGE | Mrs Hale |
| ANNE PAGE | Mrs Vincent |
| MRS QUICKLY | Mrs James |
| MRS FORD | Mrs Pritchard |

## 1747 COVENT GARDEN
*Mar. 16*

| FALSTAFF | Quin |
| FORD | Ryan |
| PAGE | Cashell |
| SHALLOW | Chapman |
| SLENDER | Woodward |
| EVANS | Hippisley |
| FENTON | Gibson |
| PISTOL | James |
| BARDOLPH | Marten |
| CAIUS | Stoppelaer |
| HOST | Rosco |
| MRS PAGE | Mrs Hale |
| ANNE PAGE | Mrs Vincent |
| MRS QUICKLY | Mrs James |
| MRS FORD | Mrs Pritchard |

## NEW WELLS, GOODMAN'S FIELDS
*Jan. 9, 13*

| FORD | Furnival |
| FALSTAFF | Paget |
| EVANS | L. Hallam |
| CAIUS | Shuter |
| PAGE | Wignell |
| SHALLOW | Dove |
| SLENDER | Cushing |
| HOST | W. Hallam |
| FENTON | Lee |
| BARDOLPH | [G.] Hallam |
| PISTOL | Brett |
| ROBIN | Master Morgan |
| SIMPLE | Miles |
| RUGBY | Baker |
| MRS PAGE | Mrs [L.] Hallam |
| ANNE PAGE | Mrs Moreau |
| MRS QUICKLY | Mrs Bambridge |
| MRS FORD | Mrs Cushing |

## THE MERRY WIVES OF WINDSOR

## 1748 COVENT GARDEN

*Jan. 12*

| | |
|---|---|
| FALSTAFF* | Bridges |
| FORD | Ryan |
| PAGE* | Ridout |
| SHALLOW | Rosco |
| SLENDER | Collins |
| FENTON | Gibson |
| PISTOL | James |
| BARDOLPH | Dunstall |
| NYM | Kennedy |
| CAIUS | Stoppelaer |
| HOST | Morgan |
| SIMPLE | Paddick |
| ROBIN | Miss Mullart |
| EVANS | Morris |
| MRS PAGE | Mrs Hale |
| ANNE PAGE* | Mrs Storer |
| MRS QUICKLY | Mrs James |
| MRS FORD | Mrs Horton |

*Mar. 21*

| | |
|---|---|
| FALSTAFF | Bridgwater |
| PAGE | Anderson |
| ANNE PAGE | Miss Haughton |

*Oct. 14, 31; Dec. 17, 30*

| | |
|---|---|
| FALSTAFF | Quin |
| FORD | Ryan |
| PAGE | Ridout |
| FENTON | Gibson |
| SHALLOW | Paget |
| CAIUS | Stoppelaer |
| SLENDER | Collins |
| HOST | Dunstall |
| BARDOLPH | Marten |
| PISTOL* | Cushing |
| SIMPLE | Bencraft |
| EVANS | Arthur |
| ROBIN | Miss Mullart |
| MRS PAGE | Mrs Hale |
| ANNE PAGE | Miss Haughton |
| MRS QUICKLY | Mrs Bambridge |
| MRS FORD | Mrs Woffington |

*Nov. 10*

| | |
|---|---|
| PISTOL | Holtom |

## 1749 COVENT GARDEN

*Jan. 27; Apr. 1*

| | |
|---|---|
| FALSTAFF | Quin |
| FORD | Ryan |
| PAGE | Ridout |
| FENTON | Gibson |
| SHALLOW* | Paget |
| CAIUS | Stoppelaer |
| SLENDER* | Collins |

*Oct. 18; Nov. 13*

| | |
|---|---|
| SHALLOW | Bransby |
| MRS PAGE | Mrs Barrington [i.e. formerly Mrs Hale] |

*Dec. 6*

| | |
|---|---|
| SHALLOW | Bransby |
| MRS PAGE | Mrs Barrington [i.e. formerly Mrs Hale] |

## 1749 COVENT GARDEN (cont.)

*Jan. 27, &c. (cont.)*

| | |
|---|---|
| HOST* | Dunstall |
| BARDOLPH* | Marten |
| PISTOL* | Cushing |
| SIMPLE* | Bencraft |
| EVANS | Arthur |
| ROBIN | Miss Mullart |
| MRS PAGE* | Mrs Hale |
| ANNE PAGE | Miss Haughton |
| MRS QUICKLY | Mrs Bambridge |
| MRS FORD | Mrs Woffington |

*Dec. 6 (cont.)*

omitted
    HOST, BARDOLPH, PISTOL, SIMPLE

*Dec. 29*

| | |
|---|---|
| SHALLOW | Collins |
| SLENDER | Bennet |
| MRS PAGE | Mrs Barrington [i.e. formerly Mrs Hale] |

omitted
    HOST, BARDOLPH, PISTOL, SIMPLE

## 1750 DRURY LANE

*Sept. 22*

| | |
|---|---|
| FALSTAFF | Berry |
| FORD | Havard |
| EVANS | Yates |
| SHALLOW | Shuter |
| CAIUS | Blakes |
| PAGE | Winstone |
| HOST | W. Vaughan |
| FENTON | Scrase |
| SIMPLE | H. Vaughan |
| BARDOLPH | Ray |
| SLENDER | Woodward |
| PISTOL | James |
| NYM | Costollo |
| RUGBY | Blakey |
| ROBIN | Miss Yates |
| MRS PAGE | Mrs Mills |
| ANNE PAGE | Miss Minors |
| MRS QUICKLY | Miss Pitt |
| MRS FORD | Mrs Pritchard |

## COVENT GARDEN

*Jan. 24*

| | |
|---|---|
| FALSTAFF | Quin |
| FORD* | Ryan |
| PAGE | Ridout |
| FENTON | Gibson |
| SHALLOW | Collins |
| CAIUS | Stoppelaer |
| EVANS | Arthur |
| SLENDER | Bennet |
| PISTOL | Cushing |
| NYM | Holtom |
| BARDOLPH | Marten |

*Mar. 26*

| | |
|---|---|
| FORD | [L.] Sparks |

*Oct. 22; Dec. 6*

| | |
|---|---|
| MRS QUICKLY | Mrs Macklin |

THE MERRY WIVES OF WINDSOR

## 1750 COVENT GARDEN (cont.)
*Jan. 24 (cont.)*

| | |
|---|---|
| HOST | Dunstall |
| ROBIN | Miss Mullart |
| MRS PAGE | Mrs Barrington |
| ANNE PAGE | Miss Haughton |
| MRS QUICKLY* | Mrs Bambridge |
| MRS FORD | Mrs Woffington |

# A MIDSUMMER-NIGHT'S DREAM

Adapted as PYRAMUS AND THISBE, by Richard Leveridge. In one act.

1716   W. Mears.

This version consists of *I. ii. 1–93; III. i. 8–81*; and *V. i. 108–362*, with about 60 new lines at the end, including an epilogue. The speeches of Theseus, Lysander, &c., in *Act V* are spoken by Crotchet, Gamut, and Semibreve. There are a few slight verbal changes, otherwise the text is verbatim. Nine songs, probably composed by Leveridge, are inserted.

See Genest, ii. 604–5; Odell, i. 232–3.

Adapted as the mock play in LOVE IN A FOREST, by Charles Johnson. See p. 90.

Adapted as PYRAMUS AND THISBE, by John Frederick Lampe. In one act.

1745   H. Woodfall.

This version consists of *V. i. 108–25, 157–369*, occasionally expanded. There is a new introduction and about 25 new lines at the end. Some of the text has been set to music and fourteen songs are introduced. The music was composed by Lampe; he may also have been responsible for the text.

See Genest, iv. 157; Odell, i. 347.

[*as* PYRAMUS AND THISBE, *by* LEVERIDGE]

## 1716 LINCOLN'S INN FIELDS
*Apr. 11*

| | |
|---|---|
| QUINCE | Bullock [Sr.] |
| BOTTOM | Spiller |
| FLUTE | H. Bullock |
| STARVELING | Coker |
| SEMIBREVE | Knapp |
| CROTCHET | H. Bullock |
| GAMUT | Coker |
| PYRAMUS | Leveridge |
| WALL | Randal |
| LION | Cook |

339

A MIDSUMMER-NIGHT'S DREAM [as LEVERIDGE'S PYRAMUS]

## 1716 LINCOLN'S INN FIELDS (cont.)

*Apr. 11 (cont.)*
- MOONSHINE  Reading
- THISBE  *Mr* Pack

[The bill gives neither the parts nor the actors' names. The above assignment is taken from the printed text. H. Bullock doubled FLUTE and CROTCHET; Coker doubled STARVELING and GAMUT.]

*Oct. 25, 26.* No parts assigned

*Oct. 29; Nov. 21, 22; Dec. 29*
- PYRAMUS  Leveridge
- WALL  Laurence
- LION  Cook
- MOONSHINE  Reading
- THISBE  *Mr* Pack

## 1717 LINCOLN'S INN FIELDS

*Jan. 25, 31*
- PYRAMUS  Leveridge
- LION*  Cook
- MOONSHINE*  Reading
- WALL*  Armstrong
- THISBE  *Mr* Pack

*Mar. 23*
omitted
LION, MOONSHINE, WALL

[*as the mock play in* LOVE IN A FOREST]

## 1723 DRURY LANE

*Jan. 9, 10, 11, 12, 14, 15*
- PYRAMUS  Penkethman
- WALL  Norris
- LION  Wilson
- MOONSHINE  Ray
- THISBE  *Mr* Miller

[See pp. 90–1.]

[*as* PYRAMUS AND THISBE, *by* LAMPE]

## 1745 COVENT GARDEN

*Jan. 25, 26, 28, 29, 31; Feb. 1, 2, 4, 5, 6, 7, 8, 11; Mar. 2, 5, 12, 25, 30; Apr. 16, 25; Sept. 27; Oct. 4, 11, 16, 28, 31; Nov. 8, 19, 28; Dec. 20*
- PYRAMUS  Beard
- LION  Reinhold
- WALL  Laguerre
- MOONSHINE  [E.] Roberts
- THISBE  Mrs Lampe

[On Jan. 26, Feb. 6, and Mar. 25 no parts are assigned; that there was any change in the cast is unlikely. On Oct. 11 the bill has merely, 'All the Vocal Parts and Dances to be perform'd as usual'.]

## A MIDSUMMER-NIGHT'S DREAM [*as* LAMPE'S PYRAMUS]

### 1746 COVENT GARDEN
*Jan. 14, 18; Feb. 7, 18*

| | |
|---|---|
| PYRAMUS | Beard |
| LION | Reinhold |
| WALL | Laguerre |
| MOONSHINE | [E.] Roberts |
| THISBE | Mrs Lampe |

### 1748 COVENT GARDEN
*Apr. 13*

| | |
|---|---|
| PYRAMUS | Beard |
| MOONSHINE | [E.] Roberts |
| LION | A Gentleman [unidentified] |
| THISBE | Mrs Lampe |

## MUCH ADO ABOUT NOTHING

Adapted as THE UNIVERSAL PASSION, by James Miller. In five acts.

1737  J. Watts.

Act I opens with about 375 new lines, taken (as are all the non-Shakespearian passages in the play) from Molière's *Princesse d'Elide*: Bellario tells of his love for Lucilia; Joculo describes his life as a court jester; Lucilia speaks mockingly of her aversion to marriage. This is followed by *I. i. 1-152*, by *II. i. 273-82, 344-52, 257-60*, and by *I. i. 160-5* and *I. iii. 1-42*. All this has been considerably altered.

Act II opens with about 30 new lines: Joculo is sarcastic about women. Then follow *I. i. 169-278* and *II. i. 248-57*, considerably reduced. The act ends with about 300 new lines, in which Lucilia tests Bellario's love, and Joculo jests with Delia. *II. i. 7-53* is partially used at the conclusion of the act.

Act III opens with about 60 new lines: an account of Bellario saving Gratiano's life. Then follow *II. i. 319-end*, reduced and the speeches rearranged, and *II. iii. 7-end*, drastically reduced. The persiflage of Protheus and Liberia at the end is expanded to about 60 lines. *III. i. 24-end* follows, put into prose and much reduced. The act ends with about 80 new lines in which Joculo and Liberia discuss Protheus.

Act IV is *III. ii. 109-26*, followed by about 30 new lines that include *The Two Gentlemen of Verona, I. iii. 84-5*; then *III. iii, IV. ii, III. iv, III. v* of the original, all of these scenes being considerably reduced. The act ends with *IV. i. 23-236*, virtually verbatim, the Friar's speeches advising the concealment of Lucilia being given to Protheus.

Act V is *IV. i. 257-end*, expanded. Then follows *Twelfth Night, I. i. 4-7*; then *V. i. 5-313* of the original, omitting *109-214*. This is followed by several lines from *The Two Gentlemen of Verona*: *III. i. 170-81, IV. iv. 161-2*, and *III. i. 225-32*. Then follow about 140 new lines: Joculo makes love to Delia. The play ends with *V. iv*, altered and enlarged.

See Genest, iii. 493-6; Odell, i. 255-7.

No acting versions of the original were published before 1750.

## MUCH ADO ABOUT NOTHING

### 1721 LINCOLN'S INN FIELDS
*Feb. 9, 10, 11*

| | |
|---|---|
| BENEDICK | Ryan |
| LEONATO | Quin |
| CLAUDIO | [J.] Leigh |
| DON PEDRO | Boheme |
| DOGBERRY | Bullock Sr. |
| DON JOHN | Egleton |
| BEATRICE | Mrs Cross |
| HERO | Mrs Seymour |
| MARGARET | Mrs Giffard |

[The bills give the actors' names only. The above assignment, with the exception of Egleton and Mrs Giffard, is suggested by Genest (iii. 59).]

### [as THE UNIVERSAL PASSION]

### 1737 DRURY LANE
*Feb. 28; Mar. 1*

| | |
|---|---|
| GRATIANO | Milward |
| BELLARIO | [W.] Mills |
| PROTHEUS | Quin |
| JOCULO | [T.] Cibber |
| BYRON | Berry |
| GREMIO | Winstone |
| LUCENTIUS | Shepard |
| PORCO | Harper |
| ASINO* | Macklin |
| LUCILIA | Mrs Butler |
| LIBERIA | Mrs Clive |
| DELIA | Mrs Pritchard |

*Mar. 3, 7, 8, 14, 21, 24, 28, 31*
added
  PRIEST  Turbutt
omitted
  ASINO

[The bills assign the parts.]

[The bills give the actors' names only. The above assignment is taken from the printed text. The bill for Feb. 28 is missing.]

### [*The original*]
### COVENT GARDEN
*Nov. 2, 3, 7*

| | |
|---|---|
| LEONATO | Johnson |
| DON PEDRO | Hale |
| DON JOHN | Bridgwater |
| CLAUDIO | [A.] Hallam |
| ANTONIO | Arthur |
| FRIAR | Rosco |
| BALTHAZAR | Salway |
| DOGBERRY | Hippisley |
| BORACHIO | Aston |
| CONRADE | Ridout |

## MUCH ADO ABOUT NOTHING

### 1737 COVENT GARDEN (cont.)
*Nov. 2, &c. (cont.)*

| TOWN CLERK | Mullart |
| SEXTON | Neale |
| VERGES | James |
| BENEDICK | Chapman |
| HERO | Mrs Templer |
| MARGARET | Mrs Mullart |
| URSULA | Mrs Stevens |
| BEATRICE | Miss Bincks |

### 1739 COVENT GARDEN
*May 25*

| LEONATO | Johnson |
| DON PEDRO | Hale |
| DON JOHN | Bridgwater |
| CLAUDIO | [A.] Hallam |
| ANTONIO | Arthur |
| FRIAR | Rosco |
| BALTHAZAR | Salway |
| DOGBERRY | Hippisley |
| BORACHIO | A. Ryan |
| CONRADE | Anderson |
| TOWN CLERK | Mullart |
| SEXTON | Neale |
| VERGES | James |
| BENEDICK | Chapman |
| HERO | Mrs Bellamy |
| MARGARET | Mrs Mullart |
| URSULA | Miss Brunette |
| BEATRICE | Mrs Vincent |

[*as* THE UNIVERSAL PASSION]

### 1741 DRURY LANE
*Mar. 14; Apr. 17*

| PROTHEUS | Quin |
| GRATIANO | Milward |
| BELLARIO | [W.] Mills |
| JOCULO | Macklin |
| LUCENTIUS | Shepard |
| BYRON | Berry |
| GREMIO | Winstone |
| ASINO | Taswell |
| PORCO | Raftor |
| LIBERIA | Mrs Clive |
| LUCILIA | Mrs Butler |
| DELIA | Mrs Pritchard |

343

## MUCH ADO ABOUT NOTHING

[*The original*]

### 1746 COVENT GARDEN
*Mar. 13, 22; Apr. 14*

| | |
|---|---|
| BENEDICK | Ryan |
| DON PEDRO | Cashell |
| DON JOHN | Ridout |
| LEONATO | Johnson |
| CLAUDIO | Hale |
| DOGBERRY | Hippisley |
| BALTHAZAR | Hayman |
| ANTONIO | Carr |
| BORACHIO | Gibson |
| CONRADE | Anderson |
| VERGES | James |
| FRIAR | Rosco |
| TOWN CLERK | Marten |
| SEXTON | Arthur |
| WATCHMAN | Stoppelaer |
| BOY | Miss Morrison |
| HERO | Mrs Hale |
| MARGARET | Miss Hippisley |
| URSULA | Mrs Vaughan |
| BEATRICE | Mrs Pritchard |

### 1748 DRURY LANE
*Nov. 14, 15, 16, 17, 18, 19, 21, 22, 30; Dec. 16*

| | |
|---|---|
| BENEDICK | Garrick |
| DON PEDRO | Havard |
| LEONATO | Berry |
| DON JOHN | Winstone |
| CLAUDIO | Lee |
| FRIAR | Bridges |
| BORACHIO | Blakes |
| DOGBERRY | Taswell |
| SEXTON | Ray |
| TOWN CLERK | James |
| VERGES | Neale |
| CONRADE | Bransby |
| 1ST WATCHMAN | Vaughan |
| 2ND WATCHMAN | Marr |
| MARGARET | Mrs Havard |
| URSULA | Miss Cole |
| HERO | Mrs Elmy |
| BEATRICE | Mrs Pritchard |

## 1749 DRURY LANE
*Jan. 19; Feb. 3; May 18*

| | |
|---|---|
| BENEDICK | Garrick |
| DON PEDRO | Havard |
| LEONATO | Berry |
| DON JOHN | Winstone |
| CLAUDIO* | Lee |
| FRIAR* | Bridges |
| BORACHIO* | Blakes |
| DOGBERRY* | Taswell |
| HERO | Mrs Elmy |
| MARGARET* | Mrs Havard |
| BEATRICE | Mrs Pritchard |

*Feb. 28*
added
    BALTHAZAR   Beard

*Mar. 30*
    DOGBERRY   James
added
    BALTHAZAR   Beard

*Apr. 29*
added
    BALTHAZAR   Beard
omitted
    FRIAR, BORACHIO, MARGARET

[Mrs Elmy acted HERO, but the bill misprints the part as AMANDA. Mrs Elmy acted Amanda in *The Relapse* on May 2.]

*Sept. 28*
added
| | |
|---|---|
| BALTHAZAR | Beard |
| VERGES | Neale |
| CONRADE | Usher |
| TOWN CLERK | James |
| SEXTON | Ray |
| URSULA | Miss Cole |

*Oct. 5; Nov. 3, 30*
    CLAUDIO   King
added
| | |
|---|---|
| BALTHAZAR | Beard |
| VERGES | Neale |
| CONRADE | Usher |
| TOWN CLERK | James |
| SEXTON | Ray |
| URSULA | Miss Cole |

## 1750 DRURY LANE
*Jan. 27*

| | |
|---|---|
| BENEDICK | Garrick |
| DON PEDRO | Havard |
| LEONATO | Berry |
| DON JOHN | Winstone |
| CLAUDIO | King |
| FRIAR* | Bridges |
| BORACHIO* | Blakes |
| DOGBERRY* | Taswell |
| BALTHAZAR | Beard |
| VERGES* | Shuter |
| CONRADE* | Usher |
| SEXTON* | Ray |
| TOWN CLERK* | Simpson |
| HERO | Mrs Elmy |

*Feb. 23*
omitted
    VERGES, CONRADE, SEXTON, TOWN CLERK

[MacMillan (293) erroneously has, 'Verges, Neale; Town Clerk, James'. Neale died on Jan. 10 of this year.]

*Mar. 29*
omitted
    FRIAR, BORACHIO, DOGBERRY, VERGES, CONRADE, SEXTON, TOWN CLERK

## 1750 DRURY LANE (cont.)

*Jan. 27 (cont.)*

| | |
|---|---|
| MARGARET | Mrs Havard |
| URSULA | Miss Cole |
| BEATRICE | Mrs Pritchard |

*Nov. 7*

| | |
|---|---|
| BENEDICK | Garrick |
| DON PEDRO | Havard |
| LEONATO | Berry |
| DON JOHN | Winstone |
| CLAUDIO | Palmer |
| FRIAR | Bridges |
| BORACHIO | Blakes |
| DOGBERRY | Shuter |
| BALTHAZAR* | Beard |
| VERGES | Vaughan |
| CONRADE | Mozeen |
| TOWN CLERK | James |
| SEXTON* | Ray |
| HERO | Mrs Willoughby |
| MARGARET | Mrs Havard |
| URSULA | Miss Minors |
| BEATRICE | Mrs Pritchard |

*Nov. 23*

| | |
|---|---|
| BALTHAZAR | Wilder |
| SEXTON | Simpson |

# OTHELLO

No acting versions appear to have been published before 1750. There are several editions (R. Wellington, 1705; John Darby, 1724; Walker, 1734, &c.) which have on their title-pages 'As it is Acted at the Theatres'. All these are, however, reading editions. Save for trivial verbal changes—seemingly attempted emendations—they are verbatim throughout.

## 1703 LINCOLN'S INN FIELDS

*May 21*

| | |
|---|---|
| OTHELLO | Betterton |
| CASSIO | Powell |
| IAGO | Verbruggen |
| RODERIGO | Pack |
| DESDEMONA | Mrs Bracegirdle |
| EMILIA | Mrs Leigh |

[Bill not in DC. The above assignment is taken from the 1695 quarto of the play in BM, in which a contemporary hand has written the actors' names, and the date '1703 the 21 of May Fryday'.]

## OTHELLO

### 1704 LINCOLN'S INN FIELDS
*Feb. 19*
    OTHELLO    Betterton
    DESDEMONA    Mrs Bracegirdle
  No other parts assigned

*Apr 27.* No parts assigned

### 1705 LINCOLN'S INN FIELDS
*Mar. 3.* No parts assigned
  [Bill in DC of Mar. 2.]

### QUEEN'S
*June 2; Dec. 22.* No parts assigned

### 1707 QUEEN'S
*Jan. 28*
    OTHELLO    Betterton
    IAGO    Verbruggen
    CASSIO    Booth
    DESDEMONA    Mrs Bracegirdle

### 1708 DRURY LANE
*Oct. 9*
    OTHELLO    Thurmond
    IAGO    Keene
    BRABANTIO    Smith
    CASSIO    Husband
    LODOVICO    Corey
    RODERIGO    Bowen
    DESDEMONA    Mrs Bradshaw
    EMILIA    Mrs Powell
    BIANCA    Mrs Finch

### 1709 DRURY LANE
*Mar. 24*
    OTHELLO    Betterton
    IAGO    Cibber
    CASSIO    Booth
    RODERIGO    Bowen
    BRABANTIO    Keene
    DESDEMONA    Mrs Bradshaw
    EMILIA    Mrs Powell

### QUEEN'S
*Sept. 15*
    OTHELLO    Betterton
  No other parts assigned

## OTHELLO

### 1710 DRURY LANE
*Jan. 21*
- OTHELLO — Booth
- CASSIO — Powell
- IAGO — Keene
- DESDEMONA — Mrs Bradshaw

*May 18*
added
- RODERIGO — Pack

### QUEEN'S
*June 22*
- OTHELLO — Wilks
- IAGO — Cibber

No other parts assigned

[IAGO appears only in the advance advertisement in DC of June 20.]

### 1711 DRURY LANE
*Jan. 18; Apr. 24; Nov. 27*
- OTHELLO — Booth
- IAGO — Cibber
- CASSIO — Powell
- RODERIGO — Bowen
- BRABANTIO — Keene
- DESDEMONA — Mrs Bradshaw
- EMILIA — Mrs Saunders

### 1712 DRURY LANE
*May 22*
- OTHELLO — Booth
- IAGO — Keene
- CASSIO — Powell
- RODERIGO — Pack
- DESDEMONA — Mrs Bradshaw

*Oct. 14*
added
- EMILIA — Mrs Saunders

### 1713 DRURY LANE
*Jan. 27*
- OTHELLO — Booth
- IAGO — Keene
- CASSIO — Powell
- RODERIGO — Pack
- DESDEMONA — Mrs Bradshaw
- EMILIA — Mrs Saunders

*Mar. 26*
- OTHELLO — Booth

No other parts assigned

*Oct. 3.* No parts assigned

### 1714 DRURY LANE
*Jan. 14; Oct. 7.* No parts assigned

348

## 1715 DRURY LANE
*Jan. 15*
- OTHELLO — Booth
- CASSIO — Wilks
- IAGO — Cibber
- RODERIGO — Bowen
- DESDEMONA — Mrs Porter
- EMILIA — Mrs Saunders

## 1716 DRURY LANE
*Jan. 7, 18*
- OTHELLO — Booth
- CASSIO — Wilks
- IAGO — Cibber
- LODOVICO — Mills
- RODERIGO — Bowen
- DESDEMONA — Mrs Santlow
- EMILIA — Mrs Saunders

*May 1; Dec. 1.* No parts assigned

## 1717 DRURY LANE
*May 2*
- OTHELLO — Booth
- IAGO — Cibber
- CASSIO — Ryan
- DESDEMONA* — Mrs Porter
- EMILIA — Mrs Saunders

*Oct. 22*
- DESDEMONA — Mrs Santlow

## 1718 DRURY LANE
*Feb. 8*
- OTHELLO — Booth
- IAGO — Cibber
- CASSIO* — Ryan
- DESDEMONA — Mrs Santlow
- EMILIA — Mrs Saunders

*Nov. 25*
- CASSIO — Wilks

## 1719 DRURY LANE
*May 6*
- OTHELLO — Booth
- RODERIGO — Miller
- IAGO — Cibber
- DESDEMONA* — Mrs Santlow
- EMILIA — Mrs Saunders

*Oct. 10*
- DESDEMONA — Mrs Thurmond

OTHELLO

### 1720 DRURY LANE
*Feb. 11; Apr. 28; Sept. 24; Oct. 24*

| | |
|---|---|
| OTHELLO | Booth |
| IAGO | Cibber |
| CASSIO | Walker |
| RODERIGO | Miller |
| DESDEMONA | Mrs Thurmond |
| EMILIA | Mrs Saunders |

### LINCOLN'S INN FIELDS

*Mar. 12*

| | |
|---|---|
| OTHELLO | Quin |
| IAGO | Ryan |
| DESDEMONA* | Mrs Seymour |

No other parts assigned

*Mar. 19*
added

| | |
|---|---|
| CASSIO | [J.] Leigh |
| BRABANTIO | Boheme |
| RODERIGO | Pack |
| EMILIA | Mrs Giffard |

*May 21*
added

| | |
|---|---|
| CASSIO | [J.] Leigh |
| BRABANTIO | Boheme |

omitted
DESDEMONA

*Oct. 20*
added

| | |
|---|---|
| CASSIO | [J.] Leigh |
| BRABANTIO | Boheme |
| EMILIA | Mrs Giffard |

### 1721 DRURY LANE

*Mar. 11*

| | |
|---|---|
| OTHELLO | Booth |
| IAGO | Cibber |
| CASSIO* | Walker |
| RODERIGO | Miller |
| DESDEMONA* | Mrs Thurmond |
| EMILIA* | Mrs Saunders |

*Nov. 18*

| | |
|---|---|
| CASSIO | Wilks |
| DESDEMONA | Mrs Porter |

omitted
EMILIA

### LINCOLN'S INN FIELDS

*Jan. 5; Feb. 23*

| | |
|---|---|
| OTHELLO | Quin |
| CASSIO* | [J.] Leigh |
| IAGO | Ryan |
| BRABANTIO | Boheme |
| DESDEMONA | Mrs Seymour |
| EMILIA* | Mrs Giffard |

*Sept. 29; Nov. 14*

| | |
|---|---|
| CASSIO | Walker |
| EMILIA | Mrs Egleton [i.e. formerly Mrs Giffard] |

OTHELLO

## 1722 DRURY LANE

*Mar. 27*

| | |
|---|---|
| OTHELLO | Booth |
| CASSIO | Wilks |
| IAGO | Cibber |
| RODERIGO | Miller |
| DESDEMONA | Mrs Thurmond |
| EMILIA* | Mrs Baker |

*Sept. 22*

omitted
    EMILIA

## LINCOLN'S INN FIELDS

*Jan. 10; May 9; Nov. 1*

| | |
|---|---|
| OTHELLO | Quin |
| IAGO | Ryan |
| CASSIO | Walker |
| RODERIGO | Egleton |
| BRABANTIO | Boheme |
| DESDEMONA | Mrs Seymour |
| EMILIA | Mrs Egleton |

## 1723 DRURY LANE

*Oct. 19*

| | |
|---|---|
| OTHELLO | Booth |
| CASSIO | Williams |
| IAGO | Cibber |
| RODERIGO | Miller |
| DESDEMONA | Mrs Thurmond |

## LINCOLN'S INN FIELDS

*Jan. 15*

| | |
|---|---|
| OTHELLO | Quin |
| IAGO | Ryan |
| BRABANTIO | Boheme |
| CASSIO | Walker |
| RODERIGO | Egleton |
| DESDEMONA* | Mrs Seymour |
| EMILIA | Mrs Egleton |

*Apr. 30*

| | |
|---|---|
| DESDEMONA | Mrs Boheme [i.e. formerly Mrs Seymour] |
| added | |
|   LODOVICO | Diggs |

*Oct. 2*

| | |
|---|---|
| DESDEMONA | Mrs Sterling |
| added | |
|   LODOVICO | Diggs |

## 1724 DRURY LANE

*Apr. 20.* No parts assigned

*Sept. 26*

| | |
|---|---|
| OTHELLO | Booth |
| CASSIO | Williams |
| IAGO | Cibber |
| RODERIGO | Miller |
| DESDEMONA | Mrs Thurmond |

351

## 1725 DRURY LANE

*Mar. 18*

| | |
|---|---|
| OTHELLO | Booth |
| CASSIO | Williams |
| IAGO | Cibber |
| RODERIGO | Miller |
| BRABANTIO* | Thurmond |
| DESDEMONA | Mrs Thurmond |

*June 14; Sept. 4; Dec. 8*

added
    EMILIA   Mrs Heron
omitted
    BRABANTIO

### LINCOLN'S INN FIELDS

*Dec. 6*

| | |
|---|---|
| OTHELLO | Quin |
| IAGO | Ryan |
| CASSIO | Walker |
| RODERIGO | Egleton |
| BRABANTIO | Boheme |
| LODOVICO | Diggs |
| EMILIA | Mrs Egleton |
| DESDEMONA | Mrs Younger |

## 1726 DRURY LANE

*Apr. 27*

| | |
|---|---|
| OTHELLO | Booth |
| IAGO | Cibber |
| CASSIO | Williams |
| RODERIGO | Miller |
| BRABANTIO | Thurmond |
| DESDEMONA | Mrs Thurmond |
| EMILIA | Mrs Butler |

*Sept. 3*

added
    MONTANO   Watson

### LINCOLN'S INN FIELDS

*Feb. 3.* No parts assigned

## 1727 DRURY LANE

*Sept. 7*

| | |
|---|---|
| OTHELLO | Booth |
| IAGO | Cibber |
| CASSIO | Williams |
| RODERIGO | Miller |
| MONTANO | Watson |
| BRABANTIO | Boman |
| LODOVICO | William Mills |
| DESDEMONA | Mrs Thurmond |
| EMILIA | Mrs Butler |

### LINCOLN'S INN FIELDS

*Oct. 6.* No parts assigned

## OTHELLO

### 1728 DRURY LANE

*Oct. 12*

| | |
|---|---|
| OTHELLO | Elrington |
| IAGO | Cibber |
| CASSIO | Williams |
| RODERIGO | Miller |
| DUKE | Corey |
| BRABANTIO | Roberts |
| LODOVICO | Wm. Mills |
| MONTANO | Watson |
| DESDEMONA | Mrs Thurmond |
| EMILIA | Mrs Butler |
| BIANCA | Miss Raftor |

*Dec. 28*

| | |
|---|---|
| OTHELLO | Elrington |

No other parts assigned

### LINCOLN'S INN FIELDS

*Oct. 7*

| | |
|---|---|
| OTHELLO | Quin |
| IAGO | Ryan |
| CASSIO | Walker |
| RODERIGO | Chapman |
| BRABANTIO | Boheme |
| LODOVICO | Milward |
| EMILIA | Mrs Egleton |
| DESDEMONA | Mrs Younger |

### 1729 DRURY LANE

*Mar. 29*

| | |
|---|---|
| OTHELLO* | Elrington |
| IAGO | Cibber |
| CASSIO | Williams |
| RODERIGO* | [T.] Cibber |
| DUKE | Corey |
| BRABANTIO | Roberts |
| LODOVICO | Wm. Mills |
| MONTANO | Watson |
| DESDEMONA | Mrs Thurmond |
| EMILIA | Mrs Butler |
| BIANCA | Miss Raftor |

*Sept. 20*

| | |
|---|---|
| OTHELLO | Mills |
| RODERIGO | Miller |

### LINCOLN'S INN FIELDS

*Feb. 3*

| | |
|---|---|
| OTHELLO | Quin |
| IAGO | Ryan |
| CASSIO | Walker |
| RODERIGO | Chapman |
| BRABANTIO | Milward |
| DESDEMONA* | Mrs Buchanan |
| EMILIA | Mrs Egleton |

*Mar. 13*

| | |
|---|---|
| DESDEMONA | Mrs Younger |

## 1730 DRURY LANE

*Jan. 7*

| | |
|---|---|
| OTHELLO | Mills |
| IAGO | Cibber |
| CASSIO | Williams |
| RODERIGO* | Miller |
| DUKE | Corey |
| BRABANTIO* | Roberts |
| LODOVICO | Wm. Mills |
| MONTANO | Watson |
| DESDEMONA | Mrs Thurmond |
| EMILIA | Mrs Butler |
| BIANCA | Miss Raftor |

*Dec. 1*

| | |
|---|---|
| RODERIGO | [T.] Cibber |
| BRABANTIO | Boman |

## LINCOLN'S INN FIELDS

*Oct. 14*

| | |
|---|---|
| OTHELLO | Quin |
| IAGO | Ryan |
| BRABANTIO | Boheme |
| LODOVICO | Milward |
| CASSIO | Walker |
| GRATIANO | Hulett |
| RODERIGO | Chapman |
| EMILIA | Mrs Egleton |
| DESDEMONA | Mrs Buchanan |

## HAYMARKET

*June 27*

| | |
|---|---|
| OTHELLO | Paget |
| IAGO | Rosco |
| RODERIGO | Reynolds |
| DUKE | Jones |
| BRABANTIO | Mullart |
| CASSIO | [Theo.] Lacy |
| LODOVICO | Stoppelaer |
| MONTANO | Dove |
| EMILIA | Mrs Mullart |
| DESDEMONA | Mrs Williamson [first appearance on the stage] |

*Dec. 17*

| | |
|---|---|
| OTHELLO | Royer |
| IAGO | Roberts |
| BRABANTIO | Mullart |
| CASSIO | [Theo.] Lacy |
| RODERIGO | Woodward [Sr.] |

## OTHELLO

**1730 HAYMARKET** (*cont.*)
*Dec. 17* (*cont.*)
| | |
|---|---|
| LODOVICO | Furnival |
| GRATIANO | Jones |
| DESDEMONA | Mrs Mullart |
| EMILIA | Mrs Woodward |

### GOODMAN'S FIELDS
*June 3*
| | |
|---|---|
| OTHELLO | A Gentleman, who never appeared on any Stage since he perform'd the Part of Castalio [in *The Orphan*, on Mar. 21, 1730] at the Theatre Royal in Drury Lane [Highmore] (Latreille, ii. 337; Genest, iii. 254–7). The GF bill is misprinted: on Mar. 21 at DL Castalio was acted by Wilks, and Highmore acted Polydore |
| CASSIO | W. Williams |
| DUKE | Bardin |
| RODERIGO | Penkethman [Jr.] |
| LODOVICO | R. Williams |
| BRABANTIO | Machen |
| MONTANO | [Theo.] Lacy |
| IAGO | Wm. Giffard |
| DESDEMONA | Mrs Giffard |
| EMILIA | Mrs Haughton |

*Oct. 19; Nov. 4*
| | |
|---|---|
| OTHELLO | Giffard |
| IAGO | Rosco |
| CASSIO | W. Williams |
| DUKE | Bardin |
| BRABANTIO | Smith |
| LODOVICO* | Woodward [Sr.] |
| MONTANO | Barret |
| GRATIANO | Machen |
| RODERIGO | Penkethman [Jr.] |
| DESDEMONA | Mrs Giffard |
| EMILIA | Mrs Haughton |

*Nov. 25*
| | |
|---|---|
| LODOVICO | R. Williams |

355

## 1731 DRURY LANE
*Nov. 15*
- OTHELLO — Mills
- IAGO — Cibber
- CASSIO — Bridgwater
- RODERIGO — [T.] Cibber
- LODOVICO — William Mills
- MONTANO — Watson
- DESDEMONA — Mrs Thurmond
- EMILIA — Mrs Butler
- BIANCA — Miss Raftor

## LINCOLN'S INN FIELDS
*Mar. 8*
- OTHELLO — Quin
- IAGO — Ryan
- BRABANTIO — Milward
- CASSIO — Walker
- RODERIGO — Chapman
- DESDEMONA — Mrs Younger

*Sept. 17*
added
- DUKE — Ogden
- MONTANO — Hulett
- EMILIA — Mrs Egleton

## GOODMAN'S FIELDS
*Mar. 16*
- OTHELLO* — Giffard
- IAGO — Rosco
- BRABANTIO — Smith
- CASSIO* — W. Williams
- DUKE — Bardin
- RODERIGO — [W.] Bullock [Jr.]
- LODOVICO* — R. Williams
- MONTANO — Havard
- DESDEMONA — Mrs Giffard
- EMILIA — Mrs Haughton

*Nov. 26, 30*
- OTHELLO — Delane
- CASSIO — W. Giffard
added
- GRATIANO — [R.] Williams
omitted
- LODOVICO

## 1732 DRURY LANE
*Aug. 4*
- OTHELLO — [T.] Cibber
- CASSIO — Bridgwater
- IAGO — Wm. Mills
- BRABANTIO — Roberts
- DESDEMONA — Miss Williams
- EMILIA — Mrs Butler

[Bill in DP of Aug. 3. DP of Aug. 4 is missing.]

*Aug. 17*
added
- LODOVICO — Paget
- MONTANO — Winstone
- GRATIANO — Ridout
- RODERIGO — Mrs Charke

# OTHELLO

## 1732 DRURY LANE (cont.)
*Dec. 4*
- OTHELLO — Mills
- IAGO — Cibber
- CASSIO — Bridgwater
- DESDEMONA — Mrs Booth
- EMILIA — Mrs Butler

[The bill for this performance is missing. The above assignment is taken from Genest (iii. 363).]

## LINCOLN'S INN FIELDS
*Jan. 24*
- OTHELLO — Quin
- IAGO — Ryan
- BRABANTIO — Milward
- CASSIO — Walker
- MONTANO* — Hulett
- RODERIGO — Chapman
- EMILIA* — Mrs Egleton
- DESDEMONA* — Mrs Buchanan

*Oct. 4*
- EMILIA — Mrs Stevens
- DESDEMONA — Mrs Younger
- omitted MONTANO

*Apr. 13*
- OTHELLO — Quin
- IAGO — Ryan
- CASSIO — Walker
- DESDEMONA — Mrs Younger
- No other parts assigned

## GOODMAN'S FIELDS
*Jan. 22; Feb. 16*
- OTHELLO — Delane
- RODERIGO* — Miller
- IAGO — Rosco
- BRABANTIO* — Smith
- CASSIO* — W. Giffard
- DUKE* — Bardin
- GRATIANO* — [R.] Williams
- MONTANO* — Havard
- DESDEMONA — Mrs Giffard
- EMILIA — Mrs Haughton

*Mar. 6*
- CASSIO — Giffard

*Apr. 17; May 19*
- CASSIO — Giffard
- omitted BRABANTIO, DUKE, GRATIANO, MONTANO

*Oct. 13; Nov. 16*
- RODERIGO — [W.] Bullock [Jr.]
- BRABANTIO — Hulett
- CASSIO — Giffard
- GRATIANO — Winstone

## 1733 COVENT GARDEN
*Jan. 13; Apr. 3; May 31*
- OTHELLO — Quin
- IAGO — Ryan
- BRABANTIO* — Milward
- CASSIO — Walker

*Sept. 15*
- RODERIGO — Neale
- DESDEMONA — Mrs Buchanan
- omitted BRABANTIO

357

## OTHELLO

**1733 COVENT GARDEN** (*cont.*)

*Jan. 13, &c.* (*cont.*)

| | |
|---|---|
| RODERIGO* | Chapman |
| EMILIA | Mrs Stevens |
| DESDEMONA* | Mrs Younger |

[The playhouse bill for Apr. 3 is in BM (Burney 937.c.5).]

*Nov. 10*

| | |
|---|---|
| BRABANTIO added | Aston |
| LODOVICO | Hale |
| MONTANO | [J.] Lacy |

## HAYMARKET

*Nov. 26*

| | |
|---|---|
| OTHELLO | Mills |
| IAGO | W. Mills |
| CASSIO | A. Hallam |
| BRABANTIO | Milward |
| RODERIGO | Miller |
| LODOVICO | Berry |
| DESDEMONA | Mrs Grace |
| EMILIA | Mrs Butler |

## GOODMAN'S FIELDS

*Apr. 2; May 16*

| | |
|---|---|
| OTHELLO | Delane |
| IAGO | Rosco |
| BRABANTIO | Hulett |
| CASSIO | Giffard |
| LODOVICO | Bardin |
| RODERIGO* | [R.] Wetherilt |
| GRATIANO* | Winstone |
| MONTANO | Havard |
| DESDEMONA | Mrs Giffard |
| EMILIA | Mrs Haughton |

*May 7*

omitted
    RODERIGO, GRATIANO

*Oct. 5*

| | |
|---|---|
| GRATIANO | Lyon |

## 1734 DRURY LANE

*May 13*

| | |
|---|---|
| OTHELLO | [T.] Cibber |
| IAGO | A. Hallam |
| RODERIGO | Mrs Charke |
| CASSIO | Hewitt |
| DUKE | Cross |
| LODOVICO | Turbutt |
| BRABANTIO | Boman |
| MONTANO | Winstone |
| GRATIANO | Corey |
| DESDEMONA | Mrs Clive |
| EMILIA | Mrs Butler |

## 1734 DRURY LANE (cont.)
*Sept. 10; Oct. 16*
| | |
|---|---|
| OTHELLO | Quin |
| CASSIO | [T.] Cibber |
| IAGO | W. Mills |
| BRABANTIO | Milward |
| RODERIGO | Miller |
| DESDEMONA | Mrs Thurmond |
| EMILIA | Mrs Butler |

## COVENT GARDEN
*Jan. 5*
| | |
|---|---|
| OTHELLO | Quin |
| IAGO | Ryan |
| CASSIO | Walker |
| BRABANTIO | Aston |
| LODOVICO | Hale |
| MONTANO | [J.] Lacy |
| RODERIGO | Chapman |
| EMILIA | Mrs Stevens |
| DESDEMONA* | Mrs Younger |

*Mar. 2.* No parts assigned

*May 22*
| | |
|---|---|
| DESDEMONA | Mrs Buchanan |

*Oct. 19, 21, 23, 24; Nov. 2*
| | |
|---|---|
| OTHELLO | Stephens [first appearance, Oct. 19, on the stage] |
| IAGO | Ryan |
| CASSIO | Walker |
| BRABANTIO* | Roberts |
| LODOVICO* | Hale |
| MONTANO* | Ridout |
| RODERIGO | Chapman |
| EMILIA | Mrs Mullart |
| DESDEMONA | Mrs Buchanan |

*Oct. 26; Nov. 18; Dec. 19*
omitted BRABANTIO, LODOVICO, MONTANO

## HAYMARKET
*Feb. 1*
| | |
|---|---|
| OTHELLO | Milward |
| IAGO | W. Mills |
| CASSIO | A. Hallam |
| BRABANTIO | Boman |
| RODERIGO | Miller |
| LODOVICO | Berry |
| DESDEMONA | Mrs Grace |
| EMILIA | Mrs Butler |

OTHELLO

## 1734 GOODMAN'S FIELDS
*Jan. 9, 25*

| | |
|---|---|
| OTHELLO | Delane |
| IAGO | Rosco |
| BRABANTIO | Hulett |
| CASSIO | Giffard |
| LODOVICO | Bardin |
| GRATIANO | Lyon |
| MONTANO | Ayres |
| RODERIGO | [R.] Wetherilt |
| DESDEMONA | Mrs Giffard |
| EMILIA | Mrs Haughton |

*Oct. 4.* No parts assigned

## VILLIERS ST., YORK BUILDINGS
*Nov. 19*

OTHELLO    The Author of the Farce [*The Mad Captain*, also acted this night: Drury]
No other parts assigned

*Nov. 29*

OTHELLO    Drury
No other parts assigned

## 1735 DRURY LANE
*Feb. 22*

| | |
|---|---|
| OTHELLO | Quin |
| CASSIO | [T.] Cibber |
| IAGO | W. Mills |
| BRABANTIO | Milward |
| RODERIGO | Miller |
| DESDEMONA | Mrs Thurmond |
| EMILIA* | Mrs Butler |

*Sept. 6*

| | |
|---|---|
| EMILIA | Mrs Cross |

## COVENT GARDEN
*Jan. 24*

| | |
|---|---|
| OTHELLO | Stephens |
| IAGO* | Ryan |
| CASSIO | Walker |
| RODERIGO | Chapman |
| DESDEMONA | Mrs Buchanan |
| EMILIA | Mrs Mullart |

*May 9*

IAGO    A. Hallam
added

| | |
|---|---|
| BRABANTIO | Ridout |
| DUKE | Wignell |
| LODOVICO | Hale |

*Oct. 3*
added

| | |
|---|---|
| BRABANTIO | Aston |
| DUKE | Wignell |
| LODOVICO | Hale |

OTHELLO

## 1735 COVENT GARDEN (cont.)
*Dec. 6*
added
| | |
|---|---|
| BRABANTIO | Aston |
| LODOVICO | Paget |

## LINCOLN'S INN FIELDS
*Apr. 19*
| | |
|---|---|
| OTHELLO | Stephens |
| IAGO | A. Hallam |
| CASSIO | Walker |
| RODERIGO | Chapman |
| DESDEMONA | Mrs Buchanan |
| EMILIA | Mrs Stevens |

## GOODMAN'S FIELDS
*Jan. 4*
| | |
|---|---|
| OTHELLO* | Delane |
| IAGO | Rosco |
| BRABANTIO* | Hulett |
| CASSIO | Giffard |
| LODOVICO* | Bardin |
| RODERIGO* | [R.] Wetherilt |
| GRATIANO* | Lyon |
| MONTANO* | Ayres |
| DESDEMONA | Mrs Giffard |
| EMILIA | Mrs Haughton |

*Mar. 27*
omitted
   LODOVICO, GRATIANO, MONTANO

*Sept. 10*
| | |
|---|---|
| OTHELLO | Hulett |
| BRABANTIO | W. Giffard |
| RODERIGO | Woodward |
| MONTANO | Havard |

added
| | |
|---|---|
| DUKE | Bardin |

omitted
   LODOVICO

## VILLIERS ST., YORK BUILDINGS
*Mar. 19*
| | |
|---|---|
| OTHELLO | Freeman |
| IAGO | Oakly |
| CASSIO | Machen |
| RODERIGO | Smith |
| DESDEMONA | Miss Stuart |
| EMILIA | Miss Turner |

## 1736 DRURY LANE
*Mar. 4*
| | |
|---|---|
| OTHELLO | Quin |
| CASSIO | [T.] Cibber |
| IAGO | W. Mills |
| BRABANTIO | Milward |
| RODERIGO | Miller |
| DESDEMONA* | Mrs Thurmond |
| EMILIA | Mrs Butler |

*Oct. 5*
| | |
|---|---|
| DESDEMONA | Mrs Cibber |

added
| | |
|---|---|
| LODOVICO | Turbutt |
| MONTANO | Winstone |

*Dec. 16*
| | |
|---|---|
| DESDEMONA | Mrs Cibber |

361

## 1736 COVENT GARDEN
*Mar. 30*

| | |
|---|---|
| OTHELLO | Stephens |
| IAGO | Ryan |
| CASSIO | Walker |
| BRABANTIO | Aston |
| RODERIGO | Chapman |
| DESDEMONA | Mrs Buchanan |
| EMILIA | Mrs Mullart |

## 1737 DRURY LANE
*Jan. 13*

| | |
|---|---|
| OTHELLO | Quin |
| CASSIO* | [T.] Cibber |
| IAGO | W. Mills |
| BRABANTIO | Milward |
| RODERIGO | Miller |
| EMILIA | Mrs Butler |
| DESDEMONA | Mrs Cibber |

*Oct. 6; Nov. 10*

| | |
|---|---|
| CASSIO | Wright |

## COVENT GARDEN
*Mar. 14*

| | |
|---|---|
| OTHELLO* | Delane |
| IAGO | Ryan |
| CASSIO | Walker |
| BRABANTIO | Aston |
| RODERIGO | Chapman |
| LODOVICO | Paget |
| EMILIA | Mrs Mullart |
| DESDEMONA* | Mrs Horton |

*Apr. 21*

| | |
|---|---|
| OTHELLO | Stephens |
| DESDEMONA | Mrs Stevens |

## LINCOLN'S INN FIELDS
*Sept. 7*

| | |
|---|---|
| OTHELLO | Stephens |
| IAGO | Rosco |
| BRABANTIO | Davis |
| RODERIGO | Yates |
| CASSIO | Stevens |
| MONTANO | [A.] Ryan |
| DESDEMONA | Mrs Stevens |
| EMILIA | Mrs Egerton |

[Bill in Harris of Sept. 6.]

## 1738 DRURY LANE
*Jan. 4; Feb. 25*

| | |
|---|---|
| OTHELLO* | Quin |
| BRABANTIO | Milward |
| CASSIO | Wright |
| IAGO | [W.] Mills |
| RODERIGO* | Miller |
| DESDEMONA* | Mrs Cibber |
| EMILIA | Mrs Butler |

*May 11*

| | |
|---|---|
| OTHELLO | Hyde |

*Sept. 26*

| | |
|---|---|
| RODERIGO | [T.] Cibber |
| DESDEMONA | Mrs Giffard |

*Nov. 13*

| | |
|---|---|
| RODERIGO | Woodward |
| DESDEMONA | Mrs Giffard |
| added | |
| LODOVICO | Ridout |

## COVENT GARDEN
*Apr. 10*

| | |
|---|---|
| OTHELLO | Delane |
| IAGO | Ryan |
| BRABANTIO | Aston |
| CASSIO | Walker |
| RODERIGO | Chapman |
| LODOVICO | Hale |
| MONTANO | Ridout |
| DESDEMONA | Mrs Horton |
| EMILIA | Mrs Mullart |

*June 27*

| | |
|---|---|
| OTHELLO | Stephens |
| IAGO | A. Hallam |
| RODERIGO | Penkethman [Jr.] |
| DUKE | W. Hallam |
| CASSIO | Stevens |
| BRABANTIO | Boman [Jr.] |
| LODOVICO | Ware |
| MONTANO | Salway |
| GRATIANO | Stoppelaer |
| EMILIA | Mrs Hamilton |
| DESDEMONA | Mrs Vincent |

## 1739 DRURY LANE
*Sept. 21; Dec. 13*

| | |
|---|---|
| OTHELLO | Quin |
| BRABANTIO | Milward |
| CASSIO | Wright |
| IAGO | [W.] Mills |
| RODERIGO | Woodward |
| LODOVICO | Ridout |
| DESDEMONA | Mrs Giffard |
| EMILIA | Mrs Butler |

## 1739 COVENT GARDEN
*Dec. 19*

| | |
|---|---|
| OTHELLO | Stephens |
| BRABANTIO | Roberts |
| CASSIO | Hale |
| IAGO | Ryan |
| RODERIGO | Neale |
| LODOVICO | Rosco |
| DUKE | Anderson |
| MONTANO | A. Ryan |
| GRATIANO | Arthur |
| DESDEMONA | Mrs Horton |
| EMILIA | Mrs Mullart |

## 1740 DRURY LANE
*Sept. 27; Dec. 16*

| | |
|---|---|
| OTHELLO | Quin |
| BRABANTIO | Milward |
| CASSIO | Wright |
| IAGO | [W.] Mills |
| RODERIGO | Woodward |
| DESDEMONA | Mrs Pritchard |
| EMILIA | Mrs Butler |

[The playhouse bill for Dec. 16 is in FSL.]

## COVENT GARDEN
*Mar. 10*

| | |
|---|---|
| OTHELLO | [T.] Cibber |
| IAGO | Ryan |
| CASSIO | Hale |
| RODERIGO | Neale |
| BRABANTIO | Roberts |
| GRATIANO | Arthur |
| LODOVICO | Rosco |
| MONTANO | A. Ryan |
| DESDEMONA | Mrs Horton |
| EMILIA | Mrs Mullart |
| BIANCA | Mrs Hale |

## GOODMAN'S FIELDS
*Oct. 23*   *Nov. 14*

| | | | | |
|---|---|---|---|---|
| OTHELLO | Walker | | CASSIO | Giffard |
| IAGO | Paget | | | |
| CASSIO* | Blakes | | | |
| RODERIGO | Yates | | | |
| DUKE | Dunstall | | | |
| BRABANTIO | Nelson | | | |

## 1740 GOODMAN'S FIELDS (cont.)

*Oct. 23 (cont.)*

| | |
|---|---|
| GRATIANO | Wallis |
| LODOVICO | Linnet |
| DESDEMONA | Mrs Giffard |
| EMILIA | Mrs Middleton |

## 1741 DRURY LANE

*Sept. 10; Oct. 26*

| | |
|---|---|
| OTHELLO | Delane |
| IAGO | [W.] Mills |
| CASSIO | Winstone |
| BRABANTIO | Berry |
| RODERIGO | Neale |
| LODOVICO | Turbutt |
| MONTANO | Havard |
| DUKE | Taswell |
| DESDEMONA | Mrs Mills |
| EMILIA | Mrs Butler |

## COVENT GARDEN

*Dec. 9*

| | |
|---|---|
| OTHELLO | Perry [first appearance on the stage] |
| IAGO | Ryan |
| CASSIO | Hale |
| BRABANTIO | Roberts |
| RODERIGO | Woodward |
| LODOVICO | Gibson |
| MONTANO | Cashell |
| DUKE | Harrington |
| GRATIANO | Lascells |
| DESDEMONA | Mrs Pritchard |
| EMILIA | Mrs Mullart |

## GOODMAN'S FIELDS

*Jan. 29*

| | |
|---|---|
| OTHELLO | A Gentleman [unidentified; first appearance on the stage] |
| IAGO | Paget |
| CASSIO | Blakes |
| RODERIGO | Yates |
| BRABANTIO | Nelson |
| GRATIANO | Julian |
| LODOVICO | Marr |

## 1741 GOODMAN'S FIELDS (cont.)

*Jan. 29 (cont.)*

| | |
|---|---|
| MONTANO | Crofts |
| DESDEMONA | Mrs Giffard |
| EMILIA | Mrs Lamball |

## 1742 DRURY LANE

*May 6*

| | |
|---|---|
| OTHELLO | Delane |
| IAGO | [W.] Mills |
| CASSIO | Winstone |
| RODERIGO | Neale |
| DUKE | Taswell |
| BRABANTIO | Berry |
| LODOVICO | Turbutt |
| MONTANO | Havard |
| EMILIA | Mrs Butler |
| DESDEMONA | Mrs Mills |

### COVENT GARDEN

*Apr. 26*

| | |
|---|---|
| OTHELLO* | Stephens |
| IAGO | Ryan |
| CASSIO | Hale |
| RODERIGO | Woodward |
| DUKE* | Harrington |
| BRABANTIO | Gibson |
| MONTANO | Cashell |
| EMILIA* | Mrs Woodward |
| DESDEMONA* | Mrs Pritchard |

*Sept. 22, 24*

| | |
|---|---|
| OTHELLO | Quin |
| EMILIA | Mrs Mullart |
| DESDEMONA | Mrs Cibber |
| added | |
| LODOVICO | Rosco |
| omitted | |
| DUKE | |

*Sept. 27; Nov. 23; Dec. 2, 13*

| | |
|---|---|
| OTHELLO | Quin |
| DESDEMONA | Mrs Cibber |
| added | |
| LODOVICO | Rosco |
| omitted | |
| DUKE | |

## 1743 COVENT GARDEN

*Feb. 5, 24; May 17*

| | |
|---|---|
| OTHELLO | Quin |
| IAGO | Ryan |
| CASSIO | Hale |
| RODERIGO* | Woodward |
| BRABANTIO | Gibson |
| LODOVICO | Rosco |
| MONTANO | Cashell |
| EMILIA* | Mrs Woodward |
| DESDEMONA* | Mrs Cibber |

*Apr. 4*

| | |
|---|---|
| RODERIGO | Chapman |

*Nov. 28, 29*

| | |
|---|---|
| EMILIA | Mrs James |
| DESDEMONA | Mrs Horton |

# OTHELLO

**1744 DRURY LANE**
*Mar. 10*

| | |
|---|---|
| OTHELLO | The Gentleman who lately perform'd it at the New Theatre in the Hay-Market [Foote (Genest, iv. 64)] |
| IAGO | Giffard |
| CASSIO | Winstone |
| RODERIGO | Neale |
| BRABANTIO | Berry |
| DUKE | Taswell |
| LODOVICO | Turbutt |
| MONTANO | Woodburn |
| DESDEMONA | Mrs Giffard |
| EMILIA | Mrs Bennet |

## COVENT GARDEN
*Jan. 12; Apr. 2; May 25; Oct. 16; Nov. 3*

| | |
|---|---|
| OTHELLO | Quin |
| IAGO | Ryan |
| CASSIO | Hale |
| RODERIGO | Woodward |
| BRABANTIO | Gibson |
| LODOVICO | Rosco |
| MONTANO | Cashell |
| EMILIA | Mrs James |
| DESDEMONA | Mrs Pritchard |

## HAYMARKET
*Feb. 6, 13, 20, 23; Mar. 2*

| | |
|---|---|
| OTHELLO | Foote [first appearance on the stage] |
| IAGO | Macklin |
| LODOVICO | Hill [first appearance on the stage] |
| MONTANO | Yorke [first appearance on the stage] |

[The bills give neither the parts nor the actors' names. The assignment of Foote, Macklin, and Hill is taken from Genest, iv. 76; of Yorke from Kirkman, *Memoirs of ... Macklin*, 1799, i. 295.]

*Apr. 26*

| | |
|---|---|
| OTHELLO | A Citizen for his diversion [unidentified] |

No other parts assigned

367

## 1744 HAYMARKET (cont.)
*Sept. 22*

| | |
|---|---|
| OTHELLO | [T.] Cibber |
| IAGO | Paget |
| BRABANTIO | Furnival |
| CASSIO | Mozeen |
| RODERIGO | Charles |
| EMILIA | Mrs Chetwood |
| DESDEMONA | Miss Jenny Cibber |

## 1745 DRURY LANE
*Mar. 7, 9*

| | |
|---|---|
| OTHELLO* | Garrick |
| IAGO | Macklin |
| BRABANTIO | Berry |
| CASSIO | Havard |
| RODERIGO | Yates |
| DUKE | Winstone |
| LODOVICO | Blakes |
| MONTANO | Mozeen |
| GRATIANO | Woodburn |
| SENATOR* | Simpson |
| OFFICER* | Green |
| EMILIA | Mrs Macklin |
| DESDEMONA* | Mrs Cibber |

*Apr. 25*

| | |
|---|---|
| OTHELLO | Sheridan |

*Oct. 1*

| | |
|---|---|
| OTHELLO | Delane |
| DESDEMONA | Miss Copin |
| omitted | |
| SENATOR, OFFICER | |

## COVENT GARDEN
*Mar. 2; Apr. 18*

| | |
|---|---|
| OTHELLO | Quin |
| IAGO | Ryan |
| CASSIO | Hale |
| RODERIGO | Woodward |
| BRABANTIO | Gibson |
| LODOVICO | Rosco |
| MONTANO | Cashell |
| EMILIA | Mrs James |
| DESDEMONA | Mrs Pritchard |

## NEW WELLS, GOODMAN'S FIELDS
*Feb. 6; May 7.* No parts assigned

*Mar. 21*

| | |
|---|---|
| OTHELLO | Townly |
| DESDEMONA | Mrs Carlisle |

No other parts assigned

## 1745 NEW WELLS, GOODMAN'S FIELDS (*cont.*)

*Nov. 29*

| | |
|---|---|
| OTHELLO | A Gentleman [unidentified; first appearance on the stage] |
| IAGO | Furnival |
| BRABANTIO | Paget |
| CASSIO | Kennedy |
| RODERIGO | L. Hallam |
| EMILIA | Mrs Bambridge |
| DESDEMONA | Mrs Phillips |

## SHEPHERD'S MARKET, MAYFAIR

*Feb. 11, 18, 20.* No parts assigned

## 1746 DRURY LANE

*Apr. 9*

| | |
|---|---|
| OTHELLO | Delane |
| IAGO | [L.] Sparks |
| BRABANTIO | Berry |
| CASSIO | Havard |
| RODERIGO | Yates |
| DUKE | Winstone |
| LODOVICO | Blakes |
| MONTANO | Bransby |
| GRATIANO | Simpson |
| EMILIA | Mrs Macklin |
| DESDEMONA | Miss Edwards |

*Oct. 4, 7, 9, 11, 14, 17, 18, 21, 28; Nov. 26*

| | |
|---|---|
| OTHELLO | Barry [first appearance, Oct. 4, in London] |
| IAGO | Macklin |
| BRABANTIO | Berry |
| CASSIO | [W.] Mills |
| RODERIGO | Yates |
| DUKE | Winstone |
| LODOVICO | Blakes |
| MONTANO | Mozeen |
| GRATIANO* | Goodfellow |
| EMILIA* | Mrs Macklin |
| DESDEMONA | Mrs Ridout |

*Dec. 5*

| | |
|---|---|
| GRATIANO | Simpson |
| EMILIA | Mrs Furnival |

## 1746 COVENT GARDEN
*Apr. 3*
| | |
|---|---|
| OTHELLO | Cashell |
| IAGO | Ryan |
| CASSIO | Hale |
| RODERIGO | Woodward |
| BRABANTIO | Gibson |
| LODOVICO | Rosco |
| DUKE | Marten |
| MONTANO | Ridout |
| EMILIA | Mrs James |
| DESDEMONA | Mrs Pritchard |

*June 20*
| | |
|---|---|
| OTHELLO | Garrick |
| IAGO | Ryan |
| CASSIO | Cashell |
| RODERIGO | Chapman |
| BRABANTIO | Philips |
| MONTANO | Marr |
| LODOVICO | Paget |
| EMILIA | Mrs Bland |
| DESDEMONA | Mrs Vincent |

*Nov. 28; Dec. 31*
| | |
|---|---|
| OTHELLO | Quin |
| IAGO | Ryan |
| CASSIO | Cashell |
| RODERIGO | Woodward |
| BRABANTIO | Gibson |
| LODOVICO | Rosco |
| MONTANO | Havard |
| EMILIA | Mrs James |
| DESDEMONA | Mrs Cibber |

## HAYMARKET
*Dec. 4*

OTHELLO    Foote
No other parts assigned

## NEW WELLS, GOODMAN'S FIELDS
*Dec. 9*
| | |
|---|---|
| OTHELLO | Goodfellow |
| IAGO | Furnival |
| CASSIO | Lee |
| RODERIGO | L. Hallam |
| BRABANTIO | Paget |
| LODOVICO | Cushing |
| DUKE | Dove |

OTHELLO

## 1746 NEW WELLS, GOODMAN'S FIELDS (cont.)
*Dec. 9 (cont.)*
| | |
|---|---|
| MONTANO | Wignell |
| GRATIANO | [G.] Hallam |
| CAPTAIN | Shuter |
| EMILIA | Mrs Bambridge |
| DESDEMONA | Mrs [L.] Hallam |

## JAMES ST., HAYMARKET
*Oct. 2.* No parts assigned

## 1747 DRURY LANE
*Jan. 1*
| | |
|---|---|
| OTHELLO | Barry |
| IAGO | Macklin |
| BRABANTIO | Berry |
| CASSIO | [W.] Mills |
| RODERIGO | Yates |
| DUKE | Winstone |
| LODOVICO | Blakes |
| MONTANO* | Mozeen |
| GRATIANO | Simpson |
| DESDEMONA* | Mrs Ridout |
| EMILIA* | Mrs Furnival |

*Feb. 4, 24*
| | |
|---|---|
| MONTANO | Bransby |

*Apr. 4, 10*
| | |
|---|---|
| MONTANO | Bransby |
| DESDEMONA | Mrs Elmy |

*Sept. 26*
| | |
|---|---|
| DESDEMONA | Mrs Elmy |
| EMILIA | Mrs Macklin |

*Oct. 22; Dec. 11*
| | |
|---|---|
| DESDEMONA | Mrs Cibber |
| EMILIA | Mrs Macklin |

## NEW WELLS, GOODMAN'S FIELDS
*Feb. 20*
| | |
|---|---|
| OTHELLO | Goodfellow |
| IAGO | Furnival |
| CASSIO | Lee |
| RODERIGO | L. Hallam |
| BRABANTIO | Paget |
| LODOVICO | Cushing |
| DUKE | Dove |
| MONTANO | Wignell |
| GRATIANO | [G.] Hallam |
| CAPTAIN | Shuter |
| EMILIA | Mrs Bambridge |
| DESDEMONA | Mrs [L.] Hallam |

## BOWLING GREEN, SOUTHWARK
*Oct. 22.* No parts assigned

## 1748 DRURY LANE

*Jan. 15; Feb. 10*

| | |
|---|---|
| OTHELLO | Barry |
| IAGO* | Macklin |
| BRABANTIO | Berry |
| CASSIO | [W.] Mills |
| RODERIGO* | Yates |
| DUKE* | Winstone |
| LODOVICO* | Blakes |
| MONTANO* | Mozeen |
| GRATIANO* | Simpson |
| EMILIA | Mrs Pritchard |
| DESDEMONA | Mrs Cibber |

*Apr. 20*

omitted
    DUKE, LODOVICO, MONTANO, GRATIANO

*Oct. 4*

| | |
|---|---|
| IAGO | [L.] Sparks |
| RODERIGO | Woodward |
| MONTANO | Bransby |

*Nov. 23*

| | |
|---|---|
| IAGO | Havard |
| MONTANO | Bransby |

## COVENT GARDEN

*Jan. 9*

| | |
|---|---|
| OTHELLO* | Sowdon |
| IAGO | Ryan |
| CASSIO | Giffard |
| RODERIGO | [T.] Cibber |
| BRABANTIO* | Bridges |
| LODOVICO | Rosco |
| MONTANO* | Anderson |
| EMILIA | Mrs James |
| DESDEMONA | Mrs Giffard |

*Oct. 28*

| | |
|---|---|
| OTHELLO | Quin |
| IAGO | Ryan |
| BRABANTIO | [L.] Sparks |
| CASSIO | Ridout |
| LODOVICO | Anderson |
| RODERIGO | Ward |
| MONTANO | Holtom |
| EMILIA | Mrs Bambridge |
| DESDEMONA | Mrs Ward |

*Jan. 11*

| | |
|---|---|
| BRABANTIO | Gibson |
| MONTANO | Ridout |
| added | |
| DUKE | Bridges |

*Apr. 6*

| | |
|---|---|
| OTHELLO | Quin |
| BRABANTIO | Gibson |
| MONTANO | Ridout |
| added | |
| DUKE | Bridges |

## HAYMARKET

*Apr. 30*

| | |
|---|---|
| OTHELLO | Scudamore |
| DESDEMONA | Mrs Daniel |

No other parts assigned

OTHELLO

## 1749 DRURY LANE
*Jan. 6*

| | |
|---|---|
| OTHELLO | Barry |
| IAGO* | Havard |
| BRABANTIO | Berry |
| CASSIO* | [W.] Mills |
| RODERIGO | Yates |
| EMILIA | Mrs Pritchard |
| DESDEMONA | Mrs Cibber |

*Nov. 2, 22, 24; Dec. 1*

| | |
|---|---|
| OTHELLO | Barry |
| BRABANTIO | Berry |
| CASSIO | Palmer |
| RODERIGO | Yates |
| DUKE | Winstone |
| LODOVICO | Blakes |
| GRATIANO | Simpson |
| OFFICER | Usher |
| IAGO | Garrick |
| DESDEMONA | Mrs Elmy |
| EMILIA | Mrs Pritchard |

*Mar. 9*

| | |
|---|---|
| IAGO | Garrick |
| CASSIO | Palmer |

## COVENT GARDEN
*Oct. 4*

| | |
|---|---|
| OTHELLO | Quin |
| IAGO | Ryan |
| BRABANTIO | [L.] Sparks |
| CASSIO | Ridout |
| LODOVICO | Anderson |
| RODERIGO | Cushing |
| MONTANO | Bransby |
| EMILIA | Mrs Bambridge |
| DESDEMONA | Mrs Woffington |

## HAYMARKET
*Oct. 17*

| | |
|---|---|
| OTHELLO | Bruodin |
| EMILIA | Mrs Hutton |

No other parts assigned
[Bill in DA of Oct. 14.]

## 1750 DRURY LANE
*Mar. 10*

| | |
|---|---|
| OTHELLO | Barry |
| BRABANTIO | Berry |
| CASSIO | Palmer |

## 1750 DRURY LANE (cont.)

*Mar. 10 (cont.)*

| | |
|---|---|
| RODERIGO | Yates |
| IAGO | Garrick |
| DESDEMONA | Mrs Elmy |
| EMILIA | Mrs Pritchard |

### COVENT GARDEN

*Oct. 17*

| | |
|---|---|
| OTHELLO* | Quin |
| IAGO* | Ryan |
| BRABANTIO | [L.] Sparks |
| CASSIO | Ridout |
| RODERIGO | Dyer |
| LODOVICO | Anderson |
| GRATIANO | Redman |
| MONTANO | Bransby |
| EMILIA* | Mrs Bambridge |
| DESDEMONA | Mrs Cibber |

*Dec. 3*

| | |
|---|---|
| OTHELLO | Barry |
| IAGO | Macklin |
| EMILIA | Mrs Macklin |

### JAMES ST., HAYMARKET

*July 23.* No parts assigned

# PAPAL TYRANNY IN THE REIGN OF KING JOHN

Colley Cibber's alteration of KING JOHN, q.v.

# PERICLES

Adapted as MARINA, by George Lillo. In three acts.

1738   John Gray.

Act I. i is *IV. i* almost verbatim. I. ii is *IV. ii*, with the dialogue between the Bawd and the Pirates considerably enlarged.

Act II. i is *IV. iii* and *iv* run together. *IV. iii* is enlarged: the Queen and Leonine are fearful of the consequences of their act. *IV. iv*, the dumb show, is written into a scene of about 125 lines. Then follows a brief new dialogue in which Leonine, dying of poison, kills the Queen. II. ii is *IV. vi* almost verbatim, with a short new scene at the end relating Marina's escape from the brothel.

Act III. i is new: Boult explains to the Bawd that Marina has been saved by Lysimachus. III. ii is *V. i* and *iii*, slightly enlarged, and interwoven.

See Genest, iii. 566–7; Odell, i. 257–9.

## PERICLES [as MARINA]

### 1738 COVENT GARDEN
*Aug. 1, 4, 8*

| PERICLES | Stephens |
| LYSIMACHUS | [A.] Hallam |
| ESCANES | Shelton |
| LEONINE | Stevens |
| VALDES | Boman [Jr.] |
| BOULT | Penkethman [Jr.] |
| THAISA | Mrs Marshall |
| PHILOTEN | Mrs Hamilton |
| MARINA | Mrs Vincent |
| MOTHER COUPLER | Mr W. Hallam |

[The bill gives the actors' names only. The above assignment is taken from the printed text. The bill omits Shelton, and also lists Stoppelaer and Dove. Their parts were probably either PIRATES or PRIESTS.]

## PYRAMUS AND THISBE

John Frederick Lampe's alteration of A MIDSUMMER-NIGHT'S DREAM, q.v.

## PYRAMUS AND THISBE

Richard Leveridge's alteration of A MIDSUMMER-NIGHT'S DREAM, q.v.

## RICHARD II

Adapted by Lewis Theobald. In five acts.

1720  G. Strahan.

Act I opens with a long series of brief passages taken at random from the original (*II. ii. 98–9; II. i. 239–62; I. ii. 4–6; II. iii. 120–2*, &c.), interspersed with new dialogue. The scene recounts Richard's weakness, Bolingbroke's power, and introduces a new element: the love between Aumerle and Lady Percy, Northumberland's daughter. With the entrance of Richard the scene continues with *III. i. 6–142* verbatim, but slightly reduced. The act ends with a new dialogue: the Queen encourages Richard. *III. ii. 54–62* is inserted.

Act II opens with a new scene: Aumerle makes love to Lady Percy. Then follow *II. iii. 59–147* almost verbatim, and *III. iii. 35–end*, somewhat reduced and slightly altered.

Act III again opens with miscellaneous passages (*V. ii. 7–21; III. ii. 155–70; V. 15–20*, &c.), and then proceeds with *IV. i. 1–30* and *107–end*, slightly revised.

Act IV is largely new, but random passages from the original are inserted. Aumerle tells Lady Percy of his loyalty to Richard and of the conspiracy against Bolingbroke. The Queen and Richard lament their fortunes. Aumerle's plot is discovered.

RICHARD II

Act V is also new, with a few passages from the original made use of (*II. i. 40–66*, &c.). Lady Percy pleads for Aumerle, but he is condemned. Richard is killed by Exton.

See Genest, iii. 32–5; Odell, i. 241–3.

No acting versions of the original were published before 1750.

[*as altered by* THEOBALD]

## 1719 LINCOLN'S INN FIELDS

*Dec. 10, 11, 12, 14, 19*

| | |
|---|---|
| RICHARD | Ryan |
| YORK | Boheme |
| AUMERLE | Smith |
| SALISBURY | Egleton |
| BISHOP OF CARLISLE | C. Bullock |
| BOLINGBROKE | [J.] Leigh |
| NORTHUMBERLAND | Ogden |
| ROSS | Diggs |
| WILLOUGHBY | Coker |
| QUEEN | Mrs Bullock |
| LADY PERCY | Mrs Spiller |

[The bills give neither the parts nor the actors' names. The above assignment is taken from the printed text.]

## 1720 LINCOLN'S INN FIELDS

*Jan. 2.* No parts assigned

*Jan. 25*

| | |
|---|---|
| RICHARD | Ryan |
| YORK | Boheme |
| AUMERLE | Smith |
| SALISBURY | Egleton |
| BISHOP OF CARLISLE | Ch. Bullock |
| BOLINGBROKE | [J.] Leigh |
| NORTHUMBERLAND | Ogden |
| QUEEN | Mrs Bullock |
| LADY PERCY | Mrs Spiller |

## 1721 LINCOLN'S INN FIELDS

*Jan. 7*

| | |
|---|---|
| RICHARD | Ryan |
| YORK | Boheme |
| AUMERLE | Quin |
| QUEEN | Mrs Seymour |
| LADY PERCY | Mrs Bullock |

*Feb. 4*
added
| | |
|---|---|
| BISHOP OF CARLISLE | Ch. Bullock |

*Oct. 24*
added
| | |
|---|---|
| BOLINGBROKE | [J.] Leigh |
| SALISBURY | Egleton |

376

## RICHARD II
*[The original]*

### 1738 COVENT GARDEN
*Feb. 6, 7*

| | |
|---|---|
| RICHARD | Delane |
| YORK | Stephens |
| GAUNT | Johnson |
| BOLINGBROKE | Ryan |
| NORFOLK | Walker |
| BISHOP OF CARLISLE | Chapman |
| AUMERLE | [A.] Hallam |
| SALISBURY* | Lyon |
| SCROOP | Aston |
| BUSHY | Rosco |
| BAGOT | Salway |
| GREEN | Arthur |
| NORTHUMBERLAND | Bridgwater |
| PERCY | Hale |
| ROSS | Ridout |
| WILLOUGHBY | A. Ryan |
| SURREY | Houghton |
| FITZWALTER* | Stevens |
| LORD MARSHAL | Mullart |
| [ATTENDANT, with looking-glass | Yates] |
| [ABBOT OF WESTMINSTER | Stoppelaer] |
| [GROOM | Clarke] |
| QUEEN | Mrs Horton |
| DUCHESS OF YORK* | Mrs Hallam |
| DUCHESS OF GLOUCESTER | Mrs James |

[ATTENDANT, ABBOT OF WESTMINSTER, and GROOM do not appear in the bills. The assignments are taken from Davies (i. 175, 180, 192 respectively).]

*Feb. 8, 9, 10, 11, 14, 21; Mar. 9*
omitted
    DUCHESS OF YORK

*May 2*

| | |
|---|---|
| SALISBURY | Stevens |

omitted
    FITZWALTER, DUCHESS OF YORK

*Nov. 30; Dec. 1, 21*

| | |
|---|---|
| RICHARD | Delane |
| YORK | Stephens |
| GAUNT | Johnson |
| BOLINGBROKE | Ryan |
| NORFOLK | Walker |
| BISHOP OF CARLISLE | Chapman |
| QUEEN | Mrs Horton |

No other parts assigned

### 1739 COVENT GARDEN
*Feb. 19*

| | |
|---|---|
| RICHARD | Delane |
| BOLINGBROKE | Ryan |
| NORFOLK | Rosco |
| GAUNT | Johnson |
| BISHOP OF CARLISLE* | Chapman |
| YORK | Stephens |
| QUEEN | Mrs Horton |

*Oct. 23*
omitted
    BISHOP OF CARLISLE

377

# RICHARD III

Adapted by Colley Cibber. In five acts.

[1700] B. Lintott.

Act I, scene i opens with about 130 new lines, consisting of a discussion of the battle of Tewkesbury. Then follows *Henry IV, Part II, I. i. 68–113*, reduced and slightly altered. Next is an account of the death of Henry VI's son, Edward: it consists of *Henry VI, Part III, V. v. 17–21*, and of *Richard II, I. iii. 294–9; V. i. 38–45*, linked with about 60 new lines. This is followed by the original, *I. i. 5–27*, and by *Henry VI, Part III, III. ii. 165–71*. The scene ends with 4 new lines. Scene ii is a rewriting of *I. iv. 1–7*, followed by *Henry VI, Part III, V. vi* entire, slightly altered, by *I. i. 148–51* of the original, and by 3 new lines.

Act II, scene i opens with about 30 new lines: Richard's wish to marry Lady Anne. Richard then has *Henry VI, Part III, III. ii. 153–64*, followed, after a few new lines, by *125–7*. About 17 new lines follow: Richard's designs on Lady Anne. Next is *Henry VI, Part I, I. i. 1–5*, followed by *I. ii. 14–end* of the original, virtually verbatim. Scene ii is *II. ii*, almost entirely rewritten.

Act III opens with *III. i*, drastically revised (*II. iv. 27–34* is used here). Then follow about 70 new lines: Richard and Lady Anne quarrel. This is succeeded by *III. vii*, almost verbatim, but abridged; and by 13 new lines: Richard rejoices that he is king.

Act IV, scene i is a rewriting of *IV. i*, with an occasional line retained verbatim. Scene ii is *IV. ii*, again almost wholly rewritten. Scene iii begins with about 50 new lines: the murder of the Princes, followed by *IV. iii*, somewhat altered; by *IV. iv. 9–18, 126–35*, slightly revised, *136–end*, much reduced and occasionally rearranged; and by 14 new lines: Richard says that he is ready for war.

Act V, scene i is *V. ii*, slightly revised (*Henry VI, Part II, III. ii. 233–5* is included). Scene ii is *V. iii. 1–116*, reduced and altered (*Henry V, IV. ii. 51–9* is included). Scene iii begins with about 50 new lines: Richard's preparations for the battle. Then follow *Henry V, Prologue to Act IV, 4–25*, reduced, and the original: *V. iii. 119–86, 208–23*, much revised (only the ghosts of Henry, Lady Anne and the Princes are retained). Scene iv opens with *V. iii. 224–37*, followed by *Henry V, III. i. 3–end*, much reduced, and by *V. iii. 278–end* and *V. iv. 1–13* of the original. Next are *Henry VI, Part II, V. ii. 13–27* and *Henry IV, Part II, I. i. 155–60*. The act ends with *V. iii. 14–end* of the original, much altered.

See Genest, ii. 195–213; Odell, i. 75–6; Spencer, 335–8.

[*as altered by* CIBBER]

## 1704 DRURY LANE

*Apr. 4*

    RICHARD  Cibber

        [The bill assigns no parts. The above is suggested by Genest (ii. 300).]

## 1710 QUEEN'S

*Jan. 28.* No parts assigned

## RICHARD III [as altered by CIBBER]

### 1710 QUEEN'S (cont.)
Mar. 27; May 13

| | |
|---|---|
| HENRY | Wilks |
| RICHARD | Cibber |
| QUEEN ELIZABETH | Mrs Porter |
| LADY ANNE | Mrs Rogers |

No other parts assigned

[Bill for Mar. 27 in DC of Mar. 20.]

### 1713 DRURY LANE
Feb. 14, 26; Apr. 27. No parts assigned

### 1714 DRURY LANE
Jan. 2; Feb. 27; Apr. 17; Oct. 15. No parts assigned

### 1715 DRURY LANE
Jan. 27. No parts assigned

Dec. 6

| | |
|---|---|
| RICHARD | Cibber |
| HENRY | Wilks |
| BUCKINGHAM | Mills |
| QUEEN ELIZABETH | Mrs Porter |

[In the edition published by W. Mears in 1718 the cast is the same as that of this performance, with the following additions:

| | |
|---|---|
| PRINCE EDWARD | Norris Jr. |
| DUKE OF YORK | Miss Lindar |
| RICHMOND | Ryan |
| NORFOLK | Boman Sr. |
| RATCLIFF | Oates |
| CATESBY | Diggs |
| TRESSEL | W. Wilks |
| OXFORD | Boman Jr. |
| LIEUTENANT | Quin |
| BLUNT | Wright |
| LORD MAYOR | Miller |
| TYRREL | Weller |
| FORREST | Wilson |
| DIGHTON | Higginson |
| LADY ANNE | Mrs Horton |
| DUCHESS OF YORK | Mrs Baker] |

[Under this date Genest (ii. 573) lists eight of these additional assignments (one erroneously: Walker, instead of Weller, as TYRREL). His source was 'the 12mo edition of Cibber's works [i.e., Tonson, 1736, Vol. ii]', in which the cast is the same as that given in Mears's 1718 edition.]

## RICHARD III [as altered by CIBBER]

### 1717 DRURY LANE
*Jan. 1; Nov. 9.* No parts assigned

### 1718 DRURY LANE
*Mar. 15.* No parts assigned

### 1719 DRURY LANE
*Feb. 12; Sept. 26.* No parts assigned

### 1720 DRURY LANE
*Feb. 13; May 19; Dec. 3.* No parts assigned

### 1721 DRURY LANE
*Dec. 26.* No parts assigned

### LINCOLN'S INN FIELDS

*Mar. 11*
| | |
|---|---|
| RICHARD | Ryan |
| HENRY | Boheme |
| BUCKINGHAM | Quin |
| RICHMOND* | [J.] Leigh |
| CATESBY* | Egleton |
| LORD MAYOR | Bullock Sr. |
| PRINCE EDWARD | Miss Stone |
| QUEEN ELIZABETH* | Mrs Seymour |
| LADY ANNE* | Mrs Spiller |
| DUCHESS OF YORK* | Mrs Giffard |

*Mar. 13*
| | |
|---|---|
| RICHMOND | Egleton |
| QUEEN ELIZABETH | Mrs Giffard |

omitted
    CATESBY, LADY ANNE, DUCHESS OF YORK

*Mar. 27*
| | |
|---|---|
| LADY ANNE | Mrs Giffard |

omitted
    DUCHESS OF YORK

*Oct. 7*
| | |
|---|---|
| RICHMOND | Walker |
| LADY ANNE | Mrs Egleton [i.e. formerly Mrs Giffard] |

omitted
    DUCHESS OF YORK

*Dec. 16*
| | |
|---|---|
| RICHMOND | Walker |
| LADY ANNE | Mrs Bullock |
| DUCHESS OF YORK | Mrs Egleton [i.e. formerly Mrs Giffard] |

omitted
    CATESBY

[The DC bill retains Egleton as CATESBY and Mrs Spiller as LADY ANNE, and omits DUCHESS OF YORK.]

### 1722 DRURY LANE
*May 14.* No parts assigned

## RICHARD III [*as altered by* CIBBER]

### 1722 LINCOLN'S INN FIELDS
*Oct. 4*

| | | | |
|---|---|---|---|
| RICHARD | Ryan | | |
| HENRY | Boheme | | |
| BUCKINGHAM | Quin | | |
| RICHMOND | Walker | | |
| CATESBY | Egleton | | |
| QUEEN ELIZABETH | Mrs Seymour | | |
| LADY ANNE | Mrs Bullock | | |
| DUCHESS OF YORK | Mrs Egleton | | |

*Nov. 15*
added
LORD MAYOR   Bullock Sr.
PRINCE EDWARD   Mrs Rogeir

### 1723 DRURY LANE
*Mar. 9.* No parts assigned

### LINCOLN'S INN FIELDS
*Oct. 11*

| | |
|---|---|
| RICHARD | Ryan |
| HENRY | Boheme |
| BUCKINGHAM | Quin |
| RICHMOND | Walker |
| CATESBY | Egleton |
| LORD MAYOR | Bullock Sr. |
| PRINCE EDWARD | Mrs Rogeir |
| QUEEN ELIZABETH | Mrs Wilson |
| LADY ANNE | Mrs Vincent |
| DUCHESS OF YORK | Mrs Knight |

### 1724 LINCOLN'S INN FIELDS
*Apr. 30.* No parts assigned
*Oct. 22*

| | |
|---|---|
| RICHARD | Ryan |
| HENRY | Boheme |
| BUCKINGHAM | Quin |
| RICHMOND | Walker |
| CATESBY | Egleton |
| STANLEY | Diggs |
| LORD MAYOR | Bullock Sr. |
| DUCHESS OF YORK | Mrs Egleton |
| LADY ANNE | Mrs Bullock |
| QUEEN ELIZABETH | Mrs Parker |

### 1725 DRURY LANE
*Feb. 6.* No parts assigned

## RICHARD III [as altered by CIBBER]

### 1725 LINCOLN'S INN FIELDS

May 1

| | |
|---|---|
| RICHARD | Ryan |
| HENRY | Boheme |
| BUCKINGHAM | Quin |
| RICHMOND | Walker |
| CATESBY | Egleton |
| STANLEY | Diggs |
| RATCLIFF* | Huddy |
| LORD MAYOR | Bullock Sr. |
| FORREST* | Spiller |
| DUCHESS OF YORK | Mrs Egleton |
| LADY ANNE | Mrs Bullock |

Nov. 9
added
    QUEEN ELIZABETH   Mrs Parker
omitted
    RATCLIFF, FORREST

[In the bill FORREST is called MURDERER.]

### 1726 DRURY LANE
Nov. 3. No parts assigned

### LINCOLN'S INN FIELDS

Oct. 17

| | |
|---|---|
| RICHARD | Ryan |
| HENRY | Boheme |
| BUCKINGHAM | Quin |
| RICHMOND | Walker |
| STANLEY | Diggs |
| LORD MAYOR | Bullock [Sr.] |
| QUEEN ELIZABETH | Mrs Berriman |
| DUCHESS OF YORK | Mrs Egleton |
| LADY ANNE | Mrs Bullock |

Dec. 29. No parts assigned

### 1727 DRURY LANE
Jan. 17. No parts assigned

### 1728 DRURY LANE

May 23

| | |
|---|---|
| RICHARD | Cibber |
| HENRY | Wilks |
| BUCKINGHAM | Mills |
| RICHMOND | Williams |
| TRESSEL | [T.] Cibber |
| PRINCE EDWARD | Mrs Cibber |
| DUKE OF YORK | Miss Robinson Jr. |
| QUEEN ELIZABETH | Mrs Porter |
| LADY ANNE | Mrs Horton |
| DUCHESS OF YORK | Mrs Butler |

Nov. 6, 20. No parts assigned

### LINCOLN'S INN FIELDS
Jan. 3. No parts assigned

## RICHARD III [as altered by CIBBER]

### 1728 HAYMARKET
*Aug. 19.* No parts assigned

### 1730 DRURY LANE
*Nov. 10.* No parts assigned

### 1732 DRURY LANE
*Oct. 14; Nov. 17*

| | |
|---|---|
| RICHARD | Cibber |

No other parts assigned

### GOODMAN'S FIELDS
*Mar. 20, 25*

| | |
|---|---|
| RICHARD | Delane |
| HENRY | Giffard |
| PRINCE EDWARD | Master Giffard |
| DUKE OF YORK | Master Huddy |
| RICHMOND | Bardin |
| BUCKINGHAM | W. Giffard |
| STANLEY | Rosco |
| RATCLIFF | Jenkins |
| CATESBY | Havard |
| TRESSEL | Huddy |
| LORD MAYOR | Morgan |
| TYRREL* | [R.] Williams |
| NORFOLK | Smith |
| BLUNT | [W.] Bullock [Jr.] |
| LADY ANNE | Mrs Giffard |
| QUEEN ELIZABETH | Mrs Roberts |
| DUCHESS OF YORK | Mrs Haughton |

*May 11*

| | |
|---|---|
| TYRREL | Norris [Jr.] |

added

| | |
|---|---|
| OXFORD | [R.] Williams |
| LIEUTENANT | Collett |

### 1733 DRURY LANE
*Feb. 12*

| | |
|---|---|
| RICHARD | Cibber |

No other parts assigned

*Oct. 17*

| | |
|---|---|
| RICHARD | Roberts |
| HENRY | Bridgwater |
| BUCKINGHAM | [W.] Giffard |
| RICHMOND | Marshall |
| LORD MAYOR | Mullart |
| PRINCE EDWARD | Miss Hughes |
| DUKE OF YORK | Miss Norris |
| QUEEN ELIZABETH | Mrs Horton |
| LADY ANNE | Miss Holliday |
| DUCHESS OF YORK | Mrs Mullart |

*Nov. 2*

added

| | |
|---|---|
| STANLEY | Corey |
| TRESSEL | Paget |

383

RICHARD III [*as altered by* CIBBER]

## 1733 COVENT GARDEN
*Dec. 15, 26*

| | |
|---|---|
| RICHARD | Ryan |
| HENRY | Chapman |
| BUCKINGHAM | Quin |
| RICHMOND | Walker |
| STANLEY | Aston |
| LORD MAYOR | Hall |
| QUEEN ELIZABETH | Mrs Hallam |
| DUCHESS OF YORK | Mrs Buchanan |
| LADY ANNE | Mrs Bullock |

## GOODMAN'S FIELDS
*Apr. 11*                                              *Apr. 12*

| | | | | |
|---|---|---|---|---|
| RICHARD | Delane | | added | |
| HENRY | Giffard | | OXFORD | Cole |
| PRINCE EDWARD | Master Giffard | | | |
| DUKE OF YORK | Miss Cole | | | |
| RICHMOND | Bardin | | | |
| BUCKINGHAM | W. Giffard | | | |
| STANLEY | Rosco | | | |
| TRESSEL | Huddy | | | |
| CATESBY | Havard | | | |
| RATCLIFF | Jenkins | | | |
| NORFOLK | Winstone | | | |
| BLUNT | James | | | |
| TYRREL | [R.] Williams | | | |
| FORREST | Dove | | | |
| LORD MAYOR | Penkethman [Jr.] | | | |
| LADY ANNE | Mrs Giffard | | | |
| QUEEN ELIZABETH | Mrs Roberts | | | |
| DUCHESS OF YORK | Mrs Haughton | | | |

## 1734 DRURY LANE
*Jan. 22*

| | |
|---|---|
| RICHARD | Roberts |
| HENRY | Bridgwater |
| BUCKINGHAM | Hewitt |
| RICHMOND | Marshall |
| LORD MAYOR | Mullart |
| STANLEY | Corey |
| TRESSEL | Paget |
| PRINCE EDWARD | Miss Hughes |
| DUKE OF YORK | Miss Norris |
| QUEEN ELIZABETH | Mrs Horton |
| LADY ANNE | Miss Holliday |
| DUCHESS OF YORK | Mrs Mullart |

## RICHARD III [as altered by CIBBER]

**1734 DRURY LANE** (cont.)

*Oct. 26, 28*

| | |
|---|---|
| RICHARD | Quin |
| HENRY | Milward |
| BUCKINGHAM | Mills |
| RICHMOND | [T.] Cibber |
| PRINCE EDWARD | Miss Brett |
| DUKE OF YORK | Miss Cole |
| NORFOLK | Boman |
| STANLEY | Berry |
| LIEUTENANT | Winstone |
| TRESSEL | Cross |
| LORD MAYOR | Harper |
| CATESBY | Oates |
| RATCLIFF | Hewitt |
| QUEEN ELIZABETH | Mrs Thurmond |
| LADY ANNE | Mrs Heron |
| DUCHESS OF YORK | Mrs Butler |

### COVENT GARDEN

*May 16*

| | |
|---|---|
| RICHARD | Ryan |
| HENRY | Chapman |
| BUCKINGHAM | Quin |
| RICHMOND | Walker |
| TRESSEL | Hale |
| LORD MAYOR | Hall |
| STANLEY | Aston |
| QUEEN ELIZABETH | Mrs Hallam |
| DUCHESS OF YORK | Mrs Buchanan |
| LADY ANNE | Mrs Bullock |

*Dec. 26*

| | |
|---|---|
| RICHARD | Ryan |
| HENRY | Walker |
| BUCKINGHAM | Bridgwater |
| RICHMOND | A. Hallam |
| TRESSEL | Chapman |
| STANLEY | Hale |
| CATESBY | Aston |
| NORFOLK | Marshall |
| LORD MAYOR | Mullart |
| RATCLIFF | Wignell |
| OXFORD | Ridout |
| QUEEN ELIZABETH | Mrs Hallam |
| DUCHESS OF YORK | Mrs Buchanan |
| LADY ANNE | Mrs Bullock |

RICHARD III [as altered by CIBBER]

## 1734 GOODMAN'S FIELDS
*Mar. 18*
    RICHARD            Hulett
    No other parts assigned

*May 8*
    RICHARD            Delane
    HENRY              Giffard
    PRINCE EDWARD      Miss Norris
    DUKE OF YORK       Miss Cole
    LADY ANNE          Mrs Giffard
    No other parts assigned

*Dec. 6*
    RICHARD            Delane
    HENRY              Giffard
    BUCKINGHAM         W. Giffard
    RICHMOND           Bardin
    NORFOLK            Harbin
    RATCLIFF           Jenkins
    STANLEY            Rosco
    CATESBY            Havard
    TRESSEL            Huddy
    OXFORD             Moore
    PRINCE EDWARD      Miss Norris
    DUKE OF YORK       Miss Haughton [first appearance on the stage]
    LORD MAYOR         Penkethman [Jr.]
    QUEEN ELIZABETH    Mrs Roberts
    LADY ANNE          Mrs Giffard
    DUCHESS OF YORK    Mrs Haughton

## 1735 DRURY LANE
*Jan. 7*
    RICHARD            Quin
    HENRY*             Milward
    BUCKINGHAM         Mills
    RICHMOND           [T.] Cibber
    PRINCE EDWARD*     Miss Brett
    DUKE OF YORK       Miss Cole
    NORFOLK            Boman
    STANLEY            Berry
    LIEUTENANT         Winstone
    TRESSEL            Cross
    LORD MAYOR         Harper
    CATESBY            Oates

*Feb. 5*
    HENRY              Hyde
    DUCHESS OF YORK    Mrs Cross

*Oct. 25*
    PRINCE EDWARD      Master Green
    RATCLIFF           Turbutt

386

RICHARD III [*as altered by* CIBBER]

## 1735 DRURY LANE (*cont.*)
*Jan. 7 (cont.)*
| | |
|---|---|
| RATCLIFF* | Hewitt |
| QUEEN ELIZABETH | Mrs Thurmond |
| LADY ANNE | Miss Holliday |
| DUCHESS OF YORK* | Mrs Butler |

## COVENT GARDEN
*Apr. 8*
| | |
|---|---|
| RICHARD | A. Hallam |
| HENRY | Chapman |
| BUCKINGHAM | Bridgwater |
| RICHMOND | Walker |
| TRESSEL | Hale |
| LORD MAYOR | Mullart |
| QUEEN ELIZABETH | Mrs Hallam |
| DUCHESS OF YORK | Mrs Buchanan |
| LADY ANNE | Mrs Bullock |

## 1736 DRURY LANE
*May 26; Sept. 18*
| | |
|---|---|
| RICHARD | Quin |
| HENRY | Milward |
| BUCKINGHAM | Mills |
| RICHMOND* | [T.] Cibber |
| QUEEN ELIZABETH | Mrs Thurmond |
| LADY ANNE | Miss Holliday |
| DUCHESS OF YORK | Mrs Butler |

*Dec. 1*
| | |
|---|---|
| RICHMOND | W. Mills |

## 1737 DRURY LANE
*Jan. 3.* The bill for this performance is missing

*Oct. 1*
| | |
|---|---|
| RICHARD | Quin |
| HENRY | Milward |
| BUCKINGHAM | [W.] Mills |
| RICHMOND | [T.] Cibber |
| PRINCE EDWARD | Green |
| DUKE OF YORK | Miss Cole |
| NORFOLK | Boman |
| STANLEY | Havard |
| RATCLIFF | Turbutt |
| CATESBY | Hill |
| TRESSEL | Cross |
| LORD MAYOR | Harper |
| QUEEN ELIZABETH | Mrs Roberts |
| DUCHESS OF YORK | Mrs Pritchard |
| LADY ANNE | Mrs Mills |

## RICHARD III [as altered by CIBBER]

### 1738 DRURY LANE

*Feb. 13*

| | |
|---|---|
| RICHARD | Quin |
| HENRY | Milward |
| BUCKINGHAM | [W.] Mills |
| RICHMOND* | [T.] Cibber |
| PRINCE EDWARD | Green |
| DUKE OF YORK | Miss Cole |
| NORFOLK | Boman |
| STANLEY | Havard |
| RATCLIFF | Turbutt |
| CATESBY | Hill |
| TRESSEL | Cross |
| LORD MAYOR | Harper |
| QUEEN ELIZABETH | Mrs Roberts |
| DUCHESS OF YORK* | Mrs Bennet |
| LADY ANNE* | Mrs Mills |

*May 23*

| | |
|---|---|
| RICHMOND | Wright |
| LADY ANNE | Mrs Pritchard |

*Sept. 30*

| | |
|---|---|
| DUCHESS OF YORK | Mrs Pritchard |

### 1739 DRURY LANE

*Jan. 31*

| | |
|---|---|
| RICHARD* | Cibber Sr. |
| HENRY | Milward |
| BUCKINGHAM | [W.] Mills |
| RICHMOND* | [T.] Cibber |
| QUEEN ELIZABETH | Mrs Roberts |
| DUCHESS OF YORK | Mrs Pritchard |
| LADY ANNE | Mrs Mills |

*Oct. 17*

| | |
|---|---|
| RICHARD | Quin |
| RICHMOND | Wright |
| added | |
| PRINCE EDWARD | Green |
| DUKE OF YORK | Miss Cole |
| STANLEY | Havard |
| TRESSEL | Ridout |
| RATCLIFF | Turbutt |
| CATESBY | Winstone |
| LIEUTENANT | Ray |
| LORD MAYOR | Taswell |

### 1740 DRURY LANE

*Jan. 14*

| | |
|---|---|
| RICHARD | Quin |
| HENRY | Milward |
| BUCKINGHAM | [W.] Mills |
| RICHMOND | Wright |
| PRINCE EDWARD | Green |
| DUKE OF YORK | Miss Cole |
| STANLEY | Havard |
| TRESSEL* | Ridout |
| RATCLIFF | Turbutt |
| CATESBY | Winstone |
| LIEUTENANT | Ray |
| LORD MAYOR | Taswell |
| QUEEN ELIZABETH | Mrs Roberts |
| DUCHESS OF YORK | Mrs Pritchard |
| LADY ANNE | Mrs Mills |

*Sept. 16*

| | |
|---|---|
| TRESSEL | Chapman |

## RICHARD III [as altered by CIBBER]

### 1741 DRURY LANE
*Feb. 12*

| | |
|---|---|
| RICHARD | Quin |
| HENRY | Milward |
| RICHMOND | Wright |
| BUCKINGHAM | [W.] Mills |
| PRINCE EDWARD | Green |
| DUKE OF YORK | Miss Cole |
| STANLEY | Havard |
| TRESSEL | Chapman |
| CATESBY | Winstone |
| RATCLIFF | Turbutt |
| LORD MAYOR | Taswell |
| LIEUTENANT | Ray |
| QUEEN ELIZABETH | Mrs Roberts |
| DUCHESS OF YORK | Mrs Pritchard |
| LADY ANNE | Mrs Mills |

*Dec. 19*

| | |
|---|---|
| RICHARD | Delane |
| HENRY | Milward |
| RICHMOND | [T.] Cibber |
| BUCKINGHAM | [W.] Mills |
| STANLEY | Havard |
| NORFOLK | Ridout |
| TRESSEL | Berry |
| RATCLIFF | Turbutt |
| CATESBY | Winstone |
| OXFORD | Woodburn |
| PRINCE EDWARD* | Miss Woodman |
| DUKE OF YORK | Miss Cibber [first appearance on the stage] |
| LIEUTENANT | Ray |
| FORREST | Gray |
| DIGHTON | Wright |
| LORD MAYOR | Taswell |
| BLUNT | Raftor |
| QUEEN ELIZABETH | Mrs Roberts |
| DUCHESS OF YORK | Mrs Bennet |
| LADY ANNE | Mrs Mills |

*Dec. 28*

| | |
|---|---|
| PRINCE EDWARD | Mrs Ridout [i.e. formerly Miss Woodman] |

added

| | |
|---|---|
| TYRREL | Woodburn |

[Woodburn doubled OXFORD and TYRREL.]

### COVENT GARDEN
*Oct. 13, 14*

| | |
|---|---|
| RICHARD | Ryan |
| HENRY | Bridgwater |
| RICHMOND | Hale |
| BUCKINGHAM | Cashell |

*Dec. 8*

| | |
|---|---|
| TRESSEL | Gibson |
| CATESBY | Roberts |

omitted
    LIEUTENANT

389

## RICHARD III [as altered by CIBBER]

### 1741 COVENT GARDEN (cont.)
Oct. 13, 14 (cont.)

| | |
|---|---|
| PRINCE EDWARD | Mrs Vincent |
| DUKE OF YORK | Miss Morrison |
| TRESSEL* | Chapman |
| STANLEY | Rosco |
| NORFOLK | Stephens |
| LORD MAYOR | Marten |
| LIEUTENANT* | Stevens |
| CATESBY* | Gibson |
| RATCLIFF | Harrington |
| OXFORD | Bencraft |
| BLUNT | Clarke |
| TYRREL | Stoppelaer |
| FORREST | Vaughan |
| QUEEN ELIZABETH | Mrs Pritchard |
| LADY ANNE | Mrs Horton |
| DUCHESS OF YORK | Mrs Mullart |

### GOODMAN'S FIELDS
Feb. 10

| | |
|---|---|
| RICHARD | Crisp [first appearance in London] |
| HENRY | Giffard |
| RICHMOND | Walker |
| PRINCE EDWARD | Mrs Dunstall |
| DUKE OF YORK | Miss Naylor |
| BUCKINGHAM | Peterson |
| NORFOLK | Blakes |
| STANLEY | Paget |
| OXFORD | Vaughan |
| TRESSEL | W. Giffard |
| CATESBY | Marr |
| RATCLIFF | Crofts |
| BLUNT | Naylor |
| TYRREL | Nelson |
| LORD MAYOR | Dunstall |
| QUEEN ELIZABETH | Mrs Steel |
| DUCHESS OF YORK | Mrs Yates |
| LADY ANNE | Mrs Giffard |

Oct. 19, 20, 21, 22, 24, 26, 27; Nov. 2, 23, 26

RICHARD    A Gentleman [Garrick (Genest, iv. 13); first appear-

Dec. 15

| | |
|---|---|
| OXFORD | Pattenden |
| TYRREL | Vaughan |

Dec. 23

| | |
|---|---|
| OXFORD | Pattenden |

## RICHARD III [as altered by CIBBER]

### 1741 GOODMAN'S FIELDS (cont.)

*Oct. 19, &c. (cont.)*

|  |  |
|---|---|
|  | ance, Oct. 19, in London] |
| HENRY | Giffard |
| RICHMOND | Marshall |
| PRINCE EDWARD | Miss Hippisley |
| DUKE OF YORK | Miss Naylor |
| BUCKINGHAM | Peterson |
| NORFOLK | Blakes |
| STANLEY | Paget |
| OXFORD* | Vaughan |
| TRESSEL | W. Giffard |
| CATESBY | Marr |
| RATCLIFF* | Crofts |
| BLUNT* | Naylor |
| TYRREL* | Pattenden |
| LORD MAYOR | Dunstall |
| QUEEN ELIZABETH | Mrs Steel |
| DUCHESS OF YORK | Mrs Yates |
| LADY ANNE | Mrs Giffard |

*Dec. 23 (cont.)*

| RATCLIFF | Naylor |
|---|---|
| BLUNT omitted | Clough |
| TYRREL |  |

[Beginning with Nov. 23 Garrick's name is in the bill. Genest erroneously assigns RATCLIFF to Mrs Crofts, and TYRREL to Puttenham.]

### 1742 DRURY LANE

*Apr. 30*

| RICHARD* | Turbutt |
|---|---|
| HENRY | Berry |
| RICHMOND | Cross |
| BUCKINGHAM | [W.] Mills |
| STANLEY | Havard |
| RATCLIFF | Woodburn |
| TRESSEL* | Ridout |
| CATESBY | Winstone |
| PRINCE EDWARD | Mrs Ridout |
| DUKE OF YORK* | Miss Cole |
| LIEUTENANT* | Ray |
| LORD MAYOR* | Taswell |
| QUEEN ELIZABETH | Mrs Roberts |
| DUCHESS OF YORK | Mrs Bennet |
| LADY ANNE | Mrs Mills |

*May 31*

| RICHARD | Garrick |
|---|---|
| DUKE OF YORK | Miss Cibber |
| LORD MAYOR added | Turbutt |
| BLUNT omitted | Raftor |
| TRESSEL, LIEUTENANT |  |

*Oct. 13*

| RICHARD | Garrick |
|---|---|
| HENRY | Berry |
| BUCKINGHAM* | [W.] Mills |
| RICHMOND | Havard |

*Oct. 15, 23*

| BUCKINGHAM | Winstone |
|---|---|
| STANLEY | Arthur |
| TRESSEL | Blakes |

[Blakes doubled NORFOLK and TRESSEL.]

391

## RICHARD III [*as altered by* CIBBER]

### 1742 DRURY LANE (*cont.*)
Oct. 13 (*cont.*)

| | |
|---|---|
| PRINCE EDWARD | Mrs Ridout |
| DUKE OF YORK* | Miss Cibber |
| STANLEY* | Winstone |
| TRESSEL* | Turbutt |
| RATCLIFF | Woodburn |
| NORFOLK* | Blakes |
| CATESBY* | Marr |
| LIEUTENANT* | Ray |
| LORD MAYOR | Taswell |
| OXFORD | Green |
| TYRREL | Vaughan |
| FORREST* | Gray |
| DIGHTON* | Wright |
| BLUNT* | Raftor |
| QUEEN ELIZABETH | Mrs Roberts |
| DUCHESS OF YORK | Mrs Bennet |
| LADY ANNE | Mrs Mills |

Oct. 28; Nov. 5, 11

| | |
|---|---|
| TRESSEL | Blakes |

[Blakes doubled NORFOLK and TRESSEL.

Dec. 20

DUKE OF YORK   Miss Macklin [first appearance on the stage]
omitted
STANLEY, TRESSEL, NORFOLK, CATESBY, LIEUTENANT, FORREST, DIGHTON, BLUNT

### COVENT GARDEN
Oct. 13

| | |
|---|---|
| RICHARD | Quin |
| HENRY | Bridgwater |
| RICHMOND | Hale |
| TRESSEL | Chapman |
| PRINCE EDWARD | Miss Hippisley |
| BUCKINGHAM | Cashell |
| STANLEY | Rosco |
| NORFOLK | Stephens |
| CATESBY | Gibson |
| RATCLIFF | Harrington |
| LIEUTENANT | Ridout |
| OXFORD | Bencraft |
| DUKE OF YORK | Miss Morrison |
| DUCHESS OF YORK | Mrs Woodward |
| LADY ANNE | Mrs Cibber |
| QUEEN ELIZABETH | Mrs Horton |

Oct. 14; Dec. 6
added

| | |
|---|---|
| TYRREL | Carr |
| LORD MAYOR | Marten |

### LINCOLN'S INN FIELDS
Dec. 27

| | |
|---|---|
| RICHARD | [T.] Cibber |
| HENRY | Giffard |
| RICHMOND | W. Giffard |
| PRINCE EDWARD | Miss Cibber |
| DUKE OF YORK | Miss Naylor |
| BUCKINGHAM | Peterson |
| NORFOLK | Freeman |

## RICHARD III [as altered by CIBBER]

### 1742 LINCOLN'S INN FIELDS (cont.)
*Dec. 27 (cont.)*

| | |
|---|---|
| STANLEY | Mozeen |
| OXFORD | Pattenden |
| CATESBY | Dighton |
| RATCLIFF | Naylor |
| BLUNT | Clough |
| TYRREL | Dove |
| LORD MAYOR | Dunstall |
| FORREST | Julian |
| QUEEN ELIZABETH | Mrs Butler |
| DUCHESS OF YORK | Mrs Bambridge |
| LADY ANNE | Mrs Giffard |

[LDP omits FORREST.]

### GOODMAN'S FIELDS
*Mar. 6*

| | |
|---|---|
| RICHARD | Garrick |

No other parts assigned

*Apr. 21*

| | |
|---|---|
| RICHARD | Garrick |
| HENRY | Giffard |
| RICHMOND | Marshall |
| BUCKINGHAM | Peterson |
| STANLEY | Paget |
| NORFOLK* | Blakes |
| RATCLIFF | Dighton |
| TRESSEL* | W. Giffard |
| OXFORD* | Pattenden |
| CATESBY | Marr |
| PRINCE EDWARD* | Mrs Dunstall |
| DUKE OF YORK | Miss Naylor |
| TYRREL* | Vaughan |
| LORD MAYOR | Dunstall |
| BLUNT | Naylor |
| QUEEN ELIZABETH | Mrs E. Giffard |
| DUCHESS OF YORK | Mrs Yates |
| LADY ANNE | Mrs Giffard |

*May 5, 14*

| | |
|---|---|
| OXFORD | Vaughan |

omitted
   NORFOLK, TYRREL

*May 21*

| | |
|---|---|
| OXFORD | Vaughan |
| PRINCE EDWARD | Miss Hippisley |

omitted
   NORFOLK, TRESSEL, TYRREL

### 1743 DRURY LANE
*Jan. 3*

| | |
|---|---|
| RICHARD | Garrick |
| HENRY | Berry |
| BUCKINGHAM | [W.] Mills |
| RICHMOND | Havard |
| PRINCE EDWARD | Mrs Ridout |
| DUKE OF YORK | Miss Macklin |

*Jan. 10, 19*

| | |
|---|---|
| QUEEN ELIZABETH | Mrs Roberts |

## RICHARD III [as altered by CIBBER]

### 1743 DRURY LANE (cont.)

**Jan. 3 (cont.)**

| | |
|---|---|
| RATCLIFF | Woodburn |
| TYRREL | Vaughan |
| LORD MAYOR | Taswell |
| OXFORD | Green |
| QUEEN ELIZABETH* | Mrs Pritchard |
| LADY ANNE | Mrs Mills |
| DUCHESS OF YORK | Mrs Bennet |

**Feb. 14**

| | |
|---|---|
| RICHARD | Garrick |
| HENRY* | Berry |
| BUCKINGHAM | [W.] Mills |
| RICHMOND | Havard |
| PRINCE EDWARD | Mrs Ridout |
| DUKE OF YORK* | Miss Macklin |
| RATCLIFF | Woodburn |
| TYRREL* | Vaughan |
| LORD MAYOR | Taswell |
| OXFORD | Green |
| STANLEY | Winstone |
| TRESSEL* | Blakes |
| CATESBY* | Marr |
| QUEEN ELIZABETH | Mrs Roberts |
| LADY ANNE* | Mrs Mills |
| DUCHESS OF YORK | Mrs Bennet |

**Apr. 16**

| | |
|---|---|
| HENRY | Blakes |
| TRESSEL | Cross |

**May 3**

| | |
|---|---|
| HENRY | Blakes |
| TRESSEL | Cross |
| LADY ANNE | Mrs Woffington |

**Dec. 17**

| | |
|---|---|
| HENRY | Giffard |
| DUKE OF YORK | Mrs Wright |
| TYRREL | Arthur |
| CATESBY | Turbutt |
| added | |
| LIEUTENANT | Ray |

### COVENT GARDEN

**Jan. 28; Mar. 7; Apr. 8**

| | |
|---|---|
| RICHARD* | Quin |
| HENRY | Bridgwater |
| RICHMOND | Hale |
| TRESSEL | Chapman |
| PRINCE EDWARD | Miss Hippisley |
| BUCKINGHAM | Cashell |
| STANLEY | Rosco |
| NORFOLK | Stephens |
| CATESBY | Gibson |
| TYRREL | Carr |
| LORD MAYOR | Marten |
| RATCLIFF* | Harrington |
| LIEUTENANT | Ridout |
| OXFORD | Bencraft |
| DUKE OF YORK | Miss Morrison |
| DUCHESS OF YORK* | Mrs Woodward |
| LADY ANNE* | Mrs Cibber |
| QUEEN ELIZABETH | Mrs Horton |

**Sept. 28; Nov. 14**

| | |
|---|---|
| RICHARD | Ryan |
| RATCLIFF | Anderson |
| LADY ANNE | Mrs Hale |

**Dec. 10**

| | |
|---|---|
| RATCLIFF | Anderson |
| DUCHESS OF YORK | Mrs James |
| LADY ANNE | Mrs Hale |

## RICHARD III [as altered by CIBBER]

### 1743 LINCOLN'S INN FIELDS
*Jan. 3, 5, 7, 14*

| | |
|---|---|
| RICHARD | [T.] Cibber |
| HENRY | Giffard |
| RICHMOND | W. Giffard |
| PRINCE EDWARD | Miss Cibber |
| DUKE OF YORK | Miss Naylor |
| BUCKINGHAM | Peterson |
| NORFOLK | Freeman |
| STANLEY | Mozeen |
| OXFORD | Pattenden |
| CATESBY | Dighton |
| RATCLIFF | Naylor |
| BLUNT | Clough |
| TYRREL | Dove |
| LORD MAYOR | Dunstall |
| FORREST | Julian |
| QUEEN ELIZABETH | Mrs Butler |
| DUCHESS OF YORK | Mrs Bambridge |
| LADY ANNE | Mrs Giffard |

[LDP omits FORREST.]

### 1744 DRURY LANE
*Jan. 3; Feb. 18; Apr. 7; May 7*

| | |
|---|---|
| RICHARD | Garrick |
| HENRY | Giffard |
| BUCKINGHAM* | [W.] Mills |
| RICHMOND* | Havard |
| PRINCE EDWARD* | Mrs Ridout |
| DUKE OF YORK* | Mrs Wright |
| RATCLIFF | Woodburn |
| TYRREL* | Arthur |
| LORD MAYOR | Taswell |
| OXFORD | Green |
| STANLEY | Winstone |
| TRESSEL | Blakes |
| CATESBY | Turbutt |
| LIEUTENANT | Ray |
| QUEEN ELIZABETH* | Mrs Roberts |
| LADY ANNE* | Mrs Mills |
| DUCHESS OF YORK | Mrs Bennet |

*May 31*

| | |
|---|---|
| LADY ANNE | Mrs Woffington |

*Nov. 3*

| | |
|---|---|
| BUCKINGHAM | Bridges |
| PRINCE EDWARD | Miss Budgell |
| TYRREL | Simpson |
| QUEEN ELIZABETH | Mrs Giffard |
| LADY ANNE | Mrs Woffington |
| omitted | |
| RICHMOND | |

*Dec. 15*

| | |
|---|---|
| BUCKINGHAM | Bridges |
| PRINCE EDWARD | Miss Budgell |
| DUKE OF YORK | Miss Yates |
| TYRREL | Simpson |
| QUEEN ELIZABETH | Mrs Giffard |
| LADY ANNE | Mrs Woffington |
| omitted | |
| RICHMOND | |

### COVENT GARDEN
*Jan. 2; Mar. 26*

| | |
|---|---|
| RICHARD* | Quin |
| HENRY | Bridgwater |
| RICHMOND | Hale |
| TRESSEL | Chapman |
| PRINCE EDWARD | Miss Hippisley |

*Apr. 5*

| | |
|---|---|
| RICHARD | Sheridan |

*Oct. 24*

| | |
|---|---|
| NORFOLK | Ridout |
| LIEUTENANT | Arthur |
| QUEEN ELIZABETH | Mrs Pritchard |

395

RICHARD III [*as altered by* CIBBER]

## 1744 COVENT GARDEN (cont.)
*Jan. 2, &c. (cont.)*

| | |
|---|---|
| BUCKINGHAM | Cashell |
| STANLEY | Rosco |
| NORFOLK* | Stephens |
| CATESBY | Gibson |
| TYRREL | Carr |
| LORD MAYOR | Marten |
| RATCLIFF | Anderson |
| LIEUTENANT* | Ridout |
| OXFORD | Bencraft |
| DUKE OF YORK | Miss Morrison |
| DUCHESS OF YORK | Mrs James |
| LADY ANNE | Mrs Hale |
| QUEEN ELIZABETH* | Mrs Horton |

[The bill for Jan. 2 in LDP is mutilated; about half the names are missing. That there were any important differences in these two bills is, however, unlikely.]

## HAYMARKET
*Feb. 15.* No parts assigned

## NEW WELLS, GOODMAN'S FIELDS
*Dec. 5, 6, 7, 8, 20*

| | |
|---|---|
| RICHARD | Goodfellow |
| QUEEN ELIZABETH | Mrs Bambridge |

No other parts assigned

## 1745 DRURY LANE
*Jan. 12*

| | |
|---|---|
| RICHARD* | Garrick |
| HENRY | Giffard |
| BUCKINGHAM | Bridges |
| RICHMOND | Havard |
| PRINCE EDWARD* | Miss Cole |
| DUKE OF YORK | Miss Yates |
| STANLEY | Winstone |
| TRESSEL | Blakes |
| CATESBY | Turbutt |
| LIEUTENANT | Ray |
| RATCLIFF | Woodburn |
| TYRREL | Simpson |
| LORD MAYOR | Taswell |
| OXFORD | Green |
| DUCHESS OF YORK | Mrs Bennet |
| LADY ANNE | Mrs Woffington |
| QUEEN ELIZABETH | Mrs Giffard |

*Feb. 12*

| | |
|---|---|
| PRINCE EDWARD | Miss Budgell |

*Mar. 5*

| | |
|---|---|
| RICHARD | Sheridan |
| PRINCE EDWARD | Miss Budgell |

added

| | |
|---|---|
| NORFOLK | Mozeen |
| BLUNT | Usher |

## RICHARD III [as altered by CIBBER]

### 1745 COVENT GARDEN
*Jan. 8*

| | |
|---|---|
| RICHARD* | Quin |
| HENRY* | Bridgwater |
| RICHMOND* | Hale |
| BUCKINGHAM | Cashell |
| TRESSEL | Chapman |
| PRINCE EDWARD | Miss Hippisley |
| DUKE OF YORK | Miss Morrison |
| STANLEY* | Rosco |
| NORFOLK* | Ridout |
| CATESBY* | Gibson |
| TYRREL* | Carr |
| LORD MAYOR* | Marten |
| RATCLIFF* | Anderson |
| LIEUTENANT* | Arthur |
| OXFORD* | Bencraft |
| DUCHESS OF YORK | Mrs James |
| LADY ANNE* | Mrs Hale |
| QUEEN ELIZABETH | Mrs Pritchard |

*Apr. 22*

| | |
|---|---|
| LADY ANNE | Mrs Horton |

omitted
    STANLEY, NORFOLK, CATESBY, TYRREL, LORD MAYOR, RATCLIFF, LIEUTENANT, OXFORD

*Nov. 28*

| | |
|---|---|
| RICHARD | Ryan |
| HENRY | Hale |
| RICHMOND | [T.] Cibber |
| LADY ANNE | Mrs Horton |

### NEW WELLS, GOODMAN'S FIELDS
*Jan. 19.* No parts assigned

*Mar. 18*

| | |
|---|---|
| RICHARD | Cushing |

No other parts assigned

*Apr. 30*

| | |
|---|---|
| RICHARD | Goodfellow |

No other parts assigned

*Dec. 16, 17*

| | |
|---|---|
| RICHARD | Lee |
| HENRY | Paget |
| RICHMOND | Cushing |
| TRESSEL | Furnival |
| DUCHESS OF YORK | Mrs Phillips |
| QUEEN ELIZABETH | Mrs Bambridge |
| LADY ANNE | Mrs [L.] Hallam |

### 1746 DRURY LANE
*Jan. 8, 9*

| | |
|---|---|
| RICHARD* | Goodfellow |
| HENRY* | Giffard |
| BUCKINGHAM | L. Sparks |
| RICHMOND | Havard |
| PRINCE EDWARD* | Miss Cole |
| DUKE OF YORK | Miss Macklin |

*Apr. 22*

| | |
|---|---|
| PRINCE EDWARD | Miss Budgell |
| RATCLIFF | Simpson |

omitted
    BLUNT, LORD MAYOR

[Simpson doubled RATCLIFF and TYRREL.]

397

## RICHARD III [as altered by CIBBER]

### 1746 DRURY LANE (cont.)
*Jan. 8, 9 (cont.)*

| | | | |
|---|---|---|---|
| STANLEY | Winstone | | |
| TRESSEL | Blakes | | |
| CATESBY | Marr | | |
| LIEUTENANT | Ray | | |
| RATCLIFF* | Woodburn | | |
| TYRREL* | Simpson | | |
| BLUNT* | Usher | | |
| LORD MAYOR* | Taswell | | |
| OXFORD | Bransby | | |
| NORFOLK | Mozeen | | |
| QUEEN ELIZABETH | Mrs Giffard | | |
| DUCHESS OF YORK | Mrs Bennet | | |
| LADY ANNE | Mrs Woffington | | |

*Apr. 29*

| | |
|---|---|
| RICHARD | [Tho.] Lacy |
| HENRY | Davies |
| PRINCE EDWARD | Miss Budgell |
| RATCLIFF | Simpson |
| TYRREL | Bransby |

[Bransby doubled TYRREL and OXFORD.]

### COVENT GARDEN
*June 16*

| | |
|---|---|
| RICHARD | Garrick |
| HENRY | Bridgwater |
| RICHMOND | Chapman |
| BUCKINGHAM | Cashell |
| PRINCE EDWARD | Mrs Vincent |
| DUKE OF YORK | Miss Morrison |
| STANLEY | Paget |
| NORFOLK | Philips |
| CATESBY | Oates |
| TYRREL | Stoppelaer |
| LORD MAYOR | Marten |
| RATCLIFF | Kennedy |
| LIEUTENANT | Beckham |
| OXFORD | Paddick |
| DUCHESS OF YORK | Mrs Daniel |
| LADY ANNE | Mrs Bland |
| QUEEN ELIZABETH | Mrs Horton |

*Oct. 20*

| | |
|---|---|
| RICHARD* | Quin |
| HENRY* | Bridgwater |
| RICHMOND | Havard |
| BUCKINGHAM | Cashell |
| TRESSEL | Chapman |
| PRINCE EDWARD | Miss Hippisley |
| DUKE OF YORK* | Miss Morrison |
| STANLEY* | Davies |
| NORFOLK | Ridout |
| CATESBY | Gibson |
| TYRREL | Carr |
| LORD MAYOR | Marten |

*Oct. 31*

| | |
|---|---|
| RICHARD | Garrick |
| HENRY | Davies |
| STANLEY | Rosco |

*Dec. 30*

| | |
|---|---|
| RICHARD | Garrick |
| HENRY | Davies |
| DUKE OF YORK | Miss Mullart |
| STANLEY | Rosco |
| LADY ANNE | Mrs Vincent |

## RICHARD III [as altered by CIBBER]

### 1746 COVENT GARDEN (cont.)
*Oct. 20 (cont.)*

| | |
|---|---|
| RATCLIFF | Anderson |
| LIEUTENANT | Arthur |
| OXFORD | Bencraft |
| DUCHESS OF YORK | Mrs James |
| LADY ANNE* | Mrs Horton |
| QUEEN ELIZABETH | Mrs Pritchard |

### NEW WELLS, GOODMAN'S FIELDS

*Mar. 3*

| | |
|---|---|
| RICHARD* | Lee |
| HENRY | Paget |
| TRESSEL | Furnival |
| RICHMOND | Cushing |
| PRINCE EDWARD* | A Gentleman [unidentified; first appearance on the stage] |
| DUCHESS OF YORK* | Mrs Phillips |
| QUEEN ELIZABETH | Mrs Bambridge |
| LADY ANNE | Mrs [L.] Hallam |

*Nov. 11*

| | |
|---|---|
| RICHARD | Lee |

No other parts assigned

*Dec. 17, 26*

| | |
|---|---|
| RICHARD | Goodfellow |
| PRINCE EDWARD | Mrs Cushing |
| DUCHESS OF YORK added | Mrs Beckham |
| DUKE OF YORK | Master Morgan |
| BUCKINGHAM | Wignell |
| STANLEY | L. Hallam |
| LIEUTENANT | Boyce |
| CATESBY | Shuter |
| LORD MAYOR | Dove |
| TYRREL | [G.] Hallam |
| BLUNT | Baker |

### 1747 DRURY LANE
*Nov. 6*

| | |
|---|---|
| RICHARD | Garrick |
| HENRY | Delane |
| BUCKINGHAM | L. Sparks |
| RICHMOND | Havard |
| STANLEY | Winstone |
| TRESSEL | Blakes |
| CATESBY | Usher |
| LIEUTENANT | Ray |
| PRINCE EDWARD | Miss Cole |
| DUKE OF YORK | Miss Yates |
| RATCLIFF | Simpson |
| TYRREL | Bransby |
| BLUNT | Burton |
| LORD MAYOR | Taswell |
| OXFORD | Bransby |
| NORFOLK | Blakes |
| QUEEN ELIZABETH | Mrs Elmy |
| DUCHESS OF YORK | Mrs Bennet |
| LADY ANNE | Mrs Woffington |

[Blakes doubled TRESSEL and NORFOLK; Bransby doubled TYRREL and OXFORD. The bill erroneously assigns BUCKINGHAM to I. Sparks. The part was regularly acted by his brother Luke; Isaac Sparks was a low comedian.]

399

# RICHARD III [as altered by CIBBER]

## 1747 COVENT GARDEN
*Dec. 28*

| | |
|---|---|
| RICHARD | Ryan |
| HENRY | Bridgwater |
| RICHMOND | Giffard |
| BUCKINGHAM | Bridges |
| TRESSEL | Ridout |
| STANLEY | Rosco |
| BLUNT | Kennedy |
| CATESBY | Gibson |
| TYRREL | Stoppelaer |
| LORD MAYOR | Dunstall |
| RATCLIFF | Anderson |
| LIEUTENANT | Storer |
| OXFORD | Bencraft |
| PRINCE EDWARD | Miss Morrison |
| DUKE OF YORK | Miss Mullart |
| DUCHESS OF YORK | Mrs James |
| LADY ANNE | Mrs Hale |
| QUEEN ELIZABETH | Mrs Horton |

## NEW WELLS, GOODMAN'S FIELDS
*Feb. 6*

| | |
|---|---|
| RICHARD | Goodfellow |
| HENRY | Paget |
| PRINCE EDWARD | Mrs Cushing |
| DUKE OF YORK | Master Morgan |
| BUCKINGHAM | Wignell |
| STANLEY | L. Hallam |
| RATCLIFF | Boyce |
| CATESBY | Shuter |
| LORD MAYOR | Dove |
| TYRREL | [G.] Hallam |
| OXFORD | Baker |
| RICHMOND | Cushing |
| TRESSEL | Furnival |
| LADY ANNE* | Mrs [L.] Hallam |
| DUCHESS OF YORK | Mrs Beckham |
| QUEEN ELIZABETH | Mrs Bambridge |

*Mar. 26*

| | |
|---|---|
| RICHARD | Cushing |
| LADY ANNE | Mrs [L.] Hallam |

No other parts assigned

400

## RICHARD III [as altered by CIBBER]

### 1748 DRURY LANE
*Jan. 27*

| RICHARD | Garrick |
| HENRY* | Delane |
| BUCKINGHAM* | L. Sparks |
| RICHMOND | Havard |
| STANLEY | Winstone |
| TRESSEL | Blakes |
| CATESBY | Usher |
| LIEUTENANT | Ray |
| PRINCE EDWARD | Miss Cole |
| DUKE OF YORK | Miss Yates |
| RATCLIFF | Simpson |
| BLUNT* | Burton |
| LORD MAYOR | Taswell |
| OXFORD | Bransby |
| NORFOLK* | Blakes |
| QUEEN ELIZABETH | Mrs Pritchard |
| DUCHESS OF YORK* | Mrs Bennet |
| LADY ANNE* | Mrs Woffington |

### COVENT GARDEN
*Feb. 29*

| RICHARD | Sowdon |
| HENRY | Bridgwater |
| RICHMOND | Giffard |
| BUCKINGHAM | Bridges |
| TRESSEL | Gibson |
| STANLEY | Rosco |
| BLUNT | Paddick |
| CATESBY | Bencraft |
| TYRREL | Stoppelaer |
| NORFOLK | Paget |
| LORD MAYOR | Dunstall |
| RATCLIFF | Anderson |
| LIEUTENANT | Storer |
| PRINCE EDWARD | Miss Morrison |
| DUKE OF YORK | Miss Mullart |
| DUCHESS OF YORK | Mrs James |
| LADY ANNE | Mrs Hale |
| QUEEN ELIZABETH | Mrs Horton |

### HAYMARKET
*Apr. 20*

RICHARD     A Gentleman [unidentified]

No other parts assigned
[Bill in GA of Apr. 19.]

*Apr. 30*
omitted
   NORFOLK

*Sept. 29*

| HENRY | Berry |
| BLUNT | Palmer |
| DUCHESS OF YORK | Mrs James |
| LADY ANNE | Mrs Mills |

omitted
   NORFOLK

[For Jan. 27, Apr. 30 and Sept. 29 MacMillan (313–14) erroneously assigns BUCKINGHAM to I. Sparks. On Jan. 27 and Apr. 30 the bills clearly have 'L. Sparks'; on Sept. 29 'Sparks'.]

*Dec. 23*

| HENRY | Berry |
| BUCKINGHAM | Bridges |
| BLUNT | Barnet |
| LADY ANNE | Mrs Mills |

omitted
   NORFOLK

[Blakes doubled TRESSEL and NORFOLK.]

RICHARD III [as altered by CIBBER]

## 1748 BOWLING GREEN, SOUTHWARK
Sept. 26

| | |
|---|---|
| RICHARD | Morgan |
| QUEEN ELIZABETH | Mrs Morgan |
| LADY ANNE | Mrs Phillips |

No other parts assigned
[Bill in DA of Sept. 24.]

## 1749 DRURY LANE
Mar. 4; Apr. 6

| | |
|---|---|
| RICHARD | Garrick |
| HENRY | Berry |
| BUCKINGHAM | Bridges |
| RICHMOND | Havard |
| STANLEY | Winstone |
| TRESSEL | Blakes |
| CATESBY | Usher |
| LIEUTENANT | Ray |
| PRINCE EDWARD | Miss Cole |
| DUKE OF YORK | Miss Yates |
| RATCLIFF* | Simpson |
| BLUNT* | Barnet |
| LORD MAYOR* | Taswell |
| OXFORD* | Bransby |
| DUCHESS OF YORK | Mrs Bennet |
| LADY ANNE | Mrs Mills |
| QUEEN ELIZABETH | Mrs Pritchard |

Nov. 16
omitted
    RATCLIFF, BLUNT, LORD MAYOR, OXFORD

## COVENT GARDEN
Oct. 2

| | |
|---|---|
| RICHARD | Quin |
| HENRY | Delane |
| RICHMOND | Ridout |
| BUCKINGHAM | [L.] Sparks |
| STANLEY | Redman |
| OXFORD | Bencraft |
| CATESBY | Gibson |
| RATCLIFF | Anderson |
| TRESSEL | Cushing |
| NORFOLK | Bransby |
| LORD MAYOR | Marten |
| TYRREL | Dunstall |
| LIEUTENANT | Oates |
| BLUNT | Holtom |
| PRINCE EDWARD | Miss Morrison |
| DUKE OF YORK | Miss Mullart |
| QUEEN ELIZABETH | Mrs Horton |
| DUCHESS OF YORK | Mrs Bambridge |
| LADY ANNE | Mrs Woffington |

402

## RICHARD III [as altered by CIBBER]

### 1749 JAMES ST., HAYMARKET
*Mar. 21.* No parts assigned

### TILED BOOTH, BOWLING GREEN, SOUTHWARK
*Oct. 16.* No parts assigned

### 1750 DRURY LANE
*Feb. 19*

| | |
|---|---|
| RICHARD | Garrick |
| HENRY | Berry |
| BUCKINGHAM | Bridges |
| RICHMOND | Havard |
| STANLEY | Winstone |
| TRESSEL | Blakes |
| CATESBY* | Usher |
| LIEUTENANT | Ray |
| PRINCE EDWARD* | Miss Cole |
| DUKE OF YORK | Miss Yates |
| DUCHESS OF YORK | Mrs Bennet |
| LADY ANNE | Mrs Mills |
| QUEEN ELIZABETH | Mrs Pritchard |

*Nov. 8*

| | |
|---|---|
| CATESBY | Marr |
| PRINCE EDWARD | Mrs Green |

### COVENT GARDEN
*Jan. 1*

| | |
|---|---|
| RICHARD* | Quin |
| HENRY* | Delane |
| RICHMOND | Ridout |
| BUCKINGHAM | [L.] Sparks |
| STANLEY | Redman |
| OXFORD* | Bencraft |
| CATESBY | Gibson |
| RATCLIFF | Anderson |
| TRESSEL* | Cushing |
| NORFOLK | Bransby |
| LORD MAYOR | Marten |
| TYRREL | Dunstall |
| LIEUTENANT* | Oates |
| BLUNT | Holtom |
| PRINCE EDWARD | Miss Morrison |
| DUKE OF YORK | Miss Mullart |
| QUEEN ELIZABETH* | Mrs Horton |
| DUCHESS OF YORK | Mrs Bambridge |
| LADY ANNE* | Mrs Woffington |

*Apr. 2*

| | |
|---|---|
| RICHARD | Lee |
| HENRY | Bridgwater |

*Oct. 26*

| | |
|---|---|
| HENRY | Ryan |
| OXFORD | [R.] Elrington |
| TRESSEL | [Tho.] Lacy |
| LIEUTENANT | Usher |
| QUEEN ELIZABETH | Mrs Cibber |
| LADY ANNE | Mrs Vincent |

RICHARD III [*as altered by* CIBBER]

1750 HAYMARKET
*Mar. 15*
   RICHARD   A Gentleman [unidentified; first appearance on the stage]
  No other parts assigned
  [Bill in GA of Mar. 14.]

# ROMEO AND JULIET

Adapted as CAIUS MARIUS, by Thomas Otway. In five acts.

1680   Tho. Flescher.

Act I is entirely new save for *I. ii. 51–8* and *I. iv. 55–89* (Queen Mab, much abridged), which are inserted about 75 lines from the end. The action is concerned with the political feud between Metellus and Old Marius, i.e. Capulet and Montague.

Act II, scene i is *I. iii. 1–76*; *III. v. 177–214*; *II. v. 38–46*. All this material is considerably revised and interspersed with new dialogue. Metellus has Lady Capulet's speeches. Scene ii is *II. i* and *ii*, with occasional new dialogue. Scene iii is new: the election of a new consul gives rise to a fight in which Old Marius's party is victorious.

Act III, scene i is largely new: Young Marius determines to aid his father. Inserted here, but much reduced, are *II. iv. 14–25, 111–221*. Scene ii is *III. ii. 1–31*, followed by *II. v. 25–66*, slightly altered. Scene iii is new: Old and Young Marius are defeated and sentenced to exile.

Act IV, scene i is *III. v. 5–59*, considerably enlarged. Scene ii is new: Lavinia follows her banished husband and father-in-law, but is captured and brought back to Rome by Metellus, who wishes to marry her to Sylla. Scene iii is *IV. i. 77–122* followed by *IV. iii. 14–59*, both somewhat reduced.

Act V, scene i is new: Old Marius returns to Rome and receives its submission. Scene ii is *IV. v. 1–32*, somewhat rewritten. Scene iii is new: Old Marius punishes Metellus's followers. Scene iv begins with *V. i*: the Apothecary lives on the outskirts of the cemetery. The scene is therefore continued directly with *V. iii*. Here the Priest has Paris's lines, and, like him, is killed by Young Marius. Lavinia awakes before Young Marius dies, and they bid farewell to one another. The remainder is new: Metellus is killed by Old Marius, who in turn is recaptured by the new consul. Young Marius's friend, Sulpitius, dies with Mercutio's speech from *III. i. 101–5*.

See Genest, i. 283–5; Odell, i. 51–3; Spencer, 293–8.

Adapted by Theophilus Cibber. In five acts.

  [1748]   C. Corbett.

Act I, scene i opens with about 30 new lines: Capulet offers Juliet to Paris. This is followed by *I. i. 81–6*. Scene ii is *I. i. 87–end*, somewhat abridged (Montague has Lady Montague's speeches, she being entirely omitted from the play), followed by about 50 lines altered from Act I of *Caius Marius*: Romeo promises his father to abjure Juliet. Scene iii is *I. ii. 1–19*, followed directly by all of *I. iii*, slightly reduced. The act ends with about 100 lines taken verbatim from Act II of *Caius Marius*: the discussion of Juliet's marriage to Paris.

Act II, scene i consists of *II. ii*, verbatim, save for brief soliloquies by Romeo at the beginning and end, both taken from Act II of *Caius Marius*. Scene ii is *II. iii*, considerably reduced. Scene iii is *II. iv. 1–5*; Queen Mab is then interpolated (*I. iv. 53–101*); and the scene resumes with *II. iv. 5–52, 113–end*, almost verbatim. Scenes iv and v are *II. v* and *vi*.

Act III consists of *III. i–iv*, slightly abridged. In scene iii Romeo has Valentine's lines in *The Two Gentlemen of Verona, III. i. 170–84*, altered.

Act IV, scene i is *III. v*. Both the opening dialogue and Juliet's closing speech are considerably expanded. Scenes ii, iii, and iv are *IV. i, ii,* and *iii*, virtually verbatim. Scene v is *IV. iv* and *v* without interruption. The musicians are omitted.

Act V, scenes i and ii are *V. i* and *ii*. Scene iii is *V. iii. 1–119*, slightly abridged, followed by about 50 lines taken verbatim from Act V of *Caius Marius* in which Romeo and Juliet lament their fortunes and take leave of one another. The scene resumes with *V. iii. 171–end*, virtually verbatim.

See Genest, iv. 167–8; Odell, i. 341–3.


'As it is performed at the Theatre Royal in Drury Lane.'

1748   J. Tonson.

Act I, scene i is *I. i. 7–109* somewhat reduced. Scene ii is *I. i. 110–58* with 10 new lines at the end. Scene iii is *I. ii. 1–23*. Scene iv is *I. i. 164–234*, slightly reduced and, without interruption, *I. iv. 48–114*. Scene v is *I. iii*. Scene vi is *I. v. 20–end*.

Acts II and III follow the original with virtually no changes.

Act IV ends at *IV. v. 89*.

Act V is untouched save for a few trivial deletions until *V. iii. 114*. Juliet then awakens and about 65 new lines follow in which she and Romeo take their last farewell of one another. The scene resumes with *V. iii. 121–end* with minor excisions.

This arrangement is by Garrick, and with slight modifications held the stage uninterruptedly until well after the middle of the nineteenth century. Garrick's addition to the tomb scene (*via* Otway) was used as late as 1875 by Charles Wyndham. It does not appear to have been abandoned until Irving's production of the play in 1882.

See Genest, iv. 262–3; Odell, i. 343–7.


'With Alterations, and an additional Scene: As it is performed at the Theatre-Royal in Drury-Lane.'

1750   J. and R. Tonson and S. Draper.

Save for occasional slight excisions, this version is identical with that published by Tonson in 1748. The 'additional Scene' is Juliet's funeral procession and its accompanying dirge, written by Garrick. It is inserted at the beginning of Act V.

ROMEO AND JULIET
[*as* CAIUS MARIUS]

### 1701 DRURY LANE
*Apr. 12.* No parts assigned

### 1703 DRURY LANE
*Dec. 18.* No parts assigned

### 1704 DRURY LANE
*Feb. 10, 24.* No parts assigned

### 1705 DRURY LANE
*Dec. 22.* No parts assigned

### 1707 QUEEN'S
*Feb. 18, 19*

| | |
|---|---|
| OLD MARIUS | Betterton |
| YOUNG MARIUS | Wilks |
| GRANIUS | Booth |
| METELLUS | Boman |
| CINNA | Keene |
| SYLLA | Husband |
| SULPITIUS | Johnson |
| 1ST CITIZEN | Cibber |
| 2ND CITIZEN | Norris |
| 3RD CITIZEN | Cross |
| 4TH CITIZEN | Trout |
| LAVINIA | Mrs Bracegirdle |
| NURSE | *Mr* Bullock |

### 1710 DRURY LANE
*Feb. 18*                               *May 17.* No parts assigned

| | |
|---|---|
| OLD MARIUS | Powell |
| YOUNG MARIUS | Booth |
| LAVINIA | Mrs Bradshaw |
| NURSE | *Mr* Norris |

No other parts assigned

### 1711 DRURY LANE
*Mar. 17*

| | |
|---|---|
| OLD MARIUS | Powell |
| YOUNG MARIUS | Booth |
| SYLLA | [C.] Bullock |
| GRANIUS | Ryan |
| METELLUS | Boman |
| 1ST CITIZEN | Penkethman |
| 2ND CITIZEN | Norris |
| 3RD CITIZEN | [F.] Leigh |
| 4TH CITIZEN | Birkhead |
| LAVINIA | Mrs Bradshaw |
| NURSE | *Mr* Bullock [Sr.] |

## ROMEO AND JULIET [as CAIUS MARIUS]

### 1712 DRURY LANE
*May 12*                              *Nov. 20.* No parts assigned

    OLD MARIUS    Powell
    YOUNG MARIUS    Booth
    LAVINIA    Mrs Bradshaw
No other parts assigned

### 1713 DRURY LANE
*June 18*                             *Oct. 31.* No parts assigned

    OLD MARIUS    Powell
    YOUNG MARIUS    Booth
    METELLUS    Boman
    1ST CITIZEN    Penkethman
    2ND CITIZEN    Norris
    LAVINIA    Mrs Bradshaw
    NURSE    *Mr* Pack

    [In the bill the CITIZENS are called CLOWNS.]

### 1714 DRURY LANE
*Oct. 30.* No parts assigned

### 1715 DRURY LANE
*Feb. 21*

    OLD MARIUS    Mills
    YOUNG MARIUS    Booth
    SYLLA    Elrington
    GRANIUS    Ryan
    SULPITIUS    Bickerstaff
    RUFFIAN    Penkethman
    APOTHECARY    Penkethman
    LAVINIA    Mrs Porter
    NURSE    *Mr* Norris

    [Penkethman doubled the RUFFIAN and APOTHECARY.]

### 1716 DRURY LANE
*Jan. 13*

    OLD MARIUS    Mills
    YOUNG MARIUS    Booth
    SYLLA    Ryan
    SULPITIUS    Bickerstaff
    RUFFIAN    Penkethman
    APOTHECARY    Penkethman
    LAVINIA    Mrs Porter
    NURSE    *Mr* Norris

    [Penkethman doubled the RUFFIAN and APOTHECARY.]

ROMEO AND JULIET [*as* CAIUS MARIUS]

## 1717 DRURY LANE
*May 10; Nov. 19*

| OLD MARIUS | Mills |
| YOUNG MARIUS | Booth |
| GRANIUS | Walker |
| SYLLA | Ryan |
| METELLUS | Boman |
| SULPITIUS | Bickerstaff |
| CINNA | Quin |
| 1ST CITIZEN | Penkethman |
| 2ND CITIZEN | Miller |
| 3RD CITIZEN | Cross |
| 4TH CITIZEN | Birkhead |
| LAVINIA | Mrs Porter |
| NURSE | *Mr* Norris |

[In the bills the CITIZENS are called the COMIC PARTS.]


## 1720 DRURY LANE
*Jan. 5*

| OLD MARIUS | Mills |
| YOUNG MARIUS | Booth |
| GRANIUS | Walker |
| 1ST CITIZEN | Penkethman |
| 2ND CITIZEN | Miller |
| LAVINIA | Mrs Porter |
| NURSE | *Mr* Norris |

[In the bill the CITIZENS and the NURSE are called the COMIC PARTS.]

*Dec. 6, 15*

added
| 3RD CITIZEN | Cross |
| 4TH CITIZEN | Birkhead |


## 1721 DRURY LANE
*May 6*

| OLD MARIUS | Mills |
| YOUNG MARIUS | Booth |
| GRANIUS* | Walker |
| 1ST CITIZEN | Penkethman |
| 2ND CITIZEN | Miller |
| 3RD CITIZEN | Cross |
| 4TH CITIZEN | Birkhead |
| LAVINIA | Mrs Porter |
| NURSE | *Mr* Norris |

[In the bill the CITIZENS are called the COMIC PARTS.]

*Dec. 1*

omitted
GRANIUS

408

## ROMEO AND JULIET [as CAIUS MARIUS]

### 1723 DRURY LANE
*Nov. 12*

| | |
|---|---|
| OLD MARIUS | Mills |
| YOUNG MARIUS | Booth |
| GRANIUS | William Mills |
| SULPITIUS | Harper |
| 1ST CITIZEN | Penkethman |
| 2ND CITIZEN | Miller |
| 3RD CITIZEN | Cross |
| 4TH CITIZEN | Ray |
| LAVINIA | Mrs Porter |
| NURSE | *Mr* Norris |

[In the bill the CITIZENS are called the COMIC PARTS.]

### 1724 DRURY LANE
*Feb. 8*         *Nov. 24.* No parts assigned

| | |
|---|---|
| OLD MARIUS | Mills |
| YOUNG MARIUS | Booth |
| GRANIUS | Will. Mills |
| SULPITIUS | Harper |
| 1ST CITIZEN | Penkethman |
| 2ND CITIZEN | Miller |
| 3RD CITIZEN | Cross |
| 4TH CITIZEN | Ray |
| LAVINIA | Mrs Porter |
| NURSE | *Mr* Norris |

[In the bill the CITIZENS are called the COMIC PARTS.]

### 1727 DRURY LANE
*Apr. 29*

| | |
|---|---|
| YOUNG MARIUS | Booth |
| OLD MARIUS | Mills |
| SYLLA | Thurmond |
| GRANIUS | Wm. Mills |
| METELLUS | Boman |
| CINNA | Williams |
| SULPITIUS | Bridgwater |
| APOTHECARY | Griffin |
| RUFFIAN | Miller |
| NURSE | *Mr* Norris |
| LAVINIA | Mrs Porter |

ROMEO AND JULIET [as CAIUS MARIUS]

## 1735 LINCOLN'S INN FIELDS
*Aug. 22*

| | |
|---|---|
| OLD MARIUS | [J.] Lacy |
| YOUNG MARIUS | Mrs Charke |
| METELLUS | Aston |
| CINNA | Turner |
| SYLLA | Walker |
| ANCHARIUS | [R.] Williams |
| CLODIUS | Lowder |
| ANTONIUS | Gerum |
| AMBASSADOR | Pearson |
| ANCHARIUS'S SON | Miss Brett |
| GRANIUS | Boothby |
| SULPITIUS | Machen |
| POMPEIUS | Richardson |
| PRIEST | Smith |
| CATULUS | Rymos |
| APOTHECARY | Whitaker |
| OLD MAN | Perkins |
| POMPEIUS'S SON | Master Littleton |
| LAVINIA | Mrs Mullart |
| NURSE | Mrs Talbot |

[*as altered by* T. CIBBER]

## 1744 HAYMARKET
*Sept. 11, 12, 14, 17, 19*

| | |
|---|---|
| ROMEO | [T.] Cibber |
| JULIET | Miss Jenny Cibber |

No other parts assigned

*Sept. 29; Oct. 2*

| | |
|---|---|
| ROMEO | [T.] Cibber |
| ESCALUS | Charles |
| CAPULET | Paget |
| MONTAGUE | Furnival |
| MERCUTIO* | Barnard |
| PARIS | Mozeen |
| BENVOLIO | Holtom |
| TYBALT* | Naylor |
| FRIAR JOHN | Michael |
| CHIEF WATCH | Wright |
| APOTHECARY* | Richards |
| BALTHAZAR* | Mrs Clark |
| PAGE* | Miss Charke |
| FRIAR LAURENCE | Hill |
| LADY CAPULET | Mrs George |

*Oct. 13*

| | |
|---|---|
| MERCUTIO | Paddick |
| APOTHECARY | Hacket |

*Nov. 1.* No parts assigned

*Dec. 17*

| | |
|---|---|
| TYBALT | [R.] Williams |
| APOTHECARY | Hacket |
| BALTHAZAR | Miss Charke |
| PAGE | Miss Tomson |

ROMEO AND JULIET [*as altered by* T. CIBBER]

## 1744 HAYMARKET (*cont.*)
*Sept. 29, &c. (cont.)*

| | |
|---|---|
| NURSE | Mrs Hill |
| JULIET | Miss Jenny Cibber |

[In the bill the CHIEF WATCH is called ALGUAZILE, and the actor's name misspelled 'Wight'. The bill assigns FRIAR LAURENCE to Johnson, evidently the stage name used by Hill. For the fact that he played the part see Henry Woodward, *Letter . . . to Dr. John Hill*, 1752, 6.]

[*The original*]

## 1748 DRURY LANE
*Nov. 29; Dec. 1*

| | |
|---|---|
| ROMEO | Barry |
| ESCALUS | Winstone |
| CAPULET | Berry |
| PARIS | Lee |
| BENVOLIO | Usher |
| TYBALT | Blakes |
| FRIAR LAURENCE | Havard |
| OLD CAPULET | Wright |
| FRIAR JOHN* | Champnes |
| GREGORY | Taswell |
| SAMPSON | James |
| BALTHAZAR | Bransby |
| ABRAHAM | Marr |
| MERCUTIO | Woodward |
| APOTHECARY* | Simpson |
| PETER* | Vaughan |
| PAGE* | Master Cross |
| 1ST GUARD* | Raftor |
| 2ND GUARD* | Gray |
| 3RD GUARD* | Ray |
| LADY CAPULET | Mrs Bennet |
| NURSE | Mrs James |
| JULIET | Mrs Cibber |

*Dec. 2, 3, 5, 6, 7, 8, 9, 10, 12, 13, 14, 15, 20, 30*
added
    MONTAGUE  Barnet
omitted
    FRIAR JOHN, APOTHECARY, PETER, PAGE, GUARDS

## 1749 DRURY LANE
*Jan. 12; Feb. 1*

| | |
|---|---|
| ROMEO | Barry |
| ESCALUS | Winstone |
| CAPULET | Berry |
| PARIS | Lee |
| BENVOLIO | Usher |

*Mar. 2; Apr. 1*
omitted
    OLD CAPULET, MONTAGUE, GREGORY SAMPSON, BALTHAZAR, ABRAHAM

## 1749 DRURY LANE (cont.)
*Jan. 12, &c. (cont.)*

| | |
|---|---|
| TYBALT | Blakes |
| FRIAR LAURENCE | Havard |
| OLD CAPULET* | Wright |
| MONTAGUE* | Barnet |
| GREGORY* | Taswell |
| SAMPSON* | James |
| BALTHAZAR* | Bransby |
| ABRAHAM* | Marr |
| MERCUTIO | Woodward |
| LADY CAPULET | Mrs Bennet |
| NURSE | Mrs James |
| JULIET | Mrs Cibber |

## 1750 DRURY LANE
*Sept. 28, 29; Oct. 1, 2, 3, 4, 5, 6, 8, 9, 10, 11, 12; Nov. 21, 26; Dec. 18*

| | |
|---|---|
| ROMEO | Garrick |
| ESCALUS | Winstone |
| CAPULET | Berry |
| PARIS | Scrase |
| BENVOLIO | Mozeen |
| TYBALT | Blakes |
| FRIAR LAURENCE | Havard |
| OLD CAPULET | Wright |
| FRIAR JOHN | Paddick |
| GREGORY | W. Vaughan |
| SAMPSON | James |
| BALTHAZAR | Ackman |
| ABRAHAM | Marr |
| MERCUTIO | Woodward |
| APOTHECARY | Simpson |
| PETER | Vaughan |
| OFFICER | Raftor |
| PAGE | Master Cross |
| [MONTAGUE | Burton] |
| LADY CAPULET | Mrs Bennet |
| NURSE | Mrs James |
| JULIET | Miss Bellamy |

[MONTAGUE does not appear in the bills. The assignment is taken from the printed text (Tonson and Draper, 1750), which also assigns PARIS to Lee.]

## COVENT GARDEN
*Mar. 1, 3, 5, 6, 8; Apr. 18*

| | |
|---|---|
| ROMEO | Lee |
| ESCALUS | Bransby |
| CAPULET | [L.] Sparks |

## 1750 COVENT GARDEN (cont.)

*Mar. 1, &c. (cont.)*

| PARIS | Anderson |
|---|---|
| BENVOLIO | Gibson |
| TYBALT | [Tho.] Lacy |
| FRIAR LAURENCE | Ridout |
| MONTAGUE | Bridgwater |
| OLD CAPULET | Redman |
| GREGORY | Arthur |
| SAMPSON | Collins |
| BALTHAZAR | Cushing |
| ABRAHAM | Dunstall |
| MERCUTIO | Dyer |
| LADY CAPULET | Mrs Horton |
| NURSE | Mrs Dunstall |
| JULIET | Miss Bellamy |

*Sept. 28, 29; Oct. 1, 2, 3, 4, 5, 6, 8, 9, 10, 11*

| ROMEO | Barry |
|---|---|
| CAPULET | [L.] Sparks |
| MONTAGUE | Bridgwater |
| ESCALUS | Anderson |
| PARIS | [Tho.] Lacy |
| BENVOLIO | Gibson |
| FRIAR LAURENCE | Ridout |
| GREGORY* | Arthur |
| SAMPSON | Collins |
| ABRAHAM | Dunstall |
| BALTHAZAR | Bransby |
| MERCUTIO | Macklin |
| TYBALT | Dyer |
| LADY CAPULET | Mrs Barrington |
| NURSE | Mrs Macklin |
| JULIET | Mrs Cibber |

*Dec. 8, 15, 17*

| GREGORY | Cushing |
|---|---|

[The playhouse bill for Sept. 28 is reproduced in Wilkinson's *Memoirs*, i. 37.]

# SAUNY THE SCOT

John Lacy's alteration of THE TAMING OF THE SHREW, q.v.

# SEE IF YOU LIKE IT

An anonymous alteration of THE COMEDY OF ERRORS, q.v.

# THE TAMING OF THE SHREW

Adapted as SAUNY THE SCOT, by John Lacy. In five acts.

1698 E. Whitlock.

Although the entire play has been rewritten into prose, a considerable number of individual lines from the original have been retained verbatim. The first four acts follow the structure of the original with reasonable fidelity; the fifth act is a drastic revision.

The Induction is omitted.

Act I is *I. i* somewhat reduced.

Act II is *I. ii* and *II. i*.

Act III begins with *III. i* and *ii*. Then follow *IV. ii*, reduced, and *IV. i*, in which Petruchio's soliloquy (*191–end*) is written out into a new scene portraying the bridal chamber.

Act IV begins with *IV. iii*, much reduced. Then follow *IV. iv*, expanded; *IV. v*; and *V. i*, which contains a new scene in which Woodall attempts to abduct Bianca.

Act V is *V. ii*, much altered and enlarged chiefly by the persistent refusal of Margaret to obey her husband.

See Genest, ii. 139; Odell, i. 39–40; Spencer, 275–81.

Adapted as THE COBLER OF PRESTON, by Charles Johnson. In two acts.

1716 W. Wilkins.

An alteration of the Induction only. An occasional speech or phrase of the original is retained; otherwise it is almost wholly new. A considerable amount of new material, current political references, &c., is introduced.

See Genest, ii. 575–6; Odell, i. 230–2.

Adapted as THE COBLER OF PRESTON, by Christopher Bullock. In one act.

1716 R. Palmer.

An alteration of the Induction only. It has been rewritten to a considerable extent and a trifling plot developed. About a third of the play is taken verbatim from the original.

See Genest, ii. 582–3; Odell, i. 229–30.

Adapted as A CURE FOR A SCOLD, by James Worsdale. In two acts.

1735 L. Gilliver.

A ballad opera written, save for two or three brief speeches, entirely in prose. It contains 23 songs. A few lines are from the original, but chiefly it is adapted from *Sauny the Scot*. The plot has been much simplified.

See Genest, iii. 448; Odell, i. 254–5.

[*as* SAUNY THE SCOT]

## 1704 DRURY LANE

*July 5; Oct. 20.* No parts assigned

## THE TAMING OF THE SHREW [as SAUNY THE SCOT]

### 1707 QUEEN'S
*July 4; Aug. 5*                    *Oct. 15.* No parts assigned

    SAUNY          Bullock
    BEAUFOY     Keene
    PETRUCHIO   Mills
    WINLOVE     Booth
    GERALDO     Husband
    WOODALL     Johnson
    JAMY          Norris
    SNATCHPENNY Pack
    TRANIO      Fairbank
    MARGARET    Mrs Bradshaw
    BIANCA      Mrs Mills

### 1708 DRURY LANE
*June 19*

    BEAUFOY     Keene
    PETRUCHIO   Mills
    GERALDO     Husband
    WINLOVE     Bickerstaff
    WOODALL     Johnson
    SIR LIONEL   Cross
    SAUNY         Bullock
    JAMY          Norris
    SNATCHPENNY Pack
    TRANIO      Fairbank
    MARGARET    Mrs Bradshaw
    BIANCA      Mrs Mills

### 1711 DRURY LANE
*July 10*

    BEAUFOY     Keene
    WOODALL     Johnson
    PETRUCHIO   Powell
    GERALDO     Husband
    WINLOVE     Bickerstaff
    TRANIO      [C.] Bullock
    SIR LIONEL   Cross
    JAMY          Norris
    SAUNY         Bullock Sr.
    MARGARET    Mrs Bradshaw

### 1712 DRURY LANE
*Feb. 6.* No parts assigned

415

## THE TAMING OF THE SHREW [as SAUNY THE SCOT]

### 1712 DRURY LANE (cont.)
*July 4*

| | |
|---|---|
| BEAUFOY | Keene |
| PETRUCHIO | Mills |
| GERALDO | Husband |
| WINLOVE | Bickerstaff |
| WOODALL | Johnson |
| JAMY | Norris |
| SAUNY | Bullock [Sr.] |
| MARGARET | Mrs Bradshaw |

### 1714 DRURY LANE
*July 13*

| | |
|---|---|
| WOODALL | Johnson |
| SIR LIONEL | Cross |
| WINLOVE | Bickerstaff |
| GERALDO | Ryan |
| JAMY | Norris |
| TRANIO | [C.] Bullock |
| SAUNY | Bullock Sr. |
| MARGARET | Mrs Bradshaw |

[*as* THE COBLER OF PRESTON, *by* JOHNSON]

### 1716 DRURY LANE
*Feb. 3, 4, 6, 8, 9, 10, 14, 16, 18, 21, 23, 25, 27; Apr. 5, 6; Oct. 25, 26*

| | |
|---|---|
| SIR CHARLES | Ryan |
| CAPTAIN JOLLY | Walker |
| CONSTABLE | [F.] Leigh |
| BUTLER | Birkhead |
| SLY | Penkethman |
| BETTY | Miss Willis |
| CICELY GUNDY | Mrs Baker |
| JOAN | Mrs Willis |

[The bills give neither the parts nor the actors' names. The above assignment is taken from the printed text.]

[*as* THE COBLER OF PRESTON, *by* BULLOCK]

### LINCOLN'S INN FIELDS
*Jan. 24, 25, 26, 27, 31; Feb. 1, 2, 4, 16, 27; Mar. 1, 3; Apr. 2, 5, 14, 19; May 21; July 13; Oct. 17; Dec. 28*

| | |
|---|---|
| SIR JASPER | Ogden |
| CLERIMONT | Coker |
| TOBY GUZZLE | Spiller |
| SNUFFLE | [C.] Bullock |
| GRIST | Bullock Sr. |
| MAID | Mrs Garnet |

## THE TAMING OF THE SHREW [as BULLOCK'S COBLER]

### 1716 LINCOLN'S INN FIELDS (cont.)

*Jan. 24, &c. (cont.)*
- DAME HACKET  Mr Hall
- DORCAS  Mr Griffin

[The bills give neither the parts nor the actors' names. The above assignment is taken from the printed text.]

*Feb. 3; July 6, 20; Aug. 15*
- TOBY GUZZLE  Spiller
- No other parts assigned

### [as SAUNY THE SCOT]
### LINCOLN'S INN FIELDS

*June 20, 27*
- SAUNY  Bullock Sr.
- No other parts assigned

*July 25; Oct. 22*
- SAUNY  Bullock Sr.
- MARGARET  Mrs Thurmond
- No other parts assigned

### 1717 LINCOLN'S INN FIELDS

*June 12.* No parts assigned

*Nov. 13*
- SAUNY  Bullock Sr.
- MARGARET  Mrs Thurmond
- No other parts assigned

### [as THE COBLER OF PRESTON, by BULLOCK]
### LINCOLN'S INN FIELDS

*June 25; July 5.* No parts assigned

*Oct. 28; Dec. 31*
- TOBY GUZZLE  Spiller
- No other parts assigned

### 1718 LINCOLN'S INN FIELDS

*Feb. 17; May 29.* No parts assigned

*May 3*
- TOBY GUZZLE  Spiller
- No other parts assigned

## THE TAMING OF THE SHREW

### [as SAUNY THE SCOT]

### 1719 LINCOLN'S INN FIELDS
*Dec. 21.* No parts assigned
*Dec. 29*
    SAUNY      Bullock Sr.
    No other parts assigned

### 1720 LINCOLN'S INN FIELDS
*Feb. 8*
    SAUNY      Bullock Sr.
    No other parts assigned

### [as THE COBLER OF PRESTON, by BULLOCK]
### LINCOLN'S INN FIELDS
*Mar. 31.* No parts assigned

### 1721 LINCOLN'S INN FIELDS
*Jan. 27*
    TOBY GUZZLE   Spiller
    No other parts assigned
*Nov. 17.* No parts assigned

### 1722 LINCOLN'S INN FIELDS
*May 3.* No parts assigned

### 1723 LINCOLN'S INN FIELDS
*May 8.* No parts assigned

### 1724 LINCOLN'S INN FIELDS
*May 8; Nov. 13*
    TOBY GUZZLE   Spiller
    No other parts assigned

### [as SAUNY THE SCOT]
### 1725 LINCOLN'S INN FIELDS
*Apr. 7*                    *May 18*
    SAUNY      Bullock Sr.    added
    BEAUFOY    Hulett        CURTIS   H. Bullock
    WINLOVE    Diggs
    TRANIO     Walker
    WOODALL    Hippisley
    SIR LIONEL   Hall
    PETRUCHIO  Ogden
    SNATCHPENNY  Spiller

### THE TAMING OF THE SHREW [as SAUNY THE SCOT]

#### 1725 LINCOLN'S INN FIELDS (cont.)
*Apr. 7 (cont.)*

| | |
|---|---|
| JAMY | Morgan |
| MARGARET | Mrs Egleton |
| BIANCA | Mrs Vincent |

[Bill in DC of Apr. 6.]

### [as THE COBLER OF PRESTON, by BULLOCK]

#### 1726 LINCOLN'S INN FIELDS
*May 18; Aug. 12, 16.* No parts assigned

#### 1730 LINCOLN'S INN FIELDS
*May 7.* No parts assigned

#### GOODMAN'S FIELDS
*July 10, 13*

| | |
|---|---|
| TOBY GUZZLE | Penkethman [Jr.] |
| SIR JASPER | Bardin |
| CLERIMONT | Mynn |
| DAME HACKET | *Mr* Pearce |
| DORCAS | *Mr* Eaton |

#### 1731 LINCOLN'S INN FIELDS
*Oct. 25*

| | |
|---|---|
| TOBY GUZZLE | Penkethman [Jr.] |
| SNUFFLE | Hippisley |
| DAME HACKET | *Mr* Hall |

No other parts assigned

#### HAYMARKET
*Mar. 17*

| | |
|---|---|
| TOBY GUZZLE | Jones |
| SIR JASPER | Furnival |
| CLERIMONT | Wathen |
| SNUFFLE | [G.] Hallam |
| GRIST | Dove |
| DAME HACKET | *Mr* Reynolds |
| DORCAS | *Mr* Ayres |

[Bill in DP of Mar. 16.]

*Apr. 20.* No parts assigned

#### GOODMAN'S FIELDS
*Feb. 8, 9*

| | |
|---|---|
| SIR JASPER | Bardin |
| CLERIMONT | Havard |

*Feb. 11, 12*

| | |
|---|---|
| SNUFFLE | W. Williams |
| GRIST | R. Williams |

THE TAMING OF THE SHREW [as BULLOCK'S COBLER]

1731 GOODMAN'S FIELDS (cont.)

Feb. 8, 9 (cont.)

| | |
|---|---|
| TOBY GUZZLE | Morgan |
| SNUFFLE* | [W.] Bullock [Jr.] |
| GRIST* | W. Williams |
| DAME HACKET | Mr Pearce |
| DORCAS | Mr Burny |
| MAID | Miss Smith |

May 15, 21

TOBY GUZZLE  Morgan
No other parts assigned

1732 LINCOLN'S INN FIELDS
May 11. No parts assigned

1735 VILLIERS ST., YORK BUILDINGS
Sept. 18. No parts assigned

[as A CURE FOR A SCOLD]

DRURY LANE

Feb. 25, 27; Mar. 1

| | |
|---|---|
| SIR WILLIAM | Shepard |
| MANLY | Macklin |
| HEARTWELL | Este |
| GAINLOVE | Cross |
| TOOTH-DRAWER | [T.] Hallam |
| ARCHER | Salway |
| DOCTOR | Turbutt |
| PETER | Raftor |
| MARGARET | Mrs Clive |
| FLORA | Mrs Pritchard |
| LUCY | Mrs Cross |

[The printed text assigns the DOCTOR to Harper, and omits PETER.]

Mar. 20. No parts assigned

May 5

MANLY     The Author [Worsdale]
MARGARET  Mrs Clive
No other parts assigned

[as SAUNY THE SCOT]

GOODMAN'S FIELDS

Dec. 8, 9, 10, 12, 13, 15

| | |
|---|---|
| SAUNY | Lyon |
| BEAUFOY | W. Giffard |
| SIR LIONEL | Norris [Jr.] |
| WINLOVE | Richardson |
| TRANIO | Woodward |
| WOODALL | Ray |
| GERALDO | Hamilton |
| JAMY | Rosco |
| CURTIS | Dove |
| PETRUCHIO | Havard |
| SNATCHPENNY | Penkethman [Jr.] |

420

## THE TAMING OF THE SHREW [as SAUNY THE SCOT]

### 1735 GOODMAN'S FIELDS (cont.)
*Dec. 8, &c. (cont.)*

| | |
|---|---|
| BIANCA | Mrs Hamilton |
| WIDOW | Miss Gerrard |
| MARGARET | Mrs Roberts |

### 1736 LINCOLN'S INN FIELDS
*Nov. 18*

| | |
|---|---|
| PETRUCHIO | Havard |
| SAUNY | Lyon |
| BEAUFOY | W. Giffard |
| SIR LIONEL | Norris [Jr.] |
| WINLOVE | Richardson |
| TRANIO | Woodward |
| GERALDO | Hamilton |
| SNATCHPENNY | Penkethman [Jr.] |
| JAMY | Rosco |
| WOODALL | Ware |
| CURTIS | Dove |
| BIANCA | Mrs Hamilton |
| MARGARET | Mrs Roberts |

### GOODMAN'S FIELDS
*Feb. 23.* No parts assigned

### [as THE COBLER OF PRESTON, by BULLOCK]
### 1737 NEW WELLS, CLERKENWELL
*June 13, 14, 15, 16, 17, 18, 20, 21, 22, 23, 24.* No parts assigned

### 1738 COVENT GARDEN
*Apr. 7*

| | |
|---|---|
| TOBY GUZZLE | Penkethman [Jr.] |
| GRIST | Salway |
| SNUFFLE | Hippisley |
| DORCAS | *Mr* Stoppelaer |
| DAME HACKET | *Mr* Mullart |

### 1741 JAMES ST., HAYMARKET
*May 11.* No parts assigned

### 1745 NEW WELLS, GOODMAN'S FIELDS
*Apr. 1, 26; May 2.* No parts assigned

## THE TAMING OF THE SHREW
### [as A CURE FOR A SCOLD]

**1750 COVENT GARDEN**

*Mar. 27*

| | |
|---|---|
| MANLY | Dunstall |
| ARCHER | Cushing |
| GAINLOVE | Wilder |
| HEARTWELL | Baker |
| SIR WILLIAM* | Stoppelaer |
| LUCY | Miss [E.] Young |
| FLORA | Miss Falkner |
| MARGARET | Mrs Dunstall |

[The bill gives the actors' names only. The above assignment is taken from the bill for Apr. 26.]

*Apr. 26*

| | |
|---|---|
| SIR WILLIAM added | Collins |
| DOCTOR | Redman |
| TOOTH-DRAWER | Hacket |
| PETER | Holtom |

[The bill assigns the parts.]

## THE TEMPEST

The first adaptation of this play was by Dryden and Davenant. It was published in 1670. Four years later Shadwell made an anonymous adaptation of this adaptation. The 1670 edition, save for the Dryden folio of 1701, was not reprinted until the twentieth century. All eighteenth-century separate editions of the play make use of Shadwell's 1674 adaptation, but with credit only to Dryden and Davenant. That this was the version used by the theatres is altogether certain.

Adapted by John Dryden and Sir William Davenant, and in turn adapted by Thomas Shadwell. In five acts.

1674    Henry Herringman.

Act I, scene i is new. It is based on *I. i*, but is half again longer than the original. An occasional brief speech is retained verbatim. Scene ii is *I. ii. 1–374*, almost verbatim. It is, however, written chiefly into prose, and contains references to the new characters introduced by the adapters. It closes with about 50 new lines: Miranda and her sister Dorinda speak of their never having seen a man.

Act II, scene i opens with about 125 new lines: Trinculo (here Trincalo) quarrels drunkenly with his companions. This is followed by *II. ii*, altered into a dialogue between Trinculo and Caliban only. Scene ii is new: it introduces Hippolito, heir to the dukedom of Mantua, who, reared by Prospero, has never seen a woman. He meets Dorinda, and they fall in love. Scene iii opens with a few speeches taken from the first half of *II. i*, and continues with a masque of devils, who upbraid Alonso. The plot against his life is omitted.

Act III, scene i is *I. ii. 375–404*. 'Full fathom five' is sung by Milcha. Scene ii opens with about 125 new lines: Dorinda tells Prospero of her love for Hippolito. Then follow *IV. i. 34–7*, and *V. i. 3–30*, slightly reduced, and 18 new lines dealing with Caliban's revolt. Scene iii is *III. iii. 18–52*, abridged, followed by about 150 new lines: Trinculo makes love to Sycorax and makes peace with Stephano; Ariel entices Ferdinand by echoing his words. Scene iv is *I. ii. 405–end*, almost verbatim, followed by 75 new lines: Prospero furthers Hippolito's love for Dorinda. Scene v is new: Ferdinand and Hippolito discuss their love for the two sisters.

# THE TEMPEST

Act IV, scene i begins with a rewriting and expansion of *III. i. 1–91*, and continues with about 175 new lines: Ferdinand and Miranda quarrel; Hippolito and Dorinda declare their love; Ferdinand challenges Hippolito to a duel. Scene ii is new: Trinculo, Stephano, and Caliban drink and fight. Scene iii is also new: Hippolito, wounded in the duel by Ferdinand, appears dead; Prospero orders Ferdinand killed; Alonso intercedes for him; Dorinda and Miranda quarrel.

Act V, which is all one scene, begins with about 175 new lines: the reconciliation of the four lovers. It closes with the reconciliation of everybody else; interspersed here are a few speeches from *V. i*. This act contains the elaborate masque of Neptune and Amphitrite.

See Genest, i. 155; Odell, i. 33–6; Spencer, 204–9.

Shadwell's alterations were mainly in the nature of scenic effects, music, &c. For Dryden's and Davenant's 1670 adaptation, see Genest, i. 76–7; Odell, i. 31–3; Spencer, 193–201.

No acting versions of the original were published before 1750.

[*as altered by* DRYDEN *and* DAVENANT *and in turn by* SHADWELL]

## 1701 DRURY LANE
*Jan. 1; Feb. 7; Mar. 4.* No parts assigned

## 1702 LINCOLN'S INN FIELDS
*Oct. 13*
    TRINCULO    Underhill
    No other parts assigned
    [Bill in DC of Oct. 10.]

## 1704 DRURY LANE
*June 19*
    PROSPERO    Powell
    No other parts assigned

## 1706 DRURY LANE
*Mar. 5*
    TRINCULO    Estcourt
    No other parts assigned

*Dec. 26.* No parts assigned

## 1707 DRURY LANE
*Jan. 1, 21*
    TRINCULO\*    Estcourt
    HIPPOLITO    Mrs Mountfort
    DORINDA\*    Mrs Cross
    No other parts assigned

*Feb. 13*
    omitted
        TRINCULO

*Nov. 20*
    omitted
        DORINDA

*Dec. 27*
    PROSPERO    Powell
    TRINCULO    Estcourt
    HIPPOLITO    Mrs Mountfort
    No other parts assigned

## THE TEMPEST [as altered by DRYDEN, et al.]

### 1708 DRURY LANE
*July 29*
| | |
|---|---|
| PROSPERO | Mills |
| ALONSO | Corey |
| FERDINAND | Smith |
| HIPPOLITO | [C.] Bullock |
| STEPHANO | Johnson |
| TRINCULO | Bullock [Sr] |
| MUSTACHO | Bickerstaff |
| VENTOSO | Fairbank |
| CALIBAN | Norris |
| SYCORAX | *Mr* Cross |
| MIRANDA | Mrs Moore |
| DORINDA | Miss Norris |

### 1710 DRURY LANE
*Jan. 20, 24; Feb. 2, 10; Apr. 13*
| | |
|---|---|
| PROSPERO | Powell |
| DORINDA | Mrs Santlow |

No other parts assigned

*May 12*
added
| | |
|---|---|
| TRINCULO | Underhill |
| VENTOSO | A Gentleman [unidentified] |

[VENTOSO appears only in the advance advertisement in DC of May 11.]

### 1712 DRURY LANE
*Jan. 7, 8, 10, 11, 15, 17, 24; Feb. 1, 15; Mar. 15; Apr. 21; May 10; Nov. 5, 21; Dec. 26.* No parts assigned

### 1713 DRURY LANE
*Jan. 1; Feb. 6; Apr. 7; Nov. 5; Dec. 26, 28.* No parts assigned

*June 23*
| | |
|---|---|
| FERDINAND | Wilks |
| MIRANDA | A Young Gentlewoman [unidentified; first appearance on the stage] |

No other parts assigned

### 1714 DRURY LANE
*Mar. 30; Nov. 25; Dec. 3, 13.* No parts assigned

*June 4*
| | |
|---|---|
| PROSPERO | Powell |
| HIPPOLITO | Mrs Mountfort |

THE TEMPEST [as altered by DRYDEN, et al.]

## 1714 DRURY LANE (cont.)

*June 4 (cont.)*

| | |
|---|---|
| ALONSO | Keene |
| FERDINAND | Ryan |
| ANTONIO | [C.] Bullock |
| CALIBAN | Johnson |
| STEPHANO | Bickerstaff |
| TRINCULO | Bullock [Sr.] |
| VENTOSO | Norris |
| MUSTACHO | [F.] Leigh |
| DORINDA | Mrs Santlow |

## 1715 DRURY LANE

*Jan. 1, 20; Feb. 2, 18; Apr. 18;
June 10; July 12; Aug. 16; Nov. 18.*
No parts assigned

## 1716 DRURY LANE

*Jan. 6; Apr. 25; June 8.* No parts assigned

*July 31*

| | |
|---|---|
| NEPTUNE | Turner |
| AMPHITRITE | Mrs Mills |
| EARTHY SPIRIT* | Renton |
| AIRY SPIRIT | Mrs Boman |

No other parts assigned

[Bill in DC of July 30.]

*Aug. 7*
added
EOLUS   Carey

*Aug. 23*
added
EOLUS   Carey
omitted
EARTHY SPIRIT

*Dec. 28*

NEPTUNE   Turner
No other parts assigned

## 1717 DRURY LANE

*Feb. 12; Apr. 22; Dec. 5.* No parts assigned

*June 10*

| | |
|---|---|
| PROSPERO | Mills |
| FERDINAND | Ryan |
| STEPHANO | Bickerstaff |
| VENTOSO | Norris |
| MUSTACHO | [F.] Leigh |
| CALIBAN | Johnson |
| SYCORAX | *Mr* Cross |
| MIRANDA | Miss Willis |
| DORINDA | Mrs Younger |

425

THE TEMPEST [as altered by DRYDEN, et al.]

## 1718 DRURY LANE

*June 11*

| | |
|---|---|
| PROSPERO | Mills |
| CALIBAN | Johnson |
| VENTOSO | Norris |
| TRINCULO | Miller |
| FERDINAND* | Thurmond |
| STEPHANO | Bickerstaff |
| MUSTACHO | [F.] Leigh |
| HIPPOLITO* | Miss Willis |
| ARIEL | Miss Lindar |
| SYCORAX* | Mr Cross |
| DORINDA* | A Young Gentlewoman [Miss Seal] |

[The only part assigned in the bill is DORINDA. It has otherwise, 'The Principal Parts by, &c.'. The above assignment is taken from the bill for Aug. 1. Bill in DC of June 9.]

*Aug. 1*
added
   MIRANDA  Miss Tenoe
omitted
   FERDINAND
[The bill assigns the parts. Miss Seal's name is in the bill.]

*Dec. 11*

| | |
|---|---|
| FERDINAND | Wilks |
| HIPPOLITO | Mrs Bicknell |
| DORINDA | Mrs Santlow |

added
   MIRANDA  Miss Willis
omitted
   SYCORAX

## 1719 DRURY LANE

*Feb. 9*

| | |
|---|---|
| PROSPERO | Mills |
| FERDINAND* | Wilks |
| TRINCULO | Miller |
| VENTOSO | Norris |
| MUSTACHO* | [F.] Leigh |
| CALIBAN | Johnson |
| HIPPOLITO* | Mrs Bicknell |
| ARIEL | Miss Lindar |
| DORINDA* | Mrs Santlow |

*Mar. 30.* No parts assigned

*July 21*
   FERDINAND  Wm. Wilks
added
   STEPHANO  Bickerstaff
omitted
   MUSTACHO, HIPPOLITO, DORINDA

## 1720 DRURY LANE
*Jan. 6; Apr. 20; June 24; Aug. 9; Dec. 26.* No parts assigned

## 1721 DRURY LANE
*May 20; Aug. 22.* No parts assigned

## 1722 DRURY LANE
*Jan. 3; Mar. 26; June 12.* No parts assigned

## THE TEMPEST [as altered by DRYDEN, et al.]

### 1723 DRURY LANE
*Jan. 7*

| PROSPERO | Mills |
| FERDINAND | William Wilks |
| STEPHANO | Shepard |
| MUSTACHO | Norris |
| VENTOSO | Harper |
| HIPPOLITO* | Theo. Cibber |
| TRINCULO | Miller |
| ARIEL* | Miss Lindar |
| MIRANDA* | Miss Willis |
| DORINDA* | Miss Seal |

*June 6*

| HIPPOLITO | Mrs Brett |
| ARIEL | Master Wetherilt |
| MIRANDA | Miss Tenoe |
| DORINDA | Miss Lindar |

### 1724 DRURY LANE
*Jan. 7; Apr. 14; May 25; Oct. 30.* No parts assigned

### 1725 DRURY LANE
*Jan. 6; May 24; Oct. 30.* No parts assigned

### 1726 DRURY LANE
*Jan. 6.* No parts assigned

### 1727 DRURY LANE
*Jan. 24; May 22; Dec. 29.* No parts assigned

### 1729 DRURY LANE
*Jan. 2*

| PROSPERO | Mills |
| FERDINAND* | Wilks |
| ANTONIO* | William Mills |
| GONZALO* | Oates |
| ALONSO* | Roberts |
| HIPPOLITO | Mrs Cibber |
| STEPHANO* | Shepard |
| MUSTACHO | Harper |
| TRINCULO | Miller |
| VENTOSO | Norris |
| ARIEL | Miss Robinson Jr. |
| MIRANDA* | Mrs Booth |
| DORINDA | Miss Raftor |

*Jan. 3, 6; Feb. 12*
added
| CALIBAN | Johnson |

*May 28*
| FERDINAND | Wm. Mills |
| ANTONIO | Corey |
| MIRANDA | Mrs Mills |

added
| CALIBAN | Johnson |

*Oct. 30*
| FERDINAND | William Mills |
| MIRANDA | Mrs Mills |

added
| CALIBAN | Johnson |

omitted
ANTONIO, GONZALO, ALONSO, STEPHANO

427

THE TEMPEST [as altered by DRYDEN, et al.]

## 1730 DRURY LANE
*Nov. 30*

| | |
|---|---|
| PROSPERO | Mills |
| HIPPOLITO | Mrs Cibber |
| TRINCULO | Harper |
| MUSTACHO | [T.] Cibber |
| VENTOSO | R. Wetherilt |
| FERDINAND | Wm. Mills |
| CALIBAN | Johnson |
| ARIEL | Miss Robinson [Jr.] |
| ALONSO | Fielding |
| GONZALO | Oates |
| NEPTUNE | Rainton |
| ANTONIO | Corey |
| MIRANDA | Mrs Mills |
| DORINDA | Miss Raftor |
| SYCORAX | *Mr* [T.] Hallam |
| AMPHITRITE | Mrs Roberts |

*Dec. 17.* No parts assigned

## 1731 DRURY LANE
*Jan. 13.* No parts assigned

*June 7*

| | |
|---|---|
| PROSPERO* | Roberts |
| HIPPOLITO | Mrs Cibber |
| MUSTACHO | [T.] Cibber |
| VENTOSO | R. Wetherilt |
| STEPHANO | Shepard |
| CALIBAN* | Wetherilt Sr. |
| ARIEL* | Miss Brett |
| FERDINAND | W. Mills |
| TRINCULO | Harper |
| ALONSO* | Fielding |
| GONZALO* | Oates |
| ANTONIO* | Berry |
| NEPTUNE | Rainton |
| SYCORAX* | *Mr* Charke |
| MIRANDA | Mrs Walter |
| DORINDA | Miss Raftor |
| MILCHA* | Mrs Boman [Jr.] |
| AMPHITRITE | Miss Raftor |

*Dec. 29*

| | |
|---|---|
| PROSPERO | Mills |
| HIPPOLITO | Mrs Cibber |
| CALIBAN | Johnson |
| ARIEL | Miss Robinson [Jr.] |
| TRINCULO | Harper |
| DORINDA | Miss Raftor |

*Dec. 2*

| | |
|---|---|
| PROSPERO | Mills |
| CALIBAN | Johnson |
| ARIEL | Miss Robinson [Jr.] |

ALONSO, GONZALO, ANTONIO, SYCORAX, MILCHA omitted

[In these two performances Miss Raftor doubled DORINDA and AMPHITRITE.]

428

## THE TEMPEST [*as altered by* DRYDEN, *et al.*]

### 1731 GOODMAN'S FIELDS
*June 2*

| ALONSO | Smith |
| FERDINAND | Bardin |
| PROSPERO | Havard |
| ANTONIO | Worsley |
| GONZALO | Machen |
| HIPPOLITO | Mrs Thomas |
| STEPHANO | Rosco |
| MUSTACHO | R. Williams |
| VENTOSO | Collett |
| TRINCULO | Morgan |
| ARIEL | Master Woodward |
| CALIBAN | W. Giffard |
| NEPTUNE | A Gentleman [unidentified] |
| SYCORAX | *Mr* Collett |
| MIRANDA | Mrs Palmer |
| DORINDA | Mrs Morgan |
| AMPHITRITE | Mrs Palmer |

[Genest (iii. 320) has, 'Master Woodward acted . . . one of the Spirits'. The DP bill clearly has, 'Ariel, a Spirit'. Collett doubled VENTOSO and SYCORAX; Mrs Palmer doubled MIRANDA and AMPHITRITE.]

### 1732 DRURY LANE
*Dec. 26*

| PROSPERO | Roberts |
| HIPPOLITO | Miss Williams |
| ARIEL | Miss Robinson [Jr.] |
| TRINCULO | Miller |
| CALIBAN | Johnson |
| DORINDA | Miss Raftor |

[Bill in DP of Dec. 25. DP of Dec. 26 is missing.]

### 1733 DRURY LANE
*Jan. 24.* No parts assigned
*Nov. 26, 27, 28, 29, 30; Dec. 3, 19, 28*

| TRINCULO | Bridgwater |
| PROSPERO | Roberts |
| FERDINAND | Marshall |
| HIPPOLITO | Miss Holliday |
| ALONSO | Hewitt |
| ANTONIO | Turbutt |
| GONZALO | Mullart |
| STEPHANO | Hewson |
| VENTOSO | Norris [Jr.] |
| MUSTACHO | Jones |
| CALIBAN | Paget |

THE TEMPEST [*as altered by* DRYDEN, *et al.*]

## 1733 DRURY LANE (*cont.*)
*Nov. 26, &c.* (*cont.*)

| | |
|---|---|
| ARIEL | Miss Norris |
| NEPTUNE | [C.] Stoppelaer |
| EARTHY SPIRIT | Waltz |
| SYCORAX | *Mr* Topham |
| MIRANDA | Mrs Walter |
| DORINDA | Mrs Clive |
| MILCHA | *Mr* Mountier |
| AMPHITRITE | Miss [C.] Young [first appearance, Nov. 26, on the stage] |

## 1734 DRURY LANE
*Jan. 1, 29*

| | |
|---|---|
| TRINCULO | Bridgwater |
| PROSPERO | Roberts |
| FERDINAND | Marshall |
| HIPPOLITO | Miss Holliday |
| ALONSO | Hewitt |
| ANTONIO | Turbutt |
| GONZALO | Mullart |
| STEPHANO | Hewson |
| VENTOSO | Norris [Jr.] |
| MUSTACHO | Jones |
| CALIBAN | Paget |
| ARIEL | Miss Norris |
| NEPTUNE | [C.] Stoppelaer |
| EARTHY SPIRIT | Waltz |
| SYCORAX | *Mr* Topham |
| MIRANDA | Mrs Walter |
| DORINDA | Mrs Clive |
| MILCHA | *Mr* Mountier |
| AMPHITRITE | Miss [C.] Young |

*May 15*

| | |
|---|---|
| PROSPERO | Mills |
| FERDINAND | W. Mills |
| TRINCULO | Miller |
| CALIBAN | Johnson |
| ALONSO | Hewitt |
| ANTONIO | Turbutt |
| GONZALO★ | Mullart |
| STEPHANO | Shepard |
| VENTOSO | Oates |
| MUSTACHO★ | Jones |
| HIPPOLITO | Miss Holliday |

*Oct. 22*

| | |
|---|---|
| GONZALO | Winstone |
| MUSTACHO | Macklin |
| NEPTUNE | Salway |
| EARTHY SPIRIT | Rainton |
| AMPHITRITE | Mrs Cantrell |

added

| | |
|---|---|
| SYCORAX | *Mr* Jones |
| MILCHA | *Mr* [E.] Roberts |

*Nov. 15.* No parts assigned

430

THE TEMPEST [as altered by DRYDEN, et al.]

## 1734 DRURY LANE (cont.)
### May 15 (cont.)

| | |
|---|---|
| ARIEL | Master Arne |
| NEPTUNE* | [C.] Stoppelaer |
| EARTHY SPIRIT* | Waltz |
| DORINDA | Mrs Clive |
| MIRANDA | Mrs Walter |
| AMPHITRITE* | Miss [C.] Young |

## 1735 DRURY LANE
### Feb. 14

| | |
|---|---|
| PROSPERO | Mills |
| FERDINAND | W. Mills |
| TRINCULO | Miller |
| CALIBAN | Johnson |
| ALONSO* | Hewitt |
| ANTONIO | Turbutt |
| GONZALO | Winstone |
| STEPHANO | Shepard |
| VENTOSO | Oates |
| MUSTACHO* | Macklin |
| HIPPOLITO | Miss Holliday |
| ARIEL* | Master Arne |
| NEPTUNE | Salway |
| EARTHY SPIRIT | Rainton |
| DORINDA | Mrs Clive |
| MIRANDA | Mrs Walter |
| MILCHA | Mr [E.] Roberts |
| AMPHITRITE | Mrs Cantrell |
| SYCORAX | Mr Jones |

### Oct. 31

| | |
|---|---|
| ALONSO | Berry |
| MUSTACHO | Este |
| ARIEL | Miss Brett |

## 1737 DRURY LANE
### Feb. 10, 11, 12, 14, 15; Apr. 11, 14, 25

| | |
|---|---|
| PROSPERO | Berry |
| FERDINAND | Este |
| CALIBAN | Johnson |
| HIPPOLITO | Miss Holliday |
| ARIEL | Miss Cole |
| TRINCULO | Miller |
| MUSTACHO | Macklin |
| STEPHANO | Cross |
| VENTOSO | Ray |
| MIRANDA | Mrs Walter |
| DORINDA | Mrs Clive |

[The bills for Feb. 11, 12 are missing. It is, however, unlikely that there were any changes in the cast. The assignment of MUSTACHO, STEPHANO, VENTOSO is conjectural. In the bills they are called SAILORS.]

THE TEMPEST [as altered by DRYDEN, et al.]

## 1739 DRURY LANE
*Dec. 26, 27*

| | |
|---|---|
| PROSPERO | Berry |
| FERDINAND | Ridout |
| TRINCULO | Macklin |
| HIPPOLITO | Mrs Mills |
| STEPHANO | Shepard |
| MUSTACHO | Woodward |
| VENTOSO | Ray |
| ANTONIO | Winstone |
| ALVAREZ | Turbutt |
| GONZALO | Woodburn |
| CALIBAN | Johnson |
| ARIEL | Miss Cole |
| MIRANDA | Mrs Walter |
| DORINDA | Mrs Clive |

[ALVAREZ seems to be a misprint for ALONSO.]

## 1740 DRURY LANE
*Jan. 4*

| | |
|---|---|
| PROSPERO | Berry |
| FERDINAND | Ridout |
| TRINCULO* | Macklin |
| HIPPOLITO | Mrs Mills |
| STEPHANO | Shepard |
| MUSTACHO* | Woodward |
| VENTOSO* | Ray |
| ANTONIO* | Winstone |
| ALVAREZ* | Turbutt |
| GONZALO | Woodburn |
| CALIBAN | Johnson |
| ARIEL | Miss Cole |
| MIRANDA* | Mrs Walter |
| DORINDA | Mrs Clive |

[For ALVAREZ, see preceding note.]

*May 14*

| | |
|---|---|
| TRINCULO | Reed |
| ANTONIO | Turbutt |
| ALONSO | Winstone |
| MIRANDA | Mrs Bennet |
| added | |
| NEPTUNE | Reinhold |
| MILCHA | Miss Edwards |
| SYCORAX | Mr Raftor |
| AMPHITRITE | Miss Jones |

[In the bill the character is ALONSO, not ALVAREZ.]

*Nov. 28*

| | |
|---|---|
| MUSTACHO | Ray |
| VENTOSO | Woodward |
| ANTONIO | Turbutt |
| ALONSO | Winstone |
| added | |
| NEPTUNE | Savage |
| SYCORAX | Mr Taswell |
| MILCHA and | |
| AMPHITRITE | Mrs Arne |

[For ALONSO, see preceding note.]

## 1741 DRURY LANE
*May 15*

| | |
|---|---|
| PROSPERO | Berry |
| CALIBAN | Johnson |
| TRINCULO | Macklin |
| FERDINAND | Ridout |
| STEPHANO | Shepard |
| VENTOSO | Ray |

## THE TEMPEST [*as altered by* DRYDEN, *et al.*]

### 1741 DRURY LANE (*cont.*)
*May 15 (cont.)*

| | |
|---|---|
| MUSTACHO | Woodward |
| ALONSO | Winstone |
| ANTONIO | Turbutt |
| GONZALO | Woodburn |
| HIPPOLITO | Green |
| ARIEL | Miss Cole |
| SYCORAX | *Mr* Taswell |
| MIRANDA | Mrs Walter |
| MILCHA | Mrs Arne |
| DORINDA | Mrs Clive |

### 1745 NEW WELLS, GOODMAN'S FIELDS

*Feb. 14, 15*

| | |
|---|---|
| PROSPERO | Furnival |
| FERDINAND* | Goodfellow |
| ALONSO | Freeman |
| ANTONIO* | Tucker |
| GONZALO* | Yorke |
| HIPPOLITO | Mrs [L.] Hallam |
| STEPHANO* | Kennedy |
| MUSTACHO | Maxfield |
| TRINCULO | L. Hallam |
| VENTOSO | Cushing |
| ARIEL | Mrs Kennedy |
| CALIBAN | Paget |
| NEPTUNE* | Brett |
| MIRANDA* | Mrs Daniel |
| DORINDA | Mrs Cushing |
| SYCORAX | *Mr* Dove |
| AMPHITRITE* | Miss Lincoln |

*Dec. 4*

| | |
|---|---|
| PROSPERO | Furnival |
| FERDINAND | Kennedy |
| HIPPOLITO | Mrs Phillips |
| ARIEL* | Mrs Kennedy |
| STEPHANO | Morgan |
| TRINCULO | L. Hallam |
| CALIBAN | Paget |
| ALONSO | Lee |
| ANTONIO | Dove |
| GONZALO | Blakey |
| VENTOSO | Cushing |
| MUSTACHO | Julian |
| SYCORAX | *Mr* [G.] Hallam |
| MIRANDA | Mrs [L.] Hallam |
| DORINDA | Mrs Cushing |

*Feb. 16, 18, 19*
omitted
NEPTUNE, AMPHITRITE

*Feb. 20, 21, 22, 23*

| | |
|---|---|
| FERDINAND | Kennedy |
| GONZALO | Townly |
| STEPHANO | Chettle |

omitted
NEPTUNE, AMPHITRITE

*Mar. 5*

| | |
|---|---|
| FERDINAND | Kennedy |
| GONZALO | Townly |
| STEPHANO | Chettle |

*Apr. 15*

| | |
|---|---|
| ANTONIO | Naylor |
| GONZALO | Townly |
| NEPTUNE | Cunningham |
| MIRANDA | Miss Haughto |
| AMPHITRITE | Mrs Carlisle |

*Dec. 5*

| | |
|---|---|
| ARIEL | Shepard |

*Dec. 26*

| | |
|---|---|
| PROSPERO | Furnival |
| ARIEL | Mrs Kennedy |

No other parts assigned

## THE TEMPEST

[*The original*]

LANE

4, 5, 18            *May 19*

[L.] Sparks      FRANCISCO Bransby
Delane           MIRANDA Mrs Mozeen [i.e. formerly
Bridges                          Miss Edwards]
Berry             omitted
Macklin           NEPTUNE, JUNO, IRIS, CERES, AMPHI-
Barrington        TRITE
I. Sparks
Marshall
Goodfellow
Woodburn
Blakes
Mrs Clive
Lowe
Miss Edwards
Mrs Arne
Miss [E.] Young
Mrs Sibilla
Mrs Arne

ubled JUNO and AMPHI-

*by* DRYDEN *and* DAVENANT *and in turn by* SHADWELL]
ELLS, GOODMAN'S FIELDS

Brett
Mrs Dove
assigned

LANE

                 *Dec. 29*

Berry             omitted
Lee                 ALONSO, GONZALO, ANTONIO, SYCORAX
Winstone
Burton
Mozeen
Mrs Clive
Arthur
Blakes
Ray
Vaughan
Macklin
I. Sparks
Mrs Woffington

THE TEMPEST [*as altered by* DRYDEN, *et al.*]

## 1747 DRURY LANE (cont.)
*Dec. 26, 28 (cont.)*

| | |
|---|---|
| SYCORAX* | *Mr* Taswell |
| MIRANDA | Mrs Mozeen |
| DORINDA | Mrs Green |

## NEW WELLS, GOODMAN'S FIELDS

*Jan. 16*

| | |
|---|---|
| PROSPERO | Furnival |
| FERDINAND | Goodfellow |
| ALONSO | Wignell |
| ANTONIO | Dove |
| GONZALO | Lee |
| HIPPOLITO | Mrs [L.] Hallam |
| STEPHANO | [W.] Hallam |
| MUSTACHO | Shuter |
| TRINCULO | L. Hallam |
| VENTOSO | Cushing |
| ARIEL | Mrs Moreau |
| CALIBAN | Paget |
| NEPTUNE | Brett |
| MIRANDA | Mrs Wignell |
| DORINDA* | Miss Budgell |
| SYCORAX | *Mr* [G.] Hallam |
| AMPHITRITE | Mrs Cushing |

*Jan. 19, 20; Feb. 9, 26*

DORINDA    Mrs Cushing
    [Mrs Cushing doubled DORINDA and AMPHITRITE. On Feb. 9, 26 DA retains Miss Budgell as DORINDA.]

*Apr. 4*

ANTONIO    The Gentleman who has the
                Benefit [unidentified]
No other parts assigned

## 1748 DRURY LANE
*Apr. 11*

| | |
|---|---|
| PROSPERO | Berry |
| FERDINAND | Lee |
| ARIEL | Mrs Clive |
| ALONSO | Winstone |
| GONZALO | Burton |
| ANTONIO | Mozeen |
| STEPHANO | Arthur |
| MUSTACHO | Blakes |
| VENTOSO | Ray |
| CLERK | Vaughan |
| TRINCULO | Macklin |
| CALIBAN | I. Sparks |
| HIPPOLITO | Mrs Woffington |
| SYCORAX | *Mr* Taswell |
| MIRANDA | Mrs Mozeen |
| DORINDA | Mrs Green |

435

THE TEMPEST [as altered by DRYDEN, et al.]

## 1748 PHILLIPS'S BOOTH, BOWLING GREEN, SOUTH-WARK

*Sept. 7, 8, 9, 10, 12*

| | |
|---|---|
| PROSPERO | Goodman |
| HIPPOLITO | Mrs Morgan |
| FERDINAND | Trye |
| ANTONIO | Brown |
| GONZALO | Betts |
| ALONSO | Machen |
| STEPHANO | Smith |
| MUSTACHO | Palmer |
| VENTOSO | Richardson |
| TRINCULO | Morgan |
| CALIBAN | Paget |
| ARIEL | Master Paget |
| SYCORAX | *Mr* Simms |
| MIRANDA | Mrs Roberts |
| DORINDA | Mrs Phillips |

[Bill in DA of Sept. 6, and reads, 'during the short Time of the [Southwark] Fair, which begins Tomorrow. To begin each Day at Twelve'. The same bill is in DA of Sept. 12, the last day of the Fair.]

## 1749 PHILLIPS'S BOOTH, SMITHFIELD

*Aug. 23, 24, 25, 26, 28*

| | |
|---|---|
| PROSPERO | Bruodin |
| ALONSO | Platt |
| ANTONIO | Reynolds |
| FERDINAND | Walker |
| GONZALO | Hall |
| VENTOSO | Smith |
| STEPHANO | Massey |
| MUSTACHO | Green |
| CALIBAN | Machen |
| TRINCULO | Morgan |
| ARIEL | Miss Platt |
| HIPPOLITO | Mrs Morgan |
| SYCORAX | Mrs Miller |
| MIRANDA | Mrs Sandum |
| DORINDA | Miss Laguerre |

[Bills in DA of Aug. 21, 23, 25, 28, and read, 'A Droll . . . Taken from the celebrated Play of Shakespeare. During the Short Time of Bartholomew Fair. To begin each Day at Twelve.']

## 1750 DRURY LANE

*Jan. 1, 2*

| | |
|---|---|
| PROSPERO* | Bridges |
| FERDINAND | King |

*Jan. 5*

omitted
MIRANDA, DORINDA

436

THE TEMPEST [as altered by DRYDEN, et al.]

## 1750 DRURY LANE (cont.)

*Jan. 1, 2 (cont.)*

| | |
|---|---|
| TRINCULO | Yates |
| HIPPOLITO | Mrs Willoughby |
| CALIBAN | Blakes |
| STEPHANO* | Shuter |
| MUSTACHO* | James |
| VENTOSO* | Ray |
| ARIEL | Mrs Clive |
| NEPTUNE* | Beard |
| SYCORAX* | *Mr* Taswell |
| MIRANDA* | Miss Cole |
| DORINDA* | Mrs Green |
| AMPHITRITE* | Miss Norris |

*Jan. 19; Feb. 12*

PROSPERO  Berry
omitted
   NEPTUNE, AMPHITRITE

*Apr. 27*

| | |
|---|---|
| PROSPERO | Berry |
| MIRANDA | Mrs Yates |
| DORINDA | Miss Cole |

omitted
   STEPHANO, MUSTACHO, VENTOSO, NEPTUNE, SYCORAX, AMPHITRITE

## TIMON OF ATHENS

Adapted by Thomas Shadwell. In five acts.

1678   Henry Herringman.

Act I opens with *I. i. 1–95*, much altered, but maintaining the structure of the original. Then follow *I. i. 95–177*, practically verbatim, and *178–249*, considerably rewritten. The rest of the act is new: Timon speaks of his love for Melissa, but promises not to abandon his mistress, Evandra.

Act II opens with a new scene: Melissa is visited by Timon. Then follow *I. i. 266–96*, somewhat altered, and the whole of *I. ii.* through the masque. The remainder is new: Evandra fears that she will lose Timon's love; Demetrius reports that his master is penniless.

Act III consists of *II. ii. 134–243*, somewhat shortened; then a new scene: Apemantus reviles the state; then *III. i–iii*, condensed into one scene. Next are two new scenes: Alcibiades declares his love for Melissa, and Timon is told of his friends' ingratitude. Then follow *III. iv. 87–end*, enlarged, and a new scene: Evandra promises to remain loyal. The act ends with *III. vi. 29–end*, considerably rewritten.

Act IV is *IV. i*, slightly rewritten; *III. v*, expanded; and *IV. iii. 1–47*, reduced. A new scene follows: Evandra insists on sharing Timon's exile. Next are *IV. iii. 198–377*, and *V. i. 1–120*, both somewhat abridged. The last scene is new: Timon spurns Melissa.

Act V opens with a new, short love-scene between Timon and Evandra. Then follow *V. i. 139–end*, somewhat reduced, and *IV. iii. 48–176*, almost verbatim. The rest of the act is new: Athens capitulates to Alcibiades; Timon dies and Evandra stabs herself; Alcibiades repudiates Melissa, pardons Apemantus, and proclaims the Athenian democracy.

See Genest, i. 247–51; Odell, i. 46–8; Spencer, 282–7.

[as altered by SHADWELL]

## 1701 DRURY LANE

*Jan. 17.* No parts assigned

## TIMON OF ATHENS [*as altered by* SHADWELL]

### 1703 DRURY LANE
*May 24; July 5; Dec. 11.* No parts assigned
[Bill for July 5 in DC of July 3.]

### 1704 DRURY LANE
*Feb. 21; Dec. 6.* No parts assigned

### LINCOLN'S INN FIELDS
*Jan. 27.* No parts assigned

### 1705 DRURY LANE
*Jan. 26.* No parts assigned

### LINCOLN'S INN FIELDS
*Oct. 19.* No parts assigned

### 1706 DRURY LANE
*Jan. 1.* No parts assigned

### 1707 DRURY LANE
*Jan. 9; Feb. 11.* No parts assigned

*Oct. 29*
| | |
|---|---|
| POET | A Comedian newly arriv'd [unidentified] |
| APEMANTUS | Captain Griffin |

No other parts assigned

*Dec. 10*
| | |
|---|---|
| TIMON | Powell |
| POET | Penkethman |

No other parts assigned

### QUEEN'S
*June 27; July 16*
| | |
|---|---|
| TIMON | Mills |
| ALCIBIADES | Booth |
| APEMANTUS | Verbruggen |
| DEMETRIUS | Corey |
| POET | Norris |
| PHAEAX | Bullock |
| AELIUS | Johnson |
| EVANDRA | Mrs Porter |
| MELISSA | Mrs Bradshaw |
| CHLOE | Mrs Mills |

## TIMON OF ATHENS [as altered by SHADWELL]

### 1708 DRURY LANE
*July 1*

| TIMON | Mills |
| ALCIBIADES | Booth |
| APEMANTUS | Keene |
| AELIUS | Johnson |
| PHAEAX | Bullock |
| POET | Norris |
| DEMETRIUS | Corey |
| EVANDRA | Mrs Porter |
| MELISSA | Mrs Bradshaw |
| CHLOE | Mrs Mills |

### 1709 DRURY LANE
*Dec. 10*

| TIMON | Powell |
| ALCIBIADES | Booth |
| APEMANTUS | Keene |
| DEMETRIUS | Corey |
| CLEON | Norris |
| NICIAS | Pack |
| ISANDER | [F.] Leigh |
| ISIDORE | Miller |
| EVANDRA | Mrs Knight |
| MELISSA | Mrs Bradshaw |

[The assignment of CLEON, NICIAS, ISANDER, ISIDORE is conjectural. In the bill they are called SENATORS.]

*Dec. 29*

| TIMON | Powell |

No other parts assigned

### 1710 DRURY LANE
*May 5*

| TIMON | Powell |
| ALCIBIADES | Booth |
| APEMANTUS | Keene |
| EVANDRA | Mrs Knight |

No other parts assigned

### 1711 DRURY LANE
*Feb. 17; Oct. 30*

| TIMON | Powell |
| ALCIBIADES | Booth |
| APEMANTUS* | Keene |
| AELIUS | Johnson |
| CLEON* | Norris |
| PHAEAX | Bullock |
| ISANDER | [F.] Leigh |
| POET* | Penkethman |

*June 22*

| APEMANTUS | Mills |
| POET | Norris |

omitted
CLEON

439

## TIMON OF ATHENS [*as altered by* SHADWELL]

### 1711 DRURY LANE (cont.)
*Feb. 17, &c. (cont.)*

| | |
|---|---|
| EVANDRA | Mrs Knight |
| MELISSA | Mrs Bradshaw |

[In the bill for Feb. 17 AELIUS, CLEON, PHAEAX, ISANDER are called SENATORS.]

### 1712 DRURY LANE
*May 17.* No parts assigned

### 1714 DRURY LANE
*May 17*            *June 16.* No parts assigned

| | |
|---|---|
| TIMON | Powell |
| ALCIBIADES | Booth |
| APEMANTUS | Husband |
| NICIAS | Pack |
| PHAEAX | Bullock |
| ISANDER | Birkhead |
| ISIDORE | [F.] Leigh |
| THRASILLUS | Cross |
| AELIUS | Johnson |
| CLEON | Norris |
| DEMETRIUS | Corey |
| DIPHILUS | Ryan |
| OLD MAN | Boman |
| POET | Bickerstaff |
| EVANDRA | Mrs Porter |
| MELISSA | Mrs Bradshaw |

### 1715 DRURY LANE
*Nov. 17; Dec. 27*      *Nov. 22.* No parts assigned

| | |
|---|---|
| TIMON | Booth |

No other parts assigned

### LINCOLN'S INN FIELDS
*Mar. 24; Apr. 22; Nov. 11.* No parts assigned

### 1716 DRURY LANE
*Feb. 28; May 16.* No parts assigned
*Oct. 18*

| | |
|---|---|
| TIMON | Booth |

No other parts assigned

440

## TIMON OF ATHENS [*as altered by* SHADWELL]

### 1716 LINCOLN'S INN FIELDS
*May 2.* No parts assigned
*Nov. 22*
   TIMON      Keene
No other parts assigned

### 1717 DRURY LANE
*Jan. 29*
   TIMON      Booth
   EVANDRA   Mrs Porter
No other parts assigned

*Oct. 11*
added
   APEMANTUS   Mills

### LINCOLN'S INN FIELDS
*Mar. 23*
   TIMON      Keene
No other parts assigned

### 1718 DRURY LANE
*May 2*
   TIMON      Booth
No other parts assigned

### LINCOLN'S INN FIELDS
*Jan. 10.* No parts assigned
*Feb. 27*
   TIMON      Keene
No other parts assigned

### 1719 DRURY LANE
*Nov. 24*
   TIMON      Booth
   APEMANTUS   Mills
   EVANDRA   Mrs Porter
No other parts assigned

### 1720 DRURY LANE
*May 20*
   TIMON      Booth
   APEMANTUS   Mills
   POET       Penkethman
   AELIUS     Johnson
   ISANDER   Miller
   CLEON     Norris
   NICIAS    Shepard
   THRASILLUS   Cross
   EVANDRA*   Mrs Porter

*Dec. 8*
   EVANDRA   Mrs Thurmond
added
   ALCIBIADES   Walker
   MELISSA   Mrs Horton

[The assignment of AELIUS, ISANDER, CLEON, NICIAS, THRASILLUS is conjectural. In the bills for May 20 and Dec. 8 they are called SENATORS.]

TIMON OF ATHENS [*as altered by* SHADWELL]

## 1720 DRURY LANE (cont.)
*Oct. 18*
    TIMON      Booth
No other parts assigned

## 1721 DRURY LANE
*May 24*
    TIMON         Booth
    APEMANTUS  Mills
    ALCIBIADES* Walker
    AELIUS      Johnson
    ISANDER     Miller
    CLEON       Norris
    NICIAS      Shepard
    THRASILLUS Cross
    POET        Penkethman
    EVANDRA   Mrs Thurmond
    MELISSA   Mrs Horton

*Oct. 10*
    ALCIBIADES  Williams
added
    DEMETRIUS   Watson

[The assignment of AELIUS, ISANDER, CLEON, NICIAS, THRASILLUS is conjectural. In both bills they are called SENATORS.]

## 1722 DRURY LANE
*May 29*
    TIMON       Booth
    APEMANTUS  Mills
    ALCIBIADES  Williams
    DEMETRIUS   Symmons
    POET        Penkethman
    AELIUS      Johnson
    ISANDER     Miller
    CLEON       Norris
    NICIAS      Shepard
    THRASILLUS Cross
    EVANDRA   Mrs Thurmond
    MELISSA   Mrs Horton

[The assignment of AELIUS, ISANDER, CLEON, NICIAS, THRASILLUS is conjectural. In the bill they are called SENATORS.]

## 1723 DRURY LANE
*May 20*
    TIMON       Booth
    APEMANTUS  Mills
    ALCIBIADES  Williams
    DEMETRIUS   Corey
    POET        Penkethman
    AELIUS      Johnson
    ISANDER     Miller
    CLEON       Norris
    NICIAS      Shepard

*Dec. 30*
omitted
    THRASILLUS

[The assignment of AELIUS, ISANDER, CLEON, NICIAS, THRASILLUS, PHAEAX is conjectural. In both bills they are called SENATORS.]

442

## 1723 DRURY LANE (cont.)
*May 20 (cont.)*

| | |
|---|---|
| THRASILLUS* | Cross |
| PHAEAX | Harper |
| EVANDRA | Mrs Thurmond |
| MELISSA | Mrs Horton |

## 1724 DRURY LANE
*May 5*

*Nov. 17.* No parts assigned

| | |
|---|---|
| TIMON | Booth |
| APEMANTUS | Mills |
| ALCIBIADES | Williams |
| DEMETRIUS | Corey |
| POET | Penkethman |
| AELIUS | Johnson |
| ISANDER | Miller |
| CLEON | Norris |
| NICIAS | Shepard |
| PHAEAX | Harper |
| THRASILLUS | Cross |
| EVANDRA | Mrs Thurmond |
| MELISSA | Mrs Horton |

[The assignment of AELIUS, ISANDER, CLEON, NICIAS, PHAEAX, THRASILLUS is conjectural. In the bill they are called SENATORS.]

## 1725 DRURY LANE
*Jan. 21; Mar. 29; Nov. 26.* No parts assigned

*May 11*

| | |
|---|---|
| TIMON | Booth |
| ALCIBIADES | Williams |
| APEMANTUS | Mills |
| DEMETRIUS | Corey |
| AELIUS | Johnson |
| CLEON | Norris |
| NICIAS | Shepard |
| ISANDER | Miller |
| PHAEAX | Harper |
| POET | [T.] Cibber |
| EVANDRA | Mrs Thurmond |
| MELISSA | Mrs Horton |

## TIMON OF ATHENS [as altered by SHADWELL]

### 1726 DRURY LANE
*Feb. 12.* No parts assigned
*May 23*

| | |
|---|---|
| TIMON | Booth |
| APEMANTUS | Mills |
| ALCIBIADES | Bridgwater |
| DEMETRIUS | Corey |
| AELIUS | Johnson |
| ISANDER | Griffin |
| CLEON | Norris |
| PHAEAX | Harper |
| NICIAS | Shepard |
| POET | [T.] Cibber |
| EVANDRA | Mrs Thurmond |
| MELISSA | Mrs Horton |
| CHLOE | Mrs Baker |

### 1729 DRURY LANE
*Apr. 23; May 26; Nov. 27*

| | |
|---|---|
| TIMON | Mills |
| ALCIBIADES | Bridgwater |
| APEMANTUS | W. Mills |
| DEMETRIUS | Corey |
| POET | [T.] Cibber |
| NICIAS | Shepard |
| PHAEAX | Harper |
| AELIUS | Johnson |
| CLEON | Griffin |
| ISANDER | Norris |
| EVANDRA | Mrs Thurmond |
| MELISSA | Mrs Horton |

### 1730 DRURY LANE
*Oct. 31; Dec. 18.* No parts assigned

### 1731 DRURY LANE
*Oct. 21*

| | |
|---|---|
| TIMON | Mills |
| ALCIBIADES | Bridgwater |
| APEMANTUS | Wm. Mills |
| AELIUS | Johnson |
| PHAEAX | Harper |
| CLEON | Griffin |
| NICIAS | Shepard |
| ISANDER | [T.] Hallam |
| ISIDORE | Wetherilt [Sr.] |
| POET | Theoph. Cibber |
| EVANDRA | Mrs Thurmond |
| MELISSA | Mrs Butler |

## TIMON OF ATHENS [as altered by SHADWELL]

### 1732 DRURY LANE
*Jan. 6.* The bill for this performance is missing

### 1733 DRURY LANE
*Apr. 18*
| | |
|---|---|
| TIMON | Mills |
| EVANDRA | Mrs Horton |

[The bill for this performance is missing. The above assignment is taken, complete, from Genest (iii. 372).]

*Nov. 23*
| | |
|---|---|
| TIMON | Bridgwater |
| ALCIBIADES | Marshall |
| APEMANTUS | William Giffard |
| AELIUS | Aston |
| PHAEAX | Mullart |
| NICIAS | Hewson |
| DEMETRIUS | Paget |
| ISANDER | Topham |
| THRASILLUS | Jones |
| POET | Norris [Jr.] |
| MELISSA | Mrs Mullart |
| CHLOE | Miss Morse |
| EVANDRA | Mrs Horton |

### COVENT GARDEN
*May 1, 29*
| | |
|---|---|
| TIMON | Milward |
| ALCIBIADES | Walker |
| APEMANTUS | Quin |
| NICIAS | Salway |
| PHAEAX | Hippisley |
| AELIUS | Neale |
| CLEON | Dyer |
| ISANDER | Hall |
| ISIDORE | H. Bullock |
| THRASILLUS | [A.] Hallam |
| DEMETRIUS | Paget |
| DIPHILUS | Houghton |
| OLD MAN | Aston |
| POET | Chapman |
| PAINTER | Wilcox |
| MUSICIAN | Ray |
| JEWELLER | Harrington |
| 1ST GENTLEMAN | Hale |
| 2ND GENTLEMAN | Clarke |
| EVANDRA | Mrs Hallam |

## TIMON OF ATHENS [as altered by SHADWELL]

### 1733 COVENT GARDEN (cont.)
*May 1, 29 (cont.)*

| | |
|---|---|
| MELISSA | Mrs Buchanan |
| CHLOE | Mrs Stevens |
| THAIS | Mrs Forrester |
| PHRYNE | Mrs Kilby |

### 1734 COVENT GARDEN
*Mar. 28*                                        *May 15*

| | | |
|---|---|---|
| TIMON | Walker | omitted |
| ALCIBIADES | Ryan | CHLOE |
| APEMANTUS | Quin | |
| POET | Chapman | |
| NICIAS | Salway | |
| PHAEAX | Hippisley | |
| AELIUS | Neale | |
| CLEON | Dawson | |
| ISANDER | Hall | |
| ISIDORE | Bullock [Sr.] | |
| THRASILLUS | [A.] Hallam | |
| DEMETRIUS | Hale | |
| DIPHILUS | Houghton | |
| OLD MAN | Aston | |
| MUSICIAN | Ray | |
| JEWELLER | Harrington | |
| 1ST GENTLEMAN | Wignell | |
| 2ND GENTLEMAN | Clarke | |
| EVANDRA | Mrs Hallam | |
| MELISSA | Mrs Buchanan | |
| CHLOE* | Mrs Stevens | |
| THAIS | Mrs Forrester | |
| PHRYNE | Mrs Kilby | |

### 1735 DRURY LANE
*Sept. 18; Dec. 8*

| | |
|---|---|
| TIMON | Milward |
| ALCIBIADES | W. Mills |
| APEMANTUS | Quin |
| AELIUS | Johnson |
| ISANDER | Miller |
| CLEON | Griffin |
| NICIAS | Shepard |
| THRASILLUS | Winstone |
| PHAEAX | Harper |
| DEMETRIUS | Turbutt |
| POET | Oates |
| EVANDRA | Mrs Thurmond |
| MELISSA | Mrs Cantrell |
| CHLOE | Mrs Cross |

446

## TIMON OF ATHENS [as altered by SHADWELL]

### 1736 DRURY LANE
*Feb. 25*

| | |
|---|---|
| TIMON | Milward |
| ALCIBIADES | W. Mills |
| APEMANTUS | Quin |
| AELIUS | Johnson |
| ISANDER | Miller |
| CLEON* | Griffin |
| NICIAS | Shepard |
| THRASILLUS | Winstone |
| PHAEAX | Harper |
| DEMETRIUS | Turbutt |
| POET | Oates |
| EVANDRA | Mrs Thurmond |
| MELISSA* | Mrs Cantrell |
| CHLOE* | Mrs Cross |

*Nov. 19*

| | |
|---|---|
| MELISSA | Mrs Pritchard |

*Dec. 27*

| | |
|---|---|
| CLEON | Macklin |
| MELISSA | Mrs Pritchard |
| CHLOE | Miss Brett |

### GOODMAN'S FIELDS
*Feb. 27, 28; Mar. 5.* No parts assigned

### 1737 DRURY LANE
*Feb. 21*

| | |
|---|---|
| TIMON | Milward |
| ALCIBIADES | W. Mills |
| APEMANTUS | Quin |
| AELIUS | Johnson |
| ISANDER | Miller |
| CLEON | Macklin |
| NICIAS | Shepard |
| THRASILLUS | Winstone |
| PHAEAX | Harper |
| DEMETRIUS | Turbutt |
| POET | Oates |
| EVANDRA | Mrs Thurmond |
| MELISSA | Mrs Pritchard |
| CHLOE | Mrs Cross |

### 1740 DRURY LANE
*Mar. 20; Apr. 7*

| | |
|---|---|
| TIMON | Milward |
| APEMANTUS | Quin |
| ALCIBIADES | [W.] Mills |
| POET | Woodward |
| AELIUS | Johnson |
| NICIAS | Shepard |

447

## 1740 DRURY LANE (cont.)

*Mar. 20, &c. (cont.)*

| | |
|---|---|
| ISANDER | Winstone |
| ISIDORE | Taswell |
| CLEON | Ray |
| PHAEAX | Marten |
| THRASILLUS | Reed |
| DEMETRIUS | Turbutt |
| PAGE | Miss Cole |
| MELISSA | Mrs Pritchard |
| EVANDRA | Mrs Butler |
| CHLOE | Mrs Bennet |

## 1741 DRURY LANE

*May 13*

| | |
|---|---|
| TIMON | Milward |
| APEMANTUS | Quin |
| ALCIBIADES | Cashell |
| AELIUS | Johnson |
| POET | Woodward |
| NICIAS | Shepard |
| ISIDORE | Taswell |
| ISANDER | Winstone |
| PHAEAX | Marten |
| THRASILLUS | Woodburn |
| DEMETRIUS | Turbutt |
| EVANDRA | Mrs Butler |
| MELISSA | Mrs Pritchard |

## GOODMAN'S FIELDS

*Mar. 19*

| | |
|---|---|
| TIMON | Marshall |
| ALCIBIADES | Walker |
| APEMANTUS | Paget |
| POET | Yates |
| NICIAS | Julian |
| PHAEAX | Dunstall |
| AELIUS | Marr |
| CLEON | Shawford |
| DEMETRIUS | Blakes |
| MELISSA | Mrs Steel |
| CHLOE | Miss Hippisley |
| THAIS | Mrs Jones |
| PHRYNE | Mrs Dunstall |
| EVANDRA | Mrs Giffard |

TIMON OF ATHENS [as altered by SHADWELL]

## 1745 COVENT GARDEN

*Apr. 20*  *Nov. 22; Dec. 30*

| | | | |
|---|---|---|---|
| APEMANTUS* | Quin | APEMANTUS | Johnson |
| TIMON | Hale | JEWELLER | Paddick |
| PHAEAX | Hippisley | MELISSA | Mrs Hale |
| POET | [T.] Cibber | omitted | |
| ALCIBIADES | Cashell | ISANDER, DIPHILUS | |
| AELIUS | Chapman | | |
| ISANDER* | Woodward | | |
| NICIAS | Marten | | |
| CLEON | Arthur | | |
| DEMETRIUS | Ridout | | |
| ISIDORE | Dunstall | | |
| THRASILLUS | Rosco | | |
| DIPHILUS* | Hayman | | |
| JEWELLER* | Anderson | | |
| PAINTER | James | | |
| OLD MAN | Gibson | | |
| MELISSA* | Mrs Clive | | |
| CHLOE | Miss Hippisley | | |
| THAIS | Mrs Bland | | |
| PHRYNE | Mrs Rowley | | |
| EVANDRA | Mrs Pritchard | | |

## TITUS ANDRONICUS

Adapted by Edward Ravenscroft. In five acts.

1687   J. Hindmarsh.

Act I, scene i is *I. i. 1–63*, almost verbatim. Scene ii begins with *I. i. 64–120*, continues with *121–56*, entirely rewritten, and ends with *157–78*, slightly reduced. Scene iii is *I. i. 179–289*, occasionally altered.

Act II consists of *I. i. 290–end*, slightly enlarged; and *II. i*, somewhat enlarged and occasionally rewritten.

Act III is *II. iii*, a little altered (Quintus and Martius do not fall into the pit, &c.); and *II. iv*, almost verbatim.

Act IV begins with *III. i. 1–233*, slightly enlarged. Then follow *IV. i. 1–80*, reduced; *III. i. 234–66*; *IV. i. 81–94*, enlarged; and *III. i. 288–end*.

Act V begins with *IV. ii. 52–end*, almost verbatim, save for the introduction of the Nurse's husband. Then follow *IV. iv* and *V. ii. 1–120*, intermingled and considerably expanded: Chiron and Demetrius are lured by gold to their deaths, which occur off stage. Then follow *V. i. 1–19*, almost verbatim; and *V. ii. 148–end*, with very slight revisions. The act ends with *V. iii*, much expanded: Aaron is tortured and finally burned to death on the stage.

See Genest, i. 232; Odell, i. 44–6; Spencer, 288–92.

## TITUS ANDRONICUS
### [as altered by RAVENSCROFT]

### 1704 DRURY LANE
*Aug. 23; Sept. 16; Nov. 17.* No parts assigned

### 1717 DRURY LANE
*Aug. 13, 16, 20, 23*

| | |
|---|---|
| TITUS | Mills |
| SATURNINUS | Thurmond |
| BASSIANUS | Walker |
| MARCUS | Boman |
| LUCIUS | Ryan |
| AARON | Quin |

### 1718 DRURY LANE
*July 8*

| | |
|---|---|
| TITUS | Mills |
| SATURNINUS | Thurmond |
| BASSIANUS | Walker |
| MARCUS | Boman |
| LUCIUS | Williams |
| AARON | Bickerstaff |

### 1719 DRURY LANE
*July 28*

| | |
|---|---|
| TITUS | Mills |

No other parts assigned

### 1720 LINCOLN'S INN FIELDS
*Dec. 21, 30*

| | |
|---|---|
| TITUS | Boheme |
| LUCIUS | Ryan |
| SATURNINUS | [J.] Leigh |
| AARON | Quin |
| TAMORA | Mrs Giffard |
| LAVINIA | Mrs Knapp |

### 1721 DRURY LANE
*June 27*

| | |
|---|---|
| TITUS | Mills |
| SATURNINUS | Thurmond |
| MARCUS | Boman |
| LUCIUS | Williams |
| AARON | Walker |

## TITUS ANDRONICUS [*as altered by* RAVENSCROFT]

### 1721 LINCOLN'S INN FIELDS
*Feb. 7*

| TITUS | Boheme |
| LUCIUS | Ryan |
| SATURNINUS | [J.] Leigh |
| AARON | Quin |
| TAMORA | Mrs Giffard |
| LAVINIA | Mrs Knapp |

### 1722 LINCOLN'S INN FIELDS
*Aug. 1*

| TITUS | Boheme |
| SATURNINUS | [J.] Leigh |
| BASSIANUS | Orfeur |
| MARCUS | Ogden |
| LUCIUS | Hulett |
| GOTH | Morgan |
| AARON | Walker |
| TAMORA | Mrs Seymour |
| LAVINIA | Mrs Morgan |

### 1724 LINCOLN'S INN FIELDS
*Mar. 19*

| AARON | Quin |
| TITUS | Boheme |
| SATURNINUS | [J.] Leigh |
| BASSIANUS | Walker |
| LUCIUS | Ryan |
| MARCUS | Ogden |
| DEMETRIUS | Diggs |
| CHIRON | Ward |
| TAMORA* | Mrs Egleton |
| LAVINIA | Mrs Sterling |

*Apr. 25*

| TAMORA | Mrs Knight |

## TROILUS AND CRESSIDA

Adapted by John Dryden. In five acts.

1679 Jacob Tonson.

Act I, scene i is *I. iii. 10–210*. Scene ii is *I. i* and *ii*. In this scene Alexander's speeches are given to Aeneas.

Act II, scene i is *II. ii*, with about 160 new lines at the end in which Andromache encourages Hector to fight. The scene ends with Hector speaking Aeneas's challenge from *I. iii. 265–83*. Scene ii is new: Pandarus abetting in turn Cressida and Troilus. The last 20 lines are *III. ii. 17–39*, almost verbatim. Scene iii begins with *I. iii. 312–end*, followed by about 125 new lines, describing Thersites, and by *II. i*.

Act III, scene i is *II. iii. 1–74*, followed by about 25 new lines, continuing the argument between Thersites and Patroclus; by *III. iii. 263–end*; and by *II. iii. 84–end*. Scene ii begins with *III. ii. 40–end*, and is followed by *III. iii. 1–37*, wholly rewritten; and by *IV. ii. 23–60*, in which Hector has Aeneas's speeches. The scene ends with a long dialogue, entirely new, between Hector and Troilus, concerning the latter's struggle between love and duty.

Act IV, scene i is *IV. ii. 77–106* and *IV. iv. 11–85*, without interruption, with about 40 new lines at the end, continuing the farewell between Troilus and Cressida. Scene ii consists of *III. iii. 37–79, 193–228*; of *IV. v. 1–11, 65–94, 116–64, 182–end*; and of *V. i* and *ii* entire. The remainder is new: Pandarus convinces Troilus that Cressida is false, and Troilus and Diomedes fight.

Act V is wholly new. Andromache fears for Hector's safety; in the battle Cressida interrupts another fight between Troilus and Diomedes, asserts that she has been faithful, and, when Troilus refuses to believe her, stabs herself; Troilus renews the fight with Diomedes; both are killed; Achilles kills Hector. An occasional passage from the original (*V. vii. 14–25*, &c.) is retained.

Throughout the play Shakespeare's dialogue is but little tampered with; it is, however, nearly always abridged.

See Genest, i. 267–9; Odell, i. 48–51; Spencer, 223–31.

[*as altered by* DRYDEN]

## 1709 DRURY LANE

*June 2*

| | |
|---|---|
| THERSITES | Betterton |
| TROILUS | Wilks |
| HECTOR | Powell |
| AGAMEMNON | Mills |
| ACHILLES | Booth |
| AJAX | Keene |
| ULYSSES | Thurmond |
| NESTOR | Corey |
| PRIAM | Fairbank |
| DIOMEDES | Husband |
| MENELAUS | Birkhead |
| AENEAS | Bickerstaff |
| PANDARUS | Estcourt |
| CRESSIDA | Mrs Bradshaw |
| ANDROMACHE | Mrs Rogers |

## 1720 LINCOLN'S INN FIELDS

*Nov. 10, 11, 12*

| | |
|---|---|
| TROILUS | Ryan |
| HECTOR | Quin |
| ACHILLES | [J.] Leigh |
| ULYSSES | Boheme |
| AGAMEMNON | Diggs |
| DIOMEDES | Egleton |

TROILUS AND CRESSIDA [*as altered by* DRYDEN]

### 1720 LINCOLN'S INN FIELDS (cont.)
*Nov. 10, 11, 12 (cont.)*

| | |
|---|---|
| AJAX | Harper |
| THERSITES | Bullock Sr. |
| PANDARUS | Spiller |
| CRESSIDA | Mrs Seymour |
| ANDROMACHE | Mrs Bullock |

### 1721 LINCOLN'S INN FIELDS
*Feb. 18*

| | |
|---|---|
| PANDARUS | Spiller |
| TROILUS | Ryan |
| HECTOR | Quin |
| ACHILLES | [J.] Leigh |
| ULYSSES | Boheme |
| AGAMEMNON | Diggs |
| DIOMEDES | Egleton |
| AJAX | Harper |
| THERSITES | Bullock Sr. |
| CRESSIDA | Mrs Seymour |
| ANDROMACHE | Mrs Giffard |

### 1723 LINCOLN'S INN FIELDS
*May 3*

| | |
|---|---|
| HECTOR | Boheme |
| TROILUS | Ryan |
| ULYSSES | Walker |
| ACHILLES* | Hulett |
| AGAMEMNON | Diggs |
| DIOMEDES | Egleton |
| PANDARUS | Hippisley |
| THERSITES | Quin |
| CRESSIDA* | Mrs Boheme |
| ANDROMACHE* | Mrs Bullock |

*May 25.* No parts assigned

*Nov. 21*

| | |
|---|---|
| ACHILLES | [J.] Leigh |
| CRESSIDA | Mrs Sterling |
| ANDROMACHE | Mrs Knight |

### 1733 COVENT GARDEN
*Dec. 20*

| | |
|---|---|
| TROILUS | Ryan |
| HECTOR | Walker |
| PRIAM | Morgan |
| AENEAS | Houghton |
| CALCHAS | Neale |
| AGAMEMNON | [J.] Lacy |
| ACHILLES | Hale |
| ULYSSES | Aston |
| DIOMEDES | Chapman |
| AJAX | Hall |

TROILUS AND CRESSIDA [as altered by DRYDEN]

## 1733 COVENT GARDEN (cont.)

*Dec. 20 (cont.)*

| | |
|---|---|
| NESTOR | Dawson |
| MENELAUS | Wignell |
| PATROCLUS | Salway |
| THERSITES | Quin |
| PANDARUS | Hippisley |
| ANDROMACHE | Mrs Buchanan |
| CRESSIDA | Mrs Bullock |

## 1734 COVENT GARDEN

*Jan. 7*

| | |
|---|---|
| TROILUS | Ryan |
| ACHILLES | Hale |
| ULYSSES | Aston |
| DIOMEDES | Chapman |
| AJAX | Hall |
| HECTOR | Walker |
| PRIAM | Morgan |
| AENEAS | Houghton |
| PANDARUS | Hippisley |
| AGAMEMNON | [J.] Lacy |
| CALCHAS | Neale |
| PATROCLUS | Salway |
| MENELAUS | Wignell |
| THERSITES | Quin |
| ANDROMACHE | Mrs Buchanan |
| CRESSIDA | Mrs Bullock |

# TWELFTH NIGHT

Adapted as LOVE BETRAYED, by William Burnaby. In five acts.

1703  D. Brown [&c.].

The plot follows that of the original with reasonable fidelity, but the dialogue has been almost wholly rewritten, chiefly in prose. About 50 lines of the original, scattered throughout the play, are retained. Among these, in Act II, are *I. i. 1–3; II. iv. 109–16; II. v. 262–3*, &c.

See Genest, ii. 291–2; Odell, i. 81–3; Spencer, 350–3.
No acting versions of the original were published before 1750.

## TWELFTH NIGHT
### [as LOVE BETRAYED]

### 1703 LINCOLN'S INN FIELDS
*n.d., probably Feb.*

| | |
|---|---|
| MORENO | Verbruggen |
| DRANCES | Powell |
| SEBASTIAN | Booth |
| TAQUILET | Dogget |
| RODOREGUE | Fieldhouse |
| PEDRO | Pack |
| VILLARETTA | Mrs Bracegirdle |
| CAESARIO | Mrs Prince |
| DROMIA | Mrs Leigh |
| LAWRA | Mrs Lawson |

[The bill for this (the first) performance is missing. The above assignment is taken from the printed text.]

### 1705 LINCOLN'S INN FIELDS
*Mar. 1.* No parts assigned

### [*The original*]

### 1741 DRURY LANE
*Jan. 15, 17, 19, 20, 21, 22, 23*      *Feb. 5; Apr. 20*

| | | | |
|---|---|---|---|
| ORSINO | [W.] Mills | SEBASTIAN | Havard |
| SEBASTIAN* | Milward | | |
| SIR TOBY | Shepard | | |
| SIR ANDREW | Woodward | | |
| MALVOLIO | Macklin | | |
| CLOWN | Chapman | | |
| ANTONIO | Cashell | | |
| FABIAN | Winstone | | |
| CAPTAIN | Turbutt | | |
| VALENTINE | Ridout | | |
| CURIO | Green | | |
| OFFICER | Marten | | |
| PRIEST | Woodburn | | |
| MARIA | Mrs Macklin | | |
| VIOLA | Mrs Pritchard | | |
| OLIVIA | Mrs Clive | | |

### 1746 DRURY LANE
*Apr. 15, 18*

| | |
|---|---|
| ORSINO | [W.] Mills |
| SEBASTIAN | Havard |
| SIR TOBY | I. Sparks |
| SIR ANDREW | Neale |
| CLOWN | Yates |
| MALVOLIO | Macklin |

455

## TWELFTH NIGHT

### 1746 DRURY LANE (cont.)
*Apr. 15, 18 (cont.)*

| | |
|---|---|
| ANTONIO | Bridges |
| VALENTINE | Usher |
| FABIAN | Winstone |
| CAPTAIN | Goodfellow |
| CURIO | Bransby |
| 1ST OFFICER | Simpson |
| 2ND OFFICER | Leigh [Jr.] |
| OLIVIA | Mrs Clive |
| MARIA | Mrs Macklin |
| VIOLA | Mrs Woffington |

### 1748 DRURY LANE
*Jan. 6, 7*

| | |
|---|---|
| ORSINO | [W.] Mills |
| SEBASTIAN | Havard |
| SIR TOBY | Berry |
| SIR ANDREW* | Neale |
| ANTONIO* | [I.] Sparks |
| VALENTINE | Usher |
| FABIAN | Winstone |
| CAPTAIN | Blakes |
| MALVOLIO* | Macklin |
| CLOWN | Yates |
| CURIO | Bransby |
| PRIEST* | Raftor |
| 1ST OFFICER* | Simpson |
| 2ND OFFICER* | Leigh [Jr.] |
| OLIVIA | Mrs Clive |
| MARIA* | Mrs Macklin |
| VIOLA | Mrs Pritchard |

[MALVOLIO appears as above. Genest (iv. 236) has 'Malvolio is omitted—the part belonged to Macklin'.]

*Nov. 9*

| | |
|---|---|
| SIR ANDREW | Woodward |
| MALVOLIO | Neale |
| MARIA | Mrs Green |

omitted
   ANTONIO, PRIEST, OFFICERS

[MALVOLIO appears as above. Genest (iv. 261) has, 'Malvolio is omitted'.]

### 1749 DRURY LANE
*Jan. 7*

| | |
|---|---|
| ORSINO | [W.] Mills |
| SEBASTIAN | Havard |
| SIR TOBY | Berry |
| SIR ANDREW | Woodward |
| CURIO* | Bransby |
| VALENTINE | Usher |
| FABIAN | Winstone |
| CAPTAIN | Blakes |
| MALVOLIO | Neale |
| CLOWN | Yates |

*Oct. 28*

| | |
|---|---|
| CURIO | Paddick |

# TWELFTH NIGHT

## 1749 DRURY LANE (cont.)
*Jan. 7 (cont.)*

| | |
|---|---|
| OLIVIA | Mrs Clive |
| MARIA | Mrs Green |
| VIOLA | Mrs Pritchard |

## THE UNIVERSAL PASSION

James Miller's alteration of MUCH ADO ABOUT NOTHING, q.v.

## THE WINTER'S TALE

No acting versions of the original were published before 1750.

### 1741 COVENT GARDEN
*Nov. 11, 12, 13*

| | |
|---|---|
| POLIXENES | Ryan |
| LEONTES | Stephens |
| FLORIZEL | Hale |
| CAMILLO | Bridgwater |
| ANTIGONUS | Rosco |
| AUTOLYCUS* | Chapman |
| DIOCLES | Cashell |
| CLEOMENES | Goodall |
| DION | Stevens |
| 1ST LORD | Lascells |
| 2ND LORD | Harrington |
| TIME | Gibson |
| SHEPHERD | Marten |
| CLOWN | Hippisley |
| HERMIONE | Mrs Horton |
| PERDITA | Mrs Hale |
| EMILIA | Mrs Mullart |
| PAULINA | Mrs Pritchard |

*Nov. 14*

omitted
AUTOLYCUS

### GOODMAN'S FIELDS
*Jan. 15, 16, 17, 19, 21, 23, 24, 26*

| | |
|---|---|
| LEONTES | Giffard |
| POLIXENES | Marshall |
| ANTIGONUS | Walker |
| FLORIZEL | W. Giffard |
| CAMILLO | Paget |
| AUTOLYCUS | Yates |
| MAMILLIUS | Miss Naylor |
| CLEOMENES | Blakes |

457

## 1741 GOODMAN'S FIELDS (cont.)

*Jan. 15, &c. (cont.)*

| | |
|---|---|
| DION | Peterson |
| OFFICER | Naylor |
| 1ST LORD | Crofts |
| 2ND LORD | Nelson |
| 3RD LORD | Marr |
| SHEPHERD | Julian |
| CLOWN | Dunstall |
| PAULINA | Mrs Steel |
| PERDITA | Miss Hippisley |
| EMILIA | Mrs Yates |
| MOPSA | Mrs Dunstall |
| DORCAS | Mrs Jones |
| HERMIONE | Mrs Giffard |

*Apr. 10*

| | |
|---|---|
| PAULINA | Mrs Steel |

No other parts assigned

## 1742 COVENT GARDEN

*Jan. 21*

| | |
|---|---|
| POLIXENES | Ryan |
| LEONTES | Stephens |
| FLORIZEL | Hale |
| CAMILLO | Bridgwater |
| ANTIGONUS | Rosco |
| DIOCLES | Cashell |
| CLEOMENES | Goodall |
| DION | Stevens |
| 1ST LORD | Lascells |
| 2ND LORD | Harrington |
| TIME | Gibson |
| SHEPHERD | Marten |
| CLOWN | Hippisley |
| AUTOLYCUS | Chapman |
| HERMIONE | Mrs Horton |
| PERDITA | Mrs Hale |
| EMILIA | Mrs Mullart |
| PAULINA | Mrs Pritchard |

## APPENDIX A

# SHAKESPEARE'S POPULARITY IN THE THEATRE, 1701-50

THE following summary must be considered as an approximation only. The records of many early performances are lost. It was not until 1708 that the *Daily Courant* began to publish with more or less dependable consistency the playbills for all the theatres. Even thereafter, an occasional performance, especially in the summer seasons that were maintained irregularly until about 1739, may not have been advertised.[1] Other matters, such as a last-minute change of play, 'dismissal', &c.—the details of which have long since perished—make it impossible to hope for a complete and definitive tabulation. And lastly the records of performances at the minor theatres (see Appendix C) are very difficult to find. These performances were frequently not announced in the newspapers at all, and, because they were unlicensed, the theatres themselves stood in constant peril of being closed—as indeed they often were, even after the audience had assembled.

The figures given below represent the number of performances at all the theatres. An analysis of each individual year seems cumbersome and needless; I present the figures, therefore, arranged in groups of five-year periods. The right-hand column includes both the original plays and their adaptations.

|         | Total number of plays performed | Number of plays by Shakespeare performed |
|---------|---------------------------------|------------------------------------------|
| 1701-5  | 1,100  | 79  |
| 1706-10 | 1,124  | 117 |
| 1711-15 | 1,184  | 163 |
| 1716-20 | 1,904  | 360 |
| 1721-5  | 1,961  | 344 |
| 1726-30 | 2,351  | 264 |
| 1731-5  | 2,838  | 434 |
| 1736-40 | 2,185  | 342 |
| 1741-5  | 2,202  | 640 |
| 1746-50 | 1,814  | 483 |
|         | 18,663 | 3,226 (of which 15 are double bills) |

At Drury Lane, Lincoln's Inn Fields, and Covent Garden the average number of plays acted each calendar year is 180; the average number of plays by Shakespeare acted each calendar year at those three theatres is 30, i.e. one in every 6. Although obviously not so in practice, this would mean that at all three theatres at least one play by Shakespeare was acted every week.

The highest figure is at Drury Lane in 1741: 93 performances of Shakespeare out of 191; the lowest is at Covent Garden in 1747: 10 out of 131.

[1] No plays at all were advertised on Dec. 8, 9, 10, 1712, on account of the cessation of publication of the *Spectator*. See p. x.

## APPENDIX B

## ORDER OF POPULARITY OF SHAKESPEARE'S PLAYS, 1701-50

FOLLOWING is a record of Shakespeare's plays in order of their relative popularity in the theatre from 1701 to 1750. After each play and each adaptation are listed the years in which it was acted and the number of performances it received. Of all the plays that were regularly in the repertory from the beginning of the century, only two, *Hamlet* and *Henry IV, Part I*, were performed uninterruptedly.

It will be observed that general favour was bestowed primarily on the tragedies. This has always been the case; it is the case today just as much as it was 200 years ago. An opinion of long standing is that Shakespeare's comedies were almost completely neglected in the first three decades of the eighteenth century. This does not appear to have been so. Several of them, it is true, were revived in the 1740's, but in various forms *The Merchant of Venice, Measure for Measure, The Tempest, The Merry Wives of Windsor, The Taming of the Shrew*, &c., had always been available to playgoers. The popularity of Falstaff was legendary on both sides of the footlights. The fact seems to be that two publishers, Tonson and Walker, were in large measure responsible for the growth of popular interest in Shakespeare that characterized the 1730's and 1740's. In 1734 they each began to issue, in very large editions and at very small cost, Shakespeare's plays in their entirety. A demand was created, and the theatres responded.

This response took two forms: the revival of many plays previously disregarded, and the gradual abandonment of altered versions. The plays that were then seen for the first time, as Shakespeare wrote them, were seven comedies: *All's Well, As You Like It, The Merchant of Venice, The Tempest, The Comedy of Errors, Twelfth Night*, and *The Winter's Tale*; five histories: *King John, Richard II, Henry IV, Part II, Henry V*, and *Henry VI, Part I*; and three tragedies: *Cymbeline, Macbeth*, and *Romeo and Juliet*. By 1746 the following alterations (at least at the patent theatres) had been shelved in favour of their originals: D'Urfey's *Cymbeline*, Betterton's *Henry IV, Part II, The Universal Passion, The Jew of Venice*, and *Caius Marius*; and Shadwell's *Timon of Athens*, Ravenscroft's *Titus Andronicus*, and Dryden's *Troilus and Cressida* had disappeared completely.

Bearing in mind the fact that the original *Merchant of Venice*, for example, and the original *Romeo and Juliet* were not revived until only a few years before 1750, one finds, I think, that the relative popularity of Shakespeare's plays in the period under discussion is by no means dissimilar to their relative popularity today.

| | |
|---|---|
| HAMLET (1703-50) | 358 |
| MACBETH | 287 |
|   As altered by Davenant (1702-46, 1749-50): 240 | |
|   The original (1744-50): 47 | |
| OTHELLO (1703-5, 1707-50) | 265 |
| HENRY IV, PART I (1704-50) | 214 |
| THE MERRY WIVES OF WINDSOR | 202 |
|   As *The Comical Gallant* (1702): 1 | |
|   The original (1704-5, 1720-50): 201 | |
| RICHARD III | 200 |
|   As altered by Cibber (1704, 1710, 1713-15, 1717-28, 1730, 1732-50) | |
| THE TEMPEST | 186 |
|   As altered by Dryden and Davenant and in turn by Shadwell (1701-2, 1704, 1706-8, 1710, 1712-27, 1729-35, 1737, 1739-41, 1745-50): 180 | |
|   The original (1746): 6 | |

# APPENDIX B

KING LEAR — 186
  As altered by Tate (1702–6, 1708–39, 1741–50)
JULIUS CAESAR (1704, 1706–7, 1709–10, 1712–29, 1732–45, 1747–50) — 163
HENRY VIII (1705, 1707–9, 1716–42, 1744–7, 1749) — 136
THE TAMING OF THE SHREW — 124
  As *Sauny the Scot* (1704, 1707–8, 1711–12, 1714, 1716–17, 1719–20, 1725, 1735–6): 29
  As Johnson's *The Cobler of Preston* (1716): 17
  As Bullock's *The Cobler of Preston* (1716–18, 1720–4, 1726, 1730–2, 1735, 1737–8, 1741, 1745): 71
  As *A Cure for a Scold* (1735, 1750): 7
THE MERCHANT OF VENICE — 115
  As *The Jew of Venice* (1701, 1706, 1711, 1715–23, 1727–32, 1734–6, 1739, 1748): 36
  The original (1741–50): 79
ROMEO AND JULIET — 96
  As *Caius Marius* (1701, 1703–5, 1707, 1710–17, 1720–1, 1723–4, 1727, 1735): 29
  As altered by T. Cibber (1744): 10
  The original (1748–50): 57
AS YOU LIKE IT — 95
  As *Love in a Forest* (1723): 6
  The original (1740–8, 1750): 89
TIMON OF ATHENS — 89
  As altered by Shadwell (1701, 1703–12, 1714–26, 1729–37, 1740–1, 1745)
HENRY IV, PART II — 88
  As altered by Betterton (1704, 1720, 1722, 1727–35, 1739–41, 1744): 45
  As *The Humours of Falstaff* (1734): 3
  The original (1736–40, 1742–7, 1749–50): 40
MEASURE FOR MEASURE — 69
  As altered by Gildon (1706): 1
  The original (1720–7, 1729–34, 1737–8, 1742–6, 1748–50): 68
A MIDSUMMER-NIGHT'S DREAM — 51
  As Leveridge's *Pyramus and Thisbe* (1716–17): 10
  As the mock play in *Love in a Forest* (1723): 6[1]
  As Lampe's *Pyramus and Thisbe* (1745–6, 1748): 35
HENRY V — 49
  As altered by Hill (1723, 1735–6, 1746): 16

The original (1738–40, 1744–8, 1750): 30
  As *The Conspiracy Discovered* (1746): 3
MUCH ADO ABOUT NOTHING — 47
  The original (1721, 1737, 1739, 1746, 1748–50): 35
  As *The Universal Passion* (1737, 1741): 12
KING JOHN — 43
  The original (1737–9, 1741, 1745, 1747, 1749): 31
  As *Papal Tyranny* (1745–6): 12
CYMBELINE — 25
  As altered by D'Urfey (1702, 1717–20, 1737–8): 22
  The original (1744, 1746): 3
RICHARD II — 25
  As altered by Theobald (1719–21): 10
  The original (1738–9): 15
ALL'S WELL THAT ENDS WELL (1741–3, 1746) — 22
TWELFTH NIGHT — 18
  As *Love Betrayed* (1703, 1705): 2
  The original (1741, 1746, 1748–9): 16
TITUS ANDRONICUS — 16
  As altered by Ravenscroft (1704, 1717–22, 1724)
THE WINTER'S TALE (1741–2) — 14
CORIOLANUS — 13
  The original (1718–22): 10
  As *The Invader of his Country* (1719): 3
THE COMEDY OF ERRORS — 12
  As *Every Body Mistaken* (1716): 3
  As *See If You Like It* (1734): 4
  The original (1741): 5
TROILUS AND CRESSIDA — 10
  As altered by Dryden (1709, 1720–1, 1723, 1733–4)
HENRY VI, PART II — 9
  As *Humfrey, Duke of Gloster* (1723)
PERICLES — 3
  As *Marina* (1738)
HENRY VI, PART I (1738) — 1
HENRY VI, PART III — 1
  As altered by T. Cibber (1723)
Total — 3,226

Plays not acted, 1701–50:
  ANTONY AND CLEOPATRA
  LOVE'S LABOUR'S LOST
  THE TWO GENTLEMEN OF VERONA

[1] In the total number of plays these six performances are counted only once, i.e. in *Love in a Forest*.

## APPENDIX C
# LONDON THEATRES IN USE BETWEEN
# 1701 AND 1750

In the following brief histories the theatres have been listed chronologically, by the date of opening.

## THE MAJOR THEATRES

### DRURY LANE

THIS theatre was opened on March 26, 1674. In 1747, when Garrick became joint patentee, the building was extensively altered. Further alterations were made in 1775. By 1791 a more modern theatre was called for, and the old one was demolished, the last performance in it being on June 4, 1791. While the new theatre was being built the Drury Lane company acted at the King's Theatre, Haymarket, and occasionally at the Theatre Royal (or Little Theatre), Haymarket. The new Theatre Royal, Drury Lane, was opened on March 12, 1794 with a performance of sacred music; the first regular play was acted on April 21, 1794. This building was destroyed by fire on February 24, 1809.

### LINCOLN'S INN FIELDS

The actual location of this theatre was in Portugal Street. It was opened on April 30, 1695, and closed on October 20, 1705. Nine years later it was entirely rebuilt and opened on December 18, 1714. It was 'officially' closed on December 5, 1732, at which time the Lincoln's Inn Fields company removed to its new theatre in Covent Garden. The old theatre was, however, occasionally used for the performance of plays as well as of concerts and operas for the next eleven years. The last play acted here was on June 3, 1743, and, following a concert by Galliard on December 11, 1744, the theatre was permanently closed. In subsequent years it was used for many purposes: in 1745 as a guard-room; in 1756 as a barracks; from about 1770 to 1778 as a dancing academy; in the 1790's as a lecture hall; and in the early nineteenth century as a china warehouse. The building was demolished in 1848.

### QUEEN'S (LATER KING'S)

The site of this, the first theatre in the Haymarket, is now occupied by His Majesty's Theatre. It was opened by the Lincoln's Inn Fields company on April 9, 1705, and used until January 10, 1708. The company then united with the Drury Lane company, at the latter's theatre, and the Queen's was used only for opera. In the autumn of 1709 the Queen's company returned to its own theatre; it was reopened on September 15, 1709, and used until November 18, 1710, after which the two companies were permanently reunited at Drury Lane. The theatre, which after the death of Queen Anne in 1714 became known as the King's Theatre, was for the remainder of the eighteenth century the principal opera house of London. It was, however, used from time to time for the performance of plays. A company from Paris acted here in the spring of 1720, and an Italian company in the season of 1726–7. In the summer of 1766 Spranger Barry acted at the King's, and throughout the seasons of 1791–2 and 1792–3 the Drury Lane company used it while its new theatre was being erected (see above). The original building had been destroyed by fire on June 17, 1789; it was rebuilt, and reopened on March 26, 1791. This theatre was burned to the ground on December 6, 1867.

### HAYMARKET

This theatre was erected in 1720 on the site directly adjoining, on the north side, the present theatre. It was generally known at first as the 'New Theatre' and was later familiarly called the 'Little Theatre' to distinguish it from the larger King's Theatre, Haymarket. It was opened by a company of French actors on December 29, 1720. It had no license, and, for many years, was therefore not in regular use. From time to time plays were performed in it by amateurs, itinerants, companies from the Continent, and by actors who had seceded from the patent theatres. It was occasionally used for operas and concerts. Beginning on June 28, 1760 Samuel Foote established a regular summer season here, in 1766 he was granted a patent to perform from May 15 to September 15 of every year. He reconstructed the theatre so as to make it virtually a new one, and opened it on May 29, 1767. The last performance in it was on October 14, 1820, after which it was demolished.

### GOODMAN'S FIELDS

This theatre was situated on the north side of Ayliffe (now Alie) Street, a short distance from Mansell Street. It was opened on October 31, 1729 and closed on May 23, 1732. It was demolished, and its new manager, Henry Giffard, constructed a new theatre on the same site, which he opened on October 2, 1732. It was used regularly until May 13, 1736; it then stood idle, probably because of the theatrical Licensing Act of 1737, until October 15, 1740, when Giffard reopened it. The following season Garrick made his debut here. On May 27, 1742, the theatre was permanently closed. It was converted into a warehouse, which was destroyed by fire on June 3, 1802.

### COVENT GARDEN

This theatre was opened by the Lincoln's Inn Fields company on December 7, 1732. From time to time it was altered and enlarged, notably in 1792, when it was almost completely rebuilt. It was burned to the ground on September 30, 1808.

## *THE MINOR THEATRES*

### JAMES STREET, HAYMARKET

This street is now called Orange Street. The theatre was in the old Tennis Court which was constructed about 1673. About 1729 the court was converted into a theatre and used as such until the late 1760's. DA of February 2, 1750, describes it as being 'sixty Feet long, and near forty Feet wide'. Until 1741 it was called in the bills the 'Tennis Court'; thereafter it was called the 'New Theatre'. About 1780 the court was again being used for tennis, and it continued to be the headquarters of the game in England until 1866 when it was dismantled. The building was later used as a warehouse. In 1936 it was drastically remodelled, and is currently occupied by the garage belonging to the Westminster City Council.

# APPENDIX C

### ST. MARTIN'S LANE

The theatre here was a temporary one. It was situated in a house near Litchfield Street and was used a few times in the spring of 1712.

### COIGNARD'S, GREEN GATE INN, CROSS STREET, HATTON GARDEN

A temporary theatre was being used here in 1719 and 1720.

### LUSSINGHAM'S GREAT ROOM, HAMPSTEAD WELLS

Bullock and Leigh had a company that acted here in the summer of 1723. The site of the Wells was in Well Walk.

### VILLIER'S STREET, YORK BUILDINGS

The earliest announcement that has come to light regarding this theatre is dated April 1731. It was also used to a considerable extent as a concert hall. It appears to have been a regular theatre, although no detailed description of it seems to have survived. PA of April 8, 1758, refers to its recent demolition, and to its 'beautiful Ceiling ... painted by Verrio'.

### WINDMILL HILL

A theatre was opened here on June 21, 1731. It was unquestionably a temporary one; no further record of its being used has survived.

### FLASK WALK, HAMPSTEAD

A company from the London theatres acted here in the summer of 1732, and in 1734 Hippisley and R. Wilks, Jr., were at the 'Playhouse'. It was almost certainly a temporary one.

### CHELSEA

A detachment of actors from Drury Lane performed here in the summer of 1733. The exact location of the theatre is not specified in the playbills.

### LEE'S BOOTH, TOTTENHAM COURT

Plays [i.e. not the drolls usually performed in the booths at the large London fairs] were being acted here in the spring of 1735.

### TILED BOOTH, BOWLING GREEN, SOUTHWARK

This booth, usually managed by the Yeates family, was from time to time opened for the performance of regular plays. The first record of such is in April 1735, the last in September 1755. For the location of the Bowling Green, see BOWLING GREEN, below.

### NEW WELLS, CLERKENWELL

This place of entertainment was located in lower Rosoman Street. Its principal attraction was its theatre, which was devoted chiefly to pantomimes, but in which plays were occasionally performed. It was opened in the spring of 1737 and closed about 1750. It was then converted into a Methodist tabernacle and demolished in 1756.

## APPENDIX C

### NEW WELLS, GOODMAN'S FIELDS

This playhouse was managed by William Hallam, who opened it on June 18, 1739, for the performance of pantomimes. It was used for this purpose until November 26, 1744, when plays began to be presented. Regular winter seasons were maintained for the next three years, after which Hallam reverted to the production of pantomimes. Plays were, however, now and then acted, the last being on November 30, 1752. On March 18, 1756, Theophilus Cibber delivered here 'two Dissertations on Theatrical Subjects', for Hallam's benefit. On October 9 of the same year Hallam was given a benefit at Sadler's Wells, being, as he stated in the playbill, 'refused the Use of [his] own house'. A letter to the editor of PA of September 27, 1765, makes it clear, however, that the Wells was still open. Of the theatre's later history nothing is known, save that in 1870 there is a record of its being occupied by a tobacco warehouseman.

### BOWLING GREEN, SOUTHWARK

The 'New Theatre' here (not to be confused with the TILED BOOTH or PHILLIPS'S BOOTH, qqv.) was used with considerable regularity from February 1743 to December 1756. It was, possibly, a regular theatre, but its subsequent history is obscure. The Bowling Green was situated on what is now Newcomen Street, opposite Guy's Hospital.

### PHILLIPS'S BOOTH, BOWLING GREEN, SOUTHWARK

There are records of regular plays being acted here from September 1741 to September 1753.

### SHEPHERD'S MARKET, MAYFAIR

The theatre here, probably a booth, was used for occasional performances of plays from 1744 to 1750.

### HICKFORD'S ROOMS, PANTON STREET

This concert hall, which had been in existence since 1713, was used for the occasional performance of plays, following Hickford's removal in 1739 to his new Rooms in Brewer Street.

### BRADLEY'S, OLD GRAVEL LANE, WAPPING

This appears to have been an inn. Plays were acted here in the autumn of 1748.

### TILED BOOTH, BLACKHEATH

A few regular plays were performed here in the autumn of 1748.

### CUSHING'S BOOTH, SMITHFIELD

*King John* was acted here in the summer of 1749.

### BLUE BOAR INN, HOLBORN

A few plays were acted at this inn in the winter of 1750. The inn was demolished in 1864.

# INDEX I
# ACTORS

ALL names in this index are those of actors unless the contrary is indicated. Each actor has been indexed according to the parts he performed. Following the names of characters (Antonio, &c.) that are common to more than one play is an abbreviation of the play, or adaptation, in which the character appears.

It will be noted that no actor is listed as 'flourishing' after 1750. This is, of course, misleading: many of the actors whose names appear below continued to flourish long thereafter. In the interests of consistency, however, I have made 1750 my terminal date. In a few cases names are given of persons who engaged in activities other than acting, for which activities they are better known today. The date of flourishing in connexion with their names has reference, however, only to their appearances on the stage.

Subjoined is a list of abbreviations used for the adaptations of Shakespeare's plays that have titles different from their originals. Complete information regarding these adaptations will be found in Part II.

C. Marius   Caius Marius (R & J)
Bullock's Cobler   The Cobler of Preston (Tam. Shrew)
Johnson's Cobler   The Cobler of Preston (Tam. Shrew)
Com. Gall.   The Comical Gallant (MWW)
Cure   A Cure for a Scold (Tam. Shrew)
Humfrey   Humfrey, Duke of Gloster (2 Hen. VI)
Humours of Fal.   The Humours of Falstaff (2 Hen. IV)
Invader   The Invader of his Country (Coriolanus)

Jew   The Jew of Venice (Merchant)
Love Bet.   Love Betrayed (Twelfth N.)
Love in For.   Love in a Forest (AYLI)
Marina   Marina (Pericles)
Papal Tyr.   Papal Tyranny (John)
Lampe's Pyramus   Pyramus and Thisbe (MND)
Leveridge's Pyramus   Pyramus and Thisbe (MND)
Sauny   Sauny the Scot (Tam. Shrew)
Univ. Pass.   The Universal Passion (Much Ado)

Ackman, Ellis, d. 1774: Balthazar (R & J) 412; Lennox 300.
Adams [unidentified], fl. 1748: 80.
Allen, *Miss*, fl. 1749: Patience 217.
Allen, Thomas [DL gallery door-keeper], d. 1738: 52.
Anderson, John(?), d. 1767: Abergavenny 214–17; Albany 266; Arundel 242–3; Balthazar (Merchant) 316; Basset 202; Cambridge (Hen. V) 196–7, 201; Chamberlain, Lord 217; Cinna the Conspirator 235–6; Colevile 189; Conrade 343–4; Donalbain 293–6; Douglas 170–4, 176–9; Duke (Merchant) 319; Duke (Othello) 364; Escalus (R & J) 413; Fenton 333; Gentleman (All's Well) 89; Gobbo 315; Gower (2 Hen. IV) 192; Gower (Hen. V) 201; Gratiano (Merchant) 316; Guildenstern 130, 134–6, 138; Hastings 193; Jaques de Bois 95–6; Jeweller 449; Leonardo 317; Lodovico 372–4; Malcolm 299–300; Marcellus 140, 142–4; Montano 372; Oliver 96–7; Page (MWW) 337; Paris 413; Peto (1 Hen. IV) 167, 169; Philario 104; Poins (1 Hen. IV) 170; Ratcliff 394, 396–7, 399–403; Trebonius 238–9. Other references 59, 170.
Armstrong, fl. 1717: Wall (Leveridge's Pyramus) 340.
Arne, Michael, fl. 1733–5: Ariel 431; Francis 159–60; Lucius (J. Caesar) 229–30; Shadow (Humours of Fal.) 185; Simple 327–8.
Arne, Thomas Augustine [composer], 1710–78: 78.
Arne, *Mrs* Thomas Augustine, Cecilia, nee Young, 1711–89: Amphitrite 430–2, 434; Juno 434; Milcha 432–3.
Arthur, John, d. 1772: Antonio (Much Ado) 342–3; Carrier 169–74, 176–9; Charles 93–4; Citizen (J. Caesar) 235, 238–9; Cleon 449; Clown (Measure) 307–8; Corin 93; Dromio of Ephesus 99;

466

# INDEX I

Essex 240–1; Evans 337–8; Fluellen 201; Gobbo 316–17; Gratiano (Othello) 364; Green 377; Gregory 413; Hecate 294–6, 299–300; King, Player 130; Launcelot 318; Lieutenant 395, 397, 399; Lucy (1 Hen. VI) 202; Mowbray 191–2; Nym (Hen. V) 200; Polonius 132, 143–4; Scroop (Betterton's 2 Hen. IV) 191; Scroop (Hen. V) 196–7; Sexton 344; Seyton 289–91; Shallow (2 Hen. IV) 193–4; Shallow (MWW) 332–3; Shylock (Jew) 313; Soldier [Interpreter] 89; Stanley 391; Stephano 434–5; Suffolk (Hen. VIII) 214–17; Touchstone 97; Tyrrel 394–5; Westmorland (1 Hen. IV) 167, 169; Witch 294, 298; Worcester 178. Other reference 61.

Aston, Walter, 1707–c. 1738: Aelius 445; Borachio 342; Brabantio 358–63; Catesby 385; Cornwall 257–8; Exeter (1 Hen. VI) 202; Gardiner 210; Gentleman Usher 256; Gloucester (Lear) 256–7; Hamlet 126; Ligarius 231; Lucius (Cymbeline) 103–4; Man, Old (Shadwell's Timon) 445–6; Metellus (C. Marius) 410; Page (MWW) 326; Pembroke 240; Scroop (Rich. II) 377; Seyton 286–9; Shylock (Jew) 312; Siward 284; Stanley 384–5; Ulysses 453–4; Westmorland (1 Hen. IV) 166; Westmorland (2 Hen. IV) 187; Westmorland (Hen. V) 196; Worcester 159, 161–2, 165. Other references 44, 49, 98.

Atkins, fl. 1750: Peto (2 Hen. IV) 193–4.

Atkins, Mrs [unidentified], fl. 1732: 39.

Atkinson [DL pit door-keeper], fl. 1748: 78.

Auguste, *Mlle* M. [dancer], fl. 1743: 65.

Ayres, James, fl. 1731–5: Cinna the Conspirator 230; Dorcas (Bullock's Cobler) 419; Montano 360–1.

Babell, William [harpsichordist], c. 1690–1723: 17.

Baggs, Zachary [DL treasurer], fl. 1704: 3.

Baily, fl. 1701: Lorenzo (Jew) 309.

Baker [DL pit door-keeper], fl. 1744: 66.

Baker, fl. 1746–50: Blunt (Cibber's Rich. III) 399; Heartwell 422; Humphrey, Prince 193–4; Montjoy 201; Murderer 298; Oxford 400; Poins (1 Hen. IV) 175; Rugby 336.

Baker, *Mrs* Catherine, fl. 1706–26: Chloe 444; Emilia (Othello) 351; Gundy, Cicely 416; York, Duchess of (Rich. III) 379. Other references 5, 10.

Baker, *Miss* Mary, later Mrs Thomas King [dancer], d. 1813: 77.

Balmerino, Arthur Elphinstone, Baron [Jacobite], 1688–1746: 199.

Bambridge, *Mrs*, fl. 1742–50: Calphurnia 239; Elizabeth, Queen 396–7, 399–400; Emilia (Othello) 369, 371–4; Goneril 261, 263, 265; Hostess (1 Hen. IV) 174, 177–9; Hostess (2 Hen. IV) 193–4; Hostess (Hen. V) 201; Isabel 202; Macduff, Lady 298; Overdone, Mrs 307–8; Queen (Hamlet) 137, 139, 141; Queen, Player 143–4; Quickly, Mrs (MWW) 336–9; Widow (All's Well) 89; York, Duchess of (Rich. III) 393, 395, 402–3.

Banberry, fl. 1746: Hamlet 138. Other reference 75.

Banks, William, d. 1776: Witch 298.

Barbier, *Mrs* [singer], d. 1737: 17, 33.

Bardin, Peter, d. c. 1788: Albany 256–7; Caius 324–8; Decius 227–8, 230, 232; Duke (Othello) 355–7, 361; Ferdinand 429; Jasper, Sir 419; Kent 254; Laertes 119–21, 123–5; Lodovico 358, 360–1; Malcolm 284–6; Osric 119; Richmond 383–4, 386; Vernon (1 Hen. IV) 157–8, 160, 162–3. Other references 40, 48–9.

Barnard, fl. 1744: Mercutio 410.

Barnet, Jervis(?), fl. 1748–50: Blunt (Cibber's Rich. III) 401–2; Duncan 300; Lennox 299–300; Montague 411–12.

Barret, fl. 1730: Fenton 324; Montano 355.

Barrington, John, d. 1773: Carrier 174–5; Citizen (J. Caesar) 237, 239; Clown (Measure) 306; Macmorris 200–1; Porter (Hen. VIII) 215–16; Trinculo 434. Other reference 73.

Barrington, *Mrs* John, formerly Mrs Sacheverel Hale, fl. 1740–50: Anne, Lady (Rich. III) 394, 396–7, 400–1; Bianca (Othello) 364; Capulet, Lady 413; Celia 93; Hero 344; Katharine 198–9, 201; Macduff, Lady 293, 295–6, 299–300; Mariana (Measure) 305–8; Melissa 449; Page, Mrs 335–9; Percy, Lady (1 Hen. IV) 170–1, 173–4, 177; Perdita 457–8. Other references 67, 71.

Barry, *Mrs* (i.e. *Miss*) Elizabeth, 1658–1713: Calphurnia 219; Katharine, Queen 205; Macbeth, Lady 268–70; Page, Mrs 320.

Barry, Spranger, 1719–77: Antony 237, 239; Hamlet 139, 141–4; Henry V 199–201; Hotspur 175–6, 179; Macbeth 296–300; Othello 369, 371–4; Romeo 411, 413. Other references 80, 83, 462.

Beard, John, 1716–91: Amiens 93, 95–7; Arviragus 104; Balthazar (Much Ado) 345–6; Lorenzo 315–18; Neptune 437; Pyramus (Lampe's Pyramus) 340–1. Other references 79–80.

Beaumont [dancer], fl. 1745: 72.

467

# INDEX I

Beckham, fl. 1731–46: Carrier 157, 175; Lieutenant 398. Other references 52, 58.

Beckham, *Mrs*, fl. 1746–7: Gentlewoman (Macbeth) 298; Hostess (1 Hen. IV) 175; York, Duchess of (Rich. III) 399–400. Other reference 77.

Beckingham, Charles [dramatist], 1699–1731: 24.

Bellamy, *Mrs*, nee Seal, later Mrs Walter, q.v.

Bellamy, *Miss* George Anne, *c.* 1727–88 [after 1754 known as Mrs Bellamy]: Blanch (Papal Tyr.) 242; Bullen, Anne 215, 217; Cordelia 266; Juliet (R & J) 412–13; Percy, Lady (1 Hen. IV) 178.

Bencraft, James, d. 1765: Abhorson 305–8; Burgundy (Lear) 260–4; Captain (Cymbeline) 104; Catesby 401; Cornwall 266; Duke (All's Well) 89; Francisco (Hamlet) 127, 130–1, 134–6; Gadshill 166–7, 169, 174, 176–9; Lepidus 235–6, 238–9; Mouldy 193–4; Murderer 293–6, 299–300; Oxford 390, 392, 394, 396–7, 399–400, 402–3; Rosencrantz 138, 140, 142–3; Salisbury (Hen. V) 201; Shadow 187; Simple 331–5, 337–8; Vernon (1 Hen. VI) 202; Witch 292. Other reference 84.

Bennet, *Mrs* (i.e. *Miss*) Elizabeth, 1714–91: Bullen, Anne 212, 216; Calphurnia 237; Capulet, Lady 411–12; Chloe 448; Courtesan 99; Elinor 242–3; Emilia (Othello) 367; Gentlewoman (Macbeth) 294–5; Goneril 260, 262–7; Isabel 200; Mariana (Measure) 307–8; Miranda 432; Nerissa 313–18; Page, Mrs 334; Phebe 91–6, 98; Queen (Hamlet) 134, 136–7, 140; Queen, Player 131–4; Tearsheet, Doll 188–91; York, Duchess of (Rich. III) 388–9, 391–2, 394–6, 398–9, 401–3. Other reference 56.

Bennet, William, d. 1768: Clarence 194; Donalbain 299–300; Slender 338.

Benson, *Mrs*, fl. 1728–30: Macduff, Lady 281; Page, Mrs 324; Percy, Lady (1 Hen. IV) 155. Other references 34, 36.

Berriman, Joseph, d. 1730: Gratiano (Jew) 311; Shallow (MWW) 323.

Berriman, *Mrs* Joseph, Anne, formerly Mrs Parker, later Mrs William Hallam, q.v.

Berrisford [DL box-keeper], fl. 1748: 78.

Berry, Edward, 1676–1760: Adam 91–7; Aegeon 99; Alonso 431; Antonio (Merchant) 317–18; Antonio (Tempest) 428; Brabantio 365–9, 371–3; Byron 342–3; Caesar 232, 234; Capulet 411–12; Casca 233–4, 237; Chamberlain, Lord 209–10; Cranmer 211–12; Duke (Measure) 306, 308; Duncan 293–4, 300; Escalus (Measure) 304; Exeter (Hen. V) 199–200; Falstaff (1 Hen. IV) 171–2, 175–6; Falstaff (2 Hen. IV) 191; Falstaff (MWW) 338; Flavius (J. Caesar) 229–30; Ghost 132, 141–3; Gloucester (Lear) 259–61, 264–6; Gonzalo 434; Hecate 294, 296–9; Henry IV (1 Hen. IV) 165, 169–70; Henry VI (Cibber's Rich. III) 391, 393–4, 401–3; Henry VIII 214–15; Hubert (John) 241, 243; Jaques 97; Kent 256–7; King (Hamlet) 127; Lafeu 88; Leonato 344–6; Lodovico 358–9; Lord Chief Justice 188–90; Marcellus 123–4; Mortimer 157; Mowbray 184; Norfolk (Hen. VIII) 211; Page (MWW) 327–9; Prospero 431–2, 434–5, 437; Seyton 285–7, 289–92; Solanio 313–17; Stanley 385–6; Toby, Sir 456; Tressel 389; Worcester 159–60, 162; York, Archbishop of 186. Other references 61, 73, 80.

Betterton, Thomas, *c.* 1635–1710: Bassanio (Jew) 309; Brutus 218; Falstaff (1 Hen. IV) 145; Falstaff (MWW) 320; Hamlet 106–7; Henry VIII 204–5; Lear 245–6; Macbeth 268–70; Marius, Old 406; Othello 346–7; Thersites 452. Other references 3–4, 6, 179, 187, 461.

Betts, fl. 1748: Gonzalo 436.

Bevil [unidentified], fl. 1730: 36.

Bickerstaff, John, fl. 1704–19: Aaron 450; Aeneas 452; Albany 246; Banquo 271; Casca 221; Citizen (Invader) 100; Kent 248; King (Hamlet) 109–10; Marcellus 107; Mustacho 424; Poet 440; Seyton 269–70; Stephano 425–6; Sulpitius 407–8; Winlove 415–16. Other references 3, 9, 12, 15.

Bicknell, *Mrs* Margaret, nee Younger, d. 1723; Hippolito 426; Nerissa (Jew) 310. Other references 9, 17.

Bincks, *Miss* Elizabeth, later Mrs Richard Vincent, q.v.

Birkhead, Matthew, d. 1722: Butler (Johnson's Cobler) 416; Citizen (C. Marius) 406, 408; Isander 440; Menelaus 452. Other references 11–12, 18, 21.

Bishop, *Mrs*, fl. 1742: Goneril 261.

Blakes, Charles, d. 1763: Boatswain 434; Borachio 344–6; Burgundy (Hen. V) 199–200; Caius 332, 334, 338; Caliban 437; Captain (Twelfth N.) 456; Cassio 364–5; Cleomenes 457; Cornwall 260–6; Dauphin (John) 241, 243; Demetrius (Shadwell's Timon) 448; Duke Senior 93–7; Dumain Sr. 88; Gloucester (Lear) 261; Hastings 191; Henry VI (Cibber's Rich. III) 394; Laertes 133–4, 136, 139–43; Lodovico 368–9, 371–3; Malcolm 294–5, 298–300; Marcellus 131, 133;

## INDEX I

Mustacho 434–5; Norfolk (Rich. III) 390–3, 399, 401; Octavius 237; Orlando 95–7; Provost 306, 308; Salarino 314–18; Seyton, 291, 296–7; Suffolk (Hen. VIII) 215–16; Tressel 391–2, 394–6, 398–9, 401–3; Tybalt 411–12; Vernon (1 Hen. IV) 171–2, 174–5; Worcester 168. Other references 63, 80.

Blakey, fl. 1743–50: Duke (All's Well) 89; Gentleman Usher 263; Gonzalo 433; Osric 137; Peto (1 Hen. IV) 173; Rugby 338.

Bland, *Mrs*, later (1) Mrs Hamilton, (2) Mrs Sweeny, d. 1787: Anne, Lady (Rich. III) 398; Emilia (Othello) 370; Francisca 305–7; Helen 104; Isabel 198–9; Juliet (Measure) 306; Mariana (All's Well) 89; Queen, Player 140, 142; Regan 264; Thais 449.

Boheme, Anthony, d. 1731: Angelo (Measure) 302–3; Arviragus(?) 103; Banquo 277–81; Brabantio 350–4; Caesar 222–3; Cassius 223–7; Duncan 276–7; Francisco (Hamlet) 112; Ghost 112–19; Hector 453; Henry IV (1 Hen. IV) 151–5; Henry VI (Cibber's Rich. III) 380–2; Hotspur 152; Lear 248–54; Ligarius 222; Pedro, Don 342; Pisanio 103; Seyton 274–5; Shallow (MWW) 320–4; Shylock (Jew) 310–12; Titus 450–1; Ulysses 452–3; Wolsey 207–8; Worcester 150–1; York (Rich. II) 376. Other references 27, 29, 32, 103, 112.

Boheme, *Mrs* Anthony [the 1st], Anna Maria, nee Seymour, d. 1723: Calphurnia 223–4; Cordelia 248–50; Cressida 453; Desdemona 350–1; Elizabeth, Queen 380–1; Hero 342; Isabella 302; Macbeth, Lady 275–7; Macduff, Lady 275; Page, Mrs 320–1; Portia (Jew) 311; Portia (J. Caesar) 223; Queen (Hamlet) 113–15; Queen (Rich. II) 376; Tamora 451. Other reference 22.

Bolton [unidentified], fl. 1730: 36.

Boman, John, Sr., c. 1665–1739: Albany 248; Brabantio 352, 354, 358–9; Clifford 204; Cluentius 100; Duncan 270, 280, 283, 285–9; Flavius (J. Caesar) 221; Ghost 108, 110, 122, 126–7; Henry IV (1 Hen. IV) 147; Ligarius 218, 229–30; Lord Chief Justice 180–7; Man, Old (Shadwell's Timon) 440; Marcus 450; Metellus (C. Marius) 406–9; Norfolk (Rich. III) 379, 385–8; Northumberland (1 Hen. IV) 145, 157, 159–60, 162, 165–6; Suffolk (Hen. VIII) 205, 208–12. Other references 9–10, 12, 23, 34, 39.

Boman, *Mrs* John, Sr., Elizabeth, nee Watson, 1677–?: Airy Spirit 425; Nerissa (Jew) 309; Portia (J. Caesar) 218.

Boman, Jr., fl. 1715–38: Austria 240; Brabantio 363; Glendower 165; Horatio 127; Host 330; Kent 258; Oxford 379; Siward 287–8; Trebonius 221; Valdes 375. Other references 12, 51.

Boman, *Mrs*, Jr., fl. 1731: Milcha 428.

Bonneval, *Mme* [dancer], fl. 1742: 62.

Booth, Barton, 1681–1733: Achilles 452; Alberto 90; Alcibiades 438–40; Banquo 272–8; Bassanio (Jew) 309; Brutus 219–26; Buckingham (Hen. VIII) 204–5; Caesar 218; Cassio 347; Coriolanus (Invader) 100; Ghost 106–16; Gloucester (Humfrey) 203; Granius 406; Gratiano (Jew) 309; Henry IV (2 Hen. IV) 180; Henry V 195; Henry VIII 206–7; Horatio 107; Hotspur 145–53; Laertes 106, 108; Lear 247–52; Lennox 268–72; Marius, Young 406–9; Othello 348–52; Sebastian (Love Bet.) 455; Timon 440–4; Vernon (1 Hen. IV) 145; Winlove 415. Other references 7–9, 12.

Booth, *Mrs* Barton [the 2nd], Hester, nee Santlow, d. 1773: Cordelia 247–53, 256; Desdemona 349, 357; Dorinda 424–6; Miranda 427; Ophelia 107–17, 119–22; Percy, Lady (1 Hen. IV) 146–57, 159; Rosalind (Love in For.) 91. Other references 7, 17, 21, 28, 34.

Boothby, fl. 1735: Granius 410.

Boucher, Thomas [GF and CG prompter and box-keeper], d. 1755: 38, 43, 57.

Boval [dancer], fl. 1721: 21.

Bowen, William, 1666–1718: Cinna the Poet 219: Gentleman Usher (probably) 245; Osric 106–8, 110; Roderigo 347–9; Witch 268. Other reference 8.

Bowen, *Mrs* William [widow of the actor], fl. 1725: 28.

Boyce, fl. 1746–7: Lieutenant 399; Ratcliff 400.

Bracegirdle, *Mrs* (i.e. *Miss*) Anne, c. 1674–1748: Cordelia 245; Desdemona 346–7; Ford, Mrs 320; Lavinia (C. Marius) 406; Ophelia 106; Portia (Jew) 309; Portia (J. Caesar) 219; Villaretta 455. Other reference 245.

Bradshaw [DL box-keeper], fl. 1743: 64.

Bradshaw, *Mrs* (i.e. *Miss*) Lucretia, later Mrs Martin Folkes, d. c. 1755: Bullen, Anne 205; Calphurnia 218; Cordelia 245, 247; Cressida 452; Desdemona 347–8; Lavinia (C. Marius) 406; Margaret (Sauny) 415–16; Melissa 438–40; Ophelia 106–8; Page, Anne 320; Percy, Lady (1 Hen. IV) 146; Portia (Jew) 310; Portia (J. Caesar) 219. Other references 4–5, 9, 146.

Bransby, Astley, d. 1789 Balthazar (R & J) 411–13; Brandon 214, 216; Capucius

# INDEX I

215–16; Chatillon 243; Conrade 344; Curio 456; Ely, Bishop of (Hen. V) 201; Escalus (R & J) 412; Francisco (Tempest) 434; Gower (Hen. V) 200; Guildenstern 143–4; Le Beau 96; Marcellus 137, 139–42; Messala 237; Metellus (J. Caesar) 238–9; Montano 369, 371–4; Murderer 296–7; Norfolk (Rich. III) 402–3; Oxford 398–9, 401–2; Poins (2 Hen. IV) 193–4; Shallow (MWW) 337; Siward 299–300; Siward, Young 298–9; Tyrrel 398–9; Westmorland (1 Hen. IV) 175; Williams 201; Worcester 178–9.

Brett, fl. 1745–7: Neptune 433–5; Pistol (MWW) 336.

Brett, *Mrs*, fl. 1723–4: Anne, Lady (Cibber's 3 Hen. VI) 204; Cordelia 251; Hippolito 427.

Brett, *Miss* Anne, later Mrs William Rufus Chetwood, q.v.

Breval, John Durant [dramatist], *c.* 1680–1738: 42.

Bride [DL machinist], fl. 1744: 66.

Bridges, William(?), fl. 1743–50: Alonso 434; Angers, Citizen of 242–3; Antonio (Twelfth N) 456; Brabantio 372; Buckingham (Rich. III) 395–6, 400–3; Canterbury, Archbishop of (Hen. V) 200; Cranmer 215–16; Decius 237; Duke (Othello) 372; Duke Senior 95; Duncan 296–7; Falstaff (MWW) 337; Friar (Much Ado) 344–6; Gloucester (Lear) 261–3; Henry IV (1 Hen. IV) 177; King (Hamlet) 134, 136–7, 139–43; Lord Chief Justice 191; Morocco 316–17; Northumberland (1 Hen. IV) 175; Peter, Friar 306; Prospero 436; Ross (Macbeth) 294–5; Witch 298–300.

Bridges, *Mrs* William(?), fl. 1746–9: Overdone, Mrs 307–8.

Bridgwater, R., d. 1754: Adam 92, 94–7; Alcibiades 444; Banquo 280, 282–3, 286–7, 289–90, 292–6, 300; Bourbon 195; Buckingham (Hen. VIII) 208–10; Buckingham (Rich. III) 385, 387; Caesar 231, 235–9; Camillo 457–8; Cassio 356–7; Constable (Hen. V) 196–9, 201; Cranmer 214–17; Decius 226; Duncan 286–9; Falstaff (1 Hen. IV) 163, 166, 169, 174; Falstaff (2 Hen. IV) 187, 189–90, 192; Falstaff (MWW) 335, 337; Ghost 116–18, 120–2; Gloucester (Lear) 257–64, 266; Gravedigger 125–6, 128; Henry IV (1 Hen. IV) 161–2, 165; Henry VI (Cibber's Rich. III) 383–4, 389, 392, 394–5, 397–8, 400–1, 403; Hotspur 157, 159; Hubert (John) 239–41; Hubert (Papal Tyr.) 242; John, Don 342–3; King (Hamlet) 129–36, 138;

Lafeu 89; Montague 413; Northumberland (Rich. II) 377; Pisanio 103–4; Reignier 202; Sulpitius 409; Timon 445; Trinculo 429–30; Vernon (1 Hen. IV) 155; Warwick (Cibber's 3 Hen. VI) 204; Westmorland (2 Hen. IV) 181–2; York, Archbishop of 193. Other references 31, 39, 54, 59.

Brooks [unidentified], fl. 1744: 66.

Brown, Dr [dramatist], fl. 1716: 98, 105.

Brown, Henry, d. *c.* 1770: Antonio (Tempest) 436.

Brown, Thomas [soldier], d. 1747: 68.

Brunette, *Miss*, fl. 1739: Ursula 343.

Bruodin, fl. 1749: Othello 373; Prospero 436. Other reference 82.

Bubb, *Mrs* [unidentified], fl. 1723: 26.

Buchanan, *Mrs* Charles, Elizabeth, d. 1736: Andromache 454; Calphurnia 227; Desdemona 353–4, 357, 359–62; Goneril 253–8; Isabella 303; Macbeth, Lady 281; Macduff, Lady 281–7; Melissa 446; Page, Mrs 329; Portia (J. Caesar) 231; Queen (Hamlet) 117–18, 122; York, Duchess of (Rich. III) 384–5, 387. Other reference 34.

Buck, Timothy, d. *c.* 1741: 16.

Budgell, *Miss*, d. *c.* 1755: Cordelia 265; Dorinda 435; Edward, Prince 395–8; Macbeth, Lady 298; Ophelia 140–1. Other reference 435.

Bullock, Christopher, *c.* 1690–1722: Antonio (Tempest) 425; Carlisle, Bishop of 376; Citizen (Coriolanus) 101; Decius 222; Donalbain 269; Gratiano (Jew) 309–11; Hippolito 424; Lucio 302; Malcolm 271; Osric 112–13; Poins (1 Hen. IV) 148, 150; Shattillion 102–3; Slender 320–1; Snuffle 416; Sylla 406; Tranio (Sauny) 415–16; Vernon (1 Hen. IV) 146; Witch 274. Other references 15, 20, 22, 24, 98, 414, 461.

Bullock, *Mrs* Christopher, Jane, nee Rogers, d. 1739: Andromache 453; Anne, Lady (Rich. III) 380–2, 384–5, 387; Bullen, Anne 207–8; Cressida 454; Eugenia 103; Macbeth, Lady 274–5, 277, 283–4; Macduff, Lady 273–80, 282; Nerissa (Jew) 310–12; Page, Mrs 321, 323, 325–6; Percy, Lady (1 Hen. IV) 149–57, 159, 161, 163; Percy, Lady (Theobald's Rich. II) 376; Portia (J. Caesar) 221, 223–7; Queen (Rich. II) 376. Other references, 13, 15, 37, 44, 47, 150, 322.

Bullock, Hildebrand, d. 1733: Barnardine 302–3; Carrier 150; Citizen (Coriolanus) 101; Citizen (J. Caesar) 223–4, 227; Cloten 103; Crotchet (Leveridge's Pyramus) 339; Curtis (Sauny) 418; Flute

470

# INDEX I

(Leveridge's Pyramus) 339; Gravedigger 114; Isidore 445; Witch 280–4. Other reference 17.
Bullock, *Mrs* Hildebrand, Ann, nee Russell [dancer], fl. 1733: 43.
Bullock, William, Sr., *c.* 1667–1742: Carrier 146, 152–5, 157, 159; Citizen (Coriolanus) 101; Citizen (J. Caesar) 219, 223–7; Dogberry 342; Falstaff (1 Hen. IV) 147–51; Gravedigger 112–23, 127; Grist 416; Host 320–6, 331; Isidore 446; Lord Mayor 380–2; Nurse (C. Marius) 406; Phaeax 438–40; Quince (Leveridge's Pyramus) 339; Sands 205; Sauny 415–18; Thersites 453; Trinculo 424–5; Witch 268–72, 274–81. Other references 8–9, 15, 17, 22, 464.
Bullock, William, Jr., d. 1733: Blunt (Cibber's Rich. III) 383; Burgundy (Lear) 254; Carrier 157–8, 160; Citizen (J. Caesar) 228; Gentleman Usher 254; Osric 114, 117, 119–21, 123; Roderigo 356–7; Slender 321, 323–6; Snuffle 420; Westmorland (1 Hen. IV) 158. Other references 32, 43.
Burgess, *Miss* Elizabeth(?), fl. 1737–41: Arthur 240; Regan 260. Other reference 52.
Burnaby, William [dramatist], *c.* 1673–1706: 267, 454.
Burny, Richard, fl. 1730–1: Dorcas (Bullock's Cobler) 420. Other reference 36.
Burton, *Mrs* [DL middle gallery boxkeeper], fl. 1728: 32, 76 n.
Burton, Edmund, d. 1772: Blunt (Cibber's Rich. III) 399, 401; Cornwall 264; Doctor (Macbeth) 299; Ghost 139; Gonzalo 434–5; Montague 412; Oliver 97; Salisbury (Hen. V) 200. Other references 81, 83.
Butler, *Mrs* Elizabeth, d. 1748: Bullen, Anne 209; Calphurnia 226, 229, 231–5; Countess (All's Well) 88–9; Elizabeth, Queen 393, 395; Emilia (Othello) 352–4, 356–66; Evandra 448; Lucilia 342–3; Macbeth, Lady 285, 287–92; Macduff, Lady 283; Melissa 444; Page, Mrs 327–32; Queen (Hamlet) 121–3, 125–32; Regan 251–2; York, Duchess of (Rich. III) 382, 385, 387.

Campbell, *Mrs*, fl. 1723: Charlotte 195; Margaret (Cibber's 3 Hen. VI) 204.
Campioni, *Signora* [dancer], fl. 1745: 71.
Cantrell, *Mrs*, fl. 1731–6: Amphitrite 430–1; Calphurnia 231; Ford, Mrs 328–9; Melissa 446–7. Other reference 37.
Carey, fl. 1716: Eolus 425.
Carey, Henry [dramatist], *c.* 1690–1743: 48.

Carlisle, *Mrs*, fl. 1745: Amphitrite 433; Desdemona 368; Macbeth, Lady 295.
Carr, Oliver, fl. 1742–7: Angers, Governor of (Papal Tyr.) 242–3; Antonio (Much Ado) 344; Hastings 192; Lord (Cymbeline) 104; Marcellus 134–6, 138; Metellus (J. Caesar) 235–6; Morocco 316; Northumberland (1 Hen. IV) 170–4, 176; Seyton 295–6; Tyrrel 392, 394, 396–8.
Cartwright, fl. 1746: Rosencrantz 139; Vernon (1 Hen IV) 173.
Cashell, Oliver, d. 1747: Alcibiades 448–9; Angelo (Measure) 305–7; Antonio (Merchant) 316; Antonio (Twelfth N.) 455; Banquo 297; Buckingham (Rich. III) 389, 392, 394, 396–8; Casca 235–6; Cassio 370; Cornwall 261–3; Cromwell 212–13; Cymbeline 104; Decius 233–4; Diocles 457–8; Edmund 264; France, King of 198; Ghost 138; Hamlet 136; Henry IV (1 Hen. IV) 172–4, 176; Henry IV (2 Hen. IV) 191–2; Horatio 129, 131–4, 138; John, King (Papal Tyr.) 242; King (All's Well) 89; Laertes 134–6; Macbeth 292, 295–6; Malcolm 290; Melun (Papal Tyr.) 242; Messala 233–4; Montano 365–8; Morocco 313; Mowbray 190–2; Norfolk (Hen. VIII) 214–17; Oliver 91–7; Othello 370; Page (MWW) 333–6; Pedro, Don 344; Poins (1 Hen. IV) 170–1; Poins (2 Hen. IV) 188–90; Siward 293–4; Vernon (1 Hen. IV) 167–9. Other references 58, 63, 71, 74.
Castleman, Richard [DL treasurer], fl. 1718–30: 16, 30, 35.
Champnes, Samuel, d. 1803: John, Friar 411.
Chapman, Henry [coachmaker], fl. 1735: 47.
Chapman, Thomas, d. 1747: Aelius 449; Albany 250; Autolycus 457–8; Benedick 343; Campeius 214–17; Canterbury, Archbishop of (Hen. V) 196–9; Carlisle, Bishop of 377; Carrier 170–1; Citizen (J. Caesar) 231, 234–7; Cloten 103–4; Clown (All's Well) 89; Clown (Twelfth N.) 455; Cornwall 252–5; Diomedes 453–4; Fenton 323–4; Ghost 118, 122–3; Glendower 166–9; Gratiano (Jew) 312–13; Henry IV (1 Hen. IV) 159, 161; Henry VI (Cibber's Rich. III) 384–5, 387; Kent 255–8, 264; Laertes 121–2, 134, 136, 138; Launcelot 313, 315–16; Lucio 303–7; Malcolm 281–4, 292, 297; Osric 117–21, 124–6, 128–9; Pandulph 239–41; Poet 445–6; Poins (1 Hen. IV) 156–7, 159, 172–4, 176; Richmond 398; Roderigo 353–4, 356–63, 366, 370;

# INDEX I

Seyton 281; Shallow (MWW) 325–6, 329–31, 333–6; Surrey (Hen. VIII) 212–13; Touchstone 91–6; Tressel 385, 388–90, 392, 394–5, 397–8; Winchester, Bishop of 202; York, Archbishop of 187, 190–2. Other references 26, 28, 42, 54, 65, 67, 98.

Charke, *Miss* Catharine Maria, later Mrs Harman, d. 1773: Balthazar (R & J) 410; Page (R & J) 410.

Charke, Richard, d. 1737: Osric 122; Sycorax 428. Other reference 41.

Charke, *Mrs* Richard, Charlotte, nee Cibber, 1713–60; Marius, Young 410; Pistol (Humours of Fal.) 185; Roderigo 356, 358. Other reference 43.

Charles, fl. 1744: Escalus (R & J) 410; Roderigo 368.

Charlton [unidentified], fl. 1730: 36.

Chettle, fl. 1745: Stephano 433.

Chetwood, William Rufus [DL prompter], d. 1766: 11, 15, 37, 43, 48, 56, 58.

Chetwood, *Mrs* William Rufus, Anne, nee Brett, fl. 1729–44: Ancharius's Son 410; Ariel 428, 431; Chloe 447; Diana 89; Edward, Prince 385–6; Emilia (Othello) 368; Falstaff's Page 181, 184; Juliet (Measure) 304; Page, Anne 330–1; Tearsheet, Doll 186–7. Other references 34, 56.

Christian, *Mrs*, nee Vaughan, fl. 1732–3: Percy, Lady (1 Hen. IV) 158, 160.

Church [unidentified], fl. 1744: 66.

Cibber, Colley, 1671–1757: Cardinal (Humfrey) 203; Citizen (C. Marius) 406; Citizen (J. Caesar) 218; Cranmer 205; Glendower 146, 150, 155–7; Gloucester (Lear) 245–9, 252–3; Iago 347–54, 356–7; Jaques (Love in For.) 91; Osric 106–7, 111–14; Pandulph (Papal Tyr.) 242; Richard III 378–9, 382–3, 388; Shallow (2 Hen. IV) 180–3, 187, 190–1; Surrey (Hen. VIII) 205; Wolsey 206–9; Worcester 145. Other references 3, 8, 12, 70, 239, 374, 378, 460.

Cibber, *Miss* Jane, 1730–?: Arthur (Papal Tyr.) 242; Desdemona 368; Edward, Prince 392, 395; Imogen 104; Juliet (R & J) 410–11; York, Duke of 389, 391–2. Other reference 69.

Cibber, Theophilus, 1703–58: Carrier 157; Casca 229–34; Cassio 359–62; Clarence 180; Dauphin (Papal Tyr.) 242–3; Falstaff (1 Hen. IV) [read by] 159; Gardiner 217; Gentleman Usher 250–3, 256–7, 259; Glendower 157, 159–60, 162, 164–6, 175–6; Gloucester (Lear) 262; Gratiano (Merchant) 316; Hamlet [read by] 132; Henry IV (1 Hen. IV) 164; Hippolito 427; Jaques 92–3; Joculo 342; Laertes 126; Le Beau (Love in For.) 91; Lennox 279–80, 282–3, 285–7, 291; Lucio 304; Macduff 283; Mustacho 428; Osric 114–18, 120–1, 123–4, 126, 140, 142; Othello 356, 358, 364, 368; Parolles 88–9; Pistol (2 Hen. IV) 181–9, 192–3; Pistol (Hen. V) 198–9; Poet 443–4, 449; Posthumus 104; Richard III 392, 395; Richmond 385–9, 397; Roderigo 353–4, 356, 363, 372; Romeo 410; Slender 327–9; Surrey (Hen. VIII) 209–12; Tressel 382; Wales, Prince of (Cibber's 3 Hen. VI) 204. Other references 21, 23, 50, 56, 71, 159, 203, 404, 461, 465.

Cibber, *Mrs* Theophilus [the 1st], Jane, nee Johnson, 1706–33; Edward, Prince 382; Hippolito 427–8.

Cibber, *Mrs* Theophilus [the 2nd], Susannah Maria, nee Arne, 1714–66: Anne, Lady (Rich. III) 392, 394; Constance 242; Cordelia 261–2, 264–6; Desdemona 361–3, 366, 368, 370–4; Elizabeth, Queen 403; Isabella 304–5, 307–8; Juliet (R & J) 411–13; Ophelia 142, 144. Other references 52, 127.

Clark, *Mrs*, fl. 1744: Balthazar (R & J) 410.

Clarke, *Mrs*, fl. 1728: 33.

Clarke, Nathaniel, 1699–1783: Blunt (Cibber's Rich. III) 390; Donalbain 290–2; Falconbridge, Robert 240–1; Gentleman (Timon) 445–6; Gloucester (Hen. V) 197; Groom (Rich. II) 377; John, Prince (1 Hen. IV) 169; Osric 127; Pistol (MWW) 332; Slender 323–5, 329–30, 333. Other references 29, 35, 59.

Clarkson [LIF pit office-keeper], fl. 1725: 29.

Clive, *Mrs* George, Catherine, nee Raftor, 1711–85: Amphitrite 428; Ariel 434–5, 437; Bianca (Othello) 353–4, 356; Celia 91–8; Desdemona 358; Dorinda 427–33; Liberia 342–3; Margaret (Cure) 420; Melissa 449; Olivia 455–7; Ophelia 137, 139–43; Portia (Merchant) 313–18. Other references 58, 67, 83.

Clough, Thomas, d. 1770: Blunt (Cibber's Rich. III) 391, 393, 395.

Coker, fl. 1716–19: Clerimont 416; Gamut (Leveridge's Pyramus) 339; Starveling (Leveridge's Pyramus) 339; Willoughby 376. Other reference 15.

Cole, *Miss*, 1728–?: Ariel 431–3; Donalbain 296–9; Dorinda 437; Edward, Prince 396–7, 399, 401–3; Falstaff's Page 185–90; Fleance 291–2, 294–5; Francisca 307–8; Henry, Prince 243; Jessica 317–18; John, Prince (1 Hen. IV) 172, 175; Miranda 437; Page

472

# INDEX I

(Shadwell's Timon) 448; Robin 328–32, 334; Ursula 344–6; York, Duke of 384–9, 391. Other references 45, 48, 52.

Cole, E. D., fl. 1720–41: Lepidus 229–30; Lord Chief Justice (Humours of Fal.) 185; Murderer 289; Oxford 384; Thomas, Friar 304–5; Wart 180; Westmorland (1 Hen. IV) 160. Other references 56, 60.

Collett, fl. 1730–3: Bardolph (1 Hen. IV) 157–8, 160; Burgundy (Lear) 254; Citizen (J. Caesar) 227 9; Lieutenant 383; Polonius 119–21, 123; Shallow (MWW) 324–6; Sycorax 429; Ventoso 429; Witch 282. Other reference 38.

Collins, William, d. 1763: Abhorson 307; Bernardo 142; Carrier 177; Citizen (J. Caesar) 237–9; Feeble 193–4; Francis 177–9; Peto (1 Hen. IV) 172, 174–5; Rugby 334; Sampson 413; Sands 217; Shallow (MWW) 338; Slender 337; William, Sir 422; Witch 299–300.

Concanen, Matthew [dramatist], 1701–49: 34.

Connelly, *Miss* [unidentified], fl. 1724: 28.

Cook, fl. 1716–17: Lion (Leveridge's Pyramus) 339–40.

Cook, *Mrs* Mary, 1665–1745: Hostess (1 Hen. IV) 150, 153.

Cooke, Philip [dancer], d. 1755: 67, 80.

Cooke, Thomas [poet], 1703–56: 64.

Copin, *Miss*, fl. 1745–8: Desdemona 368; Francisca 307.

Corey, John, fl. 1707–35: Alonso 424; Amiens (Love in For.) 91; Antonio (Tempest) 427–8; Canterbury, Archbishop of (Betterton's 2 Hen. IV) 180–2, 185; Casca 221, 225–6; Chamberlain, Lord 210–11; Demetrius (Shadwell's Timon) 438–40, 442–4; Duke (Jew) 309; Duke (Othello) 353–4; Gratiano (Othello) 358; Laertes 110–11; Lodovico 347; Malcolm 269–70; Menenius (Invader) 100; Messala 229–30; Nestor 452; Pisanio 102; Seyton 268, 271, 273–4, 278, 280, 282–4; Stanley 383–4; Worcester 149, 157; York (Hen. V) 195. Other references 5–6, 10, 13, 17, 19, 25, 28, 39.

Costollo, Patrick, d. 1766: Lennox 298; Nym (MWW) 338.

Crisp, Samuel, 1707–68: King (All's Well) 88; Richard III 390.

Crofts, fl. 1740–1: Lord (Wint. T.) 458; Montano 366; Ratcliff 390–1; Siward 291.

Cromarty, George Mackenzie, Earl of [Jacobite], c. 1703–66: 199.

Cross, fl. 1747: Duncan 297.

Cross, *Mrs* Letitia, d. 1737: Beatrice 342; Dorinda 423; Ford, Mrs 320–2; Ophelia 107, 110–11, 114–15. Other reference 26.

Cross, Richard, I, fl. 1707–24: Citizen (C. Marius) 406, 408–9; Citizen (Invader) 101; Citizen (J. Caesar) 219, 222; Lionel, Sir 415–16; Murderer 270; Polonius 106–10; Sycorax 424–6; Thrasillus 440–3; Witch 269. Other references 10, 12, 19, 21.

Cross, Richard, II, d. 1760: Albany 262; Antony's Servant 229–30; Cromwell 210 14; Duke (Othello) 358; Gainlove 420; Horatio 132; Humphrey, Prince 184; Jaques 93–4; Lorenzo 313–14, 318; Malcolm 285–9, 292, 297; Pistol (MWW) 328–30, 334; Poins (2 Hen. IV) 186; Richmond 391; Rosencrantz 124; Siward, Young 294–5; Solanio 314; Stephano 431; Tressel 385–8, 394; Vernon (1 Hen. IV) 160–2, 165–7. Other references 59, 81, 83.

Cross, *Mrs* Richard, II, Frances, née Shireburn, 1707–81: Chloe 446–7; Emilia (Othello) 360; Falconbridge, Lady 241–2; Hostess (1 Hen. IV) 160, 162, 164–7, 171–2, 174, 176; Hostess (2 Hen. IV) 184–6, 191; Lady, Old 215–16; Lucy (Cure) 420; Queen, Player 125; Quickly, Mrs (MWW) 327–30, 333–4; Regan 253, 256, 259–60, 262–7; Tearsheet, Doll 181–2, 189; Widow (All's Well) 88; York, Duchess of (Rich. III) 386. Other references 32, 34, 328.

Cross, Richard, III, fl. 1748–50: Fleance 298–300; Page (R & J) 411–12.

Cross, Thomas [LIF numberer], d. 1737: 16, 24.

Crowne, John [dramatist], c. 1640–1712: 203.

Cunningham, W., fl. 1745: Neptune 433.

Currier [DL pit office-keeper], fl. 1746: 73.

Cushing, John, 1719–90: Archer 422; Balthazar (R & J) 413; Carrier 178; Edgar 265; Gentleman Usher 266; Gregory 413; Guildford 217; Hamlet 140; Horatio 137–9; Lennox 298; Lodovico 370–1; Lucio 307–8; Macbeth 297; Osric 143–4; Pistol (2 Hen. IV) 193–4; Pistol (MWW) 337–8; Poins (2 Hen. IV) 193; Richard III 397, 400; Richmond 397, 399–400; Roderigo 373; Scroop (Hen. V) 201; Slender 336; Tressel 402–3; Tubal 319; Ventoso 433, 435; Wales, Prince of (1 Hen. IV) 173, 175–6; Witch 299–300. Other references 72, 77.

Cushing, *Mrs* John, fl. 1745–9: Amphitrite 435; Constance 244; Dorinda 433, 435; Edward, Prince 399–400; Ford, Mrs 336; Ophelia 139, 141; Queen, Player 137; Regan 265. Other reference 72.

# INDEX I

Dance, James, 1722–74 [*c.* 1751 he adopted stage name of Love]: Falstaff (1 Hen. IV) 173–4; Falstaff (MWW) 335; Ghost 137; Worcester 177.

Dancey, *Miss*, fl. 1736–9: Tearsheet, Doll 186–8.

Daniel, *Mrs* William, Mary, fl. 1741–8: Desdemona 372; Miranda 433; York, Duchess of (Rich. III) 398.

Davenant, *Sir* William [dramatist], 1606–68: 267, 301, 422, 460.

Davies, Thomas, *c.* 1712–85: Henry VI (Cibber's Rich. III) 398; Mortimer 174; Norfolk (Hen. VIII) 217; Silvius 97; Stanley 398.

Davis, fl. 1737: Brabantio 362.

Davison, *Mrs*, fl. 1723: Elizabeth, Lady 204.

Dawson, d. 1748: Cleon 446; Duncan 284; Nestor 454; Worcester 160.

Delane, Dennis, d. 1750: Antonio (Merchant) 313–17; Antony 238–9; Banquo 299; Bastard 241; Brutus 227–8, 230–2, 234, 237; Buckingham (Hen. VIII) 217; Canterbury, Archbishop of (Hen. V) 199; Falstaff (MWW) 329–30, 334; Ferdinand 434; Ghost 121, 123–6, 128–34, 136–7, 139–41, 143–4; Hamlet 132; Henry IV (2 Hen. IV) 187–9, 191, 193; Henry V 196–7, 201; Henry VI (Cibber's Rich. III) 399, 401–3; Hotspur 158, 160–1, 163, 166–7, 169–70, 172, 178–9; John, King 239–41, 243; King (All's Well) 88; Lear 256–60, 262; Macbeth 284–92, 297; Macduff 296, 298; Othello 356–8, 360–3, 365–6, 368–9; Richard II 377; Richard III 383–4, 386, 389; Talbot 202; Ursaces 103–4. Other references 40, 42, 51, 53, 56, 61, 76, 258.

Dennis, John [dramatist], 1657–1734: 18, 99–101, 218, 319.

Desnoyer, G. [dancer], fl. 1733: 41.

Desse [dancer], fl. 1739–45: 55, 70.

Destrade, d. 1754: Soldier, French 198–9. Other references 62, 71.

D'Hervigni, *Mlle* [dancer], fl. 1736: 49.

Dickinson [DL gallery office-keeper], fl. 1747: 76.

Dickinson, *Mrs* [DL middle gallery box-keeper], fl. 1747: 76.

Diggs, Richard, d. 1727: Agamemnon 452–3; Albany 248–52; Banquo 279; Catesby 379; Demetrius (Titus) 451; Escalus (Measure) 302; Horatio 115–17; Lodovico 351–2; Lucius (Cymbeline) 103; Octavius 221–2; Page (MWW) 321–2; Provost 303; Ross (Rich. II) 376; Stanley 381–2; Winlove 418. Other references 24, 26–7, 29.

Dighton, fl. 1742–3: Albany 261; Catesby 393, 395; Cornwall 261–2; Ratcliff 393.

Dogget, Thomas, *c.* 1670–1721: Evans 320; Gravedigger 108; Polonius 105; Shylock (Jew) 309; Taquilet 455; Witch 270–1. Other reference 3.

Domitilla, *Signora* [dancer], fl. 1743: 65.

Dove, Michael, d. 1747: Antonio (Tempest) 433, 435; Bardolph (1 Hen. IV) 164, 167; Bardolph (MWW) 328, 331; Bernardo 126–7; Carrier 174–5; Curtis (Sauny) 420–1; Duke (Othello) 370–1; Forrest 384; Gravedigger 137–9, 141; Grist 419; Lord Mayor 399–400; Montano 354; Murderer 298; Northumberland (1 Hen. IV) 173; Shallow (MWW) 336; Sycorax 433; Tyrrel 393, 395. Other reference 43.

Dove, *Mrs* Michael, Elizabeth, fl. 1746–7: Amphitrite 434; Arante 265.

Drury, Robert, fl. 1734–7: Othello 360. Other references 46, 52.

Dryden, John [dramatist], 1631–1700: 422, 451, 460–1.

Dubuisson [dancer], fl. 1742: 62.

Dunbar [DL box-keeper], d. 1762: 66, 73, 78.

Dunstall, John, 1717–78: Abraham 413; Bardolph (1 Hen. IV) 168; Bardolph (MWW) 337; Barnardine 308; Bullcalf 193–4; Campeius 217; Carrier 177–9; Citizen (J. Caesar) 238–9; Clown (All's Well) 89; Clown (Wint. T.) 458; Duke (Othello) 364; Gadshill 172; Gravedigger 130–1, 133–4, 143–4; Grey (Betterton's 2 Hen. IV) 191; Host 333, 337–9; Isidore 449; Jamy (Hen. V) 201; King, Player 142; Lord Mayor 390–1, 393, 395, 400–1; Manly 422; Phaeax 448; Physician (Lear) 261; Sheriff (1 Hen. IV) 177; Steward 88; Tubal 315; Tyrrel 402–3; Witch 291, 295, 299–300. Other references 79, 84.

Dunstall, *Mrs* John, Mary, d. 1758: Edward, Prince 390, 393; Ford, *Mrs* 333; Margaret (Cure) 422; Mariana (All's Well) 88–9; Mopsa 458; Nurse 413; Phryne 448; Tearsheet, Doll 191–3. Other reference 79.

Dupré, James [dancer], fl. 1733–44: 42, 47, 65, 67.

D'Urfey, Thomas [dramatist], 1653–1723: 2, 102, 218, 461.

Dyer, *Mrs*, fl. 1734: Hostess (1 Hen. IV) 161.

Dyer, Michael, d. 1774: Cleon 445; Gratiano (Merchant) 318; Mercutio 413; Mortimer 179; Osric 144; Pistol (Hen. V) 201; Roderigo 374; Shallow (MWW) 326; Tybalt 413; Witch 284.

# INDEX I

Eaton, d. 1739: Dorcas (Bullock's Cobler) 419; Evans 324.
Edwards, fl. 1746–7: Blunt (1 Hen. IV) 175–6.
Edwards, *Miss*, later Mrs Thomas Mozeen, q.v
Egerton, *Mrs*, fl. 1737–42: Audrey 91–3; Emilia (Othello) 362; Lady, Old 214.
Egleton, John, 1698–1727: Catesby 380–2; Cornwall 248–51; Diomedes 452–3; Edmund 249; Fenton 320–1; Gratiano (Jew) 311; John, Don 342; Laertes 112–14; Lucio 302–3; Malcolm 274–7; Osric 114–16; Palladour 103; Provost 302; Richmond 380; Roderigo 351–2; Salisbury (Rich. II) 376; Slender 322; Vernon (1 Hen. IV) 150–2. Other references 17, 29, 380.
Egleton, *Mrs* John, Jane, formerly Mrs Giffard, d. *c.* 1734: Andromache 453; Anne, Lady (Rich. III) 380; Calphurnia 222–3, 225–6; Elizabeth, Queen 380; Emilia (Othello) 350–4, 356–7; Goneril 248; Hostess (1 Hen. IV) 151–7, 159; Margaret (Much Ado) 342; Margaret (Sauny) 419; Queen (Cymbeline) 103; Queen (Hamlet) 112–13, 116; Quickly, Mrs (MWW) 320–6; Tamora 450–1; York, Duchess of (Rich. III) 380–2. Other references 29, 321.
Elmy, *Mrs* Mary, nee Morse, 1712–92: Chloe 445; Desdemona 371, 373–4; Elizabeth, Queen 399; Hero 344–5; Macduff, Lady 298. Other references 76, 78, 345.
Elrington, Richard, fl. 1750: Bernardo 144; Blunt (1 Hen. IV) 179; Colevile 193–4; Decius 239; Oxford 403; Westmorland (Hen. V) 201.
Elrington, Thomas, 1688–1732: Cassius 220–1; Edgar 253; Hamlet 110–11; Henry IV (2 Hen. IV) 181; Hotspur 147–9, 154–5; Macduff 273–4, 280; Othello 353; Seyton 271; Sylla 407. Other reference 34.
Elsam, *Mrs* [singer], fl. 1721: 22.
Emberton, Anthony(?) [DL stage-door-keeper], fl. 1746: 73.
Essex, John [dancer], d. 1744: 37, 52, 56, 58.
Estcourt, Richard, 1668–1712: Falstaff (1 Hen. IV) 145–6; Gravedigger 105–7; Pandarus 452; Trinculo 423. Other reference 4.
Este, William, d. 1743: Abergavenny 211; Cinna the Conspirator 229–30; Fenton 327–30; Ferdinand 431; Gadshill 161–2; Heartwell 420; Henry IV (Humours of Fal.) 185; Horatio 124, 126–7; John, Prince (2 Hen. IV) 186; Mustacho 431; Norfolk (Hen. VIII) 211.

Evans, fl. 1733–43: Barnardine 305; Trebonius 228. Other reference 45.
Evans, John, d. *c.* 1734: Falstaff (1 Hen. IV) 146–7, 149; King (Hamlet) 109. Other reference 8.
Eversman [violinist], fl. 1730–5: 36, 43, 48.
Excell, fl. 1733–5: Witch 286. Other reference 43.

Fabres, *Mlle* [dancer], fl. 1744: 67.
Fairbank, Henry, fl. 1702–9: Cornwall 246, Murderer 270; Priam 452; Tranio (Sauny) 415; Ventoso 424; Witch 269. Other references 2–3, 6.
Falkner, *Miss* Anna Maria, later Mrs William Donaldson, fl. 1750: Flora 422.
Fenn, John [DL stage-door-keeper], fl. 1743–5: 64, 70.
Fenton, *Miss* Lavinia, later Duchess of Bolton, 1708–60: Ophelia 117–18.
Ferguson, *Miss*, fl. 1738–46: Boy (Hen. V) 196–8; Gentlewoman (Macbeth) 297.
Ferrers [singer], fl. 1725: 28.
Fieldhouse, fl. 1703: Rodoregue 455.
Fielding, Timothy, 1690–1738: Abergavenny 209; Alonso 428; Cornwall 256; Douglas 159. Other reference 41.
Finch, *Mrs* Katharine, fl. 1708: Bianca (Othello) 347; Regan 245.
Fletcher, *Mrs* Elizabeth [a citizen's widow], fl. 1750: 83.
Fletcher, *Mrs* Manina, later Mrs Seedo [singer], fl. 1719: 18.
Foley [DL box-lobby-keeper], fl. 1748: 78.
Foote, Samuel, 1720–77: Othello 367, 370. Other reference 463.
Ford, Richard [LIF treasurer], fl. 1732: 39.
Forrester, *Mrs*, fl. 1719–36: Portia (J. Caesar) 222; Queen (Hamlet) 127; Regan 256; Thais 446. Other reference 42.
Freeman, fl. 1735–45: Alonso 433; Burgundy (Lear) 262; Dumain Jr. 89; Norfolk (Rich. III) 392, 395; Othello 361.
Freeman, John, fl. 1706: Gloucester (Lear) 245.
Fryar [unidentified], fl. 1746: 73.
Fuller [unidentified], fl. 1743: 64.
Fullwood [unidentified], fl. 1743: 64.
Furnival, Thomas, d. 1773: Brabantio 368; Douglas 165–7; Ford 335–6; Gloucester (Lear) 265; Hamlet 137; Henry IV (1 Hen. IV) 173, 175–6; Horatio 141; Iago 369–71; Jasper, Sir 419; Lodovico 355; Macduff 297; Montague 410; Prospero 433, 435; Tressel 397, 399–400. Other reference 72.
Furnival, *Mrs* Thomas, Fanny, fl. 1738–47: Emilia (Othello) 369, 371; Goneril

# INDEX I

259; Macbeth, Lady 296–7; Portia (J. Caesar) 233, 237; Queen (Hamlet) 139.

Gale [unidentified], fl. 1742: 62.

Gallant [LIF pit door-keeper], fl. 1720–32: 20, 26, 39.

Galliard, John Ernest [composer], c. 1687–1749: 462.

Garnet, Mrs, fl. 1716: Maid (Bullock's Cobler) 416.

Garrick, David, 1717–79: Benedick 344–6; Chorus 200–1; Ghost 131–2; Hamlet 132–4, 136, 138–9, 141–3; Hotspur 174; Iago 373–4; John, King 241; Lear 260–1, 263–6; Macbeth 293–4, 297–8, 300; Othello 368, 370; Richard III 390–1, 393–6, 398–9, 401–3; Romeo 412. Other references 63–4, 66, 70, 74, 80, 141, 405, 462–3.

George, Mrs, fl. 1744: Capulet, Lady 410.

George, Prince [consort of Queen Anne], 1653–1708: 6.

Gerrard, Miss, fl. 1735: Widow (Sauny) 421.

Gerum, fl. 1735: Antonius 410.

Gibbs [unidentified], fl. 1732: 39.

Gibbs [GF pit door-keeper], fl. 1732–3: 40, 43.

Gibson, William, 1713–71: Albany 260–4; Angers, Abbot of (Papal Tyr.) 242; Benvolio 413; Bernardo 134–6, 138; Borachio 344; Brabantio 366–8, 370, 372; Burgundy (Hen. V) 198–9; Catesby 390, 392, 394, 396–8, 400, 402–3; Donalbain 290; Dumain Jr. 89; Duncan 293–6, 300; Escalus (Measure) 307–8; Fenton 333–8; France, King of 201; Grey (Hen. V) 197; Henry IV (2 Hen. IV) 193–4; Kent 266; King, Player 138; Laertes 140, 142–4; Le Beau 92, 95–6; Lodovico 365; Man, Old (Shadwell's Timon) 449; Melun (Papal Tyr.) 243; Morton 189; Octavius 235–6, 238–9; Pandulph (Papal Tyr.) 242; Poins (1 Hen. IV) 169; Rosencrantz 130–2; Seyton 292, 294, 299–300; Siward 290–1; Solanio 315–17, 319; Surrey (Hen. VIII) 214–17; Time 457–8; Tressel 389, 401; Vernon (1 Hen. IV) 170–4, 176–9; Westmorland (2 Hen. IV) 190–4.

Giffard, Master, fl. 1732–4: Edward, Prince 383–4; Fleance 285; Lucius (J. Caesar) 228–30.

Giffard, Edward [GF box-keeper], fl. 1733: 43.

Giffard, Henry, 1699–1772: Antony 227–8, 230, 232, 237; Bertram 88–9; Cassio 357–8, 360–1, 364, 372; Dauphin (Hen. V) 195–6; Edgar 254, 256–8, 261–3; Ford 324–8, 332–4; Ghost 140–1; Hamlet 119–21, 123–5, 127–8, 130–2, 137, 139; Henry VI (Cibber's Rich. III) 383–4, 386, 390–7; Iago 367; Leontes 457; Macduff 282, 284–6, 291, 293–4, 297; Othello 355–6; Philip, King 243; Richmond 400–1; Wales, Prince of (1 Hen. IV) 153, 156, 158, 160, 162–4, 168, 172, 174–7. Other references 17, 463.

Giffard, Mrs Henry [the 2nd] Anna Marcella, nee Lyddall, 1707–77: Anne, Lady (Rich. III) 383–4, 386, 390–1, 393, 395; Constance 243; Cordelia 254, 256–8, 261–4; Desdemona 355–8, 360–1, 363, 365–7, 372; Elizabeth, Queen 395–6, 398; Evandra 448; Ford, Mrs 324–6; Helena 88–9; Hermione 458; Katharine 195–6; Katharine, Queen 215–16; Macbeth, Lady 294–5, 297; Macduff, Lady 284; Ophelia 119, 121–3; Percy, Lady (1 Hen. IV) 156, 168. Other references 60, 70, 76.

Giffard, Mrs Jane, later Mrs John Egleton, q.v.

Giffard, Mrs M., fl. 1733–5: Calphurnia 228; Page, Anne 328.

Giffard, William, c. 1712–1807: Apemantus 445; Beaufoy 420–1; Brabantio 361; Buckingham (Rich. III) 383–4, 386; Caliban 429; Casca 227–8, 230, 232; Cassio 356–7; Edmund 261–2; Falstaff (1 Hen. IV) 156, 164; Falstaff (MWW) 324–5, 328; Fenton 334; Florizel 457; France, King of 195–6; Gloucester (Lear) 254; Henry VIII 210; Horatio 130–1, 133; Hotspur 172; Iago 355; King (All's Well) 89; King (Hamlet) 119–21, 125, 127; King, Player 133–4; Laertes 122–3; Lennox 294; Macbeth 282; Malcolm 291; Poins (2 Hen. IV) 191; Richmond 392, 395; Tressel 390–1, 393; Vernon (1 Hen. IV) 168; Worcester 158, 160, 162–3. Other references 36, 38, 43, 66.

Giffard, Mrs William, Elizabeth, fl. 1742–3: Elizabeth, Queen 393; Regan 263.

Gildon, Charles [dramatist], 1665–1724: 301, 461.

Giles [unidentified], fl. 1723–40: 26, 57.

Glover [dancer], fl. 1735–7: 47, 51.

Goodall, fl. 1741–4: Cleomenes 457–8; Cromwell 214; Dauphin (Hen. V) 198; Salarino 315; Silvius 92, 94. Other references 65, 67.

Goodfellow, J., fl. 1744–7: Antonio (Tempest) 434; Blunt (1 Hen. IV) 174; Campeius 216; Captain (Twelfth N.) 456; Doctor (Macbeth) 296; Ferdinand 433, 435; Gratiano (Othello) 369; Guildenstern 136; Hamlet 135–8, 141; Hotspur 173; Lear 264–5; Macbeth

## INDEX I

297; Othello 370–1; Richard III 396–7, 399–400; Silvius 95; Surveyor 215–16. Other references 73, 77.

Goodman, fl. 1748: Prospero 436.

Goodwin, Thomas(?) [DL door-keeper], fl. 1748: 78.

Grace, *Mrs* Anne, nee Purvor, later Mrs Charles Macklin [the 1st], q.v.

Gray, James, fl. 1733–48: Bullcalf 184; Forrest 389, 392; Guard (R & J) 411; Sheriff (1 Hen. IV) 175. Other references 73, 78.

Green, fl. 1734–49: Balthazar (Merchant) 313–15; Blunt (1 Hen. IV) 171–2; Curio 455; Donalbain 291–2, 294–5; Edward, Prince 386–9; Guildenstern 131–4, 136; Henry, Prince 241; Hippolito 433; John, Prince (1 Hen. IV) 169–70; Mustacho 436; Officer (Othello) 368; Oxford 392, 394–6; Robin 327–8; Silvius 92–4; Simple 328–32, 334. Other reference 58.

Green, *Mrs* Henry, Jane, nee Hippisley, 1719–91: Blanch (Papal Tyr.) 243; Chloe 448–9; Diana 88–9; Dorinda 435, 437; Edward, Prince 391–5, 397–8, 403; Katharine 200–1; Margaret (Much Ado) 344; Maria 456–7; Nerissa 317; Ophelia 130–1, 133; Page, Anne 333; Perdita 458; Phebe 95–7.

Griffin, Benjamin, 1680–1740: Apothecary (C. Marius) 409; Butts 210–11; Carrier 148, 150; Citizen (Coriolanus) 101; Citizen (J. Caesar) 223, 229, 231–4; Cleon 444, 446–7; Dorcas (Bullock's Cobler) 417; Evans 320–1, 327–9; Feeble 181–6; Isander 444; Polonius 111–18, 120–4, 126–9; Sands 209, 212–13; Shylock (Jew) 310; Silence 182–3, 186, 188; Witch 274–5, 277–83, 285, 287–9. Other reference 15.

Griffin, 'Captain' Philip, fl. 1707–8: Apemantus 438; Lennox 269. Other reference 270.

Gulick, *Mrs*, fl. 1720: Clarinna 103; Macduff, Lady 275; Overdone, Mrs 302.

Gwinn [LIF and CG pit door-keeper], fl. 1724–43: 28, 30, 33, 44, 65.

Hacket, fl. 1744–50: Apothecary 410; Shadow 193–4; Tooth-drawer 422.

Hale, Sacheverel, d. 1746: Achilles 453–4; Albany 257–60; Antony 235–6; Banquo 291; Bardolph, Lord 187–9; Bassanio 315–16; Bastard 241; Bertram 89; Buckingham (Hen. VIII) 214–15; Cassio 364–8, 370; Claudio (Much Ado) 344; Demetrius (Shadwell's Timon) 446; Douglas 166–7, 169; Duke (Jew) 312; Edmund 260–3; Florizel 457–8; Gentleman (Timon) 445; Gower (Hen. V) 196–7; Henry V 198–9; Henry VI (Cibber's Rich. III) 397; Horatio 122–5, 128–30, 134–6; Hotspur 170–4; Iachimo (Cymbeline) 104; John, Prince (2 Hen. IV) 190–2; Laertes 131–3; Lennox 284; Lodovico 358–60, 363; Malcolm 293–6; Orlando 92–6; Pedro, Don 342–3; Percy 377; Philip, King (Papal Tyr.) 242; Poins (1 Hen. IV) 159, 161, 163; Richmond 389, 392, 394–5, 397; Siward 289–90; Somerset 202; Stanley 385; Timon 449; Tressel 385, 387. Other references 67, 71.

Hale, *Mrs* Sacheverel, later Mrs John Barrington, q.v.

Hall, fl. 1749: Gonzalo 436.

Hall, John [DL manager], fl. 1704–10: 3, 8.

Hall, John, d. 1734: Ajax 453–4; Caius 321, 323, 325–6; Carrier 152–5, 159; Citizen (Coriolanus) 101; Citizen (J. Caesar) 223–7; Elbow 302; Falstaff (1 Hen. IV) 147; Gravedigger 110–12, 116; Hacket, Dame 417, 419; Hecate 275–84; Isander 445–6; Lionel, Sir 418; Lord Mayor 384–5. Other references 11, 18, 29.

Hallam, Adam, d. 1768: Arviragus 103–4; Aumerle 377; Cassio 358–9; Claudio (Much Ado) 342–3; Cornwall 260; Dauphin (Hen. V) 196–7; Dauphin (1 Hen. VI) 202; Dauphin (John) 239–41; Edgar 256–8; Iago 358, 360–1, 363; John, Prince (2 Hen. IV) 183–4, 187–9; Laertes 120–6, 128–30, 132–3; Lysimachus (Marina) 375; Macduff 290; Malcolm 282–3, 286–91; Octavius 231; Page (MWW) 329–33; Richard III 387; Richmond 385; Thrasillus 445–6; Vernon (1 Hen. IV) 157, 159, 161, 163, 165–7, 169; Wales, Prince of (1 Hen. IV) 163. Other reference 41.

Hallam, George, fl. 1730–47: Bardolph (1 Hen. IV) 173; Bardolph (MWW) 336; Gratiano (Othello) 371; Gravedigger 119; Man, Old (Lear) 265; Mouldy 184; Northumberland (1 Hen. IV) 175–6; Polonius 139–40; Snuffle 419; Sycorax 433, 435; Tyrrel 399–400; Witch 298.

Hallam, Lewis, d. c. 1756: Evans 336; Francis 174–6; Gentleman Usher 265; Gravedigger 139, 141; Hecate 298; Lucianus 137; Roderigo 369–71; Stanley 399–400; Trinculo 433, 435. Other reference 72.

Hallam, *Mrs* Lewis, later Mrs David Douglass, d. c. 1773: Anne, Lady (Rich. III) 397, 399–400; Desdemona 371; Hippolito 433, 435; Miranda 433; Page, Mrs 336; Percy, Lady (1 Hen. IV) 174–5, 177.

477

# INDEX I

Hallam, Thomas, d. 1735: Francis 161; Isander 444; Pistol (MWW) 327–8; Silence (Humours of Fal.) 185; Sycorax 428; Tooth-drawer 420; Witch 278–9, 281–3. Other references 30–1.

Hallam, William, fl. 1735–47: Bardolph (1 Hen. IV) 166; Bardolph (2 Hen. IV) 187; Bardolph (Hen. V) 196–7; Captain (Lear) 265; Citizen (J. Caesar) 231; Coupler, Mother 375; Duke (Othello) 363; Guildenstern 127; Host 336; Stephano 435; Witch 298. Other references 72, 77, 465.

Hallam, Mrs William, Anne, formerly (1) Mrs Parker; (2) Mrs Joseph Berriman, 1696–1740: Calphurnia 231; Constance 240–1; Cordelia 251; Elizabeth, Queen 381–2, 384–5, 387; Evandra 445–6; Isabella 303–4; Joan la Pucelle 202; Katharine, Queen 207–8; Macbeth, Lady 278–90; Page, Mrs 322–3, 325, 330–1; Portia (Jew) 311–13; Queen (Cymbeline) 103–4; Queen (Hamlet) 115–26, 128–9; Regan 248; York, Duchess of (Rich. II) 377. Other references 30, 32, 54, 56.

Hamilton, fl. 1733–6: Burgundy (Lear) 257–8; Cambridge (Hen. V) 195–6; Geraldo 420–1; Guildenstern 123–7; Poins (1 Hen. IV) 162–3; Simple 328. Other reference 43.

Hamilton, Mrs, fl. 1733–8: Bianca (Sauny) 421; Emilia (Othello) 363; Macduff, Lady 285–6; Ophelia 123–8; Page, Anne 327; Percy, Lady (1 Hen. IV) 160, 162–3; Philoten 375. Other reference 43.

Harbin, Thomas, d. 1765: Douglas 160, 162–3; Norfolk (Rich. III) 386; Rosencrantz 123–5; Siward 285–6; Soothsayer 230, 232.

Harold, Mrs, fl. 1725: Calphurnia 225.

Harper, John, d. 1742: Ajax 453; Caius 320, 327–9; Casca 222; Citizen (J. Caesar) 223–6, 229–33; Elbow 304–5; Falstaff (1 Hen. IV) 152–7, 159–60, 164; Falstaff (2 Hen. IV) 181–5; Henry VIII 208–10; Host 329–30; Lord Mayor 385–8; Murderer 274, 283, 285–8; Mustacho 427; Phaeax 443–4, 446–7; Porco 342; Sulpitius 409; Trinculo 428; Ventoso 427. Other references 25, 34, 46, 159, 166, 186, 420.

Harrington, d. 1749: Bardolph (MWW) 333–4; Burgundy (Hen. V) 197; Duke (Othello) 365–6; Duncan 292; Hastings 190–1; Jeweller 445–6; King, Player 134; Lord (Wint. T.) 457–8; Marcellus 131–2; Pembroke 241; Poins (1 Hen. IV) 160; Priest (Hamlet) 130; Ratcliff 390, 392, 394; Seyton 293; Westmorland (1 Hen. IV) 170–1.

Harris, Joseph, d. c. 1715: Duke (Jew) 309.

Harrison [singer], fl. 1723: 26.

Harrison [LIF pit office-keeper], fl. 1725: 29.

Hart, fl. 1747: Siward 298.

Haughton, Mrs, fl. 1730–6: Calphurnia 229–30, 232; Emilia (Othello) 355–8, 360–1; Goneril 256–8; Macbeth, Lady 286; Page, Mrs 324–8; Queen (Hamlet) 119, 121–7; York, Duchess of (Rich. III) 383–4, 386. Other references 40, 43.

Haughton, G. [dancer], fl. 1733–8: 41, 52.

Haughton, Miss Hannah, d. 1771: Goneril 264, 266; Juliet (Measure) 307–8; Katharine 202; Macduff, Lady 297; Miranda 433; Page, Anne 337–9; Tearsheet, Doll 194; York, Duke of 386.

Havard, William, 1710–78: Adam 97; Albany 259; Angelo (Com. Err.) 99; Angelo (Measure) 306, 308; Antony 237; Banquo 293, 295, 298; Bassanio 313–18; Blunt (1 Hen. IV) 157–8; Buckingham (Hen. VIII) 216–17; Cassio 368–9; Catesby 383–4, 386; Clerimont 419; Cornwall 256–7; Dauphin (Hen. V) 199–200; Dumain Sr. 88; Edgar 260–1, 265–6; Edmund 263; Fenton 324–6, 328; Ford 338; Glendower 174; Gloucester (Lear) 264; Hamlet 132; Henry IV (1 Hen. IV) 171–2, 174; Horatio 125–34, 136–8, 140–3; Hotspur 176; Iago 372–3; John, Prince (2 Hen. IV) 186, 188–91; Laurence, Friar 411–12; Lorenzo 313; Macduff 292, 298–300; Malcolm 289–91; Marcellus 121, 123–6; Montano 356–8, 361, 365–6, 370; Mortimer 158, 160, 162–3; Norfolk (Hen. VIII) 212–14, 216; Octavius 233–4; Oliver 92–7; Orlando 96–7; Pedro, Don 344–6; Petruchio (Sauny) 420–1; Philip, King 241; Prospero 429; Provost 304–5; Richmond 391, 393–9, 401–3; Scroop (Hen. V) 195–6; Sebastian (Twelfth N.) 455–6; Seyton 285–6, 288–9; Stanley 387–9, 391; Trebonius 228, 230, 232; Vernon (1 Hen. IV) 164, 169–70; Worcester 165–9. Other references 38, 43, 61, 73, 83.

Havard, Mrs William, Elizabeth, formerly Mrs Kilby, d. 1764: Clarinna 103–4; Macduff, Lady 287; Margaret (Much Ado) 344–6; Mariana (Measure) 303; Phryne 446. Other references 37, 49, 83.

Hayman, Francis(?), fl. 1743–6: Balthazar (Merchant) 317; Balthazar (Much Ado) 344; Dauphin (Hen. V) 199; Diphilus 449; Gentleman (All's Well) 89; Gentleman, French 104; Lorenzo 316; Poins (2 Hen. IV) 192; Priest (Hamlet) 134–6;

478

# INDEX I

Silvius 94–6; Westmorland (1 Hen. IV) 171–4.
Heron, *Mrs* Mary, d. 1736: Anne, Lady (Rich. III) 385; Bullen, Anne 210; Emilia (Othello) 352; Ford, Mrs 327–8; Goneril 251. Other reference 48.
Hewitt, John, fl. 1733–6: Alonso 429–31; Buckingham (Rich. III) 384; Cassio 358; Decius 229–30; Henry IV (1 Hen. IV) 161; Mortimer 160; Norfolk (Hen. VIII) 210–11; Ratcliff 385, 387; Worcester 164.
Hewson, fl. 1733–4: Hotspur 161; Nicias 445; Stephano 429–30. Other reference 45.
Hickford, Thomas [concert manager], fl. 1713–39: 465.
Higginson, fl. 1715: Dighton 379.
Highmore, John, fl. 1730–1: Hotspur 155–6; Othello 355.
Hill, *Mrs*, fl. 1744: Nurse 411.
Hill, Aaron [actor], d. 1739: Abergavenny 211–12; Blunt (1 Hen. IV) 165–6; Catesby 387–8; Cornwall 259–60; Fenton 330; Gloucester (Hen. V) 196–7; Hastings 187; Octavius 233; Pembroke 240–1; Westmorland (1 Hen. IV) 166.
Hill, Aaron [dramatist], 1685–1750: 194–5, 461.
Hill, 'Sir' John, c. 1716–75: Laurence, Friar 410; Lodovico 367. Other reference 411.
Hilliard, *Miss*, d. 1744: Audrey 92; Juliet (Measure) 305–6; Tearsheet, Doll 190–2.
Hind, fl. 1735: Soothsayer 231.
Hippisley, *Miss* Elizabeth, later Mrs Fitzmaurice, fl. 1742–50: Arante 261; Clarence 193–4; Francisca 308; John, Prince (1 Hen. IV) 177–9.
Hippisley, *Miss* Jane, later Mrs Henry Green, q.v.
Hippisley, John, d. 1748: Carrier 174; Citizen (J. Caesar) 224–7, 231, 235–7; Clown (Measure) 303–7; Clown (Wint. T.) 457–8; Dogberry 342–4; Evans 321–6, 329–36; Fluellen 196–9; Francis 152, 156–7, 159, 161, 163, 165–7, 169–71, 173–4; Gardiner 214–17; Hecate 277; Murderer 281–92; Pandarus 453–4; Phaeax 445–6, 449; Polonius 114–26, 128–36, 138; Shallow (2 Hen. IV) 187–92; Snuffle 419, 421; Witch 277–82, 293–6; Woodall 418. Other references 26, 30, 34, 53, 55–6, 65, 71, 464.
Hobson [DL stage-door-keeper], fl. 1738–50: 52, 83.
Hodgson, *Mrs* John [singer], fl. 1710: 7.
Holliday, *Miss* Elizabeth, later Mrs William Mills [the 2nd], q.v.
Holmes, fl. 1747: Duncan 298.

Holt, fl. 1744: Marcellus 135.
Holtom, Edward, d. 1780: Benvolio 410; Blunt (Cibber's Rich. III) 402–3; Ligarius 238–9; Lovell 217; Montano 372; Nym (MWW) 338; Peter (Cure) 422; Pistol (MWW) 337; Westmorland (1 Hen. IV) 177–8.
Horsington, *Mrs* (i.e. *Miss*) Margaretta(?), fl. 1733–47: Arante 262; Audrey 93–4, 96; Page, Anne 326.
Horton, *Mrs* Christiana, 1699–1756: Anne, Lady (Rich. III) 379, 382, 390, 397, 399; Blanch 240; Bullen, Anne 207–9, 214–17; Calphurnia 220–5, 238–9; Capulet, Lady 413; Cordelia 258–60; Countess (All's Well) 89; Desdemona 362–4, 366; Elizabeth, Queen 383–4, 392, 394, 396, 398, 400–3; Evandra 445; Ford, Mrs 329–35, 337; Hermione 457–8; Isabel 201; Katharine, Queen 209–10; Macbeth, Lady 274, 282–3, 290, 292–4, 297; Macduff, Lady 272–82; Melissa 441–4; Portia (J. Caesar) 235–6; Queen (Hamlet) 138, 140, 142–4; Queen (Rich. II) 377. Other reference 19.
Hough, fl. 1740–1: Citizen (J. Caesar) 234.
Houghton, James, fl. 1726–38: Aeneas 453–4; Bernardo 117; Cambridge (Hen. V) 196; Cinna the Conspirator 231; Diphilus 445–6; Fenton 323, 325–6; Lorenzo (Jew) 312; Mortimer 163; Rosencrantz 127; Siward 281; Surrey (Rich. II) 377; Vernon (1 Hen. IV) 154, 159, 161. Other references 30, 32, 35–6.
Howard [unidentified], fl. 1745: 72.
Howard, *Mrs* [unidentified], fl. 1747: 77.
Huddy, *Master*, fl. 1732–3: Lucius (J. Caesar) 227–8; York, Duke of 383.
Huddy, Philip, fl. 1724–35: Caesar 227–8, 230, 232; Duncan 277, 284–6; Henry IV (1 Hen. IV) 156, 158, 160, 162–3; Horatio 119–21; Host 324–6; Kent 256–7; Lear 254; Page (MWW) 324, 327; Ratcliff 382; Tressel 383–4, 386. Other references 28–9, 40, 43, 48.
Hughes, *Miss*, fl. 1733–4: Edward, Prince 383–4.
Hulett, Charles, 1700–35: Achilles 453; Banquo 284–6; Beaufoy 418; Brabantio 357–8, 360–1; Casca 224; Cassius 227–8, 230, 232; Falstaff (1 Hen. IV) 158, 160–1, 163; Falstaff (MWW) 326–7; Ghost 117, 120, 126; Gloucester (Lear) 255–8; Gratiano (Othello) 354; Kent 250, 253–4; King (Hamlet) 120–1, 123–5; Lennox 275; Lucius (Titus) 451; Montano 356–7; Othello 361; Provost 303; Richard III 386; Seyton 277, 281–3; Siward 281; Worcester 155–7. Other references 20, 28–30, 39, 42, 45, 164.

479

## INDEX I

Hunt, Mrs, fl. 1716–19: Hostess (1 Hen. IV) 149. Other reference 13.
Hurst [unidentified], fl. 1724: 28.
Husband, Benjamin, 1672–c. 1752: Apemantus 440; Banquo 270–1; Cassio 347; Cromwell 205; Decius 218; Diomedes 452; Douglas 146; Edmund 246; Geraldo 415–16; Glendower 145, 149; Horatio 107; King (Hamlet) 107; Siward 268–9; Sylla 406. Other references 6, 10, 13.
Hutton, Mrs, fl. 1749: Emilia (Othello) 373. Other reference 82.
Hyde, fl. 1734–9: Falstaff (1 Hen. IV) 160; Falstaff (2 Hen. IV) 188; Henry VI (Cibber's Rich. III) 386; Lear 258; Othello 363. Other references 46, 49, 52, 55.

Irving, Sir Henry, 1838–1905: 405.

Jackson, Miss [unidentified], fl. 1747: 77.
James, Harris, d. 1751: Blunt (Cibber's Rich. III) 384; Caius 332, 335; Carrier 165–7, 169; Citizen (J. Caesar) 235–6; Corin 92, 94–7; Dogberry 345; Feeble 188–9; Francis 177; Gobbo 315; Iachimo (D'Urfey's Cymbeline) 103–4; Lucianus 127, 130–2, 134–6, 138, 140–3; Macmorris 200; Mustacho 437; Painter 449; Pistol (2 Hen. IV) 187, 190–1; Pistol (Hen. V) 196–7; Pistol (MWW) 331–8; Polonius 142; Sampson 411–12; Shallow (Humours of Fal.) 185; Shylock 315–16; Slender 330; Soothsayer 227–9; Town Clerk 344–6; Verges 343–4; Witch 286–90, 292–6. Other references 51, 68, 74, 98, 345.
James, Mrs Harris, fl. 1737–50: Audrey 95–6, 98; Calphurnia 236–7; Countess (1 Hen. VI) 202; Elinor 240–1; Emilia (Othello) 366–8, 370, 372; Gloucester, Duchess of 377; Goneril 262–4; Hostess (1 Hen. IV) 170, 174, 176–7; Hostess (2 Hen. IV) 187–93; Hostess (Hen. V) 198–9; Isabel 196–8; Lady, Old 215–17; Nurse 411–12; Queen (Cymbeline) 104; Queen (Hamlet) 134; Queen, Player 137–8; Quickly, Mrs (MWW) 330, 333–7; Widow (All's Well) 89; York, Duchess of (Rich. III) 394, 396–7, 399–401. Other reference 51.
Jarvis [CG house-keeper], fl. 1734: 44.
Jenkins, fl. 1732–5: Bernardo 123–5; Donalbain 286; Ligarius 227–30; Ratcliff 383–4, 386; Witch 285. Other reference 45.
Jervis, fl. 1744: Guildenstern 135.
Jevon, Mrs, fl. 1720: Clarinna 103.
Johnson, fl. 1749: Pembroke 243.

Johnson, 'Tall', d. 1746: Apemantus 449; Bedford (1 Hen. VI) 202; Belarius 104; France, King of 196–9; Gaunt 377; Ghost 136, 138; Henry IV (1 Hen. IV) 164, 166–7; Henry V 195–6; King (Hamlet) 128; Leonato 342–4; Northumberland (2 Hen. IV) 187–9; Pandulph (Papal Tyr.) 243.
Johnson, Benjamin, 1665–1742: Aelius 438–44, 446–8; Caliban 425–32; Carrier 146–55, 157, 159–60, 162, 164–70; Citizen (Invader) 100; Citizen (J. Caesar) 219, 221–6, 229–35; Gardiner 205–14; Gobbo 313; Gravedigger 106–24, 126–32; Hecate 268–83, 285–92; Polonius 106; Shallow (2 Hen. IV) 183–90; Shallow (MWW) 327–32; Stephano 424; Sulpitius 406; Woodall 415–16. Other references 10, 14, 27, 55, 58.
Johnson, Charles [dramatist], 1679–1748: 12, 25, 89, 98, 267, 339, 414, 461.
Jones [DL numberer and box-office-keeper], fl. 1720–48: 19, 37, 78.
Jones [LIF gallery door-keeper], fl. 1722–5: 24, 29.
Jones, Mrs, fl. 1741: Dorcas (Wint. T.) 458; Thais 448.
Jones, Miss, fl. 1740: Amphitrite 432.
Jones, Charles, fl. 1730–5: Bardolph (Humours of Fal.) 185; Carrier 157; Duke (Othello) 354; Gratiano (Othello) 355; Guzzle, Toby 419; Murderer 283; Mustacho 429–30; Nym (MWW) 327–8; Sycorax 430–1; Thrasillus 445.
Julian, Francis(?), fl. 1740–5: Carrier 168; Forrest 393, 395; Gratiano (Othello) 365; Man, Old (Lear) 261; Mustacho 433; Nicias 448; Polonius 130–1, 133, 137; Shallow (MWW) 332; Shepherd 458; Steward 89; Witch 291; Worcester 173.

Keene, Theophilus, d. 1718: Ajax 452; Alonso 425; Apemantus 439; Beaufoy 415–16; Brabantio 347–8; Brutus 220–1; Caesar 219; Casca 218–19; Cinna (C. Marius) 406; Duncan 268–72; Henry IV (1 Hen. IV) 145–9; Iago 347–8; Kent 246–7; King (Hamlet) 106–8, 110–11; Macbeth 273; Surveyor 205; Timon 441; Ursaces 102; Wolsey 205. Other references 5, 8–10, 13.
Keene, Mrs Theophilus [widow of the actor], fl. 1720–1: 20, 22.
Kelloms [unidentified], fl. 1717: 16.
Kennedy, Lawrence, 1720–86: Bernardo 138, 140; Blunt (Cibber's Rich. III) 400; Cassio 369; Donalbain 297; Ferdinand 433; Laertes 137; Nym (MWW) 337; Poins (1 Hen. IV) 173; Ratcliff 398;

480

# INDEX I

Stephano 433; Westmorland (1 Hen. IV) 176. Other reference 72.

Kennedy, *Mrs* Lawrence, E., née Orfeur, d. 1774: Ariel 433.

Kent, Thomas, fl. 1706: Ruffian (Tate's Lear) 245.

Kent, *Mrs* Thomas, Mary, fl. 1708: Goneril 245.

Kent, William [sculptor], 1684–1748: 52.

Kilby, *Mrs* Elizabeth, later Mrs William Havard, q.v.

Kilmarnock, William Boyd, Earl of [Jacobite], 1704–46: 199.

King, Daniel [DL box-keeper], d. 1731: 10–11, 25.

King, Thomas, 1730–1805: Claudio (Much Ado) 345; Ferdinand 436; Ross (Macbeth) 299–300; Solanio 317–18.

Kirby, fl. 1748: Worcester 177.

Kirk, *Mrs*, fl. 1730: Quickly, Mrs (MWW) 324.

Knapp, fl. 1706–16: Carrier 148; Semibreve (Leveridge's Pyramus) 339. Other reference 5.

Knapp, *Mrs*, d. 1734: Cordelia 249; Lavinia (Titus) 450–1. Other reference 22.

Knight, *Mrs* Frances Maria, fl. 1708–24: Andromache 453; Calphurnia 219, 221, 224; Evandra 439–40; Katharine, Queen 205; Macbeth, Lady 269–74, 277; Queen (Cymbeline) 103; Queen (Hamlet) 106–8, 110–12, 115; Tamora 451; York, Duchess of (Rich. III) 381. Other references 13, 270.

Lacy, James, 1696–1774: Agamemnon 453–4; Cornwall 255–7; Escalus (Measure) 304; Glendower 159, 161; Marius, Old 410; Montano 358–9; Seyton 283–4.

Lacy, John [dramatist], d. 1681: 413–14.

Lacy, Theophilus, fl. 1730: Cassio 354; Edmund 254; Fenton 324; Montano 355. Other reference 36.

Lacy, Thomas, fl. 1746–50: Burgundy (Hen. V) 201; Malcolm 296–7; Paris 413; Richard III 398; Tressel 403; Tybalt 413.

Laguerre, *Miss*, fl. 1749: Dorinda 436.

Laguerre, John, d. 1748: Wall (Lampe's Pyramus) 340–1. Other references 18, 29, 37.

Laguerre, *Mrs* John, Mary, formerly Mrs Rogeir, d. 1739: Edward, Prince 381; Jessica (Jew) 311; Page, Anne 321–2, 326. Other references 26, 29, 33, 37.

Lalauze, Charles, d. 1775: Shylock 316. Other references 54, 71, 74, 77, 84.

Lally, Edward [dancer], d. 1760: 29, 39.

Lamball, *Mrs*, fl. 1740–1: Emilia (Othello) 366; Macduff, Lady 291.

Lampe, John Frederick [composer], c. 1703–51: 339, 375, 461.

Lampe, *Mrs* John Frederick, Isabella, née Young, d. 1795: Thisbe (Lampe's Pyramus) 340–1. Other references 71, 79.

Lansdowne, George Granville, Baron [dramatist], 1667–1735: 218, 309.

Lanyon [dancer], fl. 1724: 28.

Larsay [unidentified], fl. 1725: 29.

Lascells, Thomas, fl. 1741–2: Gratiano (Othello) 365; Lord (Wint. T.) 457–8.

Laurence, fl. 1716–42: Wall (Leveridge's Pyramus) 340. Other references 22, 55, 63.

Law [unidentified], fl. 1747: 77.

Lawson, *Mrs* Abigail, fl. 1703: Lawra 455.

Layfield, Robert, fl. 1750: Charles 97; Hecate 300.

Lee, John, 1725–81: Alonso 433; Cassio 370–1; Claudio (Measure) 308; Claudio (Much Ado) 344–5; Dauphin (Hen. V) 201; Edmund 264–6; Fenton 336; Ferdinand 434–5; Ghost 137, 141; Gonzalo 435; Guildenstern 139; Hamlet 140; Hotspur 173–6; Malcolm 298; Montjoy 200; Paris 411; Richard III 397, 399, 403; Romeo 412; Ross (Macbeth) 298–9. Other references 73, 77, 84.

Leigh, Francis, Sr., d. 1719: Carrier 147; Citizen (C. Marius) 406; Citizen (J. Caesar) 219; Constable (Johnson's Cobler) 416; Gravedigger 110; Isander 439; Isidore 440; Mustacho 425–6; Witch 269, 272–4. Other reference 16.

Leigh, *Mrs* Francis, Sr., Elizabeth, fl. 1703–25: Dromia 455; Emilia (Othello) 346. Other references 27–8.

Leigh, Francis, Jr., fl. 1734–48: Francis 162; Francisco (Hamlet) 139; Gadshill 169, 171, 174–5; Lucilius (J. Caesar) 229–30, 237; Officer (Twelfth N.) 456; Rugby 327–32. Other reference 76.

Leigh, John, 1689–1726: Achilles 452–3; Antony 221–3; Banquo 275–7; Bassanio (Jew) 310; Bolingbroke 376; Caesar 221, 223–4; Cassio 350; Claudio (Much Ado) 342; Cymbeline 102–3; Edmund 248–9; Henry IV (1 Hen. IV) 152; Horatio 110–15; Kent 250; Macduff 273–5; Richmond 380; Saturninus 450–1; Wales, Prince of (1 Hen. IV) 148–52. Other references 17, 20, 464.

Leveridge, Richard, c. 1670–1758: Gravedigger 119, 123; Pyramus (Leveridge's Pyramus) 339–40. Other references 13, 15, 20, 27, 36, 71, 339, 375, 461.

Leviez, Charles [dancer], d. c. 1778: 51, 61, 70, 81, 83.

## INDEX I

Lillo, George [dramatist], 1693-1739: 54, 301, 374.
Lincoln, *Miss*, fl. 1745: Amphitrite 433.
Lindar, *Miss*, fl. 1715-27: Ariel 426-7; Dorinda 427; Falstaff's Page 180; Hymen (Love in For.) 91; Tearsheet, Doll 181; York, Duke of 379.
Linnet, fl. 1740: Lodovico 365.
Little [DL gallery box-keeper], fl. 1731: 37.
Littleton, fl. 1739: Bardolph (1 Hen. IV) 167.
Littleton, *Master*, fl. 1735: Pompeius's Son 410.
Longueville [unidentified], fl. 1721: 22.
Lovelace [LIF box-keeper], fl. 1725: 29.
Lowder, fl. 1735: Clodius 410; Evans 328.
Lowe, Thomas, d. 1783: Amiens 91-7; Lorenzo 313-18; Neptune 434. Other references 73, 81, 84.
Lucas [unidentified], fl. 1731: 38.
Lynham, fl. 1732-46: Vernon (1 Hen. IV) 175. Other reference 39.
Lyon, William, d. 1748: Carrier 162-3; Casca 228; Citizen (J. Caesar) 227-8, 230, 232; Glendower 164; Gratiano (Othello) 358, 360-1; Hecate 284-6; Host 328; Jamy (Hen. V) 196; Polonius 124-5, 127-8; Salisbury (1 Hen. VI) 202; Salisbury (Rich. II) 377; Sauny 420-1; York (Hen. V) 195-6.

Machen, Edward(?), fl. 1730-49: Alonso 436; Bardolph (MWW) 324; Blunt (1 Hen. IV) 161; Brabantio 355; Caliban 436; Cassio 361; Cornwall 254; Gonzalo 429; Gratiano (Othello) 355; Sulpitius 410.
Mackenzie [unidentified], fl. 1723: 26.
Macklin, Charles, *c.* 1700-97: Asino 342; Carrier 164, 166; Citizen (J. Caesar) 229, 231, 233-5; Cleon 447; Clown (All's Well) 88; Dromio of Syracuse 99; Evans 329-32; Fluellen 200-1; Francis 164-70; Ghost 135; Gravedigger 126, 132-3, 135-7, 139-41; Iago 367-9, 371-2, 374; Joculo 343; Lucio 306; Malvolio 455-6; Manly 420; Mercutio 413; Mustado 430-1; Osric 126-32; Pandulph 241, 243; Poins (1 Hen. IV) 161; Poins (2 Hen. IV) 186-7; Polonius 144; Shylock 313-18; Stephano 434; Touchstone 92-7; Trinculo 432, 434-5; Wales, Prince of (1 Hen. IV) 161; Witch 288-92, 295-7. Other references 49, 52, 58, 76, 126, 166.
Macklin, *Mrs* Charles [the 1st], Anne, nee Purvor, formerly Mrs Grace, d. 1758: Abbess 99; Desdemona 358-9; Emilia (Othello) 368-9, 371, 374; Goneril 252-3, 256; Hostess (1 Hen. IV) 167-70, 179;

Hostess (2 Hen. IV) 188-90, 193-4; Hostess (Hen. V) 199, 202; Macbeth, Lady 296; Maria 455-6; Nurse 413; Queen (Hamlet) 135; Quickly, Mrs (MWW) 330-2, 338. Other reference 76.
Macklin, *Miss* Maria, d. 1781: Arthur 242-3; York, Duke of 392-4, 397.
Maddocks [unidentified], fl. 1716: 12.
Maine, John [LIF gallery door-keeper], fl. 1722-3: 24, 26.
Male, *Miss*, fl. 1736: Ophelia 127.
Mallin, fl. 1744: Polonius 135.
Mann, *Miss* H., fl. 1733-8: Percy, Lady (1 Hen. IV) 160-1, 164; Tearsheet, Doll 184-6. Other references 46, 51.
Marr, Harry, d. 1783: Abraham 411-12; Aelius 448; Bedford (Hen. V) 200; Bernardo 140, 142-3; Burgundy (Lear) 260-1, 265-6; Catesby 390-4, 398, 403; Cinna the Conspirator 237; Gloucester (Hen. V) 199; Guildford 215-16; Herald, French 243; Jaques de Bois 94; John, Prince (1 Hen. IV) 171, 174; Laertes 135; Lennox 297; Lodovico 365; Lord (Wint. T.) 458; Montano 370; Mortimer 168; Watchman 344. Other references 60, 200.
Marshall, James(?), fl. 1731-46: Alcibiades 445; Duke Frederick 95; Ferdinand 429-30; Glendower 161, 163; Gloucester (Lear) 261; Horatio 126, 128; John, Prince (2 Hen. IV) 182; King (All's Well) 88; King (Hamlet) 124; Laertes 130-2, 136-7; Macbeth 291; Norfolk (Rich. III) 385; Polixenes 457; Richmond 383-4, 391, 393; Sebastian (Tempest) 434; Siward 286-7; Surrey (Hen. VIII) 210, 214, 216; Timon 448; Trebonius 231. Other reference 60.
Marshall, *Mrs* James(?), fl. 1736-42: Mariana (All's Well) 88; Overdone, Mrs 304-5; Percy, Lady (1 Hen. IV) 164; Thaisa (Marina) 375.
Marten, John, d. 1764: Angers, Abbot of (Papal Tyr.) 242-3; Bardolph (1 Hen. IV) 170-4, 176-9; Bardolph (2 Hen. IV) 190-4; Bardolph (Hen. V) 201; Bardolph (MWW) 334-8; Chancellor, Lord 217; Charles 92, 94-7; Citizen (J. Caesar) 234; Duke (Merchant) 315-17; Duke (Othello) 370; Elbow 307-8; King, Player 138; Lord Mayor 390, 392, 394, 396-8, 402-3; Murderer 292-6, 299-300; Nicias 449; Officer (Twelfth N.) 455; Phaeax 448; Sands 213; Shepherd 457-8; Soothsayer 235-6; Steward 89; Surveyor 214-17; Town Clerk 344; Witch 293, 297. Other references 63, 79.
Martin, *Mrs* Christopher, Elizabeth, nee Grace, formerly Mrs Barnes, later (1)

Mrs Richard Elrington; (2) Mrs Workman; (3) Mrs Richard Wilson, fl. 1733-46: Falconbridge, Lady 239-40; Hostess (1 Hen. IV) 159, 161, 163, 166, 168-9; Overdone, Mrs 305-7; Quickly, Mrs (MWW) 326.
Massey, fl. 1749: Stephano 436.
Mattocks, George, d. 1804: Donalbain 299-300.
Mawley, fl. 1733: Shadow 184.
Maxfield, fl. 1745: Mustacho 433.
May [unidentified], fl. 1722: 23.
Mechel [dancer], fl. 1742-7: 61, 76.
Mechel, *Mlle* [dancer], fl. 1742-7: 61, 76.
Merrivale, fl. 1724: Mortimer 153. Other reference 28.
Michael, fl. 1744: John, Friar 410.
Middleton, *Mrs*, fl. 1740: Emilia (Othello) 365; Page, Mrs 333.
Miles, Francis, d. 1771: Bardolph (1 Hen. IV) 175; Burgundy (Lear) 265; Doctor (Macbeth) 298; Simple 336.
Miller, *Mrs*, fl. 1749: Sycorax 436.
Miller, James [dramatist], 1706-44: 50, 341, 457.
Miller, Josias, 1684-1738: Caius 329-30; Carrier 148-55, 158-60, 162, 164-6; Citizen (C. Marius) 408-9; Citizen (Invader) 100; Citizen (J. Caesar) 222-6, 229-33; Clown (Measure) 304-5; Gravedigger 122; Host 327-9; Isander 441-3, 446-7; Isidore 439; Lord Mayor 379; Osric 112-13; Roderigo 349-54, 357-63; Ruffian (C. Marius) 409; Sands 206, 208, 210-12; Servant (Invader) 101; Silence 180-7; Thisbe (Love in For.) 91, 340; Trinculo 426-7, 429-31; Witch 285-8.
Miller, *Mrs* Josias, Henrietta Maria [widow of the actor], fl. 1738: 53.
Mills, John, d. 1736: Adam (Love in For.) 91; Agamemnon 452; Antonio (Jew) 309; Apemantus 439, 441-4; Aufidius (Invader) 100; Banquo 268-70; Buckingham (Rich. III) 379, 382, 385-7; Caesar 219-21; Cassius 222-6, 229-32; Cranmer 206-9; Douglas 145-7; Edmund 245-52; Exeter (Hen. V) 195; Falstaff (1 Hen. IV) 147-51; Falstaff (2 Hen. IV) 180; Ghost 106, 124, 126; Gloucester (Lear) 257; Hamlet 121-2, 124; Henry IV (1 Hen. IV) 147, 154-7, 159-60, 162, 164; Henry IV (2 Hen. IV) 181-6; Horatio 106-18, 120-1; Lear 245, 251, 253, 256; Lodovico 349; Mabeth 270-83, 285-6; Marius, Old 407-9; Norfolk (Hen. VIII) 204-5; Octavius 218; Othello 353-4, 356-8; Petruchio (Sauny) 415-16; Prospero 424-8, 430-1; Timon 438-9, 444-5; Titus 450; Wolsey 210-11;

York (Humfrey) 203. Other references 2, 8-9, 19, 30, 43, 46, 245, 286-7.
Mills, *Mrs* John, Margaret, fl. 1707-16: Amphitrite 425; Bianca (Sauny) 415; Chloe 438-9. Other references 9, 11.
Mills, William, d. 1750: Alcibiades 446-7; Antipholus of Ephesus 99; Antonio (Tempest) 427; Antony 232, 234; Apemantus 444; Banquo 285-92, 296-7; Bassanio 316-17; Bellario 342-3; Bertram 88; Blunt (1 Hen. IV) 155; Buckingham (Hen. VIII) 210-14; Buckingham (Humfrey) 203; Buckingham (Rich. III) 387-9, 391, 393-5; Caesar 229-34, 237; Cambridge (Hen. V) 195; Cassio 369, 371-3; Charles (Love in For.) 91; Claudio (Measure) 304, 306; Douglas 157; Duke Senior 91-3, 96-7; Duncan 293, 298-300; Edmund 251, 253, 256-7, 259-61, 263, 265; Ferdinand 427-8, 430-1; France, King of 199-200; Granius 409; Gratiano (Merchant) 313-18; Horatio 139; Iago 356, 358-66; John, Prince (2 Hen. IV) 180-2; King (Hamlet) 116-18, 120-2, 127-9, 131-4; Laertes 124, 126-7; Lodovico 352-4, 356; Malcolm 278-80; Messala 221, 226; Mowbray 180; Norfolk (Hen. VIII) 208-9; Orlando 93-5; Orsino 455-6; Richmond 387; Salisbury (John) 241, 243; Surrey (Hen. VIII) 213; Wales, Prince of (1 Hen. IV) 157, 159-60, 162, 164-71; Wales, Prince of (2 Hen. IV) 182-9, 191; Wolsey 214. Other references 25, 28, 58, 76.
Mills, *Mrs* William [the 1st], Theodosia, nee Tenoe, d. 1733: Miranda 426-8. Other reference 31.
Mills, *Mrs* William [the 2nd], Elizabeth, nee Holliday, fl. 1728-50: Anne, Lady (Rich. III) 383-4, 387-9, 391-2, 394-5, 401-3; Bullen, Anne 210-13; Cordelia 257, 259; Desdemona 365-6; Goneril 265; Hippolito 429-32; Isabel 201; Jessica (Jew) 312; Luciana 99; Macduff, Lady 285, 287-92, 294-300; Mariana (Measure) 303-5; Ophelia 118; Page, Anne 323-30; Page, Mrs 338; Percy, Lady (1 Hen. IV) 160, 162, 164-71, 174; Portia (J. Caesar) 237. Other references 76, 88, 212.
Milward, William, 1702-42: Albany 252-5; Angelo (Measure) 303-4; Antipholus of Syracuse 99; Antony 229-32; Banquo 281-4; Bassanio 313; Brabantio 353, 356-64; Cassius 232-4; Cornwall 252; Cranmer 210-11; Edgar 257, 259; Ford 327-32; Ghost 117; Gloucester (Lear) 255-6; Gratiano (Jew) 311-12; Gratiano (Univ. Pass.) 342-3; Hamlet 124, 126-30; Henry IV (1 Hen. IV) 156-7, 159;

# INDEX I

Henry IV (2 Hen. IV) 186–9; Henry VI (Cibber's Rich. III) 385–9; Horatio 117–21; Hotspur 159–60, 162, 164–9; King (All's Well) 88; King (Hamlet) 121–2, 124; Lodovico 353–4; Macduff 285–91; Malcolm 279–81; Octavius 227; Orlando 91–3; Othello 359; Sebastian (Twelfth N.) 455; Timon 445–8; Wolsey 211–13; York, Archbishop of 183–6. Other references 30, 34, 48, 55, 132.

Milward, *Mrs* William, Mary [widow of the actor], fl. 1742: 61.

Mines [CG gallery office-keeper], fl. 1743: 65.

Minns, fl. 1706: Kent 245. Other reference 5.

Minors, *Miss* Sybilla, later Mrs John Walker, 1723–1802: Blanch 242–3; Gentlewoman (Macbeth) 296–8; Jessica 315–16, 318; Page, Anne 338; Regan 265; Ursula 346.

Moffett, *Mrs*, fl. 1724–6: Cordelia 251; Ford, Mrs 322; Macduff, Lady 278. Other reference 30.

Molière, Jean Baptiste Poquelin, dit [dramatist], 1622–73: 341.

Monlass, fl. 1734–5: Bardolph (1 Hen. IV) 162–3; Citizen (J. Caesar) 230, 232; Mouldy (Humours of Fal.) 185; Murderer 286; Witch 285.

Monlass, *Mrs*, fl. 1733–5: Hostess (Humours of Fal.) 185; Queen, Player 123; Regan 257–8.

Montigny [unidentified], fl. 1727: 32.

Moore, fl. 1733–5: Francisco (Hamlet) 123–5; Metellus (J. Caesar) 230; Oxford 386; Westmorland (1 Hen IV) 160, 162–3.

Moore, *Mrs* Henrietta, fl. 1708–28: Miranda 424. Other references 6, 15, 21, 23, 32.

Moreau, *Mrs* (i.e. *Miss*), fl. 1747: Ariel 435; Donalbain 298; Page, Anne 336. Other reference 77.

Moreau, Anthony [dancer], fl. 1719: 18.

Moreau, *Mrs* Anthony, nee Schoolding [dancer], fl. 1716–19: 14, 18.

Morgan, *Master*, fl. 1746–7: Fleance 298; Robin 336; York, Duke of 399–400.

Morgan, Robert(?), fl. 1720–49: Abhorson 302; Carrier 158, 160–1, 163, 171–2, 174, 176–7; Citizen (J. Caesar) 223–9; Francis 157; Gentleman Usher 249–50, 252–4; Goth 451; Gravedigger 120–4, 137–8, 140, 142; Guzzle, Toby 420; Host 325–7, 337; Jamy (Sauny) 419; Lord Mayor 383; Nym (MWW) 334; Priam 453–4; Richard III 402; Stephano 433; Trinculo 429, 436; Witch 275–9,
281–2, 284, 297. Other references 26, 28, 30, 36, 80, 82.

Morgan, *Mrs* Robert (?), Henrietta Maria, fl. 1722–49: Dorinda 429; Elizabeth, Queen 402; Hippolito 436; Hostess (1 Hen. IV) 158, 160; Lavinia (Titus) 451; Quickly, Mrs (MWW) 325–7; Regan 256. Other references 36, 38, 80.

Morris [GF stage-door-keeper], fl. 1733: 43.

Morris, John, fl. 1748: Evans 337.

Morrison, *Miss* Ann Maria, later Mrs Thomas Hull, 1727–1805: Arthur (Papal Tyr.) 243; Boy (Hen. V) 201; Boy (Much Ado) 344; Edward, Prince 400–3; Fleance 295–7, 299–300; Page (All's Well) 89; Robin 333, 335; York, Duke of 390, 392, 394, 396–8.

Morse, *Miss* Mary, later Mrs Elmy, q.v.

Mottley, John [dramatist], 1692–1750: 22.

Mountfort, *Mrs*, fl. 1730: Page, Anne 324–5.

Mountfort, *Mrs* (i.e. *Miss*) Susannah, d. 1720: Hippolito 423–4; Ophelia 106, 108–10. Other references 10–11, 113.

Mountier, Thomas, fl. 1733–4: Milcha 430.

Mozeen, Thomas, d. 1768: Abergavenny 215–16; Albany 262, 265–6; Antonio (Tempest) 434–5; Benvolio 412; Cassio 368; Conrade 346; Douglas 175; Dumain Sr. 89; Lennox 298; Montano 368–9, 371–2; Norfolk (Rich. III) 396, 398; Oliver 96–7; Paris 410; Pembroke 241, 243; Scroop (Hen. V) 200; Silvius 96–7; Stanley 393, 395.

Mozeen, *Mrs* Thomas, nee Edwards, fl. 1740–8: Desdemona 369; Jessica 315–16; Milcha 432; Miranda 434–5. Other reference 73.

Muilment [dancer], d. 1747: 51, 61.

Mullart, *Miss* Susanna, 1735–? [c. 1761 she adopted stage name of Mrs Evans]: Falstaff's Page 190; Robin 334, 337–9; York, Duke of 398, 400–3.

Mullart, William, fl. 1730–43: Austria 239–41; Bates 196–8; Brabantio 354; Bullcalf 187; Caius 329–33; Campeius 210; Carrier 161, 163, 165–7, 169; Citizen (J. Caesar) 231; Gonzalo 429–30; Gravedigger 124–9; Hacket, Dame 421; Hecate 289; King, Player 131; Lord Mayor 383–5, 387; Marshal, Lord 377; Northumberland (1 Hen. IV) 167; Phaeax 445; Pistol (MWW) 334; Town Clerk 343; Witch 286–90, 292. Other references 63, 98.

Mullart, *Mrs* William, Elizabeth, d. 1745: Constance 241; Desdemona 355; Emilia (Othello) 354, 359–60, 362–6; Emilia (Wint. T.) 457–8; Falconbridge, Lady 240–1; Francisca 306; Goneril 258–60;

484

## INDEX I

Hostess (1 Hen. IV) 171, 173; Hostess (2 Hen. IV) 190–2; Hostess (Hen. V) 196–8; Lady, Old 214–15; Lavinia (C. Marius) 410; Margaret (Much Ado) 343; Melissa 445; Queen, Player 130–1, 134–5; Quickly, Mrs (MWW) 329–35; Regan 261–3; York, Duchess of (Rich. III) 383–4, 390.

Mynn, fl. 1730: Clerimont 419. Other reference 36.

Nailer [unidentified], fl. 1723: 25.

Naylor, fl. 1740–5: Antonio (Tempest) 433; Blunt (Cibber's Rich. III) 390–1, 393; Guildenstern 131, 133; Officer (Wint. T.) 458; Page (MWW) 332; Ratcliff 391, 393, 395; Tybalt 410.

Naylor, *Miss*, fl. 1741–3: Mamillius 457; York, Duke of 390–3, 395.

Neale, Charles, d. 1750: Aelius 445–6; Andrew, Sir 455–6; Calchas 453–4; Citizen (J. Caesar) 231, 235, 237; Gentleman Usher 256–8, 260–6; Jamy (Hen. V) 200; Launcelot 313–18; Macmorris 196–7; Malvolio 456; Michael, Don 103–4; Osric 122–3, 129–30, 132–4, 136–7, 139–41; Pinch 99; Roderigo 357, 364–7; Sands 214–16; Sexton 343; Silence 187–9, 191; Slender 326, 331–2, 334; Verges 344–5; Witch 284–90, 292, 294–9. Other references 64, 73, 345.

Nelson, fl. 1736–44: Brabantio 364–5; Douglas 168; Duke (All's Well) 88; Lord (Wint. T.) 458; Mortimer 164; Rosencrantz 135; Tyrrel 390. Other reference 60.

Newhouse [dancer], fl. 1723–31: 26, 37.

Newman, Thomas, fl. 1703–14: 2, 10.

Nivelon, Francis [dancer], fl. 1724–38: 27, 32, 53.

Norris, *Miss*, fl. 1708: Dorinda 424; Fleance 269.

Norris, *Miss*, fl. 1733–5: Ariel 430; Edward, Prince 386; John, Prince (1 Hen. IV) 163; York, Duke of 383–4.

Norris, *Miss* Elizabeth, later Mrs Chitty, fl. 1750: Amphitrite 437.

Norris, Henry, Sr., 1665–1731: Caliban 424; Citizen (C. Marius) 406–7; Citizen (Invader) 100; Citizen (J. Caesar) 219, 222–6; Cleon 439–44; Francis 146–55; Isander 444; Jamy (Sauny) 415–16; Lucianus 110; Mustacho 427; Nurse (C. Marius) 406–9; Osric 106; Pistol (2 Hen. IV) 180, 182; Poet 438–9; Servant (Invader) 101; Ventoso 425–7; Wall (Love in For.) 91, 340; Witch 268–81. Other references 7, 206.

Norris, Henry, Jr., d. *c.* 1751: Citizen (J. Caesar) 227–30, 232; Edward, Prince 379; Evans 326; Francis 154, 158, 160; Lionel, Sir 420–1; Lucianus 121; Lucius (J. Caesar) 222; Poet 445; Polonius 123; Sands 210; Shallow (MWW) 326, 328; Tyrrel 383; Ventoso 429–30; Witch 284–6. Other references 30, 43.

Norsa, *Miss* Hannah, d. 1785: Page, Anne 326, 329. Other references 39, 99.

Oakly, fl. 1735: Iago 361.

Oates [harlequin], fl. 1750: 84.

Oates, James, d. 1751: Abergavenny 217; Aedile (Invader) 100; Albany 256, 264; Bardolph (Hen. V) 198; Bernardo 143; Blunt (1 Hen. IV) 157, 159–60; Catesby 385–6, 398; Coleville 193–4; Edward (Cibber's 3 Hen. VI) 204; Feeble 182; Gonzalo 427–8; Grey (Hen. V) 195; Horatio 123; Humphrey, Prince 180–1, 184; Lieutenant 402–3; Osric 122; Pindarus 221, 229–30, 238–9; Poet 446–7; Poins (2 Hen. IV) 181–6; Ratcliff 379; Sheriff (1 Hen. IV) 178–9; Siward 297; Surveyor 210–11; Ventoso 430–1; Vernon (1 Hen. IV) 149. Other references 16, 18–19, 27, 46.

Ogden, John, d. 1732: Belarius 103; Caesar 221–2; Casca 222–3; Duke (Jew) 312; Duke (Othello) 356; Duncan 274–5, 277, 281–3; Escalus (Measure) 303; Henry IV (1 Hen. IV) 149–50; Horatio 113, 118; Jasper, Sir 416; Kent 248–52, 255; Laertes 113; Marcus 451; Northumberland (Rich. II) 376; Page (MWW) 320, 323–5; Petruchio (Sauny) 418; Shylock (Jew) 311–12; Westmorland (1 Hen. IV) 149, 156–7; Worcester 153. Other references 17, 28.

Oldfield, Mrs (i.e. *Miss*) Anne, 1683–1730; Katharine 195; Margaret (Humfrey) 203.

Orfeur, fl. 1720–2: Bassianus 451; Thomas, Friar 302.

Orpin, fl. 1746: Gadshill 175.

Otway, Thomas [dramatist], 1652–85: 98, 404.

Owen [unidentified], fl. 1746: 75.

Pack, George, fl. 1703–21: Caius 320; Citizen (Coriolanus) 101; Gentleman Usher 249; Guildford 205; Iachimo (D'Urfey's Cymbeline) 103; Nicias 439–40; Nurse (C. Marius) 407; Pedro 455; Roderigo 346, 348, 350; Snatchpenny 415; Thisbe (Leveridge's Pyramus) 340. Other references 4, 9, 11, 13, 15, 20, 22.

Paddick, fl. 1744–50: Blunt (Cibber's Rich. III) 401; Burgundy (Lear) 264, 266; Curio 456; Francisco (Hamlet) 138, 140, 142; Jeweller 449; John, Friar 412;

485

# INDEX I

Mercutio 410; Metellus (J. Caesar) 238; Oxford 398; Rosencrantz 136; Simple 337.

Padouana, *Signora* [dancer], fl. 1747: 76.

Page, fl. 1742: Rosalind 94.

Paget, *Master*, fl. 1747–8: Ariel 436; Falstaff's Page 193.

Paget, William, fl. 1730–49: Albany 258; Angers, Citizen of 240; Apemantus 448; Banquo 283, 298; Brabantio 369–71; Caliban 429–30, 433, 435–6; Camillo 457; Capulet 410; Cinna the Conspirator 238; Cranmer 210; Decius 231; Demetrius (Shadwell's Timon) 445; Douglas 165; Duncan 283, 286–7, 291; Falstaff (1 Hen. IV) 160–1, 168, 173, 175; Falstaff (2 Hen. IV) 193; Falstaff (MWW) 332–3, 336; Ghost 137; Hecate 287–8, 297; Henry VI (Cibber's Rich. III) 397, 399–400; Horatio 128; Iago 364–5, 368; Kent 261, 265; King (Hamlet) 126, 130–2, 137–8, 140; Lafeu 88; Lear 256; Lodovico 356, 361–2, 370; Mortimer 157; Mowbray 193; Norfolk (Rich. III) 401; Northumberland (1 Hen. IV) 177–8; Othello 354; Page (MWW) 325–6; Polonius 138, 140, 142; Provost 304; Shallow (MWW) 337; Stanley 390–1, 393, 398; Tressel 383–4; Vernon (1 Hen. IV) 173; Worcester 159, 177; York, Archbishop of 182. Other references 36, 39, 42–3, 63, 72, 75, 77.

Palin, *Mrs* (i.e. *Miss*), fl. 1728–9: Jessica (Jew) 311; Page, Anne 323. Other references 33, 35.

Palmer, *Mrs*, fl. 1730–2: Amphitrite 429; Hostess (1 Hen. IV) 157–8; Miranda 429; Quickly, Mrs (MWW) 325; Regan 254.

Palmer, John, 1728–68: Blunt (Cibber's Rich. III) 401; Cassio 373; Claudio (Much Ado) 346; Edmund 266; Gratiano (Merchant) 317–18; Horatio 143; Lennox 298–9; Mustacho 436; Orlando 97; Siward, Young 299–300. Other reference 83.

Papillion [singer], fl. 1731: 37.

Parker, *Mrs* Anne, later (1) Mrs Joseph Berriman; (2) Mrs William Hallam, q.v.

Parlour, fl. 1723: George 204.

Parlour, *Mrs*, fl. 1721: Jessica (Jew) 311.

Pattenden, fl. 1741–3: Duke (All's Well) 88; Oxford 390, 393, 395; Tyrrel 391.

Payne [unidentified], fl. 1745: 70.

Peacopp [DL house-keeper], fl. 1746: 73.

Pearce, fl. 1730–4: Burgundy (Lear) 254; Citizen (J. Caesar) 228–9; Evans 324–7; Gravedigger 122–4; Hacket, Dame 419–20; Murderer 284–5; Pistol (MWW) 324; Witch 282, 285.

Pearson, fl. 1735: Ambassador (C. Marius) 410.

Peddie, John [mariner], d. 1742: 56.

Peer, William, d. 1713: Ruffian (Tate's Lear) 245.

Peirson [DL treasurer], fl. 1740: 56.

Peite [unidentified], fl. 1744: 66.

Pelling [dancer], fl. 1721–3: 22, 26.

Pelling, *Mrs* [dancer], fl. 1733: 42.

Penington, fl. 1744: Osric 135.

Penkethman, William, Sr., d. 1725: Apothecary (C. Marius) 407; Caius 320; Carrier 147; Citizen (C. Marius) 406–9; Citizen (Invader) 100; Citizen (J. Caesar) 219; Feeble 180; Gentleman Usher 245–50; Poet 438–9, 441–3; Pyramus (Love in For.) 91, 340; Ruffian (C. Marius) 407; Servant (Invader) 101; Sly, Christopher (Johnson's Cobler) 416; Witch 269–71, 273–7. Other references 9, 12, 19, 206.

Penkethman, William, Jr., d. 1740: Boult (Marina) 375; Caius 331; Citizen (J. Caesar) 229–30, 232; Evans 324; Feeble 187; Francis 160, 162–4; Gentleman Usher 254–60; Gravedigger 118–19, 121, 123–8; Guzzle, Toby 419, 421; Lord Mayor 384, 386; Lucianus 123; Polonius 119; Roderigo 355, 363; Snatchpenny 420–1; Witch 281–6, 289–90. Other references 39, 118.

Penkethman, *Mrs* William, Jr. [widow of the actor], fl. 1741: 58.

Peploe, fl. 1727–33: Wart 184. Other reference 31.

Perkins, fl. 1735: Man, Old (C. Marius) 410.

Perry, Christopher, fl. 1741–6: Lear 263; Othello 365. Other references 60, 68, 75.

Pervill [unidentified], fl. 1710: 7.

Peterson, Joseph, 1717–58: Albany 261; Buckingham (Rich. III) 390–3, 395; Dion 458; Edmund 261; Henry IV (1 Hen. IV) 168, 172; Kent 262; Lafeu 89; Lennox 291; Osric 130–1, 133; Parolles 88.

Philips, Ambrose [dramatist], *c*. 1675–1749: 25, 202, 217.

Philips, Thomas, fl. 1744–6: Brabantio 370; Gentleman Usher 264; Norfolk (Rich. III) 398; Seyton 297. Other reference 68.

Phillips, William, 1699–*c*. 1775: Francis 175; Witch 293.

Phillips, *Mrs* William, fl. 1745–8: Anne, Lady (Rich. III) 402; Desdemona 369; Dorinda 436; Hippolito 433; Hostess (1 Hen. IV) 175; Ophelia 137–8; York, Duchess of (Rich. III) 397, 399.

Phipps, fl. 1721–3: Carrier 152; Citizen (J. Caesar) 223–4; Evans 320–1; Witch 275–7.

486

# INDEX I

Picq [dancer], fl. 1743–4: 65, 67.
Pilkington [DL box-office-keeper], fl. 1746: 73.
Pinner, George, fl. 1746–9: Bastard 243; Worcester 175.
Pitt, fl. 1729: Provost 303.
Pitt, *Miss* Ann, 1720–99 [after 1755 known as Mrs Pitt]: Falconbridge, Lady 243; Hostess (Hen. V) 201; Juliet (Measure) 307; Quickly, Mrs (MWW) 338. Other reference 76.
Platt, fl. 1749: Alonso 436.
Platt, *Miss*, fl. 1749: Ariel 436.
Plautus, Titus Maccius [dramatist], d. 184 B.C.: 99.
Plomer, *Mrs*, fl. 1725: Page, Mrs 322.
Poitier, Michael [dancer], fl. 1730–2: 36, 39.
Porter, *Mrs* B., fl. 1708: Fleance 270.
Porter, *Mrs* (i.e. *Miss*) Mary, d. 1765: Desdemona 349–50; Eleanor (Humfrey) 203; Elizabeth, Queen 379, 382; Evandra 438–41; Jessica (Jew) 309; Katharine, Queen 206–9, 211–12; Lavinia (C. Marius) 407–9; Macbeth, Lady 272–82, 286–7, 292; Macduff, Lady 271–2; Portia (J. Caesar) 220–1, 223–4, 233; Queen (Hamlet) 107–19; Volumnia (Invader) 101. Other references 5, 7.
Powell [CG box-keeper], fl. 1739: 55.
Powell [DL deputy treasurer], fl. 1745: 70.
Powell [unidentified], fl. 1745: 72.
Powell, George, 1668–1714: Banquo 271–2; Cassio 346, 348; Cassius 219; Drances 455; Falstaff (Com. Gall.) 319; Falstaff (1 Hen. IV) 146; Ford 320; Hamlet 107; Hector 452; Hotspur 145; Laertes 106–8; Lear 245–7; Macbeth 268–9; Macduff 269; Marius, Old 406–7; Petruchio (Sauny) 415; Prospero 423–4; Surrey (Hen. VIII) 205; Timon 438–40. Other reference 9.
Powell, *Mrs* George, Mary, fl. 1708–14: Emilia (Othello) 347; Hostess (1 Hen. IV) 146; Queen (Hamlet) 107. Other references 8, 10.
Presgrave, fl. 1735: Francisco (Hamlet) 126.
Prichard [DL upper-gallery office-keeper], fl. 1746–8: 73, 78.
Prince, Joseph [dancer], d. 1718: 15.
Prince, *Mrs* Joseph, fl. 1703: Caesario 455.
Pritchard, William [DL treasurer], d. 1763: 78.
Pritchard, *Mrs* William, Hannah, nee Vaughan, 1711–68: Anne, Lady (Rich. III) 388; Beatrice 344–6; Bullen, Anne 212–13; Constance (Papal Tyr.) 242–3; Delia 342–3; Desdemona 364–8, 370; Elizabeth, Queen 390, 394–5, 397, 399, 401–3; Emilia (Othello) 372–4; Evandra 449; Flora 420; Ford, Mrs 335–6, 338; Helena 89; Imogen 104; Isabella 306; Katharine, Queen 214–17; Macbeth, Lady 294–6, 298–300; Macduff, Lady 289–90; Melissa 447–8; Nerissa 313, 315–16; Ophelia 123; Paulina 457–8; Portia (J. Caesar) 236–7; Portia (Merchant) 317; Queen (Hamlet) 131–3, 135, 137–8, 140–3; Rosalind 91–2, 94–8; Viola 455–7; York, Duchess of (Rich. III) 387–9. Other references 58, 67, 71, 74.
Purcell, Henry [composer], c. 1658–95: 301.
Purden, *Mrs*, fl. 1724–32: Macduff, Lady 277; Page, Anne 325–6; Percy, Lady (1 Hen. IV) 157–8.

Quin, James, 1693–1766: Aaron 450–1; Antonio (Merchant) 313, 315; Antony 221; Apemantus 445–9; Aumerle 376; Brutus 221–7, 229–39; Buckingham (Rich. III) 380–2, 384–5; Cinna (C. Marius) 408; Coriolanus 101; Cymbeline 103; Duke (Measure) 302–8; Falstaff (1 Hen. IV) 151–7, 159–62, 164–74, 176–8; Falstaff (2 Hen. IV) 186–94; Falstaff (MWW) 320–38; Ghost 120–2, 124, 128–30, 132, 134–5, 137; Gloucester (Lear) 248–54; Guildenstern 110; Hector 452–3; Henry IV (1 Hen. IV) 151; Henry VIII 207–8, 210–17; Hotspur 149–50; Jaques 91–2, 94–7; John, King (Papal Tyr.) 242; King (Hamlet) 111–20, 122–4, 126–7; Lear 254–7, 259, 261–2, 266; Leonato 342; Lieutenant 379; Macbeth 273–84, 286–91, 293–4, 299–300; Othello 350–4, 356–7, 359–64, 366–8, 370, 372–4; Protheus 342–3; Richard III 385–9, 392, 394–5, 397–8, 402–3; Thersites 453–4. Other references 12, 15, 20, 26–9, 48, 50, 54–5, 58, 65, 74, 79, 81, 101, 127, 287.

Raftor, *Miss* Catherine, later Mrs George Clive, q.v.
Raftor, James, d. 1790: Abergavenny 213–14; Blunt (Cibber's Rich. III) 389, 391–2; Caesar's Servant 229–30; Cambridge (Hen. V) 200; Charles 93; Cromwell 210; Gravedigger 139; Guard (R & J) 411; Nym (MWW) 328–32; Officer (R & J) 412; Peter (Cure) 420; Peto (1 Hen. IV) 161–2, 166–7, 169–71; Pindarus 235, 237; Porco 343; Priest (Twelfth N.) 456; Sycorax 432; William 93. Other references 51, 56, 61, 73, 76.
Rainton, fl. 1730–5: Earthy Spirit 430–1; Neptune 428.
Rainton [dancer], d. 1732: 34.

487

## INDEX I

Rakestraw, Mrs [widow of an actor], fl. 1723: 26.
Randal, fl. 1716–24: Wall (Leveridge's Pyramus) 339. Other references 20, 28.
Ravenscroft, Edward [dramatist], c. 1650–c. 1700: 449, 461.
Ravenscroft, John [violinist], d. c. 1745: 36, 38, 72.
Rawlings [unidentified], fl. 1745: 71.
Ray, John, d. 1752: Antony's Servant 221, 237; Bardolph (1 Hen. IV) 165–72, 174–5; Bardolph (2 Hen. IV) 186–8, 191; Bardolph (Hen. V) 200; Bardolph (MWW) 330–2, 334, 338; Barnardine 304–5, 307–8; Burgundy (Lear) 260–4; Carrier 157; Citizen (C. Marius) 409; Citizen (J. Caesar) 233; Cleon 448; Essex 241, 243; Feeble 189–90; Francisco (Hamlet) 126; Gobbo 313–18; Gravedigger 116–25, 127–34, 136–7, 139–43; Grey (Hen. V) 195–6, 200; Guard (R & J) 411; Lieutenant 388–9, 391–2, 394–6, 398–9, 401–3; Lovell 212–16; Moonshine (Love in For.) 91, 340; Musician 445–6; Mustacho 432; Sexton 344–6; Seyton 294–5, 298–300; Shadow 180; Ventoso 431–2, 434–5, 437; William 91–5; Witch 282–5, 288, 290–2; Woodall 420. Other references 39, 51, 56, 58, 73, 76, 142.
Reading, fl. 1716–17: Moonshine (Leveridge's Pyramus) 340.
Redfern, Mrs [LIF box-keeper], fl. 1730–2: 36, 39.
Redman, fl. 1749–50: Capulet, Old 413; Cinna the Conspirator 238–9; Doctor (Cure) 422; Gratiano (Othello) 374; Grey (Hen. V) 201; John, King 243; King, Player 143–4; Mowbray 193; Northumberland (1 Hen. IV) 178–9; Stanley 402–3.
Reed, fl. 1739–40: Citizen (J. Caesar) 233–4; Murderer 290; Thrasillus 448; Trinculo 432; Witch 290.
Reeves, fl. 1744: Bernardo 135.
Reinhold, Thomas, c. 1690–1751: Lion (Lampe's Pyramus) 340–1; Neptune 432. Other references 67, 71.
Renton, Charles, 1662–1758: Earthy Spirit 425.
Reynolds, Richard, fl. 1730–49: Antonio (Tempest) 436; Hacket, Dame 419; Roderigo 354.
Rice, Mrs, fl. 1727: Ophelia 117.
Rich, Christopher Mosyer [LIF manager], c. 1693–1774: 16–17, 22, 24.
Rich, Henry [LIF pit office-keeper], fl. 1715–17: 11, 15.
Rich, John [LIF and CG manager], c. 1682–1761: 16–17, 20, 22, 26.

Richards, fl. 1744: Apothecary 410.
Richardson, Thomas, d. 1753: Bourbon 195–6; Douglas 164; Laertes 126–7; Marcellus 125; Pompeius 410; Suffolk (Hen. VIII) 210; Ventoso 436; Winlove 420–1.
Ridout, Isaac, d. 1761: Abergavenny 212; Balthazar (Com. Err.) 99; Bardolph, Lord 192; Blunt (1 Hen. IV) 161, 163, 165–74, 176–9; Brabantio 360; Burgundy (1 Hen. VI) 202; Casca 239; Cassio 372–4; Chamberlain, Lord 214; Cinna the Conspirator 234; Conrade 342; Cornwall 260, 262, 264; Cromwell 214–17; Decius 235–6, 238–9; Demetrius (Shadwell's Timon) 449; Duke Senior 93–6; Dumain Sr. 89; Dumain Jr. 88; Edmund 266; Essex 240; Exeter (Hen. V) 198–9, 201; Fenton 331–2; Ferdinand 432; Glendower 179; Gloucester (Hen. V) 196; Gratiano (Othello) 356; Hastings 184, 187–90; Horatio 140, 143–4; John, Don 344; John, Prince (2 Hen. IV) 193–4; Laertes 127, 129, 131–2, 138; Laurence, Friar 413; Le Beau 91–3; Lennox 292, 294–6, 299–300; Lieutenant 392, 394, 396; Lodovico 363; Lucius (Cymbeline) 104; Metellus (J. Caesar) 231; Montano 359, 363, 370, 372; Norfolk (Rich. III) 389, 395, 397–8; Oxford 385; Page (MWW) 337–8; Provost 305–8; Richmond 402–3; Rosencrantz 131, 134–6; Ross (Rich. II) 377; Salarino 313–16, 318; Salisbury (Papal Tyr.) 242–3; Seyton 293–4; Shylock 315; Siward 289–91; Suffolk (Hen. VIII) 213–14; Trebonius 233; Tressel 388, 391, 400; Valentine 455; Westmorland (1 Hen. IV) 160; Worcester 161. Other references 47, 54, 56, 61, 65, 67, 98.
Ridout, Mrs Isaac, nee Woodman, d. 1756: Audrey 93; Bullen, Anne 214–15; Celia 97; Desdemona 369, 371; Diana 88; Edward, Prince 389, 391–5; Jessica 313–17, 319; Macduff, Lady 293; Page, Anne 334; Percy, Lady (1 Hen. IV) 172; Regan 266.
Roberts, fl. 1750: Publius 239.
Roberts, Mrs, fl. 1748: Miranda 436.
Roberts, Ellis, fl. 1734–48: Amiens 92–3; Milcha 430–1; Moonshine (Lampe's Pyramus) 340–1. Other references 62, 67.
Roberts, John, fl. 1723–45: Alonso 427; Brabantio 353–4, 356, 359, 364–5; Catesby 389; Douglas 157; Duncan 289–91; Gloucester (Lear) 253, 256; Henry VI (Cibber's 3 Hen. VI) 204; Horatio 122; Iago 354; King (Hamlet) 137; Lennox 283; Officer, French (Hen. V)

488

# INDEX I

195; Pandulph 241; Prospero 428–30; Richard III 383–4; Roberto 91; Westmorland (2 Hen. IV) 187–9; Westmorland (Hen. V) 196–7; Wolsey 210; Worcester 159, 167; York, Archbishop of 181–2. Other reference 25.

Roberts, *Mrs* John, d. *c.* 1744: Amphitrite 428; Elizabeth, Queen 383–4, 386–9, 391–5; Ford, Mrs 326–8, 330–2; Harriet 195–6; Hostess (1 Hen. IV) 165–6; Hostess (2 Hen. IV) 186–7; Katharine, Queen 212–14; Macbeth, Lady 284–5, 291; Margaret (Sauny) 421; Ophelia 121; Portia (J. Caesar) 230, 232–5; Queen (Hamlet) 128, 133–4. Other references 42, 58.

Robertson, *Mrs* [unidentified], fl. 1717–18: 15, 17.

Robinson [DL office-keeper], fl. 1722–36: 23, 27, 48.

Robinson, Jr., *Miss*, fl. 1727–32: Ariel 427–9; Falstaff's Page 181–2; York, Duke of 382.

Rochetti [singer], fl. 1728: 33.

Rogeir, *Mrs* Mary, later Mrs John Laguerre, q.v.

Rogers [unidentified], fl. 1741: 58.

Rogers, *Mrs* Jane, fl. 1704–18: Andromache 452; Anne, Lady (Rich. III) 379; Cordelia 246; Macduff, Lady 268–70; Portia (J. Caesar) 221. Other references 3, 7.

Rogers, Thomas, fl. 1720–5: Ely, Bishop of (Betterton's 2 Hen. IV) 180. Other references 21, 29.

Roland, *Mlle* Catharine [dancer], 1714–88: 48.

Rosco, James, fl. 1730–48: Angers, Citizen of 239–41; Antigonus 457–8; Blunt (1 Hen. IV) 158, 160, 162–4, 177; Bushy 377; Chamberlain, Lord 214–17; Cornelius 104; Cornwall 254; Decius 228; Duke Frederick 92–7; Duncan 289, 294; Edmund 256–8; Escalus (Measure) 305–7; Exeter (Hen. V) 195–6; Falstaff (1 Hen. IV) 168; Friar (Much Ado) 342–4; Ghost 119–20, 125–8; Gravedigger 129, 132–6; Hecate 282, 289–90, 292–4; Horatio 121, 123–5, 142; Host 332–6; Hotspur 156; Iago 354–8, 360–2; Jamy (Sauny) 420–1; Kent 259–64; King (Hamlet) 129; King, Player 140; Lennox 284–6; Lodovico 364, 366–8, 370, 372; Lord Chief Justice 190–2; Mortimer 158; Mowbray 187; Norfolk (Rich. II) 377; Octavius 227–8, 230, 232; Page (MWW) 324–6, 328; Pembroke (Papal Tyr.) 242–3; Shallow (MWW) 327, 337; Shylock 315; Siward 295–6; Stanley 383–4, 386, 390, 392, 394, 396–8, 400–1;

Stephano 429; Surveyor 214; Thrasillus 449; Trebonius 235–6; Warwick (1 Hen. VI) 202; Williams 196–9; Worcester 166, 169–74, 176–7; York, Archbishop of 188–9. Other references 36, 55, 68.

Rowland [LIF pit door-keeper], fl. 1720: 20.

Rowley, *Mrs*, fl. 1745–7: Francisca 306; John, Prince (1 Hen. IV) 174, 176; Juliet (Measure) 307; Phebe 96; Phryne 449.

Royer, *Miss* [unidentified], fl. 1747: 76.

Royer, Lawrence, fl. 1730: Othello 354. Other reference 36.

Ryan, Anthony, d. 1740: Bedford (Hen. V) 196–7; Borachio 343; Burgundy (Lear) 259–60; Donalbain 288–9; Fenton 329–32; Henry VI (1 Hen. VI) 202; Henry, Prince 239–41; Malcolm 290; Montano 362, 364; Poins (1 Hen. IV) 165–7; Willoughby 377.

Ryan, Lacy, 1694–1760: Alcibiades 446; Antonio (Jew) 310–13; Banquo 273–5; Bassanio 318; Bastard (Papal Tyr.) 242; Benedick 342, 344; Bolingbroke 377; Buckingham (Hen. VIII) 207–8; Caesar 225–7; Cassio 349; Cassius 221–3, 231, 235–9; Charles, Sir 416; Chorus 196–9, 201; Claudio (Measure) 302–8; Cymbeline 103–4; Diphilus 440; Edgar 248–64, 266; Ferdinand 425; Ford 320–6, 329–38; Geraldo 416; Ghost 144; Gloucester (1 Hen. VI) 202; Granius 406–7; Gratiano (Merchant) 315–16; Hamlet 111–26, 128–34, 136, 138, 140–1, 143–4; Henry VI (Cibber's Rich. III) 403; Hotspur 151, 177; Iago 350–4, 356–7, 359–60, 362–8, 370, 372–4; Jaques 92–3, 95–6; Laertes 109–10; Lorenzo (Jew) 309; Lucius (Titus) 450–1; Macduff 275–84, 286–97, 299–300; Orlando 97; Philip, King 239–41; Polixenes 457–8; Posthumus 104; Richard II 376; Richard III 380–2, 384–5, 389, 394, 397, 400; Richmond 379; Shylock 316; Sylla 407–8; Troilus 452–4; Ursaces 103; Vernon (1 Hen. IV) 149–50; Wales, Prince of (1 Hen. IV) 151–7, 159, 161–2, 165–7, 169–74, 176–8; Wales, Prince of (2 Hen. IV) 187–93; Wolsey 214–17. Other references 15, 17–18, 22, 32, 49, 74, 84, 303.

Rymos, fl. 1735: Catulus 410.

Sallé [dancer], 1705–32: 39.

Sallé, *Mlle* Marie [dancer], 1707–56: 44.

Salway, Thomas, d. 1743: Abergavenny 211; Albany 255–7; Alençon 202; Amiens 92–3; Archer 420; Bagot 377;

489

# INDEX I

Balthazar (Much Ado) 342–3; Beaupré 103–4; Blunt (1 Hen. IV) 159–60, 162, 166–7, 169–71; Chatillon 240–1; Ghost 122; Gravedigger 126; Grist 421; John, Prince (2 Hen. IV) 185–6; Montano 363; Neptune 430–1; Nicias 445–6; Octavius 229–31; Patroclus 454; Poins (2 Hen. IV) 187–9; Silence 190–1. Other reference 46.

Sambre [unidentified], fl. 1734: 44.

Sandham, Jr. [dancer], 1713–?: 20.

Sandum, Mrs, fl. 1749: Miranda 436.

Santlow, Mrs (i.e. Miss) Hester, later Mrs Barton Booth [the 2nd], q.v.

Saunders [DL stage-door-keeper], fl. 1744–8: 66, 70, 73, 78.

Saunders, Mrs (i.e. Miss) Margaret, 1686–c. 1745: Emilia (Othello) 348–50. Other references 9, 67.

Savage, Richard (?), d. 1743: York (Cibber's 3 Hen. VI) 204.

Savage, William, c. 1720–89: Neptune 432.

Schoolding, fl. 1718: Northumberland (1 Hen. IV) 149.

Schoolding, Mrs (i.e. Miss), later Mrs Anthony Moreau, q.v.

Scot, Miss, and her sister [dancers], fl. 1738: 53.

Scott, Miss, fl. 1743: Arante 263.

Scrase, Henry, fl. 1750: Fenton 338; Guildenstern 143; Le Beau 97; Lennox 300; Paris 412.

Scudamore, fl. 1748: Othello 372. Other reference 80.

Seal, Mrs (i.e. Miss), later (1) Mrs Bellamy; (2) Mrs Walter, q.v.

Settle, Elkanah [dramatist], 1648–1724: 15.

Seymour, Mrs (i.e. Miss) Anna Maria, later Mrs Anthony Boheme [the 1st], q.v.

Shadwell, Thomas [dramatist], c. 1642–92: 422, 437, 460–1.

Shaw, John [dancer], d. 1725: 13, 16, 23.

Shawford, d. 1763: Cleon 448. Other reference 73.

Shelton, fl. 1738: Escanes (Marina) 375.

Shepard, fl. 1745: Ariel 433; Blunt (1 Hen. IV) 173.

Shepard, Charles, 1675–1748: Artemidorus 229–30, 233–5; Bardolph (1 Hen. IV) 160–2; Bardolph (2 Hen. IV) 180–6, 189–90; Bardolph (MWW) 327–9; Campeius 211–14; Chancellor, Lord 209; Decius 221; Falstaff (1 Hen. IV) 170; Lucentius 342–3; Marcellus 110; Nicias 441–4, 446–8; Provost 304; Shylock 314; Stephano 427–8, 430–2; Toby, Sir 455; William, Sir 420; Witch 274–6, 280, 282–3, 285, 287, 289–92. Other references 16, 32, 34, 39, 41, 61, 66.

Shepheard, F. [GF treasurer], fl. 1735: 48.

Sherburn, Mrs (i.e. Miss), fl. 1711: Cordelia 246; Jessica (Jew) 310.

Sheridan, Thomas, 1719–88: Brutus 236; Hamlet 134–5; Macbeth 294; Othello 368; Richard III 395–6. Other references 67, 70.

Sherman [unidentified], fl. 1710: 7.

Shireburn, Mrs (i.e. Miss) Frances, later Mrs Richard Cross, II, q.v.

Short [unidentified], fl. 1737: 51.

Shuter, Edward, c. 1728–76: Caius 336; Captain (Othello) 371; Catesby 399–400; Corin 97; Cornwall 265; Dogberry 346; Gentleman Usher 266; Launcelot 318; Mustacho 435; Osric 138–9, 141; Polonius 140; Shallow (MWW) 338; Stephano 437; Verges 345; Vernon (1 Hen. IV) 176; William 96; Witch 297–300. Other reference 83.

Sibilla, Mrs, stage name of Sibilla Gronamann, later Mrs Thomas Pinto [the 1st], d. c. 1765: Ceres 434.

Simms, fl. 1748: Sycorax 436.

Simons, fl. 1746: Peto (1 Hen. IV) 175.

Simpson, d. 1758: Angus 293, 295, 298–300; Apothecary 411–12; Balthazar (Merchant) 315–17; Burgundy (Lear) 263; Falconbridge, Robert 242–3; Gratiano (Othello) 369, 371–3; Horatio 135; Hubert (John) 243; Jaques de Bois 98; Murderer 297; Officer (Twelfth N.) 456; Ratcliff 397–9, 401–2; Rosencrantz 136–7, 139–43; Senator (Othello) 368; Sexton 346; Thomas, Friar 306, 308; Town Clerk 345; Tyrrel 395–6, 398; Westmorland (Hen. V) 200.

Simpson, Mrs Elizabeth, fl. 1749: Juliet (Measure) 308.

Smith, fl. 1735–49: Citizen (J. Caesar) 231, 236–7; Francisco (Hamlet) 135; Priest (C. Marius) 410; Roderigo 361; Stephano 436; Traveller (1 Hen. IV) 178; Ventoso 436.

Smith, Miss [dancer], fl. 1717: 16.

Smith, Miss, fl. 1731: Maid (Bullock's Cobler) 420; Page, Anne 325.

Smith, Thomas, fl. 1708–33: Alonso 429; Arviragus 103; Aumerle 376; Brabantio 347, 355–7; Douglas 149–50; Ferdinand 424; Osric 110–11, 119; Lennox 273–5; Norfolk (Rich. III) 383; Trebonius 222, 227–8; Westmorland (1 Hen. IV) 158; Worcester 156, 158. Other references 13, 15, 26.

Smithies, Mrs, fl. 1726: 30.

Sowdon, John, d. 1789: Banquo 298–300; Ghost 143; Othello 372; Richard III 401. Other references 79, 143.

Sparks, Isaac, d. 1776: Antonio (Twelfth

N.) 456; Bardolph (Hen. V) 200; Butts 215–16; Caliban 434–5; Carrier 174–5; Charles 95–6; Elbow 307; Morocco 317; Soothsayer 237; Toby, Sir 455. Other references 73, 399, 401.

Sparks, Luke, 1711–68: Angelo (Measure) 307–8; Antonio (Merchant) 318; Banquo 300; Bastard 243; Brabantio 372–4; Buckingham (Rich. III) 397, 399, 401–3; Caesar 239; Canterbury, Archbishop of (Hen. V) 201; Capulet 412–13; Casca 238–9; Cassius 237; Constable (Hen. V) 199–200; Duncan 298–300; Ford 338; Gratiano (Merchant) 316–17; Henry IV (1 Hen. IV) 175–8; Iago 369, 372; Jaques 95–7; King (Hamlet) 140–1, 143–4; Lennox 296–7; Lord Chief Justice 193–4; Norfolk (Hen. VIII) 217; Prospero 434; Wolsey 214–15. Other references 73, 76, 78, 84, 399, 401.

Sparling [unidentified], fl. 1725: 29.

Spicer, *Mrs*, fl. 1723: Portia (J. Caesar) 224.

Spiller, James, 1692–1730: Bottom (Leveridge's Pyramus) 339; Caius 320–2; Citizen (Coriolanus) 101; Citizen (J. Caesar) 223–7; Clown (Measure) 302; Forrest 382; Francis 148–55; Gentleman Usher 248–9, 251–3; Gravedigger 110–18; Guzzle, Toby 416–18; Iachimo (D'Urfey's Cymbeline) 103; Murderer 274, 277–80; Pandarus 453; Pistol (MWW) 320–1; Snatchpenny 418. Other references 13, 20, 321.

Spiller, *Mrs* James, fl. 1716–22: Anne, Lady (Rich. III) 380; Macduff, Lady 274; Mariana (Measure) 302; Percy, Lady (1 Hen. IV) 152; Percy, Lady (Theobald's Rich. II) 376; Portia (Jew) 310; Portia (J. Caesar) 222; Queen (Hamlet) 112. Other references 13, 380.

Starkey, Richard [unidentified], fl. 1746–7: 75, 77.

Steddy [unidentified], fl. 1727: 32.

Stede, John [LIF and CG prompter], 1687–1768: 29, 36, 44, 47, 65.

Stede, *Mrs* John [wife of LIF and CG prompter], fl. 1729: 34.

Steel, *Mrs*, fl. 1740–2: Countess (All's Well) 88; Elizabeth, Queen 390–1; Macbeth, Lady 291; Melissa 448; Paulina 458; Queen (Hamlet) 130–1, 133. Other reference 60.

Stephens [DL gallery box-keeper], fl. 1744: 66.

Stephens, Samuel, d. 1764: Belarius 103–4; Casca 231; Duke Senior 92–4; Exeter (Hen. V) 196–8; Falstaff (1 Hen. IV) 165, 167; Falstaff (MWW) 331–3; Ghost 124–5, 127, 131–4; Henry IV (1 Hen. IV) 163, 169–71; Henry IV (2 Hen. IV) 190–1; Lear 257–8; Lennox 286–94; Leontes 457–8; Lord Chief Justice 187–9; Norfolk (Rich. III) 390, 392, 394, 396; Othello 359–64, 366; Pericles (Marina) 375; Salisbury (John) 240–1; Suffolk (Hen. VIII) 214; York (1 Hen. VI) 202; York (Rich. II) 377. Other references 47, 49, 51, 55, 63, 67.

Sterling, *Mrs* James, née Lyddall, fl. 1723–4: Cressida 453; Desdemona 351; Lavinia (Titus) 451; Ophelia 115.

Stevens, fl. 1737–42: Cassio 362–3; Dion 457–8; Douglas 168; Fitzwalter 377; Grey (Hen. V) 196–7; Guildenstern 131–2; Jaques de Bois 92; Leonine (Marina) 375; Lieutenant 390; Mortimer 166; Morton 187; Palladour 104; Pistol (MWW) 332; Salisbury (Rich. II) 377; Talbot, John 202.

Stevens, *Mrs*, stage name of Priscilla Wilford, later Mrs John Rich [the 3rd], d. 1783: Blanch 240–1; Bullen, Anne 214; Chloe 446; Desdemona 362; Emilia (Othello) 357–9, 361; Macduff, Lady 288–90, 292–4; Ursula 343. Other references 38, 51, 67.

Stevens, George Alexander, 1710–84: Cromwell 215–16; Hamlet 136.

Stone, *Miss* Anne, d. c. 1724: Edward, Prince 380; Jessica (Jew) 310; Juliet (Measure) 302; Ophelia 113–14; Page, Anne 320–1.

Stoppelaer, Charles, fl. 1733–40: Neptune 430–1. Other reference 56.

Stoppelaer, Michael, fl. 1730–50: Bardolph (1 Hen. IV) 169; Bardolph (2 Hen. IV) 190; Barnardine 306–8; Butts 214–17; Caius 334–8; Citizen (J. Caesar) 228–9, 235–9; Dorcas (Bullock's Cobler) 421; Gratiano (Othello) 363; Gravedigger 132–6, 138, 140, 142–4; Lodovico 354; Mouldy 187; Murderer 293–4, 297; Nym (Hen. V) 196–9, 201; Nym (MWW) 331; Peto (1 Hen. IV) 177–8; Silence 192–4; Tubal 315–17; Tyrrel 390, 398, 400–1; Watchman 344; Westminster, Abbot of 377; William, Sir 422; Witch 285–6. Other references 74, 98.

Storer, Charles, d. c. 1765: Guildenstern 140, 142; Lieutenant 400–1; Westmorland (1 Hen. IV) 177.

Storer, *Mrs* Charles, Elizabeth, née Clark, d. 1767: Ophelia 140, 142; Page, Anne 337.

Stuart, *Miss*, fl. 1735: Desdemona 361.

Swinny, Owen [DL manager], d. 1754: 3, 51.

Symmons, fl. 1722: Demetrius (Shadwell's Timon) 442. Other reference 23.

# INDEX I

Talbot, *Mrs*, fl. 1734–5: Nurse (C. Marius) 410; Tearsheet, Doll (Humours of Fal.) 185.

Taswell, d. 1759: Asino 343; Caius 332; Cambridge (Betterton's 2 Hen. IV) 191; Corin 91–6; Doctor (Macbeth) 294–5, 298–300; Dogberry 344–5; Duke (Othello) 365–7; Elbow 308; Gardiner 215–16; Gregory 411–12; Harfleur, Governor of 200; Isidore 448; King, Player 129, 132; Ligarius 234–5, 237; Lord Mayor 388–9, 391–2, 394–6, 398–9, 401–2; Man, Old (Lear) 262; Messenger (Com. Err.) 99; Murderer 290–2, 296–7; Northumberland (1 Hen. IV) 167–72; Nym (Hen. V) 200; Polonius 129, 131–4, 136–7, 139–43; Shallow (MWW) 334; Silence 189–90; Surveyor 214; Sycorax 432–3, 435, 437; Tubal 313–18. Other reference 76.

Tate, Nahum [dramatist], 1652–1715: 244, 461.

Taverner, William [dramatist], d. 1731: 98, 105.

Taylor [LIF box-keeper], fl. 1725: 29.

Taylor, *Miss*, fl. 1744: Queen, Player 135.

Temple [GF box-keeper], fl. 1732–3: 40, 43.

Templer, *Mrs*, fl. 1729–39: Eugenia 103–4; Ford, Mrs 326; Hero 343; Mariana (Measure) 304; Percy, Lady (1 Hen. IV) 165; Regan 253–5, 257–60.

Tench, Henry, fl. 1734: Feeble (Humours of Fal.) 185.

Tenoe, *Miss* Theodosia, later Mrs William Mills [the 1st], q.v.

Theobald, Lewis [dramatist], 1688–1744: 18, 43, 375, 461.

Thomas, *Mrs*, fl. 1730–1: Goneril 254; Hippolito 429; Regan 254.

Thompson, Edward, d. 1748: Drawer (Humours of Fal.) 185. Other reference 44.

Thurmond, John, Sr., d. 1727: Brabantio 352; Caesar 222–5; Cominius (Invader) 100; Ferdinand 426; France, King of 195; Gloucester (Lear) 248–51; Hamlet 107; Henry IV (1 Hen. IV) 147–54; Kent 248; King (Hamlet) 111–16; Laertes 107; Lennox 270–1, 278; Macduff 269; Oliver (Love in For.) 91; Othello 347; Salisbury (Humfrey) 203; Saturninus 450; Sylla 409; Ulysses 452; York, Archbishop of 180. Other references 6, 12–13, 21, 27, 30, 206.

Thurmond, John, Jr., fl. 1708–24: Osric 107. Other reference 27.

Thurmond, *Mrs* John, Jr., Sarah, nee Lewis, d. 1762: Celia (Love in For.) 91; Cordelia 250; Desdemona 349–54, 356, 359–61; Elizabeth, Queen 385, 387; Eugenia 103; Evandra 441–4, 446–7; Ford, Mrs 330; Harriet 195; Katharine, Queen 211–12; Macduff, Lady 274–5, 282; Margaret (Sauny) 417; Ophelia 110, 115, 118; Portia (Jew) 310; Portia (J. Caesar) 222, 224–6, 228–32; Queen (Hamlet) 112, 120–1; Virgilia (Invader) 101. Other references 19, 23, 28, 39, 46.

Tillman [LIF gallery door-keeper], fl. 1722–5: 24, 29.

Tollett, *Miss* Henrietta Maria, later Mrs Samuel Crisp, 1709–80: Charlotte 195–6; Juliet (Measure) 305.

Tomson, *Miss*, fl. 1744: Page (R & J) 410.

Topham, fl. 1719–34: Bardolph (1 Hen. IV) 161; Butts 210; Isander 445; Sycorax 430. Other reference 18.

Topham, H. [dancer], fl. 1720: 20.

Townly, fl. 1744–5: Gonzalo 433; King (Hamlet) 135; Othello 368. Other reference 72.

Triquet, John [soldier], fl. 1741: 60.

Trout, fl. 1707: Citizen (C. Marius) 406.

Trye, fl. 1748: Ferdinand 436.

Tucker, fl. 1745: Antonio (Tempest) 433.

Turbutt, Robert, d. 1746: Albany 260–1, 263–4; Alonso 432; Ambassador, French 188–90; Angus 294; Antonio (Tempest) 429–33; Arragon 313; Campeius 212, 215; Captain (Twelfth N.) 455; Capucius 211; Catesby 394–6; Chatillon 242; Cornwall 259; Cranmer 214; Demetrius (Shadwell's Timon) 446–8; Doctor (Cure) 420; Falstaff (Humours of Fal.) 185; Glendower 171–2; Host 331–2, 334; Jaques de Bois 91–4; King, Player 125, 131–4; Lennox 293, 295; Lodovico 358, 361, 365–7; Lord Mayor 391; Marcellus 133–4, 136; Merchant (Com. Err.) 99; Metellus (J. Caesar) 229–30, 233–5; Murderer 287–92; Priest (Univ. Pass.) 342; Ratcliff 386–9; Richard III 391; Salarino 314; Steward 88; Surveyor 210; Tressel 392; Westmorland (1 Hen. IV) 160–2, 165–70; York, Archbishop of 191. Other references 49, 52, 54, 61, 64.

Turner, fl. 1735: Cinna (C. Marius) 410.

Turner, *Miss*, fl. 1735: Emilia (Othello) 361.

Turner, William, 1651–1740: Neptune 425.

Tyfer [LIF gallery door-keeper], fl. 1725: 29.

Tynte, *Miss*, fl. 1726: 30.

Underhill, Cave, 1634–c. 1710: Gravedigger 107; Trinculo 423–4. Other references 2, 7.

Usher, N. L., fl. 1744–50: Albany 265–6; Bedford (Hen. V) 199; Benvolio 411;

# INDEX I

Blunt (1 Hen. IV) 175; Blunt (Cibber's Rich. III) 396, 398; Captain (Macbeth) 296–7; Catesby 399, 401–3; Conrade 345; Dauphin (Hen. V) 201; Douglas 174; Gloucester (Hen. V) 200; Gower (2 Hen. IV) 191; Guildenstern 137, 139–42; Herald, English 242–3; Jaques de Bois 95–6; Lieutenant 403; Ligarius 239; Marcellus 134; Metellus (J. Caesar) 237; Officer (Othello) 373; Peter, Friar 308; Rosencrantz 144; Sergeant (Hen. VIII) 215–16; Seyton 300; Valentine 456; Westmorland (1 Hen. IV) 179; Westmorland (2 Hen. IV) 193–4. Other reference 200.

Vallois, Jovan de [dancer], fl. 1736–8: 50, 53.
Vaughan, *Miss*, later Mrs Christian, q.v.
Vaughan, *Mrs*, fl. 1746: Ursula 344.
Vaughan, Henry, d. 1779: Abhorson 308; Charles 97; Citizen (J. Caesar) 234–7; Clerk 434–5; Corin 95; Falstaff (1 Hen. IV) 161–2; Forrest 390; Gravedigger 135, 141–2; Oxford 390–1, 393; Peter (R & J) 411–12; Pistol (MWW) 335; Rosencrantz 131, 133; Simple 335, 338; Slender 333; Tubal 315; Tyrrel 390, 392–4; Verges 346; Watchman 344; William 92, 95–6, 98; Witch 291. Other reference 56.
Vaughan, M. [LIF and CG box-keeper], fl. 1726: 30.
Vaughan, William, fl. 1750: Gregory 412; Host 338.
Verbruggen, John Baptista, d. 1708: Antonio (Jew) 309; Apemantus 438; Cassius 218; Edgar 245; Horatio 106; Hotspur 145; Iago 346–7; Moreno 455; Page (MWW) 320; Wolsey 205.
Verhuyck, John [CG pit door-keeper], fl. 1743: 65.
Verrio, Antonio [painter], c. 1639–1707: 464.
Villeneuve [dancer], fl. 1739: 55.
Vincent, *Mrs*, fl. 1723–31: Anne, Lady (Rich. III) 381; Bianca (Sauny) 419; Ford, Mrs. 323; Ophelia 115–20; Percy, Lady (1 Hen. IV) 152–4. Other references 28, 36.
Vincent, *Mrs* Richard, Elizabeth, nee Bincks, fl. 1732–50: Anne, Lady (Rich. III) 398, 403; Arthur 239–41; Beatrice 343; Celia 92, 94–7; Cordelia 262–4; Desdemona 363, 370; Edward, Prince 390, 398; Jessica (Jew) 312; Jessica (Merchant) 315–17; Katharine 198; Marina (Marina) 375; Nerissa 319; Ophelia 121–6, 128–34, 136, 138, 143–4; Page, Anne 330–6; Percy, Lady (1 Hen. IV) 174, 176, 178–9. Other references 71, 99.

Walker, fl. 1735–49: Chatillon 243; Ferdinand 436; Sylla 410.
Walker [DL numberer], fl. 1743: 64.
Walker, Thomas, 1698–1744: Aaron 450–1; Alcibiades 441–2, 445, 448; Angelo (Measure) 304; Antigonus 457; Antony 223–7, 231; Banquo 284, 286–9, 291; Bassanio (Jew) 310–13; Bassianus 450–1; Bastard 239, 41; Brutus, Junius (Invader) 100; Burgundy (Hen. V) 196–7; Cassio 350–4, 356–7, 359–63; Cornwall 248; Cromwell 207; Edmund 249–60; Ghost 124, 130–1; Granius 408; Hector 453–4; Henry VI (Cibber's Rich. III) 385; Horatio 113–14, 121–2, 129; Hotspur 151–7, 159, 161–3, 165, 168; John, Prince (2 Hen. IV) 180; Jolly, Captain 416; King (Hamlet) 125–6, 128; Laertes 112, 114–23; Lennox 276–84, 286–7; Norfolk (Rich. II) 377; Octavius 221–2; Othello 364; Richmond 380–2, 384–5, 387, 390; Shattillion 103–4; Suffolk (1 Hen. VI) 202; Timon 446; Tranio (Sauny) 418; Ulysses 453; Vernon (1 Hen. IV) 149–50. Other references 15, 17, 19, 24, 44, 54, 379.
Wallis, fl. 1740: Glendower 168; Gratiano (Othello) 365.
Walter, *Mrs*, fl. 1729–41: Miranda 428, 430–3. Other references 34, 41.
Walter, *Mrs*, nee Seal, formerly Mrs Bellamy, d. 1771: Dorinda 426–7; Goneril 254; Grey, Lady 204; Hero 343; Macduff, Lady 288; Nerissa (Jew) 313; Page, Mrs 332–5; Regan 251.
Waltz, Gustavus, fl. 1733–4: Earthy Spirit 430–1.
Ward, Henry, fl. 1748: Roderigo 372.
Ward, *Mrs* Henry, Sarah, d. 1771: Cordelia 266–7; Desdemona 372.
Ward, John, 1704–73: Chiron 451; Douglas 169; Duke Frederick 92–3; Laertes 130; Merchant (Com. Err.) 99; Trebonius 235; Vernon (1 Hen. IV) 153. Other references 26, 28, 30.
Ware, fl. 1736–8: Lodovico 363; Woodall 421.
Ware, *Mrs*, fl. 1738–41: Katharine 196–8; Margaret (1 Hen. VI) 202; Percy, Lady (1 Hen. IV) 166, 168–9.
Warner [DL box-lobby-keeper], fl. 1748: 78.
Wathen, fl. 1731: Clerimont 419.
Watson, Pleasaunce, fl. 1720–32: Cromwell 209; Demetrius (Shadwell's Timon) 442; Hastings 180–2; Horatio 121; Montano 352–4, 356; Octavius 226;

INDEX I

Orleans 195; Poins (1 Hen. IV) 155, 157; Siward 283; Suffolk (Humfrey) 203. Other references 21, 25.

Webb [unidentified], fl. 1723: 26.

Weller, fl. 1715–16: Tyrrel 379. Other references 12, 379.

Welsted, Leonard [dramatist], 1688–1747: 30.

Wetherilt, Henry, fl. 1720–37: Bullcalf 180; Caliban 428; Citizen (J. Caesar) 228–30, 232; Gravedigger 126, 128; Isidore 444; Murderer 284–6. Other reference 48.

Wetherilt, Mrs Henry, Elizabeth, fl. 1723–36: Hostess (1 Hen. IV) 162–4; Hostess (2 Hen. IV) 181–2; Quickly, Mrs (MWW) 328. Other reference 25.

Wetherilt, Robert, c. 1708–43: Ariel 427; Carrier 160, 162–3; Citizen (J. Caesar) 227–8; Francis 157; Metellus (J. Caesar) 229; Osric 123, 125; Roderigo 358, 360–1; Slender 327; Ventoso 428; Witch 282–3.

Whitaker, Thomas, fl. 1735: Apothecary (C. Marius) 410.

White, fl. 1749: Pandulph 244.

White, James [CG treasurer], fl. 1741–8: 59, 79.

Whittingham, John, fl. 1743: Hotspur 171.

Wignell, John, d. 1774: Albany 265; Alonso 435; Buckingham (Rich. III) 399–400; Duke (Othello) 360; Gentleman (Timon) 446; Laertes 139–40; Menelaus 454; Montano 371; Page (MWW) 336; Provost 304; Ratcliff 385; Salerio (Jew) 312; Seyton 298; Westmorland (1 Hen. IV) 163; Worcester 176. Other reference 47.

Wignell, Mrs John, fl. 1747: Miranda 435.

Wilcox, fl. 1724–33: Painter 445. Other reference 28.

Wilder, James, 1724–?: Balthazar (Much Ado) 346; Doctor (Macbeth) 300; Gainlove 422.

Wilks, Master, fl. 1746: Fleance 296.

Wilks, Robert, Sr., 1665–1732: Antony 218–26; Buckingham (Hen. VIII) 206–7; Cassio 349–51; Dauphin (Hen. V) 195; Edgar 245–53; Ferdinand 424, 426–7; Hamlet 106–18, 120–1; Henry VI (Cibber's Rich. III) 379, 382; Macduff 268–83; Marius, Young 406; Orlando (Love in For.) 91; Othello 348; Troilus 452; Wales, Prince of (1 Hen. IV) 145–57; Wales, Prince of (2 Hen. IV) 180–1. Other references 2, 5–6, 207, 355.

Wilks, Robert, Jr., fl. 1734: 464.

Wilks, William, Sr. [DL office-keeper], fl. 1716–23: 12, 21, 25.

Wilks, William, Jr., fl. 1715–24: Clifford, Young 204; Edmund 249; Ferdinand 426–7; Laertes 114–15; Metellus (J. Caesar) 221; Poins (2 Hen. IV) 180; Rosencrantz 110; Sicinius (Invader) 100; Tressel 379. Other references 12, 19, 23, 27.

Williams [unidentified], fl. 1718: 16.

Williams, Miss, fl. 1731–2: Desdemona 356; Hippolito 429. Other reference 37.

Williams, Charles, 1693–1731: Alcibiades 442–3; Banquo 278–81; Caesar 226; Cassio 351–4; Cinna (C. Marius) 409; Douglas 149, 155; Duke Frederick (Love in For.) 90; Kent 249–53; Laertes 115–18; Lartius (Invader) 100; Lucius (Titus) 450; Mortimer 149; Octavius 222–5; Richmond 382; Scroop (Hen. V) 195; Soothsayer 221; Surrey (Hen. VIII) 208; Wales, Prince of (2 Hen. IV) 180–2; Warwick (Humfrey) 203; Westmorland (2 Hen. IV) 180. Other references 16, 18–19, 30, 206.

Williams, Robert, fl. 1726–44: Albany 254; Ancharius 410; Cinna the Conspirator 227–9; Gratiano (Othello) 356–7; Gravedigger 119–21; Grist 419; Guildenstern 119; Host 324; Lodovico 355–6; Mustacho 429; Northumberland (1 Hen. IV) 157–8; Oxford 383; Rosencrantz 119; Rugby 326; Tybalt 410; Tyrrel 383–4. Other references 30–1, 40, 119.

Williams, William, fl. 1730–1: Cassio 355–6; Edmund 254; Gravedigger 119; Grist 420; Laertes 119; Snuffle 419. Other references 36, 119.

Williamson, Mrs, fl. 1730–3: Calphurnia 228; Desdemona 354; Goneril 256.

Willis, Miss Mary, fl. 1709–23: Betty 416; Cordelia (probably) 246; Hippolito 426; Miranda 425–7; Ophelia 112; Tearsheet, Doll 180. Other reference 246.

Willis, Mrs Richard, Elizabeth, d. 1739: Hostess (1 Hen. IV) 147–55, 157, 159; Hostess (2 Hen. IV) 180; Joan (Johnson's Cobler) 416; Lady, Old 206, 210. Other references 5–6, 25, 27–8, 30, 246.

Willoughby, Mrs, d. 1768: Hero 346; Hippolito 437.

Wilmer [LIF and CG box-keeper], fl. 1730–9: 36, 55.

Wilson [LIF box-keeper], fl. 1721: 22.

Wilson, Mrs, fl. 1723: Elizabeth, Queen 381; Macduff, Lady 277.

Wilson, Thomas, fl. 1715–23: Cinna the Conspirator 221; Forrest 379; Lion (Love in For.) 91, 340; Mouldy 180; Richard (Cibber's 3 Hen. VI) 204.

Winstone, Richard, 1699–1787: Alonso 432–5; Antonio (Tempest) 432; Austria 241, 243; Bernardo 134, 136–7, 139; Buckingham (Hen. VIII) 214, 216;

494

## INDEX I

Buckingham (Rich. III) 391; Casca 233–4; Cassio 365–7; Catesby 388–9, 391; Chamberlain, Lord 211–13, 215; Charles 91–2; Decius 234; Douglas 158–62, 167–8; Duke (Com. Err.) 99; Duke (Merchant) 313–18; Duke (Othello) 368–9, 371–3; Duke Frederick 93–4, 96–7; Duncan 289–92; Ely, Bishop of (Hen. V) 199–200; Escalus (Measure) 306, 308; Escalus (R & J) 411–12; Fabian 455–6; Gonzalo 430–1; Gratiano (Othello) 357–8; Gremio (Univ. Pass.) 342–3; Guildenstern 124, 131; Isander 448; John, Don 344–6; Kent 259–63, 265–6; King, Player 140–3; Lieutenant 385–6; Metellus (J. Caesar) 227–8; Montano 356, 358, 361; Norfolk (Rich. III) 384; Page (MWW) 330–2, 334, 338; Peter, Friar 304–5; Poins (1 Hen. IV) 166–9; Siward 284–9, 294–300; Soldier [Interpreter] 88; Stanley 392, 394–6, 398–9, 401–3; Thrasillus 446–7; Trebonius 229–30, 234, 237; Westmorland (2 Hen. IV) 184, 186–91; Worcester 169–72, 174–5. Other references 43, 48, 61, 73.

Woffington, *Mrs* (i.e. *Miss*) Margaret, *c.* 1714–60: Adriana 99; Anne, Lady (Rich. III) 394–6, 398–9, 401–3; Cordelia 260, 262; Desdemona 373; Ford, Mrs 334, 337–9; Helena 88; Hippolito 434–5; Isabella 307–8; Katharine, Queen 217; Macbeth, Lady 299–300; Nerissa 313–14; Ophelia 133–4, 136; Percy, Lady (1 Hen. IV) 176, 178; Portia (J. Caesar) 238–9; Portia (Merchant) 315, 319; Queen (Hamlet) 144; Rosalind 92–7; Viola 456. Other reference 88.

Wood, Thomas [LIF and CG treasurer], d. 1748: 28, 42, 51, 54.

Woodburn, E., fl. 1734–46: Brandon 215; Canterbury, Archbishop of (Betterton's 2 Hen. IV) 191; Chamberlain, Lord 214, 216; Douglas 170–2; Duke (All's Well) 88; Francisco (Tempest) 434; Gonzalo 432–3; Gratiano (Othello) 368; Herald, French 242; Le Beau 93–5; Montano 367; Morocco 313–16; Murderer 290; Officer (Com. Err.) 99; Oxford 389; Popilius 229–30; Priest (Twelfth N.) 455; Ratcliff 391–2, 394–6, 398; Rosencrantz 131–4, 136; Siward 292; Thrasillus 448; Tyrrel 389.

Woodman, *Miss*, later Mrs Isaac Ridout, q.v.

Woodward, Sr., fl. 1730: Lodovico 355; Roderigo 354.

Woodward, *Mrs*, Sr., fl. 1730–43: Calphurnia 235–6; Emilia (Othello) 355, 366; Goneril 254, 261–2; Queen (Hamlet) 130, 132–4; York, Duchess of (Rich. III) 392, 394. Other reference 65.

Woodward, Henry, 1714–77: Andrew, Sir 455–6; Ariel 429; Carrier 166–74; Citizen (J. Caesar) 233–7; Dauphin (Hen. V) 198–9; Donalbain 284–5; Feeble 187–8; Francis 174, 176; Gentleman Usher 261–4; Guiderius 104; Isander 449; John, Prince (1 Hen. IV) 162; Lucio 305, 308; Marcellus 126; Mercutio 411–12; Mustacho 432–3; Octavius 234; Orleans 195–6; Osric 126 f, 131 f, 13f, 141–3; Parolles 89; Pistol (2 Hen. IV) 189–92; Pistol (Hen. V) 198–200; Poet 447–8; Poins (1 Hen. IV) 164; Roderigo 361, 363–8, 370, 372; Sands 214–17; Silvius 91–2; Simple 325–7; Slender 328, 330–6, 338; Touchstone 92, 94–6, 98; Tranio (Sauny) 420–1; Ventoso 432; Witch 292–6. Other references 58, 65, 67, 74, 77, 429.

World [unidentified], fl. 1733: 43.

Worsdale, James, *c.* 1692–1767: Manly 420. Other references 46, 102, 414.

Worsley, fl. 1731: Antonio (Tempest) 429.

Wrexham, Samuel [DL treasurer], fl. 1728: 33.

Wright, fl. 1741–50: Capulet, Old 411–12; Chief Watch 410; Dighton 389, 392; Publius 237.

Wright, d. 1753: Blunt (Cibber's Rich. III) 379; Davy 180. Other references 25, 70.

Wright, *Mrs* [singer], fl. 1730–7: 36, 51.

Wright, *Mrs* (i.e. *Miss*) Christiana, d. 1744: Page, Anne 332; Phebe 92, 94; York, Duke of 394–5.

Wright, Thomas, 1707–*c.* 1760: Antony 233–4; Cassio 362–4; Cranmer 212–13; Duke Frederick 91–2; Escalus (Measure) 304–5; Gloucester (Lear) 259; Henry IV (1 Hen. IV) 165–9; Laertes 127–9; Lennox 288–91; Richmond 388–9; York, Archbishop of 186, 188–90. Other references 30, 35, 37, 54, 56, 58.

Wyndham, *Sir* Charles, 1837–1919: 405.

Yates, *Miss*, fl. 1744–50: Arthur 244; Boy (Hen. V) 200; Robin 338; York, Duke of 395–6, 399, 401–3.

Yates, Richard, *c.* 1706–96: Attendant (Rich. II) 377; Autolycus 457; Citizen (J. Caesar) 233–4, 237; Clown (All's Well) 88; Clown (Measure) 308; Clown (Twelfth N.) 455–6; Evans 333–4, 338; Fluellen 200; Francis 168, 171–2, 174–5; Gentleman Usher 261; Gravedigger 130–1, 133–4, 141–3; Hecate 291; Lucianus 132–3, 136–7, 139–40; Pistol (2 Hen. IV) 188, 191; Pistol (Hen. V) 200; Pistol (MWW) 331; Poet 448;

495

Roderigo 362, 364–5, 368–9, 371–4; Shylock 317–18; Trinculo 437; Wart 187; Witch 294–300.

Yates, *Mrs* Richard [the 1st], d. 1753: Emilia (Wint. T.) 458; Gentlewoman (Macbeth) 298–300; Hostess (1 Hen. IV) 168; Miranda 437; Queen, Player 134, 136–7, 139–43; Quickly, Mrs (MWW) 333; Regan 261, 264–5; Widow (All's Well) 88; York, Duchess of (Rich. III) 390–1, 393.

Yeates, Thomas, Jr. [harlequin], fl. 1748: 80, 464.

Yorke, fl. 1744–5: Gonzalo 433; Montano 367.

Young, *Miss* Cecilia, later Mrs Thomas Augustine Arne, q.v.

Young, *Miss* Esther, later Mrs John Jones, fl. 1746–50: Iris 434; Lucy (Cure) 422. Other reference 79.

Younger, *Mrs* (i.e. *Miss*) Elizabeth, later the Hon. Mrs John Finch, 1699–1762: Cordelia 252–7; Desdemona 352–3, 356–9; Dorinda 425; Ford, Mrs 323–6.

# INDEX II
# CHARACTERS

This index lists all the characters that appear in the playbills. Under each character will be found the names of all the performers who undertook that particular part. In many instances actresses appeared in the same part both before and after their marriage. In such instances I have given both their maiden and married names. If, however, an actress appeared in a part only under her maiden name or only under her married name, that name alone is listed.

For the abbreviations of the adaptations of Shakespeare's plays as given here, see the foreword to Index I.

Aaron (Titus). *See* Bickerstaff, Quin, T. Walker.
Abbess (Com. Err.). *See* Mrs Macklin.
Abergavenny (Hen. VIII). *See* Anderson, Este, Fielding, A. Hill, Mozeen, Oates, Raftor, Ridout, Salway.
Abhorson (Measure). *See* Bencraft, Collins, Morgan, H. Vaughan.
Abraham (R & J). *See* Dunstall, Marr.
Achilles (Troilus). *See* Booth, Hale, Hulett, J. Leigh.
Adam (AYLI). *See* Berry, Bridgwater, Havard. In Johnson's alteration (Love in For.), *see* J. Mills.
Adriana (Com. Err.). *See* Mrs Woffington.
Aedile (Coriolanus). In Dennis's alteration (Invader), *see* Oates.
Aegeon (Com. Err.). *See* Berry.
Aelius. In Shadwell's Timon the name given to one of the Senators, q.v.
Aeneas (Troilus). *See* Bickerstaff, Houghton.
Agamemnon (Troilus). *See* Diggs, J. Lacy, J. Mills.
Airy Spirit (Dryden and Davenant's Tempest). A character not in the original play. *See* Mrs Boman Sr.
Ajax (Troilus). *See* J. Hall, Harper, Keene.
Albany (Lear). *See* Anderson, Bardin, Bickerstaff, Boman Sr., Chapman, R. Cross II, Diggs, Dighton, Gibson, Hale, Havard, Milward, Mozeen, Oates, Paget, Peterson, Salway, Turbutt, Usher, Wignell, R. Williams.
Alberto. In Johnson's alteration of AYLI (Love in For.) the name given to Duke Senior, q.v.
Alcibiades (Timon). *See* Booth, Bridgwater, Cashell, Marshall, W. Mills, L. Ryan, T. Walker, C. Williams.
Alençon (1 Hen. VI). *See* Salway.
Alonso (Tempest). *See* Berry, Bridges, Corey, Fielding, Freeman (fl. 1735–45), Hewitt, Keene, Lee, Machen, Platt, J. Roberts, T. Smith, Turbutt, Wignell, Winstone.
Ambassador (C. Marius). A character not in the original play. *See* Pearson.
Ambassador, French (Betterton's 2 Hen. IV). A character not in the original play. *See* Turbutt.
Amiens (AYLI). *See* Beard, Lowe, E. Roberts, Salway. In Johnson's alteration (Love in For.), *see* Corey.
Amphitrite (Dryden and Davenant's Tempest). A character not in the original play. *See* Mrs Arne, Mrs Cantrell, Mrs Carlisle, Mrs Cushing, Mrs Dove, Miss Jones, Miss Lincoln, Mrs J. Mills, Miss E. Norris, Mrs Palmer, Miss Rafor, Mrs J. Roberts, Miss C. Young [i.e. later Mrs Arne].
Ancharius (C. Marius). A character not in the original play. *See* R. Williams.
Ancharius's Son (C. Marius). A character not in the original play. *See* Miss Brett.
Andrew, Sir (Twelfth N.). *See* Neale, H. Woodward.
Andromache (Troilus). *See* Mrs Buchanan, Mrs Bullock, Mrs J. Giffard, Mrs Knight, Mrs Rogers.
Angelo (Com. Err.). *See* Havard.
Angelo (Measure). *See* Boheme, Cashell, Havard, Milward, L. Sparks, T. Walker.
Angers, Abbot of. In Cibber's alteration of John (Papal Tyr.) the name given in part [II. i. 363–560] to the Citizen of Angers, q.v.
Angers, Citizen of (John). *See* Bridges, Paget, Rosco. In Cibber's alteration (Papal Tyr.) this character's speeches given (1) to Governor of Angers, *see* Carr; and (2) to Abbot of Angers, *see* Gibson, Marten.
Angers, Governor of. In Cibber's alteration of John (Papal Tyr.) the name given in

## INDEX II

part [II. i. 200–333] to the Citizen of Angers, q.v.

Angus (Macbeth). *See* Simpson, Turbutt.

Anne, Lady (Cibber's 3 Hen. VI). A character not in the original play. *See* Mrs Brett.

Anne, Lady (Rich. III). *See* Mrs Bland, Mrs Bullock, Mrs S. M. Cibber, Mrs Egleton, Mrs H. Giffard, Mrs J. Giffard [i.e. later Mrs Egleton], Mrs Hale, Mrs L. Hallam, Mrs Heron, Miss Holliday [i.e. later Mrs W. Mills the 2nd], Mrs Horton, Mrs W. Mills the 2nd, Mrs Phillips, Mrs Pritchard, Mrs Rogers, Mrs Spiller, Mrs Vincent (fl. 1723–31), Mrs R. Vincent, Mrs Woffington.

Antigonus (Wint. T.). *See* Rosco, T. Walker.

Antipholus of Ephesus (Com. Err.). *See* W. Mills.

Antipholus of Syracuse (Com. Err.). *See* Milward.

Antonio (Merchant). *See* Berry, Cashell, Delane, Quin, L. Sparks. In Granville's alteration (Jew), *see* J. Mills, L. Ryan, Verbruggen.

Antonio (Much Ado). *See* Arthur, Carr.

Antonio (Tempest). *See* Berry, Brown, C. Bullock, Corey, Dove, Goodfellow, W. Mills, Mozeen, Naylor, Reynolds, Tucker, Turbutt, Winstone, Worsley.

Antonio (Twelfth N.). *See* Bridges, Cashell, I. Sparks. In Burnaby's alteration (Love Bet.) this character named Rodoregue. *See* Fieldhouse.

Antonius (C. Marius). A character not in the original play. *See* Gerum.

Antony (J. Caesar). *See* Barry, Delane, H. Giffard, Hale, Havard, J. Leigh, W. Mills, Milward, Quin, T. Walker, R. Wilks, T. Wright.

Antony's Servant (J. Caesar). *See* R. Cross II, Ray.

Apemantus (Timon). *See* W. Giffard, P. Griffin, Husband, 'Tall' Johnson, Keene, J. Mills, W. Mills, Paget, Quin, Verbruggen.

Apothecary (R & J). *See* Hacket, Richards, Simpson. In Otway's alteration (C. Marius), *see* B. Griffin, Penkethman Sr., Whitaker.

Arante (Tate's Lear). A character not in the original play. *See* Mrs Dove, Miss E. Hippisley, Mrs Horsington, Miss Scott.

Archer. In Worsdale's alteration of Tam. Shrew (Cure) the name given to Grumio, q.v.

Ariel (Tempest). *See* Arne, Miss Brett, Mrs Clive, Miss Cole, Mrs Kennedy, Miss Lindar, Mrs Moreau, Miss Norris (fl. 1733–35), Master Paget, Miss Platt, Miss Robinson Jr., Shepard (fl. 1745), R. Wetherilt, H. Woodward.

Arragon (Merchant). *See* Turbutt.

Artemidorus (J. Caesar). *See* C. Shepard.

Arthur (John). *See* Miss Bincks [i.e. later Mrs R. Vincent], Miss Burgess, Miss Macklin, Mrs R. Vincent, Miss Yates. In Cibber's alteration (Papal Tyr.), *see* Miss Cibber, Miss Morrison.

Arundel (Papal Tyr.). A character not in the original play. *See* Anderson.

Arviragus (Cymbeline). *See* Beard, Boheme (?), A. Hallam, T. Smith.

Asino. In Miller's alteration of Much Ado (Univ. Pass.) the name given to Verges, q.v.

Athenian, Old (Timon). In Shadwell's alteration this character named Old Man. *See* Aston, Boman Sr., Gibson.

Attendant (Rich. II). *See* Yates.

Audrey (AYLI). *See* Mrs Egerton, Miss Hilliard, Mrs Horsington, Mrs James, Mrs Ridout.

Aufidius (Coriolanus). In Dennis's alteration (Invader), *see* J. Mills.

Aumerle (Rich. II). *See* A. Hallam, Quin, T. Smith.

Austria (John). *See* Boman Jr., Mullart, Winstone.

Autolycus (Wint. T.). *See* Chapman, Yates.

Bagot (Rich. II). *See* Salway.

Balthazar (Com. Err.). *See* Ridout.

Balthazar (Merchant). *See* Anderson, Green, Hayman, Simpson.

Balthazar (Much Ado). *See* Beard, Hayman, Salway, Wilder.

Balthazar (R & J). *See* Ackman, Bransby, Miss Charke, Mrs Clark, Cushing. In Otway's alteration (C. Marius) this character named Catulus. *See* Rymos.

Banquo (Macbeth). *See* Bickerstaff, Boheme, Booth, Bridgwater, Cashell, Delane, Diggs, Hale, Havard, Hulett, Husband, J. Leigh, J. Mills, W. Mills, Milward, Paget, Powell, L. Ryan, Sowdon, L. Sparks, T. Walker, C. Williams.

Baptista (Tam. Shrew). In Lacy's alteration (Sauny) this character named Beaufoy. *See* W. Giffard, Hulett, Keene. In Worsdale's alteration (Cure) this character named Sir William. *See* Collins, C. Shepard, M. Stoppelaer.

Bardolph (1 Hen. IV). *See* Collett, Dove, Dunstall, G. Hallam, W. Hallam, Littleton, Marten, Miles, Monlass, Ray, C. Shepard, M. Stoppelaer, Topham.

Bardolph (2 Hen. IV). *See* W. Hallam, Marten, Ray, C. Shepard, M. Stoppelaer.

## INDEX II

In the anonymous alteration (Humours of Fal.), see Jones.
Bardolph (Hen. V). See W. Hallam, Marten, Oates, Ray, I. Sparks.
Bardolph (MWW). See Dove, Dunstall, G. Hallam, Harrington, Machen, Marten, Ray, C. Shepard.
Bardolph, Lord (2 Hen. IV). See Hale, Ridout.
Barnardine (Measure). See H. Bullock, Dunstall, Evans (fl. 1733–43), Ray, M. Stoppelaer.
Bassanio (Merchant). See Hale, Havard, W. Mills, Milward, L. Ryan. In Granville's alteration (Jew), see Betterton, Booth, J. Leigh, T. Walker.
Basset (1 Hen. VI). See Anderson.
Bassianus (Titus). See Orfeur, T. Walker.
Bastard (John). See Delane, Hale, Pinner, L. Sparks, T. Walker. In Cibber's alteration (Papal Tyr.), see L. Ryan.
Bates (Hen. V). See Mullart.
Bawd (Pericles). In Lillo's alteration (Marina) this character named Mother Coupler. See W. Hallam.
Beatrice (Much Ado). See Miss Bincks [i.e. later Mrs R. Vincent], Mrs L. Cross, Mrs Pritchard, Mrs R. Vincent. In Miller's alteration (Univ. Pass.) this character named Liberia. See Mrs Clive.
Beaufoy. In Lacy's alteration of Tam. Shrew (Sauny) the name given to Baptista, q.v.
Beaupré. In D'Urfey's Cymbeline the name given to Philario, q.v.
Bedford (Hen. V). See Marr, A. Ryan, Usher.
Bedford (1 Hen. VI). See 'Tall' Johnson.
Belarius (Cymbeline). See 'Tall' Johnson, Ogden, Stephens.
Bellario. In Miller's alteration of Much Ado (Univ. Pass.) the name given to Claudio, q.v.
Benedick (Much Ado). See Chapman, Garrick, L. Ryan. In Miller's alteration (Univ. Pass.) this character named Protheus. See Quin.
Benvolio (R & J). See Gibson, Holtom, Mozeen, Usher. In Otway's alteration (C. Marius) this character named Granius. See Booth, Boothby, W. Mills, L. Ryan, T. Walker.
Bernardo (Hamlet). See Collins, Dove, R. Elrington, Gibson, Houghton, Jenkins, Kennedy, Marr, Oates, Reeves, Winstone.
Bertram (All's Well). See H. Giffard, Hale, W. Mills.
Betty. In Johnson's alteration of the induction to Tam. Shrew (Cobler) the name given to the Page, q.v.
Bianca (Othello). See Mrs Finch, Mrs Hale, Miss Raftor.
Bianca (Tam. Shrew). In Lacy's alteration (Sauny), see Mrs Hamilton, Mrs J. Mills, Mrs Vincent (fl. 1723–31). In Worsdale's alteration (Cure) this character named Flora. See Miss Falkner, Mrs Pritchard.
Biondello (Tam. Shrew). In Lacy's alteration (Sauny) this character named Jamy. See Morgan, Norris Sr., Rosco.
Blanch (John). See Mrs Horton, Miss Minors, Mrs Stevens. In Cibber's alteration (Papal Tyr.), see Miss Bellamy, Miss J. Hippisley.
Blunt (1 Hen. IV). See Edwards, R. Elrington, Goodfellow, Green, Havard, A. Hill, Machen, W. Mills, Oates, Ridout, Rosco, Salway, Shepard (fl. 1745), Usher.
Blunt (Cibber's Rich. III). See Baker, Barnet, W. Bullock Jr., Burton, Clarke, Clough, Holtom, James, Kennedy, Naylor, Paddick, Palmer, Raftor, Usher, Wright (d. 1753).
Boatswain (Tempest). See Blakes.
Bolingbroke (Rich. II). See J. Leigh, L. Ryan.
Borachio (Much Ado). See Aston, Blakes, Gibson, A. Ryan. In Miller's alteration (Univ. Pass.) this character named Gremio. See Winstone.
Bottom (MND). In Leveridge's alteration (Pyramus), see Spiller.
Boult (Pericles). In Lillo's alteration (Marina), see Penkethman Jr.
Bourbon (Hen. V). See Bridgwater, Richardson.
Boy (Hen. V). See Miss Ferguson, Miss Morrison, Miss Yates.
Boy (Much Ado). See Miss Morrison.
Brabantio (Othello). See Aston, Berry, Boheme, Boman Sr., Boman Jr., Bridges, Davis, Furnival, Gibson, W. Giffard, Hulett, Keene, Machen, Milward, Mullart, Nelson, Paget, Philips, Ridout, J. Roberts, T. Smith, L. Sparks, Thurmond Sr.
Brandon (Hen. VIII). See Bransby, Woodburn.
Brutus (J. Caesar). See Betterton, Booth, Delane, Keene, Quin, Sheridan.
Brutus, Junius (Coriolanus). In Dennis's alteration (Invader), see T. Walker.
Buckingham (Hen. VIII). See Booth, Bridgwater, Delane, Hale, Havard, W. Mills, L. Ryan, R. Wilks, Winstone.
Buckingham (2 Hen. VI). In Philips's alteration (Humfrey), see W. Mills.
Buckingham (Rich. III). See Bridges,

499

## INDEX II

Bridgwater, Cashell, W. Giffard, Hewitt, J. Mills, W. Mills, Peterson, Quin, L. Sparks, Wignell, Winstone.
Bullcalf (2 Hen. IV). *See* Dunstall, Gray, Mullart, H. Wetherilt.
Bullen, Anne (Hen. VIII). *See* Miss Bellamy, Mrs Bennet, Mrs Bradshaw, Mrs Bullock, Mrs Butler, Mrs Heron, Miss Holliday [i.e. later Mrs W. Mills the 2nd], Mrs Horton, Mrs W. Mills the 2nd, Mrs Pritchard, Mrs Ridout, Mrs Stevens.
Burgundy (Hen. V). *See* Blakes, Gibson, Harrington, Tho. Lacy, T. Walker.
Burgundy (1 Hen. VI). *See* Ridout.
Burgundy (Lear). *See* Bencraft, W. Bullock Jr., Collett, Freeman (fl. 1735–45), Hamilton, Marr, Miles, Paddick, Pearce, Ray, A. Ryan, Simpson.
Bushy (Rich. II). *See* Rosco.
Butler (Johnson's Cobler). A character not in the original play. *See* Birkhead.
Butts (Hen. VIII). *See* B. Griffin, I. Sparks, M. Stoppelaer, Topham.
Byron, In Miller's alteration of Much Ado (Univ. Pass.) the name given to Don John, q.v.

Caesar (J. Caesar). *See* Berry, Boheme, Booth, Bridgwater, Huddy, Keene, J. Leigh, J. Mills, W. Mills, Ogden, L. Ryan, L. Sparks, Thurmond Sr., C. Williams.
Caesario. In Burnaby's alteration of Twelfth N. (Love Bet.) the name given to Viola, q.v.
Caesar's Servant (J. Caesar). *See* Raftor.
Caius (MWW). *See* Bardin, Blakes, J. Hall, Harper, James, Miller, Mullart, Pack, Penkethman Sr., Penkethman Jr., Shuter, Spiller, M. Stoppelaer, Taswell.
Calchas (Troilus). *See* Neale.
Caliban (Tempest). *See* Blakes, W. Giffard, B. Johnson, Machen, Norris Sr., Paget, I. Sparks, H. Wetherilt.
Calphurnia (J. Caesar). *See* Mrs Bambridge, Mrs Barry, Mrs Bennet, Mrs Boheme, Mrs Bradshaw, Mrs Buchanan, Mrs Butler, Mrs Cantrell, Mrs Egleton, Mrs J. Giffard [i.e. later Mrs Egleton], Mrs M. Giffard, Mrs W. Hallam, Mrs Harold, Mrs Haughton, Mrs Horton, Mrs James, Mrs Knight, Mrs Seymour [i.e. later Mrs Boheme], Mrs Williamson, Mrs Woodward.
Cambridge (Betterton's 2 Hen. IV). A character not in the original play. *See* Taswell.
Cambridge (Hen V). *See* Anderson, Hamilton, Houghton, W. Mills, Raftor.

Camillo (Wint. T.). *See* Bridgwater, Paget.
Campeius (Hen. VIII). *See* Chapman, Dunstall, Goodfellow, Mullart, C. Shepard, Turbutt.
Canterbury, Archbishop of (Betterton's 2 Hen. IV). A character not in the original play. *See* Corey, Woodburn.
Canterbury, Archbishop of (Hen. V). *See* Bridges, Chapman, Delane, L. Sparks.
Captain (Cymbeline). *See* Bencraft.
Captain (Lear). *See* W. Hallam.
Captain (Macbeth). *See* Usher.
Captain (Othello). *See* Shuter.
Captain (Twelfth N.). *See* Blakes, Goodfellow, Turbutt.
Capucius (Hen. VIII). *See* Bransby, Turbutt.
Capulet (R & J). *See* Berry, Paget, L. Sparks. In Otway's alteration (C. Marius) this character named Metellus. *See* Aston, Boman Sr.
Capulet, Lady (R & J). *See* Mrs Barrington, Mrs Bennet, Mrs George, Mrs Horton.
Capulet, Old (R & J). *See* Redman, Wright (fl. 1741–50).
Cardinal (2 Hen. VI). In Philips's alteration (Humfrey), *see* C. Cibber.
Carlisle, Bishop of (Rich. II). *See* C. Bullock, Chapman.
Carrier (1 Hen. IV). *See* Arthur, Barrington, Beckham, H. Bullock, W. Bullock Sr., W. Bullock Jr., Chapman, T. Cibber, Collins, Cushing, Dove, Dunstall, B. Griffin, J. Hall, Hippisley, James, B. Johnson, Jones, Julian, Knapp, F. Leigh Sr., Lyon, Macklin, Miller, Morgan, Mullart, Penkethman Sr., Phipps, Ray, I. Sparks, R. Wetherilt, H. Woodward.
Casca (J. Caesar). *See* Berry, Bickerstaff, Cashell, T. Cibber, Corey, W. Giffard, Harper, Hulett, Keene, Lyon, Ogden, Ridout, L. Sparks, Stephens, Winstone.
Cassio (Othello). *See* Blakes, Booth, Bridgwater, Cashell, T. Cibber, H. Giffard, W. Giffard, Hale, A. Hallam, Havard, Hewitt, Husband, Kennedy, Theo. Lacy, Lee, J. Leigh, Machen, W. Mills, Mozeen, Palmer, Powell, Ridout, L. Ryan, Stevens (fl. 1737–42), T. Walker, R. Wilks, C. Williams, W. Williams, Winstone, T. Wright.
Cassius (J. Caesar). *See* Boheme, T. Elrington, Hulett, J. Mills, Milward, Powell, L. Ryan, L. Sparks, Verbruggen.
Catesby (Rich. III). *See* Aston, Bencraft, Diggs, Dighton, Egleton, Gibson, Havard, A. Hill, Marr, Oates, J. Roberts, Shuter, Turbutt, Usher, Winstone.
Catulus. In Otway's alteration of R & J (C. Marius) the name given to Balthazar, q.v.

500

# INDEX II

Celia (AYLI). *See* Mrs Clive, Mrs Hale, Mrs Ridout, Mrs R. Vincent. In Johnson's alteration (Love in For.), *see* Mrs Thurmond.
Ceres (Tempest). *See* Mrs Sibilla.
Chamberlain, Lord (Hen. VIII). *See* Anderson, Berry, Corey, Ridout, Rosco, Winstone, Woodburn.
Chancellor, Lord (Hen. VIII). *See* Marten, C. Shepard.
Charles (AYLI). *See* Arthur, Layfield, Marten, Raftor, I. Sparks, H. Vaughan, Winstone. In Johnson's alteration (Love in For.), *see* W. Mills.
Charles, Sir. In Johnson's alteration of the induction to Tam. Shrew (Cobler) the name given to the Lord, q.v.
Charlotte (Hill's Hen. V). A character not in the original play. *See* Mrs Campbell, Miss Tollett.
Chatillon (John). *See* Bransby, Salway, Turbutt, Walker (fl. 1735–49).
Chief Watch (R & J). *See* Wright (fl. 1741–50).
Chiron (Titus). *See* J. Ward.
Chloe (Shadwell's Timon). A character not in the original play. *See* Mrs Baker, Mrs Bennet, Miss Brett, Mrs R. Cross, Miss J. Hippisley, Mrs J. Mills, Miss Morse, Mrs Stevens.
Chorus (Hen. V). *See* Garrick, L. Ryan.
Cinna (C. Marius). A character not in the original play. *See* Keene, Quin, Turner (fl. 1735), C. Williams.
Cinna the Conspirator (J. Caesar). *See* Anderson, Ayres, Este, Houghton, Marr, Paget, Redman, Ridout, R. Williams, Wilson.
Cinna the Poet (J. Caesar). *See* Bowen.
Citizen (C. Marius). A character not in the original play. *See* Birkhead, C. Cibber, R. Cross I, F. Leigh Sr., Miller, Norris Sr., Penkethman Sr., Ray, Trout.
Citizen (Coriolanus). *See* C. Bullock, H. Bullock, W. Bullock Sr., B. Griffin, J. Hall, Pack, Spiller. In Dennis's alteration (Invader), *see* Bickerstaff, R. Cross I, B. Johnson, Miller, Norris Sr., Penkethman Sr.
Citizen (J. Caesar). *See* Arthur, Barrington, H. Bullock, W. Bullock Sr., W. Bullock Jr., Chapman, C. Cibber, Collett, Collins, R. Cross I, Dunstall, B. Griffin, J. Hall, W. Hallam, Harper, Hippisley, Hough, James, B. Johnson, F. Leigh Sr., Lyon, Macklin, Marten, Miller, Monlass, Morgan, Mullart, Neale, Norris Sr., Norris Jr., Pearce, Penkethman Sr., Penkethman Jr., Phipps, Ray, Reed, Smith (fl. 1735–49), Spiller, M. Stoppelaer, H. Vaughan, H. Wetherilt, R. Wetherilt, H. Woodward, Yates.
Clarence (2 Hen. IV). *See* Bennet, T. Cibber, Miss E. Hippisley.
Clarinna. In Durfey's Cymbeline the name given to Helen, q.v.
Claudio (Measure). *See* Lee, W. Mills, L. Ryan.
Claudio (Much Ado). *See* Hale, A. Hallam, King, Lee, J. Leigh, Palmer. In Miller's alteration (Univ. Pass.) this character named Bellario. *See* W. Mills.
Cleomenes (Wint. T.). *See* Blakes, Goodall.
Cleon. In Shadwell's Timon the name given to one of the Senators, q.v.
Clerimont (Bullock's Cobler). A character not in the original play. *See* Coker, Havard, Mynn, Wathen.
Clerk (Dryden and Davenant's Tempest). A character not in the original play. *See* H. Vaughan.
Clifford (Cibber's 3 Hen. VI). *See* Boman Sr.
Clifford, Young (Cibber's 3 Hen. VI). *See* W. Wilks.
Clodius. In Otway's alteration of R & J (C. Marius) the name given to Peter, q.v.
Cloten (Cymbeline). *See* H. Bullock, Chapman.
Clown (All's Well). *See* Chapman, Dunstall, Macklin, Yates.
Clown (Measure). *See* Arthur, Barrington, Hippisley, Miller, Spiller, Yates.
Clown (Twelfth N.). *See* Chapman, Yates.
Clown (Wint. T.). *See* Dunstall, Hippisley.
Cluentius (Invader). A character not in the original play. *See* Boman Sr.
Colevile (2 Hen. IV). *See* Anderson, R. Elrington, Oates.
Cominius (Coriolanus). In Dennis's alteration (Invader), *see* Thurmond Sr.
Conrade (Much Ado). *See* Anderson, Bransby, Mozeen, Ridout, Usher.
Constable (Hen. V). *See* Bridgwater, L. Sparks.
Constable (Johnson's Cobler). A character not in the original play. *See* F. Leigh Sr.
Constance (John). *See* Mrs S. M. Cibber, Mrs Cushing, Mrs H. Giffard, Mrs W. Hallam, Mrs Mullart. In Cibber's alteration (Papal Tyr.), *see* Mrs Pritchard.
Cordelia (Lear). *See* Miss Bellamy, Mrs Boheme, Mrs Booth, Mrs Bracegirdle, Mrs Bradshaw, Mrs Brett, Miss Budgell, Mrs S. M. Cibber, Mrs H. Giffard, Miss Holliday [i.e. later Mrs W. Mills the 2nd], Mrs Horton, Mrs Knapp, Mrs W. Mills the 2nd, Mrs Moffett, Mrs Parker, Mrs Rogers, Mrs Santlow [i.e. later Mrs Booth], Mrs Seymour [i.e. later Mrs

## INDEX II

Boheme], Mrs Sherburn, Mrs Thurmond, Mrs R. Vincent, Mrs Ward, Miss Willis (probably), Mrs Woffington, Mrs Younger.

Corin (AYLI). *See* Arthur, James, Shuter, Taswell, H. Vaughan.

Coriolanus (Coriolanus). *See* Quin. In Dennis's alteration (Invader), *see* Booth.

Cornelius (Cymbeline). *See* Rosco.

Cornwall (Lear). *See* Aston, Bencraft, Blakes, Burton, Cashell, Chapman, Dighton, Egleton, Fairbank, Fielding, A. Hallam, Havard, A. Hill, J. Lacy, Machen, Milward, Ridout, Rosco, Shuter, Turbutt, T. Walker.

Countess (All's Well). *See* Mrs Butler, Mrs Horton, Mrs Steel.

Countess (1 Hen. VI). *See* Mrs James.

Coupler, Mother. In Lillo's alteration of Pericles (Marina) the name given to the Bawd, q.v.

Courtesan (Com. Err.). *See* Mrs Bennet.

Cranmer (Hen. VIII). *See* Berry, Bridges, Bridgwater, C. Cibber, J. Mills, Milward, Paget, Turbutt, T. Wright.

Cressida (Troilus). *See* Mrs Boheme, Mrs Bradshaw, Mrs Bullock, Mrs Seymour [i.e. later Mrs Boheme], Mrs Sterling.

Cromwell (Hen. VIII). *See* Cashell, R. Cross II, Goodall, Husband, Raftor, Ridout, G. A. Stevens, T. Walker, Watson.

Crotchet (Leveridge's Pyramus). A character not in the original play. *See* H. Bullock.

Curio (Twelfth N.). *See* Bransby, Green, Paddick.

Curtis (Tam. Shrew). In Lacy's alteration (Sauny), *see* H. Bullock, Dove. In Worsdale's alteration (Cure) this character named Peter. *See* Holtom, Raftor.

Cymbeline (Cymbeline). *See* Cashell, J. Leigh, Quin, L. Ryan.

Dauphin (Hen. V). *See* H. Giffard, Goodall, A. Hallam, Havard, Hayman, Lee, Usher, R. Wilks, H. Woodward.

Dauphin (1 Hen. VI). *See* A. Hallam.

Dauphin (John). *See* Blakes, A. Hallam. In Cibber's alteration (Papal Tyr.), *see* T. Cibber.

Davy (2 Hen. IV). *See* T. Wright.

Decius (J. Caesar). *See* Bardin, Bridges, Bridgwater, C. Bullock, Cashell, R. Elrington, Hewitt, Husband, Paget, Ridout, Rosco, C. Shepard, Winstone.

Delia. In Miller's alteration of Much Ado (Univ. Pass.) the name given to Margaret, q.v.

Demetrius (Titus). *See* Diggs.

Demetrius. In Shadwell's Timon the name given to Flavius, q.v.

Desdemona (Othello). *See* Mrs Boheme, Mrs Booth, Mrs Bracegirdle, Mrs Bradshaw, Mrs Buchanan, Mrs Carlisle, Miss Cibber, Mrs S. M. Cibber, Mrs Clive, Miss Copin, Mrs Daniel, Miss Edwards, Mrs Elmy, Mrs H. Giffard, Mrs Grace, Mrs L. Hallam, Mrs Horton, Mrs W. Mills the 2nd, Mrs Mullart, Mrs Phillips, Mrs M. Porter, Mrs Pritchard, Mrs Ridout, Mrs Santlow [i.e. later Mrs Booth], Mrs Seymour [i.e. later Mrs Boheme], Mrs Sterling, Mrs Stevens, Miss Stuart, Mrs Thurmond, Mrs R. Vincent, Mrs Ward, Miss Williams, Mrs Williamson, Mrs Woffington, Mrs Younger.

Diana (All's Well). *See* Mrs Chetwood, Miss J. Hippisley, Mrs Ridout.

Dighton (Cibber's Rich. III). A character not in the original play. *See* Higginson, Wright (fl. 1741–50).

Diocles (Wint. T.). *See* Cashell.

Diomedes (Troilus). *See* Chapman, Egleton, Husband.

Dion (Wint. T.). *See* Peterson, Stevens (fl. 1737–42).

Dionyza (Pericles). In Lillo's alteration (Marina) this character named Philoten. *See* Mrs Hamilton.

Diphilus. In Shadwell's Timon the name given to Lucilius, q.v.

Doctor (Cure). A character not in the original play. *See* Redman, Turbutt.

Doctor (Macbeth). *See* Burton, Goodfellow, Miles, Taswell, Wilder.

Dogberry (Much Ado). *See* W. Bullock Sr., Hippisley, James, Shuter, Taswell. In Miller's alteration (Univ. Pass.) this character named Porco. *See* Harper, Raftor.

Donalbain (Macbeth). *See* Anderson, Bennet, C. Bullock, Clarke, Miss Cole, Gibson, Green, Jenkins, Kennedy, Mattocks, Mrs Moreau, A. Ryan, H. Woodward.

Dorcas (Bullock's Cobler). A character not in the original play. *See* Ayres, Burny, Eaton, B. Griffin, M. Stoppelaer.

Dorcas (Wint. T.). *See* Mrs Jones.

Dorinda (Dryden and Davenant's Tempest). A character not in the original play. *See* Miss Budgell, Mrs Clive, Miss Cole, Mrs L. Cross, Mrs Cushing, Mrs Green, Miss Laguerre, Miss Lindar, Mrs Morgan, Miss Norris (fl. 1708), Mrs Phillips, Miss Raftor [i.e. later Mrs Clive], Mrs Santlow, Mrs Seal, Mrs Younger.

Douglas (1 Hen. IV). *See* Anderson, Fielding, Furnival, Hale, Harbin, Husband, J.

## INDEX II

Mills, W. Mills, Mozeen, Nelson, Paget, Richardson, J. Roberts, T. Smith, Stevens (fl. 1737-42), Usher, J. Ward, C. Williams, Winstone, Woodburn.

Drances. In Burnaby's alteration of Twelfth N. (Love Bet.) the name given to Sir Toby, q.v.

Drawer (2 Hen. IV). In the anonymous alteration (Humours of Fal.), see Thompson.

Dromia. In Burnaby's alteration of Twelfth N. (Love Bet.) the name given to Maria, q.v.

Dromio of Ephesus (Com. Err.). See Arthur.

Dromio of Syracuse (Com. Err.). See Macklin.

Duke (All's Well). See Bencraft, Blakey, Nelson, Pattenden, Woodburn.

Duke (Com. Err.). See Winstone.

Duke (Measure). See Berry, Quin.

Duke (Merchant). See Anderson, Marten, Winstone. In Granville's alteration (Jew), see Corey, Hale, Harris, Ogden.

Duke (Othello). See Anderson, Bardin, Bridges, Corey, R. Cross II, Dove, Dunstall, W. Hallam, Harrington, Jones, Marten, Ogden, Taswell, Wignell, Winstone.

Duke Frederick (AYLI). See Marshall, Rosco, J. Ward, Winstone, T. Wright. In Johnson's alteration (Love in For.), see C. Williams.

Duke Senior (AYLI). See Blakes, Bridges, W. Mills, Ridout, Stephens. In Johnson's alteration (Love in For.) this character named Alberto. See Booth.

Dumain Jr. (All's Well). See Freeman (fl. 1735-45), Gibson, Ridout.

Dumain Sr. (All's Well). See Blakes, Havard, Mozeen, Ridout.

Duncan (Macbeth). See Barnet, Berry, Boheme, Boman Sr., Bridges, Bridgwater, Cross (fl. 1747), Dawson, Gibson, Harrington, Holmes, Huddy, Keene, W. Mills, Ogden, Paget, J. Roberts, Rosco, L. Sparks, Winstone.

Earthy Spirit (Dryden and Davenant's Tempest). A character not in the original play. See Rainton, Renton, Waltz.

Edgar (Lear). See Cushing, T. Elrington, H. Giffard, A. Hallam, Havard, Milward, L. Ryan, Verbruggen, R. Wilks.

Edmund (Lear). See Cashell, Egleton, W. Giffard, Hale, Havard, Husband, Theo. Lacy, Lee, J. Leigh, J. Mills, W. Mills, Palmer, Peterson, Ridout, Rosco, T. Walker, W. Wilks, W. Williams.

Edward (Cibber's 3 Hen. VI). See Oates.

Edward, Prince (Rich. III). See Miss Brett, Miss Budgell, Miss Cibber, Mrs J. Cibber, Miss Cole, Mrs Cushing, Mrs Dunstall, Master Giffard, Green, Mrs Green, Miss J. Hippisley [i.e. later Mrs Green], Miss Hughes, Miss Morrison, Norris Jr., Miss Norris (fl. 1733-35), Mrs Ridout, Mrs Rogeir, Miss Stone, Mrs R. Vincent, Miss Woodman [i.e. later Mrs Ridout].

Elbow (Measure). See J. Hall, Harper, Marten, I. Sparks, Taswell.

Eleanor (2 Hen. VI). In Philips's alteration (Humfrey), see Mrs M. Porter.

Elinor (John). See Mrs Bennet, Mrs James.

Elizabeth, Lady (Cibber's 3 Hen. VI). A character not in the original play. See Mrs Davison.

Elizabeth, Queen (Rich. III). See Mrs Bambridge, Mrs Berriman [i.e. later Mrs W. Hallam], Mrs Butler, Mrs S. M. Cibber, Mrs Elmy, Mrs E. Giffard, Mrs H. Giffard, Mrs. J. Giffard, Mrs W. Hallam, Mrs Horton, Mrs Morgan, Mrs Parker [i.e. later (1) Mrs Berriman; (2) Mrs W. Hallam], Mrs M. Porter, Mrs Pritchard, Mrs J. Roberts, Mrs Seymour, Mrs Steel, Mrs Thurmond, Mrs Wilson.

Ely, Bishop of (Betterton's 2 Hen. IV). A character not in the original play. See Rogers.

Ely, Bishop of (Hen. V). See Bransby, Winstone.

Emilia (Othello). See Mrs Baker, Mrs Bambridge, Mrs Bennet, Mrs Bland, Mrs Butler, Mrs Chetwood, Mrs R. Cross, Mrs Egerton, Mrs Egleton, Mrs Furnival, Mrs J. Giffard [i.e. later Mrs Egleton], Mrs Hamilton, Mrs Haughton, Mrs Heron, Mrs Hutton, Mrs James, Mrs Lamball, Mrs Leigh, Mrs Macklin, Mrs Middleton, Mrs Mullart, Mrs Powell, Mrs Pritchard, Mrs Saunders, Mrs. Stevens, Miss Turner, Mrs Woodward.

Emilia (Wint. T.). See Mrs Mullart, Mrs Yates.

Eolus (Dryden and Davenant's Tempest). A character not in the original play. See Carey.

Escalus (Measure). See Berry, Diggs, Gibson, J. Lacy, Ogden, Rosco, Winstone, T. Wright.

Escalus (R & J). See Anderson, Bransby, Charles, Winstone. In Otway's alteration (C. Marius) this character named Pompeius. See Richardson.

Escanes (Pericles). In Lillo's alteration (Marina), see Shelton.

Essex (John). See Arthur, Ray, Ridout.

503

## INDEX II

Eugenia. In D'Urfey's Cymbeline the name given to Imogen, q.v.

Evandra (Shadwell's Timon). A character not in the original play. See Mrs Butler, Mrs H. Giffard, Mrs W. Hallam, Mrs Horton, Mrs Knight, Mrs M. Porter, Mrs Pritchard, Mrs Thurmond.

Evans (MWW). See Arthur, Dogget, Eaton, B. Griffin, L. Hallam, Hippisley, Lowder, Macklin, Morris, Norris Jr., Pearce, Penkethman Jr., Phipps, Yates.

Exeter (Hen. V). See Berry, J. Mills, Ridout, Rosco, Stephens.

Exeter (1 Hen. VI). See Aston.

Fabian (Twelfth N.). See Winstone.

Falconbridge, Lady (John). See Mrs R. Cross, Mrs Martin, Mrs Mullart, Miss Pitt.

Falconbridge, Robert (John). See Clarke, Simpson.

Falstaff (1 Hen. IV). See Berry, Betterton, Bridgwater, W. Bullock Sr., T. Cibber [read by], Dance, Estcourt, J. Evans, W. Giffard, J. Hall, Harper, Hulett, Hyde, J. Mills, Paget, Powell, Quin, Rosco, C. Shepard, Stephens, H. Vaughan.

Falstaff (2 Hen. IV). See Berry, Bridgwater, Harper, Hyde, J. Mills, Paget, Quin. In the anonymous alteration (Humours of Fal.), see Turbutt.

Falstaff (MWW). See Berry, Betterton, Bridges, Bridgwater, Dance, Delane, W. Giffard, Hulett, Paget, Quin, Stephens. In Dennis's alteration (Com. Gall.), see Powell.

Falstaff's Page (2 Hen. IV). See Miss Brett, Miss Cole, Miss Lindar, Miss Mullart, Master Paget, Miss Robinson Jr.

Feeble (2 Hen. IV). See Collins, B. Griffin, James, Oates, Penkethman Sr., Penkethman Jr., Ray, H. Woodward. In the anonymous alteration (Humours of Fal.), see Tench.

Fenton (MWW). See Anderson, Barret, Chapman, Egleton, Este, Gibson, W. Giffard, Havard, A. Hill, Houghton, Theo. Lacy, Lee, Ridout, A. Ryan, Scrase.

Ferdinand (Tempest). See Bardin, Delane, Este, Goodfellow, Kennedy, King, Lee, Marshall, W. Mills, Ridout, L. Ryan, T. Smith, Thurmond Sr., Trye, Walker (fl. 1735–49), R. Wilks, W. Wilks.

Fitzwalter (Rich. II). See Stevens (fl. 1737–42).

Flavius (J. Caesar). See Berry, Boman Sr.

Flavius (Timon). In Shadwell's alteration this character named Demetrius. See Blakes, Corey, Hale, Paget, Ridout, Symmons, Turbutt, Watson.

Fleance (Macbeth). See Miss Cole, R. Cross III, Master Giffard, Master Morgan, Miss Morrison, Miss Norris (fl. 1708), Mrs B. Porter, Master Wilks.

Flora. In Worsdale's alteration of Tam. Shrew (Cure) the name given to Bianca, q.v.

Florizel (Wint. T.). See W. Giffard, Hale.

Fluellen (Hen. V). See Arthur, Hippisley, Macklin, Yates.

Flute (MND). In Leveridge's alteration (Pyramus), see H. Bullock.

Ford (MWW). See Furnival, H. Giffard, Havard, Milward, Powell, L. Ryan, L. Sparks.

Ford, Mrs (MWW). See Mrs Bracegirdle, Mrs Cantrell, Mrs L. Cross, Mrs Cushing, Mrs Dunstall, Mrs H. Giffard, Mrs Heron, Mrs Horton, Mrs Moffett, Mrs Pritchard, Mrs J. Roberts, Mrs Templer, Mrs Thurmond, Mrs Vincent (fl. 1723–31), Mrs Woffington, Mrs Younger.

Forrest (Cibber's Rich. III). A character not in the original play. See Dove, Gray, Julian, Spiller, H. Vaughan, Wilson.

France, King of (Hen. V). See Cashell, Gibson, W. Giffard, 'Tall' Johnson, W. Mills, Thurmond Sr.

Francis (1 Hen. IV). See Arne, Collins, L. Hallam, T. Hallam, Hippisley, James, F. Leigh Jr., Macklin, Morgan, Norris Sr., Norris Jr., Penkethman Jr., Phillips, Spiller, R. Wetherilt, H. Woodward, Yates.

Francisca (Measure). See Mrs Bland, Miss Cole, Miss Copin, Miss E. Hippisley, Mrs Mullart, Mrs Rowley.

Francisco (Hamlet). See Bencraft, Boheme, F. Leigh Jr., Moore, Paddick, Presgrave, Ray, Smith (fl. 1735–49).

Francisco (Tempest). See Bransby, Woodburn.

Friar (Much Ado). See Bridges, Rosco. In Miller's alteration (Univ. Pass.) this character named Priest. See Turbutt.

Gadshill (1 Hen. IV). See Bencraft, Dunstall, Este, F. Leigh Jr., Orpin.

Gainlove. In Worsdale's alteration of Tam. Shrew (Cure) the name given to Lucentio, q.v.

Gamut (Leveridge's Pyramus). A character not in the original play. See Coker.

Gardiner (Hen. VIII). See Aston, T. Cibber, Hippisley, B. Johnson, Taswell.

Gaunt (Rich. II). See 'Tall' Johnson.

Gentleman (All's Well). See Anderson, Hayman.

Gentleman (Timon). See Clarke, Hale, Wignell.

504

# INDEX II

Gentleman, French (Cymbeline). *See* Hayman. In D'Urfey's alteration this character named Don Michael. *See* Neale.

Gentleman Usher. In Tate's Lear the name given to Oswald, q.v.

Gentlewoman (Macbeth). *See* Mrs Beckham, Mrs Bennet, Miss Ferguson, Miss Minors, Mrs Yates.

George (Cibber's 3 Hen. VI). *See* Parlour.

Geraldo. In Lacy's alteration of Tam. Shrew (Sauny) the name given to Hortensio, q.v.

Ghost (Hamlet). *See* Berry, Boheme, Boman Sr., Booth, Bridgwater, Burton, Cashell, Chapman, Dance, Delane, Garrick, H. Giffard, Hulett, 'Tall' Johnson, Lee, Macklin, J. Mills, Milward, Paget, Quin, Rosco, L. Ryan, Salway, T. Smith, Sowdon, Stephens, T. Walker.

Glendower (1 Hen. IV). *See* Boman Jr., Chapman, C. Cibber, T. Cibber, Havard, Husband, J. Lacy, Lyon, Marshall, Ridout, Turbutt, Wallis.

Gloucester (Hen. V). *See* Clarke, A. Hill, Marr, Ridout, Usher.

Gloucester (1 Hen. VI). *See* L. Ryan.

Gloucester (2 Hen. VI). In Philips's alteration (Humfrey), *see* Booth.

Gloucester (Lear). *See* Aston, Berry, Blakes, Bridges, Bridgwater, C. Cibber, T. Cibber, J. Freeman, Furnival, W. Giffard, Havard, Hulett, Marshall, J. Mills, Milward, Quin, J. Roberts, Thurmond Sr., T. Wright.

Gloucester, Duchess of (Rich. II). *See* Mrs James.

Gobbo (Merchant). *See* Anderson, Arthur, James, B. Johnson, Ray.

Goneril (Lear). *See* Mrs Bambridge, Mrs Bennet, Mrs Bishop, Mrs Buchanan, Mrs Furnival, Mrs J. Giffard, Mrs Grace, Mrs Haughton, Miss Haughton, Mrs Heron, Mrs James, Mrs Kent, Mrs W. Mills the 2nd, Mrs Mullart, Mrs Seal, Mrs Thomas, Mrs Williamson, Mrs Woodward.

Gonzalo (Tempest). *See* Berry, Betts, Blakey, Burton, Hall (fl. 1749), Lee, Machen, Mullart, Oates, Townly, Winstone, Woodburn, Yorke.

Goth (Titus). *See* Morgan.

Gower (2 Hen. IV). *See* Anderson, Usher.

Gower (Hen. V). *See* Anderson, Bransby, Hale.

Granius. In Otway's alteration of R & J (C. Marius) the name given to Benvolio, q.v.

Gratiano (Merchant). *See* Anderson, T. Cibber, Dyer, W. Mills, Palmer, L. Ryan, L. Sparks. In Granville's alteration (Jew), *see* Berriman, Booth, C. Bullock, Chapman, Egleton, Milward.

Gratiano (Othello). *See* Arthur, Corey, Goodfellow, G. Hallam, Hulett, Jones, Julian, Lascells, Lyon, Machen, Redman, Ridout, Simpson, M. Stoppelaer, Wallis, R. Williams, Winstone, Woodburn.

Gratiano. In Miller's alteration of Much Ado (Univ. Pass.) the name given to Leonato, q.v.

Gravedigger (Hamlet). *See* Bridgwater, H. Bullock, W. Bullock Sr., Dogget, Dove, Dunstall, Estcourt, J. Hall, G. Hallam, L. Hallam, B. Johnson, F. Leigh Sr., Leveridge, Macklin, Miller, Morgan, Mullart, Pearce, Penkethman Jr., Raftor, Ray, Rosco, Salway, Spiller, M. Stoppelaer, Underhill, H. Vaughan, H. Wetherilt, R. Williams, W. Williams, Yates.

Green (Rich. II). *See* Arthur.

Gregory (R & J). *See* Arthur, Cushing, Taswell, W. Vaughan.

Gremio (Tam. Shrew). In Lacy's alteration (Sauny) this character named Woodall. *See* Hippisley, B. Johnson, Ray, Ware.

Gremio. In Miller's alteration of Much Ado (Univ. Pass.) the name given to Borachio, q.v.

Grey (Betterton's 2 Hen. IV). A character not in the original play. *See* Dunstall.

Grey (Hen. V). *See* Gibson, Oates, Ray, Redman, Stevens (fl. 1737-42).

Grey, Lady (Cibber's 3 Hen. VI). *See* Mrs Seal.

Grist (Bullock's Cobler). A character not in the original play. *See* W. Bullock Sr., Dove, Salway, R. Williams, W. Williams.

Groom (Rich. II). *See* Clarke.

Grumio (Tam. Shrew). In Lacy's alteration (Sauny) this character named Sauny. *See* W. Bullock Sr., Lyon. In Worsdale's alteration (Cure) this character named Archer. *See* Cushing, Salway.

Guard (R & J). *See* Gray, Raftor, Ray.

Guiderius (Cymbeline). *See* H. Woodward. In D'Urfey's alteration this character named Palladour. *See* Egleton, Stevens (fl. 1737-42).

Guildenstern (Hamlet). *See* Anderson, Bransby, Goodfellow, Green, W. Hallam, Hamilton, Jervis, Lee, Naylor, Quin, Scrase, Stevens (fl. 1737-42), Storer, Usher, R. Williams, Winstone.

Guildford (Hen. VIII). *See* Cushing, Marr, Pack.

Gundy, Cicely. In Johnson's alteration of the induction to Tam. Shrew (Cobler) the name given to the Hostess, q.v.

Guzzle, Toby. In Bullock's alteration of the

505

# INDEX II

induction to Tam. Shrew (Cobler) the name given to Christopher Sly, q.v.

Hacket, Dame. In Bullock's alteration of the induction to Tam. Shrew (Cobler) the name given to the Hostess, q.v.

Hamlet (Hamlet). *See* Aston, Banberry, Barry, Betterton, Cashell, T. Cibber [read by], Cushing, Delane, T. Elrington, Furnival, Garrick, H. Giffard, Goodfellow, Havard, Lee, J. Mills, Milward, Powell, L. Ryan, Sheridan, G. A. Stevens, Thurmond Sr., R. Wilks.

Harfleur, Governor of (Hen. V). *See* Taswell.

Harriet (Hill's Hen. V). A character not in the original play. *See* Mrs J. Roberts, Mrs Thurmond.

Hastings (2 Hen. IV). *See* Anderson, Blakes, Carr, Harrington, A. Hill, Ridout, Watson.

Heartwell. In Worsdale's alteration of Tam. Shrew (Cure) the name given to Hortensio, q.v.

Hecate (Macbeth). *See* Arthur, Berry, J. Hall, L. Hallam, Hippisley, B. Johnson, Layfield, Lyon, Mullart, Paget, Rosco, Yates.

Hector (Troilus). *See* Boheme, Powell, Quin, T. Walker.

Helen (Cymbeline). *See* Mrs Bland. In D'Urfey's alteration this character named Clarinna. *See* Mrs Gulick, Mrs Jevon, Mrs Kilby.

Helena (All's Well). *See* Mrs H. Giffard, Mrs Pritchard, Mrs Woffington.

Henry IV (1 Hen. IV). *See* Berry, Boheme, Boman Sr., Bridges, Bridgwater, Cashell, Chapman, T. Cibber, Furnival, Havard, Hewitt, Huddy, 'Tall' Johnson, Keene, J. Leigh, J. Mills, Milward, Ogden, Peterson, Quin, L. Sparks, Stephens, Thurmond Sr., T. Wright.

Henry IV (2 Hen. IV). *See* Booth, Cashell, Delane, T. Elrington, Gibson, J. Mills, Milward, Stephens. In the anonymous alteration (Humours of Fal.), *see* Este.

Henry V (Hen. V). *See* Barry, Booth, Delane, Hale, 'Tall' Johnson.

Henry VI (1 Hen. VI). *See* A. Ryan.

Henry VI (Cibber's 3 Hen. VI). *See* J. Roberts.

Henry VI (Cibber's Rich. III). A character not in the original play. *See* Berry, Blakes, Boheme, Bridgwater, Chapman, Davies, Delane, H. Giffard, Hale, Hyde, Milward, Paget, L. Ryan, T. Walker, R. Wilks.

Henry VIII (Hen. VIII). *See* Berry, Betterton, Booth, W. Giffard, Harper, Quin.

Henry, Prince (John). *See* Miss Cole, Green, A. Ryan.

Herald, English (John). *See* Usher.

Herald, French (John). *See* Marr, Woodburn.

Hermione (Wint. T.). *See* Mrs H. Giffard, Mrs Horton.

Hero (Much Ado). *See* Mrs Bellamy, Mrs Elmy, Mrs Hale, Mrs Seymour, Mrs Templer, Mrs Willoughby. In Miller's alteration (Univ. Pass.) this character named Lucilia. *See* Mrs Butler.

Hippolito (Dryden and Davenant's Tempest). A character not in the original play. *See* Mrs Bicknell, Mrs Brett, C. Bullock, Mrs J. Cibber, T. Cibber, Green, Mrs L. Hallam, Miss Holliday [i.e. later Mrs W. Mills the 2nd], Mrs W. Mills the 2nd, Mrs Morgan, Mrs S. Mountfort, Mrs Phillips, Mrs Thomas, Miss Williams, Miss Willis, Mrs Willoughby, Mrs Woffington.

Horatio (Hamlet). *See* Boman Jr., Booth, Cashell, R. Cross II, Cushing, Diggs, Este, Furnival, W. Giffard, Hale, Havard, Huddy, Husband, J. Leigh, Marshall, J. Mills, W. Mills, Milward, Oates, Ogden, Paget, Palmer, Ridout, J. Roberts, Rosco, Simpson, Verbruggen, T. Walker, Watson.

Hortensio (Tam. Shrew). In Lacy's alteration (Sauny) this character named Geraldo. *See* Hamilton, Husband, L. Ryan. In Worsdale's alteration (Cure) this character named Heartwell. *See* Baker, Este.

Host (MWW). *See* Boman Jr., W. Bullock Sr., Dunstall, W. Hallam, Harper, Huddy, Lyon, Miller, Morgan, Rosco, Turbutt, W. Vaughan, R. Williams.

Hostess (1 Hen. IV). *See* Mrs Bambridge, Mrs Beckham, Mrs Cook, Mrs R. Cross, Mrs Dyer, Mrs Egleton, Mrs Grace [i.e. later Mrs Macklin], Mrs Hunt, Mrs James, Mrs Macklin, Mrs Martin, Mrs Morgan, Mrs Mullart, Mrs Palmer, Mrs Phillips, Mrs Powell, Mrs J. Roberts, Mrs Shireburn [i.e. later Mrs R. Cross], Mrs Wetherilt, Mrs Willis, Mrs Yates.

Hostess (2 Hen. IV). *See* Mrs Bambridge, Mrs R. Cross, Mrs Grace [i.e. later Mrs Macklin], Mrs James, Mrs Macklin, Mrs Mullart, Mrs J. Roberts, Mrs Shireburn [i.e. later Mrs R. Cross], Mrs Wetherilt, Mrs Willis. In the anonymous alteration (Humours of Fal.), *see* Mrs Monlass.

Hostess (Hen. V). *See* Mrs Bambridge, Mrs James, Mrs Macklin, Mrs Mullart, Miss Pitt.

Hostess (Tam. Shrew). In Johnson's altera-

## INDEX II

tion of the induction (Cobler) this character named Cicely Gundy. *See* Mrs Baker. In Bullock's alteration of the induction (Cobler) this character named Dame Hacket. *See* J. Hall, Mullart, Pearce, Reynolds.
Hotspur (1 Hen. IV). *See* Barry, Boheme, Booth, Bridgwater, Delane, T. Elrington, Garrick, W. Giffard, Goodfellow, Hale, Havard, Hewson, Highmore, Lee, Milward, Powell, Quin, Rosco, L. Ryan, Verbruggen, T. Walker, Whittingham.
Hubert (John). *See* Berry, Bridgwater, Simpson. In Cibber's alteration (Papal Tyr.), *see* Bridgwater.
Humphrey, Prince (2 Hen. IV). *See* Baker, R. Cross II, Oates.
Hymen (AYLI). In Johnson's alteration (Love in For.), *see* Miss Lindar.

Iachimo (Cymbeline). *See* Hale. In D'Urfey's alteration this character named Shattillion. *See* C. Bullock, T. Walker.
Iachimo. In D'Urfey's Cymbeline the name given to a Lord [companion to Cloten], q.v.
Iago (Othello). *See* C. Cibber, Furnival, Garrick, H. Giffard, W. Giffard, A. Hallam, Havard, Keene, Macklin, W. Mills, Oakly, Paget, J. Roberts, Rosco, L. Ryan, L. Sparks, Verbruggen.
Imogen (Cymbeline). *See* Miss Cibber, Mrs Pritchard. In D'Urfey's alteration this character named Eugenia. *See* Mrs Bullock, Mrs Templer, Mrs Thurmond.
Iris (Tempest). *See* Miss E. Young.
Isabel (Hen. V). *See* Mrs Bambridge, Mrs Bennet, Mrs Bland, Mrs Horton, Mrs James, Mrs W. Mills the 2nd.
Isabella (Measure). *See* Mrs Berriman [i.e. later Mrs W. Hallam], Mrs Boheme, Mrs Buchanan, Mrs S. M. Cibber, Mrs W. Hallam, Mrs Parker [i.e. later (1) Mrs Berriman; (2) Mrs W. Hallam], Mrs Pritchard, Mrs Seymour [i.e. later Mrs Boheme], Mrs Woffington.
Isander. In Shadwell's Timon the name given to one of the Senators, q.v.
Isidore. In Shadwell's Timon the name given to one of the Senators, q.v.

Jamy (Hen. V). *See* Dunstall, Lyon, Neale.
Jamy. In Lacy's alteration of Tam. Shrew (Sauny) the name given to Biondello, q.v.
Jaques (AYLI). *See* Berry, T. Cibber, R. Cross II, Quin, L. Ryan, L. Sparks. In Johnson's alteration (Love in For.), *see* C. Cibber.

Jaques de Bois (AYLI). *See* Anderson, Marr, Simpson, Stevens (fl. 1737–42), Turbutt, Usher. In Johnson's alteration (Love in For.) this character named Roberto. *See* J. Roberts.
Jasper, Sir. In Bullock's alteration of the induction to Tam. Shrew (Cobler) the name given to the Lord, q.v.
Jessica (Merchant). *See* Miss Cole, Miss Edwards, Miss Minors, Mrs Ridout, Mrs R. Vincent, Miss Woodman [i.e. later Mrs Ridout]. In Granville's alteration (Jew), *see* Miss Bincks, Miss Holliday, Mrs Laguerre, Mrs Palin, Mrs Parlour, Mrs M. Porter, Mrs Rogeir [i.e. later Mrs Laguerre], Mrs Sherburn, Miss Stone.
Jeweller (Timon). *See* Anderson, Harrington, Paddick.
Joan (Johnson's Cobler). A character not in the original play. *See* Mrs Willis.
Joan la Pucelle (1 Hen. VI). *See* Mrs W. Hallam.
Joculo (Univ. Pass.). A character not in the original play. *See* T. Cibber, Macklin.
John, Don (Much Ado). *See* Bridgwater, Egleton, Ridout, Winstone. In Miller's alteration (Univ. Pass.) this character named Byron. *See* Berry.
John, Friar (R & J). *See* Champnes, Michael, Paddick.
John, King (John). *See* Delane, Garrick, Redman. In Cibber's alteration (Papal Tyr.), *see* Cashell, Quin.
John, Prince (1 Hen. IV). *See* Clarke, Miss Cole, Green, Miss E. Hippisley, Marr, Miss Norris (fl. 1733–35), Mrs Rowley, H. Woodward.
John, Prince (2 Hen. IV). *See* Este, Hale, A. Hallam, Havard, Marshall, W. Mills, Ridout, Salway, T. Walker.
Jolly, Captain (Johnson's Cobler). A character not in the original play. *See* T. Walker.
Juliet (Measure). *See* Mrs Bland, Miss Brett, Miss Haughton, Miss Hilliard, Miss Pitt, Mrs Rowley, Mrs Simpson, Miss Stone, Miss Tollett.
Juliet (R & J). *See* Miss Bellamy, Miss Cibber, Mrs S. M. Cibber. In Otway's alteration (C. Marius) this character named Lavinia. *See* Mrs Bracegirdle, Mrs Bradshaw, Mrs Mullart, Mrs M. Porter.
Juno (Tempest). *See* Mrs Arne.

Katharina (Tam. Shrew). In Lacy's alteration (Sauny) this character named Margaret. *See* Mrs Bradshaw, Mrs Egleton, Mrs J. Roberts, Mrs Thurmond. In

507

## INDEX II

Worsdale's alteration (Cure) this character named Margaret. *See* Mrs Clive, Mrs Dunstall.

Katharine (Hen. V). *See* Mrs Barrington, Mrs H. Giffard, Mrs Green, Mrs Hale [i.e. later Mrs Barrington], Miss Haughton, Mrs Oldfield, Mrs R. Vincent, Mrs Ware.

Katharine, Queen (Hen. VIII). *See* Mrs Barry, Mrs Berriman, Mrs H. Giffard, Mrs Horton, Mrs Knight, Mrs Parker [i.e. later Mrs Berriman], Mrs M. Porter, Mrs Pritchard, Mrs J. Roberts, Mrs Thurmond, Mrs Woffington.

Kent (Lear). *See* Bardin, Berry, Bickerstaff, Boman Jr., Chapman, Gibson, Huddy, Hulett, Keene, J. Leigh, Minns, Ogden, Paget, Peterson, Rosco, Thurmond Sr., C. Williams, Winstone.

King (All's Well). *See* Cashell, Crisp, Delane, W. Giffard, Marshall, Milward.

King (Hamlet). *See* Berry, Bickerstaff, Bridges, Bridgwater, J. Evans, W. Giffard, Hulett, Husband, 'Tall' Johnson, Keene, Marshall, W. Mills, Milward, Paget, Quin, J. Roberts, Rosco, L. Sparks, Thurmond Sr., Townly, T. Walker.

King, Player (Hamlet). *See* Arthur, Dunstall, Gibson, W. Giffard, Harrington, Marten, Mullart, Redman, Rosco, Taswell, Turbutt, Winstone.

Lady, Old (Hen. VIII). *See* Mrs R. Cross, Mrs Egerton, Mrs James, Mrs Mullart, Mrs Willis.

Laertes (Hamlet). *See* Bardin, Blakes, Booth, Cashell, Chapman, T. Cibber, Corey, Egleton, Gibson, W. Giffard, Hale, A. Hallam, Kennedy, Marr, Marshall, W. Mills, Ogden, Powell, Richardson, Ridout, L. Ryan, Thurmond Sr., T. Walker, J. Ward, Wignell, W. Wilks, C. Williams, W. Williams, T. Wright.

Lafeu (All's Well). *See* Berry, Bridgwater, Paget, Peterson.

Lartius (Coriolanus). In Dennis's alteration (Invader), *see* C. Williams.

Launcelot (Merchant). *See* Arthur, Chapman, Neale, Shuter.

Laurence, Friar (R & J). *See* Havard, J. Hill, Ridout. In Otway's alteration (C. Marius) this character named Priest. *See* Smith (fl. 1735-49).

Lavinia (Titus). *See* Mrs Knapp, Mrs Morgan, Mrs Sterling.

Lavinia. In Otway's alteration of R & J (C. Marius) the name given to Juliet, q.v.

Lawra (Love Bet.). A character not in the original play. *See* Mrs Lawson.

Lear (Lear). *See* Betterton, Boheme, Booth, Delane, Garrick, Goodfellow, Huddy, Hyde, J. Mills, Paget, Perry, Powell, Quin, Stephens.

Le Beau (AYLI). *See* Bransby, Gibson, Ridout, Scrase, Woodburn. In Johnson's alteration (Love in For.), *see* T. Cibber.

Lennox (Macbeth). *See* Ackman, Barnet, Booth, T. Cibber, Costollo, Cushing, W. Giffard, P. Griffin, Hale, Hulett, Marr, Mozeen, Palmer, Peterson, Ridout, J. Roberts, Rosco, Scrase, T. Smith, L. Sparks, Stephens, Thurmond Sr., Turbutt, T. Walker, T. Wright.

Leonardo (Merchant). *See* Anderson.

Leonato (Much Ado). *See* Berry, 'Tall' Johnson, Quin. In Miller's alteration (Univ. Pass.) this character named Gratiano. *See* Milward.

Leonine (Pericles). In Lillo's alteration (Marina), *see* Stevens (fl. 1737-42).

Leontes (Wint. T.). *See* H. Giffard, Stephens.

Lepidus (J. Caesar). *See* Bencraft, Cole.

Liberia. In Miller's alteration of Much Ado (Univ. Pass.) the name given to Beatrice, q.v.

Lieutenant [of the Tower] (Cibber's Rich. III). *See* Arthur, Beckham, Boyce, Collett, Oates, Quin, Ray, Ridout, Stevens (fl. 1737-42), Storer, Usher, Winstone.

Ligarius (J. Caesar). *See* Aston, Boheme, Boman Sr., Holtom, Jenkins, Taswell, Usher.

Lion (MND). In Leveridge's alteration (Pyramus), *see* Cook. In Lampe's alteration (Pyramus), *see* Reinhold. In the mock play in Johnson's alteration of AYLI (Love in For.), *see* Wilson.

Lionel, Sir. In Lacy's alteration of Tam. Shrew (Sauny) the name given to Vincentio, q.v.

Lodovico (Othello). *See* Anderson, Bardin, Berry, Blakes, Corey, Cushing, Diggs, Furnival, Gibson, Hale, J. Hill, Linnet, Marr, J. Mills, W. Mills, Milward, Paget, Ridout, Rosco, M. Stoppelaer, Turbutt, Ware, R. Williams, Woodward Sr.

Lord (Cymbeline). *See* Carr. In D'Urfey's alteration this character named Iachimo. *See* James, Pack, Spiller.

Lord (Tam. Shrew). In Johnson's alteration of the induction (Cobler) this character named Sir Charles. *See* L. Ryan. In Bullock's alteration of the induction (Cobler) this character named Sir Jasper. *See* Bardin, Furnival, Ogden.

## INDEX II

Lord (Wint. T.). *See* Crofts, Harrington, Lascells, Marr, Nelson.

Lord Chief Justice (2 Hen. IV). *See* Berry, Boman Sr., Bridges, Rosco, L. Sparks, Stephens. In the anonymous alteration (Humours of Fal.), *see* Cole.

Lord Mayor (Rich. III). *See* W. Bullock Sr., Dove, Dunstall, J. Hall, Harper, Marten, Miller, Morgan, Mullart, Penkethman Jr., Taswell, Turbutt.

Lorenzo (Merchant). *See* Beard, R. Cross II, Havard, Hayman, Lowe. In Granville's alteration (Jew), *see* Baily, Houghton, L. Ryan.

Lovell (Hen. VIII). *See* Holtom, Ray.

Lucentio (Tam. Shrew). In Lacy's alteration (Sauny) this character named Winlove. *See* Bickerstaff, Booth, Diggs, Richardson. In Worsdale's alteration (Cure) this character named Gainlove. *See* R. Cross II, Wilder.

Lucentius (Univ. Pass.). A character not in the original play. *See* C. Shepard.

Luciana (Com. Err.). *See* Mrs W. Mills the 2nd.

Lucianus (Hamlet). *See* L. Hallam, James, Norris Sr., Norris Jr., Penkethman Jr., Yates.

Lucilia. In Miller's alteration of Much Ado (Univ. Pass.) the name given to Hero, q.v.

Lucilius (J. Caesar). *See* F. Leigh Jr.

Lucilius (Timon). In Shadwell's alteration this character named Diphilus. *See* Hayman, Houghton, L. Ryan.

Lucio (Measure). *See* C. Bullock, Chapman, T. Cibber, Cushing, Egleton, Macklin, H. Woodward.

Lucius (Cymbeline). *See* Aston, Diggs, Ridout.

Lucius (J. Caesar). *See* Arne, Master Giffard, Master Huddy, Norris Jr.

Lucius (Titus). *See* Hulett, L. Ryan, C. Williams.

Lucy (Cure). A character not in the original play. *See* Mrs R. Cross, Miss E. Young.

Lucy (1 Hen. VI). *See* Arthur.

Lysimachus (Pericles). In Lillo's alteration (Marina), *see* A. Hallam.

Macbeth (Macbeth). *See* Barry, Betterton, Cashell, Cushing, Delane, Garrick, W. Giffard, Goodfellow, Keene, Marshall, J. Mills, Powell, Quin, Sheridan.

Macbeth, Lady (Macbeth). *See* Mrs Barry, Mrs Berriman [i.e. later Mrs W. Hallam], Mrs Boheme, Mrs Buchanan, Miss Budgell, Mrs Bullock, Mrs Butler, Mrs Carlisle, Mrs Furnival, Mrs H. Giffard, Mrs W. Hallam, Mrs Haughton, Mrs Horton, Mrs Knight, Mrs Macklin, Mrs Parker [i.e. later (1) Mrs Berriman; (2) Mrs W. Hallam], Mrs M. Porter, Mrs Pritchard, Mrs J. Roberts, Mrs Seymour [i.e. later Mrs Boheme], Mrs Steel, Mrs Woffington.

Macduff (Macbeth.) *See* T. Cibber, Delane, T. Elrington, Furnival, H. Giffard, A. Hallam, Havard, J. Leigh, Milward, Powell, L. Ryan, Thurmond Sr., R. Wilks.

Macduff, Lady (Macbeth). *See* Mrs Bambridge, Mrs Barrington, Mrs Bellamy, Mrs Benson, Mrs Buchanan, Mrs Bullock, Mrs Butler, Mrs Elmy, Mrs H. Giffard, Mrs Gulick, Mrs Hale [i.e. later Mrs Barrington], Mrs Hamilton, Miss Haughton, Miss Holliday [i.e. later Mrs W. Mills the 2nd], Mrs Horton, Mrs Kilby, Mrs Lamball, Mrs W. Mills the 2nd, Mrs Moffett, Mrs M. Porter, Mrs Pritchard, Mrs Purden, Mrs Ridout, Mrs Rogers, Mrs Seymour, Mrs Spiller, Mrs Stevens, Mrs Thurmond, Mrs Wilson.

Macmorris (Hen. V). *See* Barrington, James, Neale.

Maid (Bullock's Cobler). A character not in the original play. *See* Mrs Garnet, Miss Smith.

Malcolm (Macbeth). *See* Anderson, Bardin, Blakes, C. Bullock, Cashell, Chapman, Corey, R. Cross II, Egleton, W. Giffard, Hale, A. Hallam, Havard, Tho. Lacy, Lee, W. Mills, Milward, A. Ryan.

Malvolio (Twelfth N.). *See* Macklin, Neale. In Burnaby's alteration (Love Bet.) this character named Taquilet. *See* Dogget.

Mamillius (Wint. T.). *See* Miss Naylor.

Man, Old (C. Marius). A character not in the original play. *See* Perkins.

Man, Old (Lear). *See* G. Hallam, Julian, Taswell.

Man, Old. In Shadwell's Timon the name given to the Old Athenian, q.v.

Manly. In Worsdale's alteration of Tam. Shrew (Cure) the name given to Petruchio, q.v.

Marcellus (Hamlet). *See* Anderson, Berry, Bickerstaff, Blakes, Bransby, Carr, Harrington, Havard, Holt, Richardson, C. Shepard, Turbutt, Usher, H. Woodward.

Marcus (Titus). *See* Boman Sr., Ogden.

Margaret (1 Hen. VI). *See* Mrs Ware.

Margaret (2 Hen. VI). In Philips's alteration (Humfrey), *see* Mrs Oldfield.

Margaret (Cibber's 3 Hen. VI). *See* Mrs Campbell.

Margaret (Much Ado). *See* Mrs J. Giffard, Mrs Havard, Miss J. Hippisley, Mrs Mullart. In Miller's alteration (Univ.

# INDEX II

Pass.) this character named Delia. *See* Mrs Pritchard.

Margaret. In Lacy's and in Worsdale's alterations of Tam. Shrew (Sauny and Cure) the name given to Katharina, q.v.

Maria (Twelfth N.). *See* Mrs Green, Mrs Macklin. In Burnaby's alteration (Love Bet.) this character named Dromia. *See* Mrs Leigh.

Mariana (All's Well). *See* Mrs Bland, Mrs Dunstall, Mrs Marshall.

Mariana (Measure). *See* Mrs Barrington, Mrs Bennet, Mrs Hale [i.e. later Mrs Barrington], Miss Holliday [i.e. later Mrs W. Mills the 2nd], Mrs Kilby, Mrs W. Mills the 2nd, Mrs Spiller, Mrs Templer.

Marina (Pericles). In Lillo's alteration (Marina), *see* Mrs R. Vincent.

Marius, Old. In Otway's alteration of R & J (C. Marius) the name given to Montague, q.v.

Marius, Young. In Otway's alteration of R & J (C. Marius) the name given to Romeo, q.v.

Marshal, Lord (Rich. II). *See* Mullart.

Melissa (Shadwell's Timon). A character not in the original play. *See* Mrs Bradshaw, Mrs Buchanan, Mrs Butler, Mrs Cantrell, Mrs Clive, Mrs Hale, Mrs Horton, Mrs Mullart, Mrs Pritchard, Mrs Steel.

Melun (John). In Cibber's alteration (Papal Tyr.), *see* Cashell, Gibson.

Menelaus (Troilus). *See* Birkhead, Wignell.

Menenius (Coriolanus). In Dennis's alteration (Invader), *see* Corey.

Merchant (Com. Err.). *See* Turbutt, J. Ward.

Mercutio (R & J). *See* Barnard, Dyer, Macklin, Paddick, H. Woodward. In Otway's alteration (C. Marius) this character named Sulpitius. *See* Bickerstaff, Bridgwater, Harper, B. Johnson, Machen.

Messala (J. Caesar). *See* Bransby, Cashell, Corey, W. Mills.

Messenger (Com. Err.). *See* Taswell.

Metellus (J. Caesar). *See* Bransby, Carr, Moore, Paddick, Ridout, Turbutt, Usher, R. Wetherilt, W. Wilks, Winstone.

Metellus. In Otway's alteration of R & J (C. Marius) the name given to Capulet, q.v.

Michael, Don. In D'Urfey's Cymbeline the name given to the French Gentleman, q.v.

Milcha (Dryden and Davenant's Tempest). A character not in the original play. *See* Mrs Arne, Mrs Boman Jr., Miss Edwards, Mountier, E. Roberts.

Miranda (Tempest). *See* Mrs Bennet, Mrs Booth, Miss Cole, Mrs Daniel, Miss Edwards [i.e. later Mrs Mozeen], Mrs L. Hallam, Miss Haughton, Mrs W. Mills the 1st, Mrs Moore, Mrs Mozeen, Mrs Palmer, Mrs Roberts (fl. 1748), Mrs Sandum, Miss Tenoe [i.e. later Mrs W. Mills the 1st], Mrs Walter (fl. 1729–41), Mrs Wignell, Miss Willis, Mrs Yates.

Montague (R & J). *See* Barnet, Bridgwater, Burton, Furnival. In Otway's alteration (C. Marius) this character named Old Marius. *See* Betterton, J. Lacy, J. Mills, Powell.

Montano (Othello). *See* Anderson, Ayres, Barret, Bransby, Cashell, Crofts, Dove, Havard, Holtom, Hulett, J. Lacy, Theo. Lacy, Marr, Mozeen, Ridout, A. Ryan, Salway, Watson, Wignell, Winstone, Woodburn, Yorke.

Montjoy (Hen. V). *See* Baker, Lee.

Moonshine (MND). In Leveridge's alteration (Pyramus), *see* Reading. In Lampe's alteration (Pyramus), *see* E. Roberts. In the mock play in Johnson's alteration of AYLI (Love in For.), *see* Ray.

Mopsa (Wint. T.). *See* Mrs Dunstall.

Moreno. In Burnaby's alteration of Twelfth N. (Love Bet.) the name given to Orsino, q.v.

Morocco (Merchant). *See* Bridges, Carr, Cashell, I. Sparks, Woodburn.

Mortimer (1 Hen. IV). *See* Berry, Davies, Dyer, Havard, Hewitt, Houghton, Marr, Merrivale, Nelson, Paget, Rosco, Stevens (fl. 1737–42), C. Williams.

Morton (2 Hen. IV). *See* Gibson, Stevens (fl. 1737–42).

Mouldy (2 Hen. IV). *See* Bencraft, G. Hallam, M. Stoppelaer, Wilson. In the anonymous alteration (Humours of Fal.), *see* Monlass.

Mowbray (2 Hen. IV). *See* Arthur, Berry, Cashell, W. Mills, Paget, Redman, Rosco.

Murderer (Macbeth). *See* Baker, Bencraft, Bransby, Cole, R. Cross I, Dove, Fairbank, Harper, Hippisley, Jones, Marten, Monlass, Pearce, Reed, Simpson, Spiller, M. Stoppelaer, Taswell, Turbutt, H. Wetherilt, Woodburn.

Musician (Shadwell's Timon). A character not in the original play. *See* Ray.

Mustacho (Dryden and Davenant's Tempest). A character not in the original play. *See* Bickerstaff, Blakes, T. Cibber, Este, Green, Harper, James, Jones, Julian, F. Leigh Sr., Macklin, Maxfield, Norris Sr., Palmer, Ray, Shuter, R. Williams, H. Woodward.

510

# INDEX II

Neptune (Dryden and Davenant's Tempest). A character not in the original play. *See* Beard, Brett, Cunningham, Lowe, Rainton, Reinhold, Salway, W. Savage, C. Stoppelaer, W. Turner.

Nerissa (Merchant). *See* Mrs Bennet, Miss J. Hippisley, Mrs Pritchard, Mrs R. Vincent, Mrs Woffington. In Granville's alteration (Jew), *see* Mrs Bellamy, Mrs Bicknell, Mrs Boman Sr., Mrs Bullock.

Nestor (Troilus). *See* Corey, Dawson.

Nicias. In Shadwell's Timon the name given to one of the Senators, q.v.

Norfolk (Hen. VIII). *See* Berry, Cashell, Davies, Este, Havard, Hewitt, J. Mills, W. Mills, L. Sparks.

Norfolk (Rich. II). *See* Rosco, T. Walker.

Norfolk (Rich. III). *See* Blakes, Boman Sr., Bransby, Freeman (fl. 1735-45), Harbin, Marshall, Mozeen, Paget, Philips, Ridout, T. Smith, Stephens, Winstone.

Northumberland (1 Hen. IV). *See* Boman Sr., Bridges, Carr, Dove, G. Hallam, Mullart, Paget, Redman, Schoolding, Taswell, R. Williams.

Northumberland (2 Hen. IV). *See* 'Tall' Johnson.

Northumberland (Rich. II). *See* Bridgwater, Ogden.

Nurse (R & J). *See* Mrs Dunstall, Mrs Hill, Mrs James, Mrs Macklin. In Otway's alteration (C. Marius), *see* W. Bullock Sr., Norris Sr., Pack, Mrs Talbot.

Nym (Hen. V). *See* Arthur, M. Stoppelaer, Taswell.

Nym (MWW). *See* Costollo, Holtom, Jones, Kennedy, Morgan, Raftor, M. Stoppelaer.

Octavius (J. Caesar). *See* Blakes, Diggs, Gibson, A. Hallam, Havard, A. Hill, J. Mills, Milward, Rosco, Salway, T. Walker, Watson, C. Williams, H. Woodward.

Officer (Com. Err.). *See* Woodburn.

Officer (Othello). *See* Green, Usher.

Officer (R & J). *See* Raftor.

Officer (Twelfth N.). *See* F. Leigh Jr., Marten, Simpson.

Officer (Wint. T.). *See* Naylor.

Officer, French (Hen. V). *See* J. Roberts.

Oliver (AYLI). *See* Anderson, Burton, Cashell, Havard, Mozeen. In Johnson's alteration (Love in For.), *see* Thurmond Sr.

Olivia (Twelfth N.). *See* Mrs Clive. In Burnaby's alteration (Love Bet.) this character named Villaretta. *See* Mrs Bracegirdle.

Ophelia (Hamlet). *See* Miss Bincks [i.e. later Mrs R. Vincent], Mrs Booth, Mrs Bracegirdle, Mrs Bradshaw, Miss Budgell, Mrs S. M. Cibber, Mrs Clive, Mrs L. Cross, Mrs Cushing, Miss Fenton, Mrs H. Giffard, Mrs Hamilton, Miss J. Hippisley, Miss Holliday, Miss Male, Mrs S. Mountfort, Mrs Phillips, Mrs Pritchard, Mrs Rice, Mrs J. Roberts, Mrs Santlow [i.e. later Mrs Booth], Mrs Sterling, Miss Stone, Mrs Storer, Mrs Thurmond, Mrs Vincent (fl. 1723-31), Mrs R. Vincent, Miss Willis, Mrs Woffington.

Orlando (AYLI). *See* Blakes, Hale, Havard, W. Mills, Milward, Palmer, L. Ryan. In Johnson's alteration (Love in For.), *see* R. Wilks.

Orleans (Hen. V). *See* Watson, H. Woodward.

Orsino (Twelfth N.). *See* W. Mills. In Burnaby's alteration (Love Bet.) this character named Moreno. *See* Verbruggen.

Osric (Hamlet). *See* Bardin, Blakey, Bowen, C. Bullock, W. Bullock Jr., Chapman, Charke, C. Cibber, T. Cibber, Clarke, Cushing, Dyer, Egleton, Macklin, Miller, Neale, Norris Sr., Oates, Penington, Peterson, Shuter, Thurmond Jr., R. Wetherilt, H. Woodward.

Oswald (Lear). In Tate's alteration this character named Gentleman Usher. *See* Aston, Blakey, Bowen (probably), W. Bullock Jr., T. Cibber, Cushing, L. Hallam, Morgan, Neale, Pack, Penkethman Sr., Penkethman Jr., Philips, Shuter, Spiller, H. Woodward, Yates.

Othello (Othello). *See* Barry, Betterton, Booth, Bruodin, Cashell, T. Cibber, Delane, Drury, T. Elrington, Foote, Freeman (fl. 1735-45), Garrick, H. Giffard, Goodfellow, Highmore, Hulett, Hyde, J. Mills, Milward, Paget, Perry, Quin, Royer, Scudamore, Sheridan, Sowdon, Stephens, Thurmond Sr., Townly, T. Walker, R. Wilks.

Overdone, Mrs (Measure). *See* Mrs Bambridge, Mrs Bridges, Mrs Gulick, Mrs Marshall, Mrs Martin.

Oxford (Rich. III). *See* Baker, Bencraft, Boman Jr., Bransby, Cole, R. Elrington, Green, Moore, Paddick, Pattenden, Ridout, H. Vaughan, R. Williams, Woodburn.

Page (All's Well). *See* Miss Morrison.

Page (MWW). *See* Anderson, Aston, Berry, Cashell, Diggs, A. Hallam, Huddy, Naylor, Ogden, Paget, Ridout, Rosco, Verbruggen, Wignell, Winstone.

## INDEX II

Page (R & J). *See* Miss Charke, R. Cross III, Miss Tomson.

Page (Tam. Shrew). In Johnson's alteration of the induction (Cobler) this character named Betty. *See* Miss Willis.

Page (Shadwell's Timon). A character not in the original play. *See* Miss Cole.

Page, Anne (MWW). *See* Miss Bincks [i.e. later Mrs R. Vincent], Mrs Bradshaw, Miss Brett [i.e. later Mrs Chetwood], Mrs Chetwood, Mrs M. Giffard, Mrs Hamilton, Miss Haughton, Miss J. Hippisley, Miss Holliday, Mrs Horsington, Mrs Laguerre, Miss Minors, Mrs Moreau, Mrs Mountfort (fl. 1730), Miss Norsa, Mrs Palin, Mrs Purden, Mrs Ridout, Mrs Rogier [i.e. later Mrs Laguerre], Miss Smith, Miss Stone, Mrs Storer, Mrs R. Vincent, Mrs Wright.

Page, Mrs (MWW). *See* Mrs Barrington, Mrs Barry, Mrs Bellamy [i.e. later Mrs Walter], Mrs Bennet, Mrs Benson, Mrs Berriman [i.e. later Mrs W. Hallam], Mrs Boheme, Mrs Buchanan, Mrs Bullock, Mrs Butler, Mrs Hale [i.e. later Mrs Barrington], Mrs L. Hallam, Mrs W. Hallam, Mrs Haughton, Mrs Middleton, Mrs W. Mills the 2nd, Mrs Parker [i.e. later (1) Mrs Berriman; (2) Mrs W. Hallam], Mrs Plomer, Mrs Seymour [i.e. later Mrs Boheme], Mrs Walter (née Seal).

Painter (Timon). *See* James, Wilcox.

Palladour. In D'Urfey's Cymbeline the name given to Guiderius, q.v.

Pandarus (Troilus). *See* Estcourt, Hippisley, Spiller.

Pandulph (John). *See* Chapman, Macklin, J. Roberts, White. In Cibber's alteration (Papal Tyr.), *see* C. Cibber, Gibson, 'Tall' Johnson.

Paris (R & J). *See* Anderson, Tho. Lacy, Lee, Mozeen, Scrase. In Otway's alteration (C. Marius) this character named Sylla. *See* C. Bullock, T. Elrington, Husband, L. Ryan, Thurmond Sr., Walker (fl. 1735–49).

Parolles (All's Well). *See* T. Cibber, Peterson, H. Woodward.

Patience (Hen. VIII). *See* Miss Allen.

Patroclus (Troilus). *See* Salway.

Paulina (Wint. T.). *See* Mrs Pritchard, Mrs Steel.

Pedant (Tam. Shrew). In Lacy's alteration (Sauny) this character named Snatchpenny. *See* Pack, Penkethman Jr., Spiller.

Pedro (Love Bet.). A character not in the original play. *See* Pack.

Pedro, Don (Much Ado). *See* Boheme, Cashell, Hale, Havard.

Pembroke (John). *See* Aston, Harrington, A. Hill, Johnson (fl. 1749), Mozeen. In Cibber's alteration (Papal Tyr.), *see* Rosco.

Percy (Rich. II). *See* Hale.

Percy, Lady (1 Hen. IV). *See* Miss Bellamy, Mrs Benson, Mrs Booth, Mrs Bradshaw, Mrs Bullock, Mrs Christian, Mrs H. Giffard, Mrs Hale, Mrs L. Hallam, Mrs Hamilton, Miss Holliday [i.e. later Mrs W. Mills the 2nd), Miss Mann, Mrs Marshall, Mrs W. Mills the 2nd, Mrs Purden, Mrs Ridout, Mrs Santlow [i.e. later Mrs Booth], Mrs Spiller, Mrs Templer, Miss Vaughan [i.e. later Mrs Christian], Mrs Vincent (fl. 1723–31), Mrs R. Vincent, Mrs Ware, Mrs Woffington.

Percy, Lady (Theobald's Rich. II). A character not in the original play. *See* Mrs. Bullock, Mrs Spiller.

Perdita (Wint. T.). *See* Mrs Hale, Miss J. Hippisley.

Pericles (Pericles). In Lillo's alteration (Marina), *see* Stephens.

Peter (R & J). *See* H. Vaughan. In Otway's alteration (C. Marius) this character named Clodius. *See* Lowder.

Peter. In Worsdale's alteration of Tam. Shrew (Cure) the name given to Curtis, q.v.

Peter, Friar (Measure). *See* Bridges, Usher, Winstone.

Peto (1 Hen. IV). *See* Anderson, Blakey, Collins, Raftor, Simons, M. Stoppelaer.

Peto (2 Hen. IV). *See* Atkins.

Petruchio (Tam. Shrew). In Lacy's alteration (Sauny), *see* Havard, J. Mills, Ogden, Powell. In Worsdale's alteration (Cure) this character named Manly. *See* Dunstall, Macklin, Worsdale.

Phaeax. In Shadwell's Timon the name given to one of the Senators, q.v.

Phebe (AYLI). *See* Mrs Bennet, Miss J. Hippisley, Mrs Rowley, Mrs Wright.

Philario (Cymbeline). *See* Anderson. In D'Urfey's alteration this character named Beaupré. *See* Salway.

Philip, King (John). *See* H. Giffard, Havard, L. Ryan. In Cibber's alteration (Papal Tyr.), *see* Hale.

Philoten. In Lillo's alteration of Pericles (Marina) the name given to Dionyza, q.v.

Phryne. In Shadwell's Timon the name given to Phrynia, q.v.

Phrynia (Timon). In Shadwell's alteration this character named Phryne. *See* Mrs Dunstall, Mrs Kilby, Mrs Rowley.

Physician (Lear). *See* Dunstall.

Pinch (Com. Err.). *See* Neale.

## INDEX II

Pindarus (J. Caesar). *See* Oates, Raftor.
Pirate (Pericles). In Lillo's alteration (Marina) this character named Valdes. *See* Boman Jr.
Pisanio (Cymbeline). *See* Boheme, Bridgwater, Corey.
Pistol (2 Hen. IV). *See* T. Cibber, Cushing, James, Norris Sr., H. Woodward, Yates. In the anonymous alteration (Humours of Fal.), *see* Mrs Charke.
Pistol (Hen. V). *See* T. Cibber, Dyer, James, H. Woodward, Yates.
Pistol (MWW). *See* Brett, Clarke, R. Cross II, Cushing, T. Hallam, Holtom, James, Mullart, Pearce, Spiller, Stevens (fl. 1737–42), H. Vaughan, Yates.
Poet (Timon). *See* Bickerstaff, Chapman, T. Cibber, Norris Sr., Norris Jr., Oates, Penkethman Sr., H. Woodward, Yates.
Poins (1 Hen. IV). *See* Anderson, Baker, C. Bullock, Cashell, Chapman, Gibson, Hale, Hamilton, Harrington, Kennedy, Macklin, A. Ryan, Watson, Winstone, H. Woodward.
Poins (2 Hen. IV). *See* Bransby, Cashell, R. Cross II, Cushing, W. Giffard, Hayman, Macklin, Oates, Salway, W. Wilks.
Polixenes (Wint. T.). *See* Marshall, L. Ryan.
Polonius (Hamlet). *See* Arthur, Collett, R. Cross I, Dogget, B. Griffin, G. Hallam, Hippisley, James, B. Johnson, Julian, Lyon, Macklin, Mallin, Norris Jr., Paget, Penkethman Jr., Shuter, Taswell.
Pompeius. In Otway's alteration of R & J (C. Marius) the name given to Escalus, q.v.
Pompeius's Son (C. Marius). A character not in the original play. *See* Master Littleton.
Popilius (J. Caesar). *See* Woodburn.
Porco. In Miller's alteration of Much Ado (Univ. Pass.) the name given to Dogberry, q.v.
Porter (Hen. VIII). *See* Barrington.
Portia (J. Caesar). *See* Mrs Boman Sr., Mrs Bracegirdle, Mrs Bradshaw, Mrs Buchanan, Mrs Bullock, Mrs Forrester, Mrs Furnival, Mrs Horton, Mrs W. Mills the 2nd, Mrs M. Porter, Mrs Pritchard, Mrs J. Roberts, Mrs Rogers, Mrs Seymour, Mrs Spicer, Mrs Spiller, Mrs Thurmond, Mrs Woffington.
Portia (Merchant). *See* Mrs Clive, Mrs Pritchard, Mrs Woffington. In Granville's alteration (Jew), *see* Mrs Berriman [i.e. later Mrs W. Hallam], Mrs Bracegirdle, Mrs Bradshaw, Mrs W. Hallam, Mrs Seymour, Mrs Spiller, Mrs Thurmond.

Posthumus (Cymbeline). *See* T. Cibber, L. Ryan. In D'Urfey's alteration this character named Ursaces. *See* Delane, Keene, L. Ryan.
Priam (Troilus). *See* Fairbank, Morgan.
Priest (Hamlet). *See* Harrington, Hayman.
Priest (Twelfth N.). *See* Raftor, Woodburn.
Priest. In Miller's alteration of Much Ado (Univ. Pass.) the name given to the Friar, q.v.
Priest. In Otway's alteration of R & J (C. Marius) the name given to Friar Laurence, q.v.
Prospero (Tempest). *See* Berry, Bridges, Bruodin, Furnival, Goodman, Havard, J. Mills, Powell, J. Roberts, L. Sparks.
Protheus. In Miller's alteration of Much Ado (Univ. Pass.) the name given to Benedick, q.v.
Provost (Measure). *See* Blakes, Diggs, Egleton, Havard, Hulett, Paget, Pitt, Ridout, C. Shepard, Wignell.
Publius (J. Caesar). *See* Roberts (fl. 1750), Wright (fl. 1741–50).
Pyramus (MND). In Leveridge's alteration (Pyramus), *see* Leveridge. In Lampe's alteration (Pyramus), *see* Beard. In the mock play in Johnson's alteration of AYLI (Love in For.), *see* Penkethman Sr.

Queen (Cymbeline). *See* Mrs J. Giffard, Mrs W. Hallam, Mrs James, Mrs Knight.
Queen (Hamlet). *See* Mrs Bambridge, Mrs Bennet, Mrs Berriman [i.e. later Mrs W. Hallam], Mrs Boheme, Mrs Buchanan, Mrs Butler, Mrs Egleton, Mrs Forrester, Mrs Furnival, Mrs J. Giffard [i.e. later Mrs Egleton], Mrs W. Hallam, Mrs Haughton, Mrs Horton, Mrs James, Mrs Knight, Mrs Macklin, Mrs Parker [i.e. later (1) Mrs Berriman; (2) Mrs W. Hallam], Mrs M. Porter, Mrs Powell, Mrs Pritchard, Mrs J. Roberts, Mrs Seymour [i.e. later Mrs Boheme], Mrs Spiller, Mrs Steel, Mrs Thurmond, Mrs Woffington, Mrs Woodward.
Queen (Rich. II). *See* Mrs Bullock, Mrs Horton, Mrs Seymour.
Queen, Player (Hamlet). *See* Mrs Bambridge, Mrs Bennet, Mrs Bland, Mrs R. Cross, Mrs Cushing, Mrs James, Mrs Monlass, Mrs Mullart, Miss Taylor, Mrs Yates.
Quickly, Mrs (MWW). *See* Mrs Bambridge, Mrs R. Cross, Mrs Egleton, Mrs J. Giffard [i.e. later Mrs Egleton], Mrs Grace [i.e. later Mrs Macklin], Mrs James, Mrs Kirk, Mrs Macklin, Mrs Martin, Mrs Morgan, Mrs Mullart, Mrs Palmer, Miss Pitt, Mrs Shireburn [i.e.

later Mrs R. Cross], Mrs Wetherilt, Mrs Yates.

Quince (MND). In Leveridge's alteration (Pyramus), see W. Bullock Sr.

Ratcliff (Rich. III). See Anderson, Boyce, Crofts, Dighton, Harrington, Hewitt, Huddy, Jenkins, Kennedy, Naylor, Oates, Simpson, Turbutt, Wignell, Woodburn.

Regan (Lear). See Mrs Bland, Miss Burgess, Mrs Butler, Mrs R. Cross, Mrs Cushing, Mrs Finch, Mrs Forrester, Mrs E. Giffard, Miss Minors, Mrs Monlass, Mrs Morgan, Mrs Mullart, Mrs Palmer, Mrs Parker, Mrs Ridout, Mrs Seal, Mrs Shireburn [i.e. later Mrs R. Cross], Mrs Templer, Mrs Thomas, Mrs Yates.

Reignier (1 Hen. VI). See Bridgwater.

Richard (Cibber's 3 Hen. VI). See Wilson.

Richard II (Rich. II). See Delane, L. Ryan.

Richard III (Rich. III). See C. Cibber, T. Cibber, Crisp, Cushing, Delane, Garrick, Goodfellow, A. Hallam, Hulett, Tho. Lacy, Lee, Morgan, Quin, J. Roberts, L. Ryan, Sheridan, Sowdon, Turbutt.

Richmond (Rich. III). See Bardin, Chapman, T. Cibber, R. Cross II, Cushing, Egleton, H. Giffard, W. Giffard, Hale, A. Hallam, Havard, J. Leigh, Marshall, W. Mills, Ridout, L. Ryan, T. Walker, C. Williams, T. Wright.

Roberto. In Johnson's alteration of AYLI (Love in For.) the name given to Jaques de Bois, q.v.

Robin (MWW). See Miss Cole, Green, Master Morgan, Miss Morrison, Miss Mullart, Miss Yates.

Roderigo (Othello). See Bowen, W. Bullock Jr., Chapman, Mrs Charke, Charles, T. Cibber, Cushing, Dyer, Egleton, L. Hallam, Miller, Neale, Pack, Penkethman Jr., Reynolds, Smith (fl. 1735-49), H. Ward, R. Wetherilt, Woodward Sr., H. Woodward, Yates.

Rodoregue. In Burnaby's alteration of Twelfth N. (Love Bet.) the name given to Antonio, q.v.

Romeo (R & J). See Barry, T. Cibber, Garrick, Lee. In Otway's alteration (C. Marius) this character named Young Marius. See Booth, Mrs Charke, R. Wilks.

Rosalind (AYLI). See Mr Page, Mrs Pritchard, Mrs Woffington. In Johnson's alteration (Love in For.), see Mrs Booth.

Rosencrantz (Hamlet). See Bencraft, Cartwright, R. Cross II, Gibson, Harbin, Houghton, Nelson, Paddick, Ridout, Simpson, Usher, H. Vaughan, W. Wilks, R. Williams, Woodburn.

Ross (Macbeth). See Bridges, King, Lee.

Ross (Rich. II). See Diggs, Ridout.

Ruffian (C. Marius). A character not in the original play. See Miller, Penkethman Sr.

Ruffian (Tate's Lear). A character not in the original play. See Kent, Peer.

Rugby (MWW). See Baker, Blakey, Collins, F. Leigh Jr., R. Williams.

Salarino (Merchant). See Blakes, Goodall, Ridout, Turbutt.

Salerio (Jew). A character not in the original play. See Wignell.

Salisbury (Hen. V). See Bencraft, Burton.

Salisbury (1 Hen. VI). See Lyon.

Salisbury (2 Hen. VI). In Philips's alteration (Humfrey), see Thurmond Sr.

Salisbury (John). See W. Mills, Stephens. In Cibber's alteration (Papal Tyr.), see Ridout.

Salisbury (Rich. II). See Egleton, Lyon, Stevens (fl. 1737-42).

Sampson (R & J). See Collins, James.

Sands (Hen. VIII). See W. Bullock Sr., Collins, B. Griffin, Marten, Miller, Neale, Norris Jr., H. Woodward.

Saturninus (Titus). See J. Leigh, Thurmond Sr.

Sauny. In Lacy's alteration of Tam. Shrew (Sauny) the name given to Grumio, q.v.

Scroop (Betterton's 2 Hen. IV). A character not in the original play. See Arthur.

Scroop (Hen. V). See Arthur, Cushing, Havard, Mozeen, C. Williams.

Scroop (Rich. II). See Aston.

Sebastian (Tempest). See Marshall.

Sebastian (Twelfth N.). See Havard, Milward. In Burnaby's alteration (Love Bet.), see Booth.

Semibreve (Leveridge's Pyramus). A character not in the original play. See Knapp.

Senator (Othello). See Simpson.

Senators (Timon). In Shadwell's alteration these characters are named: (1) Aelius: see Aston, Chapman, B. Johnson, Marr, Neale; (2) Cleon: see Arthur, Dawson, Dyer, B. Griffin, Macklin, Norris Sr., Ray, Shawford; (3) Isander: see Birkhead, B. Griffin, J. Hall, T. Hallam, F. Leigh Sr., Miller, Norris Sr., Topham, Winstone, H. Woodward; (4) Isidore: see H. Bullock, W. Bullock Sr., Dunstall, F. Leigh Sr., Miller, Taswell, H. Wetherilt;(5) Nicias: see Hewson, Julian, Marten, Pack, Salway, C. Shepard; (6) Phaeax: see W. Bullock Sr., Dunstall, Harper, Hippisley, Marten, Mullart; (7) Thrasil-

# INDEX II

lus: *see* R. Cross I, A. Hallam, Jones, Reed, Rosco, Winstone, Woodburn.

Sergeant (Hen. VIII). *See* Usher.

Servant (Coriolanus). In Dennis's alteration (Invader), *see* Miller, Norris Sr., Penkethman Sr.

Sexton (Much Ado). *See* Arthur, Neale, Ray, Simpson.

Seyton (Macbeth). *See* Arthur, Aston, Berry, Bickerstaff, Blakes, Boheme, Carr, Chapman, Corey, T. Elrington, Gibson, Harrington, Havard, Hulett, J. Lacy, Philips, Ray, Ridout, Usher, Wignell.

Shadow (2 Hen. IV). *See* Bencraft, Hacket, Mawley, Ray. In the anonymous alteration (Humours of Fal.), *see* Arne.

Shallow (2 Hen. IV). *See* Arthur, C. Cibber, Hippisley, B. Johnson. In the anonymous alteration (Humours of Fal.), *see* James.

Shallow (MWW). *See* Arthur, Berriman, Boheme, Bransby, Chapman, Collett, Collins, Dove, Dyer, B. Johnson, Julian, Norris Jr., Paget, Rosco, Shuter, Taswell.

Shattillion. In D'Urfey's Cymbeline the name given to Iachimo, q.v.

Shepherd (Wint. T.). *See* Julian, Marten.

Sheriff (1 Hen. IV). *See* Dunstall, Gray, Oates.

Shylock (Merchant). *See* James, Lalauze, Macklin, Ridout, Rosco, L. Ryan, C. Shepard, Yates. In Granville's alteration (Jew), *see* Arthur, Aston, Boheme, Dogget, B. Griffin, Ogden.

Sicinius (Coriolanus). In Dennis's alteration (Invader), *see* W. Wilks.

Silence (2 Hen. IV). *See* B. Griffin, Miller, Neale, Salway, M. Stoppelaer, Taswell. In the anonymous alteration (Humours of Fal.), *see* T. Hallam.

Silvius (AYLI). *See* Davies, Goodall, Goodfellow, Green, Hayman, Mozeen, H. Woodward.

Simple (MWW). *See* Arne, Bencraft, Green, Hamilton, Miles, Paddick, H. Vaughan, H. Woodward.

Siward (Macbeth). *See* Aston, Boman Jr., Bransby, Cashell, Crofts, Gibson, Hale, Harbin, Hart, Houghton, Hulett, Husband, Marshall, Oates, Ridout, Rosco, Watson, Winstone, Woodburn.

Siward, Young (Macbeth). *See* Bransby, R. Cross II, Palmer.

Slender (MWW). *See* Bennet, C. Bullock, W. Bullock Jr., T. Cibber, Clarke, Collins, Cushing, Egleton, James, Neale, H. Vaughan, R. Wetherilt, H. Woodward.

Sly, Christopher (Tam. Shrew). In Johnson's alteration of the induction (Cobler), *see* Penkethman Sr. In Bullock's alteration of the induction (Cobler) this character named Toby Guzzle. *See* Jones, Morgan, Penkethman Jr., Spiller.

Snatchpenny. In Lacy's alteration of Tam. Shrew (Sauny) the name given to the Pedant, q.v.

Snuffle (Bullock's Cobler). A character not in the original play. *See* C. Bullock, W. Bullock Jr., G. Hallam, Hippisley, W. Williams.

Solanio (Merchant). *See* Berry, R. Cross II, Gibson, King.

Soldier, French (Hen. V). *See* Destrade.

Soldier [Interpreter] (All's Well). *See* Arthur, Winstone.

Somerset (1 Hen. VI). *See* Hale.

Soothsayer (J. Caesar). *See* Harbin, Hind, James, Marten, I. Sparks, C. Williams.

Stanley (Rich. III). *See* Arthur, Aston, Berry, Corey, Davies, Diggs, Hale, L. Hallam, Havard, Mozeen, Paget, Redman, Rosco, Winstone.

Starveling (MND). In Leveridge's alteration (Pyramus), *see* Coker.

Stephano (Tempest). *See* Arthur, Bickerstaff, Chettle, R. Cross II, W. Hallam, Hewson, B. Johnson, Kennedy, Macklin, Massey, Morgan, Rosco, C. Shepard, Shuter, Smith (fl. 1735-49).

Steward (All's Well). *See* Dunstall, Julian, Marten, Turbutt.

Suffolk (1 Hen. VI). *See* T. Walker.

Suffolk (2 Hen. VI). In Philips's alteration (Humfrey), *see* Watson.

Suffolk (Hen. VIII). *See* Arthur, Blakes, Boman Sr., Richardson, Ridout, Stephens.

Sulpitius. In Otway's alteration of R & J (C. Marius) the name given to Mercutio, q.v.

Surrey (Hen. VIII). *See* Chapman, C. Cibber, T. Cibber, Gibson, Marshall, W. Mills, Powell, C. Williams.

Surrey (Rich. II). *See* Houghton.

Surveyor (Hen. VIII). *See* Goodfellow, Keene, Marten, Oates, Rosco, Taswell, Turbutt.

Sycorax (Dryden and Davenant's Tempest). A character not in the original play. *See* Charke, Collett, R. Cross I, Dove, G. Hallam, T. Hallam, Jones, Mrs Miller, Raftor, Simms, Taswell, Topham.

Sylla. In Otway's alteration of R & J (C. Marius) the name given to Paris, q.v.

Talbot (1 Hen. VI). *See* Delane.

Talbot, John (1 Hen. VI). *See* Stevens (fl. 1737-42).

Tamora (Titus). *See* Mrs Egleton, Mrs J. Giffard [i.e. later Mrs Egleton], Mrs Knight, Mrs Seymour.

## INDEX II

Taquilet. In Burnaby's alteration of Twelfth N. (Love Bet.) the name given to Malvolio, q.v.

Tearsheet, Doll (2 Hen. IV). *See* Mrs Bennet, Miss Brett, Mrs R. Cross, Miss Dancey, Mrs Dunstall, Miss Haughton, Miss Hilliard, Miss Lindar, Miss Mann, Mrs Shireburn [i.e. later Mrs R. Cross], Miss Willis. In the anonymous alteration (Humours of Fal.), *see* Mrs Talbot.

Thais. In Shadwell's Timon the name given to Timandra, q.v.

Thaisa (Pericles). In Lillo's alteration (Marina), *see* Mrs Marshall.

Thersites (Troilus). *See* Betterton, W. Bullock Sr., Quin.

Thisbe (MND). In Leveridge's alteration (Pyramus), *see* Pack. In Lampe's alteration (Pyramus), *see* Mrs Lampe. In the mock play in Johnson's alteration of AYLI (Love in For.), *see* Miller.

Thomas, Friar (Measure). *See* Cole, Orfeur, Simpson.

Thrasillus. In Shadwell's Timon the name given to one of the Senators, q.v.

Timandra (Timon). In Shadwell's alteration this character named Thais. *See* Mrs Bland, Mrs Forrester, Mrs Jones.

Time (Wint. T.). *See* Gibson.

Timon (Timon). *See* Booth, Bridgwater, Hale, Keene, Marshall, J. Mills, Milward, Powell, T. Walker.

Titus (Titus). *See* Boheme, J. Mills.

Toby, Sir (Twelfth N.). *See* Berry, C. Shepard, I. Sparks. In Burnaby's alteration (Love Bet.) this character named Drances. *See* Powell.

Tooth-drawer (Cure). A character not in the original play. *See* Hacket, T. Hallam.

Touchstone (AYLI). *See* Arthur, Chapman, Macklin, H. Woodward.

Town Clerk (Much Ado). *See* James, Marten, Mullart, Simpson.

Tranio (Tam. Shrew). In Lacy's alteration (Sauny), *see* C. Bullock, Fairbank, T. Walker, H. Woodward.

Traveller (1 Hen. IV). *See* Smith (fl. 1735–49).

Trebonius (J. Caesar). *See* Anderson, Boman Jr., Evans (fl. 1733–43), Havard, Marshall, Ridout, Rosco, T. Smith, J. Ward, Winstone.

Tressel (Cibber's Rich. III). A character not in the original play. *See* Berry, Blakes, Chapman, T. Cibber, R. Cross II, Cushing, Furnival, Gibson, W. Giffard, Hale, Huddy, Tho. Lacy, Paget, Ridout, Turbutt, W. Wilks.

Trinculo (Tempest). *See* Barrington, Bridgwater, W. Bullock Sr., Estcourt, L. Hallam, Harper, Macklin, Miller, Morgan, Reed, Underhill, Yates.

Troilus (Troilus). *See* L. Ryan, R. Wilks.

Tubal (Merchant). *See* Cushing, Dunstall, M. Stoppelaer, Taswell, H. Vaughan.

Tybalt (R & J). *See* Blakes, Dyer, Tho. Lacy, Naylor, R. Williams.

Tyrrel (Rich. III). *See* Arthur, Bransby, Carr, Dove, Dunstall, G. Hallam, Nelson, Norris Jr., Pattenden, Simpson, M. Stoppelaer, H. Vaughan, Weller, R. Williams, Woodburn.

Ulysses (Troilus). *See* Aston, Boheme, Thurmond Sr., T. Walker.

Ursaces. In D'Urfey's Cymbeline the name given to Posthumus, q.v.

Ursula (Much Ado). *See* Miss Brunette, Miss Cole, Miss Minors, Mrs Stevens, Mrs Vaughan.

Valdes. In Lillo's alteration of Pericles (Marina) the name given to a Pirate, q.v.

Valentine (Twelfth N.). *See* Ridout, Usher.

Ventoso (Dryden and Davenant's Tempest). A character not in the original play. *See* Collett, Cushing, Fairbank, Harper, Norris Sr., Norris Jr., Oates, Ray, Richardson, Smith (fl. 1735–49), R. Wetherilt, H. Woodward.

Verges (Much Ado). *See* James, Neale, Shuter, H. Vaughan. In Miller's alteration (Univ. Pass.) this character named Asino. *See* Macklin, Taswell.

Vernon (1 Hen. IV). *See* Bardin, Blakes, Booth, Bridgwater, C. Bullock, Cartwright, Cashell, R. Cross II, Egleton, Gibson, W. Giffard, A. Hallam, Havard, Houghton, Lynham, Oates, Paget, L. Ryan, Shuter, T. Walker, J. Ward.

Vernon (1 Hen. VI). *See* Bencraft.

Villaretta. In Burnaby's alteration of Twelfth N. (Love Bet.) the name given to Olivia, q.v.

Vincentio (Tam. Shrew). In Lacy's alteration (Sauny) this character named Sir Lionel. *See* R. Cross I, J. Hall, Norris Jr.

Viola (Twelfth N.). *See* Mrs Pritchard, Mrs Woffington. In Burnaby's alteration (Love Bet.) this character named Caesario. *See* Mrs Prince.

Virgilia (Coriolanus). In Dennis's alteration (Invader), *see* Mrs Thurmond.

Volumnia (Coriolanus). In Dennis's alteration (Invader), *see* Mrs M. Porter.

Wales, Prince of (1 Hen. IV). *See* Cushing, H. Giffard, A. Hallam, J. Leigh, Macklin, W. Mills, L. Ryan, R. Wilks.

# INDEX II

Wales, Prince of (2 Hen. IV). *See* W. Mills, L. Ryan, R. Wilks, C. Williams.

Wales, Prince of (Cibber's 3 Hen. VI). *See* T. Cibber.

Wall (MND). In Leveridge's alteration (Pyramus), *see* Armstrong, Laurence, Randal. In Lampe's alteration (Pyramus), *see* Laguerre. In the mock play in Johnson's alteration of AYLI (Love in For.), *see* Norris Sr.

Wart (2 Hen. IV). *See* Cole, Peploe, Yates.

Warwick (1 Hen. VI). *See* Rosco.

Warwick (2 Hen. VI). In Philips's alteration (Humfrey), *see* C. Williams.

Warwick (Cibber's 3 Hen. VI). *See* Bridgwater.

Watchman (Much Ado). *See* Marr, M. Stoppelaer, H. Vaughan.

Westminster, Abbot of (Rich. II). *See* M. Stoppelaer.

Westmorland (1 Hen. IV). *See* Arthur, Aston, Bransby, W. Bullock Jr., Cole, Harrington, Hayman, A. Hill, Holtom, Kennedy, Moore, Ogden, Ridout, T. Smith, Storer, Turbutt, Usher, Wignell.

Westmorland (2 Hen. IV). *See* Aston, Bridgwater, Gibson, J. Roberts, Usher, C. Williams, Winstone.

Westmorland (Hen. V). *See* Aston, R. Elrington, J. Roberts, Simpson.

Widow (All's Well). *See* Mrs Bambridge, Mrs R. Cross, Mrs James, Mrs Yates.

Widow (Tam. Shrew). In Lacy's alteration (Sauny), *see* Miss Gerrard.

William (AYLI). *See* Raftor, Ray, Shuter, H. Vaughan.

William, Sir. In Worsdale's alteration of Tam. Shrew (Cure) the name given to Baptista, q.v.

Williams (Hen. V). *See* Bransby, Rosco.

Willoughby (Rich. II). *See* Coker, A. Ryan.

Winchester, Bishop of (1 Hen. VI). *See* Chapman.

Winlove. In Lacy's alteration of Tam. Shrew (Sauny) the name given to Lucentio, q.v.

Witch (Macbeth). *See* Arthur, Banks, Bencraft, Bowen, Bridges, C. Bullock, H. Bullock, W. Bullock Sr., Collett, Collins, R. Cross I, Cushing, Dogget, Dunstall, Dyer, Excell, Fairbank, B. Griffin, G. Hallam, T. Hallam, W. Hallam, Hippisley, James, Jenkins, Julian, F. Leigh Sr., Macklin, Marten, Miller, Monlass, Morgan, Mullart, Neale, Norris Sr., Norris Jr., Pearce, Penkethman Sr., Penkethman Jr., Phillips, Phipps, Ray, Reed, C. Shepard, Shuter, M. Stoppelaer, H. Vaughan, R. Wetherilt, H. Woodward, Yates.

Wolsey (Hen. VIII). *See* Boheme, C. Cibber, Keene, J. Mills, W. Mills, Milward, J. Roberts, L. Ryan, L. Sparks, Verbruggen.

Woodall. In Lacy's alteration of Tam. Shrew (Sauny) the name given to Gremio, q.v.

Worcester (1 Hen. IV). *See* Arthur, Aston, Berry, Blakes, Boheme, Bransby, C. Cibber, Corey, Dance, Dawson, W. Giffard, Havard, Hewitt, Hulett, Julian, Kirby, Ogden, Paget, Pinner, Ridout, J. Roberts, Rosco, T. Smith, Wignell, Winstone.

York (Hen. V). *See* Corey, Lyon.

York (1 Hen. VI). *See* Stephens.

York (2 Hen. VI). In Philips's alteration (Humfrey), *see* J. Mills.

York (Cibber's 3 Hen. VI). *See* [R.?] Savage.

York (Rich. II). *See* Boheme, Stephens.

York, Archbishop of (2 Hen. IV). *See* Berry, Bridgwater, Chapman, Milward, Paget, J. Roberts, Rosco, Thurmond Sr., Turbutt, T. Wright.

York, Duchess of (Rich. II). *See* Mrs W. Hallam.

York, Duchess of (Rich. III). *See* Mrs Baker, Mrs Bambridge, Mrs Beckham, Mrs Bennet, Mrs Buchanan, Mrs Butler, Mrs R. Cross, Mrs Daniel, Mrs Egleton, Mrs J. Giffard [i.e. later Mrs Egleton], Mrs Haughton, Mrs James, Mrs Knight, Mrs Mullart, Mrs Phillips, Mrs Pritchard, Mrs Woodward, Mrs Yates.

York, Duke of (Rich. III). *See* Miss Cibber, Miss Cole, Miss Haughton, Master Huddy, Miss Lindar, Miss Macklin, Master Morgan, Miss Morrison, Miss Mullart, Miss Naylor, Miss Norris (fl. 1733-35), Miss Robinson Jr., Mrs Wright, Miss Yates.

PRINTED IN
GREAT BRITAIN
AT THE
UNIVERSITY PRESS
OXFORD
BY
CHARLES BATEY
PRINTER
TO THE
UNIVERSITY

## Date Due

| JAN 13 | | | |
|---|---|---|---|
| | | | |
| | | | |
| | | | |
| | | | |
| | | | |
| | | | |
| | | | |
| | | | |
| | | | |
| | | | |
| | | | |
| | | | |
| | | | |
| | | | |
| | | | |
| | | | |

Library Bureau Cat. No. 1137